SIR NICHOLAS HARRIS NICOLAS was born in 1799, and served in the Royal Navy in the Mediterranean from 1808 to 1816 under Admiral Duckworth and Lord Exmouth. Retired on half-pay at the end of the Napoleonic Wars, he turned to antiquarian and literary pursuits after a brief legal career, compiling and editing a large number of scholarly works. This seven-volume annotated compilation of Nelson's correspondence was originally published by Henry Colburn between 1844 and 1847, and was to be followed by his ambitious *A History of the British Navy, from the Earliest Times to the Wars of the French Revolution*, but when he died in France in 1848, only the first two volumes, covering up to the year 1422, had been completed.

THE

DISPATCHES AND LETTERS

OF

VICE ADMIRAL

LORD VISCOUNT NELSON

WITH NOTES BY

SIR NICHOLAS HARRIS NICOLAS, G.C.M.G.

" The Nation expected, and was entitled to expect, that while Cities vied with each other in consecrating Statues in marble and brass to the memory of our NELSON, a Literary Monument would be erected, which should record his deeds for the immortal honour of his own Country, and the admiration of the rest of the World." — QUARTERLY REVIEW.

THE SECOND VOLUME.

1795 TO 1797.

CHATHAM PUBLISHING

LONDON

Published in 1997 by
Chatham Publishing,
1 & 2 Faulkner's Alley, Cowcross Street,
London EC1M 6DD

Chatham Publishing is an imprint of
Gerald Duckworth and Co Ltd

First Published in 1845
by Henry Colburn

ISBN 1 86176 049 3

A catalogue record for this book is available
from the British Library

Printed and bound in Great Britain by
Redwood Books, Trowbridge, Wiltshire

PREFACE.

THIS Volume contains the DISPATCHES and LETTERS of NELSON from the beginning of the year 1795 to the end of the year 1797. They relate principally to Admiral Hotham's Actions with the French Fleet on the 13th and 14th of March, and 13th of July 1795; to his proceedings when in command of a small Squadron on the Coast of Genoa, acting in co-operation with the Austrian General de Vins; to the Blockade of Leghorn; to the Capture of Porto Ferrajo in July, and of the Island of Capraja in September 1796; to the Evacuation of Corsica; to the Action with, and Capture of, a Spanish Frigate in December of that year; to the Battle of St. Vincent in February, the bombardment of Cadiz, and engagement with the Spanish Gun-boats, and to the unsuccessful attack on Santa Cruz in Teneriffe, in July 1797, where he lost his right arm. Some of the events described in these Letters are among the most brilliant and interesting of his Life.

During this period NELSON was promoted to the rank of COMMODORE of the Second, then of the First Class, and afterwards to that of REAR-ADMIRAL, was made a KNIGHT OF THE BATH, and obtained a Pension for his wounds and services. He returned to England for the recovery of his health in September 1797, and remained on shore until March following, when he hoisted his Flag in the Vanguard, and commenced a new career of glory, by his unparalleled Achievement at the Nile, in August 1798, the particulars of which will be found in his Correspondence in the next Volume.

Although it is by no means wished that the Notes to this work should be of a controversial nature, it has nevertheless been thought expedient to shew that the statement in James's "Naval History of Great Britain," respecting the proceedings of the "Agamemnon," NELSON'S Ship, in Admiral Hotham's Action on the 13th and 14th of March 1795, is both imperfect and unjust; and that his implied derogation from the merit of NELSON'S exploits at the Battle of St. Vincent, is altogether unfounded.

It will be seen that numerous Letters in this Volume were addressed to Admiral Sir John Jervis, K.B., (afterwards Earl of St. Vincent,) then Commander-in-Chief in the Mediterranean, and that the only authority for most of them is Clarke and M'Arthur's "Life of Nelson."

The incorrect manner in which those Writers have printed documents, imposed upon the Editor the duty of using every means in his power to inspect the originals;

and he feels it due to the Public and to himself to prove that he did not neglect it, in a case where, from the number and importance of the Letters, it was, perhaps, more necessary than in any other.

After making application to various members of the late Earl of St. Vincent's family, in reply to which he was assured that the Papers were not in their possession, he learned that they belonged to the Countess of St. Vincent's nephew, Vice-Admiral Sir William Parker, Bart. G.C.B., and that they were in the hands of Jedediah Stephens Tucker, Esq., the author of " Memoirs of Admiral the Earl of St. Vincent." As Sir William Parker was abroad, the Editor wrote to Mr. Jedediah Tucker, stating his wishes, and pointing out the importance of enabling him to verify the Letters given in Clarke and M'Arthur's work, in justice alike to the Earl of St. Vincent, to Lord Nelson, and to the Public. Mr. Jedediah Tucker's reply, in October last, stated that he was unable to inform him of the address of any relative of Lord St. Vincent, who may have letters from Lord Nelson, except Sir William Parker, " neither can Mr. Tucker place the Letters he " may possess from Lord Nelson in Sir Harris Nicholas's " hands, for Mr. Tucker does not think it advisable that " Sir Harris Nicholas should publish them. Attention " is given to the state in which the Letter from Lord " St. Vincent appear, and should it be thought expe- " dient to take any steps, the proper ones will be re- " sorted to."

From the Writer of a Note in which little was intelligible except discourtesy, it was obvious that nothing useful could be expected.

On the return to England of Vice-Admiral Sir William Parker, the Editor lost no time in writing to him; and though he did not succeed in obtaining access to the Papers, he received a courteous answer, the purport of which was, that though the Earl of St. Vincent had bequeathed to Sir William Parker Lord Nelson's Correspondence, yet, from particular circumstances, those Letters had never been actually in his possession, that they were then in a distant part of the country, that it was absolutely necessary that he himself should peruse them before they could be published, and that, whenever it might be in his power, he would gladly afford any assistance to the Editor, as no individual existed who could be more anxious to promote any authentic work which would enhance the reputation of those bright examples of the Naval Profession.   This reply precluded all hope of accomplishing the Editor's object, at least until a remote and indefinite period, and compelled him, though with indescribable reluctance, to print many Letters of the greatest importance to the fame of two of England's most celebrated Admirals, written at the most eventful period of their services, exactly as he found them, well knowing as he, and the possessor of the originals do, that the copies to which he is obliged to trust, are interpolated, and imperfect.

In consequence of there being a few Letters in Clarke and M'Arthur's work, from NELSON to the late Earl Spencer, while First Lord of the Admiralty, the Editor requested the present Earl to permit him to see the originals; but his Lordship informed him that he has no Letters from Lord Nelson which could be of any use to him, or he would willingly allow him to see them.

In the "Advertisement" to the Second Edition of the First Volume, the Editor expressed his obligations to many persons for contributions since its publication; and to that List, and to the List in the Preface, he now adds, with very great satisfaction, the name of EARL NELSON, whose interest in the fame of the Great Founder of his Honours is alike earnest and becoming. The Editor also begs leave to thank Rear-Admiral Samuel Hood Inglefield, C.B., for some valuable Letters.

The rapid sale of the First Volume of this Work having made it necessary to reprint it, advantage was taken of the circumstance to insert in the new Edition such Letters as had been sent to the Editor since its appearance; but, in justice to the purchasers of the First Edition, all those Letters have been reprinted, and are inserted, with the "Advertisement" to the new Edition, at the end of this Volume. It may be proper to add that the large impression which has been struck of the present, and will be taken of the subsequent Volumes, renders a new Edition of them improbable.

Torrington Square,
14*th February,* 1845.

(Vide p. 435. Vol. II.)

Thorns Aug't 16th: 1797,

My Dear Sir /

    Sojourn at Thorns &c &c more

in sight of your flag, and with your far-

you my respects. If the time ... and ... I
know my wishes, a ... handed Removal will
... ... be considered as useful. Therefore
the sooner I get to a very humble cottage the better
And no other room for a better man to serve the State.
but whatever be my ... Believe me with the most
... ... be whether ... than your most faithful

Horatio Nelson

The papers I sent by Walter were I

neither correct or all which

sent. I send you the

CONTENTS.

LETTERS.

1795.

PAGE

To Mrs. Nelson . . . . Fiorenzo, 17th January   1
To H. R. H. the Duke of Clarence . . . Fiorenzo, 19th January   1
To Mrs. Nelson . . . . Fiorenzo, 31st January   2
To William Suckling, Esq. Agamemnon, Fiorenzo, 1st February   3
To Thomas Pollard, Esq. . . . . . Agamemnon, 6th February   4
To William Suckling, Esq. . . . . St. Fiorenzo, 7th February   4
To Mrs. Nelson . . . . St. Fiorenzo, 7th February   7
To Mrs. Nelson . . . . Leghorn, 25th February   8
To Daniel Williams, Esq. . . . . . . Leghorn, 27th February   9
Transactions on board his Majesty's Ship Agamemnon, and of the
    Fleet, as seen and known by Captain Nelson,
                      From the 8th to the 14th March 10
To Mrs. Nelson . . . . . . Agamemnon, at Sea, 10th March 17
To Vice-Admiral Goodall . . . . . Agamemnon, 12th March 18
To Vice-Admiral Goodall . . . . . Agamemnon, 15th March 19
To H. R. H. the Duke of Clarence . . . . 15th March 19
To William Locker, Esq. Agamemnon, Porto Especia, 21st March 20
To William Suckling, Esq., Agamemnon, Porto Especia, 22nd March 22
To the Rev. Mr. Nelson, Hilborough
            Agamemnon, Porto Especia, 25th March 23
To Thomas Pollard, Esq. . . . . Agamemnon (*torn*) 25
To Mrs. Nelson . . . . Fiorenzo, 1st April 25
To Sir Gilbert Elliot, Vice-Roy of Corsica
           Agamemnon, St. Fiorenzo, 5th April 27
To the Right Hon. Sir Gilbert Elliot . . . . 8th April 28
To Mrs. Nelson . . . . St. Fiorenzo, 12th April 28
To the Right Honourable Sir Gilbert Elliot, Agamemnon, 16th April 30
To H. R. H. the Duke of Clarence . . . St. Fiorenzo, 16th April 30
To H. R. H. the Duke of Clarence
          Agamemnon, of Cape Corse, 24th April 31

1795, *continued.*

PAGE

To the Rev. Mr. Nelson, Bath . Agamemnon, at Sea, 24th April 32
To William Suckling, Esq. . . Agamemnon, at Sea, 24th April 33
To Mrs. Nelson . . . . Leghorn, 28th April 34
To William Locker, Esq. . . . Agamemnon, Leghorn, 4th May 34
To William Suckling, Esq. . . . . Leghorn, 4th May 36
To . . . . Leghorn, 5th May 37
To Daniel Williams, Esq. . . . Agamemnon, Leghorn, 5th May 38
To Thomas Pollard, Esq. . . . . 22nd May 38
To Mrs. Nelson . . . . Off Minorca, 29th May 39
To Thomas Pollard, Esq. . . . . 29th May 40
To William Suckling, Esq. . . . . Off Port Mahon, 7th June 40
To the Right Hon. William Windham, Secretary at War, 8th June 41
To the Rev. Mr. Nelson, Hilborough . . Off Minorca, 8th June 42
To Thomas Pollard, Esq. . . . . 8th June 43
To William Locker, Esq. . . . . . . Off Minorca, 18th June 43
To William Suckling, Esq. . . . . . Off Minorca, 20th June 44
To the Rev. Dixon Hoste . . . . . . Off Minorca, 22nd June 45
To the Rev. Mr. Nelson, Hilborough,
                    Agamemnon, off Minorca, 22nd June 46
To Mrs. Nelson . . . . St. Fiorenzo, 1st July 48
To William Locker, Esq. . Agamemnon, off Cape Corse, 8th July 49
To H. R. H. the Duke of Clarence . . . . 15th July 52
To his Excellency Francis Drake, Esq., Minister at Genoa
                    Agamemnon, Genoa Mole, 18th July 53
To Earl Spencer, First Lord of the Admiralty . . . . 19th July 56
To Admiral Hotham . . . Agamemnon, Vado Bay, 22nd July 57
To Mrs. Nelson . . . . Off Vado Bay, 24th July 59
To the Right Hon. Sir Gilbert Elliot
                    Agamemnon, Leghorn, 27th July 60
To William Suckling, Esq. . . . . . . Leghorn, 27th July 61
To Admiral Hotham . Agamemnon, Leghorn Roads, 28th July 62
To the Rev. Mr. Nelson, Hilborough
                    Agamemnon, Gulf of Genoa, 29th July 63
To Mrs. Nelson . . . . Vado Bay, 2nd August 65
To Francis Drake, Esq . . . . 4th August 65
To Francis Drake, Esq. . . . . 6th August 66
To Captain Cockburn . . . . 8th August 67
To the Right Hon. Sir Gilbert Elliot . . Vado Bay, 13th August 67
To William Locker, Esq. . . . . . . Vado Bay, 19th August 69
To J. Harriman, Esq. . . . . Vado Bay, 23rd August 71
To the Commander of a French Corvette . Alassio, 26th August 72
To Admiral Hotham . . . . Vado Bay, 27th August 73
To Admiral Hotham . . . . Agamemnon, at Sea, 27th August 75
To Admiral Hotham . . Agamemnon, Vado Bay, 30th August 76
To Captain Collingwood . . . . . . Vado Bay, 31st August 77

1795, *continued.*

PAGE

To John M'Arthur, Esq. . . . . . . Vado Bay, 31st August 78
To Mrs. Nelson . . . . Vado Bay, 1st September 79
To Francis Drake, Esq. . . Agamemnon, at Sea, 9th September 79
Memoir sent to General de Vins . . . . About 9th September 80
To his Excellency Baron de Vins
     Agamemnon, Vado Bay, 14th September 81
To Mrs. Nelson . . . . Vado Bay, 15th September 82
To General de Vins . . . . Genoa Mole, 17th September 83
To Admiral Hotham . . . . Genoa, 17th September 83
To his Excellency Francis Drake, Esq.
     Agamemnon, Genoa Mole, 18th September 85
To Admiral Hotham . . . . 20th September 86
To Mrs. Nelson . . . . 21st September 86
To the Right Hon. Sir Gilbert Elliot
     Agamemnon, Leghorn, 24th September 87
To the Rev. Mr. Nelson, Bath . . . . Leghorn, 29th September 89
To the Commander of the Neapolitan Flotilla . . . 1st October 90
To Mrs. Nelson . . . . Vado Bay, 5th October 91
To William Suckling, Esq. . . . Off Marseilles, 27th October 92
To . . . . Agamemnon, Vado Bay, 6th November 94
To General Count Wallis, of the Austrian Army
     Agamemnon, Vado Bay, 7th November 95
To Baron de Vins . . . Agamemnon, Vado Bay, 8th November 96
To Francis Drake, Esq. . Agamemnon, Vado Bay, 12th November 96
To John M'Arthur, Esq., John Udney, Esq., and Thomas Pollard,
 Esq., Prize Agents . Agamemnon Vado Bay, 12th November 98
To Evan Nepean, Esq., Secretary to the Admiralty
     Agamemnon, Genoa Mole, 13th November 98ª
To H. R. H. the Duke of Clarence, Genoa Roads, 18th November 99
To H. R. H. the Duke of Clarence . . . . . . 19th November 101
To Vice-Admiral Sir Hyde Parker,
     Agamemnon, Genoa Road, 20th November 102
To Lord Grenville, Secretary of State for Foreign Affairs
     Agamemnon, Genoa Road, 23rd November 103
To the Reverend Mr. Nelson, Hilborough
     Agamemnon, Genoa Road, 25th November 106
To Admiral Sir John Jervis, K.B. . . . . About 25th November 107
To his Excellency Francis Drake, Esq.
     Agamemnon, Genoa Road, 27th November 108
To John William Brame, Esq., Consul at Genoa . 30th November 110
To Mrs. Nelson . . . . 2nd December 110
To Vice-Admiral Sir Hyde Parker . . . . . 2nd December 111
To the Right Hon. Sir Gilbert Elliot
     Agamemnon, at Sea, 4th December 112
To his Excellency Francis Drake, Esq. . Leghorn, 8th December 114

1795, *continued.*

PAGE

To Mr. Thomas Pollard . . . . . . Leghorn, 10th December 115
To the Rev. Dixon Hoste . Agamemnon, Leghorn, 12th December 115
To his Excellency Francis Drake . . . Leghorn, 16th December 117
To Mrs. Nelson . . . . 18th December 119
To Admiral Sir John Jervis, K.B., Commander-in-Chief in the Me-
    diterranean . . . . . . Leghorn Roads, 21st December 120
To the Reverend Mr. Nelson, Hilborough
        Agamemnon, Leghorn, 26th December 121

1796.

To Mrs. Nelson . . . . . Agamemnon, Leghorn, 6th January 123
To Mrs. Nelson . . . Agamemnon, St. Fiorenzo, 20th January 124
To Admiral Sir John Jervis, K.B. . . . . 23rd January 125
To Mrs. Nelson . . . . Gulf of Genoa, 27th January 126
To Mrs. Nelson . . . . Leghorn, 12th February 127
To Thomas Pollard, Esq. . . . . . . Leghorn, 17th February 128
To the Hon. John Trevor, Minister at Turin. About the 2nd March 128
To H. R. H. the Duke of Clarence . . . Genoa Mole, 3rd March 129
To William Locker, Esq. . . Agamemnon, Genoa Mole, 4th March 130
To the Rev. Mr. Nelson, Hilborough . . Genoa Mole, 4th March 132
To the Hon. John Trevor . Agamemnon, Genoa Mole, 4th March 133
To Admiral Sir John Jervis, K.B. . . . . Leghorn, 10th March 134
To the Right Hon. Sir Gilbert Elliot, Bart. Leghorn, 10th March 134
To the Right Hon. Sir William Hamilton, K.B., Minister at Naples
        Agamemnon, Leghorn, 11th March 134
To Francis Drake, Esq., Minister at Genoa . . . . 15th March 136
To Admiral Sir John Jervis, K.B. . . . . At Sea, 16th March 137
To Admiral Sir John Jervis, K.B. . . . . 16th March 137
    (In continuation) . . Off the Hieres Islands, 18th March 139
To his Excellency Francis Drake, Esq. . . . . . 25th March 140
To Mrs. Nelson . . . . 25th March 140
To Admiral Sir John Jervis, K.B. . . Agamemnon, 28th March 141
To his Excellency Francis Drake, Esq. . . . Genoa, 6th April 142
To Admiral Sir John Jervis, K.B. . . . . Off Genoa, 7th April 143
To Admiral Sir John Jervis, K.B.
        Agamemnon, Gulf of Genoa, 8th April 143
To Admiral Sir John Jervis, K.B. . . . . . Genoa, 9th April 148
To General Beaulieu, Commander-in-Chief of the Austrian Army
        About 9th April 149
To his Excellency Francis Drake, Esq. . . . . . . 11th April 150
To Admiral Sir John Jervis, K.B. . . . . 13th April 151
To Admiral Sir John Jervis, K.B. . . . . 15th April 152
To Captain Collingwood . . . . Genoa, 16th April 154
To Admiral Sir John Jervis, K.B. . . . Genoa Mole, 18th April 155

1796, *continued.*

PAGE

To H. R. H. the Duke of Clarence
Agamemnon, off Genoa, 18th April 156
To Francis Drake, Esq. . Agamemnon, Genoa Road, 19th April 157
To Francis Drake, Esq. . Agamemnon, off Vado Bay, 22nd April 159
To the Hon. John Trevor . . . . 22nd April 160
To Mrs. Nelson . . . . Gulf of Genoa, 24th April 161
To Admiral Sir John Jervis, K.B. . . . Off Loano, 25th April 161
To Admiral Sir John Jervis, K.B. . . . . 26th April 162
To Captain Collingwood . . . . 1st May 163
To Admiral Sir John Jervis, K.B. . . . . Genoa Mole, 1st May 164
To his Excellency Francis Drake, Esq. . . . . . . No date 166
To Admiral Sir John Jervis, K.B. . . . Off Cape Noli, 4th May 167
To Admiral Sir John Jervis, K.B. . . . . 8th May 167
Memorandum delivered to Mr. Brame, British Consul at Genoa
About 15th May 170
To the Right Hon. Sir Gilbert Elliot, Bart.
Agamemnon, at Sea, 16th May 171
To Admiral Sir John Jervis, K.B. . . . Leghorn Roads, 18th May 172
To Mrs. Nelson . . . . Leghorn, 20th May 173
To Admiral Sir John Jervis, K.B. . . . . 23rd May 174
To Admiral Sir John Jervis, K.B. . . . . 30th May 175
To Admiral Sir John Jervis, K.B.
Agamemnon, off Oneglia, 31st May 176
A List of Prizes taken between the 1st of June, 1794, and the 1st of
June, 1796 178
To Admiral Sir John Jervis, K.B. . . . . Off Nice, 2nd June 179
To Admiral Sir John Jervis, K.B. . . . . 3rd June 180
To Thomas Pollard, Esq. . . . . . . St. Fiorenzo, 4th June 181
To Admiral Sir John Jervis, K.B. . . . . Fiorenzo, 4th June 181
To Admiral Sir John Jervis, K.B. . . . . 5th June 182
To the Right Hon. Sir Gilbert Elliot, ... 9th June 183
To the Right Hon. Sir Gilbert Elliot
Agamemnon, San Fiorenzo, 10th June 183
To the Right Hon. Sir Gilbert Elliot . . . Captain, 12th June 184
To Mrs. Nelson . . . . Captain at Sea, 13th June 184
To William Locker, Esq. . . . . . Captain at Sea, 20th June 185
To the Rev. Mr. Nelson, Hilborough . Captain at Sea, 20th June 186
To the French Minister at Genoa . . . Genoa Mole, 22nd June 188
To Admiral Sir John Jervis, K.B. . . Genoa Mole, 23rd June 189
To Admiral Sir John Jervis, K.B. . Captain at Sea, 24th June 189
To Admiral Sir John Jervis, K.B. . . . . 25th June 193
To (apparently) Francis Drake, Esq. . . . About 25th June 194
To Admiral Sir John Jervis, K.B. . Leghorn Roads, 28th June 194
To Sir Gilbert Elliot . . . . Captain, San Fiorenzo, 1st July 195
Memoranda sent in the preceding Letter 196

b

1796, *continued.*

PAGE

To Sir Gilbert Elliot . . . . Captain, San Fiorenzo, 2nd July   198

To Sir Gilbert Elliot . . Captain, San Fiorenzo, 2nd July, A.M.   199

To Admiral Sir John Jervis, K.B. Captain, San Fiorenzo, 3rd July   200

To David Heatly, Esq. . . . Captain, San Fiorenzo, 4th July   202

To Sir Gilbert Elliot . . . . Captain, San Fiorenzo, 5th July   203

To Sir Gilbert Elliot . . . . Captain, San Fiorenzo, 5th July   204

To Admiral Sir John Jervis, K.B. . . . . 5th July   205

To Joseph Brame, Esq. . . . . . . Captain at Sea, 6th July   205

To the Consuls of the different Nations at Leghorn

Captain, off Leghorn, 7th July   206

To Sir Gilbert Elliot . . . Captain, off Porto Ferrajo, 9th July   206

To Admiral Sir John Jervis, K.B., Captain, Porto Ferrajo, 9th July   207

To Admiral Sir John Jervis, K.B., Captain, Porto Ferrajo, 10th July   208

To Sir Gilbert Elliot . . . . Captain, Porto Ferrajo, 10th July   210

To his Excellency, the Hon. William F. Wyndham

Captain, Porto Ferrajo, 11th July   210

To Admiral Sir John Jervis, K.B. Captain, off Leghorn, 15th July   211

To Sir Gilbert Elliot . . . . Captain, off Leghorn, 15th July   213

To the Danish Consul at Leghorn

Captain, Leghorn Roads, 17th July   214

To Sir Gilbert Elliot . . . Captain, Leghorn Roads, 18th July   215

To Admiral Sir John Jervis, K.B. . Leghorn Roads, 18th July   216

Memorandum . . . . About the 20th July   217

To H. R. H. the Duke of Clarence

Captain, Leghorn Roads, 20th July   218

To the Right Hon. Sir Gilbert Elliot . Captain at Sea, 26th July   219

To Admiral Sir John Jervis, K.B. . . . . 27th July   222

To the Right Hon. Sir Gilbert Elliot, Bart.

Captain, Leghorn Roads, 28th July   222

Memorandum . . . . . Captain, Leghorn Roads, 31st July   223

To Captain Collingwood . . Captain, Leghorn Roads, 1st August   223

To Admiral Sir John Jervis, K.B. . . . . . . 1st August   225

In continuation . . . . 2nd August   225

In continuation . . . . 3rd August   226

To Sir Gilbert Elliot . . . Captain, Leghorn Roads, 1st August   227

List of Commodore Nelson's Squadron, and how disposed of

1st August   228

To William Locker, Esq. Captain, Leghorn Roads, 2nd August   229

To Mrs. Nelson . . . . 2nd Augnst   230

To the Marquis de Silva, Naples . . . . 3rd August   231

To Sir Gilbert Elliot . . . Captain, Leghorn Roads, 3rd August   232

To the Right Hon. Sir Gilbert Elliot . Leghorn Roads, 4th August   233

To Sir Gilbert Elliot . . . Captain, Leghorn Roads, 5th August   233

To Sir Gilbert Elliot . . . Captain, Leghorn Roads, 5th August   233

To Admiral Sir John Jervis, K.B. . . Leghorn Roads, 5th August   235

1796, *continued.*

PAGE

To . . . . Captain, Leghorn Roads, 5th August 237
To Sir Gilbert Elliot . . . Captain, Leghorn Roads, 10th August 238
To Sir Gilbert Elliot . . . Captain, Leghorn Roads, 11th August 239
To Admiral Sir John Jervis, K.B. . . . . 15th August 240
 Apparently in continuation . . . . Bastia, 17th August 241
To the Rev. Mr. Nelson, Hilborough
   Captain, between Bastia and Leghorn, 18th August 241
To the Right Hon. Sir Gilbert Elliot . Captain, at Sea, 18th August 243
To Sir Gilbert Elliot . . . . Captain, off Bastia, 18th August 244
To the Rev. Mr. Nelson, Bath . . . . . Captain, 19th August 244
To His Royal Highness the Duke of Clarence . . . 19th August 245
To the Swedish Consul at Leghorn . . . . . . 20th August 247
To Sir Gilbert Elliot . . Captain, Leghorn Roads, 20th August 248
To Admiral Sir John Jervis, K.B.   Leghorn Roads, 20th August 248
 Apparently in continuation . . . . 22nd August 249
To Signor Jaques de Lavelette, Governor of Leghorn
      Leghorn Roads, 22nd August 250
To Sir Gilbert Elliot . . Captain, Leghorn Roads, 22nd August 251
To Mrs. Nelson . . . . Leghorn Roads, 23rd August 252
To Sir Gilbert Elliot . . Captain, Leghorn Roads, 23rd August 253
To Sir Gilbert Elliot . . Captain, Leghorn Roads, 25th August 253
To Sir Gilbert Elliot . . Captain, off the Gorgona, 27th August 255
To Sir Gilbert Elliot . . Captain, Leghorn Roads, 3rd September 258
To Admiral Sir John Jervis, K.B.   Leghorn Roads, 3rd September 258
Note addressed to the Genoese Government
    Captain, Mole of Genoa, 4th September 259
Note addressed to the Genoese Government,   About September 260
To his Excellency Francis Drake, Esq. . . . . 9th September 261
To the Genoese Secretary of State
   Captain, Genoa Mole, 10th September 261
To Mrs. Nelson . . . . 10th September 262
To Admiral Sir John Jervis, K.B.
   Captain, off Genoa, 11th September 262
To Admiral Sir John Jervis, K.B. ·
   Captain, off Genoa, 11th September 264
To Joseph Brame, Esq., British Consul at Genoa, 11th September 265
Facts respecting his conduct towards the Genoese Government
     11th September 266
To his Excellency Francis Drake, Esq.
   Captain at Sea, 12th September 266
To Admiral Sir John Jervis, K.B. . . . . . 14th September 269
 In continuation . . . . 15th September 270
To . . . . (About 17th September) 270
To Admiral Sir John Jervis, K.B.
   Captain, Harbour of Capraja, 19th September 270

1796, *continued.*

PAGE

To the Governor of the Fortress and Island of Capraja 272
To the Governor of the Fortress and Island of Capraja
      Camp, before the Town of Capraja, 18th September 273
Capitulation of the Fort and Island of Capraja 273
To the Right Honourable Sir Gilbert Elliot . . 19th September 274
To the Captain of a Spanish Frigate, Captain, at Sea, 20th September 276
Reply of the Captain of the Spanish Frigate
      La Fregate Espagnole, La Vengeance, la 20 7bre 276
To Don Juan de Sannava, Captain of the Spanish Frigate La
    Vengeance . . . . . . Captain, at Sea, 20th September 277
Don Juan de Sannava to Commodore Nelson
      La Vengeance, la 20 7bre 277
To Don Juan de Sannava . . . Captain, at Sea, 20th September 278
Don Juan de Sannava to Commodore Nelson
      La Vengeance, la 20 7bre 279
To Admiral Sir John Jervis, K.B., Captain, at Sea, 21st September 279
To Sir Gilbert Elliot . Captain, off Porto Ferrajo, 24th September 280
To Sir Gilbert Elliot . . . . Leghorn Roads, 25th September 282
To the Right Honourable Sir Gilbert Elliot . . 26th September 282
To Admiral Sir John Jervis, K.B., Diadem, at Sea, 28th September 283
To Admiral Sir John Jervis, K.B. . . Bastia, 30th September 285
Memoranda respecting the Evacuation of Corsica 287
To Admiral Sir John Jervis, K.B. . . . . . . 15th October 288
In Continuation . . . . 17th October 289
To Messrs. Heath and Co., Genoa . . . . . Bastia, 17th October 290
To Mrs. Nelson . . . . About 17th October 290
To Admiral Sir John Jervis, K.B. . . . . . . 19th October 291
To Admiral Sir John Jervis, K.B., Captain, Port Ferrajo, 21st October 292
To H. R. H. the Duke of Clarence . . . Captain, 25th October 293
To the Genoese Government . . . About October or November 294
To Joseph Brame, Esq. . . . . Captain, at Sea, 4th November 296
To William Locker, Esq. . . . Captain, at Sea, 5th November 298
To Mrs. Nelson . . . . 7th November 300
To H. R. H. the Duke of Clarence, Captain, at Sea, 11th November 300
To Captain Collingwood . . . . 20th November 304
To the Reverend Dixon Hoste . . Captain, at Sea, 25th November 304
To William Suckling, Esq.
      Captain, off Gibraltar Bay, 29th November 306
To Captain Collingwood . . . . 1st December 307
To Admiral Sir John Jervis, K.B., Gibraltar Bay, 3rd December 308
To Mrs. Nelson . . . . About 10th December 311
To Admiral Sir John Jervis, K.B. . . . . . 20th December 312
To Admiral Sir John Jervis, K.B. . . . . . 20th December 314
To his Excellency Don Miguel Gaston, Captain General of the
    Department of Carthagena, La Minerve, at Sea, 24th December 315

1796, *continued.*

PAGE

To Admiral Don Juan Morino . Apparently about 24th December 316
To Admiral Sir John Jervis, K.B. . . . . . . 24th December 317
To Admiral Sir John Jervis, K.B. . . . . . . 24th December 317
To the Right Honourable Sir Gilbert Elliot
        La Minerve, East side of Sardinia, 24th December 318
To . . . . Apparently 24th December 319
To Sir Gilbert Elliot . . . . . . La Minerve, 27th December 320
To Admiral Sir J. Jervis, K.B. . . . . . . 29th December 321
To the Captain General of Carthagena
        La Minerve, Port Ferrajo, 29th December 321
To Admiral Sir John Jervis, K.B.
        La Minerve, Port Ferrajo, 29th December 321
To Lieutenant-General de Burgh . . . . . . 29th December 322
To Lieutenant-General de Burgh . . La Minerve, 30th December 323

1797.

Memoranda 324
To the Reverend Edmund Nelson . . . La Minerve, 1st January 325
To Mrs. Nelson . . . . Porto Ferrajo, 13th January 325
To the Reverend Mr. Nelson, Hilborough
        La Minerve, Port Ferrajo, 13th January 326
To Mrs. Pollard, Naples . . . . . La Minerve, 20th January 327
To Lieutenant-General de Burgh
        La Minerve, Porto Ferrajo, about 20th January 328
To Admiral Sir John Jervis, K.B.
        La Minerve, Porto Ferrajo, 25th January 329
To Mrs. Nelson . . . . 27th January 330
To Edward Harman, Esq., Private Secretary to Sir Gilbert Elliot
        La Minerve, 11th February 330
A Few Remarks relative to myself, in the Captain, in which my
   Pendant was flying on the most glorious Valentine's Day, 1797 340
A Few Remarks relative to myself, in the Captain, in which my
   Pendant was flying on the most glorious Valentine's Day, 1797 344
To Captain Collingwood, H. M. Ship Excellent
        Irresistible, 15th February 347
To Sir Gilbert Elliot, Bart. . . . . Irresistible, 15th February 349
To Sir Gilbert Elliot . . . . . . Irresistible, 16th February 350
To the Rev. Mr. Nelson . Irresistible, Lagos Bay, 17th February 351
To the Rev. Dixon Hoste, Irresistible, Lagos Bay, 17th February 352
To William Locker, Esq. . Irresistible, Lagos Bay, 21st February 353
To William Suckling, Esq., Irresistible, off Lagos Bay, 23rd February 355
To Wadham Windham, Esq., M.P. for Norwich
        Irresistible, off Lisbon, 26th February 356
To the Mayor of Norwich . Irresistible, off Lisbon, 26th February 357

CONTENTS.

1797, *continued.*

PAGE

To Mrs. Nelson . . . . . . Irresistible, Lisbon, 28th February 358
To Sir James Saumarez, Captain of H. M. Ship Orion
                        Irresistible, Lisbon, 2nd March 360
Memoranda respecting Prize Money . . Apparently about March 360
To Vice-Admiral the Honourable William Waldegrave, 5th March 361
To Admiral Sir John Jervis, K. B. . . . . . About 12th March 362
To John M'Arthur, Esq., Irresistible, off Lagos Bay, 16th March 363
To H. R. H. the Duke of Clarence, Off Cape St. Vincent, 22nd March 364
Services performed this War by Captain Nelson
                        Apparently written in March 365
To Earl Spencer, First Lord of the Admiralty
                   Captain, off Cape St. Mary's, 2nd April 368
To H. R. H. the Duke of Clarence . . . . 2nd April 369
To Mrs. Nelson . . . . April 369
To the Rev. Mr. Nelson, Hilborough
                 Captain, off Cape St. Vincent's, 6th April 369
To John M'Arthur, Esq. . . . Captain, off Cadiz, 10th April 371
To John M'Arthur, Esq. . . . Captain, off Cadiz, 10th April 372
To John M'Arthur, Esq. 372
To Admiral Sir John Jervis, K. B. . . . . 11th April 376
To the American and Danish Consuls at Cadiz
                 Captain, off Cadiz, 11th April 377
To the Captains under the Orders of Rear-Admiral Nelson
                 Off Cadiz, 11th April 378
To Admiral Sir John Jervis, K.B. . . : . . . . . 12th April 378
To Sir James Saumarez, Commander of his Majesty's Ship Orion
                 Captain, off Cadiz, 12th April 381
To Admiral Sir John Jervis, K.B. . . . . 21st April 381
To H. R. H. the Duke of Clarence Off Cape de Gatte, 30th April 383
To Admiral Sir John Jervis, K.B., Captain, off Cape Pallas, 1st May 384
To James Simpson, Esq., American Consul at Malaga
                 Gibraltar, 20th May 385
To Captain Ralph Willett Miller . . . Ville de Paris, 24th May 386
To H. R. H. the Duke of Clarence . . . Off Cadiz, 26th May 386
To Mrs. Nelson . . . . 27th May 388
To Admiral Don Josef de Mazaredo, Cadiz . Theseus, 30th May 388
To Admiral Sir John Jervis, K.B. . . . . Theseus, 31st May 389
Case for the Opinion of Counsel, Apparently written in May or June 390
To John M'Arthur, Esq. . . . . Theseus, 1st June 391
To Sir James Saumarez, Captain of His Majesty's Ship Orion
                 Theseus, 1st June 391
To Admiral Sir John Jervis, K.B. . . . . . About 6th June 392
To Admiral Sir John Jervis, K.B. . . . . 7th June 392
To Vice-Admiral Moreno, of the Spanish Navy, Theseus, 8th June 393

1797, *continued.*

PAGE

To Admiral Sir John Jervis, K.B. . . . .   Theseus, 9th June   393
To Sir James Saumarez . . . . 9th June   395
To Admiral Sir John Jervis, K.B. . . . .   10th June   395
To Admiral Sir John Jervis, K.B. . H. M. S. Theseus, 12th June   396
To Admiral Sir John Jervis, K.B. . . . .   13th June   396
To Admiral Sir John Jervis, K.B. . H. M. S. Theseus, 13th June   397
To Mrs. Nelson . . . .   15th June   397
To Admiral Sir John Jervis, K.B. . . . .   Theseus, 21st June   398
To Admiral Sir John Jervis, K.B. . . . .   29th June   398
To Mrs. Nelson . . . .   29th June   399
To George Naylor, Esq., York Herald, and Genealogist of the Order
    of the Bath . . . .   Theseus, off Cadiz, 29th June   400
To the Rev. Dixon Hoste . . . .   Theseus, 30th June   401
To Admiral Don Josef de Mazaredo . . . . . .   30th June   402
To Admiral Sir John Jervis, K.B. . . . .   3rd July   403
To Admiral Sir John Jervis, K.B. . . . . .   Theseus, 4th July   403
To Admiral Sir John Jervis, K.B. . . . .   5th July   406
To Admiral Sir John Jervis, K.B. . . H. M. S. Theseus, 7th July   407
To Admiral Sir John Jervis, K.B. . . . . .   Theseus, 9th July   408
To Sir Robert Calder, Knight, First Captain to Admiral the Earl
    of St. Vincent, K.B. . . . .   Theseus, 9th July   409
To Admiral Sir John Jervis, K.B. . . . .   9th July   410
To Admiral Sir John Jervis, K.B. . . . . .   Theseus, 10th July   410
To Sir James Saumarez . . . .   Theseus, 10th July   411
To Captain John Nicholson Inglefield . . . . 11th July   411
To Mrs. Nelson . . . .   12th to 14th July   412
Memoranda respecting the attack on Teneriffe   413
Memorandum respecting the attack on Teneriffe   414
Questions which appear to have been submitted to one or more of the
    Captains of the Squadron destined to attack Teneriffe   415
Regulations respecting the attack on Santa Cruz   415
To Thomas Troubridge, Esq., Captain of H. M. Ship Culloden, and
    Commander of the Forces ordered to be landed for taking Santa
    Cruz . . . .   Theseus, at Sea, 20th July   416
Memorandum relative to Teneriffe . . . . . Theseus, 20th July   417
To Lieutenant Baynes, Royal Artillery, . . . Theseus, 20th July   418
To Captain Thomas Oldfield, Senior Captain of the Marines ordered
    to disembark . . . . Theseus, 20th July   418
To the Governor or Commanding Officer of Santa Cruz
                                    Theseus, 20th July   419
To Admiral Sir John Jervis, K.B.
                        Theseus, off Santa Cruz, 24th July   421
To his Excellency Don Antonio Gutierrez, Commandant-General of   421
    the Canary Islands . . .   H. M. Ship Theseus, 26th July   421

1797, *continued.*

PAGE

To Admiral Sir John Jervis, K.B., Theseus, off Santa Cruz, 27th July 423

List of Killed, Wounded, Drowned, and Missing, in Storming Santa Cruz, in Teneriffe, on the night of the 24th July, 1797 . . . 424

A Detail of the Proceedings of the Expedition against Santa Cruz, in Teneriffe . . . 425

Journal of Proceedings of H.M. Ship Theseus . 14th to 27th July 429

To Admiral Sir John Jervis, K.B. . . . . . Theseus, 27th July 434

To Admiral Sir John Jervis . . . . . Theseus, 16th August 435

To Lady Nelson . . . . . Theseus, at Sea, 3rd to 16th August 436

To Rear-Admiral William Parker . . . . 19th August 438

To Admiral Sir John Jervis, K.B.
Between the 20th and 30th August 438

To William Suckling, Esq. . . Seahorse, off Scilly, 30th August 438

To Evan Nepean, Esq. . . . . Seahorse, Spithead, 1st September 439

To John Palmer, Esq. . . . . Bath, 4th September 440

To the Rev. Mr. Nelson, Hilborough . . . Bath, 6th September 440

To H. R. H. the Duke of Clarence . . . . 7th September 441

To —— Manley, Esq. . . . . . . Bath, 8th September 442

To the Rev. Dixon Hoste . . . . Bath, September 442

To Sir Andrew Snape Hamond, Bart. . . . Bath, 8th September 443

To Admiral the Earl of St. Vincent, K.B., London, 18th September 444

To Major Suckling . . . . Bond Street, about 24th September 446

Memorial to the King . . . . About October 447

To Admiral the Earl of St. Vincent, K.B. . . London, 6th October 448

To Evan Nepean, Esq., Admiralty . . . London, 9th October 448

To Lieutenant-Governor Locker . . . . . . 11th October 449

To the Lord Chancellor . . . . Bond Street, 12th October 449

To John Halkett, Esq., Secretary to the Lord Chancellor
Bond Street, 23rd October 450

To the Rev. Mr. Weatherhead, Sedgeford, Norfolk
Bond Street, 31st October 451

To Captain Knight, H. M. Ship Montagu . About 1st November 451

To the Rev. Henry Crowe, Smallburgh, Norwich
Bond Street, 16th November 452

To the Chamberlain of the City of London . . . 22nd November 452

To Captain Edward Berry, R.N. . . . . . . 28th November 453

To Evan Nepean, Esq., Admiralty . . London, 28th November 454

To the Lord Chancellor . . . . Bond Street, 2nd December 455

Thanksgiving in St. George's Church, Hanover Square, 8th December 455

To Captain Edward Berry, R.N. . . . . . . 8th December 456

To Captain Ralph Willett Miller . . . . . 11th December 456

To the Rev. Mr. Morris . . . . 11th December 457

To Captain Albemarle Bertie . . . Bond Street, 11th December 458

To William Marsden, Esq., Secretary to the Admiralty
13th December 458

1797, *continued.*

PAGE

Proposed agreement of the Admirals serving under the Earl of St. Vincent, to institute Legal Proceedings for the recovery of Prize and Freight Money . . . October and 13th December 459
To Evan Nepean, Esq., Admiralty . . . . . . 14th December 460
To Earl Spencer, First Lord of the Admiralty, About 18th December 461

APPENDIX.

Copy of the Log of the Agamemnon on the 13th and 14th March 1795 463
Memoir of Captain Ralph Willett Miller 465
Remarks on the Order of the Bath 467
Rear Admiral Sir William Parker's Letter and Statement respecting the Battle of St. Vincent 470

LETTERS INSERTED IN THE SECOND EDITION OF THE FIRST VOLUME, WHICH DO NOT OCCUR IN THE FIRST EDITION, VIZ. :— .

Advertisement to the Second Edition of the First Volume 475

1784.

To William Suckling, Esq. . . . . 14th January 481

1793.

To Commodore Linzee . . . . 24th October 481

1794.

To Admiral Lord Hood . . . . . . Porto Novo, 8th February 480
To Admiral Lord Hood . . . . . Agamemnon, 22nd February 481
To Admiral Lord Hood . . . . Agamemnon, 7th June 483
To Admiral Lord Hood . . Agamemnon, near Calvi, 19th June 484
To Admiral Lord Hood . . . . Camp, 21st June 485
To Admiral Lord Hood . . . . Camp, 23rd June 487
To the Hon. Lieutenant-General Stuart . . . . . 23rd June 488
To Admiral Lord Hood . . . . Camp, 25th June 489
To Admiral Lord Hood . . . . Camp, 30th June 490
To Admiral Lord Hood . . . . Battery, 31st July 491
To Admiral Lord Hood . . . . Camp, 2nd August 492
To Admiral Lord Hood, Agamemnon, Genoa Mole, 23rd September 493
To John M'Arthur, Esq. Agamemnon, Leghorn, 28th November 494

ANALYSIS

LIFE OF NELSON,

FROM 1795 TO 1797.

YEAR.	MONTH.	FACTS.
1795.		In command of the *Agamemnon*.
—	January 17th to February 7th	With the Fleet under Admiral Hotham at St. Fiorenzo in Corsica.
—	— —	.........Cruising with the Fleet.
—	February 24th to March 6th	...With the Fleet at Leghorn
—	March 6th	...........Sailed in Pursuit of the French Fleet.
—	— 13th — 14th	Present in Admiral Hotham's Action with the French Fleet, and distinguished himself on the 13th in engaging the Ça Ira.
—	— 21st to — 25th	...At Port Especia.
—	— 30th to April 16th	...At St. Fiorenzo.
—	— — 4th	...........Ordered to Hoist a DISTINGUISHING PENDANT.
—	— — 25th	...........Off Cape Corse.
—	— — 28th to May 5th	...At Leghorn.
—	— 22nd to June 22nd	...With the Fleet off Minorca.
—	— — 1st	...............Appointed Colonel of Marines.

YEAR.	MONTH.	FACTS.

1795, *continued* .... In command of the *Agamemnon*, wearing a Distinguishing Pendant.

— July 1st ....At Fiorenzo.

— — 8th...............Off Cape Corse.

— — 13th ....Present in Admiral Hotham's second Action with the French Fleet.

— — 15th ....Sent with a small Squadron to co-operate with the Austrian General, De Vins, against the Enemy, on the Coast of Genoa.

— — 18th ....At Genoa.

— — 22nd ⎱
— — 24th ⎰ ...Off Vado Bay

— — 27th ....At Leghorn.

— — 29th ....In the Gulf of Genoa.

— August 2nd ⎱
    to ⎰ ...In Vado Bay.
— — 23rd

— — 11th ....Appointed a COMMODORE, with a Captain under him.

— — 26th ....Captured a French Corvette, some Gun-boats, and their Convoy at Alassio.

— — 29th ....Sent his Boats to cut out a Ship at Oneglia; meeting three Turkish vessels on their way they boarded them, but were defeated with great loss.

— — 30th ....In Vado Bay.

— September 1st ⎱
    to ⎰ ...In Vado Bay or its vicinity.
— — 15th

— — 17th ......At Genoa.

— — 24th ⎱
    to ⎰ ...At Leghorn.
— — 29th

— October 5th ....In Vado Bay.

— — 27th ....Off Marseilles.

— November 6th ⎱
    to ⎰ ...In Vado Bay.
— — 12th

— — 18th ⎱
    to ⎰ ...At Genoa.
— — 27th

— December 8th ⎱
    to ⎰ ...At Leghorn.
1796. January 6th

— — 20th.........At St. Fiorenzo.

— — 27th.........In the Gulf of Genoa.

— February 12th.........At Leghorn

YEAR. MONTH. FACTS.

1796, *continued* .... In command of the *Agamemnon*, wearing a
Broad Pendant.

— February 17th ......Off the Hieres Islands.

— March 2nd ⎫
⁣⁣ to ⎬...At Genoa.
— — 4th ⎭

— — 10th ⎫...At Leghorn.
— — 11th ⎭

— — 16th.............At Sea.

— — 18th.............Off the Hieres Islands.

— April 6th ⎫
⁣⁣ to ⎬...Off Genoa.
— — 24th ⎭

— — 25th ....Attacked and brought out some Vessels at
Loano.

— May 1st ....At Genoa.

— — 4th ....Off Cape Noli.

— — 8th ....Took two Vessels from under the batteries
of Pietra.

— — 18th ....At Leghorn.

— — 31st ....Attacked and Captured a Ketch, Gun-boats,
and Transports, at Torre dell' Arena.

— June 2nd...............Off Nice.

— — 4th ⎫
⁣⁣ to ⎬...St. Fiorenzo.
— — 10th ⎭

— — 11th ....Shifted his Broad Pendant from the *Agamemnon* to the *Captain*.

— — 13th ....At Sea.

— — 22nd ⎫...At Genoa.
— — 23rd ⎭

— — 24th ....At Sea.

— — 28th ....At Leghorn, which Port he was employed in
blockading.

— July 1st ⎫
⁣⁣ to ⎬...At St. Fiorenzo.
— — 5th ⎭

— — 6th ....At Sea.

— — 10th ....Took Porto Ferrajo in Elba.

— — 10th ⎫
⁣⁣ to ⎬...At Porto Ferrajo.
— — 11th ⎭

— — 15th ⎫
⁣⁣ to ⎬...Off Leghorn.
— — 20th ⎭

— — 21st ....Proceeded to Genoa.

YEAR.   MONTH.   FACTS.

1796, *continued* .... In command of the *Captain*, wearing a Broad Pendant.

— July 28th
     to   } ...At Leghorn.
— August 15th

— — 17th ....At Bastia.

— — 20th
     to   } ......At Leghorn.
— — 27th

— September 3rd ......In Leghorn Roads.

— — 10th ......At Genoa.

— — 11th ......Fired at by the batteries of Genoa.

— — 14th ......At Bastia.

— — 18th ......Took the Island of Capraja.

— — 20th ......On his Passage to Leghorn, met a Spanish Frigate; but did not detain her, being doubtful whether War was declared with Spain.

— — 24th ......Off Porto Ferrajo.

— — 25th ......In Leghorn Roads.

— — 30th
     to   } At or near Bastia, being employed in the Evacuation of Corsica.
— October 19th

— — 21st ....At Porto Ferrajo.

— November 1st .... At Genoa, to demand satisfaction for various aggressions.

— — 2nd ......Sailed with the Fleet from Mortella Bay, in Corsica, for Gibraltar.

— — 4th ....At Sea.

— — 11th ......Off Minorca.

— December 1st
     to   } At Gibraltar, and shifted his Broad Pendant from the *Captain* to *La Minerve* Frigate.
— — 10th

— — 15th ......Sailed in *La Minerve*, with the *Blanche*, for Porto Ferrajo, to bring away the English Troops and Stores, but the Troops did not embark.

— — 19th ......Captured *La Sabina*, Spanish Frigate, off Carthagena.

— — 20th ......Fought the *Santa Matilda*, Spanish Frigate.

— — 23rd ......Off the South End of Sardinia, captured a French Privateer.

— — 26th
     to   } ...At Porto Ferrajo.
1797. January 29th

— February 9th ....Arrived at Gibraltar.

— — 11th ......Sailed from Gibraltar.

YEAR.   MONTH.   FACTS.

1797, *continued* .... In command of the *Captain*, wearing a Broad Pendant.

— February 13th ......Joined Admiral Sir John Jervis's Fleet off Cape St. Vincent, and Rehoisted his Broad Pendant in the *Captain*.

—   —   14th ......BATTLE OF CAPE ST. VINCENT, after which he shifted his Broad Pendant to the *Irresistible*.

—   —   15th   ⎫
            to   ⎬...With the Fleet in Lagos Bay.
—   —   23rd   ⎭

—   —   20th ......Appointed a REAR-ADMIRAL OF THE BLUE.

—   —   28th ......Anchored with the Fleet in the Tagus.

— March 2nd ....Sent with a small Squadron to cruise off Cadiz, to intercept the Viceroy of Mexico.

—   —   16th............Off Lagos Bay.

—   —   17th............Appointed a KNIGHT OF THE BATH.

—   —   22nd   ⎫
            to   ⎬...Off Cadiz.
— April 11th   ⎭

—   —   12th ....Proceeded to Porto Ferrajo to bring down the Troops left there.

—   —   21st ....Off the South End of Corsica, fell in with the Convoy having the Troops from Porto Ferrajo on board.

—   —   30th ....Off Cape de Gatte.

— May 1st ....Off Cape Pallas.

—   —   20th ....At Gibraltar.

—   —   24th ....Rejoined the Admiral, Sir John Jervis, off Cadiz. Hoisted his Flag in the *Theseus*, and commanded the Inshore Squadron off Cadiz.

— July 3rd ....Bombarded Cadiz, and was desperately engaged in his Barge with a Spanish Gunboat.

—   —   5th ....Again bombarded Cadiz.

—   —   15th ....Proceeded with a Squadron to attack Santa Cruz, in Teneriffe.

—   —   24th ....Attacked Santa Cruz ; severely wounded, and suffered amputation of his right arm. The attack failed.

— August 16th ....Rejoined Admiral the Earl of St. Vincent off Cadiz.

—   —   20th ....Struck his Flag in the *Theseus* ; hoisted it in the *Seahorse*, and proceeded to England.

— September 1st.........Arrived at Spithead; struck his Flag, and proceeded to Bath.

YEAR.	MONTH.	FACTS.

1797, *continued* ....

— September 1st
      to   } ...At Bath.
   About 15th

— — 18th.........In London.

— — 27th.........Invested with the Ensigns of the Order of the Bath.

— December 17th ......Went to Chatham to inspect the *Vanguard*, 74, the Ship appointed to receive his Flag.

— — 19th ......Attended the Ceremony of the King's returning thanks at St. Paul's for the Naval Victories.

ILLUSTRATIONS TO VOL. II.

Fac-simile of Nelson's Autograph, in August 1797, soon after he lost his arm ... ... To face the Title

Fac-simile of Nelson's Autograph, in July 1797, immediately before he lost his arm .. .. To face p. 419

Fac-simile of Sir Horatio and Lady Nelson's Autograph, in October 1797... ... ... To face p. 451

PUBLISHER'S NOTE
The three facsimile letters listed above appear in this edition following pages vii, 419 and 449.

LETTERS.

1795—ÆT. 36.

TO MRS. NELSON.

[From Clarke and M'Arthur, vol. i. p. 198.]

Fiorenzo, 17th January, 1795.

We have had nothing but gales of wind, but in Agamemnon we mind them not: she is the finest Ship I ever
sailed in, and, were she a seventy-four, nothing should induce
me to leave her whilst the war lasted; for not an hour this
war will I, if possible, be out of active service; much as I
shall regret being so long parted from you, still we must
look beyond the present day, and two or three months may
make the difference of every comfort, or otherwise, in our income. I hope we have many happy years to live together;
and if we can bring £2000 round, I am determined to purchase some neat cottage, which we should never have occasion
to change. As for Josiah,[1] I have no doubt but he will be a
comfort to both of us: his understanding is excellent, and his
disposition really good: he is a seaman every inch of him.
The Fleet is on the eve of going to sea again, to cover our
reinforcements. Yours, &c.

HORATIO NELSON.

TO HIS ROYAL HIGHNESS THE DUKE OF CLARENCE.

[From Clarke and M'Arthur, vol. i. p. 198.]

Sir, Fiorenzo, 19th January, 1795.

Our last cruise from 21st December 1794, to January the
10th, when we arrived in this Port, was such a series of storms

---

[1] Josiah Nisbet, his step-son, a midshipman of the Agamemnon. Vide vol. i. p. 217.

and heavy seas, as I never before experienced: the Fleet were
twelve days under storm stay-sails. Our Ships, although short
of complement, are remarkably healthy, as are the Troops in this
Island. There is already a difference to be perceived in the
cultivation of the land since last year. Many hundred acres
of pasture are now covered with wheat; and as the Corsicans
will find a ready sale for their corn, wine, and oil, (the two last
articles the French suppressed as much as possible,) every
year will doubtless increase the growth. The Fleet goes to
sea on the 22nd or 23rd, thirteen Sail of the Line. The
French have fifteen in the outer road of Toulon, and fifty Sail
of large Transports ready at Marseilles; therefore it is certain
they have some Expedition just ready to take place, and I
have no doubt but Porto Especia is their object. We expect
soon to be joined by some Neapolitan Ships and Frigates:
I have no idea we shall get much good from them: they are
not seamen, and cannot keep the sea beyond a passage.

I beg your Royal Highness to believe, that I ever am your
most faithful servant,

HORATIO NELSON.

TO MRS. NELSON.

[From Clarke and M'Arthur, vol. i. p. 199.]

Fiorenzo, 31st January, 1795.

It is with inexpressible pleasure I have received within these
two days past your letters, with our father's of January the 1st.
I rejoice that my conduct gives you pleasure, and I trust I
shall never do anything which will bring a blush on your face,
or on that of any of my friends. It is very true that I have
ever served faithfully, and ever has it been my fate to be
neglected; but that shall not make me inattentive to my duty.
I have pride in doing my duty well, and a self-approbation,
which if it is not so lucrative, yet perhaps affords more pleasing
sensations. I trust the time will come when I may be rewarded,
though really I don't flatter myself it is near. Lord Hood
told me that my loss of an eye should be represented to the
King. Lord Chatham carried my papers to the King; but

now he is out,[2] all hopes will be done away. My eye is grown worse, and is in almost total darkness, and very painful at times; but never mind, I can see very well with the other.

I believe I shall inform Lord Hood, what I never told him yet, that after everything was fixed for the attack of Bastia, I had information given me of the enormous number of Troops we had to oppose us; but my own honour, Lord Hood's honour, and the honour of our Country, must have all been sacrificed, had I mentioned what I knew; therefore, you will believe, what must have been my feelings during the whole Siege, when I had often proposals made to me by men, now rewarded, to write to Lord Hood to raise the Siege. Remember me kindly to our friends at Bristol. I also beg to present my best compliments at Wolterton. Yours, &c.

HORATIO NELSON.

TO WILLIAM SUCKLING, ESQ.

[From " The Athenæum."]

Agamemnon, Fiorenzo, February 1st, 1795.

My dear Sir,

Your letter, without date, but which I guess to be written about Christmas, I received two days ago; and although I have not very frequently been favoured with a sight of your writing, except on the outside of letters, yet I am always sure of your continued regard for me, a circumstance which I ever hold dear, and which it will ever be my pride to deserve. I don't think, at present, Agamemnon has any chance of coming home: we are too inferior to the Enemy. Our Admiral[3] is careful of us, and will not suffer a Line-of-Battle Ship to get out of his sight. We sail the day after to-morrow, but I do not expect to do any good. I have taken advantage of your offer, and enclose a letter for Mrs. Nelson. With kindest

---

[2] Lord Chatham was succeeded as First Lord of the Admiralty, by Earl Spencer, in December 1794.

[3] Vice-Admiral, afterwards Lord Hotham.

remembrances to Mrs. Suckling, Miss Suckling, and family,
believe me ever

    Your much obliged and affectionate
                    HORATIO NELSON.

Best respects at Hampstead.

TO THOMAS POLLARD, ESQ., LEGHORN.

[Autograph, in the possession of John Luxford, Esq.]

Agamemnon, February 6th, 1795.

Dear Pollard,

We shall never get out of this d——d place :[4] I had rather
remain at sea for ever than return here, where nothing is to
be had for love or money. Lord Beauclerk[5] will allow a few
trifles to be received on board, for I have sent back the fowl-
coop by him. I have wrote you by Tartar, and all may have
sent letters ; God knows if they arrive. Reports are current
with everybody that we return to Leghorn after a short cruise.
I sincerely hope it. Believe me ever your much obliged,

                    HORATIO NELSON.

TO WILLIAM SUCKLING, ESQ.

[Autograph, in the possession of John Young, Esq.]

Agamemnon, St. Fiorenzo, February 7th, 1795.

My dear Sir,

This day twelvemonth saw the British troops land at this
place, for the purpose of turning the French out of the Island,
and the more I see of its produce, and convenient Ports for
our Fleets, the more I am satisfied of Lord Hood's great wisdom
in getting possession of it; for had his Lordship not come
forward with a *bold plan,* all our trade and political consequence would have been lost in Italy ; for, after the evacuation
of Toulon, to what place were we to look for shelter for our
Fleet, and the numerous attendants of Victuallers, Store-ships,
and Transports ? Genoa was inimical to us, and, by treaty,

---

[4] Porto Ferrajo in Elba.
[5] The present Admiral Lord Amelius Beauclerk, G.C.B., who was then Captain of
the Juno, 32.

only five Sail of the Line could enter their Ports at the same
time. If we look at Tuscany, she was little better than forced
to declare for us, and ever since wishing to get her Neutrality
again. Even the French Consul, though not officially received,
has not left Leghorn. All our trade, and of our Allies, to
Italy, must all pass close to Corsica: the Enemy would have
had the Ports of this Island full of Row-galleys; and, from the
great calms near the land, our Ships of War could not have
protected the trade—they can always be taken under your eye:
therefore, on this account only, every man of common sense
must see the necessity of possessing this Island. The Spanish
Ports and Neapolitan are so improper, and (except Minorca,
which is now only a fishing Town, with a few slips for
Ship-building, everything being destroyed,) the distance from
the scene of war, so distant that they could not have been
used, even would the Dons have made us welcome, which I
doubt.

The loss to the French has been great indeed: all the Ships
built at Toulon have their sides, beams, decks, and straight
timbers from this Island. The pine of this Island is of the
finest texture I ever saw; and the tar, pitch, and hemp,
although I believe the former not equal to Norway, yet were
very much used in the yard at Toulon. So much for the
benefit of it to us during the war; and, in peace, I see no
reason but it may be as beneficial to England as any other
part of the King's Dominions. Every article of this Island
was suppressed, as it interfered with the produce of the South
of France. The large woods of olives must produce great
quantities of fine oil, and the wines are much preferable to the
wines of Italy. Our Naval yards will be supplied with excellent wood; and, I dare say, the expense of keeping the Island
will be very trifling, and its importance to us very great.
Other Powers will certainly envy us; and the inhabitants will
grow rich, and, I hope, happy, under our mild Government.
The difference is already visible; before, every Corsican
carried his gun, for every district was at enmity with the other;
many parts at war with the French, and none friendly with
them; no single Frenchman could travel in this Island—his
death was certain. Now, not one man in fifty carries arms;
their swords are really turned into ploughshares; and we travel

everywhere with only a stick. This day I have walked over
300 acres of fine wheat, which last year only served to feed a
few goats ; and if these great alterations are to be seen in the
least fertile part of the Island, what must be the change in the
more fruitful ?

And when I reflect that I was the cause of re-attacking
Bastia, after our *wise* Generals gave it over, from not knowing
the force, fancying it 2000 men ; that it was I, who, landing,
joined the Corsicans, and with only my Ship's party of Marines,
drove the French under the walls of Bastia ; that it was I, who,
knowing the force in Bastia to be upwards of 4000 men, as I
have now only ventured to tell Lord Hood, landed with
only 1200 men, and kept the secret till within this week
past ;—what I must have felt during the whole Siege may be
easily conceived. Yet I am scarcely mentioned. I freely
forgive, but cannot forget. This and much more ought to
have been mentioned. It is known that, for two months, I
blockaded Bastia with a Squadron : only fifty sacks of flour
got into the Town. At St. Fiorenzo and Calvi, for two months
before, nothing got in, and four French frigates could not get
out, and are now ours. Yet my diligence is not mentioned ;
and others, for keeping succours out of Calvi for a few summer
months, are handsomely mentioned. *Such things are.*

I have got upon a subject near my heart, which is full when
I think of the treatment I have received : every man who had
any considerable share in the reduction, has got some place
or other—I, only I, am without reward. The taking of Corsica,
like the taking of St. Juan's,[6] has cost me money. St. Juan's
cost near £500 ; Corsica has cost me £300, an eye, and a cut
across my back ; and my money, I find, cannot be repaid me.
Nothing but my anxious endeavour to serve my Country makes
me bear up against it ; but I sometimes am ready to give
all up.

We are just going to sea, and I hope to God we shall meet
the French Fleet, which may give us all gold Chains[7]—who

---

[6] Vide vol. i., p. 9, ante.

[7] Medals with gold Chains were given to the Admirals present at Lord Howe's
victory, of the 1st of June, 1794 ; and some of the Captains received a Medal, suspended from a riband, white, with blue edges, which was worn at the button-hole
of their uniform coats.

knows? Remember me most kindly to Mrs. Suckling, and
Miss Suckling; and, believe me, in every situation, I feel
myself

Your much obliged and affectionate

HORATIO NELSON.

Best respects to Mr. Rumsey and family, and to Mr. Mentz.
Forgive this letter: I have said a great deal too much of myself;
but indeed it is all too true.

TO MRS. NELSON.

[From Clarke and M'Arthur, vol. i. p. 199.]

St. Fiorenzo, 7th February, 1795.

This day twelve months, my dear Fanny, our Troops landed
here to attempt the conquest of the Island, at least of those
parts which the French were in possession of; and, however
lightly the acquisition of Corsica may be deemed by many in
England, yet I take upon me to say, it was a measure founded
on great wisdom; and during the war must be ever of the
most essential service to us, and very detrimental to our
Enemies. After the evacuation of Toulon, we had no place
whatever of our own for the Fleet to anchor in: Tuscany was
wavering, and, although since declared for us, yet we are not
certain of her alliance from one day to another. The French
Consul at Leghorn, though not received officially, has never
quitted that place, and we know that attempts have been made
to get Tuscany again acknowledged by the French as a Neutral Power; in which case what security have we for our Fleet,
and the numerous Victuallers and Storeships attendant on it?
Corsica has always supplied Toulon with all the straight
timbers, beams, decks, and sides for their Ships; they are now
deprived of that supply, which would have enabled them by
this time to have built a small Fleet; and besides, the Corsican tar and hemp formed by no means an inconsiderable
resource for the dock-yard at Toulon. Moreover, all our trade,
with that of our Allies, is obliged to make the Coasts of this
Island, the Ports of which would have been so full of Row-
galleys, that no commerce could have been carried on: nor

could our Men-of-War have prevented the evil, for half the twenty-four hours is calm, when these Vessels would take the Merchant-men, though the whole of the British Navy were in sight. So much for the value of Corsica—I have done ; the recollection of one short year brings it to my mind. It was Lord Hood's plan, and it was accomplished chiefly by seamen.

Yours, &c.,

HORATIO NELSON.

TO MRS. NELSON.

[From Clarke and M'Arthur, vol. i. p. 200.]

Leghorn, 25th February.

We arrived here last night after a very bad cruise. This Country, I understand, will in a very few days declare its Neutrality ; therefore, as all Powers give up the contest, for what has England to fight ? I wish most heartily we had peace, or that all our Troops were drawn from the Continent, and only a Naval war carried on, the war where England can alone make a figure.

March 2nd. The French have one hundred and twenty-four Transports full of Troops ; something they certainly mean to attempt. Tuscany has just concluded a peace, and this Port is now open to the French, as well as ourselves. The Berwick is refitted,[8] so we are again fourteen Sail of the Line, and one Neapolitan Ship of the Line[9] has joined us ; we are therefore strong. I wish Lord Hood would make haste out.

Leghorn, March 6th. The Admiral has just got some information which has induced him to go to sea immediately.[1] I sincerely hope it is for a good purpose. We are taken rather

---

[8] Vide vol. i., p. 348.

[9] The Tancredi, commanded by Captain Caraccioli, whose wretched fate is so well known.

[1] In his Dispatch of the 16th of March, Admiral Hotham stated that on the 8th he received an express from Genoa, announcing that the French fleet from Toulon, consisting of fifteen Sail of the Line and three Frigates, had been seen off the Isle of Marguerite, and as that intelligence corresponded with a signal from the Mozelle, then in the offing, for a Fleet in the N.W. quarter, he immediately caused the Squadron to be unmoored, and at daylight on the following morning they put to sea.

suddenly, but are got off pretty tolerably as to order. My
health is perfectly good, as is Josiah's. Remember me to my
good father. I have only to pray God to bless you.

Yours, &c.

HORATIO NELSON.

TO DANIEL WILLIAMS, ESQ., CHURCH STREET, SPITALFIELDS.

[From the "European Magazine," vol. xlix. p. 101. Lieutenant Charles David
Williams, (son of Daniel, afterwards Sir Daniel, Williams, a Police Magistrate,) then
belonged to the Agamemnon, and had shortly before been taken prisoner under the
circumstances mentioned in this Letter.]

Dear Sir,   Leghorn, February 27th, 1795.
I only received your letter of December 29th yesterday, on
the return of the Fleet from sea.

I had some time learnt with pleasure that your son was a
prisoner, and not lost, which I feared was the case from the
bad account I had heard of the Vessel. I at that time made
inquiries if any little money could be got to him ; but was told
at this place it was impossible : however, I will make further
inquiry, and, if possible, get a remittance to him. I shall have,
I assure you, great pleasure in doing it on your son's account,
who is a very good young man, and who at a future time I
shall be glad to serve. I need no reference to any person for
your character ; Mr. Prestwood's recommendation of him to
me was sufficient for every purpose.

I can acquit myself of his misfortune. I was at sea ; and
the English Consul thought fit, which I never should have
consented to, to desire your son and others, belonging to the
Agamemnon and other Ships, to navigate a Vessel with
bullocks to Toulon ; a Vessel by no means proper for the purpose ; and left no doubt in my mind of his being lost. However, in case we cannot send him money, his case is not
singular : a great number of English are in the same situation.
I will not willingly miss the post, although it may be long in
reaching you ; and you shall hear from me again before I leave
Leghorn. I beg my compliments to Mr. Prestwood ; and be
assured, Dear Sir, I am,

Your very faithful Servant,

HORATIO NELSON.

TRANSACTIONS ON BOARD HIS MAJESTY'S SHIP AGAMEMNON, AND OF THE FLEET, AS SEEN AND KNOWN BY CAPTAIN NELSON.

[Autograph, in the Nelson Papers. Though this Narrative was printed by Clarke and M'Arthur, and is referred to by Southey, yet Mr. James, in his "Naval History," (Ed. Chamier, vol. i. pp. 256—263,) has disregarded it. The omission is the more extraordinary, since Mr. James justly complained of the want of precision in Admiral Hotham's Dispatch, and sneers, *more suo*, at other writers, for not being properly informed on the subject. His account of the Agamemnon's services seems to be almost wilfully unjust; and it has, therefore, been thought right, in confirmation of the statements in Nelson's Narrative, and in his Letters, to insert a copy of the Agamemnon's Log of the 13th and 14th of March, 1795, and likewise the account given of her proceedings on those days by Mr. Hoste, one of her Midshipmen, in a letter to his father. Vide Note A, at the end of this volume, where Mr. James' account of the Affair will also be found.]

From the 8th to the 14th of March, 1795.

On Sunday, March 8th, at five P.M., the Mozelle[2] being near the Gorgona, made the signal for a Fleet to the westward. The Admiral made the signal to unmoor, and to prepare to weigh after dark.

On the 9th, at five A.M., the signal to weigh, the wind blowing a fine breeze from the eastward. At eight o'clock, every Ship was without the Melora. Signal for the Inconstant[3] to look out, W.S.W., Meleager,[4] N.W., and the Tarleton[5] to proceed to St. Fiorenzo, to order the Berwick to join the Fleet. At four P.M., Cape Corse W.S.W. four or five leagues; little wind; the Fleet hauled up to the N.W. At half-past five the Meleager made the signal for the Enemy's Fleet, eighteen Sail. At eight, the Admiral made the signal that the Enemy's Fleet were supposed to be near.

March 10th.—At daylight, the Tarleton joined, and gave information that a boat came off from Cape Corse, and told them that the Berwick had been taken on Saturday, the 7th.[6]

[2] Mozelle, 24, Captain Charles Dudley Pater: he died a Flag officer.

[3] Inconstant, 36, Captain Fremantle, afterwards Vice Admiral Sir Thomas Francis Fremantle, Bart., G.C.B.

[4] Meleager, 32, Captain George Cockburn, now the Right Hon. Admiral Sir George Cockburn, G.C.B.

[5] Tarleton, Fireship, Captain Brisbane, afterwards Rear Admiral Sir Charles Brisbane, K.C.B. He died in December, 1829.

[6] The Berwick was captured by the French Fleet, after a gallant resistance, her Captain, Littlejohn, being slain; " by which misfortune his Majesty has lost a most valuable and experienced Officer, who has left a widow and four small children."— *Vice-Admiral Hotham's Dispatch.*

At about half-past nine A.M., signal for all Flag Officers: at ten, A.M., the Mozelle made the signal for a Fleet, twenty-five sail, in the N.W. : signal for a general chase in that quarter. All day very light airs : in the evening a light breeze westerly. At half-past five P.M., the Mozelle made the Signal that the Enemy were upon a wind on the starboard tack. At six signal to form in two divisions. Stood to the northward till midnight, when the Admiral made the signal to form in the Order of Battle.

March 11th.—At daylight nothing in sight. All day, light airs and variable, with a heavy swell from the S.W. In the afternoon saw a French brig to the westward making signals.[7] Nearly calm all night, but at times the wind all round the compass.

March 12th.—At daylight saw near us the Princess Royal,[8] Fortitude,[9] and Egmont ;[1] at the distance of four or five miles to the northward, Captain,[2] Illustrious,[3] and Tancredi :[4] to the E.S.E. a number of Ships with the foot of their topsails out of the water ; and south, a number of Ships, their hulls just rising out of the water. At six, the Egmont made the signal for a strange Fleet ; at the same time the Princess Royal made the signal for the Enemy's Fleet, south. We endeavoured to join the Princess Royal, which we accomplished at nine A.M. Light airs, southerly : the Enemy's Fleet nearing us very fast, our Fleet nearly becalmed. At a quarter past

[7] James says that the Enemy's Fleet were descried in the afternoon of the 11th, in the south or windward quarter, by the Princess Royal, and several Ships then near her, who were five or six miles from the main body of our Fleet.—(*Naval History*, vol. i. p. 257.) Admiral Hotham, in his *Dispatch*, says, " Although the French Ships were seen by our advanced Frigates daily, yet the two Squadrons did not get sight of each other until the 12th, when that of the Enemy was discovered to windward."

[8] Princess Royal, 90, Captain John Child Purvis, bearing the Flag of Vice-Admiral of the White, Samuel Cranston Goodall.

[9] Fortitude, 74, Captain Young, (afterwards Admiral Sir William Young, G.C.B.) bearing the Flag of Vice-Admiral Sir Hyde Parker.

[1] Egmont, 74, Captain Sutton, afterwards Admiral Sir John Sutton, K.C.B.

[2] Captain, 74, Captain Samuel Reeve : he was made a Rear-Admiral of the Red, in June, 1795, and died a Vice-Admiral of the White, in May, 1803.

[3] Illustrious, 74, Captain Thomas Lenox Frederick, who commanded the Blenheim, 98, at the battle of St. Vincent, and died a Flag Officer.

[4] A Neapolitan 74, commanded by Captain Caraccioli.

nine, Admiral Goodall made the signal for the Ships near, to
form ahead and astern of him, as most convenient: Admiral
Hotham[5] made the same signal. The Egmont stood from us
to join Admiral Hotham. Our Ships endeavouring to form a
junction, the Enemy pointing to separate us, but under a very
easy sail. They did not appear to me to act like Officers who
knew anything of their profession. At Noon they began to
form a Line on the larboard tack, which they never accomplished. At two P.M. they bore down in a Line ahead, nearly
before the wind, but not more than nine sail formed. They
then hauled the wind on the larboard tack; about three miles
from us, the wind southerly, Genoa Light-house N.N.E. about
five leagues; saw the Town very plain. At a quarter past
three P.M., joined Admiral Hotham, who made the signal to
Prepare for Battle, the body of the Enemy's Fleet about three
or four miles distant. At six minutes past four, signal to form
the Order of Battle on the larboard tack: half past four,
signal for each Ship to carry a light during the night. At
sixteen minutes past five, signal for each Ship to take suitable
stations for their mutual support, and to Engage the Enemy as
they came up. Our Fleet at this time was tolerably well
formed, and with a fine breeze easterly, which, had it lasted
half-an-hour, would certainly have led us through the Enemy's
Fleet about four Ships from the Van ship, which was separated
from the Centre about one mile. At three-quarters past five,
the Fleet hoisted their Colours. At dark, the wind came
fresh from the westward. At fifty-five minutes past six, the
signal to wear together. A fresh breeze all night: stood to
the southward all night, as did the Enemy.

March 13th.—At daylight the Enemy's Fleet in the S.W.
about three or four leagues with fresh breezes. Signal for a
General chase. At eight A.M. a French Ship of the Line[6] carried
away her main and fore topmasts. At a quarter-past nine, the
Inconstant frigate fired at the disabled Ship, but receiving
many shot, was obliged to leave her. At ten A.M., tacked and
stood towards the disabled Ship, and two other Ships of

---

[5] The Commander-in-Chief, in the Britannia.

[6] The Ça Ira ran foul of La Victoire, and carried away her own fore and main-
topmasts.

the Line.　The disabled Ship proved to be the Ça Ira of
84 guns $\begin{cases} 36 \ldots 24 \ldots 12 \text{ Pounders French weight} \\ 42 \ldots 27 \ldots 14 \quad \text{do. English do.} \end{cases}$ 1300 men;
Sans Culotte, one hundred and twenty guns; and the Jean
Barras,[7] seventy-four guns.　We could have fetched the Sans
Culotte by passing the Ça Ira to windward, but on looking
round I saw no Ship of the Line within several miles to support me: the Captain was the nearest on our lee quarter.　I
then determined to direct my attention to the Ça Ira, who,
at a quarter-past ten, was taken in tow by a Frigate; the Sans
Culotte and Jean Barras keeping about gun-shot distance on
her weather bow.　At twenty minutes past ten the Ça Ira
began firing her stern-chasers.　At half-past ten the Inconstant
passed us to leeward, standing for the Fleet.　As we drew up [8]
with the Enemy, so true did she fire her stern-guns, that not a
shot missed some part of the Ship, and latterly the masts were
struck every shot, which obliged me to open our fire a few
minutes sooner than I intended, for it was my intention to
have touched his stern before a shot was fired.　But seeing
plainly from the situation of the two Fleets, the impossibility
of being supported, and in case any accident happened to our
masts, the certainty of being severely cut up, I resolved to fire
so soon as I thought we had a certainty of hitting.　At a
quarter before eleven A.M., being within one hundred yards of
the Ça Ira's stern, I ordered the helm to be put a-starboard,
and the driver and after-sails to be braced up and shivered,
and as the Ship fell off, gave her our whole broadside, each
gun double-shotted.　Scarcely a shot appeared to miss.　The
instant all were fired, braced up our after-yards, put the helm
a-port, and stood after her again.　This manœuvre we prac-

[7] Jean Bart.

[8] " The signal was made for a General chase, in the course of which, the weather
being squally, and blowing very fresh, we discovered one of their Line-of-Battle
Ships to be without her topmasts, which afforded to Captain Fremantle, of the Inconstant Frigate (who was then far advanced on the chase) an opportunity of shewing a good proof of British enterprise, by his attacking, raking, and harassing her
until the coming up of the Agamemnon, when he was most ably seconded by Captain Nelson, who did her so much damage as to disable her from putting herself
again to rights; but they were at this time so far detached from our own Fleet, that
they were obliged to quit her, as other Ships of the Enemy were coming up to her
assistance, by one of which she was soon after taken in tow."—*Vice-Admiral Hotham's Dispatch.*

tised till one P.M., never allowing the Ça Ira to get a single
gun from either side to fire on us. They attempted some of
their after-guns, but all went far ahead of us. At this time the
Ça Ira was a perfect wreck, her sails hanging in tatters, mizen
topmast, mizen topsail, and cross jack yards shot away. At
one P.M., the Frigate hove in stays, and got the Ça Ira round.[9]
As the Frigate first, and then the Ça Ira, got their guns to bear,
each opened her fire, and we passed within half pistol-shot.
As soon as our after-guns ceased to bear, the Ship was hove
in stays, keeping, as she came round, a constant fire, and the
Ship was worked with as much exactness, as if she had been
turning into Spithead. On getting round, I saw the Sans
Culotte, who had before wore with many of the Enemy's Ships,
under our lee bow, and standing to pass to leeward of us,
under top-gallant sails. At half-past one P.M., the Admiral made the signal for the Van-ships to join him. I instantly bore away, and prepared to set all our sails, but the
Enemy having saved their Ship, hauled close to the wind, and
opened their fire, but so distant as to do us no harm ; not a
shot, I believe, hitting. Our sails and rigging were very much
cut, and many shot in our hull and between wind and water,
but, wonderful, only seven men were wounded. The Enemy
as they passed our nearest Ships opened their fire, but not a
shot, that I saw, reached any Ship except the Captain, who
had a few passed through her sails. Till evening, employed
shifting our topsails and splicing our rigging. At dark, in our
Station : signal for each Ship to carry a light. Little wind :
south-westerly all night : stood to the westward, as did the
Enemy.

March 14th.—At daylight, taken aback with a fine breeze
at N.W., which gave us the weather-gage, whilst the Enemy's
Fleet kept the southerly gage. Saw the Ça Ira, and a Line of
Battle ship[1] who had her in tow about three and a half miles

---

[9] The following passage, in Nelson's hand, occurs as a Note to the Narrative :
—N.B. I observed the guns of the Ça Ira to be much elevated, doubtless laid
for our rigging and distant shots, and when she opened her fire in passing, the elevation not being altered, almost every shot passed over us, very few striking our
hull. The Captain of the Ça Ira told Admiral Goodall and myself, that we had
killed and wounded one hundred and ten men, and so cut his rigging to pieces, that
it was impossible for him to get up other topmasts.

[1] " At daylight the next morning, (the 14th,) being about six or seven leagues to

from us, the body of the Enemy's Fleet about five miles.
Quarter past six A.M., signal for the Line of Battle, S.E. and
N.W. Forty minutes past six, for the Captain and Bedford[2]
to attack the Enemy. At seven A.M., signal for the Bedford
to engage close; Bedford's signal repeated for close Action.
Five minutes past seven, for the Captain to engage close.
Captain's and Bedford's signals repeated: at this time, the shot
from the Enemy reached us, but at a great distance. Quarter-
past seven, signal for the Fleet to come to the wind on the
larboard tack. This signal threw us and the Princess Royal
to the leeward of the Illustrious, Courageux,[3] and Britannia.
At twenty minutes past seven the Britannia hailed, and
ordered[4] me to go to the assistance of the Captain and Bedford.
Made all sail: Captain lying like a log on the water, all her

the south-west of Genoa, we observed the Enemy's disabled Ship, with the one that
had her in tow, to be so far to leeward, and separated from their own Squadron,
as to afford a probable chance of our cutting them off. The opportunity was not
lost; all sail was made to effect that purpose, which reduced the Enemy to the
alternative of abandoning those Ships, or coming to battle. Although the latter did
not appear to be their choice, they yet came down (on the contrary tack to which
we were) with the view of supporting them; but the Captain and Bedford, whose
signals were made to attack the Enemy's disabled Ship and her companion, were so
far advanced, and so closely supported by the other Ships of our van, as to cut them
off effectually from any assistance that could be given them; the conflict ended in
the Enemy's abandoning them, and firing upon our Line as they passed with a light air
of wind. The two Ships that fell, proved to be the Ça Ira, (formerly the Couronne,)
of eighty guns, and the Censeur, of seventy-four. Our Van-ships suffered so
much by this attack, particularly the Illustrious and Courageux, (having each lost
their main and mizen-masts,) that it became impossible for anything further to
be effected. I have, however, good reason to hope, from the Enemy's steering to the
westward, after having passed our Fleet, that whatever might have been their design,
their intentions are for the present frustrated."—*Vice-Admiral Hotham's Dispatch.*

[2] Bedford, 74, Captain Gould, who commanded the Audacious at the Battle of the
Nile, now Admiral Sir Davidge Gould, G.C.B.

[3] Courageux, 74, Captain Augustus Montgomery: he died in command of the
Theseus, in February 1796.

[4] The Commander-in-Chief. No allusion to this *order* occurs in Admiral Hotham's *Dispatch*, in which neither the Agamemnon nor Captain Nelson are mentioned, except in the extract already given, describing the engagement with the Ça
Ira on the previous day, whereas it appears that so conspicuous were the services of
the Agamemnon on the 14th, that both the Ça Ira and Le Censeur, 74, surrendered to, and were taken possession of by her. Admiral Hotham's reason for
not naming any Captain who had distinguished himself, except his Flag Captain,
John Holloway, (after expressing his "cordial commendation of all ranks collec-
tively,") was, that "it is difficult to specify particular desert where emulation was common to all, and zeal for his Majesty's service the general description of the Fleet."

sails and rigging shot away: Bedford on a wind on the larboard tack. Quarter past seven, signal to annul coming to
the wind on the larboard tack. Thirty-five minutes past
seven, signal for the Illustrious and Courageux to make more
sail. Forty minutes past seven, ditto signal repeated. Forty-
two minutes past seven, Bedford to wear, Courageux to get in
her station. At this time, passed the Captain; hailed Admiral
Goodall, and told him Admiral Hotham's orders and desired
to know if I should go ahead of him? Admiral Goodall desired me to keep close to his stern. The Illustrious and
Courageux took their stations ahead of the Princess Royal,
the Britannia placed herself astern of me, and Tancredi
lay on the Britannia's lee quarter. At eight A.M., the
Enemy's Fleet began to pass our line to windward, and
the Ça Ira and Le Censeur were on our lee side; therefore the Illustrious, Courageux, Princess Royal, and Agamemnon were obliged to fight on both sides of the Ship. The
Enemy's Fleet kept the southerly wind, which enabled them
to keep their distance, which was very great. From eight to
ten, engaging on both sides. About three-quarters past eight,
the Illustrious lost her main and mizen masts. At a quarter
past nine, the Courageux lost her main and mizen masts. At
twenty-five minutes past nine, the Ça Ira lost all her masts,
and fired very little. At ten, Le Censeur lost her main-mast. At
five minutes past ten they both struck. Sent Lieutenant George
Andrews[5] to board them, wh o hoisted English colours, and
carried the Captains, by order of Admiral Hotham, on board
of the Princess Royal, to Admiral Goodall.[6] By computation
the Ça Ira is supposed to have about three hundred and fifty
killed and wounded on both days, and Le Censeur about two
hundred and fifty killed and wounded. From the lightness of
the air of wind, the Enemy's Fleet and our Fleet were a very
long time in passing, and it was past one, P.M., before all firing
ceased, at which time the Enemy crowded all possible sail to

---

[5] Vide vol. i. p. 91.

[6] James is as silent as Admiral Hotham about the surrender of the Ça Ira and
Le Censeur, and his whole account of the Fleets on the 14th of March, is very unsatisfactory. He seems to have judged of the conduct of our Ships by the vulgar and
erroneous estimate of their losses; and he does not even mention the Agamemnon.

the westward, our Fleet laying with their heads to the south east and east.

A List of Killed and Wounded in our Fleet:
Seventy-three killed: two hundred and seventy-two wounded.[7]
Lieutenants Rathbone and Miles; Masters, Wilson, and Blackburn, and Hawker, wounded.[8]

ENGLISH FLEET.		FRENCH FLEET.	
Captain	74	Le Duquésne	74
Bedford	74	La Victoire	80
Tancredi	74	Le Guerrier	74
Princess Royal	90	Le Conquérant	74
Agamemnon	64	Le Mercure	74
Illustrious	74	Le Barras	74
Courageux	74	Le Tonnant	80
Britannia	100	Le Sans Culotte	120
Egmont	74	Le Timoleon	74
Windsor Castle	90	Le Généreux	74
Diadem	64	Le Heureux	74
St. George	90	Le Censeur	74
Terrible	74	L'Alcide	74
Fortitude	74	Le Souverain	74
		Le Ça Ira	80
	1090		1174

7650 Men.   16,900 Men.

TO MRS. NELSON.

[From Clarke and M'Arthur, vol. i. p. 200.]

Agamemnon at Sea, 10th March, 1795.

We are just in sight of the French Fleet, and a signal is out for a general chase. We have but little wind, and unfor-

---

[7] The Official Return, by Vice-Admiral Hotham, gave seventy-five killed, and two hundred and eighty wounded.

[8] The Officers wounded were, Lieutenants Robert Honeyman, of the St. George; Robert Hawker, of the Windsor Castle; and Miles, of the Bedford: and Messrs. William Hunter, John Blackburn, and John Wilson, Masters of the Captain, Courageux, and Agamemnon.—*London Gazette.*

tunately the Enemy are in-shore of us; however, I hope the
Admiral will allow us to go on, and if the French do not skulk
under their batteries, I trust we shall give a good account of
them. Whatever may be my fate, I have no doubt in my own
mind but that my conduct will be such, as will not bring a
blush on the face of my friends : the lives of all are in the
hands of Him, who knows best whether to preserve mine or
not; to His will do I resign myself. My character and good
name are in my own keeping. Life with disgrace is dreadful.
A glorious death is to be envied ; and if anything happens to
me, recollect that death is a debt we must all pay, and whether
now, or a few years hence, can be but of little consequence.
God bless you, and believe me ever your most faithful and
affectionate husband,

HORATIO NELSON.

TO VICE-ADMIRAL GOODALL.[9]

[Autograph, in the possession of John Dillon, Esq. This letter was written when in
sight of the French Fleet. The Agamemnon belonged to Vice-Admiral Goodall's
Division, and was next in succession to his Flag-Ship, the Princess Royal.]

Agamemnon, March 12th, 1795.

My dear Admiral,
    I most heartily congratulate you on our being so near the
Enemy's Fleet, and have only to assure you that the Agamemnon shall ever most faithfully support you. I wish we
had a hundred, or at least should have, fifty good men. Should
any of our Frigates get near you, I hope you will order some
men for us, even should Admiral Hotham forget us. Believe
me ever, but never more than on the present occasion,

Your most faithful
HORATIO NELSON.

[9] Vice-Admiral Goodall left the Mediterranean towards the end of the year
1795, being much hurt that, on Admiral Hotham's leaving the Station, the command was not entrusted to him. He died an Admiral of the White, in 1801.

TO VICE-ADMIRAL GOODALL.

[Autograph, in the possession of John Dillon, Esq.]

Agamemnon, March 15th, 1795.

My dear Admiral,

I have sent Officers and men to get the powder out of the Censeur, and you may be assured I will afford her all assistance in my power, consistent with the greater object of putting the Agamemnon in good order again. We are rather short of eighteen-pound, twenty-four pound and nine-pound shot, not having more than six hundred of each of the two former, and very few of the latter. If Illustrious or Courageux could spare us some eighteen-pound shot, it would be useful; but unless the large Ships, or Diadem,[1] can give us twenty-four pound shot, none are to be had in this country. I have sent a list of our wounded men, some of whom are very bad, distinguishing which were wounded on the 13th, and which on the 14th; also our defects.

I hope you are quite well. The Enemy are fled and we are not running after them: their orders, from what I hear, were to defeat the English Fleet if they chose to fight, and then to land and retake Corsica. The Ça Ira has the carriages for the battering cannon on board: ten thousand men are embarked on board the Transports at Toulon.

I hope we shall get rid of these Prizes and Lame Ducks this day, and get to the westward to secure our Convoy, which may, notwithstanding our victory, be in great danger.

Believe me, ever your most faithful,

HORATIO NELSON.

TO HIS ROYAL HIGHNESS THE DUKE OF CLARENCE.

[From Clarke and M'Arthur, vol. i. p. 205.]

March 15th, 1795.

Our Fleet closed with Ça Ira and Censeur, who defended themselves in the most gallant manner; the former lost 400, the latter 350 men; the rest of the Enemy's Ships behaved very ill. Martini, the Admiral, and St. Michael, the Commis-

---

[1] Diadem, 64, Captain Tyler, afterwards Admiral Sir Charles Tyler, G.C.B. Vide vol. i. p. 412.

sioner, were on board a Frigate. The orders of the French
were, to defeat us, and to retake Corsica: I believe they will
in no respect obey their orders. Every Ship fired red-hot shot;
but we now know, from experience, they are useless on board a
Ship. Frederick behaved exceedingly well, as did Montgomery in the Courageux, and Reeve in the Captain; and I
must not forget Goodall, who is as gallant an Officer as ever
lived. These Ships being the van, had more than their share
of the Action. Every Officer, I am sure, would have been
happy, had the Enemy given them equal opportunities. The
French bore away towards Toulon in the afternoon, and are
now out of sight. I am, &c.

HORATIO NELSON.

TO WILLIAM LOCKER, ESQ., LIEUTENANT-GOVERNOR OF
GREENWICH HOSPITAL.

[Autograph, in the Locker Papers.]

Agamemnon, Porto Especia, March 21st, 1795.

My dear Friend,

You will have heard of our brush with the French Fleet,
a Battle it cannot be called, as the Enemy would not give us
an opportunity of closing with them; if they had, I have no
doubt, from the zeal and gallantry endeavoured to be shewn
by each individual Captain, one excepted, but we should have
obtained a most glorious conquest. Admiral Hotham has had
much to contend with, a Fleet half manned, and in every respect
inferior to the Enemy;[2] Italy calling him to her defence, our

------

[2] James gives the annexed Table of the Comparative Force of the two Fleets on
the 12th, 13th, and 14th of March; but he does not include the troops embarked
in the French Ships.

COMPARATIVE FORCE OF THE TWO FLEETS.

		British.	French.		
			March.		
			12	13	14
Ships . . . . . . No.		14	15	14	13
Broadside Guns . .	No.	557	587	550	490
	lbs.	12711	14587	13680	12307
Crews . . . . Agg. No.		8810	11320	10620	9520
Size . . . . . . Tons		23996	29012	27212	24612

newly-acquired Kingdom[3] calling might and main, our reinforcements and Convoy hourly expected ; and all to be done
without a force, by any means adequate to it.　The French
were sent out as for certain conquest ; their orders were positive
to search out our Fleet, and to destroy us, of which they had
no doubts, if we presumed to come to Action with them ; then,
their troops were to have been landed, and Corsica retaken :
however, thank God, all is reversed.　I firmly believe they
never would have fought us, had not the Ça Ira lost her topmasts, which enabled the Agamemnon and Inconstant to close
in with her, and so cut her up that she could not get a top-
mast up during the night, which caused our little brush the
next day.　Providence, in a most miraculous manner, preserving my poor brave fellows, who worked the Ship in manœuvring
about his stern and quarters, with as much exactness as if she
had been working into Spithead.　The Action never ceasing
for upwards of two hours, one hundred and ten of the Enemy
were killed and wounded on that day, and only seven of ours
wounded.　Agamemnon had only three hundred and forty-
four at quarters, myself included.　I am flattered by receiving
the approbation of my own Fleet, as well as the handsomest
testimony by our Enemies.　The Sans Culotte at last bore
down, when the Admiral called me off.　A gale of wind came
on two days after the Action, which forced us in here, and most
unluckily put the Illustrious on shore, where she lays in great
danger.　Our Fleet, except Courageux and Illustrious, is perfectly refitted, and ready for sea : we sail to-morrow for Leghorn to join Blenheim,[4] and Bombay Castle,[5] when the Admiral
will immediately put to sea, to see if we can find any of these
crippled fellows ; for some went off towed by Frigates, and
some without bowsprits.　The Sans Culotte is in Genoa, others
are in Vado Bay.　I think we are quite up again in these seas,
and had we only a breeze, I have no doubt but we should
have given a destructive blow to the Enemy's Fleet : however,
it is very well.　I beg my best and kindest remembrances to

---

[3] Corsica.

[4] Blenheim, 98, Captain John Bazeley : he died a Flag-officer.

[5] Bombay Castle, 74, Captain Charles Chamberlayne : he was made a Rear-
Admiral in June following, and died an Admiral of the Blue in 1810.

all your family.   Josiah is a fine young man, and a brave
fellow.

Believe me ever

Your most faithful friend,

HORATIO NELSON.

All the Enemy's Ships are fitted with forges, and fired from
some guns constantly hot shot and shells, but they appear
ashamed of their orders, which are positive from the Convention,
and find nothing superior to the old mode of fighting.   I only
[wish] some of their own Ships will suffer by having such a
furnace in their cockpit, which will end such a diabolical
practice.   If you see Admiral Lutwidge, or ever write Kingsmill, remember me to him, as also to Mr. Bradley.

TO WILLIAM SUCKLING, ESQ.

[From " The Athenæum."]

Agamemnon, Porto Especia, March 22nd, 1795.

My dear Sir,

The event of our brush with the French Fleet you will know
long before this reaches you, and I know you will participate
in the pleasure I must have felt in being the great cause of our
success.   Could I have been supported, I would have had
Ça Ira on the 13th, which might probably have increased our
success on the next day.   The Enemy, notwithstanding their
red-hot shot and shells, must now be satisfied (or we are ready
to give them further proofs) that England yet reigns Mistress
on the Seas; and I verily believe our seamen have lost none
of their courage; and sure I am, that had the breeze continued,
so as to have allowed us to close with the Enemy, we should
have destroyed their whole Fleet.   They came out to fight us,
and yet, when they found us, all their endeavours were used
to avoid an Action.

But accidents will happen to us as to others : a few days
after the action we met with a very heavy gale of wind, which
has driven the Illustrious[6] on shore; but we have some faint

------

[6] The Illustrious, 74, Captain Frederick, having lost her main and mizen masts
in the Action, was taken in tow by the Meleager, and separated from the Fleet in a
violent gale, on the night of the 17th of March.   The tow-rope broke, and she

hopes she may yet be saved. Our Prizes are almost refitted ; and to-morrow we sail for Corsica. I beg leave to trouble you with a letter for Mrs. Nelson, and have to beg you will give my kindest remembrances to Mrs. Suckling, Miss Suckling, and all the family, not forgetting Mr. Rumsey and family.

Believe me ever your most affectionate,

HORATIO NELSON.

TO THE REV. MR. NELSON, HILBOROUGH.

[Autograph, in the Nelson Papers.]

Agamemnon, Porto Especia, March 25th, 1795.

My dear Brother,

Although you will have read as much of our late Action with the French Fleet as I can tell you, yet I know from experience there is no pleasure equal to that of hearing from our friends at a distance, therefore I take up the pen merely to say I am most perfectly well, as is Josiah, and that Agamemnon is as ready as ever to give the French another meeting ; and I really believe the Convention will again force these people out to fight us. Sure it is that the Enemy had no idea of our meeting them on the seas, if it was possible to have got into port, and so certain were they of our easy conquest, that the Mayor and all the Municipality of Bastia were on board the Sans Culotte to resume their Stations at that place—not that I am certain Corsica is safe, if they undertake the Expedition with proper spirit. The Enemy's Fleet are anchored in Hieres Bay, where in a week or ten days we shall be also.

Fortune in this late affair has favoured me in a most extraordinary manner, by giving me an opportunity which seldom offers of being the only Line-of-Battle Ship who got singly into Action on the 13th, when I had the honour of engaging the Ça Ira, absolutely large enough to take Agamemnon in her hold. I never saw such a Ship before. That Being who has

drove on shore in Valence Bay, between Spezia and Leghorn, on the 18th, and it being impossible to get her off, was set on fire and destroyed. The particulars will be found in the *Naval Chronicle*, vol. xxxvii. p. 355. Captain Frederick and his Officers were (as is usual) tried by a Court-martial for the loss of their Ship, but were honourably acquitted.

ever in a most wonderful manner protected me during the
many dangers I have encountered this war, still shielding
me, and my brave Ship's company. I cannot account for
what I saw : whole broadsides within half-pistol shot missing
my little Ship, whilst ours was in the fullest effect. The French
Captain has paid me the highest compliments—much more
flattering than those of my own Fleet, as they must have been
true. We killed on board Ça Ira on the 13th, one hundred
and ten, whilst only seven were slightly wounded on board
Agamemnon. On the 14th, although one of the Van-ships, and
in close Action on one side and distant Action on the other for
upwards of three hours, yet our neighbours suffered most exceedingly, whilst we comparatively suffered nothing. We had
only six men slightly wounded. Our sails were ribbons, and
all our ropes were ends. Had our good Admiral have followed
the blow, we should probably have done more, but the risk was
thought too great. If you see Hoste's father in your travels,
I beg you will say what a good young man—I love him dearly,
and both him and Josiah are as brave fellows as ever walked.
Certain it is Agamemnon has given experience to her crew ;
five times my Ship has been engaged, three at sea, two against
Bastia, three Actions in boats, and two Sieges, ought to make
us stand fire, but we are too far from home to be noticed. Our
Actions are not known, beyond this country and our immediate friends. How does Mrs. Nelson, my Aunt, and all our
Swaffham friends ? Is Robert Rolfe married ?[7] Remember
me kindly to all, not forgetting Charlotte[8] and my namesake.[9]

Believe me ever

Your most affectionate brother,

HORATIO NELSON.

Blenheim and Bombay Castle joined.

St. Fiorenzo, March 30th.—We are got here, and are fitting
our Ships for sea, where we shall be in about one week.

We are all well.

---

[7] His Cousin, the present Rev. Robert Rolfe, of Norwich, whom, when made a
Peer, he appointed one of his Chaplains.

[8] Mr. Nelson's daughter, the present Lady Bridport.

[9] His son, Horatio, afterwards Viscount Trafalgar.

TO THOMAS POLLARD, ESQ., LEGHORN.

[Autograph, in the possession of John Luxford, Esq.　Indorsed, "31 March, 1795."]

Agamemnon, [*torn.*]

My dear Sir,

We had a meeting yesterday to nominate Agents for our Prizes taken on the 14th, and the majority of Captains in this Port have nominated the four Admirals' Secretaries and the Consul, only Captain Foley[1] and myself adding you to the other number; but as the Captains and Admirals can only dispose of their own Agency, I still hope you will be nominated by the Lieutenants' Class, and probably Warrant Officers. All those Classes in the Agamemnon are for inserting your name, but you must know that the majority in each Class have the power of nomination. I consider myself . . . . [*torn*] . . . . both by you and . . . . Consul, that . . . should have felt a . . . . not to have remembered both on the present occasion : to be sure, the amount with six Agents will not be much, but the compliment would have been the same ; but we shall take more, and I hope you will be considered. You know what my determination was respecting Agency long ago : and had I taken a Frigate or Man of War by myself, the Commander-in-Chief's Secretary, the Consul, and yourself, I intended to fix as Agents. I have thought it right to say thus much, that you may not for a moment suppose me ungrateful for your many kindnesses to [*torn off.*]

TO MRS. NELSON.

[From Clarke and M'Arthur, vol. i. p. 206.]

Fiorenzo, 1st April, 1795.

I am absolutely, my dearest Fanny, at this moment in the horrors, fearing, from our idling here, that the active Enemy may send out two or three Sail of the Line, and some Frigates,

---

[1] Of the St. George, 90, afterwards Admiral Sir Thomas Foley, G.C.B., who was Nelson's Flag-Captain at Copenhagen.

to intercept our Convoy, which is momentarily expected. In short, I wish to be an Admiral, and in the command of the English Fleet; I should very soon either do much, or be ruined. My disposition cannot bear tame and slow measures. Sure I am, had I commanded our Fleet on the 14th, that either the whole French Fleet would have graced my triumph, or I should have been in a confounded scrape. I went on board Admiral Hotham as soon as our firing grew slack in the Van, and the Ça Ira and Censeur had struck, to propose to him leaving our two crippled Ships, the two Prizes, and four Frigates, to themselves, and to pursue the Enemy; but he, much cooler[2] than myself, said, ' We must be contented, we have done very well.' Now, had we taken ten Sail, and had allowed the eleventh to escape, when it had been possible to have got at her, I could never have called it well done. Goodall backed me; I got him to write to the Admiral, but it would not do: we should have had such a day, as I believe the Annals of England never produced. I verily think if the Admiral can get hold of them once more, and he does but get us close enough, that we shall have the whole Fleet. Nothing can stop the courage of English seamen.

I may venture to tell you, but as a secret, that I have a Mistress given to me, no less a Personage than the Goddess Bellona; so say the French verses made on me, and in them I am so covered with laurels, that you would hardly find my sallow face. At one period I am ' the dear Nelson,' ' the amiable Nelson,' ' the fiery Nelson:' however nonsensical these expressions are, they are better than censure, and we are all subject and open to flattery. The French Admiral is to be tried, and some of the Captains are under arrest: it is reported that the Captain of the Sans Culotte has run away. The Toulonese will not allow the French Fleet to enter their port, but make them remain in Hieres Bay, telling them, ' To get out and execute their former orders, or never to enter the ports of the Republic.' They were very much alarmed in Corsica at the appearance of the Enemy's Fleet. So certain were the

---

[2] " I can, *entre nous*," said Sir William Hamilton, in a Letter to Captain Nelson, "perceive that my old friend, Hotham, is not quite awake enough for such a command as that of the British Fleet in the Mediterranean, although he is the best creature imaginable."—*Southey's Life of Nelson.*

French of defeating us, that the Mayor and all the Municipality of Bastia were on board the Sans Culotte, to resume their Stations.

Yours, &c.
HORATIO NELSON.

TO THE RIGHT HONOURABLE SIR GILBERT ELLIOT, BART., VICEROY OF CORSICA.

[Autograph, in the Minto Papers.]

Agamemnon, St. Fiorenzo, April 5th, 1795.

My dear Sir,

Our worthy young man, Lieutenant George Andrews,[3] has received letters from his friend in England, who recommended him to Mr. Pelham, and was the cause of Mr. Pelham's recommendation of him to you, that Lord Spencer had been spoken to, and that it was probable he would be recommended to Admiral Hotham, which, if it was to give him the first vacancy, might be well; but if at this time, to go youngest into the Britannia, the prospect of promotion is too distant even for *hope*. Mr. Andrews is fearful that Mr. Pelham, not knowing your inability to serve him in this Country, should suppose that he had not merited your notice. He requests, therefore, if, from what you have heard of him, you think him worthy of your interest, that you will write Mr. Pelham that it has been want of ability and not want of inclination. You know my opinion of Mr. Andrews too well to render it necessary for me to speak again of his merits, but I must add, that if the conduct of the Agamemnon on the 13th was by any means the cause of our success on the 14th, that Lieutenant Andrews has a principal share in the merit, for a more proper opinion was never given by an Officer than the one he gave me on the 13th, in a situation of great difficulty.

Believe me, dear Sir,
Your most faithful, humble servant,
HORATIO NELSON.

[3] Vide vol. i. p. 91. Since the publication of the First Volume, (to which this Note would properly belong,) it has been ascertained that the Miss Andrews to whom Nelson was attached in 1783, married, first, a clergyman of the name of Farror; and second, Colonel Warne, of the East India Company's Service, and died a few years ago.

TO THE RIGHT HONOURABLE SIR GILBERT ELLIOT, BART.,
VICEROY OF CORSICA.

[Autograph, in the Minto Papers.]

April 8th, 1795.

My dear Sir,

Mr. Andrews is much obliged by your kind intentions towards him, and I yet hope to see him a Captain before the conclusion of the war. I trust and sincerely hope we shall very soon see Lord Hood:[3] it is said we are to sail to-morrow; I hope it is so, and that we shall intercept these Ships said to be cruising on the coast of Spain. My letters I took the liberty of sending to Bastia by the Officer who escorted over the French Officers first landed, and I shall beg leave to trouble you to order them to be sent to Mr. Udney,[4] to go by post from Leghorn.

Believe me, dear Sir, with the greatest respect,

Your most faithful servant,

HORATIO NELSON.

His Excellency the Viceroy.

TO MRS. NELSON.

[From Clarke and M'Arthur, vol. i. p. 208.]

St. Fiorenzo, 12th April, 1795.

Rest assured, my dear Fanny, you are never absent from my thoughts.—If the folks will give me the Colonelcy of Marines,[5]

---

[3] Lord Hood, while lying at Spithead with a small Squadron, about to resume the command in the Mediterranean, thought it his duty to remonstrate strongly with the Admiralty on the inadequacy of the force on that Station. His correspondence proving unsatisfactory, he was, on the 2nd of May, most unexpectedly ordered to strike his Flag, which was never again hoisted. Admiral Sir John Jervis, K.B., was appointed to succeed him, and he sailed in the Lively Frigate, on the 11th of November, 1795.

[4] The English Consul at Leghorn.

[5] Colonelcies of Marines were then conferred upon three, and afterwards upon four, old Post Captains, and were, in fact, honourable sinecures, which they relinquished on obtaining their Flags. One Admiral was also a General, another a Lieutenant-General, and a third a Major-General of Marines. These appointments were discontinued a few years ago, and " Good Service Pensions" substituted for them. The only Naval officer now holding a Marine commission, is Admiral Sir George Cockburn, G.C.B., who was made a Major-General in April 1821.

I shall be satisfied; but I fear my interest is not equal to get it: although I will never allow that any man whatever has a claim superior to myself.[6]　We have just got the thanks of the Corsican[7] Parliament and Viceroy, for our gallant and good conduct on the 13th and 14th day of March, which they say, and truly, has saved them from an invasion.　The Viceroy's private letter to me has a very flattering compliment, that cannot but be pleasing to you: ' I certainly consider the business of the 13th of March as a very capital feature in the late successful contest with the French Fleet; and the part which the Agamemnon had in it must be felt by every one to be one of the circumstances that gave lustre to this event, and rendered it not only useful, but peculiarly honourable to the British Arms.　I need not assure you of the pleasure with which I constantly see your name foremost in everything that is creditable and serviceable; nor of my sincere regard and affection.'

So far, all hands agree in giving me those praises,[8] which cannot but be comfortable to me to the last moment of my life.　The time of my being left out here by Lord Hood, I may call well spent; had I been absent, how mortified should I now be.　What has happened may never happen to any one again, that only one Ship of the Line out of fourteen, should get into Action with the French Fleet, and for so long a time as two hours and a half, and with such a Ship as the Ça Ira.　Had I been supported, I should certainly have brought the

---

[6] Captain Nelson was then within forty-six of the top of the list of Post Captains, and he here compares his own services with those of the Captains who stood above him.

[7] Dated March 24th, 1795. " All his Majesty's faithful subjects in this Kingdom acknowledge, on this successful occasion, the powerful munificence of the King, and that they are in a similar degree sensible of the signal merits of the Vice-Admiral. Resolved that the Thanks of the House, &c. Signed, Giafferi, President. Muselli, Secretary."—*Clarke and M'Arthur.*

[8] The praises which are always dearest to a son's heart—those of his father—were conveyed to him in a letter from Bath, on the 5th of May, 1795.—" I can now, my dear Horatio, address you in the language of our University, *Bene et optimé fecisti,* and I do most heartily rejoice at your acquisition of a fresh, never-fading laurel, obtained in a consciousness of having discharged the duties of your station, and by a religious sense of that over-ruling Providence who maketh all things work together for good to those who love Him. It is said with confidence, that Lord Hood will not go to the Mediterranean : having reached St. Helen's, he is returned to Spithead. This is the news of the day. God bless you ! Farewell."—*Clarke and M'Arthur,* vol. i. p. 210.

Sans Culottes to battle, a most glorious prospect. A brave man runs no more risk than a coward, and Agamemnon to a miracle has suffered scarcely anything: three or four of our wounded are dead, the others are in a fair way of doing well. We have got accounts of the French Fleet, the troops are landed, and their Expedition is given up; the Ships have suffered much, many at this time are shifting their masts. Our Fleet was never in better order. My kindest remembrances to my father.

Yours, &c.
HORATIO NELSON.

TO THE RIGHT HONOURABLE SIR GILBERT ELLIOT, BART., VICEROY OF CORSICA.

[Autograph, in the Minto Papers.]

Agamemnon, April 16th, 1795.

Dear Sir,

From the present prospect of affairs, it is not impossible that an attack may be made on this Island; and should Admiral Hotham judge it most advisable to remain at anchor to assist in the defence of it, I beg leave, should no other person be judged more proper, to offer myself for the command of such seamen as might be judged proper to be landed. Believe me, dear Sir, ever, but never more than in a time like the present,

Yours most faithfully,
HORATIO NELSON.

His Excellency the Viceroy.

TO HIS ROYAL HIGHNESS THE DUKE OF CLARENCE.

[From Clarke and M'Arthur, vol. i. p. 207.]

St. Fiorenzo, 16th April, 1795.

Sir,

The arrival of a reinforcement from Brest, at Toulon, of six Sail of the Line, two Frigates, and two Cutters,[9] has, for the present moment, rather altered the complexion of affairs in

---

[9] Under Rear-Admiral Rénaudin: they arrived at Toulon on the 4th of April.

this Country; but I have no doubt Administration has taken care to send us at least an equal number of Ships, although unfortunately they are not yet arrived. The Enemy have now actually ready to sail from Toulon twenty Sail of the Line, and two Sail of the Line are launched, and will be ready in fourteen days from this date. We have ready for sea, and in perfect good order, fourteen Sail of the Line; five Three-deckers, six Seventy-fours, and two Sixty-fours, English, one Seventy-four Neapolitan. The Courageux is sent for from Leghorn,[1] and will be ready in about three weeks, as will the Censeur, who is to be manned, if necessary, to fight the Enemy, superior as they are, out of the Frigates; so that we shall be sixteen Sail of the Line, a force by no means possible for the Enemy to injure. The late Captain of the Vengeur commands the Ships from Brest, and all our prisoners told us of this reinforcement; but it was not thought right to believe them. Should the attempts of the Enemy be against this Island, I have no doubt but they will fail, provided the Corsicans are true to their country; a doctrine and practice, I own, not much in fashion in the present day: but I believe the Corsicans are not yet civilized enough to adopt the contrary; they love their country. I own myself to be rather of opinion, that the attempt of the Enemy will be against Italy; their Fleet to anchor in Telamon Bay, and their troops to land at Orbitella, about sixty-five miles from Rome, just on the frontiers of the Tuscan Dominions. May health and every blessing attend your Royal Highness.

I am, &c.
HORATIO NELSON.

TO HIS ROYAL HIGHNESS THE DUKE OF CLARENCE.

[From Clarke and M'Arthur, vol. i. p. 208.]

Agamemnon, at Sea, off Cape Corse, 24th April, 1795.

Sir,

We sailed a week past from Fiorenzo, and are to call off Minorca, to know what our Allies, the Spaniards, intend to do with twenty-one Sail of the Line, which are lying in Mahon.

---

[1] Where she remained to repair the damages sustained on the 14th of March.

Contrary winds have kept us here, and every moment we expect the Enemy's Fleet to heave in sight. We are thirteen English Sail of the Line, and two Neapolitan seventy-fours, one of which joined this morning; and, I am sorry to say, was matter of exultation to an English Fleet: the Courageux is not yet ready to join us.

I hope, and believe, if we only get three Sail from England, that we shall prevent this Fleet of the Enemy from doing further service in the Mediterranean, notwithstanding the red-hot shot and combustibles, of which they have had a fair trial, and found them useless. They believed that we should give them no quarter; and it was with some difficulty we found the combustibles, which are fixed in a skeleton like a carcass; they turn into a liquid, and water will not extinguish it. They say the Convention sent them from Paris, but that they did not use any of them, only hot shot.

I am, &c.
HORATIO NELSON.

TO THE REV. MR. NELSON, BATH.

[Autograph, in the Nelson Papers.]

Agamemnon, at Sea, April 24th, 1795.

My dear Father,

I received your letter of March 20th, several days past, therefore I hope the channel of communication is again open, and that you will more frequently hear of us than of late. We are proceeding to look out for Lord Hood, for although I have doubts that the Enemy, superior as they are, could make any impression upon an English Fleet of our numbers, however, all must wish to have that force as almost to make a victory on our side certain. What the new Lords of the Admiralty are after, to allow such a reinforcement to get out here, surprises us all. Lord Chatham did better than this sleeping. Nothing this war has ever been half so badly managed as we find the new Admiralty. As I write you, and the signal is just thrown out for a Ship to go to Leghorn, I shall not write Mrs. Nelson this day. After this campaign we must have peace at all events: next autumn shall carry me to England.

I hope my brother will like his purchase, and that it will be for the mutual benefit of all parties concerned. We are in want of news, and anxious to hear of Lord Hood's sailing from England. Remember me with the sincerest affection to my dear wife, and say Josiah is very well, and a very good boy. Hoste, Mather,[2] Lead, &c., are all well. Believe me,

Ever your most dutiful son,

HORATIO NELSON.

TO WILLIAM SUCKLING, ESQ.

[From " The Athenæum."]

Agamemnon, at Sea, April 24th, 1795.

My dear Sir,

A signal is just made, signifying that a Frigate will be sent to Leghorn this afternoon; therefore, I cannot allow her to leave us without writing you a line to say we are yet in being, and not swallowed up by the French.

We are put to sea, not only as being more honourable, but also as much safer, than skulking in Port: nor do I think that our small Fleet would be a very easy conquest; but our zeal does not in the least justify the gross neglect of the new Admiralty Board. Lord Chatham was perhaps bad: in this Fleet we find, from woful experience, that this is ten times worse. Our Merchants are ruined for want of Convoy, which it has never been in our power to grant them. Had not our late Action proved more distressing to the Enemy than the Admiralty had any right to suppose, we should before this time have been driven out of the Mediterranean. Every moment I expect to see the Enemy's Fleet; for they must be as badly managed as ourselves, if they do not embrace the present favourable moment for any enterprise they may have in their heads. We hope soon to see Lord Hood, or some small reinforcement: the junction of a single Neapolitan Ship of the Line has this morning been to the English Fleet absolutely matter for exultation—so much neglected and forgotten

---

[2] Apparently William Mather, who was made a Lieutenant in 1799, and died a Post Captain.

are we at home. However, after all my complaints, I have no
doubt but, if we can get close to the Enemy, we shall defeat
any plan of theirs; but we ought to have our ideas beyond
mere defensive measures.

Pray forward the enclosed to Bath; and remember me most
kindly to Mrs. Suckling, Miss Suckling, every part of the
family, and our friends at Hampstead, whom, next October
I hope to see as cheerful as ever. Believe me,

My dear Sir, your much obliged and affectionate

HORATIO NELSON.

TO MRS. NELSON.

[From Clarke and M'Arthur, vol. i. p. 209.]

Leghorn, 28th April, 1795.

We have been trying these ten days past to get to the
westward, to join our expected reinforcements from England;
but the winds have been so contrary that we every day lost
ground. Yesterday, to our surprise, our Storeships and Victuallers from Gibraltar arrived in the Fleet: their escape from
the Enemy has been wonderful, and, had we lost them, our
game was up here. This I suppose has induced the Admiral
to bear up for this place, and by it we shall get the Courageux
ready for sea.

Yours, &c.,

HORATIO NELSON.

TO WILLIAM LOCKER, ESQ. LIEUTENANT-GOVERNOR OF GREENWICH HOSPITAL.

[Autograph, in the Locker Papers.]

Agamemnon, Leghorn, May 4th, 1795.

My dear Friend,

We have been here a whole week, expecting every hour to
hear something from England, but nothing comes to us, neither
messenger, nor post; surely the people at home have forgot us.
The Admiral has not the scratch of a pen for a month past;
no reinforcements arrived, nor have we heard of their having

sailed, and yet the six Ships of the Enemy left Brest last December with the Grand Fleet, and have been arrived six weeks in Toulon harbour; and but fortunately we so much crippled the masts of the Enemy in the Action, we should have been left here in a very inferior state. The King of Naples has sent us one more Seventy-four, and the Courageux will be finished to-morrow, or we should only have fourteen Sail of the Line to twenty, now we shall be sixteen—fourteen English, two Neapolitans. But if, as reported by the French Minister at Genoa, that the preliminaries of peace are actually signed with Spain,[3] we shall of course lose our Naples friends, which will, in our present state, be a very heavy stroke upon us; for our Minister at Naples tells us, ' as do Spain, so do Naples.' Reports of the day say, that the French Fleet sailed on the 1st of May from Toulon, eighteen or twenty Sail of the Line; we shall hear more, if it is true, in twenty-four hours: if only the former, I have no doubts but we shall obtain a complete victory; if the latter, we cannot expect it; and what is worse, a battle without a complete victory is destruction to us, for we cannot get another mast this side Gibraltar: but Providence will, I trust, order all for the best. We are likely to get an exchange of prisoners; and Vessels are ready to sail from Toulon with English, who are to be exchanged at this place; we sail certainly from here on Friday the 8th, even should the French Fleet be still in port, and are to proceed to the westward to look for Lord Hood, or some reinforcements.

You mention your son John having wrote me a letter; I am sorry never to have received it. Pray remember me kindly to him and William, with the rest of the family. Admiral Hotham is very well, but I believe heartily tired of his temporary command; nor do I think he is intended by nature for a Commander-in-Chief, which requires a man of more active turn of mind. When I am to see England, God knows! I have in the present situation of affairs determined on staying here till the autumn, or another Action takes place, when all active service will probably be over, in these seas. Remember me to our Naval friends, or such others as inquire after me. I flatter myself, if

---

[3] The Treaty of Peace between France and Spain was signed at Brussels on the 22nd of July, 1795.

the promotion of Flags comes very soon, I shall stand a fair
chance for the Marines;[4] if services this War may be allowed
a claim, I may stand to a certainty. One hundred and ten
days I have been actually engaged at Sea and on shore
against the Enemy; three Actions against Ships, two against
Bastia, in my Ship, four Boat Actions, and two Villages taken,
and twelve Sail of Vessels burned. I don't know any one has
done more, and I have had the comfort to be ever *applauded*
by my Commander-in-Chief, but never *rewarded;* and what
is more mortifying, for services in which I have been slightly
wounded, others have been praised, who at the time were
actually in bed, far from the scene of Action. But we shall, I
hope, talk my opinion of men and measures over the fire next
winter at Greenwich. Believe me ever,

Your obliged and affectionate

HORATIO NELSON.

TO WILLIAM SUCKLING, ESQ.

[From " The Athenæum."]

Leghorn, May 4th, 1795.

My dear Sir,

Here we have been exactly one week, and can hear no
accounts from England, nor have we for upwards of three
weeks past. It is extraordinary that neither messenger nor
post should arrive; but the great folks at home forget us at a
distance. We hear nothing of our reinforcements, and yet
six Sail of the Enemy have arrived upwards of five weeks at
Toulon. Fortunately for us, we so much damaged the masts
of the Fleet in the last Action, that they have not hitherto been
able to get their Fleet to sea before ours has been completely
refitted. Reports of this day say that the French are sailed
from Toulon with eighteen or twenty Sail of the Line : if only
the former, we shall be very happy to meet them, and I doubt
not of obtaining a complete Victory : if the latter, we shall
come to no harm, but cannot, in the common course of events,
expect any success against such a great superiority: fourteen

---

[4] The Colonelcy of the Chatham Division of Marines, which he obtained on the
Promotion of Flags on the 1st of June following, when he became the seventh on
the list of Captains.

English, and two Neapolitans, is our force. We are waiting impatiently for more authentic accounts, which twenty-four hours will certainly give us.

What can the new Board of Admiralty be after? Hotham is very much displeased with them, and certainly with reason. These Ships left Brest in December last with the French Grand Fleet: had the Fleet at Toulon only waited for this reinforcement, what a state we should have been in! at this time most probably have lost Corsica, and the French would certainly have been at Rome, and our Fleet retired in disgrace. Providence has ordered it otherwise, and every scheme of the Enemy has hitherto been defeated in this Country; and I hope will continue so, for it cannot be very long before Lord Hood arrives.

The Enemy have a great many small Privateers at sea, and many of our Merchant-ships are taken: one from Zante to London has just been brought in by a row-boat Privateer, and, to the westward, great numbers are carried into Marseilles and Toulon. We are just on the eve of an exchange of prisoners; three Vessels, full of English, being ready to sail from Toulon for this place, where the exchange is to be made: they will be of very great use to our weak Fleet. The French Minister at Genoa has given out that the preliminaries of peace with Spain are signed—if so, I suppose it is the same with Naples, and we shall lose our two Sail of the Line, which will be a heavy stroke upon us at the present moment.

Pray remember me kindly to Mrs. Suckling, Miss Suckling, and family, also at Hampstead; and believe me ever

Your most affectionate and obliged

HORATIO NELSON.

I have not written to Mrs. Nelson by this post.

TO . . . .

[From the " European Magazine," vol. xlix. p. 101.]

Leghorn, May 5th, 1795.

My dear Sir,

Pray be so good as to send the enclosed to Mr. Williams:

it is just to say that I expect his son[5] here every day in a Cartel from Toulon, to be exchanged for the people taken in our Prizes. We expect the French Fleet to be at sea every hour.

I am, dear Sir, &c.

HORATIO NELSON.

If any of my old friends in the Office recollect me, pray remember me to them.

TO DANIEL WILLIAMS, ESQ.

[Autograph, in the possession of William Upcott, Esq. Vide p. 9, ante.]

Agamemnon, Leghorn, May 5th, 1795.

Dear Sir,

The last time I was here, the neutrality of Tuscany being but just settled, I could not send to your son the £20, which you desired, and which I should, had it been possible, have had the greatest satisfaction in sending ; and at this time three Cartels are expected from Toulon [with] sick prisoners ; amongst whom I hope, and have little doubt, is your son. I therefore have not sent the money, but have desired Mr. Udney, the Consul, to advance him £20 immediately on his arrival, to get him those things which he must want; and assure you I shall, with his other friends, be very glad to see him. I think that this account of your son will be acceptable.

I am, dear Sir, &c.

HORATIO NELSON.

I beg my compliments to Mr. Prestwood.

TO THOMAS POLLARD, ESQ. LEGHORN.

[Autograph, in the possession of John Luxford, Esq.]

May 22nd, 1795.

Dear Pollard,

I should have liked to have heard by La Flèche, who joined yesterday, that you were quite recovered, but I hope you are.

---

³ Vide p. 9, ante.

⁶ La Flèche, 14, Captain Gore, afterwards Vice-Admiral Sir John Gore, K.C.B.

We are waiting off Minorque, doing nothing, waiting for Lord Hood, and with continued foul winds for his Lordship, from the day of our sailing from Leghorn : the moment he arrives we shall be off for Toulon, and only have to hope we shall fall in with the Enemy's Fleet before they do any harm, for I must believe they are at sea. We chase nothing, although we see many Vessels who may be French for aught we can tell. Pray send the enclosed and let me hear from you, and if possible send me a newspaper.

Believe me ever your obliged
HORATIO NELSON.

TO MRS. NELSON.

[From Clarke and M'Arthur, vol. i. p. 210.]

Off Minorca, 29th May, [to June 15th,] 1795.

As yet we have no accounts of Lord Hood's having actually sailed from St. Helen's : and what they can mean by sending him with only five Sail of the Line, is truly astonishing; but all men are alike, and we in this Country do not find any amendment, or alteration, from the old Board of Admiralty. They should know that half the Ships in this Fleet require to go to England, and that long ago they ought to have reinforced us. At this moment our operations are at a stand, for want of Ships to support the Austrians in getting possession of the Sea-coast of the King of Sardinia; and behold, our Admiral does not feel himself equal to shew himself, much less to give assistance in their operations.

June 7th.—We have been off here very nearly a month, expecting first Lord Hood, then Admiral Dickson. We have lost much by Lord Hood's going to England, and much more, probably, by his not returning.

June 15th.—Yesterday, Admiral Man[7] joined us, with a Squadron from England. Lord Hood enclosed me a copy of a letter from Lord Spencer about me, acknowledging my pre-

---

[7] Robert Man, Rear Admiral of the Blue, whose Flag was flying in the Cumberland, 74, Captain Bartholomew Samuel Rowley. The Squadron consisted of seven Sail of the Line.

tensions to favour and distinction, when proper opportunities offer. This letter was written before the account of our Action had arrived ; that may throw an additional weight into the scale for me. However, I hope to save my pay, which, with a little addition, will buy us a very small cottage, where I shall be as happy as in a house as large as Holkham.

Yours, &c.

HORATIO NELSON.

TO THOMAS POLLARD, ESQ. LEGHORN.

[Autograph, in the possession of John Luxford, Esq.]

May 29th, 1795.

Dear Pollard,

Pray be so good as to forward the enclosed for me. . I sincerely hope you are quite recovered. I hear from a man in the Fleet, who joined the Fleet by La Flèche, that in the Post Office are lying three letters for me ; be so kind as to inquire [and get] hold of them. The Argo[8] joined yesterday, but none of us, except the Admiral, has any communication with her, therefore we are ignorant if she has any letters for us. I wrote you by La Flèche.

Believe me, ever yours truly,

HORATIO NELSON.

If any opportunity offers, you will be so good as to order me some green almonds, and whatever else will keep : all will be acceptable.

TO WILLIAM SUCKLING, ESQ.

[From " The Athenæum."]

June 7th, off Port Mahon.

My dear Sir,

I have really not a moment to say, 'pray send the enclosed to Mrs. Nelson, as probably she has left Bath.' No reinforcements, nor do we hear of any arriving, yet in the Mediter-

---

[8] The Argo, 44, Captain Richard Rundell Burgess, who was slain in command of the Ardent, at Camperdown.

ranean.[9] The French have not yet sailed from Toulon, but all ready—twenty-one Sail of the Line, thirteen Frigates. Truly sorry am I that Lord Hood does not command us: he is a great Officer; and were he here, we should not now be skulking. With kindest remembrances, believe me

Your affectionate

HORATIO NELSON.

TO THE RIGHT HON. WILLIAM WINDHAM, SECRETARY AT WAR.

[Autograph draught, in the Nelson Papers.]

8th June, 1795.

Sir,

I have been in waiting for Lord Hood's arrival in these seas, that his Lordship might have supported my application for an allowance, which I believe, from my great length of service on shore, will be considered as just.

I was landed on the 4th of April, [1794,] to command the seamen assisting in the reduction of Bastia, and remained in that Command till every cannon and store was embarked for the siege of Calvi, which was the 6th of June, [1794.] Between that day and the 10th, I went in the Command of my Ship with Lord Hood in search of the French Squadron then at sea, which got into Gourjean Bay, when Lord Hood sent me to carry on the expedition in concert with General Stuart against Calvi. I embarked the Troops &c. from Bastia, and landed with them and a number of seamen under my Command on the 19th of June, and served on shore until the surrender of the place; and on the 12th of August, I embarked by order of Lord Hood with the seamen, and sailed from Calvi so soon as I had, in obedience to my orders from his Lordship, embarked the garrison for Toulon. I trust I do not ask an improper thing when I request that the same allowance may be made to me as would be made to a land Officer of my rank, which, situated as I was, would have been that of a Brigadier General, or my additional expenses paid me.

---

[9] The reinforcement arrived on the 14th of June. Vide p. 39, ante.

I have stated my case, Sir, plainly, and leave it to your
wisdom to act in it as is proper.[1]

I am, Sir, &c.

HORATIO NELSON.

[The following paragraph also occurs on the same draught, but it is not certain
that it formed part of the letter itself:—]

This is my case, which I have stated plainly, and have only
to request that the same allowance may be made to me as would
have been to a Land Officer of equal rank, which I understand is that of Brigadier General, the same as Sir Roger
Curtis had at Gibraltar.

TO THE REV. MR. NELSON, HILBOROUGH.

[Autograph, in the Nelson Papers.]

June 8th, 1795, off the Island of Minorque.

My dear Brother,

We have been cruising off here for a long month, every moment in expectation of reinforcements from England. Our
hopes are now entirely dwindled away, and I give up all expectation : then comes accounts of Lord Hood's resignation.[2]
Oh, miserable Board of Admiralty! They have forced the
first Officer in our Service away from his command. The
late Board may have lost a few Merchant-vessels by their
neglect: this Board has risked a whole Fleet of Men-of-War.
Great good fortune has hitherto saved us, what none in this
Fleet could have expected for so long a time. Near two
months we have been skulking from them. Had they not got
so much cut up on the 14th of March, Corsica, Rome, and
Naples would, at this moment, have been in their possession,
and may yet, if these people[3] do not make haste to help us. I
am out of spirits, although never better in health. With
kindest regards to Mrs. Nelson and my Aunt, believe me
ever

Your most affectionate brother,

HORATIO NELSON.

[1] He was informed by Mr. Windham, on the 21st of July, 1795, in reply to this
letter, " That no pay has ever been issued under the direction, or to the knowledge of
this Office, to Officers of the Navy serving with the Army on shore."—*Original*, in
the Nelson Papers.

[2] Vide p. 28, ante.   [3] The Admiralty.

TO THOMAS POLLARD, ESQ.

[Autograph, in the possession of Josiah French, Esq.]

June 8th, 1795.

Dear Pollard,

Be so good as to send the inclosed as directed, and you will pay forty zechins on the 1st of July, as by my order sent this day; but before that I hope we shall have defeated the Enemy's Fleet, and I shall be at Leghorn.

Believe me ever your obliged

HORATIO NELSON.

TO WILLIAM LOCKER, ESQ., LIEUT.-GOVERNOR, ROYAL HOSPITAL, GREENWICH.

[Autograph, in the Locker Papers.]

Off Minorca, June 18th, 1795.

My dear Friend,

I received your kind letter of April 15, on the 14th of June, when Admiral Man joined, and my friend Williams yesterday, with a book, by Mr. Summers,[4] who I shall be glad to be attentive to. Great changes have taken place in this Fleet, and more are on the eve of taking place, as the Admiral expects a messenger every day, with the account of the promotion of several Captains here : perhaps the Admiralty may commission me for some Ship here; if so, provided they give me the Marines, I shall feel myself bound to take her, much as I object to serving another winter campaign without a little rest. We are now waiting for the Convoy's arrival from Gibraltar, and as the winds hang easterly, they may be some time before they arrive. The French say they will fight us again, provided we are not more than two or three Ships superior; I can hardly believe they are such fools : pray God they may! All is squabbles at Toulon, one party in possession of the great Fort, Le Malgue, the Jacobins of the Arsenal and Town. The Fleet came to sea for two days, but are gone back, and joined the Jacobins; the Austrians and Piedmontese are

---

[4] Mr. James Summers, who was made a Lieutenant in the following year.

waiting only for our getting to the eastward to take Vado Bay,
which will be a fine anchorage for us. We have our wants and
our wishes in the Fleet; but, upon the whole, I believe we are
much more comfortable than the Home Fleet, and our people
very healthy ; the scurvy not known; we eat very little salt
meat. From the little I have seen of Mr. Charnock's[5] book, I
think it a good thing. It will perpetuate the name of many a
brave Officer whose services would be forgot. I intend to send
[by] the Argo, or one of the Ships of the Convoy, your
quarter-cask of sherry, but how it is to be got from Portsmouth
to Greenwich is the greatest difficulty. I shall keep this letter
open till I hear of a Vessel going to Leghorn ; but our Admiral
gives us but very little notice.

June 19th.—Mr. Summers is recommended by Lord Hood
to Admiral Hotham, and Holloway has put your good wishes
for the young man against his name; and he will certainly be
very soon made a Lieutenant.

June 20th.—A Vessel going to Leghorn, no Convoy in sight.
With kindest remembrance to your family, and Mr. Bradley,
believe me ever your

Most obliged, affectionate
HORATIO NELSON.

Hotham desires his compliments.

TO WILLIAM SUCKLING, ESQ.

[From " The Athenæum."]

Off Minorca, June 20th, 1795.

My dear Sir,

I am almost afraid that, by the new regulations of post, I
may be wrong to send you an enclosure : if so, will you have
the goodness to tell me ? Our reinforcements of Men-of-War
joined us on the 14th; but we are now awaiting the Convoy,
which, as the wind is fair, may be every hour expected. They

---

[5] " Biographia Navalis, or, Impartial Memoirs of the Lives and Characters of
Officers of the Navy of Great Britain, from the year 1660 to the present time ; by
John Charnock, Esq." Six volumes 8vo. The first volume of the " Biographia
Navalis" was published in 1794; the second, in 1795 ; the third, fourth, and fifth,
in 1797 ; and the sixth, in 1798.

say the Enemy will come out, although we have got our reinforcements : if so, I do not think they will all go back again—
so God send us a good and speedy meeting! I have some
reason to expect I shall have the Marines, or my Flag. If
they give me the last, I shall be half ruined : unless I am immediately employed in this Country, I should, by the time I
landed in England, be a loser, several hundred of pounds out
of pocket. The former would be very pleasant, as it would
give me additional pay, and not take me from actual service,
which would distress me much, more especially as I almost
believe these people will be mad enough to come out ; for I
own nothing could give me more pleasure than a good drub-
bing to them ; and, in Agamemnon, we are so used to service,
that there is not a man in the Ship but what wishes to meet
them.

How is Mr. Rumsey ? Remember me kindly to him ; the
war over, I shall have great pleasure in taking him by the
hand. My best wishes attend Mrs. Suckling, Miss Suckling,
and every part of your family, and believe me ever

Your most affectionate nephew,

HORATIO NELSON.

TO THE REVEREND DIXON HOSTE, GODWICK HALL, NORFOLK.

[Autograph, in the possession of Captain Sir William Hoste, Bart.]

Agamemnon, off Minorca, June 22nd, 1795.

My dear Sir,

Although your good son writes the day of receiving a letter
from you, yet I will not let the opportunity slip of sending a
line to thank you for your news. The changes and politics
of Ministers and men are so various, that I am brought to
believe all are alike ; the loaves and fishes are all the look out.
The ins and outs are the same, let them change places. The
extraordinary circumstance of the Prince of Wales's debts is
much more lamentable : his best friends must be hurt, and the
others are, as far as I hear, as much in debt as people will
trust them. They are of an age to know better, and if they
will not practise what they know, they ought to be punished,
by letting them feel that want they are making others so

severely partake of. However, I trust if this debt is once more paid, that he will be acquainted by the Nation they will pay no more for him. What a figure would the Duke of Clarence have made had he served, out of debt and beloved by the nation; in short, our profession, *in war*, is so popular, that he might have done what he pleased.

We have just got accounts that the French Fleet is at sea, twenty-two Sail of the Line. Sir Sydney Smith did not burn them all[6]—Lord Hood mistook the man: there is an old song, *Great talkers do the least, we see.* Admiral Hotham is waiting here with twenty English and two Neapolitan Ships of the Line, for our invaluable Convoy of Stores, Provisions, and Troops from Gibraltar. I hope the Enemy will not pass us to the westward, and take hold of them. This Fleet must regret the loss of Lord Hood, the best Officer, take him altogether, that England has to boast of. Lord Howe certainly is a great Officer in the management of a Fleet, but that is all. Lord Hood is equally great in all situations which an Admiral can be placed in. Our present Admiral is a worthy, good man, but not by any means equal to either Lord Hood or Lord Howe. Fame says I am to have my Flag or the Marines; I hope the latter. The former will most likely throw me out of service, which I should very much regret: I long for one more good Action with this Fleet, and then peace. I beg my best respects to Mrs. Hoste, and also to Mr. and Mrs. Coke:[7] I hope a son will come forth.

I am, dear Sir,

Your very faithful servant,

HORATIO NELSON.

TO THE REVEREND MR. NELSON, HILBOROUGH.

[Autograph, in the Nelson Papers.]

Agamemnon, off Minorca, June 22nd, 1795.

My dear Brother,

I have this moment received your letter of May 13th, and as

---

[6] At Toulon, in 1793. Sir Sidney Smith's exalted opinion of his own services, (however justified by his undoubted gallantry and zeal,) seems to have given offence to many eminent Officers both of the Navy and Army.

[7] Of Holkham.—No Son did "come forth" until after Mr. Coke's second marriage, in 1822, with Lady Anne Keppel, by whom he had the present Earl of Leicester.

the Admiral has made a Ship's signal for Leghorn, I write you a line. I wrote you some time ago about the Action, and believe have wrote since. I shall only write you heads: nothing particular. I need not say I am not Captain of the Ça Ira. She required too much repair for me to remain inactive whilst she was fitting. At present she is a Prison-ship.[8] The Censeur[9] goes home next Convoy. The particulars of the Action I must defer till we meet in England, when I can shew you my account of it, with plans &c.   Ça Ira is on two-decks,

$$\left.\begin{array}{l}\text{84 guns, 36 ... 24 ... 12 French weight}\\\text{English } 42 ... 27 ... 14\end{array}\right\}1300 \text{ men.}$$

Agamemnon killed and wounded 110 men, more by seamanship than fighting. We lost only seven men wounded, three of whom are since dead. Had not the Sans Culotte bore down and fired on me, I would have taken her. She is the largest two-decker I ever saw.

Admiral Man joined us on the 14th, with six Sail of the Line, so that we are now twenty Sail of the Line, English, and two Neapolitans. We have this day accounts of the French Fleet's being at sea with twenty-two Sail of the Line, and innumerable Frigates, &c. We are waiting for our valuable Convoy from Gibraltar, expected every moment; are totally ignorant which way the Enemy's Fleet are gone: hope sincerely they will not fall in with our Convoy, but our Admiral takes things easy. Lord Hood's absence is a great National loss; but if we have the good fortune to fall in with the Enemy's Fleet, the event will be what no Englishman can doubt.

As you seem so anxious about Hilborough, I am truly sorry any impediment should be in the way of a final settlement. Fame says I am likely to be an Admiral; I hope not: the Colonelcy of Marines would suit me much better at present. Many thanks to Mrs. Nelson, my Aunt, and all our Swaffham friends, for their kind congratulations. If 1 am unfortunately an Admiral, I shall soon see them, for we have more already than is wanted. I am glad to hear Miss Charlotte and Horace are got so forward as to think of going to school: give my kind love to them. I assure you I shall return again to the farm

---

[8] At St. Fiorenzo. She was burnt by accident on the 11th of April, 1796.

[9] This Ship was retaken off Cape St. Vincent, on her passage to England, by a French Squadron on the 7th of October following.

with no small degree of satisfaction: it is the happiest of lives if people will but be contented.

Believe me ever,

Your most affectionate Brother,

HORATIO NELSON.

I shall write to Suckling very soon.

I have to boast, what no Officer can this war, or any other that I know of, being, in 15 months, 110 days in Action at Sea and on Shore.

TO MRS. NELSON.

[From Clarke and M'Arthur, vol. i. p. 211.]

St. Fiorenzo, 1st July, 1795.

Our Convoy having joined us on the 22nd, we made sail for this Port, and arrived all safe on the 29th; so far we are fortunate. The French Fleet of seventeen Sail of the Line are out, but only to exercise their men, at least our good Admiral says so: however, they may make a dash, and pick up something. We have Zealous, seventy-four,[1] and three Ordnance Ships expected daily from Gibraltar. I hope they will not look out for them. Two French Frigates were for ten days very near us, as we are informed by Neutral Vessels. I requested the Admiral to let me go after them; but he would not part with a Ship of the Line. When the Fleet bore away for this place, he sent two small Frigates, Dido and Lowestoffe, to look into Toulon; and the day after they parted from us, they fell in with the two Frigates. It was a very handsome done thing in the Captains, who are Towry and Middleton,[2]

---

[1] Commodore Christopher Mason, Captain J. Young.

[2] The following account of this gallant action is given by Clarke and M'Arthur, from the Letter of Lieutenant George Clarke, first Lieutenant of the Lowestoffe. The Dido was commanded by Captain George Henry Towry, and the Lowestoffe, by Captain Robert Gambier Middleton. "On the 24th of June, 1795, the Dido, a little eight and twenty, of nine-pounders, and the Lowestoffe, a two and thirty, of twelve-pounders, had to contend with the superior force of La Minerve, forty-two eighteen-pounders, and L'Artemise, of thirty-six twelve-pounders: each having on board 350 men. The Dido had 200, the Lowestoffe, 220. Can you credit our having gained a complete victory, with such odds against us? and further, that the Lowestoffe had not a man hurt? The Dido had six men killed, and twenty-one

and much credit must be due to these Officers, and their Ships' company.

Thank God, the superiority of the British Navy remains, and I hope ever will: I feel quite delighted at the event. Had our present Fleet but one good chance at the Enemy, on my conscience, without exaggeration, I believe that if the Admiral would let us pursue, we should take them all.

Yours, &c.,
HORATIO NELSON.

TO WILLIAM LOCKER, ESQ., LIEUTENANT-GOVERNOR
ROYAL HOSPITAL, GREENWICH.

[Autograph, in the Locker Papers.]

Agamemnon, off Cape Corse, July 8th, 1795.

My dear Friend,

Mr. Summers is now fourth Lieutenant of the Agamemnon, but as the vacancy is not by death, but in the room of an Officer invalided, it may be necessary to have a friend to say a word at the Admiralty for his immediate confirmation: not that it is likely they will send out Lieutenants to such vacancies. I told Admiral Hotham of your good wishes for the young man.

We are now at sea, looking for the French Fleet, which chased myself and two Frigates into Fiorenzo, yesterday afternoon. The Admiral had sent me, and some Frigates,[3] to co-

wounded: she was the Commodore, and led on; the French Commodore ran aboard her, in consequence of which the Dido's mizen-mast was carried away; and in this close engagement, the chief part of the men above mentioned were killed and wounded. At this juncture the Lowestoffe came up, and raked the Frenchman; the Dido still at him on the lee-bow. Away went Minerve's fore-mast, bowsprit, main top-mast, and mizen-mast. The other fellow, a most abominable coward, after fighting a little, sheered off, and the Lowestoffe made after him; but, owing to superior sailing, he unfortunately got away. In the meantime, the Dido, who had hauled off to repair damages, made our signal to return, so Lowestoffe tacked, and stood again towards Minerve: when we favoured her so plentifully with shot, that she ordered the National flag to be struck—what three hearty cheers we gave!" In transmitting Captain Towry's Official Letter, Admiral Hotham described the affair as "a most gallant and spirited action," which "reflected the highest honour on the Captains, Officers, and Crews."

[3] "I dispatched on the 4th Instant from St. Fiorenzo, the Ships named in the margin, [Agamemnon, Meleager, Ariadne, Moselle, Mutine, Cutter,] under the

operate with the Austrian General[4] in the Riviera of Genoa, when off Cape delle Melle I fell in with the Enemy, who, expecting to get hold of us, were induced to chase us over, not knowing, I am certain, from their movements, that our Fleet was returned into Port.[5] The chase lasted twenty-four hours, and, owing to the fickleness of the winds in these seas, at times was hard pressed; but they being neither Seamen nor Officers, gave us many advantages. Our Fleet had the mortification to see me seven hours almost in their possession; the shore was our great friend, but a calm and swell prevented our Fleet from getting out till this morning.[6] The Enemy went off yesterday evening, and I fear we shall not overtake them; but in this country no person can say anything about winds. If we have that good fortune, I have no doubt but we shall give a very good account of them, seventeen Sail of the Line, six Frigates; we twenty-three of the Line, and as fine a Fleet as ever graced the seas.

July 14th.—Yesterday we got sight of the French Fleet; our flyers were able to get near them, but not nearer than half gun-shot: had the wind lasted ten minutes longer, the six Ships would have each been alongside six of the Enemy. Man[7] commanded us, and a good *man* he is in every sense of the word.[8] I had every expectation of getting Agamemnon

orders of Captain Nelson, whom I directed to call off Genoa for the Inconstant and Southampton Frigates that were lying there, and to take them with him, if from the intelligence he might there obtain he should find it necessary. On the morning of the 7th, I was much surprised to learn that the above Squadron was seen in the offing returning into Port, pursued by the Enemy's Fleet, which, by General de Vins' letter, (the latest account I had received,) I had reason to suppose were certainly in Toulon."—*Admiral Hotham's Dispatch*, 14th July, 1795.

  [4] General de Vins.

  [5] St. Fiorenzo, in Corsica.

  [6] James (*Naval History*, i., 266, 267,) states that the pursuit of the French Fleet began on the 7th of July, that they chased the Agamemnon within sight of Admiral Hotham's fleet in San Fiorenzo Bay, at 9, 30 A.M., on the 8th, but that they were prevented from sailing immediately, by the wind blowing right into the Bay, and by most of the Ships being employed in watering and refitting. With great exertions, however, they put to sea at nine in the evening.

  [7] Rear-Admiral Robert Man, who hoisted his Flag in the Victory on that occasion.

  [8] James (i. 269) has added to his own account of this unsatisfactory, or as Nelson (p. 63) calls it, "miserable" Action, and (p. 70) "our very little business," a long Note, written by "as gallant an Admiral as the service can boast," (but withholds his name,) who was then a Lieutenant of the Victory, bearing Admiral Man's Flag, which contains severe reflections on the conduct of that Ship, and consequently on the Rear-Admiral.

close alongside an eighty-gun Ship, with a Flag, or Broad
Pendant; but the west wind first died away, then came east,
which gave them the wind, and enabled them to reach their
own Coast, from which they were not more than eight or nine
miles distant. Rowley[9] and myself[1] were just again getting
into close Action, when the Admiral made our signals to call
us off.[2] The Alcide, seventy-four, struck, but soon afterwards
took fire, by a box of combustibles in her fore-top, and she
blew up; about two hundred French were saved by our Ships.
In the morning I was certain of taking their whole Fleet,
latterly of six Sail. I will say no Ships could behave better
than ours,[3] none worse than the French; but few men are killed,
but our sails and rigging are a good deal cut up. Agamemnon,
with her usual good luck, has none killed, and only one badly
wounded; by chance, for I am sure they only fired high, they
put several shot under water, which has kept [us] ever since at
the pumps. The Enemy anchored in Frejus, and we are
steering for Fiorenzo.

　　　　　　　　　Believe me ever yours,
　　　　　　　　　HORATIO NELSON.

The Culloden lost his main top-mast as he was getting alongside a Seventy-four.

Victory, Admiral Man; Captain, Reeve; Agamemnon,
Nelson; Defence, Wells; Culloden, Troubridge; Cumber-
land, Rowley; Blenheim, Bazeley; I think was every Ship.[4]
If I have omitted any, I beg their pardons.

[9] Captain Bartholomew Samuel Rowley, of the Cumberland, seventy-four: he died
an Admiral of the Blue while Commanding-in-Chief at Jamaica, in 1811.

[1] James says the signal was once if not twice repeated with the Cumberland's
pendants, before that Ship would see it; and that the Blenheim, Gibraltar, Captain,
and a few other Ships, were then closing with the Enemy's rear, but he does not
here mention the Agamemnon, though it would appear that she was as close to the
Enemy as the Cumberland.

[2] "Those of our Ships which were engaged had approached so near to the shore,
that I judged it proper to call them off by signal."—*Admiral Hotham's Dispatch.*
The English Fleet lost one Midshipman, and ten seamen and marines, and one
Lieutenant and twenty-three seamen wounded. The Victory suffered most. Admiral
Hotham spoke of "the most distinguished and honourable manner" in which the
advanced Ships availed themselves of their position; but named no other officer in
his Dispatch than Rear-Admiral Man.

[3] Nelson does not, as on a former occasion, (vide p. 20, ante) make any exception:
hence the justice of Mr. James's pointed censure of the Defence (i. 269) may be
doubtful.

[4] *i. e.*, every Ship engaged with the Enemy.

TO H. R. H. THE DUKE OF CLARENCE.

[From Clarke and M'Arthur, vol. i. p. 215.]

15th July, 1795.

Sir,

Not having had any signification to the contrary, I still presume to suppose, that an account from me of the operations of this Fleet is acceptable to your Royal Highness.

The Agamemnon was sent from Fiorenzo with a small Squadron of Frigates to co-operate with the Austrian General de Vins, in driving the French out of the Riviera of Genoa, at the beginning of July. On the 6th, I fell in with the French Fleet of seventeen Sail of the Line and six Frigates ; they chased me twenty-four hours, and close over to St. Fiorenzo, but our Fleet could not get out to my assistance. However, on the 8th, in the morning, Admiral Hotham sailed with twenty-three Sail of the Line ; and on the 13th, at daylight, got sight of the Enemy, about six leagues south of the Hieres Islands. A signal was then made for a general chase. At noon, the Victory, Admiral Man, with Captain, Agamemnon, Cumberland, Defence, and Culloden, got within gun-shot of the Enemy ; when the west wind failed us, and threw us into a line abreast. A light air soon afterwards coming from the Eastward, we laid our heads to the northward, as did the Enemy, and the Action commenced.

It was impossible for us to close with them, and the smoke from their Ships and our own made a perfect calm ; whilst they, being to windward, drew in shore ; our Fleet was becalmed six or seven miles to the westward. The Blenheim and Audacious got up to us during the firing. The Alcide struck about half-past two, and many others were almost in as bad a state ; but she soon afterwards took fire, and only two hundred men were saved out of her. At half-past three the Agamemnon and Cumberland were closing with an eighty-gun ship with a Flag, the Berwick, and Heureux, when Admiral Hotham thought it right to call us out of Action, the wind being directly into the Gulf of Frejus, where the Enemy anchored after dark.

Thus has ended our second meeting with these gentry. In the forenoon we had every prospect of taking every Ship in the Fleet; and at noon, it was almost certain we should have had the six near Ships. The French Admiral, I am sure, is not a wise man, nor an Officer: he was undetermined whether to fight or to run away: however, I must do him the justice to say, he took the wisest step at last. Indeed, I believe this Mediterranean Fleet is as fine a one as ever graced the Ocean.

John Holloway [5] is Captain of the Fleet, a good man. The Enemy will have still twenty-one Sail at sea in a month, but I do not believe they can ever beat us in their present undisciplined state: the prisoners we have seen are stanch Royalists, and I really believe the war is almost at an end. I am going to Genoa, to see Mr. Drake, our Minister, and to consult about what assistance the Admiral can afford the Austrians in the Riviera of Genoa. We have just got accounts of Vado Bay being taken from the French.

I am, &c.

HORATIO NELSON.

TO HIS EXCELLENCY FRANCIS DRAKE, ESQ.,
MINISTER AT GENOA.

[Original, in the possession of Mrs. Davies, the daughter of Mr. Drake.]

Agamemnon, Genoa Mole, 18th July, 1795.

Sir,

From the conversation I had the honour to hold with your Excellency last evening, it appeared to you, as I own it does to myself, that the great use of the co-operation between His Majesty's Squadron under my command, and the Allied Army under General de Vins, is to put an entire stop to all trade between Genoa, France, and places occupied by the Armies of France; and without which trade is stopped, your Excellency tells me it is almost impossible for the Allied Army to hold their present situation, and much less possible for them to make any progress in driving the French out of the Riviera of Genoa; and by the paper you gave me to read, it also appears to be your opinion, that probably Nice itself might fall

---

[5] Of this gallant Officer, who was an intimate friend of Nelson, and who died a full Admiral, a Memoir is given in the nineteenth volume of the *Naval Chronicle.*

for want of a supply of provisions, forage, and ammunition coming from Genoa.

I have the honour to transmit you a copy of Admiral Hotham's orders to me, on my coming on this service : as, also, a copy of an order dated June 17th,[6] which, from the impossibility of being complied with in this Country, amounts to a prohibition of similar orders which have been given in England. I beg, therefore, to submit to your Excellency whether it will not be proper for you to write to Admiral Hotham on this subject, stating the absolute necessity of stopping all the trade which may pass between Genoa, France, and places occupied by the Armies, and that Ventimiglia must be considered as a place under that description ; for if a Genoese Vessel may pass with impunity to that place, nothing can prevent their going to Nice, and every French Port to the westward of it.

However, Sir, so sensible am I of the necessity of vigorous measures, that if your Excellency will tell me that it is for the benefit of His Majesty's service, and for the reasons which you have stated, that I should stop all trade between the Neutral Towns and France, and places occupied by the Armies of France, considering Ventimiglia in that situation, I will give

---

[6] Admiral Hotham's Order of the 15th July, 1795, was in these words :—" You are hereby required, and directed to proceed forthwith, in the Ship you command, with the Ships, Sloop, and Cutter named in the margin, [Meleager, Ariadne, Tarleton, Resolution Cutter, whose Captains have my orders to follow your directions,] off Genoa, where, upon your arrival, you are to confer with Mr. Drake, his Majesty's Minister at that place, on such points as may be deemed essential towards your co-operating with General de Vins, the Commander-in-Chief of the Allied Armies in Italy, for the benefit of the common Cause against the Enemy, carrying the same into execution as expeditiously as possible. You will receive his Excellency Mr. Drake on board the Agamemnon, for his passage with you to Vado, should he be desirous of it. Given on board the Britannia, Martello Bay, the 15th day of July, 1795. W. Hotham."

Admiral Hotham's Order of the 17th June, 1795, was as follows :—" (Circular Instructions.) You are hereby required and directed to take all possible care not to give any just cause of offence to the Foreign Powers in amity with His Majesty, and whenever any Ships or Vessels belonging to the Subjects of those Powers shall be detained or brought by you into Port, you are to transmit to the Secretary of the Admiralty a complete specification of their cargoes, by the first opportunity that may offer, and not to institute any legal process against such Ships or Vessels until their Lordships' further pleasure shall be known. Given on board the Britannia, off Minorca, 17th June, 1795. W. Hotham."

proper directions to the Squadron under my command for that purpose.

I have the honour to remain,
Your Excellency's most obedient, humble Servant,
HORATIO NELSON.

[An autograph draught of this Letter is in the Nelson Papers, which, except in a few unimportant words, agrees with the above ; but after the words, " for that purpose," the following passages are added :—]

And the Vessels and their cargoes lay in Vado Bay, until I can receive my Commander-in-Chief's directions about them ; or, if your Excellency thought it proper, to send an express to England, until that answer could return.

The great obstacles, Sir, which lie before me, as a Captain in the Navy, are briefly, the being liable to prosecution for detention and damage, and the danger of Agents becoming bankrupts. Suppose I stop a Genoese Vessel, loaded with corn for France, or places occupied by her Armies, considering Ventimiglia in that situation ; what can I do with her ? By my orders of the 17th June, I am not to institute any legal process against her, until their Lordships' further pleasure shall be known : I am to send a complete specification of her cargo to the Secretary of the Admiralty. This is a measure of impossibility in this Country ; for the cargoes, probably chiefly of corn, would be spoiled long before their Lordships' pleasure could reach me ; and in case the Vessel and cargo should be released by their Lordships' orders, it is to me the owners would look for damages.

Even supposing that, in consequence of your Excellency's statement, I should stop the Vessels before described ; and, to avoid unnecessary expense, that I direct the corn, or other cargo, to be taken out of such Vessel, the freight to be paid for, and the Vessel released, I might, notwithstanding, be unfortunate in the choice of an Agent, and, the value of these cargoes be not forthcoming, then the Captain would naturally be looked to for the money. Such things have happened ; therefore, there is only one measure to be taken—to bear the Officer harmless from prosecution on this new occasion—which is, that the Officer sends the Neutral Vessels and cargoes to such person or persons as you may think proper to appoint, that he or they

may pay for the freight and release the Vessel, selling the cargo
and holding the amount, until legal process is had on it;
your Excellency pledging yourself, that Government would
prevent any prosecution from falling on the Officer, who may
stop Vessels as before described. Should this meet your
Excellency's approbation, I have no objection to avoid the
possibility of a bad choice of an Agent by the Officer, that
the Vessels and cargoes should be delivered to such person or
persons as you may judge proper and responsible people, till
legal adjudication can be had on the value of cargoes restored
by order of Administration.

I hope you will excuse the length of this letter; but when
your Excellency considers the responsibility of a Captain in
the Navy in these cases, I trust you will think it right for me
to state my opinion fully.

TO EARL SPENCER, FIRST LORD OF THE ADMIRALTY.

[Original Draught, in the Nelson Papers.]

Agamemnon, July 19th, 1795.

My Lord,

I have seen in the newspapers that I am appointed one of the
Colonels of Marines,[7] an appointment certainly most flattering
to me, as it marks to the world an approbation of my conduct.
To your Lordship I beg leave to express my gratification, more

---

[7] On the 6th June, 1795. Captain Nelson's appointment as Colonel of Marines,
was thus announced to him by his father, in a letter from Bath, on the 4th of
June, 1795:—" My dear Horatio, I have this moment received full authority to
say, that you are appointed one of the Colonels of Marines, vacated by the promotion to Flags. God bless you with all the prosperity this pleasing and much-
wished-for event can bring with it. It marks your public conduct as highly honourable, and worthy of the notice of your Country: it is the general voice that
it was well and properly given. How eminently does such a situation appear above
whatever is obtained by interest or bribery! Myself and your good wife are full of
joy, and we often amuse ourselves in fixing on the cottage retirement, to which you
are looking forward. Lord Hood, you will find, is totally retired; yet I verily believe he came forward as your friend in this business. All allow him judgment
as well as long experience in his profession. I have only to add, that so affectionate a son merits all that a kind father can bestow—his fervent prayers that God
may long preserve him. Farewell, my dear son.—EDMUND NELSON."—*Clarke
and M'Arthur*, vol. i. p. 213.

especially as, by a letter from your Lordship to Lord Hood,[8] you declared your intention to represent my services in the most favourable point of view to the King ; for which I beg leave to return your Lordship my most sincere thanks. In the same letter the doubts which had arisen respecting the damage my eye had sustained at the Siege of Calvi, made it, your Lordship said, impossible to say whether it was such as amounted to the loss of a limb. I have only to tell your Lordship, that a total deprivation of sight for every common occasion in life, is the consequence of the loss of part of the crystal of my right eye.

As I mean not to press on your Lordship the propriety of considering my loss, I shall conclude by assuring you, that my endeavours shall never be wanting to merit a continuance of your good opinion, and that I shall ever consider myself your Lordship's most obliged, humble servant,

HORATIO NELSON.

Being appointed with a small Squadron of Frigates to co-operate with the Austrian General de Vins, I cannot allow my letter to go, without saying that it appears to me that General de Vins is an Officer who perfectly knows his business, and is well disposed to act with vigour on every proper occasion. The Enemy are throwing up strong works near Albinga ; but before three days are past, I expect the Army will be to the westward of them.

TO ADMIRAL HOTHAM.

[From Clarke and M'Arthur, vol. i. p. 220.]

Agamemnon, Vado Bay, 22nd July, 1795.

Sir,

I have the honour to inform you, that I arrived at Genoa on the evening of the 17th, and found there two French

[8] A copy of Earl Spencer's answer to Lord Hood's application for a pension for Captain Nelson, for the loss of his eye, dated 27th of March, 1795, is in the Nelson Papers. After expressing a doubt whether any remuneration could be granted for a wound, unless it were equivalent to the loss of a limb, his Lordship added— " I am sure, however, from the general character of Captain Nelson, and his acknowledged services at all times, that his Majesty cannot fail to approve his being most favourably noticed ; and I shall feel extremely happy in availing myself of whatever proper opportunity may offer, to testify the sense which must be entertained of his pretensions to favour and distinction."

frigates, La Vestale of 32 guns, La Brune of 26 guns, and two brigs, the Scout and Alert. I sailed with Mr. Drake from Genoa at daylight on the 20th, and arrived here yesterday morning, where I found Mr. Trevor waiting for Mr. Drake. I have had a conference with the Austrian General De Vins, who seemed extremely glad to see us. At present I do not perceive any immediate prospect of their getting on to the westward, it appearing to be the General's opinion, that the Enemy must be reduced in their provisions, before the Austrians can make advances; and that for the present, famine is to do more than the sword. You will see, Sir, by my correspondence with Mr. Drake, the necessity I felt myself under to give the orders of which I have the honour to enclose you a copy, together with my correspondence, and I flatter myself you will approve what I have done.

I sail this evening with Mr. Drake and Mr. Trevor, for Genoa, at which place it is not my present intention to anchor, but to return here with all expedition. The Austrian General having fitted out many Privateers, has taken several Vessels laden with corn for France; and I trust, with the disposition of the Ships under my command, I shall be able to stop all intercourse with France from the eastward, hoping you will approve of the measures that have been recommended by the British Ministers at Genoa and Turin.

The Meleager, Captain Cockburn, brought in yesterday a valuable prize:[9] I have no doubt that her cargo is French property; the gold, silver, and jewels, which were found in the cabin, are on board the Agamemnon; but things of much more consequence, I understand, are in the hold: indeed I cannot guess at the value[1] of the cargo. She was deserted by the Master and all the crew; two passengers remained on board, who were left in the hurry. The Southampton[2] joined yesterday evening. The Tarleton was very active; I should

[9] Called " Nostra Signora di Belvedere :" the taking of this vessel was made a great cause of complaint by the Genoese Government, and Captain Cockburn was obliged to vindicate his conduct in a letter to Lord Grenville, then Secretary of State for Foreign Affairs. She sailed fom Marseilles, and was bound to Genoa.—*Clarke and M'Arthur.*

[1] In another Letter he stated, that report had valued her at £160,000 when she left France.—*Ibid.*

[2] Captain, afterwards Lord Edward O'Bryen, brother of William, second Marquis of Thomond: he died a Post-Captain in March, 1824.

be glad to have her again. In respect to Vado Bay, had it not been called a Bay, I should never have named it one : it is a bend in the land, and since I have been here by no means good landing. The water is deep, good clay bottom, and plenty of fresh water; open from E. to S. To the east the land is at a great distance ; but I think a Fleet may ride here for a short time in the summer months. General De Vins returned my visit yesterday afternoon, and was received with all the honour due to his rank. I am, &c.

HORATIO NELSON.

TO MRS. NELSON.

[From Clarke and M'Arthur, vol. i. p. 221. Captain Nelson was sent with a small Squadron, to co-operate with the Austrian and Sardinian Armies, under General de Vins, in driving the French from the Riviera of Genoa.]

Off Vado Bay, 24th July, 1795.

What changes in my life of activity ! Here I am, having commenced a co-operation with an old Austrian General, almost fancying myself charging at the head of a troop of horse. Nothing will be wanting on my part towards the success of the Common Cause. I have eight sail of Frigates[3] under my command ; the service I have to perform is important, and, as I informed you a few days ago from Genoa, I am acting, not only without the orders of my Commander-in-Chief, but in some measure contrary to them. However, I have not only the support of his Majesty's Ministers, both at Turin and Genoa, but a consciousness that I am doing what is right and proper for the service of our King and Country. Political courage in an Officer abroad is as highly necessary as military courage.

The above-mentioned Ministers want the Admiral to give me an order to wear a Distinguishing Pendant. The Austrian Army is composed of 32,000 of the finest Troops I ever saw ; and the General when he gets to Nice will have the baton of

---

[3] Apparently the Inconstant, Captain Fremantle; Meleager, Captain Cockburn ; Tartar, Captain the Honourable Charles Elphinstone ; Southampton, Captain Edward O'Bryen; Ariadne, Captain Robert Gambier Middleton, and afterwards Captain Robert Plampim ; Lowestoffe, Captain Benjamin Hallowell; Romulus, Captain George Hope; Speedy, Captain T. Elphinstone ; and Tarleton, Captain Charles Brisbane.

a Field-Marshal: what shall I get? However, this I can say,
that all I have obtained I owe to myself, and to no one else,
and to you I may add, that my character stands high with
almost all Europe; even the Austrians knew my name perfectly. When I get through this campaign, I think myself
I ought to rest. I hope to God the war will be over, and
that I may return to you in peace and quietness. A little
farm, and my good name, form all my wants and wishes.

Yours, &c.
HORATIO NELSON.

TO THE RIGHT HONOURABLE SIR GILBERT ELLIOT,
VICE-ROY OF CORSICA.

[Autograph, in the Minto Papers.]

Agamemnon, Leghorn, 27th July, 1795.

My dear Sir,

A merchant in this place . . . . whose name I am
confident you will keep secret, has just told me, and intends
to tell the Consul, that gunpowder is sold out of the magazine
at St. Fiorenzo. A Vessel, he says, has just arrived, which
brought over 2000 barrels, and that many others have brought
small quantities. He did not choose to disclose his informer's
name, but I understood he was in the Vessel. As the information can do no harm if false, and a great deal of service if
true, I think it right to send it your Excellency.

A gale of wind has blown me in here from off Genoa, on
which Coast I am stationed to co-operate with the Austrian
army; the advanced posts of that Army are at Loana, 12,000
men, the other part is at Vado, 20,000; a finer body of men I
never saw, and the General seems inclined to go forward, if
England will perform her part, which I hope she will; but the
co-operation expected of us is the putting a stop to all supplies going to France, a measure Admiral Hotham may possibly hesitate complying with. Mr. Trevor and Mr. Drake
have both wrote to him on the absolute necessity of the
measure; in the meantime, in consequence of similar representations, I have directed the Squadron under my orders to
detain all Vessels, to whatever Nation they may belong, bound

to France, or to any place occupied by the armies of France.
This good effect has already resulted from the measure, that
the Genoese are alarmed, and will be careful how they send
their Vessels to an almost certain capture. Insurance is not
at present to be had; the capture of a Tuscan Vessel or two
will stop the Leghorn trade. The only fears that seem to
me to strike England, are of the Barbary States; but, Sir, is
England to give up the almost certainty of finishing this war
with honour, to the fear of offence to such beings? Forbid it
Honour and every tie which can bind a great Nation. If supplies are kept from France for six weeks, I am told, most probably the Austrian Army will be at Nice, which will be a great
event for us, we having guaranteed the repossession of Nice to
the King of Sardinia.

A word for myself; the Colonelcy of Marines has been
given me in a handsome manner, but, in good truth, I am
almost worn out. I find my exertions have been beyond
my strength. I have a complaint in my breast, which will
probably bear me down ; but please God if I see this campaign out, if Agamemnon does not go to England, I must,
the medical people tell me, be on shore for a month or two,
without the thoughts of service. With kindest wishes for your
Excellency's health,

Believe me ever
Your most faithful and obedient
HORATIO NELSON.

His Excellency the Vice-Roy.

TO WILLIAM SUCKLING, ESQ.

[From " The Athenæum."]

Leghorn, July 27th, 1795.

My dear Sir,
I have, I hear, so many letters gone to the Fleet and to
Genoa, that I hope to have one of yours amongst them, and
to hear that all my worthy friends at Kentish Town are well.
I was blown in here yesterday morning by a heavy gale of
wind, from my station off Genoa; at which place I am fixed
to co-operate with the Austrian Army, with eight Frigates under

my command.   The orders I have given, by the advice of the
Ministers of Turin and Genoa, are strong ; and I know not
how my Admiral will approve of them, for they are, in a great
measure, contrary to those he gave me ; but the service requires strong and vigorous measures to bring the war to a conclusion.

My orders are to take and detain all Vessels (to whatever
Nations they may belong) bound to France.   The Genoese
begin to quake ; Tuscany will do the same ; and the Dey of
Algiers seems the only Power which England fears ; but if we
are to finish the war with France, we must not be disposed to
stop at trifles : it has already continued much too long ; more
by an opposition, and fear of an opposition at home, than a
want of power in England.   We have much power here at present to do great things, if we know how to apply it.   Hotham
must get a new head : no man's heart is better, but that will
not do without the other.   If my conduct is approved of, in
September we shall be at Nice, and perhaps across the Var,
for Provence will, I am sure, declare for us the first opportunity.

The weather is turning moderate, and I hope to get to sea
this night, therefore I must conclude, begging you to present
my kindest remembrances to Mrs. Suckling, Miss Suckling,
and our friends at Hampstead.   Believe me ever

Your most obliged and affectionate

HORATIO NELSON.

TO ADMIRAL HOTHAM.

[Autograph, in the Nelson Papers.]

Agamemnon, Leghorn Roads, July 28th, 1795.

Sir,

On the 24th, in the evening, I landed Mr. Drake[4] and Mr.
Trevor[5] in Genoa, and kept towards Vado Bay the whole night.
On the morning of the 25th, a very heavy gale of wind came
on at S.W. ; I endeavoured to clear the Gulf by standing to

---

[4] Francis Drake, Esq., Minister Plenipotentiary at Genoa.

[5] The Honourable John Trevor, Envoy Extraordinary, and Minister Plenipotentiary at Turin.

the W.N.W., but found that was impossible, and it was only by carrying an extraordinary press of sail that I was enabled to weather Cape Rapallo. As I was in great want of wood, instead of going into Port Especia, which I otherwise should have done, I made for this place, where I arrived in the night. Both Saturday and Sunday it blew so hard that not a boat has been able to get off with our wood, oxen, &c., but as this morning is fine, four hours I hope will finish our business, and that I shall get away with Inconstant and Ariadne, the latter having brought the Convoy from Genoa. I am the less uneasy at being blown off my station with a westerly than with an easterly gale, for in the latter case the Enemy I fear would get supplies in spite of us.

There are several Vessels here loaded with corn for France, and some of them under passports from the Dey of Algiers. However, they must be stopped if met with by the Squadron under my orders, and the Ministers of Genoa and Turin must be solely answerable for what may be the result. But, Sir, the whole of the necessity of stopping all the Vessels is comprised in a very few words; that, if we will not stop supplies of corn, &c. going to France, the Armies will return from whence they came, and the failure of this Campaign, from which so much is expected, will be laid to our want of energy; for the only use of the Naval co-operation is the keeping out a supply of provisions, which, if done for six weeks, the Ministers tell me the Austrian Army will be in possession of Nice, and ready to carry on a winter campaign in Provence. But by that time I pray God the war may be finished.

Believe me, Sir, with the highest esteem, your most obedient servant,

HORATIO NELSON.

TO THE REVEREND MR. NELSON, HILBOROUGH.

[Autograph in the Nelson Papers.]

Agamemnon, Gulf of Genoa, July 29th, 1795.

My dear Brother,

I have not, I believe, wrote you since our miserable Action of the 13th. To say how much we wanted Lord Hood at that

time, is to say, will you have all the French Fleet or no
Action? for the scrambling distant fire was a farce; but if one
fell by such a fire, what might not have been expected had
our whole Fleet engaged? Improperly as the part of the
Fleet which fired got into Action, we took one Ship, but
the subject is unpleasant, and I shall have done with it. I am
now co-operating with the Austrian Army, under General de
Vins, and hope we shall do better there. If the Admiral will
support the measures I have proposed, I expect, by the middle
of September, we shall be in Nice, and of course have the harbour of Ville Franche for our Squadron. But Hotham has no
head for enterprise, perfectly satisfied that each month passes
without any losses on our side. I almost, I assure you, wish
myself an Admiral, with the command of a Fleet. Probably,
when I grow older, I shall not feel all that alacrity and anxiety
for the Service which I do at present.

August 3rd.—I have just received your letter of June 11th,
for which I thank you. The Marines certainly came to me in
the most pleasant way, unknown except from services, and
without interest or any one to say a word for me. But I do
not expect to keep them long: they are too good not [to] make
it certain they will take the first opportunity of making me an
Admiral. From the vigorous measures I am taking with the
Genoese, I am most unpopular here. I cannot perhaps, with
safety, land at Genoa, but half measures will never do when I
command. All war or all peace is my idea, and the old
Austrian General is entirely of my way of thinking. Hotham
is coming to look at us, with the Fleet, but the command rests
with me; and very probably I shall be ordered to hoist a Distinguishing Pendant. Do not be surprised if you hear that
we are once more in possession of Toulon. Had Lord Hood
been here, I have no doubt but we should have been there at
this moment.

I beg you will give my kindest remembrances to Mrs.
Nelson, my Aunt, and all our Swaffham friends, and kindest
love to Charlotte and my namesake. He had much better be
a Parson than a Sailor—it is a much quieter trade. I am now
pointed out as having been this war *one hundred and twelve*
times engaged against the French, and always successful to a
certain degree. No Officer in Europe can say as much. I

wish Captain Wickey[6] had a Ship. He is a good man, and
many very indifferent ones are employed. I expect this
autumn will carry Agamemnon to England. Believe me ever
your most affectionate brother,

HORATIO NELSON.

Lieutenant Allison[7] is gone home [in] bad health.

TO MRS. NELSON.

[From Clarke and M'Arthur, vol. i. p. 223.]

Vado Bay, August 2nd, 1795.

At the time we got possession of it before, the Royalists
were by no means so strong at Toulon as they are at this
moment. . . . I have been very negligent, Fanny, in writing to my father, but I rest assured he knows I would have
done it long ago, had you not been under the same roof. At
present I do not write less than from ten to twenty letters
every day; which, with the Austrian General, and Aide-de-
Camps, and my own little Squadron, fully employ my time:
this I like ; active service, or none. Pray draw for £200, my
father and myself can settle our accounts when we meet;
at present, I believe I am the richer man, therefore I desire
you will give my dear father that money.

Yours, &c.

HORATIO NELSON.

TO FRANCIS DRAKE, ESQ., MINISTER AT GENOA.

[From Clarke and M'Arthur, vol. i. p. 224.]

4th August, 1795.

Should the French Ships sail from Toulon, and be bound
to the Archipelago, the Admiral will have a very good chance
of falling in with them ; but I rather am inclined to hope they
are bound to Genoa, to cover their Convoy; and if that be

---

[6] Captain John Wickey: he died an Admiral.

[7] Lieutenant John Allison; he was not promoted until October, 1825, and died a
Commander.

their intention, you may rest assured they shall never do it as long as Agamemnon is above water. Should you hear of their sailing from Toulon, be so good as to let me know it, that if they are coming this way, I may fight them before the Ships from Genoa join.

I am, &c.
Horatio Nelson.

TO FRANCIS DRAKE, ESQ., MINISTER AT GENOA.

[From Clarke and M'Arthur, vol. i. p. 224.]

6th August, 1795.

The disposition and acts of my Cruisers will soon prove incontestably that Genoa is not blockaded, as all Vessels will arrive in perfect security which are not French, or laden with French property. Cruisers off Cape Corse, or the Straits of Bonifaccio, would not stop the trade so well as where I have placed them; were I to remove those Ships on the Especia side of the Gulf, nothing could prevent the escape of the French Squadron, and any Convoy they might choose to carry with them. It ever has been customary to endeavour to intercept Enemy's Vessels coming from Neutral Ports, and the Cruisers off Port Especia are very little nearer Genoa than Leghorn, and are at the utmost extremity of the Genoese Territory'; for I have been most careful to give no offence to the Genoese Territory or Flag. Were I to follow the example which the Genoese allow the French, of having some small Vessels in the Port of Genoa, that I have seen towed out of the Port, and board Vessels coming in, and afterwards return into the Mole, there might then certainly be some reason to say their Neutral Territory was insulted; but the conduct of the English is very different. I take the liberty, Sir, of writing thus fully, which I hope you will excuse, as it may help to furnish you with strong arguments, should the Genoese Government complain: and another cogent reason why British Cruisers are necessary, even on the Coast and before the Port of Genoa, is the necessity of protecting our own trade, and that of our Allies, from the numerous French privateers, which cover the Gulf every night from the Ports of the Republic. I am almost blind, and it is with very great pain I write this letter.

I am, &c.
HORATIO NELSON.

TO CAPTAIN COCKBURN, H.M. SHIP MELEAGER.

[From Clarke and M'Arthur, vol. i. p. 224.]

8th August, 1795.

The Lowestoffe has just joined me: I shall order her to keep about four miles off Port Vado, to prevent the French Ships passing in-shore, and the Agamemnon is kept ready to sail at a moment's notice. I have been ill several days, and this day am alive, and that's all.

I am, &c.
HORATIO NELSON.

TO THE RIGHT HONOURABLE SIR GILBERT ELLIOT,
VICE-ROY OF CORSICA.

[Autograph, in the Minto Papers.]

Vado Bay, August 13th, 1795.

My dear Sir,
  Your kind letter[8] of the 7th I have just received, by the Speedy. I shall answer those parts which relate to business first, and if my health and eyes, which are both almost worn

---

[8] In that Letter Sir Gilbert Elliot said—" Give me leave, my dear Sir, to congratulate you on the Agamemnon's supporting uniformly, on all occasions, the same reputation which has always distinguished that Ship since I have been in the Mediterranean. I know that it was not Agamemnon's fault, if more was not done on the late cruise. It gives me great pleasure also to see you employed in your present important service, which requires zeal, activity, and a spirit of accommodation and co-operation, qualities which will not be wanting in the Commodore of your Squadron. I consider the business you are about, I mean the expulsion of the Enemy from the Genoese and Piedmontese Territories, as the most important feature in the southern campaign, and you cannot bestow a greater favour on me than by giving me intelligence of what is going forward, by as many opportunities as occur." . . . . . . " I am lately returned from a six weeks' tour through the Island, which afforded me the highest satisfaction, both from the improvable nature of the country, and from the general spirit of loyalty, and attachment of the King's country, which manifested itself wherever I went. I may tell you in confi-

F 2

out, will allow, shall endeavour to tell you our little occurrences. Corsica is never from my thoughts; I have entered thirteen or fourteen very fine young men, soldiers, deserters from the Genoese, being Corsicans, for Smith's corps. Mons. Sajet has sent three French deserters for Dillon's corps, and I have put these on board the Tarleton Brig, who shall carry them to Corsica the first opportunity. I received from Mr. Murray, when at Genoa, a few recruits for Smith's corps, which I sent by Vanneau from Leghorn, and told him, and have told Mr. Drake, to send me the men, and I will take care of them. I had letters from good Lord Hood: however wrong he might have been in writing so strongly (he allows he has) to the Admiralty, the Nation has suffered much by his not coming to this Country, for an abler head, or heart more devoted to the service of his Country, is not readily to be met with. When I think of what Lord Bridport did under L'Orient,[9] I cannot but sigh.

Respecting our movements here, they are very slow. General De Vins has been long expecting, but I fear in vain, an attack by General Calli with the Piedmontese, near Ormea, directly back from Ventimiglia. This is the great point to be carried, as the Piedmontese Army would then get Ventimiglia, and, of course, the Enemy's very strong posts near Alberga be useless, and probably, unless they are very active, their retreat to Nice cut off. De Vins says he has flattered and abused the Piedmontese and Neapolitans, but nothing will induce them to act. A plan is now concerted between the General and myself, but unknown to even a Minister, therefore pray do not mention it, to embark (if these other people will not act) 5 or

dence, that Paoli has been endeavouring to stir up mischief, during my absence, in this part of the Island; and by lies, and inventions, some disturbance has been created in the districts adjoining to his own residence. But by perfect firmness and proper temper on my part, these attempts to disturb us are sure of ending in the disgrace of their authors, as in truth this one has already pretty nearly done. It seems that Paoli is not great enough to reconcile himself to the station of a private man and that he still hankers after the Crown, which he gave to the King at a time, indeed, when he could no longer keep it for himself."—*Original*, in the Nelson Papers.

[9] Lord Bridport attacked the French Fleet close in with the Port of L'Orient, on the 24th of June, 1795, and captured L'Alexandre, Le Formidable, and Le Tigre Ships of the Line.

6000 men, and to make a landing between St. Remo and Ventimiglia. Some risk must be run, and the General seems a man who will venture when it is proper. I think I need scarcely say the greatest harmony subsists between us. Admiral Hotham is daily expected, and my humble plans may be put aside, or carried into execution by other Officers, which I should not altogether like; however, I think the Admiral will stay here as little while as possible. The strong orders which I judged it proper to give on my first arrival, have had an extraordinary good effect; the French Army is now supplied with almost daily bread from Marseilles; not a single boat has passed with corn. The Genoese are angry, but that does not matter.

I am truly concerned that Paoli should be troublesome. I had heard it, but could not give credit to such an apparent absurd conduct on his part. I fully trust and believe that your Excellency's mild and equitable administration will leave the good Corsicans little to hope or fear from Paoli and his adherents. Poor Agamemnon is as near worn out as her Captain: we must both soon be laid up to repair. The Marines have been given to me in the handsomest manner. The answer given to many was, the King knew no Officer who had served so much for them as myself. This goes in a packet to Mr. Drake, who I shall request to forward it. I beg my best remembrances to Governor Villettes,[1] and that you will believe me,

Ever your obliged and affectionate
HORATIO NELSON.

To his Excellency the Vice-Roy.

TO WILLIAM LOCKER, ESQ.

[Autograph, in the Locker Papers.]

Vado Bay, August 19th, 1795.

My dear Friend,

I have received your letter of July 8th, with a very late newspaper. I hope Lord Bridport's success and the appearances of the *émigrés* landed in Brittany, will bring this war to

---

[1] Colonel Villettes, Governor of Calvi, vide vol. i. p. 378.

a happy conclusion. The peace with Spain is unfortunate, insomuch as it lets loose an additional Army against the Austrian Army here; for certainly, from the [in]activity of the Spaniards, no benefit whatever arose to the Common Cause. As the conditions of the peace are not to be made public till September 23rd, we may suppose there are some of the Articles by no means pleasant to the Allied Powers I own myself[2]—besides money, the Spaniards have consented to give Ships. I know the French long since offered Spain peace for fourteen Sail of the Line fully stored, I take for granted not manned, as that would be the readiest way to lose them again. My command here of thirteen Sail of Frigates and Sloops is not altogether unpleasant; with the Fleet we do nothing, not a Frigate is allowed to chase out of sight. As I have been so much in the habit of soldiering this war, the moment that it was known the Austrian Army was coming, it was fixed the *Brigadier* must go. However, I have succeeded in all my attempts, and I trust I shall not fail in our present undertaking; nothing shall, as far as my force goes, be wanting on our parts; but Hotham hates this co-operation, and I cannot get him here. The Mediterranean command has ever so much business, compared to any other, that a man of business ought to be here. The Nation has lost much by the dismissal of Lord Hood, probably the whole French Fleet, and certainly again the possession of Toulon. Far be it from me to detract from Admiral Hotham's merits, for a better heart no man possesses, and he is ever kind and attentive to me; but between the abilities of him and Lord Hood can be no comparison. I know not absolutely if Hotham has accepted for a continuance this command, but we expect Sir John Jervis, who, I understand, is a man of business. It is with real sorrow that I should appear to you so negligent in not sending you wine, which I fully intended, by Captain Burgess, of the Argo; but my short history, I hope, will plead my excuse. On the 4th of July the Argo came into Fiorenzo from Leghorn, and I sailed for Genoa the same night: I was chased back on the 7th by the French Fleet, but did not go into Fiorenzo. After our very little business,[3] we anchored at St. Fiorenzo on the 16th, at one P.M., and I

---

[2] *Sic.* 　　[3] "The miserable Action" of the 13th of July. Vide p. 63, ante.

sailed at dark; the Argo was then at Leghorn, for a Convoy: this is the truth, and it must plead my excuse for apparent neglect. If an opportunity offers, will you have the goodness to send me Mr. Charnock's other book.[4] Do you ever hear from Kingsmill? If you write or see him, remember me to him. I thank you for your remembrance of me to Simon Taylor. West India affairs seem to look but black, but I hope they are at the worst, and that no more blood will be shed there. Admiral Ford,[5] I am told, has made £180,000—what a fortune! Remember me most kindly to your sons, and all the family; and believe me, with the sincerest affection,

Ever yours most truly,
HORATIO NELSON.

August 23.

TO J. HARRIMAN, ESQ., CLERK TO MR. UDNEY,
THE BRITISH CONSUL AT LEGHORN.

[Autograph, in the Nelson Papers. It is doubtful if this letter was forwarded.]

Vado Bay, August 23rd, 1795.

My dear Sir,

I return you very many thanks for your kind letter, full of news, and for the enclosure from England, which I received at a time I was most exceedingly ill. But I am now quite recovered. The Admiral, I have no doubt, will have left Leghorn before you receive this letter, as Mr. Drake, who is now here, tells me the Fleet arrived on the 18th. No doubt but the Neapolitan Flotilla would have been of the greatest service here, as we want Vessels of that description very much, but the season is almost past for their acting. A few weeks more and they will not stay a night at sea to save an Empire. We are sorry to hear such very bad accounts from the Coast of Brittany,[6] but somehow on shore we have never been successful for a continuance this war. But I hope this Army will commence our success by land: there is a good man, and I verily believe a good General, at the head of it, but these Piedmontese will not

---

[4] Vide p. 44, ante.
[5] Vice-Admiral of the Blue, John Ford, Commander-in-Chief at Jamaica.
[6] The failure of the Quiberon expedition, in July of that year.

do their utmost to defend, or expel the Enemy from their own Country, and what good can be expected from acting for such a set of people?

I hope the new Governor of Leghorn is a change for the better: as he has been in our service and acting with us, he must know the disposition of the English. I beg you will make my best respects to the Consul, and

Believe me your much obliged

HORATIO NELSON.

August 27th, 1795.

P.S.—I can add a Postscript worth a hundred such letters. Yesterday, I went with part of my Squadron to Alassio and Languelia, places in possession of the French Army, where I did not take the Vessels loaded with corn, as they had landed it, but I took one National Corvette, two small Galleys, one large Gun-boat, and six or seven other Vessels, one fully laden. Had I the Flotilla, nothing should be on this Coast, but the season is almost past for their acting. Pray make my best remembrances to Mr. Udney. I almost despair of seeing the Admiral here.

TO THE COMMANDER OF THE NATIONAL CORVETTE.

[Autograph draught, in the Nelson Papers.]

Agamemnon, Alassio, August 26th, 1795.

Sir,

The French having taken possession of the Town and Coast of Alassio, I cannot but consider it as an Enemy's Coast; therefore, to prevent destruction to the Town, and to avoid the unnecessary effusion of human blood, I desire the immediate surrender of your Vessel. If you do not comply with my desire, the consequences must be with you and not with

Your very humble Servant,

HORATIO NELSON.

TO ADMIRAL HOTHAM.

[Original, in the Admiralty: published in the London Gazette, of October 3rd, 1795. In transmitting Captain Nelson's Dispatch to the Admiralty, Admiral Hotham said, "His officer-like conduct upon this, and, indeed, upon every occasion where his services are called forth, reflects upon him the highest credit."]

Agamemnon, Vado Bay, August 27th, 1795.

Sir,

Having received information from General de Vins, that a Convoy of provisions and ammunition was arrived at Alassio, a place in possession of the French Army, I yesterday proceeded with the Ships named in the margin[7] to that place, where, within an hour, we took the Vessels named in the enclosed list. There was but a very feeble opposition from some of the Enemy's cavalry, who fired on our boats after Boarding the Vessels near the shore, but I have the pleasure to say no man was killed or wounded. The Enemy had two thousand horse and foot Soldiers in the Town, which prevented my landing and destroying their magazines of provisions and ammunition. I sent Captain Fremantle of the Inconstant, with the Tartar, to Languelia, a Town on the west side of the Bay of Alassio, where he executed my orders in the most officer-like manner; and I am indebted to every Captain and Officer of the Squadron for their activity, but most particularly so to Lieutenant George Andrews, first Lieutenant of the Agamemnon, who by his spirited and officer-like conduct saved the French Corvette from going on shore.

I have the honour to be, Sir,

With the highest respect,

Your most obedient Servant

HORATIO NELSON.

---

[7] Inconstant, Meleager, Southampton, Tartar, Ariadne, Speedy.

INCLOSURE, No. 1:—

A List of Vessels taken by his Majesty's Squadron under the Command of Horatio Nelson, Esquire, in the Bay of Alassio and Languelia, August 26th, 1795.

VESSELS' NAMES.	HOW RIGGED.	CARGO. Guns.	Swivels.	Men.	TO WHAT NATION BELONGING.
La Résolve (Corvette)	Polacca Ship { 6 guns thrown overboard	10	4	87	French
La Republique	Gun-boat	6	0	49	French
La Constitution	Galley	Brass 1	4	30	French
La Vigilante	Galley	Boat 1	4	29	French
Name unknown	Brig, 100 tons . . .	Ballast			French
Ditto	Bark, 70 tons	Powder and Shells			French
La Giuletta	Brig, 100 tons . . .	Wine			French
Name unknown	Galley, 50 tons . . .	Ballast			Unknown
Ditto	Tartan, 35 tons . . .	Wine			Unknown
Destroyed	One.				
Name unknown	Bark	Powder			Drove on shore
Ditto	Bark	Provisions . . .			Burned

HORATIO NELSON.

INCLOSURE, No. 2:—

Dimensions of the Resolve:

	Feet.	Inches.
Length from the after-part of the stern to the fore-part of the stern-post . . . . }	84	9
Extreme breadth from outside to outside . .	26	1
Depth of the hold	11	10

	Feet.	Inch.	
Draught of water . . . . . {	8	10	Aft.
	7	10	Forward.

206 Tons.

Guns on board:—Four nine-pounders, iron; four brass swivels. Hove overboard—two twelve-pounders, four nine-pounders.

Very well stowed.

Vado Bay, August 28th, 1795.

TO ADMIRAL HOTHAM.

[Autograph draught, in the Nelson Papers.]

Agamemnon, at Sea, August 27th, 1795.

Dear Sir,

As it is perfectly understood by the Genoese Republic that the part of the Riviera in the possession of the French Army will be considered, whilst they remain in it, as an Enemy's Country by the Allied Powers, I thought it much better not to say anything about it in my Public Letter, for I do not believe there will be any representation from the deed I did yesterday, for not a boat or message came from the Town, during my stay. On my approach, Genoese colours were hoisted on a small battery of two brass guns, which I laid the Agamemnon within pistol-shot of. The French lined the beach, with their colours at the head of their battalions, but humanity to the poor inhabitants would not allow me to fire on them. The same motives induced me to summons the Corvette to surrender, as our fire must have greatly injured the Town. My Summons induced the crew to abandon her. Latterly the French cavalry fired so hot on our Boats at the West end of the Town that I was obliged to order the Meleager to fire a few shot to protect them, and I have reason to believe the Enemy suffered some loss.

The Ariadne by the great zeal of Captain Plampin to do much, having already taken the two small Gallies got on shore, but she was got off without any damage; but it retarded our operations a little, and gave the Enemy an opportunity of landing more of their cargoes than I intended by our Boats being employed in assisting her. The Corvette is the long black polacca Ship which kept close alongside the Sans Culotte on the 13th of July, and outsails us all. The Gallies and Gun-boat I shall sell to the Austrian General, or the King of Sardinia, if he will buy them.

I have only to conclude by saying that Mr. Drake, who I left at Vado, much approved of my Expedition. The Meleager joined me on the 24th with your letters, which I communicated to the General. He was to set off last night to view the Enemy's position, and to return in about three days, when probably I shall hear more of his intentions of proceeding to the westward.

I am, &c.

HORATIO NELSON.

TO ADMIRAL HOTHAM.

[Original, in the Admiralty.]

Agamemnon, Vado Bay, August 30th, 1795.

Sir,

Having received information that a Ship loaded with provisions had arrived at Oneglia, I yesterday afternoon manned the two small Gallies (taken on the 26th) with forty-four Officers and men from the Agamemnon, and ten men belonging to the Southampton, under the command of Lieutenant George Andrews and Lieutenant Peter Spicer,[8] of the Agamemnon, and ordered Lieutenant Andrews to proceed to Oneglia, and to endeavour to take the said Ship. On his way down, about nine o'clock at night, he fell in with three large Vessels, with lateen sails, which he engaged at ten o'clock. One of these was carried by boarding, the men belonging to her retiring to the others, and cut her adrift (the three Vessels being made fast to each other.) At half-past ten, the attack on the other two was renewed with the greatest spirit, but the number of men in the vessels was too great, united with the height of the Vessels, for our force; and my gallant Officers and men, after a long contest, were obliged to retreat; and it is with the greatest pain I have to render so long a list of killed and wounded.

The spirited and officer-like conduct of Lieutenants Andrews and Spicer I cannot sufficiently applaud; and every praise is due to each individual for their exceeding bravery and good conduct.

I have the honour to be, &c.,

HORATIO NELSON.

N.B. The Vessels had no Colours hoisted, but a Greek Flag has been found on board the Prize.

---

[8] Afterwards a Post-Captain.

List of Killed and Wounded.

AGAMEMNON.

Killed, 3 ; mortally wounded, 3 ; wounded, 7.

Officers' names.—Mr. Thomas Withers,[9] Mate, wounded ;
Mr. William D. Williams, Midshipman, mortally wounded ;
Mr. Samuel Gamble, wounded.

SOUTHAMPTON.

Killed, 1 ; mortally wounded, none ; wounded, 3.

Total.—Killed, 4 ; mortally wounded, 3 ; wounded, 10.

HORATIO NELSON.

TO CAPTAIN COLLINGWOOD.

[Autograph, in the possession of the Honourable Mrs. Newnham Collingwood.]

Vado Bay, August 31st, 1795.

My dear Coll.,

I cannot allow a Ship to leave me without a line for my old
friend, who I shall rejoice to see ; but I am afraid the Admiral
will not give me that pleasure at present. You are so old a
Mediterranean man, that I can tell you nothing new about the
Country. My command here is so far pleasant as it relieves
me from the inactivity of our Fleet, which is great indeed, as
you will soon see. From the event of Spain making peace,
much may be looked for,—perhaps a war with that Country :
if so, their Fleet (if no better than when our Allies) will soon
be done for. Reports here say, they mean to protect Genoese
and other Vessels from search by our Cruisers, in the Gulf of
Genoa. If so, the matter will soon be brought to issue ; for I
have given positive directions to search such Vessels, denying
the right of the Spaniard to dictate to us what Ships we shall
or shall not search. The Genoese are going, it is said, to
carry a Convoy with provisions to their Towns in the Riviera of
Genoa, in possession of the French Army. However cruel it
may appear to deprive poor innocent people of provisions, yet
policy will not allow it to be done, for if the inhabitants have
plenty, so will the Enemy, and therefore I have directed them

[9] He died a Post-Captain, in 1843.

to be brought into Vado. So far have I gone; and trust I
have acted, and shall act, so as to merit approbation. Our
Admiral, *entre nous*, has no political courage whatever, and is
alarmed at the mention of any strong measure; but, in other
respects, he is as good a man as can possibly be.

I hope, my dear friend, you left Mrs. Collingwood well.
How many children have you? Did you see Mrs. Moutray
lately? Her dear, amiable son was lost by serving under me.
I have a stone on board, which is to be erected in the church
of St. Fiorenzo to his memory.[1] I hardly ever knew so amiable
a young man. Believe me, ever, my dear Collingwood,

Your most affectionate Friend,

HORATIO NELSON.

Tell me a great deal.

TO JOHN MACARTHUR, ESQ., LEGHORN.

[Autograph, in the possession of Mrs. Conway.]

Vado Bay, August 31st, 1795.

My dear Sir,

We send you and Pollard, but you are my Agent, a Brig
with wine. She is French, we are sure. If the Admiral does
not buy the Corvette,[2] the King of Sardinia probably will; and
as I intend to take a number of Prizes, I sincerely wish we
had an Agent resident here, to take all the trouble off my
hands. I have Gallies, Gun-boats, Transports, &c. to sell,
and I manage all.

The money for the corn I have on board: it must be condemned, if there is any justice. Our Allies to supply our
Enemies is too much. Two others who sailed from Cagliari
are arrived at Nice. I have paid freight, and liberated the
Vessel, she being Genoese.

I have 110 barrels of gunpowder to sell. What is the price
[per] barrel of 130 or 40 lbs.?

Yours truly,

HORATIO NELSON.

The head-money you must get us for the Corvette and Gun-
boat: for the Gallies, perhaps they are not worth the condem-
nation.

---

[1] Vide the Inscription in vol. i. p. 482.   [2] Taken at Alassio. Vide p. 73.

TO MRS. NELSON.

[From Clarke and M'Arthur, vol. i. p. 229.]

Vado Bay, 1st September, 1795.

We have made a small Expedition with the Squadron, and taken a French Corvette and some other Vessels, in which affair I lost no men; but since, I have not been so successful. I detached Mr. Andrews to cut off a Ship from Oneglia: on his passage, he fell in with three Turkish Vessels, as it has since turned out, who killed and wounded seventeen of my poor fellows. Seven are already dead, and more must be lost by the badness of their wounds; and I am sorry to add, that the Turks got into Genoa, with six millions of hard cash: however, they who play at bowls must expect rubs; and the worse success now, the better, I hope, another time. Our Fleet is still at Leghorn. Collingwood I hear is arrived in the Excellent, 74, with the Convoy from England. I am almost afraid that the campaign in this Country will end in a very different manner from what might have been expected; but I will do my best until it finishes.

Yours, &c.

Horatio Nelson.

TO HIS EXCELLENCY FRANCIS DRAKE, ESQ.

[Original, in the possession of Mrs. Davies.]

Agamemnon, at Sea, September 9th, 1795.

Dear Sir,

I am just favoured by your letter of September 1st, by a Ship from Vado. I was induced to go to the westward for the reasons I had the honour of writing you before I sailed, and, in addition, to make my own observations. I send you a copy of a paper I shall give to General De Vins, which I hope you will approve. I trust you will give me credit that no idle speculative advantages are in my view, but that my opinion is formed from experience and knowledge of what my Squadron can perform.

If General De Vins will not move to the westward, the fault does not lay with his Majesty's Fleet, who undertakes everything which can be expected from it.

I have no doubt in my mind, but the whole French Army to the eastward of St. Remo would fall, or they must instantly quit their strong works at St. Espirito, and retreat, if possible, by the mountains; and Oneglia could be retaken whenever the General thought proper to send a body of men which I could land close to it, and in a situation which would instantly command the Town.

On the subject of the Genoese supplying their Town with provisions, I will do myself the honour of writing you a separate letter.

I have the honour to be, &c.

HORATIO NELSON.

MEMOIR SENT TO GENERAL DE VINS.

[From Clarke and M'Arthur, vol. i. p. 229.]

[About 9th of September.]

Having been down the Coast to the westward, as far as Nice, the following is the result of my observation; and the service which I can undertake to perform with his Majesty's Squadron, should you, Sir, be inclined to think it right to get to the westward of your present situation.

I can embark four or five thousand men, with their arms and a few days' provisions, on board the Ships of the Squadron, and will engage to land them within two miles of St. Remo, with their field-pieces. It is necessary for me to point out the necessity of possessing St. Remo, and its situation with respect to the sea; as it is the only place between Vado and Ville Franche, where the Squadron can lie in safety. The Town is situated in the middle of a small Bay, where the Squadron can anchor in almost all winds: in some respects it is as good as Vado Bay; in others, for the security of large Ships, it certainly is not so. It has a Mole, where all small Vessels can lie and load and unload their cargoes: an advantage which Vado has not. Secondly, respecting provisions for the Austrian Army, I will undertake to provide sufficient Convoys, that they shall arrive in safety: and, thirdly, there can be no doubt but an embarkation of the Troops, should such a measure prove necessary, might always be covered by the Squadron.

The possession of St. Remo, as Head-quarters for Magazines of stores and provisions, would enable General de Vins to turn his Army to the eastward or westward ; the Enemy at Oneglia would be cut off from provisions, and a body of men could be landed to attack it, whenever it might be judged necessary. Nice, from the vicinity of St. Remo, would be completely blockaded by sea; and the British Fleet, twenty-three Sail of the Line, are now off Toulon.

TO HIS EXCELLENCY BARON DE VINS.

[From a Copy, in the possession of Mrs. Davies. This Letter was a reply to General de Vins' answer to the preceding Memoir, dated on the 14th of September, wherein the General said, " I have received with much pleasure, your Memoir, concerning an attack in the neighbourhood of St. Remo, which you have been pleased to communicate. You are well aware that in all enterprises it is necessary to calculate the advantages that would accrue, if entirely successful, or only partially so ; and also the disadvantages that might arise, if it terminated unsuccessfully. You say in the Memoir that the Bay of St. Remo is equally good with that of Vado. I am not a seaman, but from the information I have collected respecting the different anchorages along the coast of the Riviera, I have been led to conclude, that Vessels of a certain size could not approach St. Remo nearer than at the distance of a mile, or thereabouts, and that even then they were exposed, whilst at anchor, to every wind that blows ; whereas, on the contrary, in Vado Bay, as we have it on record, the English Fleet, under the orders of Admiral Matthews, passed a great part of the winter there, during the years 1745 and 1746. In the Military Commission that was held at Milan on the 22nd of June 1794, it was said that the Allies ought to make themselves Masters of the Road and Port of Vado, it being the only anchorage of the Riviera, where an English Fleet could remain during the winter, and prevent the Enemy from making any attempt on Italy ; si cependant Monsieur le Commandant Nelson est assuré qu'une partie de la Flotte puisse y passer l'hiver, il n'y a aucun risque auquel je ne m'exposerai avec plaisir pour procurer des abris assurés aux Vaisseaux de S.M. Britannique."—*Clarke and M'Arthur*, vol. i. p. 230.]

Agamemnon, Vado Bay, September 14th, 1795.

Sir,

I am honoured with your Excellency's letter of this day's date: my reason for the necessity of possessing St. Remo, was not that it was a better anchorage than Vado, as I say the contrary in my Observations, but that it is the best between Vado and Nice, and perfectly safe for all small Vessels.

I cannot, or do not, pretend to judge of the movements your Excellency may think proper to make ; but I wished to inform you of the support and assistance it is in my power to

give you, and on which you may depend in any arrangement
making, for getting to the westward.

I beg leave to transmit you a copy of Admiral Hotham's
letter[2] to me of August 19th, which I believe is a full answer to
one part of your letter. I beg leave to assure your Excellency
that I am ever ready to give you every assistance in my power,
and that I am,

With the greatest truth, your Excellency's

Most faithful obedient servant,

HORATIO NELSON.

TO MRS. NELSON.

[From Clarke and M'Arthur, vol. i. p. 231.]

Vado Bay, 15th September, 1795.

I am not, Fanny, quite so well pleased as I expected with
this Army, which is slow beyond all description; and I begin
to think, that the Emperor is anxious to touch another four
millions of English money.[3] As for the German Generals,
war is their trade, and peace is ruin to them; therefore we
cannot expect that they should have any wish to finish the
war. I have just made some propositions to the Austrian
General to spur him on, which I believe he would have been
full as well pleased had I omitted: in short, I can hardly
believe he means to go any farther this winter. I am now

---

[2] Clarke and M'Arthur (i. 227,) have given the following copy of Admiral Hotham's Letter to Captain Nelson, of the 19th of August:—" I have received your
letter of the 16th, [this Letter has not been found] informing me of General de
Vins' desire, to have clear answers to the propositions therein stated. To the first
of which, viz.: 'Will the Admiral return to Vado from Leghorn?' I answer, Uncertain; but I rather think I shall not have an opportunity of returning there,
owing to the intelligence I have received from the Admiralty, which renders my
presence immediately necessary in another place. To the second proposition, viz.,
'Will the Admiral assist, and cover the landing of from six to ten thousand men, on
the Coast of Provence?' I answer, That it will not be in my power so to do, on
account of the Fleet being required for another service, as stated in the preceding
answer. To the third proposition, viz., 'Will the Admiral undertake to prevent the
Toulon fleet from molesting my operations?' I answer, Yes, most certainly."

[3] By a Convention signed at Vienna, on the 4th of May, 1795, between the King
of Great Britain and the Emperor, it was agreed that 4,600,000l. should be raised
in England on account of his Imperial Majesty, who engaged to employ in his different Armies in the campaign of this year, at least 200,000 effective men.

under sail, on my way to Genoa, to consult with our Minister on the inactivity of the Austrians; and he must take some step to urge these people forward. The small Flotilla from Naples has just joined; but the season is almost too late for their acting. However, if they will act, I can find them plenty of employment; though I doubt their inclination. I hope my dear father is as well as I sincerely pray he may be.

Yours, &c.
HORATIO NELSON.

TO GENERAL DE VINS.

[From Clarke and M'Arthur, vol. i. p. 231.]

Genoa Mole, 17th September, 1795.

Your Excellency having doubtless suggested a much better plan than the debarkation of the Troops at St. Remo, which, I again take the liberty of reminding you, was mentioned as the only place proper for landing stores and provisions: if you would have the goodness to let me know the time, and the number of Troops ready to embark, I will immediately dispatch a Ship to Admiral Hotham, to request he will order a sufficient number of Transports; which, if at Corsica, I am sure he will instantly do, and I trust that your Excellency's plan would be successful in its fullest extent. Your Excellency will see by the Admiral's letter of August 19th, of which I had the honour to send you a copy, that the Admiral insures you from any molestation in your operations by the French Fleet.

I am, &c.
HORATIO NELSON.

TO ADMIRAL HOTHAM.

[From Clarke and M'Arthur, vol. i. p. 231.]

Genoa, 17th September, 1795.

Sir,

I came here yesterday morning for the purpose of communicating with his Majesty's Minister[4] on several very important

---

[4] On the 13th of September, Mr. Drake wrote to Captain Nelson : " General de Vins' excuse, about the Court of Turin having made Peace is a mere pretext : to

points, and, amongst others, on the appearance of the inactivity of the Austrian General de Vins, who, at my first coming on this station, seemed very anxious to get to Nice ; and indeed I had very little doubts as to the accomplishment of it. However, week after week has passed, without his Army having removed one foot to the westward of where I found them. You know, Sir, his desire to have answers to three questions I had the honour to send you—which you gave him; and, in the last, you declared, that the French Fleet should not molest his operations : this answer was certainly all he could have wished.

As I perceived that every idea of an attack on the Enemy's works at St. Espirito was given over, I proceeded down the Coast to the westward as far as Nice, and the only place where I found it practicable to land the Troops, was near St. Remo, a Genoese Town in possession of the French troops, except the Citadel. You will see, the General's answer to my letter goes totally wide from what I could have meant. As it had for some time appeared to me that the General intended to go no farther than his present 'position, and meant to lay the miscarriage of the enterprise against Nice, which I had always been taught to believe was the great object of this Army, to the non-cooperation of the British Fleet and the Sardinian Army; to leave the General no room to insinuate such a want on our part, has been the object of my Memoir, which I hope you will approve. In concert with Mr. Drake, I have written this day to the General. If his answer should be the desire of Transports, I think we have them—a passage of twenty-four hours is the outside ; but I suspect he will now find other excuses, and were you to grant the whole Fleet for Transports, I verily believe some excuse would be found. This, Sir, is my public opinion, and which I wish not to conceal : happy shall I be to find myself mistaken, and with what ardour would I give the General every support, should such a favourable change take place.   I am, &c.

HORATIO NELSON.

P.S.—I have just received the General's answer to my

leave him no loop hole, I have written to him to-day, to assure him formally and ministerially, that it is not true; and you are fully at liberty to repeat to the General, in the strongest manner, these assurances from me."

letter written in concert with Mr. Drake. As I know not the place of debarkation, I cannot say anything about it; but believe it is between Nice and the Var, where the Country people have never been subjected to the French; and it is expected they will take the batteries on the Coast, and hold them until a landing is effected. If the General is in earnest, which I still doubt, I have no fear for the success, and we shall yet have Ville Franche.

TO HIS EXCELLENCY FRANCIS DRAKE, ESQ.

[Autograph, in the possession of John Bullock, Esq.]

Agamemnon, Genoa Mole, September 18th, 1795.

My dear Sir,

The occasion of the Inconstant's having been fired upon by the Battery, as reported to the Officer commanding the Agamemnon in my absence, by the Captain of the Port, is as follows :—

That when I came in I was told that no other Ship of War could enter the Port, to which I said, none other was coming in; that the first gun was only with powder, and as she still came in, the other was with shot fired ahead of her, and that he requested I would make a signal for the Ships not to enter the Port. Having said this, he went on shore. The Inconstant wanted [to have communication with me[5]] therefore stood round the Agamemnon. This case can hardly be called coming into Port—at least, we do not understand it so.

These are the facts as stated to me. I should like to know one thing, on which must hinge the propriety or impropriety, of the conduct of [the] Republic : Would the Republic, in no situation of danger whatever, admit more than five Ships inside the Mole-head? If they answer ' No,' I have but little to say ; but if they answer ' Yes,' how could they tell that the Inconstant was not necessitated from some cause to make for a Port? No inquiries were made, but the first notice is a shot—to say, whatever may be your distress, you shall not enter here, or find protection in Genoa Mole. [Much more[5]]

---

[5] The original being torn in these places, the lacunæ are supplied from the copy in Clarke and M'Arthur, vol. i. p. 232.

might be said, but I am sure you will do what is right. The demanding an explanation may one day serve our turn by the answer they may give.

If I was to chase a French Ship of War, and she went into Genoa Mole, at a time when there were more than five Ships in the Mole, and they did not fire on her, and turn her out, I would instantly attack her on their own reasoning, 'We will protect five, and no more.'

TO ADMIRAL HOTHAM.

[From Clarke and M'Arthur, vol. i. p. 234.]

September 20th, 1795.

I have had a meeting with General de Vins this morning, who informed me, that yesterday his Troops carried a Post of the Enemy in the centre of the mountain St. Espirito, and that the Austrians are now within half musket-shot of some other point, which, if possible, he means to attack : he is going to the advanced post himself. The General also told me, that the moment he knows the Transports are ready, he will head the Troops, and has no doubt of being successful.—Four or five thousand peasantry are ready to take a battery of eight guns, where the landing is to be effected : for such a short voyage, a few Ships will carry the men ; and if the Dolphin is at hand, or the Camel cleared, they would take a great number. I hope, Sir, the General will be left without any excuse.

I am, &c.

HORATIO NELSON.

TO MRS. NELSON.

[From Clarke and M'Arthur, vol. i. p. 234.]

September 21st, 1795.

I have been, in concert with his Majesty's Minister, very hard at work in pushing the Austrian General forward; and yesterday morning got them to make an attack, that has been successful, and they have carried the centre Post, on the ridge of mountains occupied by the French Troops. The Action lasted ten hours, and if the General will carry one other point, we shall gain thirty-three miles of Country. Another plan is in agitation, which, if the Admiral will give me Transports to carry a certain number of Troops, will astonish the French, and perhaps the English. The General, if he can be brought to move, is an Officer of great abilities ; but the politics of his Court so constantly tie his hands, that he cannot always do what he thinks proper. However, if the Army does not move, our Minister, who is fixed at Head-quarters, will endeavour to withhold the remainder of the Emperor's loan—say gift : this is an all-powerful motive with a German Court, and for which the lives of their Subjects are held in no estimation : I am become a politician, almost fit to enter the Diplomatic line.

September 24th.—I am just arrived at Leghorn, and have received a most honourable testimony of my conduct, which has been transmitted from the Austrian General to our Minister.[6]. It has not, indeed, been in my power to perform much ; but I have done all I could to serve the Cause.

Yours, &c.

HORATIO NELSON.

TO THE RIGHT HONOURABLE SIR GILBERT ELLIOT,
VICE-ROY OF CORSICA.

[Autograph, in the Minto Papers.]

Agamemnon, Leghorn, September 24th, 1795.

My dear Sir,

The news I can tell you is very little. The General seemed to make excuses for his not going on, apparently to me very frivolous, and I am sure it was his intention to have laid part of the blame of the want of success in this campaign to the non-cooperation of the British Fleet ; and as it was, he said, impossible to force the Enemy's works at St. Esprit, he seemed very much inclined to rest for the winter at Vado. However, to leave him without an excuse on my part, I went down the Coast to the westward, as far as Nice, and sounded and ex-

6 Vide p. 89, post.

amined every Port. On my return, I offered to carry five thousand men at one time, and to land them, bag and baggage, with their field-pieces, and to ensure their safe Convoys of provisions. This would have cut off all supplies for the Enemy to the Eastward, and they must, in my opinion, have abandoned their stupendous works at St. Esprit. To this paper the General gave me another plan, which he thought would be better; but as this requires a small degree of assistance from Admiral Hotham, it cannot be carried into execution till I hear from the Admiral. I only want Transports, and if he gave me one Seventy-four, I verily believe we shall yet possess Nice. Mr. Drake perhaps tells you how we are obliged to manœuvre about the General, but the politics of Courts are, my dear Sir, (I see,) so mean, that private people would be ashamed to act in the same way : all is trick and finesse, to which is sacrificed the Common Cause.

The General wants a loop-hole, but I hope he will not have one ; he shall not, if I can help it, for I want Ville Franche for a good anchorage this winter. From what motives I don't know,—I hope, from a good one,—the General sent orders to attack the Enemy's strongest post at St. Esprit. After an attack of ten hours, it was carried. The General seems pleased, and says, if he can carry one other, the Enemy must retire, which would give us the Country as far as Oneglia. Then comes another objection, which I am preparing against— viz., he will say I cannot hold an extent of Sea-coast of forty miles. I must give up Vado, for the Enemy at Ormea are on my left flank, and the Piedmontese will not attack them ; however, time and opportunity may do much.

Mr. Drake has just received his appointment to reside at the Head-quarters of the Austrian Army. I rejoice at it. The loss of the Austrians in the last attack was 1000 killed and wounded. The Austrians have a battery of six 24-pounders in the centre of the Enemy's posts. I send over nine men for Colonel Smith's corps, which I entered for him at Genoa and Vado. I have on board, for their passage to Leghorn, three Officers of Dillon's, who have been obliged to leave Genoa. It gives me pain to hear such bad accounts of the behaviour of many of the Corsicans. What they can mean, is impossible for me to guess, unless French gold has found its way amongst

some of their Chiefs; but I hope they will yet be quiet, and
no longer troublesome to your Administration, which has done
so much for them. I beg my best compliments to Governor
Villettes, and believe me, dear Sir,

> Most faithfully yours,
> HORATIO NELSON.

TO THE REVEREND MR. NELSON, BATH.

[Autograph, in the Nelson Papers.]

Leghorn, September 29th, 1795.

My dear Father,

I am this moment receiving the pleasure of your letter of
September 3rd, and should be glad, did circumstances so turn
out, that I could get to England in the Agamemnon, for in no
other way can I get home with honour or propriety ; and I
must say, except the being at home, I know of no Country
so pleasant to serve in as this, or where my health is so good.
My command at Vado is honorary though expensive, for all
Foreigners only consider our rank and not our pay. I have
the satisfaction to have received the handsomest testimony of
conduct, and as I know you will partake with me that satisfaction,
I send you a copy of the Minister's Note to the Admiral—viz.,
' I cannot in justice to the abilities, judgment, and activity of
Captain Nelson, omit mentioning to your Excellency, the
very high opinion in which that Officer is held by General de
Vins and the other Austrian General-Officers; and I have
thought it my duty to transmit to his Majesty's Ministers at
Home this handsome testimony which our Allies bear to the
zeal and good conduct of that Officer, whom your Excellency
was pleased to select to command the Squadron co-operating
with them. This unprejudiced testimony is no less flattering
to Captain Nelson than to your Excellency's discernment in
having made choice of him for this service.'

I have nothing to write about but myself, for none else
attempts to do anything. If our plan can be carried into
execution, we shall take Nice, but much must be left to
chance : the plan well laid is most likely, but never certain, of
success. I came in here four days past and am now under
sail for Vado. Our Fleet has arrived at Corsica from a

cruize off Toulon, where they permitted six Sail of the Line and eight Frigates to escape out of Toulon,[7] and I believe they have left the Mediterranean. Having talked of myself, I have nothing more to add, except that Admiral Hotham is just going to send six Sail of the Line after the French Ships escaped from Toulon,[8] and supposed to be gone to the West Indies. Josiah is well, never ill. Hoste has almost recovered his broken leg.[9] Parted with Frank[1] for drunkenness, and when so, mad : never will keep a drunkard another hour. Agamemnon almost worn out, must go home shortly. With best love to my wife, believe me

Your most affectionate and dutiful Son,

HORATIO NELSON.

I was not much surprised to hear of Mr. Raven's departure, but very much of poor Edmund Rolfe.[2]

TO THE COMMANDER OF THE NEAPOLITAN FLOTILLA.

[From Clarke and M'Arthur, vol. i. p. 235.]

1st October, 1795.

Sir,

The Enemy's Gun-boats having very much annoyed the Austrian Camp, near Loano, I must desire that you will, until further orders, consider the preventing of these Boats from an-

[7] Under Rear-Admiral Richery.

[8] James says (*Naval History*, vol. i. p. 273,) that Admiral Hotham heard of the escape of the French Squadron by a Cartel, on the 22nd of September; and that it was not until the 5th of October that he detached Rear-Admiral Man, with six Sail of the Line, after them.

[9] Mr. Hoste broke his leg on board of one of the Vessels taken out of Alassio on the 27th of August, by falling down the scuttle. He gave a humorous account of the accident in a letter to his brother, on the 14th of September, wherein he said—" Captain Nelson often comes down to see me, and tells me to get everything I want from him."—*Memoirs of Sir William Hoste*, vol. i. p 44.

[1] Frank Lepée, his old servant. Frank Lepée was frequently mentioned in Mrs. Nelson's letters to her husband; and it appears from her letter of the 10th of December, 1794, that he had fallen into disgrace : — " Poor Frank ! I own I was afraid something was the matter—that he was not so good as formerly; I am very sorry that he is in so deplorable a way; I hope he never is with you; you may be able to get him in Greenwich Hospital. You are sure of Captain Locker."

[2] His first cousin, son of the Reverend Robert Rolfe by Alice Nelson, vide vol. i. p. 18.

noying the Austrian Camp, as the greatest and only service which I at present wish you to perform; and I hope, from the zeal which the Officers of the King of Naples have always shown, that you will soon find an opportunity of attacking and destroying these Gun-boats.

If you can spare any of the Feluccas from this service, I shall be glad to have two of them stationed between Vado and Genoa, to prevent the Enemy's row-boats, from Genoa, molesting the Vessels with provisions for the Army at Vado.

I am, &c.

HORATIO NELSON.

TO MRS. NELSON.

[From Clarke and M'Arthur, vol. i. p. 236.]

Vado Bay, October 5th, 1795.

Nothing has occurred, since I wrote last, except the sailing of the French Squadron from Genoa. As soon as they knew of my absence, they made a push, and I fear are all got off. Two of our Frigates were seen firing at them; but I have not much expectation of their success. It was a near touch, for I came back the next morning, after they had sailed on the preceding evening. I am vexed and disappointed; but the best laid schemes, if obliged to be trusted to others, will sometimes fail. I must submit, and hope for better luck another time: yet a Squadron of French Ships would have so graced my triumph! In the opinion of the Genoese, my Squadron is constantly offending: so that it almost appears a trial between us, who shall first be tired, they of complaining, or me of answering them. However, my mind is fixed; and nothing they can say will make me alter my conduct towards them.

Our Armies are very close to the French, every hour I expect an attack from them; as the General, from some cause or other, does not just now seem to be in the humour to begin the attack.—I have just received a very affectionate letter from his Royal Highness the Duke of Clarence,[3] and he appears to remember our long acquaintance with much satisfaction: one of his expressions is, ' I never part with a letter of yours, they

[3] Vide p. 97.

are to me highly valuable.' He finds me unalterable, which I
fancy he has not always done in those he has honoured with a
preference.

Yours, &c.,

HORATIO NELSON.

TO WILLIAM SUCKLING, ESQ.

[From "The Athenæum." The Agamemnon was sent to reconnoitre Toulon,
in company with the Flora, towards the end of October, but she returned to her
station off Vado early in the following month.]

Agamemnon, off Marseilles, October 27th, 1795.

My dear Sir,

Although I seldom have the pleasure of hearing immediately
from yourself, yet Mrs. Nelson never fails of telling me of your
health, the goodness of which, she well knows, gives me real
satisfaction.

The campaign of our Allies, the Austrians and Piedmontese,
is, I suppose, almost over, not that I am in the secret when it
commenced. My situation with this Army has convinced me,
by ocular demonstration, of the futility of Continental Alliances.
The conduct of the Court of Vienna, whatever may be said by
the House of Commons to the contrary, is nothing but deception : I am certain, if it appears to that Court to be their interest
to make peace with France, it will be instantly done. What is
Austria better than Prussia, or *vice versâ ?*—in one respect,
Prussia perhaps may be better than Austria : the moment he
got our money he finished the farce. Austria, I fear, may induce us to give her more, for to a certainty she will not carry
on another campaign without more money ; but it appears to
me that the continuance or cessation of the war depends entirely on the French Nation themselves : it will now be seen
whether they are willing to receive and join the Count d'Artois
and have Royalty ; or if they oppose him, that they are determined to be a Republic. If the first, at this moment of writing
all must be nearly finished : if they destroy the Emigrants
landed at Charente, it is clear the French Nation wish to be a
Republic ; and the best thing we can do, is to make the best
and quickest peace we can : the landing the Emigrants is our
last trial ; and if that fail, we have done our utmost to place

Louis upon the Throne. To me, I own, all Frenchmen are alike : I despise them all. They are (even those who are fed by us) false and treacherous : even Louis XVIII. receives our money, and will not follow our advice, and keep up the dignity of the King of France at Verona.

Fame, with her wings and long tongue, has proclaimed that prizes (and, of course, riches are imagined,) have fallen most abundantly on the Agamemnon. I wish I could tell you it is true ; if the Golden Fleece is condemned, which I very much doubt, from the number who share for her—nine of us,--if I get 5 or 600 pounds, what a valuable prize she must be ! My others, although pretty numerous, are scarcely anything ; for I assure you, that if, at the conclusion of the war, I save my pay for the Agamemnon, I shall feel myself extremely fortunate. Everything is by comparison : except one or two Line of Battle Ships, we are the only one who has got a pound ; and they must, from the expenses of a Fleet, have spent a little fortune—so far I feel highly fortunate.

As the Armies are quiet, the Admiral has given me directions to look after the French Fleet at Toulon (whilst he lies quiet in Leghorn Roads) ; and as I know of no person so active as myself, here I am with one Frigate off Marseilles—not a Vessel to be seen ; but before I close my letter I hope to say we have a prize.

Remember me most kindly to Mrs. Suckling, Miss Suckling, and every part of the family. Is Captain Suckling still on the Continent ?　　　November 2nd.[3]

No success, although I have been indefatigable. The seamen have all deserted the Ships in Toulon, therefore as a Fleet, they cannot come to sea again. In France they had a very fine harvest, and bread is by no means dear or scarce. The Spanish Vessels now fill Marseilles with every comfort and luxury. Peace, I believe, will yet be with us before next January ; at least I hope so, if it can be had on honourable terms. Believe me

Your most obliged and affectionate Nephew,
HORATIO NELSON.

[3] At Noon, " East End of the Isle of Levant, (near Toulon,) N.W. ¼ W. six leagues."—*Agamemnon's Log.*

TO . . . . . .

[From " The Athenæum." The Address of this Letter is not given.]

Agamemnon, Vado Bay, November 6th, 1795.

Dear Sir,

I have just received your letter of September 29th, and will
be open and sincere in my declaration, that I will not attempt
to come into Parliament[4] but in support of the real Whig interest—I mean the Portland interest; and I must know that
those principles are truly acceptable to that party which you
conceive would give me its support.

My pretensions are only a long series of services performed
for my Country; and if that part of my Country who may
honour me with their confidence in Parliament, think me an
eligible person to serve them in the House of Commons, the
same zeal shall manifest itself there as it has done so repeatedly
in their service in Action against the French. I have only to
say, that I have been more than one hundred times actually
engaged in Battle, at sea and on shore, against the French, since
the commencement of this war, and that I have been twice
wounded. If these gentlemen are satisfied, the Duke of Portland must be applied to, through Lord Walpole and Lady
Walpole; for although I have so often seen the French shot, yet
truly I have seen little of their money. I can have no doubt of
Lord Hood's good wishes to serve me, and I will write to him
on the subject; nor will Admiral Cornwallis, I am confident,
withhold his assistance. Lord Conway[5] is my friend and acquaintance, and a more honourable man, I am confident, does
not grace the Navy of England; therefore, if I am joined with
him, the same Admiralty interest will support us both. If it
is necessary that I should be in England, the Duke of Portland must make application for the Agamemnon to be ordered
home : but I should hope that, being now actually in the most
active service in the Mediterranean, it will not be necessary,
(for I should not much like a land voyage,) therefore, if it is
necessary, I should hope Agamemnon will be ordered home.

---

[4] Nothing more is known of the proposition to bring Nelson into Parliament: he
never sat in the House of Commons.

[5] Vice-Admiral Lord Hugh Seymour Conway, vide vol. i. p. 323.

Thus, my dear Sir, I have been plain, and cannot well be misunderstood.　Believe me ever,

Your most obliged, humble servant,

HORATIO NELSON.

TO GENERAL COUNT WALLIS, OF THE AUSTRIAN ARMY.

[From Clarke and M'Arthur, vol. i. p. 236.]

Agamemnon, Vado Bay, 7th November, 1795.

Sir,

I was honoured last night with your letter of yesterday's date.　I hope every General Officer in the Army will give me credit for my desire of doing whatever is in my power to render them assistance.　I will immediately order a Frigate and a Brig to cruise off Cape Noli, in order to keep these Gunboats in some check; but the Captains of the Ships who have anchored off Pietra declare to me, that it is impossible to lie there in the least swell, as it is a quicksand; and the Frigate and Brig were with difficulty saved, when there a few days ago.

Indeed, Sir, though I shall order the Ships off Noli, as you seem to wish it, yet I must apprise you, that the first strong wind off the land may drive them to sea, and that the same wind is favourable to the Enemy's Gun-boats; and I am sorry to observe, that Languelia and Alassio are good places to ride at anchor in, when the same wind would drive any Vessel on shore which may be at Pietra.　The moment I hear of an attack, you may be assured I shall come round in the Agamemnon, and render you every assistance in my power.　I wish the Neapolitan Gallies would ever keep in Vado Bay, when they would be nearer to you, but they are always in Savona Mole.　I truly lament his Excellency General De Vins' bad state of health, and I beg leave to send my sincere wishes for his speedy recovery.

I am, &c.

HORATIO NELSON.

TO HIS EXCELLENCY BARON DE VINS.

[From a Copy, in the possession of Mrs. Davies.]

Agamemnon, Vado Bay, November 8th, 1795.

Sir,

As you are in expectation of a general attack by the French, and that the Enemy's Gun-boats may be very troublesome by coming on your flank, and as I hold my Ships in momentary readiness to come to your assistance, I beg leave to suggest as the quickest means of my knowing of the attack, that signals by guns (if possible) may be established from Pietra to the Fort in Vado.

You may rest assured that the moment I know of the attack that a very short time shall carry the Agamemnon and every Vessel I can collect to Pietra; for believe me, I have the most sincere disposition to co-operate with your Excellency in the destruction of our Enemies, and that I am, with the highest respect and esteem,

Your Excellency's
Most Obedient Servant,
HORATIO NELSON.

TO HIS EXCELLENCY FRANCIS DRAKE, ESQ.

[From Clarke and M'Arthur, vol. i. p. 237.]

Agamemnon, Vado Bay, 12th November, 1795.

My dear Sir,

I was only yesterday favoured with yours of the 5th, enclosing a Bulletin relative to the Coast near St. Remo. I had yesterday morning a letter from General de Vins, informing me that the Tartans were withdrawn from Borghetto, and that he thinks his position too strong for the French to succeed in any attack they may make. Nothing, I am sure you will believe, will be wanting on the part of my Squadron, to cover the General's flank by sea. I have requested the General to establish signals by guns, when I should be with him, before they got well warm in the attack. Flora and a Brig are now cruising off Noli and Pietra; but I fear they may be blown off the Coast. The weather is so severe, that either the French or Austrians must quit the hills; and as some Austrian soldiers

have died with the cold on their posts, the Enemy cannot be
very comfortable. A few days must, I think, give a turn to
the face of affairs. Kellerman, I understand, visits every post
once in twenty-four hours, and says everything to encourage
the soldiers. Last night brought a report, that the French
privateers from Genoa had landed at Voltri, and taken money
and other effects belonging to the Austrians. If this account
be true, it must alter the system of Genoese neutrality : pray,
tell me something about it : you must of course be informed of
the circumstance, or know it to be a fabrication. I am un-
mooring, and intend, if the weather be tolerable, to go to-
morrow to Pietra for a few hours, to pay my respects to General de Vins, who has been very ill.

Reports say, and I believe it is true, that Admiral Hotham
has struck his Flag and given up the command, as also Admiral
Goodall; and that Sir Hyde Parker commands the Fleet until
Sir John Jervis's arrival. Captain Frederick[6] has hoisted a
Distinguishing Pendant, and commands the third Division of
the Fleet. This cannot, my dear Sir, but make me feel, that
I am the first Officer commanding a Squadron, destined to
co-operate with the Austrians and Sardinians, who has been
without a Distinguishing Pendant : most have had a Broad
Pendant,[7] but that I neither expected, nor wished for ; yet I
think, as I have had the pleasure to give satisfaction to our
Allies, that the Ministry, if you thought proper to represent it,
would order me a Distinguishing Pendant from my having
this command, or some other mark of their favour. Pray excuse
this part of my letter : I am assured you will do what is right
for me.

I am, &c.
HORATIO NELSON.

[6] Captain Nelson was then within seven of the top of the List of Post Captains,
and the name of Captain Thomas Lenox Frederick stood next below his own.
[7] See a Note on the subject of Flags, Distinguishing Pendants, &c., at the end of
this or of a subsequent Volume. Nelson did not obtain his wish until the following
year.

TO JOHN M'ARTHUR, ESQ., JOHN UDNEY, ESQ., AND THOMAS
POLLARD, ESQ., AGENTS FOR THE CAPTORS.

[Autograph, in the possession of John Luxford, Esq.]

Gentlemen,   Agamemnon, Vado Bay, November 12th, 1795.

You will herewith receive depositions relative to the taking
a Ship laden with corn, bound to a place occupied by the
Armies of France or to France. If it is necessary, you will send
these papers to England, but really I see but little a Court of
Admiralty has to decide upon. The confiscation of the cargo
does not depend on proving it the property of our Enemies,
but by a mutual agreement between the Genoese Government,
the English Minister at Genoa, and the Austrian General,
that all corn necessary for the use of the inhabitants of the
Republic should be allowed to pass without molestation, it
being certified by the Genoese Secretary of State, the English
Minister giving a passport, and also the Austrian General,—all
other cargoes were to be considered as liable to confiscation.
All the corn for the use of the inhabitants has been passed
for two months with the proper papers, therefore I beg you to
consider what is proper to be done in this case. From what is
the Court of Admiralty to judge?—the freight is to be paid by
an order on the French Corn-agent at Genoa, the house of
Gheraldi; most probably the cargo will not be claimed, but if
it is, our Proctor must have proper notice how matters stand
here. The Austrians sell instantly, and share the money; our
poor sailors are kept a long time out of their money. Is there
no Court of Admiralty established in Corsica? England is a
great way off: however, I trust you will be as expeditious as
possible; the corn being liable to be spoiled, I had it surveyed,
and have [*illegible*] it paid the Master his freight, and shall
liberate the Vessel so soon as the cargo is delivered. Her
damages, occasioned by our heavy fire on her, in consequence
of her running away from us, I shall not make good; the Captain brought it on himself. I have only to hope you will do
the best, and am   Your very humble servant,

HORATIO NELSON.

Mr. Thomas Fellows has a great deal of trouble in seeing
the cargo delivered, for which I conceive he ought to be
allowed something out of the five per cent. agency.

TO EVAN NEPEAN, ESQ. SECRETARY TO THE ADMIRALTY.

[From a Copy in the State Paper Office.]

Sir,　　　　　Agamemnon, Genoa Mole, November 13th, 1795.

As Sir Hyde Parker is sailed from Leghorn with the Fleet,
I think it my duty to acquaint you, for their Lordships' information, of the situation of affairs connected with my command on this Coast. The situation of the French Army
from Borghetta Point along the Mountains of St. Esprit, is
almost impregnable, their numbers amounting to full 28,000
men. The Austrian Army is likewise possessed of such
posts as to render an attack on them by the French (as
General De Vins tells me) impracticable, and almost without
a possibility of being successful. Thus both armies remain to
see who can stand the cold longest; at present it is intense,
what could not have been expected in this country, without
snow, but most intense frosts and northerly winds, blowing
hard. A few days ago, I scoured the coast between Monacoa
and Borghetta so completely, that although I was only able to
take one Ship loaded with corn, yet I forced the others into
the Bay of Alassio and Languelia, where they are so completely under the protection of formidable batteries, that not
less than three Sail of the Line could attempt to take or
destroy them. I have wrote to the Admiral on the subject,
but I believe he was sailed before my Letter could reach him.
The number of Vessels loaded and unloaded at those places
are near 100, the greater part loaded with corn and stores for
France. The French General has laid an embargo on them
all, and it would not surprise me, should any particular events
take place, but that he quits this part of the Riviere. An
event new and rather extraordinary has called for my presence here; on the night of the 10th, the boats of the Brune
French Frigate and a number of Privateers, embarked about
300 men in this Port, and landed them at a place called
Voltri, about nine miles from Genoa, where the Austrians
had a post of a very few men, and a magazine of corn: of
course they succeeded in possessing themselves of the corn,
and also unfortunately of £10,000 sterling, which the Austrian Commissary was carrying from hence to Savona. On
the 11th the Austrians regained the post and took a Lieutenant-Colonel, the Commander, prisoner, and pursued the
French to St. Pierre d'Arena, the suburbs of Genoa. On

the night of the 11th, the French attacked a Salt Magazine belonging to the King of Sardinia, within 150 yards of the guns of Genoa, which was plundered, and the contents given to the lower order of Genoese, who enjoyed the riot. Yesterday, an additional number of men were raised here by the French, recruiting absolutely on the Exchange at four livres per day for the expedition, and forty-eight livres bounty; about 700 men were raised during the days of the 11th and 12th, and embarked in the Brune, a large Brig, and other Vessels. 1000 men were to have been sent from the Army at Borghetta, in gun-boats and feluccas, and they were to have taken a post between Savona and Voltri, on strong ground, and to have fortified themselves; the Genoese have cannon near the place. I don't think the plan would have succeeded, but such it was. I have stationed a Frigate at Vado, for at this season it is impossible to keep the shore aboard, without anchoring; therefore, should they pass, I hope we shall have them. After going to Voltri, I anchored here yesterday evening, which changed the face of affairs; the Brune and Transports were employed warping all night, from the outer to the inner Mole, and now she is without guns or powder, and hauled inside ten or twelve Merchant Ships. Although, His Majesty's Minister has nothing to do officially with the breach of neutrality committed against the Austrians and Sardinians, yet from my situation, as co-operating with those powers, it became necessary for me to take steps that this breach of neutrality and forfeiture of the Word of Honour of the French Captain should not be detrimental to our Allies. Mr. Drake has been with me to the Austrian and Sardinian Ministers, and they will demand of the Republic that the Brune shall be disarmed and not permitted to depart the Port, till satisfaction be given for the glaring breach of neutrality. If they cannot succeed in this point, I must either stay here, or always keep a superior force in this Port, till General de Vins can take such measures as may be necessary to secure his Army from having an Enemy in their rear.

I could not think it right to allow events of this importance to reach their Lordships' ears but from their own Officers; therefore, as the Admiral is absent, I hope their Lordships will think I have done right in giving them this information, without its coming through the Admiral, which is the proper channel. I have the honour to be, &c.

HORATIO NELSON.

TO H.R.H. THE DUKE OF CLARENCE.[8]

[From Clarke and M'Arthur, vol. i. p. 238.]

Genoa Roads, 18th November, 1795.

Sir,

Almost every day produces such changes in the prospect of our affairs, that in relating events I hardly know where to begin. The two Armies are both so strongly posted, that neither is willing to give the attack; each waits to see which can endure the cold longest. The French General has laid an embargo on all the Vessels on the Coast, near a hundred Sail, and it would not surprise me if he is meditating a retreat, in case his plans do not succeed; which I hope they will not, as the prevention of them, in a great measure, depends on our Naval force under my orders. This has called me here, where a circumstance has arisen, that has given us the alarm sooner than was intended.

An Austrian Commissary was travelling from Genoa towards Vado, with £10,000 sterling, and it was known he was to sleep at a place called Voltri, about nine miles from Genoa. This temptation was too great for the French Captain of the Brune, in concert with the French Minister, to keep his word of honour; and the Boats of that Frigate, with some Privateers, went out of the Port, landed, and brought back the money. The next day, the 11th of November, recruiting was publicly carried on in the Town of Genoa, and numbers enlisted; and

[8] His Royal Highness had written to Captain Nelson from St. James's, on the 24th of August, 1795.

"Dear Nelson,

"Understanding that a Messenger goes to-morrow evening for the Mediterranean, I cannot allow this opportunity to escape without my writing my old Friend a few lines. Your letters are to me so truly interesting, that I have kept every one, and shall look forward to your future correspondence as highly interesting.

"Having been through life acquainted with you, I was not surprised to read your name in every account from Hotham, but I rejoice in the defeat you have given your Enemies. Since your last letter, Spain has made peace, and consequently, must materially alter your situation. I think if we have not peace with France, which God grant! we *must* have war with Spain. In all cases, I rely on the Mediterranean Fleet under Hotham and Holloway, to whom I wish to be kindly remembered. As for you I say nothing: you well know my opinion of yourself, which every action of yours this war has strengthened. Till we meet, adieu! which I hope, for the sake of this Country, will be soon; and ever believe me, dear Sir, yours sincerely, WILLIAM."—*Autograph*, in the Nelson Papers.

on the 13th at night, as many men as could be collected were
to sail under Convoy of the Brune, and to land, and take a
strong post of the Genoese, between Genoa and Savona. A
hundred men were to have been sent from the French Army
at Borghetto, and an insurrection of the Genoese peasantry
was to have been encouraged; which I believe would have
succeeded for several miles up the Country. General de Vins
must have sent four or five thousand men, probably, from his
Army, which would have given the Enemy a fairer prospect of
success in their intended attack. The scheme was bold, but I
do not think it would have succeeded in all points.

However, my arrival here on the 13th in the evening, caused
a total change: the Frigate, knowing her deserts, and what
had been done here before with the Transports and Privateers,
hauled from the outer to the inner Mole, and is got inside the
Merchant Ships, with her powder out, for no Ships can go
into the inner Mole with powder on board; and, as I have long
expected an embarkation from the French Army from the
westward, to harass General de Vins, there I was fully on my
guard. Whilst I remain here, no harm can happen, unless,
which private information says is likely to take place, that four
Sail of the Line and some Frigates are to come here, and take
Agamemnon and her Squadron. What steps the Austrian
Generals, and Ministers, will adopt to get redress, for this (I
fear allowed) breach of neutrality, on the part of the Genoese
Government, I cannot yet tell. It is a very extraordinary circumstance, but a fact, that since my arrival, respect to the
Neutral Port has not been demanded of me : if it had, my
answer was ready, ' that it was useless and impossible for me
to give it.' As the breach of the Neutrality has not been
noticed, I fancy they are aware of my answer, and therefore
declined asking the question.

A superior force to the French must now always be kept
here; but, I own, I think the French will make a push from
Toulon to drive us away, that they may do something, and
they have no time to lose. Sir Hyde Parker is gone to the
westward, and my force is very much reduced, at a time I
humbly conceive it wants addition. Admiral Hotham is
travelling until the spring; as is Admiral Goodall, who feels
much hurt at not getting the command; a braver or better

Officer is seldom to be found. I am in expectation of being ordered to England; the Ship, Ship's company, and myself, are all out of repair.

I beg leave to subscribe myself, your Royal Highness's most attached and faithful

HORATIO NELSON.

TO H. R. H. THE DUKE OF CLARENCE.

[From Clarke and M'Arthur, vol. i. p. 239.]

19th November, 1795.

The new Doge is now elected, and we hope to get some answer from the Government. My situation is the more awkward, as what has happened does not relate to the English Minister, the breach of Neutrality being an Austrian business; but, as I am co-operating with the Austrians, it has made me a party. My line of conduct is very clear, as I shall signify at a proper time, ' that if the Genoese Government have not the power, nor the inclination, to prevent these Expeditions sailing from their Ports, it then becomes my business, as far as in me lies, to prevent it; which must be done by keeping a superior force in the Port, to sail with them.' I hope for the best; but to say the truth, I think I shall be attacked very soon by a much superior force from Toulon, and I have long begged for two Sail of the Line to be added to my Squadron : certainly I had no more substantial reason, than what was strongly impressed on my mind, from various reports and conversations. I pray God I may be mistaken, and that Sir Hyde may keep them in Port. The number of Gun-boats collecting, both at Toulon and Nice, can be for no other purpose than to force a landing on this Coast; and it would surprise me, should they get a Squadron up here, if they did not seize Genoa ; and then fourteen days would decide the campaign.

I am, &c.,

HORATIO NELSON.

TO VICE-ADMIRAL SIR HYDE PARKER.[9]

[From Clarke and M‘Arthur, vol. i. p. 240.]

Agamemnon, Genoa Road, November 20th, 1795.

Sir,

Upon consultation with his Excellency Mr. Drake, I have determined on sending a Vessel to you, with the enclosed reports of the state of the Ships in Toulon. It is needless for me to make any further observations on their contents; but if the Enemy's Squadron comes on this Coast, and lands from three to four thousand men between Genoa and Savona, I am confident that either the whole Austrian Army will be defeated, or must inevitably retreat into Piedmont, and abandon their artillery and stores. We are acquainted with the French plans, and of the well-founded expectation they have of raising an insurrection of the Genoese peasantry, in a particular valley between this and Vado. I have not, which probably you know, been on former occasions backward in representing my thoughts to Admiral Hotham, that at one time or another, the French would make a push for this Coast, as also my wishes for a reinforcement of two 74-gun Ships, and that the Frigates should not be diminished; the latter, I am sorry to say, is done.

The extraordinary events which have taken place here, and the Expedition which would now sail from this Port, were I to withdraw the Agamemnon, will always render it a measure of necessity to keep a superior force to the French at this place, with orders to attack the Enemy, if they presume to sail: they broke the Neutrality, and the Genoese have not called on me for my word to respect it.

November 21st.

I am sorry to add, that the weather is so very bad in this Gulf, that neither sails, nor ships, nor people, can remain at sea for a long time. This morning, at daylight, the Austrians took possession of the French empty magazines at St. Pierre d'Arena, and the sentinels are now close to the gates of Genoa. We think General de Vins has done wrong in this instance. He demanded satisfaction and payment of the Genoese Government, and, without waiting for the answer, has taken satisfaction

---

[9] Admiral Hotham struck his Flag on the 1st of November, when the temporary command of the Fleet devolved on Vice-Admiral Sir Hyde Parker.

himself. Had the General done so first, he would have found
full magazines, instead of empty ones: by his conduct he has
liberated the Genoese from their difficulties. You may be
assured I shall pursue a steady, moderate line of conduct.

I am, &c.,

HORATIO NELSON.

TO THE RIGHT HONOURABLE LORD GRENVILLE, SECRETARY
OF STATE FOR FOREIGN AFFAIRS.

[Autograph Draught, in the Nelson Papers. Mr. Drake having informed Captain
Nelson that a report was circulated among the Allies, to which the King of Sardinia
had been induced to give credence, that the British Cruisers connived with the Enemy
to permit the Coasting Vessels to land their Cargoes for the supply of the French
Army in the Riviera of Genoa, Nelson immediately wrote the following indignant
Letter to Lord Grenville. Clarke and M'Arthur do not say where the Letter actually
forwarded was preserved; but they state that as it was of so delicate and extraordinary a nature, they had deemed it expedient, before publication, to submit it, through
the Viscountess Perceval, to Mr. Trevor, who was Minister at Turin at the time it
was written; and they have printed Mr. Trevor's reply to Lady Perceval, which will
be found in the Note.[1]]

Agamemnon, Genoa Road, 23rd November, 1795.

My Lord,

Having received, from Mr. Drake, a copy of your Lordship's
letter to him of October, enclosing a paper highly reflecting
on the honour of myself and other of His Majesty's Officers

---

[1] Mr. Trevor's letter to the Viscountess Perceval.—" I return to you the very
energetic letter of my late Noble Friend: it was no doubt addressed to Lord Grenville, from whom the paper alluded to must have been officially sent to Mr. Drake.
A scandalous and calumniating suspicion prevailed at that time amongst the Allies
that there existed a criminal connivance between the British cruisers in the Mediterranean, and the Coasting vessels of the Enemy; whereby they were permitted to
land their cargoes for the supply of the French Army in the Riviera of Genoa.
The fact was, that the French Army was most provokingly supplied by sea, notwithstanding the British ships who were stationed off the coast: but it was by no
means for want of every exertion on their part, much less from any treachery.
Without condescending to repel an accusation, as groundless as it was injurious, the
thing spoke for itself upon a moment's reflection: for neither we, nor the Allies, had
any small Craft that could approach the shore; whilst the supplies were smuggled
along the coast by night, in light Vessels, in spite of everything which our Frigates,
or Sloops of War, could do to prevent it. I was sent to Milan to confer with the
Austrian General and Admiral Goodall, on this subject, and other matters of co-
operation. We suggested the only remedy that could be devised, which was that of
getting some Galleys and Row-boats, from Genoa or Civita Vecchia. I never saw
the injurious Paper in question: from his ignorance of Naval affairs, the

employed on this Coast under my Orders, it well becomes me,
as far as in my power lies, to wipe away this ignominious stain
on our characters. I do, therefore, in behalf of myself, and
much-injured Brethren, demand, that the person, whoever he
may be, that wrote, or gave that paper to your Lordship, do
fully, and expressly bring home his charge; which, as he
states that this agreement is made by numbers of people on
both sides, there can be no difficulty in doing. We dare him,
my Lord, to the proof. If he cannot, I do most humbly im-
plore, that His Majesty will be most graciously pleased to
direct his Attorney-General to prosecute this infamous libeller
in His Courts of Law; and I likewise feel, that, without impropriety, I may on behalf of my brother Officers, demand the
support of His Majesty's Ministers: for as, if true, no punish-
ment can be too great for the traitors; so, if false, none can be
too heavy for the villain, who has dared to allow his pen to
write such a paper. Perhaps I ought to stop my letter here;
but I feel too much to rest easy for a moment, when the
honour of the Navy, and our Country, is struck at through
us; for if nine [ten] Captains, whom chance has thrown

Austrian Commander, who felt the effects of the misfortune without sufficiently
attending to its cause, easily listened to the misrepresentations that were made
to him upon the subject, and transmitted them to his Court; whence, or through
the medium of that of Turin, they reached England. The accusation was probably
vague and general; it does not appear that any names were mentioned; the nature
and the channel of the information did not admit of any public refutation of it; and
Commodore Nelson's letter, as well as Mr. Drake's answer, would have been more
than sufficient to obliterate in a moment any attention that might have been given to
it by Government. With regard to the mention, made in Nelson's letter, of my
approbation of his conduct, I cannot help adding a little on that subject, because
it belongs to one of the circumstances in my life, which I recollect with the greatest
pleasure. It was, I think, in 1795, that this great man, with whom I had been in
official correspondence, and with whom and Mr. Drake many conferences had been
held on board the Agamemnon, and whom I even then looked up to with admiration,
sent me a letter expressive of uneasiness and disappointment, that his ardour and
faithful services had not been more favourably attended to by Government, and
requesting me to furnish him with a letter to Ministers expressive of my sense of
his services, as far as they had fallen within the sphere of my observation or knowledge. I have often regretted that this letter, which subsequent events have since
made a curious and interesting document, was burnt with my papers at Turin; but
I possess a copy of my answer to it, which concluded with these words—'And I
shall ever consider it as the proudest circumstance in my life, that such a character
as Commodore Nelson's should have thought a testimonial of mine could add anything to its lustre.'"—*Clarke and M'Arthur*, vol. i. p. 224.

together, can instantly join in such a traitorous measure, it is fair to conclude we are all bad.

As this traitorous agreement could not be carried on but by concert of all the Captains, if they were on the Stations allotted them, and as they could only be drawn from those Stations by orders from me, I do most fully acquit all my brother Captains from such a combination, and have to request, that I may be considered as the only responsible person for what is done under my command, if I approve of the conduct of those under my orders, which in this most public manner I beg leave to do: for Officers more alert, and more anxious for the good, and honour, of their King and Country, can scarcely ever fall to the lot of any Commanding Officer: their Names I place at the bottom of this letter.

For myself, from my earliest youth I have been in the Naval service ; and in two Wars, have been in more than one hundred and forty Skirmishes and Battles, at Sea and on shore ; have lost an eye, and otherwise blood, in fighting the Enemies of my King and Country ; and, God knows, instead of riches, my little fortune has been diminished in the Service: but I shall not trouble your Lordship further at present, than just to say—that at the close of this Campaign, where I have had the pleasure to receive the approbation of the Generals of the Allied Powers ; of his Excellency Mr. Drake, who has always been on the spot; of Mr. Trevor, who has been at a distance ; when I expected and hoped, from the representation of His Majesty's Ministers, that His Majesty would have most graciously condescended to have favourably noticed my earnest desire to serve Him, and when, instead of all my fancied approbation, to receive an accusation of a most traitorous nature —it has almost been too much for me to bear. Conscious innocence, I hope, will support me.

I have the honour to be
My Lord,
Your Lordship's most obedient, humble servant,
Horatio Nelson.

N.B.—Captains Fremantle, Hope, Cockburn, Hon. Charles Elphinstone, Shields, Middleton, Plampin, Brisbane, Thomas Elphinstone, Macnamara.

TO THE REVEREND MR. NELSON, HILBOROUGH.

[Autograph, in the Nelson Papers.]

Agamemnon, Genoa Road, November 25th, 1796 [1795.]

My dear Brother,

Although my mind is pretty fully employed in the events which have taken place on this Coast within the last week, yet this evening I give up an hour to private affection.

You will have heard of an Expedition going from this Port attacking an Austrian Post and taking about £10,000 sterling. Another and more important event was to take place, the landing and possessing a strong post between Genoa and Vado, which, if accomplished, would have had the worst effects—probably nothing less than the retreat of the whole Austrian Army, if not the defeat. The latter, however, I prevented, by laying Agamemnon across the harbour's mouth of Genoa, and suffering no French vessel to sail out of the Port. Yesterday morning, at four o'clock, the French made a grand attack on all the Austrian Posts, near Borghetta, about forty miles from hence. The Action cannot be said to be finished at this time of writing. The friends of each party say what they wish: the French, that 3000 Austrians are killed at Loano, and 1500 taken, and that all the other parts attacked were equally successful. The other side say, the French are repulsed with great slaughter. I am very anxious and uneasy, as you will believe. A part of the Austrian Army is now at the gates of Genoa, where they have taken possession of the French magazines of corn and flour. What these events may produce in the Republic of Genoa, time only can discover. The Government must feel severely its degradation. Our Fleet is gone far away, and left me here very much unprotected. If the French Squadron, which is ready at Toulon, and with Troops on board, come here, which is expected, the safety of poor Agamemnon becomes very precarious. I feel I am left in a shameful way; but I hope, when Sir John Jervis arrives, to be better taken care of than in this interregnum.[2] We expect, and may expect, orders every day for England.

---

[2] Between the departure of Admiral Hotham and the arrival of Sir John Jervis.

My Ship and Ship's Company are worn out, but the folks at Home do not feel for us.

December 4th.

I am on my way to Leghorn, to refit. The campaign is finished by the defeat of the Austrians, and the French are in full possession of Vado Bay. The losses of either side are lessened, but much blood has been shed. I think the Admiral will be hauled over the coals for not letting me have Ships. All my Squadron was taken away, except two, and they unfortunately were blown off the Coast; therefore I was left alone, and not being able to do all myself, could not prevent the Enemy's gun-boats from harassing the left flank of the Austrians, which I have no doubt the General will make the most of, although they were more beaten on the right, and I verily believe by inferior numbers.

Leghorn, December 7th.

We arrived here yesterday, and found that Sir John Jervis had joined the Fleet, at St. Fiorenzo, on the 29th November. I hope he has brought orders for us to proceed to England. Pray remember me kindly to my Aunt, Mrs. Nelson, and your children; and do not forget me to the Rolfes, and our friends at Swaffham. Believe me, ever

Your most affectionate Brother,
HORATIO NELSON.

TO ADMIRAL SIR JOHN JERVIS, K.B.

[From Clarke and M'Arthur, vol. i. p. 242. Sir John Jervis arrived at San Fiorenzo, in the Lively frigate, on the 30th of November, and it appears that Captain Nelson immediately made a written report of his proceedings, of which report the following passages formed the conclusion. The " visit" to Admiral Hotham appears to have been made about the middle of October.]

[About 25th November, 1795.]

The object of my visit[3] was to ask the Admiral to give me two 74-gun Ships, and as many Transports as he had in Leg-

---

[3] On the 26th of October, Mr. Drake, in a letter to Captain Nelson, thus alluded to his communication with the Admiral:—" I am just returned from Genoa, from my military excursion: I had intended to have gone from Turin to Savona; but I was so fully persuaded, from everything I heard and saw, whilst on my tour, that there was no hope of stimulating the Austrian General to any active operations during the campaign, that I thought it better to return to Genoa. I shall be very anxious to hear the result of your visit to the Admiral; and I hope he will have adopted your proposition."—*Clarke and M'Arthur*, vol. i. p. 242.

horn, with the Camel and Dolphin, to have carried the ten
thousand men, as desired; the Admiral, however, did not
think it right to send a Ship. On the 1st of November I
chased a very large convoy into Alassio, and by the 8th, they
were increased to full one hundred sail, including Gun-boats,
and other Vessels of War; but they were too well protected
for me to make any attempt with my small Squadron. On
the 10th, the French took the Austrian post at Voltri; on the
11th it was retaken; on the 12th the French were making
every exertion for a most vigorous and bold attempt to establish
themselves in a strong post between Voltri and Savona, and
were in hopes of causing an insurrection of the Genoese peasantry. My presence was required at Genoa to prevent this
Expedition, by Mr. Drake, the Austrian Minister, and by the
Austrian General commanding at Vado. On the 13th, I went
to Genoa, and was kept there, contrary to my inclination,
until after the defeat of the Austrian Army on the 23rd November. However I have the consolation, that to the Agamemnon's staying at Genoa, so many thousands owe their
safety, by the pass of the Bocchetta being kept open, and
amongst others, General de Vins himself.

I am, &c.,

HORATIO NELSON.

TO HIS EXCELLENCY FRANCIS DRAKE, ESQ.

[From Clarke and M'Arthur, vol. i. p. 245.]

Agamemnon, Genoa Road, 27th November, 1795.

Sir,
    As I have heard from reports that the retreat of the Austrian
Army is laid to want of co-operation on the part of the British
Squadron, it becomes me to state a few facts, by which your
Excellency can form a judgment of my conduct; and in which
I flatter myself it will appear, that nothing has been wanting
on my part to give every possible energy to the operations of
the Austrians. A Frigate was always anchored near Pietra,
until the season was such as to render that measure no longer
possible; for it was persevered in until two of his Majesty's
Ships were nearly lost. When this defence was taken away,

in the first week in November, I stationed the Flora and
Speedy Brig off Cape Noli, within six miles of Pietra ; but at
the same time I informed General de Vins, that I considered
them by no means so ready to afford assistance in case of an
attack, as if they lay at a greater distance in Vado. The event
has justified my fears ; for the Speedy has never since been
heard of,[4] and the Flora, from some cause which I am at present unacquainted with, is gone to Leghorn.

The Agamemnon lay at single anchor in Vado Bay, with
the two Neapolitan Gallies, ready to proceed on the first gun
being fired by the Enemy ; and so anxious was I to render every
assistance to our Allies, that I requested General de Vins to
establish a signal by guns from Pietra to Vado, that I might
be with him, if the wind was fair, long before any messenger
could have reached Vado. On the 9th of November, General
de Vins sent me word, that he believed the French thought his
position too strong to be attacked, and that, as he was coming
from Savona in a few days, we would talk over the subject of
signals. The demand made of my assistance here, I shall not
enter into ; the cause of it, of my remaining here, and the sal-
vation of many thousand Austrian troops, and of General de
Vins himself, are fully known to your Excellency. I shall
therefore only state further, that the Lowestoffe, Inconstant,
and Southampton have been taken from my Squadron, and
the Ship that was ordered to replace them has never yet come
under my orders.

I therefore trust it will appear in this short statement, that
nothing has been wanting on my part to give full effect to
every operation of the Austrians ; and that the force under my
command has been so employed as will meet the approbation
of our Sovereign, your Excellency, and his Majesty's Ministers.
Whenever a more full or more particular account of my conduct is demanded, I have no doubt but I shall be found not
only free from blame, but worthy of approbation.

I am, &c.

HORATIO NELSON.

---

[4] The Speedy, 14, Captain Thomas Elphinstone, was, however, safe.

TO JOHN WILLIAM BRAME, ESQ., CONSUL AT GENOA.

[Autograph, in the possession of J. Benjamin Heath, Esq., His Sardinian Majesty's
Consul-General in London.]

November 30th, 1795.

My dear Sir,

If you have any letters for me, pray send them off, as I do
not intend to anchor. I shall also be glad to hear any news
you may please to send me.

                    I am, dear Sir,
                         Your very humble servant,
                              HORATIO NELSON.

As I am yet ignorant when the Austrians left Vado, or if
they have left it, pray tell me. You will hear of my Boat
being detained at Savona. Recollect it is near night, and I
am anxious for my Boat to be on board.

TO MRS. NELSON.

[From Clarke and M'Arthur, vol. i. p. 246.]

December 2nd, 1795.

Lord Hood will have discovered, that, from my last letter to
him respecting the defeat of the Austrians on the 23rd of
November, the loss of Vado would consequently follow. Tell
him, the French had collected full a hundred sail of Vessels,
in case of failure, to carry off their troops; they had also ten
or twelve Gun-vessels, as many Privateers, and a Man-of-War
Brig. I described to the Admiral the great service that the
destruction of these Vessels would be of, many of them being
laden with corn, on which the French General had laid an
embargo; and, as I had not force enough, I begged of the
Admiral, if he came to sea, to look at this Fleet himself,
offering, if he would permit me the honour, to lead the Culloden and Courageux to the attack, and, with my then Squadron
of Frigates, to take or destroy the whole. I pretend not to
say the Austrians would not have been beat, had not the Gun-
boats harassed them, for on my conscience I believe they
would; but I believe the French would not have attacked, had
we destroyed all the Vessels of War, Transports, &c. The

Austrians, by all accounts, did not stand firm. The French, half naked, were determined to conquer or die; and had I not, though I own against my inclination, been kept at Genoa, from eight to ten thousand men would have been taken prisoners, and amongst the number General De Vins himself. For the French plan, well laid, was to possess a Post in the road these people fled by, retreat it could not be called, for, except a part of the Army under General Wallis, of about ten thousand men, it was, ' the devil take the hindmost.' I had a Lieutenant, two Midshipmen, and sixteen men taken at Vado; the Purser of the Ship, who was there, ran with the Austrians eighteen miles without stopping, the Men without any arms whatever, Officers without soldiers, Women without assistance. Thus has ended my campaign. . . . . Let the blame be where it may, I do not believe any party will seriously lay it at my door; and if they do, I am perfectly easy as to the consequences. I sincerely hope an inquiry may take place, the world would then know how hard I have fagged. The weather has been most intensely cold. Sir John Jervis arrived at St. Fiorenzo on the 29th of November, to the great joy of some, and sorrow of others.

Yours, &c.
HORATIO NELSON.

TO VICE-ADMIRAL SIR HYDE PARKER.

[From Clarke and M'Arthur, vol. i. p. 247.]

December 2nd, 1795.

I assure you, Sir, I never more regretted the not being able to divide the Agamemnon: I was in Vado Bay on the 9th of November, and saw the French in full possession. Meleager joined on the 30th, when I directed Captain Cockburn to cruise off the Bay, to prevent any of our Ships from going in; and to perform such other services off the Port of Genoa, as, on consultation with his Excellency Mr. Drake, may be found most beneficial for his Majesty's service.

I am, &c.
HORATIO NELSON.

TO THE RIGHT HONOURABLE SIR GILBERT ELLIOT,
VICE-ROY OF CORSICA.

[Autograph, in the Minto Papers.]

Agamemnon, at Sea, December 4th, 1795.

My dear Sir,

My campaign is closed by the defeat of the Austrian Army,
and the consequent loss of Vado and every place in the Riviera
of Genoa, and I am on my way to refit poor Agamemnon and
her miserable Ship's company at Leghorn. We are, indeed,
Sir, worn out; except six days I have never been one hour off
the station. I have to regret, but mean not to complain, that
my force was too small for the services which I wished to perform. If I had been favoured with the two 74-gun Ships, which
I have often asked for, I am fully persuaded that the last attack
never would have been made. Instead of this increase of force,
my Frigates were withdrawn from me without my knowledge, and
I had only Flora and Speedy, Brig, left with me; these were,
I fancy, blown off the coast, and only Agamemnon remained.
The extraordinary events which have taken place near Genoa,
and the plan which was laid by the French to take post between
Voltri and Savona, perhaps you are acquainted with; if not, I
will tell you.

Seven hundred men were enlisted and embarked on board
the Brune French frigate in Genoa, (seven thousand stand of
arms,) and on board many small Privateers and one Brig;
these were on a certain night to have landed in a strong post
between Voltri and Savona, to be joined in small Feluccas by
1000 men from Borghetta. An insurrection of the Genoese
peasantry, we have every reason to believe, would have been
made for forty miles up a valley towards Piedmont. The money
going from Genoa tempted these people to make an attack
before their time, which certainly caused the plan to miscarry.
On the great preparation at Genoa, Agamemnon was called
for, might and main, to prevent the plan, which I most effectually did, and so fearful was the Imperial Minister and General
of my leaving Genoa, that I was told that if I quitted Genoa,
the loss of 3000 Austrians was the certain consequence; thus
I was put in the cleft stick. If I left Genoa, the loss of 3000
men would be laid to my charge; if I was not at Pietra, the

gun-boats would, unmolested, harass the left flank of the Army ; and the defeat may very probably be laid to the want of assistance of the Agamemnon. However, my being at Genoa, although contrary to my inclination, has been the means of saving from 8000 to 10,000 men, and amongst others, General de Vins himself, who escaped by the road, which, but for me, the Enemy would have occupied. I must, my dear Sir, regret not having more force.

My orders left at Vado, for the station of Southampton and Inconstant, taken from me, will shew, if, on inquiry by Ministry, for I know not who else can inquire, that not a Gunboat, if my orders had been obeyed, could have annoyed the Army. Mr. Drake, who has been on the spot, and Mr. Trevor, who has known all my proceedings, are pleased to highly approve my conduct; and I also have had, to the 9th of November, the full approbation of every General in the Army. That the Gun-boats harassed them I am truly sorry for ; it only becomes me to shew I could not help it,—not that I believe they would not have been beat without the Gun-boats, for the right wing, twelve miles from the shore, was entirely defeated, and the left retreated, but not in much order. I fancy, from what I hear, no defeat was ever more complete ; on the other hand, I know all the Generals wished for nothing more than orders to quit the Coast. They say, and true, they were brought on it, at the express desire of the English, to co-operate with the Fleet, which Fleet nor Admiral they never saw. There certainly are other and much better Posts to prevent the Invasion of Italy than Vado. I verily believe the Austrians are glad to quit the Coast on any pretence. General de Vins complains heavily of not seeing the Admiral. So much for my story—you are tired with it, and so am I.

I sincerely hope all is quiet in Corsica, and that you are enjoying that good health I sincerely wish you. Apropos, I have just received an order from Sir Hyde Parker, to receive on board such recruits as might be raised for Dillon's Corps in Corsica ; this implies that they had been refused. I wrote you, Sir, long ago, and I am sure you credit me, that whatever I could do to be of service to Corsica, no man was readier. I have raised and sent over many more men than the Officers raised ; but the fact is, if any complaint has been made by these impertinent people, that one man was taken with a malignant fever, and gave it to my Ship's company. I then told the Officer that he must keep his recruits on shore, and that whenever a Ship went to Leghorn or Corsica they should certainly take them on board. Admiral Hotham and Mr. Drake, who I told of the circumstance, approved of my conduct. I sent two fine young men for Smith's Corps; but you have no conception of the troublesome impertinence of these people. Now, my dear Sir, I know you took a young man by hand, a Mr. Pierson,[5] from Naples; he is now a Lieutenant in the 69th Regiment, and embarked on board the Agamemnon: he is a very good and amiable lad, and I am sure whatever farther notice you may be pleased to shew him, that his future conduct will convince you he merits it. I own I shall feel a pleasure to see your Excellency favour him. Believe me, dear Sir,

Your Excellency's most faithful servant,

HORATIO NELSON.

I expect Mr. Drake very soon at Leghorn. Mrs. Drake is gone to Milan; and Mr. Drake is returned, for security, to the town of Genoa from the country.

His Excellency the Vice-Roy.

TO HIS EXCELLENCY FRANCIS DRAKE, ESQ.

[From Clarke and M'Arthur, vol. i. p. 248.]

Leghorn, 8th December, 1795.

We have just heard, Sir, of your arrival at Alessandria. I have two requests to make, which I trust you will grant; the one is, a copy of the Paper I sent you by the Genoese Secretary of State, containing the number of inhabitants in the Riviera, and the quantity of provisions wanted for their use for two months; and such other Papers as may shew clearly to the Court of Admiralty, that it was perfectly understood by the Genoese Government, that all Vessels which were bound to any place in possession of the French, who had not passports from the Government, or from your Excellency and General de Vins, would be taken, and their cargoes made prizes.

The next request much more concerns my honour, than the

---

[5] This gallant young Officer is again often mentioned.

other does my interest—it is to prove to the World, to my own
Admiral, or to whoever may have a right to ask the question,
why I remained at Genoa. I have therefore to desire that
you will have the goodness to express, in writing, what you
told me, that the Imperial Minister and yourself were assured,
if I left the Port of Genoa unguarded, not only the Imperial
troops at St. Pierre d'Arena and Voltri would be lost, but that
the French plan for taking Post between Voltri and Savona
would certainly succeed; and also, that if the Austrians should
be worsted in the advanced Posts, the retreat by the Bocchetta
would be cut off: to which you added, that if this happened,
the loss of the Army would be laid to my leaving Genoa, and
recommended me most strongly not to think of it. The Imperial Minister's wanting more force, is needless to mention,
unless you think it right. I am anxious, as you will believe,
to have proofs in my possession, that I employed to the last
the Agamemnon as was judged most beneficial to the Common
Cause.
I am, &c.
HORATIO NELSON.

TO MR. THOMAS POLLARD.

[Autograph, in the possession of — Safe, Esq.]

~~By G~~[6]

Mr. Egar must be paid all his expenses incurred in the
necessary duty of the Vessel, in which must certainly be included his very necessary Journey to Leghorn; and considering his great attention, I think that not less than ten
pounds should be given him as a present.
HORATIO NELSON.

Leghorn, December 10th, 1795.

TO THE REVEREND DIXON HOSTE.

[Autograph, in the possession of Captain Sir William Hoste, Bart.]

Agamemnon, Leghorn, December 12th, 1795.

My dear Sir,
Your letter of November 1st, I received a few days past,
and your good son tells me he has answered his letter. William

---

[6] Sic in Orig.

I 2

will have served his two years as rated Mid on the 1st of
February next. This time as Mid, is absolutely necessary as
a part of the long six years. You had better get out his Time
from the Navy Office, and when his six years draw towards an
end, I would have him strongly recommended to Sir John
Jervis ; for whenever peace comes it will be very difficult, with
the best interest, to get him made a Lieutenant. I hope he
has more than one year's Time : if not, two years is very long
to look forward for a continuance of the war. You will have
heard of the Austrians being defeated on the Coast of Genoa,
and a part of the defeat attributed to a want of a sufficient Naval
force. However, on inquiry, things may turn out, I have still
had the good fortune, individually, to meet with approbation
from our Ministers and the Generals. Our Admirals will
have, I believe, much to answer for in not giving me that force
which I so repeatedly called for, and for at last leaving me
with Agamemnon alone.

I was put in a cleft stick : if I quitted where I was at
anchor, the French would have landed in the rear of the
Austrian Army, and the total defeat of that Army must have
been the consequence : if I remained at anchor, the Enemy's
Gun-boats in the general attack would harass the left wing
of the Austrian Army. Much against my inclination, I took
the plan of laying quiet, instead of attacking their Gun-boats ;
and most fortunate it has been for the Army I did so, for
eight or ten thousand men made their escape by the road I
protected, and amongst others, General de Vins himself.
The Austrians will make the most of a want of Naval force
for all purposes. Admiral Hotham kept my Squadron too
small for its duty ; and the moment Sir Hyde took the command of the Fleet he reduced it to nothing—only one Frigate
and a Brig, whereas I demanded two Seventy-four Gun-
ships and eight or ten Frigates and Sloops to ensure safety to
the Army. However, on inquiry, which I trust and sincerely
hope will take place, on my own account, it will turn out that
the centre and right wing gave way, and that although it must
have been very unpleasant to have a number of Gun-boats
firing on them, the left was the only part that was not defeated, but retreated in a body ; whereas the others fled.
General de Vins, from ill-health, as he says, gave up the com-

mand in the middle of the Battle, and from that moment, not
a soldier stayed in his post, and many thousands ran away
who had never seen the Enemy—some of them thirty miles
from the advanced posts. So much for my history.

I tremble at your account of want of bread for our poor.
Pray God send us peace. We have established the French
Republic, which, but for us, I verily believe would never have
been settled by such a volatile, changeable people. I hate a
Frenchman. They are equally objects of my detestation,
whether Royalists or Republicans—in some points, I believe the
latter are the best. Sir John Jervis took the command of the
Fleet on the 29th of November, at St. Fiorenzo, but I have not
yet heard from him, or has anybody here. We sincerely hope
he has orders to send Agamemnon home. We are worn out.
I beg you will present my respects to Mr. and Mrs. Coke,
also, though unknown, to Mrs. Hoste and your family, and
believe me, Dear Sir,

Yours very faithfully,
HORATIO NELSON.

TO HIS EXCELLENCY FRANCIS DRAKE, ESQ.

[From Clarke and M'Arthur, vol. i. p. 249.]

Leghorn, December 16th, 1795.

My dear Sir,

The Prince of Esterhazy, one of General de Vins' Aide-de-
Camps, is here; he brought, as I understand, a letter from
General Wallis to Sir Hyde Parker, declaring, that the check
of the Austrian Army was owing to the non-cooperation of the
English; and the Prince, it seems, asserts this everywhere. I
met him yesterday, when he was pleased to say, that they were
assured, if I had possessed the means, it would not have happened. I did not choose to enter deeply on the subject. I
think we have a strong hold on General Wallis, and in my
opinion we ought not to let it slip : this has been my inducement for writing to him; therefore, if you see no impropriety
in the letter, may I beg you will forward it to him ? I sincerely
hope it will produce an answer. However, I request, if you
think it improper for me to write to General Wallis, and to

allow his own or his Army's unrepelled assertions to keep their ground, (which, by the bye, if they do, it is more than they did,) I then, Sir, hope you will suppress the letter.

If the General's public letter should reflect on me, I must, in my own defence, write to the Admiralty; for I will not sit quiet, and hear what I do every day. My health is but so so; to say the truth, my mind is uneasy, although I feel a clear conscience that no part of the evil is owing to my want of exertion. Our Fleet is gone to the westward; and two Sail of the Line, and three Frigates are sent up the Levant; L'Aigle and Cyclops escaped very narrowly, and we have our fears for the Nemesis. Flora was detached from my command about the time of the Action, and Sir Hyde intended to take every large Frigate from me; and, in short, except Meleager, to send nothing that could be useful. The language held after Admiral Hotham's departure, was less inclinable to come near us, or assist us, than ever; so you see blame must have fallen on the Navy some time or other; and, as Commanding Officer, I must have ever been held up to the Army as the responsible person. Excuse all the latter part of this letter; my mind is uneasy.[7]

I am, &c.,

HORATIO NELSON.

[7] In reply to this letter, Mr. Drake wrote on the 7th of January:—

"With respect to your request, I cannot possibly have any difficulty in repeating to you in writing, what I had so frequently the honour of stating to you in person, whilst the Agamemnon was at Genoa: the substance of these statements was, that by the express solicitations of the Imperial Chargé d'Affaires, I wrote to desire your presence at Genoa, in order to prevent the crew of the French frigate, and the Corps Franc of Jauffier, from making a second attempt to land at Voltri, and thereby to cut off the communication of the Austrian army with Genoa, and with the road of the Bocchetta. Your continuance at Genoa was in compliance with the wishes of the Austrian Chargé d'Affaires, of the Colonel commanding the Austrian troops at S. Pier d'Arena, and of myself. It is to the presence of the Agamemnon, that the corps stationed at S. Pier d'Arena owes its safety; and it was that cause alone, which enabled several thousands of Austrian soldiers, as well as the Commander-in-Chief himself, to effect their retreat by way of Voltri, Rivarola, and the Bocchetta. It certainly was unfortunate that your Squadron should have been so reduced, as to have rendered it impossible for you to provide for every service which was required of you by the Austrian generals: but I am entirely persuaded, that on this, as well as on every other occasion, you employed the force, which you had, in the manner the most beneficial to the common cause; and it is with great satisfaction I assure you, that anxious as the Austrian generals are, to transfer the

TO MRS. NELSON.

[From Clarke and M'Arthur, vol. i. p. 249.]

December 18th, 1795.

I have had letters from my poor Lieutenants and Midshipmen,[8] telling me that few of the French soldiers are more than twenty-three or twenty-four years old ; a great many do not exceed fourteen years, all without clothes ; and my Officers add, they are sure my Barge's crew would have beat a hundred of them, and that, had I seen them, I should not have thought, if the world had been covered with such people, that they could have beat the Austrian Army. The oldest Officers say, they never heard of so complete a defeat, and certainly without any reason. The King of Sardinia was very near concluding a hasty peace in the panic : however, I believe we shall now make peace, when the Emperor must do the same. I only hope we shall, if possible, keep St. Domingo ; if we can, the expenses of the war are nothing to what we shall gain. The French have detached a Squadron towards Constantinople, and many think the Turks will join them : Captain Troubridge is sent on this service with some Ships ; if he gets hold

blame of the misfortunes of the 23rd of November from themselves to us, they have always done ample justice to your zealous and able conduct : their complaints turn upon the insufficiency of the force under your command, and not upon the mode in which that force was employed. . . . .

" I have not yet sent your letter to General Wallis, as I wish to submit to your consideration, whether it would be proper either for you, or me, to offer any justification of our conduct to a Foreign General ; when it is to our Sovereign and his ministers alone, that we are accountable. I have already written to Lord Grenville on the subject of the complaints of the Austrian officers ; and I have on this, as well as on every other occasion, borne testimony to the zeal, activity, and prudence, which so eminently distinguished the whole of your conduct during the term of your command at Vado ; and I have assured his lordship, that both you, and myself, will be ready to give any further explanations of our conduct that may be required of us, or which the assertions of the Austrian generals may render necessary. It appears to me, therefore, that we should rest here, and that we ought to remain silent, until some specific charges are brought forward by the Austrian generals. If, however, you should think differently, I will either send your letter to General Wallis, or make any other communication to him which you may point out."— *Clarke and M'Arthur*, vol. i. p. 250. Captain Nelson was convinced by Mr. Drake's arguments ; for on the 15th of January he wrote to him—" My feelings ever alive, perhaps, to too nice a sense of honour are a little cooled."—*Ibid*.

[8] Taken prisoners by the French at Vado. Vide, ante.

of them, they will not easily escape. Mr. Hinton,[9] who was
my first Lieutenant, and Andrews, have both been promoted
from the services of Agamemnon. Reports say I am to be
offered the St. George, 90, as Sir Hyde Parker is going into
the Britannia; or else the Zealous, 74, as 'Lord Hervey wants
a 90-gun Ship. Sir John Jervis seems determined to be active,
and I hope he will continue so. My kindest remembrances
to my father.

Yours, &c.
HORATIO NELSON.

TO ADMIRAL SIR JOHN JERVIS, K.B., COMMANDER-IN-CHIEF
IN THE MEDITERRANEAN.

[From Clarke and M'Arthur, vol. i. p. 250.]

Leghorn Roads, December 21st ,1795.

Sir,

I cannot allow the Lively, Captain Lord Garlies,[1] to have a
chance of falling in with you, without bringing some account
of the state of the Agamemnon. We are getting on very fast
with our caulking; our head is secured; our rigging nearly
overhauled; and our other wants in as great a state of forwardness as I could expect at this season of the year; and by
the first week in January, I hope that Agamemnon will be as
fit for sea, as a rotten Ship can be.[2]

I have written to Genoa, directing Captain Cockburn to
take the Ships in that Port under his protection to Leghorn;
but should they, from any change of circumstances, not wish
to leave Genoa, the Meleager is then to join me here, by the
31st of December, when I shall order Captain Cockburn to
be ready for sea. By letters from Mr. Drake, of December 8th,
from Milan, it appears that the French, after having attempted
to get into the plain of Piedmont, in which they failed, had

---

[9] Captain Martin Hinton.

[1] Afterwards John, eighth Earl of Galloway, K.T.: he died an Admiral of the
Blue, in March, 1834.

[2] When the Agamemnon came into dock to be refitted, there was not a mast,
yard, sail, nor any part of the rigging, but was obliged to be repaired, owing to the
shot she had received. Her hull had been long secured by cables served round.—
Clarke and M'Arthur.

retired into winter-quarters. The loss of the Austrian Army is not yet ascertained, but it is supposed to exceed 4500 men, killed, wounded, and deserters. General Wallis has 18,000 men with him, and stragglers are joining their corps very fast: he is near Acqui, in a very good position for the defence of Piedmont. I understand the General has written to Sir Hyde Parker, since his defeat, but which I hear he is pleased to call a check, complaining of a want of co-operation on our parts. I take for granted, Sir, neither Sir Hyde nor yourself will fully answer his letter, until I have an opportunity of explaining the whole of my conduct. His Excellency Mr. Drake, his Majesty's Minister at the Head-Quarters of the Army, to whom I always communicated all my proceedings, has borne to Lord Grenville the fullest approbation of my conduct. I shall only trouble you with one observation, that will almost furnish an answer to any letter General Wallis may have written :—That part of the Austrian Army which had to sustain an attack in front, as well as the *terrible fire* of the Gunboats, was the only part of the Army that was not forced, and the only part which retreated in a body; a clear proof to my mind, that either the Gun-boats did little or no mischief, or that the other parts of the line were not equally well defended. I have written to General Wallis to congratulate him, that (under the great misfortune) where he commanded all went well. I have been long on my guard against these gentlemen; and months ago apprised them of what would one day happen; but they believed themselves invincible.

I am, &c.

HORATIO NELSON.

TO THE REVEREND MR. NELSON, HILBOROUGH.

[Autograph, in the Nelson Papers.]

Agamemnon, Leghorn, December 26th, [1795.]

My dear Brother,

I had the pleasure of your letter of November 20th, yesterday, and most heartily wish you, Mrs. Nelson, my Aunt, and all our friends near you, a merry Christmas, and many happy returns of the Season. It must give me satisfaction to find that

from all quarters of England, from my King to the lowest
order, all join in acknowledging my services. Certainly I
may say to you, that none in this Country can be put in com-
petition with what I have gone through; and had it not been
for the neglect of my Admiral,[3] I should have quitted my
command with more pleasure to myself, as I should have had
a battle with the French Gun-boats which harassed the left
wing of the Austrian Army. However, that, from the fault of
my Admiral, (too long to enter into,) not being the case, it will
afford satisfaction to my friends, that no blame has been
attempted to attach itself to my want of exertion ; on the contrary, His Majesty's Minister, at the Head-Quarters of the
Austrian Army, has borne to Lord Grenville the fullest approbation of my conduct : nor do I believe that, as far as relates
[to] me or my conduct, the Generals have wrote a word
against me; although I know they have complained of a want
of a sufficient Naval force—not that I believe all our Fleet
would have served them, unless they fought better than they
did. But they wish, if possible, to throw the cause of their defeat
to the molestation of the Enemy's Gun-boats ; but it is as extraordinary as true, that the right and centre were the only
part totally defeated ; and the left, the part attacked by sea
and land, was the only part which resisted the Enemy, and
the only part which retreated in a body—a plain proof that
either the other parts of the Line were not equally well defended,
or that the Enemy's Gun-boats (which I own I believe) did
no great harm. But the Austrians ran away from some post,
twenty [or] twenty-five miles from the Enemy, by fright.
General de Vins is said to be dead. I think it very probable
that grief, added to his bad health, may have shortened his
days.

Our new Admiral[4] is at sea. I fear he is willing to keep me
with him. He has wrote me, I am sorry to say, a most flattering letter, and I hear I am to be offered St. George or Zealous,
but, in my present mind, I shall take neither. My wish is to
see England once more, and I want a few weeks' rest, as do
every one in my Ship. Mr. Andrews, my late First-Lieutenant is now a Captain, made by the Admiralty, for the

---

³ Hotham.   ⁴ Sir John Jervis.

services of the Agamemnon. I have been fortunate in getting two First-lieutenants made since I left England. You say I don't write. I assure you, I believe I have wrote you from Genoa, no very long time ago. However that may be, I always have you in affectionate remembrance.

December 28th.

A signal is now out for a Fleet, which I take to be the Convoy from England, and I believe Sir John Jervis is amongst them. We have nothing new here: no battles, no defeats. With kindest remembrances, believe me,

Your most affectionate Brother,

HORATIO NELSON.

TO MRS. NELSON.

[From Clarke and M'Arthur, vol. i. p. 252.]

Agamemnon, Leghorn, 6th January,[5] 1796.

The French, I am certain, will, this Spring, make a great exertion to get into Italy, and I think Sir John Jervis must be active to keep them out. By the 1st of February, fifteen Sail of the Line will be ready at Toulon, with 140 Transports, and 200 Flat boats adapted for the coast of Italy. The prevention of the intentions of the Enemy requires great foresight; for, if once landed, our Fleet is of no use, and theirs would retire into Toulon, or some secure Port: had they done so last year,

---

[5] On the 4th of that month, Captain Nelson's Father wrote the following beautiful letter to his distinguished Son:—

" The commencement of a new year calls on a Father's tender and affectionate feelings, to rejoice with you on the many extraordinary escapes you have experienced, which do evidence a Providential hand that has guarded you from impending dangers : may that great and good Being still be your shield and defender! I have also further joy in perceiving those self-approving reflections, which arise from a consciousness of having done all, that the great trust reposed in you could require ; and this you must feel in the highest degree. May you, my dear Son, add year to year through a long life, with the indescribable delight, that your own heart condemns you not. It is difficult, within the narrow limits of an epistle, sufficiently to gratify a son who claims every mark of parental regard that language can express ; and little more than verbal expressions has ever been within the compass of my abilities and very confined sphere of action to bestow. God has blessed me infinitely, even beyond hope, by length of days, to see my posterity in possession of what is more durable than riches or honours—a good name, an amiable disposition, upright conduct, and pure

where would have been the advantage of our action? The French will improve on their last year's folly: I am convinced in my own mind, that I know their very landing-place: if they mean to carry on the war, they must penetrate into Italy. Holland and Flanders, with their own Country, they have entirely stripped; Italy is the gold mine, and, if once entered, is without the means of resistance.

January 8th.—Our news, that the French are retiring from Holland, confirms in my mind their intention to force Italy: nothing else can save them, in any peace that may be near at hand. My Officers and people who are prisoners in France, are exceedingly well treated, particularly so by the Naval Officers; and, as they say, because they belong to the Agamemnon, whose character is well known throughout the Republic.

Yours, &c.
HORATIO NELSON.

TO MRS. NELSON.

[From Clarke and M'Arthur, vol. i. p. 255. On the 19th of January, the Agamemnon joined the Fleet in Fiorenzo Bay, when Captain Nelson had his first inter- view with Admiral Sir John Jervis, K.B., the Commander-in-Chief.]

Agamemnon, St. Fiorenzo, 20th January, 1796.

We were received, not only with the greatest attention, but with much apparent friendship. Sir John Jervis's offer of either the St. George, 90, or Zealous, 74, was declined;

religion: these must be the supporters of public fame, and they will fight in its defence against envy and calumny. The almost daily proofs of your faithful observance of your various professional duties, are pleasing compensations for your long absence: every disappointment has its consolation, every storm its succeeding sunshine, and we bring this home immediately to ourselves. You are now in the very meridian of life, and have daily opportunities of growing rich in knowledge, of filling your honest and well-disposed heart with the stores of good grain, which in time to come, when the mental powers shall decay, shall prove a treasure, and make good what time has stolen away. Old age is only made pleasant by happy reflections, and by reaping the harvest we have sown in youth. Be assured, my good Son, I now regret to find, that my stock in this respect is low: my education, situation in life, and opportunities of improvement, have been all against me. But, thank God! I still retain some sources of delight. My setting sun is clearer, than when it was mid-day. My blessings are innumerable; my wishes most abundantly fulfilled. God bless you, and prosper all you undertake! Farewell. EDMUND NELSON."—*Clarke and M'Arthur*, vol. i. p. 256.

but with that respect, and sense of obligation on my part, which such handsome conduct demanded of me. I found the Admiral anxious to know many things, which I was a good deal surprised to find had not been communicated to him from others in the Fleet; and it would appear, that he was so well satisfied with my opinion of what is likely to happen, and the means of prevention to be taken, that he had no reserve with me respecting his information and ideas of what is likely to be done: he concluded by asking me if I should have any objection to serve under him, with my Flag. My answer was, that if I were ordered to hoist my Flag, I should certainly be happy in serving under him; but if Agamemnon were ordered to go home, and my Flag were not arrived, I should on many accounts wish to return to England; yet still, if the war continued, I should be very proud of the honour of hoisting my Flag under his command: and, I rather believe, Sir John Jervis writes home this day, that if the Fleet is kept here, my Flag, on a promotion, may be sent to the Mediterranean. The credit I derive from all these compliments must be satisfactory to you; and, should I remain until peace, which cannot be very long, you will, I sincerely hope, make your mind easy. Yet, sometimes, notwithstanding all I have said, I think my promotion will be announced, and that I shall have a land voyage: be it as it may, I shall take it easy. Agamemnon is just going to sea, and I can assure you that my health was never better than at this moment.

Yours, &c.

HORATIO NELSON.

TO ADMIRAL SIR JOHN JERVIS, K.B.

[From Clarke and M'Arthur, vol. i. p. 257.]

23rd January, 1796.

Sir,

I yesterday, joined the Meleager and Blanche, but the weather was too bad to have any communication until this morning: there is no appearance of any number of Vessels being collected, from Nice to Genoa, and no Vessel of war; therefore, any large embarkation cannot at present be intended on this Coast. As to a mere plundering party, in a few Feluccas, it is perhaps out of the power of our whole Squadron to prevent it; but I shall do my best. I sent the Blanche to Genoa, with letters for Mr. Trevor and Mr. Drake, requesting them to give me all the information in their power, respecting the Austrian and Sardinian as well as the French Armies, and also the Toulon Fleet.

I am, &c.

HORATIO NELSON.

TO MRS. NELSON.

[From Clarke and M'Arthur, vol. i. p. 257.]

Gulf of Genoa, 27th January, 1796.

I sent you a line just as I was getting under sail from St. Fiorenzo. The Fleet was not a little surprised at my leaving them so soon, and, I fancy, there was some degree of envy attached to the surprise ; for one Captain told me, ' You did just as you pleased in Lord Hood's time, the same in Admiral Hotham's, and now again with Sir John Jervis;[6] it makes no difference to you who is Commander-in-Chief.' I returned a pretty strong answer to this speech. My command here is to prevent any small number of men from making a descent in Italy. I hear no more of this promotion, and I sincerely hope they will put it off a little longer ; unless, which I cannot well expect, they should send me out my Flag. My health was never better.

Yours, &c.

HORATIO NELSON.

---

[6] Sir John Jervis's high opinion of Nelson was thus expressed to Mr. Trevor, Minister at Turin, as early as the 11th of February, 1796 :—" I am very happy to learn that Captain Nelson, whose zeal, activity, and enterprise cannot be surpassed, stands so high in your good opinion. I have only to lament the want of means to give him the command of a Squadron equal to his merit."—*Tucker's Memoirs of Earl St. Vincent,* vol. i. p. 172.

TO MRS. NELSON.

[From Clarke and M'Arthur, vol. i. p. 257.]

Leghorn, 12th February, 1796.

The French are making great preparations for opening the campaign in Italy; and if the Austrians and Piedmontese do not exert themselves, Turin will be lost, and of course all Piedmont: Sardinia is in rebellion. I now see no prospect of peace. Before the King's speech[7] appeared, I had hope; but from that moment I gave it up. Our new Admiral will not land at Leghorn.

[In continuation.]

Off the Hieres Islands, 17th February.

Time, my dear Fanny, will soon wear away, when we shall, I doubt not, possess a cottage of our own, and an ample income to live on; if not in luxury, at least in comfort. As yet, I appear to stand well with Sir John Jervis, and it shall not be my fault if I do not continue to do so: my conduct has no mystery. I freely communicate my knowledge and observations, and only wish, that whatever Admiral I serve under may make a proper use of it. God forbid, I should have any other consideration on service, than the good of my Country. I am now sent to examine the state of the Ships in Toulon; their numbers we know full well, but the accounts of the state they are in are so contradictory, as to leave us uncertain. Sir John Jervis is at present inferior to the French: they have built five Sail of the Line since we left Toulon.

---

[7] His Majesty met Parliament on the 29th of October, 1795, and the Speech from the Throne contained the following passage in reference to France:—" The distraction and anarchy which have so long prevailed in that country have led to a crisis. of which it is as yet impossible to foresee the issue, but which must in all human probability produce consequences highly important to the interests of Europe. Should this crisis terminate in any order of things compatible with the tranquillity of other countries, and affording a reasonable expectation of security and permanence in any treaty which might be concluded, the appearance of a disposition to negotiate for general Peace on just and suitable terms will not fail to be met on my part with an earnest desire to give it the fullest and speediest effect. But I am persuaded that you will agree with me, that nothing is so likely to endure and accelerate this desirable end, as to shew that we are prepared for either alternative, and are determined to prosecute the war with the utmost energy and vigour, until we have the means of concluding, in conjunction with our Allies, such a peace as the justice of our cause and the situation of the Enemy may entitle us to expect."

February 28th.

I am now on my way to Genoa, having been joined by the Admiral on the 23rd, off Toulon. The French have thirteen Sail of the Line and five Frigates ready for sea; and four or five, which are in great forwardness, are fitting in the arsenal. Sir John Jervis, from his manner, as I plainly perceive, does not wish me to leave this station. He seems at present to consider me more as an associate than a subordinate Officer; for I am acting without any orders. This may have its difficulties at a future day; but I make none, knowing the uprightness of my intentions. He asked me, if I had heard any more of my promotion; I told him, 'No:' his answer was, ' You must have a larger Ship, for we cannot spare you, either as Captain or Admiral.'   Yours, &c.

HORATIO NELSON.

TO THOMAS POLLARD, ESQ., LEGHORN.

[Autograph, in the possession of John Luxford, Esq.]

Leghorn, February 17th, 1796.

Sir,

Please to send by my Cockswain, ten Tuscan crowns for Mr. Bolton,[8] which place to my account. Pray send our people on board from the prizes. I hope they have pratique, if not, get it for them directly. The Ship is unmoored, and only waiting for our people, who must have pratique.

Yours truly,

HORATIO NELSON.

TO THE HONOURABLE JOHN TREVOR,[9] MINISTER AT TURIN.

[From Clarke and M'Arthur, vol. i. p. 258.]

[About the 2nd March, 1796.]

[In this Letter, Captain Nelson mentioned his arrival at Genoa on the 2nd of March, and then said]—

I hope to hear of some intended movements of the Austrian Army towards Vado. I am certain, from Sir John Jervis's

---

[8] Midshipman of the Agamemnon, afterwards Captain Sir William Bolton.

[9] The Honourable John Trevor, second son of Robert first Viscount Hampden. On the 20th of August, 1824, he succeeded his brother, as third Viscount Hampden, but died on the 9th of September following, when all his titles became extinct.

own assertion, that nothing will be wanting on his part towards an effectual co-operation, consistent with the other services which you so well know are required of an English
Admiral; and I can take upon me to say, that he will come to
Vado Bay, when future plans may be better concerted. I
cannot help thinking that the taking of Vado would be a great
object, and that it must be done early in the spring; or the
Enemy's Fleet may with ease cover a body of troops in Transports, and land them in Italy. I was six days in sight of
Toulon; and could each day see a visible getting forward of
their Ships. I believe we shall have a battle before any Convoy sails, and which pray God send; for the event, under so
active and good an Admiral, who can doubt of? I am just
favoured with your letters of February 6th, 13th, and 18th:
if the Admiral had small Vessels, he could not venture to un-
man his Fleet.

I am, &c.

HORATIO NELSON.

TO HIS ROYAL HIGHNESS THE DUKE OF CLARENCE.

[From Clarke and M'Arthur, vol. i. p. 258.]

Genoa Mole, 3rd March, 1796.

Sir,

I left Sir John Jervis off Toulon on the 23rd of February,
and sincerely hope he has not suffered in the very severe gale
of easterly wind which I have experienced; our stern is stove
in, and several of our quarter planks started. If the Admiral
unfortunately should be crippled, the French Fleet would be
at sea in a week; and, at all events, I do not believe they will
remain longer in Port than till after the equinox. It is said
the campaign will open against Italy with 80,000 men; if
the Enemy's fleet should be able to cover the landing of 20,000
men, between Port Especia and Leghorn, where I have always
been of opinion they would attempt it, I know of nothing to
prevent their fully possessing the rich mine of Italy. I hope
the Austrians will again take possession of Vado Bay, which
would of course impede not only the along-shore voyage of
the French, and afford our Fleet an opportunity of falling in

with the Enemy, and of giving, I hope, a decisive blow to their
Fleet; but would also prevent them from getting into the
Milanese, by possessing the strong passes of the Bocchetta.
They have desired of the Genoese the fortress of Savona, as a
place for arms; which although the Republic has refused, yet
of course they will take it when convenient, and without opposition, as a great friend of theirs is Governor of it, the Marquis
of Spinola. They have also desired the loan of thirty millions
of livres, to which this Republic has pleaded poverty.

Genoa is full of corn for the use of the French; but, possessing the whole Coast, it is almost impossible to take any of
their Vessels: I have taken three lately; yet the Vessels and
cargoes being Neutral, I suppose they will not be condemned.
None but Neutral vessels navigate to France: not a French
Merchant-vessel appears on the sea. Whatever may occur
within my knowledge, your Royal Highness may depend on
knowing.

I am, &c.
HORATIO NELSON.

TO WILLIAM LOCKER, ESQ., LIEUTENANT-GOVERNOR OF
GREENWICH HOSPITAL.

[Autograph, in the Locker Papers.]

Agamemnon, Genoa Mole, March 4th, 1796.

My dear Friend,

I received the day before I last left Leghorn your letter of
December 30th, for which I thank you. As to my sailing for
England, it is impossible to say when it is to happen; for
so many Ships are in a bad state, that I know not who is
to have the preference. The Convoy must, I suppose, sail
next month, but the French are so nearly equal to us, that
the Admiral will not part with many Ships. I am just come
from looking into Toulon, where thirteen Sail of the Line
and five Frigates are ready for sea, and some others fitting in
the Arsenal: I think by the end of this month the Enemy's
Fleet will be at sea, and as they have a great number of Transports ready at Marseilles, I firmly believe the Fleet from
Cadiz, perhaps joined by some from L'Orient or Brest, will

join them, when one week's very superior Fleet will effect a
landing between Port Especia and Leghorn, I mean on that
coast of Italy, when they will of course possess themselves of
Leghorn, and there is nothing to stop their progress to Rome
and Naples: we may fight their Fleet, but unless we can
destroy them, their Transports will push on and effect their
landing. What will the French care for the loss of a few
Men-of-war? it is nothing if they can get into Italy. This
[is] the gold-mine, and what, depend on it, they will push for.
The little I have seen of Sir John, I like; and he seems
pleased with my conduct, and does not seem very willing to
let me go home, even if Agamemnon does. I left the Admiral on the 23rd ult., to the westward of Toulon. I told
him of your remembrances to him. Mr. Summers has sent
home his commission, and although the Officer in whose room
he came, was only invalided, yet the vacancy ought to be a
good one, as he died very soon afterwards; therefore the list
is not increased by his appointment. I suppose Admiral
Hotham will be thinking of homeward steering; he has spent
the winter at Naples, and been well received.

How unfortunate Admiral Christian has been![1] I hope our
West India Islands will not suffer more than they have done ;
but I see Wilberforce is meddling again with the slave-trade.
I feel very much obliged by Simon Taylor's remembrances ;
pray do not forget me to him when you write. Was I an
Admiral, there is no station I should like so well in a war, as
Jamaica; I think I could give satisfaction by keeping the
Island free from privateers, which I know is the general complaint against our Admirals. I have got your quarter cask of
sherry very safe, and it ought to be very good. I shall, if I
come home, order a hogshead from Mr. Duff, as you say you

---

[1] On the 16th of November, 1795, Rear-Admiral Hugh Cloberry Christian, his
Flag in the St. George, 98, sailed from St. Helen's with a Squadron of Ships of
War, and 200 Sail of Transports and West Indiamen, having 16,000 troops on
board, to act against the French and Dutch Settlements in the West Indies; but
two days after they sailed, the Fleet was dispersed by a heavy gale, in which many
of the Transports and Merchantmen foundered. Having repaired their damages, the
Fleet sailed from St. Helen's on the 9th of December, but it was again dispersed by
a heavy gale of wind, which compelled the Rear-Admiral and some of the Ships of
war and Merchant vessels to return to Spithead.

want mine. We are this day covered with snow, and intensely
cold; this will make the campaign later in opening, but
every day fresh troops are arriving to reinforce the French
army. I have my fears for Piedmont, unless the Emperor
orders many more troops than he has at present. I beg you
will remember me kindly to every part of your family, and do
not forget me to such of our friends as you may meet with,
Mr. Bradley, &c. Believe me

Yours most truly,

Horatio Nelson.

TO THE REVEREND MR. NELSON, HILBOROUGH.

[Autograph, in the Nelson Papers.]

Genoa Mole, March 4th, 1796. Deep snow, and intensely cold.

My dear Brother,

I am truly sorry to find, by my letters from Bath, that poor
Aunt Mary[2] has been very ill. I feel much for her, and shall
truly rejoice to hear she has got better, and may be comfortable
for several years. I am just come from looking into Toulon,
where there are thirteen Sail of the Line and five Frigates,
ready for sea, and some others fitting in the Arsenal; therefore, probably we shall soon have another battle in the Mediterranean; and I have little doubt but it will, if the French give
us as good opportunities, be destructive to the Fleet of France.
But I own myself rather of opinion, that a Squadron from
L'Orient will join Citizen Richery,[3] at Cadiz, and they will
have a very superior Fleet to us. But fight we must, or Italy
will be lost this summer; for not less than 80,000 men are to
open the campaign; and if their Transports can land, under
cover of their Fleet, 20,000 men in the plain country of Italy,
nothing remains to stop their march to Rome and Naples—
probably both ripe for a revolt.

Our Convoy is to sail next month: whether I am to be of
the party seems very doubtful. Sir John does not appear very
willing to part with me ; but some of us must go : perhaps

---

[2] Miss Mary Nelson, his father's eldest sister. She died, unmarried, in 1800.

[3] The Rear-Admiral commanding the French Squadron in Cadiz.

Ships may be coming out to relieve us. I shall not be *very* sorry to see England again. I am grown old and battered to pieces, and require some repairs. However, on the whole, I have stood the fag better than could have been expected. I am sorry to tell you, the fancied rich prize is not likely to be condemned: I believe the captor will be glad to give her up again. However, I never built much on her: if I return not poorer than I set out, I shall be perfectly satisfied; but I believe the contrary. Mine is all *honour:* so much for the Navy! I have not heard from you for a long time. I now look daily for a letter. How does Robert Rolfe[4] do? You will remember me to him. I dare say he is happy, because I believe he deserves to be so: and do not forget my remembrances to our friends at Swaffham. Josiah is very well, and often inquires after you. Remember me kindly to Mrs. Nelson and my Aunt. Your children are not yet, I suppose, correspondents, although I know they can write. Believe me, ever

Your most affectionate Brother,

HORATIO NELSON.

TO THE HONOURABLE JOHN TREVOR, MINISTER AT TURIN.

[From Clarke and M'Arthur, vol. i. p. 259.]

Agamemnon, Genoa Mole, 4th March, 1790.

Is the whole Island[5] in rebellion, and friendly to the French, and would it be dangerous for an English Ship to anchor in Oristan, or any other port in Sardinia? Should the Vessels belonging to the Sardinians be seized? In short, Sir, pray tell me, in what light the King of Sardinia considers the inhabitants of that Island, and how you think I should consider them. I did not, I own, rejoice at the snow, and the very bad weather we have had, until you told me how beneficial it may prove to our good Ally the King of Sardinia, whom I shall always respect.

I am, &c.,

HORATIO NELSON.

[4] His cousin, the Reverend Robert Rolfe, so often mentioned.
[5] Sardinia.

TO ADMIRAL SIR JOHN JERVIS, K.B.

[From Clarke and M'Arthur, vol. i. p. 259; who state that, in this letter, Captain Nelson sent a general account of his correspondence with their Excellencies Mr. Trevor and Mr. Drake, and concluded by saying]—

Leghorn, 10th March, 1796.

Mr. Wyndham's letter from Florence, shows that if the Tuscan Government are ready to receive a French garrison, it will be very difficult to prevent it until we possess Vado. The points for us to look to, are a small Squadron off Port Especia, with one on the other side of the Gulf, for the present embarkation will be in small Vessels; but if the Genoese will not oppose their passage, there is nothing to prevent, in a march of forty-eight hours, the arrival of the French at Leghorn.

I am, &c.

HORATIO NELSON.

TO THE RIGHT HON. SIR GILBERT ELLIOT, BART.

[Autograph, in the Minto Papers.]

Leghorn, March 10th, 1796.

Dear Sir,

As I think you will like to know my proceedings, which I can truly say are always employed to the best of my knowledge for the Public good, I send you my letter to Sir John Jervis for your perusal, which be so good, when read as to seal up.[6]

Believe me, dear Sir,

Your most faithful

To his Excellency the Vice-Roy.   HORATIO NELSON.

TO THE RIGHT HON. SIR WILLIAM HAMILTON, K.B., MINISTER AT NAPLES.

[From the "Letters of Lord Nelson to Lady Hamilton," vol. ii. p. 227. It is also printed by Clarke and M'Arthur, but with their usual incorrectness.]

Agamemnon, Leghorn, 11th March, 1796.

Sir,

Mr. Wyndham having communicated to Mr. Udney, the conversation of the French Minister with the Tuscans, I cannot,

---

[6] Apparently the preceding Letter.

being entrusted by the Admiral with the command of the small
Squadron in the Gulf of Genoa, but think it right for me to
beg that your Excellency will apply for such Vessels of War
belonging to his Sicilian Majesty, as may be judged proper to
cruise in the Gulf of Genoa, and particularly off the Point of the
Gulf of Especia. Zebecs, Corvettes, and Frigates are the fittest
to cruise; and the first have the great advantage of rowing, as
well as sailing, I am told, very fast. General [Acton[7]] knows,
full as well as myself, the Vessels proper to prevent the
disembarkation of Troops on this Coast; therefore I shall not
particularly point them out. Last campaign, the word Flotilla
was misunderstood : I can only say, that all Vessels which can
sail, and row, must be useful; and for Small-craft, Port
Especia is a secure harbour.

Whatever is to be done, should be done speedily; for by
Mr. Wyndham's account, we have no time to lose. If we
have the proper Vessels, I am confident the French will not
be able to bring their 10,000 men by sea; and should they
attempt to pass through the Genoese territories, I hope the
Austrians will prevent them. But, however, should all our
precautions not be able to prevent the Enemy's possessing
themselves of Leghorn, yet we are not to despair. Fourteen
days from their entry, if the Allied Powers unite heartily, I
am confident we shall take them all prisoners. I am confident
it can, and therefore—(should such an unlucky event take place,
as their possessing themselves of Leghorn)—I hope will be
done. I have sent to the Admiral. I am very lately from
off Toulon, where thirteen Sail of the Line, and five Frigates
are ready for sea, and others fitting. With my best respects
to Lady Hamilton, believe me, dear Sir, your Excellency's
most obedient servant,

HORATIO NELSON.

---

[7] His Sicilian Majesty's Prime Minister.

TO FRANCIS DRAKE, ESQ., MINISTER AT GENOA.

[From Clarke and M'Arthur, vol. i. p. 262.]

March 15th, 1796.

Having received information, on which I am told I may
depend, that Salicetti[8] is now here, with other Commissioners,
for the express purpose of expediting the operations of the
French Army towards the invasion of Italy; and that one of
the three columns, into which that Army is to be divided, is
either to penetrate through the Genoese territory, or to be
conveyed coastways to take possession of Port Especia; which
will instantly give them the flat country as far as Leghorn;
and no doubt but a small Army appearing before Leghorn,
would, without any difficulty, make themselves masters of it:
I therefore feel it my duty, as Commanding Officer of his
Majesty's Squadron employed on this Coast, and in the absence
of the Naval Commander-in-Chief, to state clearly the fatal
consequences which will attend this plan of the French Commissioners.   The possession of Port Especia will always give
an easy access to every part of Italy, even to the Kingdom of
Naples, and also security to Transports, Ships of War, and
small Vessels; and I moreover beg it may be understood, that
if the French Flotilla proceeds along the Coast, our Ships-of-
war cannot molest them; not being able to approach the
Coast, from the shallowness of the water.   I must besides observe, that the Enemy possessing Leghorn, cuts off all our
supplies; and of course our Fleet cannot always be looked for
on the northern Coast of Italy.   I therefore beg leave to state,
that to obviate these misfortunes, two plans are necessary to be
attended to; the first, and best, is the possession of Vado Bay;
this done, as far as human foresight can discern, Italy is safe:
the next is the taking of Port Especia; and, as a Sea-officer,
I beg leave to say, that unless one of these plans is adopted,

---

[8] Commissary of the French Government with the Armies of Italy and the Alps.
After the evacuation of Corsica, he was sent to that Island from Leghorn by Buonaparte, on the 17th of October; and his Address to the Corsicans, dated on the 24th
of November, 1796, is in the *Annual Register* of that year.   Vide vol. xxxviii. *State
Papers*, pp. 253, 259.

my Admiral, and Commander-in-Chief of his Majesty's Fleet, cannot answer for the safety of Italy, from any attempts that may be made on it Coastways.

I am, &c.

HORATIO NELSON.

TO ADMIRAL SIR JOHN JERVIS, K.B.

[From Clarke and M'Arthur, vol. i. p. 259.]

At Sea, 16th March, 1796.

Sir,

I beg leave to transmit copies of all the letters that have passed between me and His Majesty's Ministers at Turin, Genoa, and Naples; that you may be in full possession of my conduct, and know whether I am worthy the honour of commanding the Squadron intrusted to my direction. My last letter to Mr. Drake, dated yesterday, is of so very important a nature, and the opinion I have given so very decisive, that I must request you will send me your ideas of my conduct, as soon as possible: should it unfortunately be disapprobation, I have only to regret that my abilities are not equal to my zeal.

I am, &c.,

HORATIO NELSON.

TO ADMIRAL SIR JOHN JERVIS, K.B.

[From Clarke and M'Arthur, vol. i. p. 262.]

March 16th, 1796.

Mr. Drake having expressed a wish to see me, to communicate many things which he did not think it right to trust to paper, I arrived yesterday morning at Genoa, with Meleager and Blanche, and held a conference with him. The same cause, which prevented him from writing, prevents me from entering fully on the part of the plan intimated in his letter, and which at present is submitted to the consideration of Ministers: but, when I have the honour of meeting you, I am at full liberty to communicate it; for I would receive no information, or plans, which I might not freely communicate to you. Mr. Drake expressed himself pleased at your deter-

mination to give the Austrian General a meeting, whenever he
chose to bring his Army on the coast; but, at the same time,
he said, he found it extremely difficult to make them hear of
the Riviera, although he had pressed very much to have the
plan of the last year carried into execution; with the exception, in the first instance, of penetrating into Provence. The
Commander-in-Chief of the Army was not yet fixed on; but
it was understood that the Archduke was to be the nominal,
and General Beaulieu the active Commander-in-Chief, that
Beaulieu wished to meet the French in the plains of Lombardy,
and then to follow up the blow, which he had no doubt would
be decisive.

I could not help observing, that the very reason why the
General wished to meet them in a particular place, would of
course be the reason why the French would not penetrate by
that route; and that respecting the information, which I had
received, of the intention of the Directory to order the movement of their Army in three columns, one by Ceva, another
by the pass of the Bocchetta, and another to march through
the Genoese territory, or be carried coastways to Port Especia,
which would give them an easy entry into the plains of Italy;
I had no doubt the two first would be feints, and the last the
real plan. I must here observe, that before night, Mr. Drake
had the same information communicated to him; and also,
that a body of troops would be embarked on board the Fleet,
the moment Richery arrived from Cadiz, and a push be made
for Port Especia. This information induced me, and, if possible, more strongly than ever, to press the measure of taking
Vado, or Port Especia, without delay; and I added, that
without one or the other was done, you could not answer for
the safety of Italy coastways, it being now perfectly clear for
what the two hundred Flat boats were built, and the numerous
Gun-boats fitted out. Mr. Drake told me, that he had already
urged the measure of taking Vado, and would continue to do
it, and would also instantly press the necessity of possessing
Port Especia, if I would declare, that our Naval force should
support the Austrians from attacks by sea; which, I said,
there could be no doubt of, for it would be the home of our
Squadron employed on this coast. He then desired me to
give my opinion in writing, as the authority of a Sea-officer

would have more weight than all he could urge; and this was
the cause of my writing the letter, on which I am so anxious
to obtain your sentiments.

Salicetti has failed in his demand for the loan of thirty
millions of livres. On his first demand, when it was generally
understood, that five millions would be given him to get rid of
it, Mr. Drake came to Genoa, and, with all the Ministers of
the coalesced Powers, joined in a Note to the Serene Republic,
stating, ' they had heard of the demand made by the French,
yet could not believe that the Republic would so far forget her
neutrality, as to comply with it: that if She did, the coalesced
Powers could no longer recognise her as a neutral State, but
as the ally of France.' The demand of Salicetti was taken
into consideration on the night of the 12th, and was rejected
by 142 against 34.—Information from Toulon was received
yesterday by Mr. Drake, that an embargo has been laid on
that Port; the gates were shut, and no person was suffered to
go out of the Town. This is an additional inducement for my
looking into that Port, which being done, I will despatch a
Frigate to you.

[Apparently in continuation.]

Off the Hieres Islands, 18th March.

I wish much to have the honour of seeing you, and the
moment I hear of your arrival at St. Fiorenzo, I shall go there.
When you did me the honour to offer me the Zealous, you
was acquainted with my reasons for not accepting her. In
any situation, if you approve of my conduct, I beg leave to
assure you, I shall feel pleasure in serving under your command; and in case a promotion of Flags should take place, I
am confident that your mention of me to Lord Spencer would
be sufficient to have my Flag ordered to be hoisted in this
Country. The Zealous, most probably, is disposed of long
before this: if not, and you approve of me for this command,
either as Captain or Admiral, I am at your disposal. Mr.
Drake, in his conversation, on my telling him that I thought
the Agamemnon would go home, and that probably the
Zealous was disposed of, said, ' as I last year represented to
Admiral Hotham the propriety of ordering you a Distinguishing Pendant, and also did the same to Lord Grenville,
the Admiral will perhaps direct you to hoist it on board

l'Aigle, which will make her as good as Agamemnon.' On
these, Sir, and many other points, I shall take the first opportunity of consulting you. The opening of this campaign will
be warm, and most important: everything will be risked on
the part of the French, to get into Italy. Mr. Grey's motion
for peace, on the 15th February, was lost by 189 to 50.[9]

I am, &c.,

HORATIO NELSON.[1]

TO HIS EXCELLENCY FRANCIS DRAKE, ESQ.

[From Clarke and M'Arthur, vol. i. p. 264.]

March 25th, 1796.

I do not know when I have been so ill, as during this cruise,
but I hope a good opening to the campaign will set me quite
to rights. Whilst I receive from your Excellency, from Mr.
Trevor, and my Admiral, every approbation of my conduct, I
should be a wretch not to exert myself.

I am, &c.,

HORATIO NELSON.

TO MRS. NELSON.

[From Clarke and M'Arthur, vol. i. p. 264.]

[In a previous paragraph, Captain Nelson appears to have said that he would
send her the following extract from Sir John Jervis' Letter to him:—]

25th March, 1796.

' I have received by the Blanche, your two letters, of the
16th and 19th instant, together with the several enclosures,
and copies of your correspondence at Turin, Genoa, and
Naples ; and I feel the greatest satisfaction in communicating

---

[9] Mr. (now Earl) Grey's motion was for an Address to the King, stating the desire
of the House of Commons that his Majesty would take such steps as he thought
proper for communicating directly to the Executive Government of the French
Republic his Majesty's readiness to meet any disposition to negotiate on the part of
that Government with an earnest desire to give it the fullest and speediest effect.

[1] Admiral Sir John Jervis, in acknowledging the receipt of those letters on the
21st of March, said, " I feel the greatest satisfaction in communicating this public
testimony of my thorough approbation of your late and recent correspondence and
conduct."—*Tucker's Memoir of Earl of St. Vincent*, vol. i. p. 173.

this public testimony of my thorough approbation of your late conduct, and recent correspondence.' In his private letter, Sir John Jervis added, ' No words can express the sense I entertain of every part of your conduct, and I shall be very happy to manifest it in the most substantial manner : a Distinguishing Pendant you shall certainly wear, and I will write to Lord Spencer about you : in short, there is nothing within my grasp, that I shall not be proud to confer on you.' All this, my dear Fanny, is certainly flattering and pleasant ; and these blossoms may one day bring forth fruit. I have just read in the papers, that Admiral Christian has a Red ribbon ;[2] and it has given me pleasure to see, that merit, although unfortunate, is not always neglected. God bless you, and give us a happy meeting, and soon, is the sincere wish of your most affectionate husband,

HORATIO NELSON.

TO ADMIRAL SIR JOHN JERVIS, K.B.

[From " Memoirs of the Earl of St. Vincent," by Jedediah Stephens Tucker, Esq. vol. i. p. 175.]

H.M.S. Agamemnon, March[3] 28, 1796.

Sir,

The Blanche is returned,[3] but with very few stores; not canvass enough to mend our sails—10lbs. of twine, no tar, not a spar. We have, literally speaking, no top-gallant yards, no steering-sail booms, those we have up, are fished, not an ounce of paint, and many other things, the Commissioner[4] tells me; but I send his letters. We want much, and I must beg you will give me your order to purchase stores. I assure you, Sir, not an article shall be got but what is absolutely necessary.

I am, Sir, your very humble Servant,
HORATIO NELSON.

[2] Rear Admiral Christian (vide p. 131. ante) was Invested with the Order of the Bath on the 17th of February, 1796 ; he proceeded to the West Indies soon after, and died in November, 1798.

[3] In Mr. Jedediah Tucker's work, this Letter is said to have been dated on the 28th of April; but this is evidently a typographical error. Vide p. 140, ante.

[4] The Commissioner of the Navy at Gibraltar.

TO HIS EXCELLENCY FRANCIS DRAKE, ESQ.

[From Clarke and M'Arthur, vol. i. p. 268.]

Genoa, 6th April, 1796.

My dear Sir,

I was favoured on the 1st of this month, with your letter of March 29th, and on Saturday I went to Fiorenzo to talk with Sir John Jervis. We may rely on every support and effectual assistance from him: we have only to propose, and, if possible, it will be done. I hope the Galleys and Gun-boats will be sent in abundance, and I have a plan for forcing them to be useful; which is, to buy two Tartans, fit them as heavy Gun-boats, and occasionally man them from the Shipping of my Squadron. This will enable me to go myself, or send a Captain to command the whole, in which case I shall be sure that the service will be performed: when the time approaches, we must talk more on this subject. The Transport-ships Sir John Jervis will find; but troops from Corsica we must not expect. You may, Sir, assure General Beaulieu, that on whatever part of the Coast he comes, I shall never quit him. If he is able, and willing, and expeditious, I am sure we shall do much; but whenever that time comes, I shall hope to see you. The Admiral has directed me to wear a Broad Pendant,[5] and this was done in the handsomest manner;—he will come off Vado.

I am, &c.

HORATIO NELSON.

P.S. The Diadem[6] has just joined, and we only wish for an opportunity of acting. Yesterday I received a letter from Naples, in answer to my request of March the 11th; and I have the pleasure to say, that the Galleys and Gun-boats are fitting.

[5] On the 20th of April, Mr. Hoste, then a Midshipman of the Agamemnon, writing to his mother from Genoa said—"Our Squadron at present consists of two Sail of the Line and four Frigates; but it is to be increased in the summer, when we shall not want for amusement, I make no doubt, as our Commodore does not like to be idle. I suppose your curiosity is excited by the word *Commodore* Nelson. It gives me infinite pleasure to be able to relieve it, by informing you that our good Captain has had this additional mark of distinction conferred on him, which I dare say you will agree with me, that his merit richly deserves. His Broad Pendant is now flying; therefore I must beg my dear father to draw an additional cork in honour of our gallant countryman."—*Memoirs of Captain Sir William Hoste*, vol. i. p. 52.

[6] Captain Charles Tyler.

TO ADMIRAL SIR JOHN JERVIS, K.B.

[From Clarke and M'Arthur, vol. i. p. 265.]

Off Genoa, 7th April, 1796.

Lieutenant Pierson of the 69th Regiment informs me, that he expects to be ordered on board the Britannia, there being but one subaltern there, and that Major Saunderson[7] is to be embarked on board the Agamemnon, to which it would seem I could have no manner of objection. But I think, from a very particular circumstance, that Mr. Pierson will not be removed from me, and I hope Sir Hyde Parker[8] will agree with me in the propriety of his staying here, abstracted from my regard for him, as he was brought forward in the 69th Regiment, under the auspices of Colonel Villettes and myself, having come to us at the Siege of Bastia, as a volunteer from the Neapolitan service, and never having served with any one but ourselves. Yet this I should lay no stress upon, were I not so particularly situated. We are likely, I hope, to have a numerous Neapolitan Flotilla, which of course will be under my command: this Officer was my Aide-de-Camp to them last year, as well as to the Austrian Generals: I will only suppose, in an attack on the Enemy's flank, that I want to send particular directions; I know of no person so qualified as Lieutenant Pierson, to prevent mistakes and confusion in my orders, both from his acquaintance with the Neapolitan service, and his knowledge of the Italian language.

I am, &c.

HORATIO NELSON.

TO ADMIRAL SIR JOHN JERVIS, K.B.

[Original, in the Admiralty.]

Agamemnon, Gulf of Genoa, April 8th, 1796.

Sir,

I am honoured with your letter of the 4th Instant, transmitting one from Mr. Nepean to you, and directing you to cause

---

[7] Major Alexander Saunderson of the 69th Regiment: he was made a Lieutenant Colonel in 1797: but either retired from the Army or died before 1803.

[8] Vice-Admiral Sir Hyde Parker, the second in command.

inquiry to be made into certain circumstances stated by the
Marquis of Spinola, the Genoese Minister at the Court of
London, as insulting, and a breach of Neutrality, to the Republic of Genoa, and which you have directed me to give my
answer to, as all the circumstances alluded to are supposed to
have been committed by the Squadron under my orders.

I shall endeavour, Sir, to be as brief as possible consistent
with clearness in my answer to every circumstance stated by
the Genoese Minister.

As to the political situation of Genoa, the reason why
Foreign Armies took possession of certain parts of the Republic,
does not come within the supposed sphere of my knowledge ;
therefore I shall proceed to the accusation against his Majesty's Ships, reserving myself to draw a conclusion very different from the Marquis.

The first complaint is, the distress of the western Coast of
the Republic from want of provisions: to this I answer, that
the Genoese Government having proposed a plan for the supplying their Towns with provisions, the same was arranged
with his Majesty's Minister at Genoa, and acceded to by the
Austrian General and myself, although those Towns were in
possession of the French troops; and the Marquis does not
even pretend to state, that any Vessels furnished with the
documents arranged with his Government, were molested or
detained on their voyage.

The next hostile act stated to have been committed, was on
the 26th of August 1795, at Alassio, when the place was
threatened with demolition and conflagration, a Genoese
vessel burnt, and another seized, together with some of the
same Flag, under cannon-shot of the castle, having Genoese
colours flying.

To this I beg leave to reply by facts. The French Army
occupied the Town, to the number of 2000 horse and foot,
having cannon mounted on different parts of it: a Convoy of
warlike stores arriving at this place for the French Army, I
anchored in the Bay of Alassio and Langueglia, and took a
French Corvette, four other Vessels of war, and five or six
French vessels, laden with powder, shot, shells, and provisions. It is true, that Genoese colours were flying on a castle

in the Town; but the French colours were laid over the wall, and the French troops, with their colours flying, were drawn up in the Castle, in front of the Castle, and in front of the Town, on the beach, and fired from the beach on our Boats employed in cutting out the Vessels; and my forbearance will be considered as great, when I assert, that fifteen musket-balls passed through my Barge, yet I would not suffer the Town to be fired upon. A Vessel, whose cable was cut, and ran on shore, was burned, in opposition to all the French troops: and I here affirm, on the honour of an Officer, that no Genoese or other Neutral vessel was kept possession of; and indeed it is acknowledged by my conduct to the Adriot vessels, that Neutrals had only to declare their Neutrality, to claim respect from me. As to the threats of demolition and conflagration to the Town, I have to say, that I neither received, nor sent any message, nor had any communication with the Town whatever; therefore this must be wilful misrepresentation.

To the circumstance of August 27th, 1795, where it is stated, that the English pursued another Vessel, and chased her into a little Bay, and cannonaded her upon the Territory of the Republic, I must here observe, that although the Genoese may claim, and have undoubted right to, the possession of their Territory, yet the French having taken possession of every foot of ground from Ventimiglia to Voltri, erected batteries at whatever places they thought proper, ordered requisitions of provisions, mules, and drivers; firing on the Ships of their Enemies, although they may be friends of the Genoese. Are not these acts, which the Marquis must acknowledge to be every day committed, proof sufficient that the French, and not the Genoese, are Masters of the Country? Nor can the French allowing Genoese flags to be hoisted on some of the fortifications, alter the case: the Vessel alluded to was a French Gun-boat, which had fired on his Majesty's Ship, and received the chastisement she so highly merited; but this happened on a beach where not a house belonging to the Genoese could be injured.

The next accusation is, that, on the 6th of September, an English Ship of the Line, &c., having captured a Brig off St. Remo put an English crew on board, and sent her in, threatening to burn seven Adriot and Genoese vessels, and another,

which was a Frenchman, in the very Port of St. Remo. I
have only to say, that not having captured a Brig off the Port
of St. Remo, I could not send in any message by her: and I
also declare, that I never sent any message into St. Remo.
Had I acted as they say, my line of conduct must have taken
a sudden change; for only on the 26th of August, eleven
days before, it is asserted what respect I paid to Adriot vessels,
then in my power. It is true, I chased ten Sail into St. Remo;
but there it ended.

On the 9th of September it is stated, that an English Ship
of the Line, &c. anchored on the Coast off Della Riva, and
took two Genoese Tartans, and that, when a signal was made
from the shore, no other answer was returned, than showing
their guns; and that on the same day, the same Boats seized
another Vessel at anchor off St. Stephano. It is true I anchored on the Coast, as stated ; but as to my taking two Vessels, it is an untruth. Our Boats examined two Tartans, and
finding them actually Genoese, left them: a French boat was
taken on the coast of St. Stephano, the crew having fired on
our boats. As to the signals made from the shore, or the
Agamemnon showing her guns, the first I could not understand; and respecting the last, I never heard of a Man of
War's guns being hid.

As the Marquis of Spinola appears to have been well furnished with accounts of our proceedings, I wonder he did not
relate a fact, which it is natural to suppose came to his knowledge, as a representation of it was made by Mr. Drake to the
Genoese Government—viz., that the Boats of the Agamemnon,
with English colours flying, going to examine three Vessels,
on their coming alongside the Vessels, were fired upon, and
seventeen of his Majesty's Subjects killed and wounded.[3] A
representation was made at Genoa of this barbarous act, but I
believe the Vessels could not be found out. The similar circumstance, acknowledged by the Marquis on the 13th, is a
proof of the barbarity of these Adriot Vessels, when they had
the superiority. It is said, that two English Long-boats would
have captured two Adriot Vessels proceeding for Genoa, had
they not been prevented by the fire of the Ottomans. That

---

[3] Vide, ante.

the English Ships will, if possible, examine every Vessel they meet with, is certain, and in this they do their duty. The pieces of iron fired on shore, most probably came from the Ottomans; as it is well known, that English Ships of war are furnished with no such ammunition as langrage. How can the Marquis think that we can know what Vessels are, or their lading, and to what place they are bound, without examination? I shall only say, that no Vessel belonging to any Nation whatever was taken or detained (except for the act of examining her papers) during the time of my command, which includes the whole period stated by the Marquis, that was laden with provisions for the City of Genoa. It is next stated, that two Frigates continually remained at anchor, in sight of the mouth of the Port of Genoa. I shall only assert, that this is a most notorious misrepresentation and falsehood ; and I do further declare, that if at any time a Frigate anchored in Genoa road, her Boats never boarded any Vessel whilst in that situation.

Having answered every part of the accusation made by the Genoese Minister, I beg leave to say a few words on his conclusion, which is certainly a most extraordinary one. To pretend to assert, that although our Enemies take possession of, and continue in the Republic of Genoa, we are not, by every means in our power, to attack them both at sea and on shore, will [not] bear reasoning upon ; but I can with truth assert, that in the act of distressing our Enemies in the Republic of Genoa, the greatest forbearance, and even acts of kindness, have been constantly shown to individual Genoese.

The Republic of Genoa has now had six months unmolested Fraternization with the French Army ; and I am assured, that the inhabitants of the Republic had rather again encounter our fancied breaches of Neutrality, and violation of Territory, than the Fraternal embraces of the French troops, which have been given to their women, their churches, and their olive trees.

I am, &c.
HORATIO NELSON.

TO ADMIRAL SIR JOHN JERVIS, K.B.

[From Clarke and M'Arthur, vol. i. p. 268.]

Genoa, April 9th, 1796.

On my arrival off here, yesterday morning, I was so strongly pressed by the Sardinian and Imperial Ministers to come into the Port, in order that they might have some conversation with me, that, although rather against my inclination of anchoring, I could not refuse; and I am just going on shore to meet them. There has been some little skirmishing between the advanced Piquets of the two Armies in the vicinity of Voltri; but it is generally thought the French will retire to Savona, Vado, &c. Ceva and Ormea are to be the two places attacked by them; but I hope General Beaulieu on his passing the heights of Vado, may find an opportunity of taking them, and give us the anchorage of Vado Bay. We are on the best terms with the Genoese; and as far as a private communication to the Secretary of State, through Mr. Brame,[4] they are certain of our good disposition towards them, and of our sincere wishes to see the Republic really enjoying her Neutrality. At the same time, I desired Mr. Brame to signify that Vessels to whatever Nation they belonged, bound to France with provisions or stores, would be seized; that I wished this to be understood; and that the seizures of Vessels belonging to Genoese subjects, in the situation alluded to, ought not to be considered as hostile to the Genoese flag, for all other Nations were precisely in the same situation. To this the Secretary replied, in his private character, that if Merchants would run the risk, it rested with them; and that he did not think the Government had any concern in it; that he should acquaint the Doge of the conversation, and was very happy to see me here with a Broad Pendant, which was saluted. The Secretary was full of praises of the late Austrian Army: not a sixpence of debt had been left behind, nor an individual injured by their stay in the Riviera; contrasting it with the conduct of the French. Salicetti is gone from Genoa.

I am just returned on board; and enclosed send you a copy

4 The English Consul at Genoa.

of my Note, which is gone off by express to General Beaulieu.
The Ministers of the Emperor, and King of Sardinia, were
pleased with it; and I hope it will meet with your approbation also.   I have found from experience, that we cannot be
too clear with these gentlemen; and I am determined to leave
no room for them to say, ' We thought you could do this
thing, or the other.'   These Ministers tell me, that a general
attack may be expected, on the same day, from Voltri to
Finale.   Your appearance off the Coast would most certainly
have a good effect.   The line of Austrians and Piedmontese
is full 40,000 ; the French, I am assured, not more : they yesterday got cannon on the strong post of St. Giacomo, and will
defend Vado, but I hear they tremble.

I am, &c.

HORATIO NELSON.

TO GENERAL BEAULIEU, COMMANDER-IN-CHIEF OF THE
AUSTRIAN ARMY.

[From Clarke and M'Arthur, vol. i. p. 269.]

[About April 9th, 1796.]

Does General Beaulieu wish the English Squadron should
cruise off any particular point of the Coast, whence it may be
satisfactory for the General to see it from the mountains, and
of course be discouraging to the French?—It would be
attended with this risk, that calms, or contrary winds, might
put the Squadron at a distance, at the time General Beaulieu
may arrive on the Coast: would the General, therefore, rather
have us remain at Genoa, with a moral certainty of joining him
in ten or twelve hours, after the news of his arrival on the
Coast is sent to me.

Next consideration : If General Beaulieu sends me notice,
at what particular time and place it is probable he may attack
the French, in that case it is almost certain I could be very
near at hand, and act as opportunity might offer : for instance,
suppose the attack is on the heights over Savona, the
Squadron, if the weather be moderate, could anchor about five
or six miles from Savona, instead of waiting at Genoa.   These

considerations are submitted to General Beaulieu, who has
only to express his wishes to have them, as far as is possible,
complied with.

HORATIO NELSON.

TO HIS EXCELLENCY FRANCIS DRAKE, ESQ.

[From Clarke and M'Arthur, vol. i. p. 270.]

11th April, 1796.

It has been well, but might have been better; for if I had
been fully acquainted with the movements of the Army, I am
sure not many of the French would have returned to Savona:
our Ships command every foot of the road. I beg you will
endeavour to impress on those about the General, the necessity
of punctuality in a joint operation, for its success to be complete. I received yesterday afternoon, at five o'clock, a Note
from the Baron de Malcamp, to tell me, that the General had
resolved to attack the French at daylight this morning, and on
the right of Voltri: yet by the Austrians getting too forward
in the afternoon, a slight Action took place, and during the
night the French retreated. My movements I kept secret;
and, after the shutting of the gate, weighed the Squadron from
Genoa, and at half-past nine I anchored within half gun-shot
of the Austrian Army, sending Diadem and Blanche to anchor
between Voltri and Savona: but the French were aware of
their perilous situation, and passed our Ships in the night. I
do not mean this as any complaint, but to show the necessity
of punctuality; for had the Austrians kept back, very few of
the French could have escaped. I have a Ship off Voltri; the
rest of my little Squadron are off Vado. As the difficulty will
now be increased for the French to get supplies, the Genoese
will of course employ deception, and clear all Vessels as for
their own people in the Riviera, although possibly for the use
of the French Army. How, Sir, shall we manage? Will you
turn this in your mind?

I am, &c.

HORATIO NELSON.

TO ADMIRAL SIR JOHN JERVIS, K.B.

[From Clarke and M'Arthur, vol. i. p. 270.]

13th April, 1796.

Sir,

As it is impossible to be too particular in all my communications with the Austrian General, I think it right to note
down the conversation which I held last evening, in the presence of Mr. Brame, with the Baron de Malcamp, nephew
and Aide-de-Camp to General Beaulieu, whom the General
had desired to communicate with me.

The Baron began by returning thanks from his General,
for our well-timed co-operation, and for the assurances I had
given of every support and assistance ; that the General wished
to know, what was the particular object of my Squadron, and
in what manner his operations could be serviceable to me.
To this I replied, that the co-operation was my duty, and
which I had the greatest pleasure in performing; and I begged
he would assure the General, that my Squadron had no object
whatever in view but the co-operation with his Army. Whenever he came down on the Sea-coast, there he would be sure
to find me.

The Baron then asked, if I could anchor in any other place
than Vado Bay ? I replied, that for these five months to
come, for nineteen days out of twenty, whenever the General
was on the Coast, there I should always be, at either Finale,
Albenga, Alassio, Oneglia, St. Remo, and the whole Coast
of Nice; and I would anchor the Squadron opposite his
Army : that Vado was the only place where our Fleet could
lie in safety ; but as for my Squadron, all places would suit it.
I therefore begged it might be perfectly and clearly understood, that if the General thought it better to cut down to the
Sea-coast, to the westward of Vado, he would do so, for Vado
was not necessary for my Squadron ; that I had understood
St. Giacomo was strongly fortified ; and if six or seven thousand men were to be lost in getting it, merely for the immediate possession of Vado Bay, it was no object to us, if the
General chose to leave them to the eastward. This point I
pressed on the Baron three different times, and he said he
perfectly understood me; that he should go to the General, as

this day, the 13th, and the General would send me a *tableau*
of his plan of operations. The General also desired him to
assure me, on his part, that the most perfect harmony would
be kept up with me; and that from my character, as well as
from my exactness on the 11th, he was assured all would go
well for the Common Cause; and this would have the happiest
effect, as our Enemies would be convinced of the most perfect
harmony subsisting between the Allies.

I assured the Baron he might depend on my openness of
conduct, and that what I had promised, should, if possible, be
performed : nor had I promised anything but what I had a
moral certainty of being able to perform; and I desired he
would assure his General, I was authorized by Sir John Jervis
to promise the most sincere and cordial co-operation, for that
nothing should be omitted on his part, to convince the General
and our Allies, as well as our Enemies, and the Neutral
Powers, how much the Admiral had the good of the Common
Cause at heart ; and further, that as soon as Sir John Jervis
knew of the General's being on the Coast, he would come
there. I also desired the Baron to acquaint the General, that
I would undertake to furnish proper Convoys, for their provisions being carried coastways from Genoa, Voltri, &c. Upon
which he asked me, two or three times, if there were not a risk
that my Squadron might be lost on the Coast : to this I constantly replied, That should these Ships be lost, my Admiral
would find others, and we should risk the Squadron at all times
to assist the General ; and I requested he would give me credit
for my sincere disposition to contribute all in my power towards
the success of the common cause. I am, &c.,

                                   HORATIO NELSON.

TO ADMIRAL SIR JOHN JERVIS, K.B.

[From Clarke and M‘Arthur, vol. i. p. 271.]

                                        15th April, 1796.
Sir,
I anchored here, in Genoa Road, this morning, and shall
immediately proceed to the information which I have received
from the Imperial and Sardinian Ministers, both of whom I

immediately waited upon. General Beaulieu's letter to the Minister was dated Acqui, the 14th, in which he says, ' Yesterday, Generals Argenteau and Leichtein attacked a post of the Enemy at Montenotte; they did not succeed, and returned to their first position.' I beg, Sir, you will not believe the reports of the ill-disposed at Genoa, though I cannot say I like this account; but you will form the same conjectures as myself: no loss is mentioned, and the word *first* conveys to my mind a great deal. Argenteau has ever failed; they fell, report says, into an ambuscade. The Minister at Turin writes thus to Mr. Nomis, Sardinian Minister here: ' The snow still lies so much on the mountains near Ceva, that neither party can take possession of those posts they wish. The Enemy made an attack on one of our posts, but were repulsed with some loss.' Mr. Nomis expects an express from Alessandria, with an account of the attack at Montenotte, and I shall know the contents as soon as they arrive. Salicetti sent from Savona, two days past, for thirty thousand pair of shoes: the Consul[5] sent off this intelligence to Captain Towry,[6] who had his boats out all night, but without success: eight thousand pair are gone to Savona.

I send you Mr. Trevor's original letters. Anxious as I am to do everything, we cannot equip Vessels quite so fast as his Excellency wishes. The Sardinian sailors manning two or three, would be of great use. England, I know, must pay for them, and probably victual them. This measure must have a little further thought. Heavy gun-boats will not do as cruisers, and, on the contrary, we must have a place to keep them in; but I shall see you very soon, when I shall enlarge upon this subject; and, I am afraid, time enough will remain to equip our vessels, if not, so much the better. The firing I saw last night on the hills, between Voltri and Savona, was, I hope, an advance of the General.

Seven o'clock, P.M.—We have no particulars, but it is said the French have been beat from some of the hills above Savona, and many wounded have been carried thither.

I am, &c.,

HORATIO NELSON.

⁵ Mr. Brame.   ⁶ Of the Dido.

TO CAPTAIN COLLINGWOOD.

[Autograph, in the possession of the Hon. Mrs. Newnham Collingwood. Captain Collingwood had shortly before joined the Mediterranean Fleet in command of the Excellent, 74 guns.]

My dear Coll.,   Genoa, April 16th, 1796.

I have desired a basket of vegetables for you and Pakenham.[7] If you will send me a list of what you want by Peterel,[8] if we join again, I will bring them.

As to news—what shall I tell you? The Austrians and the French have been fighting at different places for these last two days. Thousands have fell on each side, but no advantage gained. They suffered the French to escape at Voltri, by not adhering to their plan or time of attack, which they sent me. Four thousand men escaped, which, on the 13th, beat back the Austrians, at Montenotte. However, although, in my opinion, they did not do [as] much as they ought on the 11th, yet the matter was so managed, that, with my usual good fortune, I have received praises from the General, who has wrote very handsomely to the King of Sardinia and the Emperor, about me.

From England, Royal Sovereign put back much damaged; a Transport run on board her.[9] The Fleet gone on, under Captain Drury.[1] The Abolition of the Slave Trade, lost by four.[2] Our Fleet seen nothing of the Dutch.[3]

[7] Captain John Pakenham, of the Gibraltar, of 80 guns.

[8] Commanded by the present Admiral Sir Charles Ogle, Bart.

[9] On the 29th of February, 1796, Vice-Admiral the Honourable William Cornwallis sailed from Portsmouth, in the Royal Sovereign, and a Squadron of three Sail of the Line and two Frigates, with a Convoy of Transports and Merchantmen, for the West Indies; but on the 14th of March, the Vice-Admiral returned to Spithead in the Royal Sovereign, very much disabled, she having run foul of the Belisarius Transport, in a gale of wind. The Transport had on board upwards of 300 persons, 130 of whom got on board the Royal Sovereign, but many fell between the Ships in their attempt to jump on board, and were crushed to death. It was for some time believed that the rest had perished with the Transport, but with much difficulty she reached Corunna, in a crippled condition.

[1] Captain Thomas Drury, in the Alfred, 74.

[2] Mr. Wilberforce attempted to enforce the resolution of the House of Commons, that it was expedient to abolish the Slave Trade, by moving that the abolition should take place on the 1st of January, 1796; but the motion was negatived by a majority of four. It appears that Nelson, who had served long in the West Indies, did not approve of the measure.

[3] A Treaty of Alliance, offensive and defensive, between France and Holland, was

Leda,[4] I fear it is too true she is gone!　With compliments to Pakenham,

Ever yours, most faithfully,

HORATIO NELSON.

Send back the basket by Peterel.

TO ADMIRAL SIR JOHN JERVIS, K.B.

[From Clarke and M'Arthur, vol. i. p. 275.]

Sir,　　　　　　　　　　　Genoa Mole, 18th April, 1796.

Captain Cockburn will convey to you all the news, certainly none of it is pleasing; and I own I regret more the good fortune of the Enemy in getting their Convoy into Vado, than all which has happened on shore. By the time I sail, I will make myself master of the exact force of the Enemy that has escaped us; report says, two Frigates and sixteen Transports. They may be alarmed for a night or two, and it may go off: if you therefore think, Sir, that the attempt to take the Frigates and Transports is proper by Boats, I beg leave to offer myself for that distinguished Command. The Barges and Pinnaces will be more than thirty. I think it may be done; at least, if you approve of the measure, nothing shall be wanting on my part for its complete success. My idea is, for ten Barges to attack each Frigate, one Boat to be especially appointed with a most confidential Officer, to cut the cable of each Frigate; if the wind is off the land, in ten minutes they must drive out of soundings, and ten Boats would be left for the attack of the Transports. I should wish you, Sir, to consider the matter, and I am then certain, what is proper will be done. To-morrow evening, at dark, I shall sail from hence, and will be with you on Wednesday morning. I grieve when the French have any good fortune by sea.

I am, &c.

HORATIO NELSON.

concluded at the Hague on the 15th May, 1795; and a Proclamation was soon after issued, ordering all Dutch vessels in the Ports of Great Britain to be stopped. The Dutch Fleet was defeated by Admiral Duncan off Camperdown, in October, 1797.

[4] The Leda, of 36 guns, Captain John Woodley, foundered near Madeira, on the 11th of February, 1796, with nearly all her crew.

TO HIS ROYAL HIGHNESS THE DUKE OF CLARENCE.

[From Clarke and M'Arthur, vol. i. p. 273.]

Agamemnon, off Genoa, 18th April, 1796.

Sir,

I wish it had been in my power to send your Royal Highness a good account of the opening of the campaign; but as
the news, good or bad, must be known, I think it is proper
for me to give you an exact relation of what has passed.

I shall first call to your recollection a letter of mine, during
the winter,[5] wherein I told you, that I was informed from the
French themselves, they would open the Campaign with
80,000 men; and, by the first of May, would lay Siege to
Turin, or Milan. I shall now give your Royal Highness a
brief account of this campaign, as far as report goes; for we
have no official information from the General.

On Monday, 11th April, the Austrians took possession of
Voltri, with 10,000 men; nearly 300 of the Enemy were
killed, wounded, or made prisoners. About 4000 men effected
their retreat, from the attack having commenced twelve hours
before the time fixed by General Beaulieu, and previous to
the General's arrival; or I am satisfied not a Frenchman could
have escaped; and, by what has followed, the disasters commenced from the retreat of those troops. Our Ships so entirely commanded the road, that had the General's concerted
time and plan been attended to, I again assert, none of the
Enemy could have escaped. These troops retired during
the day and night of the 11th, to Montenotte, about eight or
nine miles on the back of Savona, where the Enemy had about
2000 men posted. At daybreak General Argenteau attacked
this post with about 4000 men, not knowing of the reinforcement. He was repulsed, and pursued with great loss; 900
Piedmontese troops, 500 Austrians, field-pieces, &c. fell into
the Enemy's hands. The killed we know not, but it was
hard fought. On the 13th and 14th, the French forced the
gorges of Millesimo, and the village of Dego, which were well
defended; but they were carried by superior numbers. On
the morning of the 15th, the Austrian troops, under Colonel
Waskanovick, posted at Sassello, on the right flank, and rather

5 Vide, ante.

in the rear of the Enemy, or as we should say, on the starboard quarter, attacked the Enemy at Speigno, and totally
routed them ; and not only retook the twenty pieces of cannon which the Austrians had lost, but also all belonging to
the Enemy; when unfortunately the Colonel, pursuing his
advantage too far, fell in with the main body of the French,
who, after an obstinate resistance of four hours, totally defeated him. To add to this misfortune, General Beaulieu
had sent five battalions from Acqui to support this brave
Colonel Waskanovick; but, alas, they arrived too late, and
added to the triumph of the Enemy.

By the best accounts I can learn, the Austrians have not
lost less than 10,000 men killed, wounded, and prisoners.
The French loss has also been great, but they can better spare
the men than the Austrians. General Beaulieu has now withdrawn all his Troops from the mountains, and is encamped at
a place called Boseo, on a plain between Novi and Alessandria. I am yet in hopes, if the French attack him on the
plain, he may still get on by giving them a total defeat. The
Austrians seem to have been ruined by loss of posts; but I
dare say it was necessary to possess them ; and they were lost
owing to the superior numbers of the Enemy. A column of
20,000 French is on the side of Ceva, one of the passes into
the plain of Piedmont; if they carry this post, the road to
Turin is open.

Genoa, two o'clock. The mails are just arrived from
Milan, and I rejoice that affairs are not so bad as was reported. General Argenteau is arrested, and sent prisoner to
Pavia, on strong suspicion of treason. Reports say, the
French are repulsed at Ceva with great loss; but the Turin
post is not yet arrived. Believe me ever your Royal Highness's most faithful servant,

　　　　　　　　　　　　　　　　　HORATIO NELSON.

TO HIS EXCELLENCY FRANCIS DRAKE, ESQ.

[Autograph, in the possession of Mrs. Davies.]

　　　　　　　　　　　　　Agamemnon, Genoa Road, April 19th, 1796.
My dear Sir,
　　I grieve at the account I hear, which indeed is all from the
French, for the Imperial Minister has not received a line from

the General, or other person, of what is passing. To increase
the measure of sorrow, a number of Vessels under convoy of
some Gun-boats, got into Savona Mole and Vado Bay, on
Sunday Evening. I was on board the Victory and saw them
myself; Polaccas, Brigs, and Galleys,—the Imperial Minister
and Mr. Noni I believe, fancy that because our Fleet saw
them it was very possible for us to stop them; they know
nothing of what a Fleet can do, therefore, in some measure, they are excusable. These Vessels came down very close
to the shore, and from to windward, the wind at W.N.W. It
is perhaps necessary to repel the argument of these Gentlemen: to suppose that our large Ships can approach the Coast
so as to stop these supplies, is ridiculous. You know the impossibility of it, therefore I shall not enlarge on that head.
Our Fleet is sent into these seas to oppose the French at sea;
and, at the present time, should the Admiral to stop a Tartan
or two, or a hundred, lose two or three Sail of the Line, or get
them dismasted, the Enemy would be as much masters of the
sea as it appears they are of the land, and Italy would be
lost without a blow. This argument, I am sure, you will
make a much better use of than I can: but they are always
ready to blame England. Believe me, dear Sir,

Your most faithful servant,
HORATIO NELSON.

[ENCLOSURE.]

Disposition of the Frigates between Toulon and Cape Dell
Melle.

Boston and Tartar.—Off Toulon, which chased this Convoy
into Hieres Bay.

Flora.—Off Cape Taillat, chased this Convoy into Frejus,
and afterwards into Nice.

Lively.—Between Nice and Dell Melle the Convoy put into
Monaco.

I send you this to shew that every means in the Admiral's
power have been taken to prevent the passage of Vessels, and
the Ships have not been able to take one, of two or three
hundred of different sizes which must have passed them.

TO HIS EXCELLENCY FRANCIS DRAKE, ESQ.

[Autograph, in the possession of Mrs. Davies.]

Agamemnon, off Vado Bay, April 22nd, 1796.

My dear Sir,

After the disastrous events which have taken place within these ten days past, the Admiral and myself are very anxious to hear the extent of the misfortune from you and Mr. Trevor. We have none but French accounts, which we hope are exaggerated, but from the Imperial Minister I know nothing; I am now on my way to Genoa, hoping to receive letters by to-morrow's post. I cannot learn even the number *of the Austrian Army*,[6] nor *of their loss*. A great firing was heard from the Fleet, Sunday or Monday, which must have been towards Ceva. From what I hear at Genoa, I suppose there is nothing to stop the Enemy from getting to *Turin*. Had not the *General troops* [*enough*]? if not, it is lamentable. *Sir John Jervis* waits until he can hear something, and form an opinion; we are in total ignorance. The *French reinforce seamen at Toulon*, to which *Sir John Jervis* will proceed. He was in hopes the presence of the Fleet might have been of service, but if that has not been the case, he is better away, for then no blame or improper language can be attached to him. I have wrote you, last post, on the subject, and you will recollect that Admiral Goodall, from judgment, and myself from experience, have uniformly held out that it was not in the power of our large Ships to stop this coasting business. We must have a point of land to act from; give us that, and if supplies get to the Enemy, except in Row-boats, then we are to blame. I was placed in the Gulf to meet the General on the Sea Coast, and my Squadron would have been risked to have supported him; but as he has not been able to get to the Coast, do not let us be blamed. You will recollect, if *Vado* could not be got, that we both agreed the other place ought. If the *French Fleet* get in there by any accident, or their troops possess themselves of it, I look upon Italy as lost. Pray, write me particulars as to numbers, loss, &c., and what is likely to be done. Do the Austrians mean to stop? I

---

[6] The words in *italics* were in cipher.

have great hopes yet from General Beaulieu. Will these Neapolitan troops be of no service? Has the General wrote about landing them at any particular place? Were the English troops and supplies wished to be prevented from getting to the French Army, they might perhaps be landed near St. Remo, where at this season we could always embark them if a superior force came against them. This would cut off all supplies by land as well as by sea, and if they drew many men from inland to attack them, then Beaulieu might be able to get on. This is pretty much your plan, which might be executed if we had the proper troops and a good General to command them. I am sure you will say and act everything which is proper. I am anxious in the extreme to hear from you. I wish we had all these French at Sea; there, as yet, we have never failed. Believe me ever with the greatest truth,

Yours most faithfully,

HORATIO NELSON.

TO THE HONOURABLE JOHN TREVOR, MINISTER AT TURIN.

[From Clarke and M'Arthur, vol. i. p. 276, who state that in this letter Captain Nelson mentioned his sorrow and astonishment at what had happened, and the impossibility of the Enemy's convoy being stopped by Line-of-Battle Ships, and then said—]

April 22nd, 1796.

Therefore, Sir, the getting in with them was impossible, before they would have anchored under such batteries as must have crippled our Fleet; and had such an event happened, in the present state of the Enemy's navy, Tuscany, Naples, Rome, Sicily, &c. would have fallen as fast as their Ships would have sailed along the Coast: our Fleet is the only protector at present of those Countries. Sir John Jervis has cruised close up to the shore in this Gulf, where I will venture to say no Fleet ever cruised before, with the hope of drawing some of the French troops from the inland countries; and I believe it has had its effect, or the Austrians would have been worse off than at present.

I am, &c.

HORATIO NELSON.

TO MRS. NELSON.

[From Clarke and M'Arthur, vol. i. p. 276.]

Gulf of Genoa, 24th April, 1796.

You will be informed, from my late letters, that Sir John Jervis has such an opinion of my conduct, that he is using every influence, both public and private, with Lord Spencer, for my continuance on this station; and I am certain you must feel the superior pleasure of knowing, that my integrity and plainness of conduct are the cause of my being kept from you, to the receiving me as a person whom no Commander-in-Chief would wish to keep under his Flag. Sir John was a perfect stranger to me, therefore I feel the more flattered; and when I reflect that I have had the unbounded confidence of three Commanders-in-Chief, I cannot but feel a conscious pride, and that I possess abilities. Rest assured, my dearest Fanny, of my unabated and steady affection, which, if possible, is increasing by that propriety of conduct which you pursue. Whilst the war lasts, I must serve somewhere, and for health, and nearness to England, I know of none to equal this. In case Admiral Linzee returns, Sir John Jervis informed me, that I am to hoist a Broad Pendant, with a Captain under me, and to command a Division of the Fleet, though he can ill spare us from our present important service.

Yours, &c.,

HORATIO NELSON.

TO ADMIRAL SIR JOHN JERVIS, K.B.

[From a Copy in the Admiralty, and the " London Gazette," of 28th June, 1796.]

Off Loano, 25th April, 1796.

Sir,

This morning, having received information that a Convoy, laden with stores for the French Army, had anchored at Loano, I lost no time in proceeding off that place with the Ships named in the margin.[7] On my approach, I was sorry to observe, that instead of a Convoy, only four Vessels were lying under the batteries, which opened on our approach, and the

[7] Meleager, Diadem, Peterel.

fire was returned as our Ships got up, under cover of which, our Boats boarded the four Vessels, and brought them off: the vessels lying very near the shore, a heavy fire of musketry was kept up on our boats; and it is with the greatest grief I have to mention, that Lieutenant James Noble,[8] of the Agamemnon, a most worthy and gallant Officer, is, I fear, mortally wounded. From our Ships keeping under the fire of their batteries, we sustained no damage; the Agamemnon was, I believe, the only Ship struck by shot. The principal part of this service fell on our Boats, whose conduct and gallantry could not on any occasion have been exceeded, and I wish fully to express the sense I entertain of the gallantry of every Officer and man[9] employed on this occasion. Herewith I transmit a list of wounded, and of the Vessels taken; none of which had any colours hoisted, nor was there a man on board when they were captured.

I am, &c.,
HORATIO NELSON.

TO ADMIRAL SIR JOHN JERVIS, K.B.

[From Clarke and M'Arthur, vol. i. p. 278.]

26th April, 1796.

Sir,

Captain Towry rejoined me yesterday morning, with letters from Mr. Drake and Mr. Trevor, which I beg leave to transmit to you. Captain Towry brought me the unpleasant news, which I also enclose; and he tells me, that Mr. Brame has no doubt but the King of Sardinia is endeavouring to negotiate a peace with the French. We had several Boats on board yesterday, from Cape Noli, the people of which informed us, that although the French had taken Ceva, and killed, wounded, or made pri-

---

[8] Mr. Noble was severely, but not mortally wounded, by a ball in the throat; and was again wounded at the capture of La Sabina by Nelson, in La Minerve, in December of the same year: he was made a Post Captain in April, 1802, and is now a Rear-Admiral of the Red.

[9] The Officers employed in the Boats were: Lieutenants of the Agamemnon, Suckling, Noble, Compton. Lieutenant Culverhouse, Meleager. Lieutenant Ryder, Diadem. Wounded: Lieutenant James Noble; and two seamen of the Meleager. Vessels taken: One Ship laden with corn and rice, eight guns, four of which were brass; twenty brass patteraroes. One Ketch laden with muskets and powder. One Galley laden with wine. Another Galley laden with corn.

soners, above 5000 Piedmontese, yet that the French had lost not less than 11,000 men. The fort of Ceva is not yet taken, but the Town was plundered, and the Enemy passed on to Mondovi, leaving a strong post of Piedmontese in their rear; they also plundered Mondovi, and every house between it and Ceva. If the King of Sardinia does not make peace, I should hope that such conduct of the French would rouse the whole Nation to arms. As to my going to Naples, I need only say, that the Neapolitans, especially Mr. Forteguerri, would not like the interference of a foreigner : he is at the head of their Marine, and fancies himself equal to any Officer in Europe. I am so anxious to examine the Ports along the Coast, to see if the Convoy is in any of them, that I hope you will excuse my sending a Vessel to you immediately : at whatever place I find their Ships, I am determined not to let the first favourable moment for attacking them escape. I wish sincerely for the Neapolitan vessels; I would clear the Coast in a week of fine weather, if they would act, and I flatter myself I should manage them to their liking.

April 28th.—There are no Vessels of consequence in any bay from Monaco to Vado; but not less than a hundred Genoese are every day passing, which may or may not have stores for the French.

I am, &c.,

HORATIO NELSON.

TO CAPTAIN COLLINGWOOD.

[Autograph, in the possession of the Hon. Mrs. Newnham Collingwood.]

May 1st, 1796.

My dear Coll.,

I cannot let a Ship go to the Fleet without a line, just to say how bad we are. Peace is concluded between the Sardinians and the French—most likely hostile to us. The King has given up Cuneo and Suza, or Alessandria, to the French, as a security for his performance of the treaty, and an armistice is agreed till the return of the courier from Paris, with the ratification of the five Kings. I think, in case of a Spanish war, Naples is preparing to desert us also, and Spain is certainly going to war with somebody. Cornwallis's[1] trial was to come on the 5th of April. How extraordinary! he was the last man I could have supposed would have done a wrong thing, and I cannot, with all my partiality for him,[2] bring myself to think it right that he deserted his command. But I suspect some ill-treatment of the Admiralty after he sailed, which induced him to return.

General Beaulieu is at Valenza, with a bridge over the Po, to secure his retreat into the Milanese. God bless you! I hope Mrs. Collingwood and your little ones were well when you last heard from home. Believe me, though I write in haste, for ever

Your most faithful Friend,
HORATIO NELSON.

TO ADMIRAL SIR JOHN JERVIS, K.B.

[From Clarke and M'Arthur, vol. i. p. 278.]

Genoa Mole, 1st of May, 1796.

Sir,

I am still of opinion that my presence at Naples can be of no use; but should you think otherwise, I am perfectly ready to proceed there, and do my best. When these troops arrive at Leghorn, I will attend to their debarkation at La Venza, or Port Especia, as may be most proper. I have written to Mr. Drake, to have his ideas, whether, if more convenient from weather and other causes, we should force a landing at Port Especia? I told him it was a question you would naturally ask, and I therefore desired his answer. This, I am assured, is the last gale, and therefore I shall be very glad to get the Neapolitan vessels over to this Coast. You will observe the

---

[1] Vide vol. i. p. 30.

[2] Vice-Admiral the Honourable William Cornwallis was tried by a Court-martial, at Portsmouth, on the 17th of April, 1796, for having returned to England in the Royal Sovereign, instead of proceeding to the West Indies with his Convoy, (vide p. 154, ante,) and for disobedience of orders after his return, in not hoisting his Flag on board the Astrea frigate, and proceeding to his destination. The Court determined that " misconduct was imputable" to the Vice-Admiral for not having shifted his Flag to the Minotaur, when the Royal Sovereign was disabled, but it acquitted him of disobedience of orders.

Report of the Commissioners, as they call themselves, at Toulon : I have long had reason to suspect great part is fabricated at Genoa. My channel of information says, this day, if the wind is fair, two small Frigates, two Cutters, and thirty-three Sail of Transports, will sail from Marseilles, laden with ammunition, provisions, and clothing. I feel distressed beyond measure at being kept here, and at present there is no sign of a change of wind. If you are of opinion that the Report of these Commissioners is true, you may probably think it proper to reinforce me with a Ship of the Line; for they may slip past you in a strong westerly wind : but I cannot bring myself to believe that the French will trust six Sail of the Line to the eastward, even for the certainty of destroying my Squadron ; and yet they do at times act so contrary to all reasonable ideas, that we must not judge of them as of other people.

I have thus, Sir, got to the end of our Naval business, and shall therefore now take up the accounts of the proceedings of General Beaulieu, and the Sardinians, where Mr. Drake leaves off. The treaty is finished, and an armistice is agreed on, until the return of the courier from Paris. I never had much faith in the Sardinian Minister, after their extraordinary request to me last year, and I much fear they have not done their utmost to defend Piedmont, and the French seem to have understood them. Neither Ceva, nor the strong posts, were then taken, as I sent you word in a former letter, nor are they to this day. Twenty thousand French pushed forward to within six miles of Turin : General Beaulieu advancing with celerity from Acqui, was on one side of the plain, and next day would have attacked the French Army. The French had already begun to retreat, when an express reached him, that an armistice, and most probably a peace, had taken place between the Sardinians and French. Mr. Trevor, with the Imperial, Neapolitan, and Russian Ministers, waited on the King, to desire that Alessandria and Tortona might be delivered up to the Germans, which was peremptorily refused : upon this the Ministers quitted the Kingdom, without taking leave, and it is very probable we have now an additional Enemy. General Beaulieu is retreating, I am told, towards the Milanese; but how far he has fallen back, I do not hear. The French near Acqui are very ill supplied, and the Convoy

expected is of the greatest importance to their future operations; I am told if it does not reach them, they must come
again to the Sea-coast.   I learn with pleasure that we knocked
to pieces the largest of the batteries at Loano, and killed
twenty-five French in it.   The place is also very much damaged, which I regret; but these things must happen where
batteries are situated in a Town.   I have authorized Mr. Brame
to declare, should any conversation with the Secretary of State
here turn that way, that I will never fire the first shot; and,
therefore, if the inhabitants of the Genoese towns prevent the
French from firing, which they can do if they please, their
Towns are safe; if they do not, the act rests with them.

I am, &c.

HORATIO NELSON.

P.S. I have great pleasure in saying my poor Lieutenant,
Noble, is still alive, and we have some hopes.

2nd May.—General Beaulieu's Army has taken post at
Valenza, and between that place and Alessandria.   The King
of Sardinia, if the Convention ratifies the Treaty, is to give up
Cuneo and Alessandria, some say Suza; the latter place, I believe,
as security for his punctual adherence to the treaty.   I have
written to Mr. Drake what I have desired Mr. Brame to say.

TO HIS EXCELLENCY FRANCIS DRAKE, ESQ.

[From a Copy in the Nelson Papers.   No date is affixed to this Note, but it perhaps refers to the communication mentioned in the preceding Letter.]

Scribbled in Mr. Brame's room.   He will send [it to] you,
but I have charged him to give nothing that will come with
more propriety through your orders.   I pray God, General
Beaulieu may yet make head against these miscreants.   I
sincerely wish I could assist him.   Ever believe me,

Dear Sir,

Your most obliged and affectionate

HORATIO NELSON.

I shall not fail to constantly write you.

TO ADMIRAL SIR JOHN JERVIS, K.B.

[From Clarke and M'Arthur, vol. i. p. 281.]

Off Cape Noli, 4th of May, 1796.

Sir,

I got out of Genoa yesterday forenoon, and this morning joined Blanche. It is said, that on the 1st Instant the French took possession of Alessandria. I have still hopes from General Beaulieu; should these people follow him into the plain, his force is very respectable. The French are levying contributions of money, bread, &c. all over Piedmont, and the Piedmontese are said to have paid more already than they used to give their King for several years. I expect to hear you are far westerly after the Enemy. It is not improbable that they may be bound for Cadiz, to engage Admiral Man off that Port, and be joined at the same time by Richery; but all must be conjecture, they may also be bound to Sicily, where everything is not right.

I am, &c.

HORATIO NELSON.

TO ADMIRAL SIR JOHN JERVIS, K.B.

[From Clarke and M'Arthur, vol. i. p. 281.]

8th May, 1796.

Sir,

Since writing to you on the 4th, but little has occurred. I send you a copy of the Treaty of suspension of Arms, and of Mr. Trevor's letter to Mr. Brame. From the first, it appears, that the King of Sardinia was to accept of what the five Kings may direct; for the Minister, and Salicetti, &c. would not hear of a Treaty of Peace, without orders from Paris. I cannot but observe, between ourselves, that a Minister may be continued too long at a particular Court; he thus becomes imperceptibly the friend of that Court, when he ought to be the jealous observer of their conduct.

The Meleager has joined me from Leghorn. The Vice-Roy has bought the 1600 stand of arms, and all the ammunition: we expect that the hulls of the Vessels will also be condemned, for they are hired Transports. Yesterday evening we chased into Loano a French Gun-boat, two light Brigs, and one deep one; they came last from the anchorage at Alassio; but we are rather inclined to believe they sailed at first from Vado. It fell stark calm as we got within shot, and dark. Several shots struck the Blanche, and one a hot one, which set her on fire, but we soon got the shot cut out, and towed off; her sails and rigging were also cut, but not a man was killed or wounded. With our general good luck, not a shot struck us, and only one gun was fired from the Squadron; we were long gun-shot distant, and it would have been merely a waste of powder and shot. The Enemy have at least 500 men at work building a new battery, and I am waiting for a good wind to get at them, when I shall fully expect the deep-laden Brig.

Two Brigs, and several Tartans, having got into Finale, which we supposed to be French, I took the opportunity of the Enemy's fancying we were looking at them, to send the Boats of the Squadron, under Lieutenants Culverhouse,[3] Compton, and Drummond,[4] belonging to the Meleager, Agamemnon, and Peterel, and also Lieutenant Grant, of the Blanche, to cut out the Vessels at Finale, which they did without a person in the Town, or Vessels, knowing it; but they were all Genoese, and I released them this morning, sending a Note to the Governor of Finale, which I trust can do no harm, and may be of some use to us.

May 14th, Gulf of Genoa.—The Diadem joined me yesterday, after ten days' absence, not having been able to get out of Genoa Mole. We have had, and now have, extraordinary weather—fogs, heavy swells, and calms. I send you Mr. Trevor's letter to me.[5] The French, by Captain Towry's

---

[3] He was First Lieutenant of La Minerve, when she captured the Spanish Frigate La Sabina, in December, 1796, for which action he was promoted; and he attained Post rank in 1802. His fate was remarkably unfortunate : while Agent for Transports at the Cape of Good Hope, in 1809, he and his wife were drowned in going on shore in Table Bay.

[4] Now Sir Adam Drummond, K.C.H., Vice-Admiral of the White.

[5] " Mr. Trevor, in his letter, written in cipher, desired the Commodore to acquaint Sir John Jervis of the desperate state of the Kingdom of Sardinia, which, added to the insurrection in Corsica, required all the vigilance and vigour we could exert; he also begged that a watchful eye might be kept on the plan of operations of the Spanish Minister."—*Clarke and M'Arthur.*

account, have crossed the Po, and with little or no opposition. Reports say, General Beaulieu is retreating to Mantua, and that Milan has presented its keys to the Enemy. Where, or when is the progress of these people to be stopped? If the Emperor has not troops to face them, peace seems the only alternative. . . . . I must now revert to a subject as unpleasant for you to hear as for me to write. The miserable state of the Agamemnon, who, with Meleager, are like two tubs floating on the water. I have every reason to believe that our ground-tier has given way; we know that some of the casks fell in. I am glad Captain Smith got good rope at Ajaccio. What has been sent us is, without exception, the worst I ever saw, the twice-laid we make on board is far preferable; indeed, I never saw any so bad in my life. How can a Commander-in-Chief form a true judgment from such directly opposite assertions? I must suppose that the Ship going to the Fleet was intended to be well served, and as to us, it was of no consequence, being too far from the ear of the Commander-in-Chief. This may be politic, but cannot be proper.

May 15th.—I send you Salicetti's account of the defeat of Beaulieu; but Captain Elphinstone[6] tells me it is not believed; pray God it may not be true. I have now before me complaints from the Genoese Secretary of State, for taking their Vessels even out of a French Port. I have also complaints, that we allowed a French Convoy to pass us. Indeed, my dear Sir, you may perceive I feel distressed. Do you really think we are of any use here? if not, we may serve our Country much more by being in other places. The Levant, and Coast of Spain, call aloud for Ships, and they are, I fancy, employed to no purpose here; for unless the Austrians get possession of a point of land, we cannot stop the Coasting trade.

I am, &c.
HORATIO NELSON.

---

[6] Captain Thomas Elphinstone, of the Speedy Sloop.

MEMORANDUM DELIVERED TO MR. BRAME,
BRITISH CONSUL AT GENOA.

[From Clarke and M'Arthur, vol. i. p. 280.]

[About 15th May, 1796.]

The papers from the Secretary of State, I am astonished at; but before I answer a word, I wish to receive, and officially, if it be proper for you to communicate in that way with the Genoese Government, which I think you told me it was not, a plain answer, ' Yes,' or ' No.' Are all the batteries on the coast manned by, and belonging to the Genoese? Should the reply be ' Yes;' then I have a most heavy complaint to make, and I doubt not but England is fully equal to repel the insult which every day is offered to her Flag. Should the reply be ' No,' they are in the possession of the French; then of course I shall consider it as an Enemy's coast. It may, however, be said, and truly, ' The French have built batteries along the coast, within shot of each other ; but the Genoese have some fortresses which still remain in their possession, and yet we know that these batteries fire on the approach of any English Ship, nor have we the means or power of preventing it. If an English Ship comes into any of the Genoese Ports or Roads to the westward, we are certain she will be fired at and destroyed, unless she is able to batter down the fortifications : it must therefore be acknowledged, that the Genoese Ports to the westward are not neutral for the English.' As this should be the language of the Secretary of State here, can he for a moment fancy, that I will receive shot and shells from every part of the Coast, and not consider it as a hostile one ? This, indeed, he may be assured of, that I never have, nor ever will fire the first shot; but if shot are fired, I will do my utmost to destroy the batteries firing at the English flag, although in doing this I shall guard as much as possible against injuring any individual Genoese, a Nation which I respect on many accounts. The Secretary, however, must be sensible, that the fire of cannon, once opened, is terrible to a Town.

HORATIO NELSON.

TO THE RIGHT HON. SIR GILBERT ELLIOT, BART.

[Autograph, in the Minto Papers.]

Agamemnon, at Sea on her passage to Leghorn, May 16th, [1796.]

Sir,

You will know so well from Mr. Trevor and Mr. Drake the melancholy prospect of affairs in Italy, that it would be only a trouble to your Excellency, were I to attempt to repeat what comes from a much better informed quarter. One of my Squadron joined me yesterday from Genoa, and brought me letters from Mr. Trevor, of May 11th. By his desire I have deciphered a part for your information, viz:—' And Vice-Roy of Corsica, that I am afraid that the French will soon oblige Sardinia to be their Ally,[7] and that they are disposed to treat Tuscany as an Enemy. These considerations added to the Insurrection in Corsica, and to the designs the Enemy may have on Sardinia, seem to me to require all the vigilance and vigour of the King's Agents in the Mediterranean. A watchful eye must be kept in the present moment upon the plan of operations of the Spanish Minister, who must also be considered as [one of] the Allies of France.'

Mr. Drake's letter is dated Milan, May 8th. I sent both to the Admiral last night, or I should forward these to you. Mr. D. says General Beaulieu's Army is 38,000 men, and he hopes no battle will happen to him till he gets reinforcements, I am sorry to say, Mr. Brame sent me a letter published by Salicetti, saying that the French had defeated Beaulieu, on the 11th were at Lodi, and taken all the artillery and camp of the Austrians. The story is very ill told, and I should doubt much had I not unfortunately been in the habit of believing accounts of French victories.

The French have lost great numbers in passing the Po and another river, but they have enough left, for the Emperor has not reinforced his Army. I very much believe that England, who commenced the war with all Europe for her Allies, will finish it by having nearly all Europe for her Enemies.[8] Should

---

[7] A Treaty of Peace between France and Sardinia, was signed at Paris on the 15th of May, 1796.

[8] This remarkable prediction was not, however, completely fulfilled until after Nelson's death.

all the Powers in this Country make peace, the French possess themselves of Leghorn and other places to cut off our supplies, Corsica will be the only tie to keep our great Fleet in the Mediterranean; how far the conduct of those Islanders, taken in a general scale, deserves that a Fleet and Army should be kept for their security, is well deserving of serious consideration. I beg pardon for the readiness of my pen, it has, I fear, gone further to your Excellency on this subject than it ought. The loan from Genoa, I suppose, will now take place: it is demanded by Salicetti, thirty-six millions of Livres. That your Excellency may be successful in quieting the disturbances in Corsica, and enjoying that happiness in that Island, which every inhabitant ought from gratitude to endeavour to give you, is the most sincere wish of your obliged and faithful servant,

HORATIO NELSON.

His Excellency the Vice-Roy.

TO ADMIRAL SIR JOHN JERVIS, K.B.

[From Clarke and M'Arthur, vol. i. p. 283.]

Leghorn Roads, 18th of May, 1796.

The Comet joined me off Cape Noli, the night of the 15th, and I left the Squadron with Captain Cockburn, who I am sure will do everything that is proper. We arrived here yesterday morning in a gale of wind, and I hope to have my Ship ready for sea by the 20th or 21st. One of the Neapolitan flotilla is now here, the others are at Port Longone in Elba, and I do not much expect they will get further than Leghorn before Naples is at peace; a measure that seems absolutely necessary for that Court to adopt. The French say they will go to Rome, and the distance to Naples is then but little. As the French cannot want supplies to be brought into the Gulf of Genoa, for their grand Army, I am still of opinion, that if our Frigates are wanted for other services, they may very well be spared from the Gulf. Money, provisions, and clothes the Enemy have in abundance; and they command arsenals to supply their wants in arms and ammunition.

I have felt, and do feel, Sir, every degree of sensibility and gratitude, for your kind and flattering attention, in directing me to hoist a Distinguishing Pendant;[9] but as the service, for which it was intended to be useful, is nearly, if not quite at an end, I assure you I shall have no regret in striking it; for it will afford me an opportunity of serving nearer your Flag, and of endeavouring to shew, by my attention in a subordinate station, that I was not unworthy of commanding. Reports are afloat that a promotion is certainly very near ; and, if so, the Admiralty will either direct my Flag to be hoisted here, or I shall have a land voyage.

I must now, dear Sir, take the liberty of saying a word respecting my health. It certainly is not bad ; on the contrary, I believe it is better than what medical people assert; but, I believe, a little rest, and the baths of Pisa, the same nearly as those of Bath, would render me great benefit. If I could, without any impediment to the service, take twenty days to fit me for another winter, I should not dislike it; and yet, perhaps, I shall do without it. I do. not much like what I have written.

　　　　　　　　　　　　　　　　I am, &c.

　　　　　　　　　　　　　HORATIO NELSON.

TO MRS. NELSON.

[From Clarke and M‘Arthur, vol. i. p. 283.]

Leghorn, 20th of May, 1796.

This may possibly find you at Mr. Suckling's; if so, I beg you will say every kind thing for me. We are certainly under greater obligations to him than to any one. He is a good man, and a respectable character. If I am ordered to hoist my Flag in this Country, the compliment is great ; and therefore we must both rest contented for a little time. The French must soon be tired, and I believe all our Allies are so already. The Dukes of Parma and of Modena have both made treaties with the French, paying large sums of money; and, in their treaties it is specified, that certain pictures are to be delivered, to be sent to Paris. The Palace of the Louvre is to have the finest

gallery of pictures in the world. The Pope has offered ten
millions of crowns, to prevent their coming to Rome; and it is
said they have refused it, unless the famous statue of the Apollo
Belvidere is sent to Paris. What a race of people! but they
have done wonders. Reinforcements are coming to join
General Beaulieu; and the inhabitants of the Tyrol, a hardy and
warlike Nation, are rising to join the General. If all the States
of Italy make peace, we have nothing to look to but Corsica;
which, in the present state of the inhabitants, is not, in my
opinion, an object to keep us in the Mediterranean : we shall,
I hope quit it, and employ our Fleet more to our advantage.

I am, &c.

HORATIO NELSON.

TO ADMIRAL SIR JOHN JERVIS, K.B.

[From Clarke and M'Arthur, vol. i. p. 284, who state that in the first part of this
letter, Commodore Nelson informed the Admiral that the whole of the Neapolitan
flotilla had not yet joined, nor even left Naples.]

23rd May, 1796.

I believe there is a struggle between the Courts of Vienna
and Spain, which shall dictate to that of Naples. The advances of the French have been certainly much facilitated by
the defection of our Allies, brought on, in this part, by their
fears. Report says, the Pope has accommodated matters with
the French; however, that will not stop them, if the Austrian
Army is unable. General Beaulieu is certainly getting reinforcements, and the French have not for one week advanced.
The castle of Milan has twice repulsed the French, who now
only blockade it. I hope to sail at daylight. I again beg, Sir,
if you think I can be in any way useful by coming to you,
without the Pendant,[1] that you will order it to be struck without hesitation. I do not believe my health is such as to require
Pisa just now, at least I am willing to believe so.

I am, &c.

HORATIO NELSON.

[1] Non-professional readers may require the following explanation of this passage.
A Broad Pendant is always struck when the Officer who wears it comes into the
presence of a Senior Captain, or when the special service for which he was authorized to hoist it, is concluded. Vide vol. i. p. 118.

TO ADMIRAL SIR JOHN JERVIS K.B.

[From Clarke and M'Arthur, vol. i. p. 284.]

30th May, 1796.

I send Captain Cockburn, as I believe his anxiety to get into La Minerve[2] is great. Your cruise off Toulon is no doubt tedious, but not uninteresting in its consequences; for if any plan, which the Directory have laid, is defeated for three or four months, there is no calculating what benefit may arise to our Country from it : I think they are bound to the westward, I cannot bring myself to believe they will venture eastward ; if they do, I have no doubt but we shall get at them. I know not what opinion to give about my Squadron ; I have written to Mr. Drake on the subject, and much will depend on his account of what the Austrian Army is likely to do. If it can again make head, and this insurrection of the peasantry be encouraged, we may be of some use ; but the Austrians have now no object to bring them on the sea-coast.

Lieutenant Berry[3] joined me in the Comet, and I have, as far as I have seen, every reason to be satisfied with him, both as a gentleman and an officer. I had a few days ago a plan for taking the French Brig of War out of Vado, and intrusted the execution of it to him : it miscarried from an unforeseen and improbable event, but I was much pleased by Mr. Berry's strict attention to my instructions.

The Meleager joined me yesterday ; and I send you, Sir, all the letters and information received by her. Mr. Trevor seems to think a Spanish war is almost unavoidable, and that the French, after all their protestations, will take possession of Leghorn. My mind is clear, if they have force to penetrate further into Italy, they will possess themselves of that place. The Toulon information is, as I always thought, pleasant to know, but never to be depended upon ; all is guess, they may go east, west, north, or south. These Commissioners know

---

[2] Captain Cockburn was removed from the Meleager to La Minerve, the frigate captured by the Dido and Lowestoffe.

[3] Afterwards Rear-Admiral Sir Edward Berry, Bart., K.C.B.: of this most distinguished Officer, who will be often mentioned, an account will be found in a subsequent part of this work.

nothing, they write a history to get money, and in this, I fancy, they succeed wonderfully well. I hope to hear from Mr. Drake of the actual situation of the Armies, and if he has hopes: should he have none, (for he will have them, if within probability, however distant,) I shall not have the smallest.

I am, &c.

HORATIO NELSON.

TO ADMIRAL SIR JOHN JERVIS, K.B.

[From " The London Gazette" of the 16th of July, 1796. In transmitting this letter to the Admiralty, Sir John Jervis wrote:—" Their Lordships are so thoroughly acquainted with the vigilance and enterprise of Commodore Nelson, that I forbear to repeat his merits on this occasion."]

Agamemnon, off Oneglia, May 31st, 1796.

Sir,

At two P.M., yesterday, seeing some Vessels running along shore which I believed to be French, and knowing the great consequence of intercepting the cannon and ordnance stores which I had information were expected from Toulon, to be landed at St. Pierre d'Arena for the siege of Mantua, I made the signal for a general chase, when the Vessels got close under a battery and anchored. Three o'clock, the Meleager and Agamemnon anchored; as, soon afterwards, did the Peterel and Speedy. After a short resistance from the battery and Vessels, we took possession of them. It is impossible I can do justice to the alacrity and gallantry ever conspicuous in my little Squadron. Our Boats boarded the National Ketch in the fire of three eighteen pounders, and of one eighteen pounder in a Gun-boat. The Blanche and Diadem being to leeward, the former could not anchor until the Vessels had struck; but the Boats of all the Ships were active in getting them off the shore, the Enemy having cut their cables when they surrendered. The Agamemnon's masts, sails, and rigging are a little cut, but of no material consequence.

Much as I feel indebted to every Officer in the Squadron, yet I cannot omit the mention of the great support and assistance I ever receive from Captain Cockburn. He has been under my command near a year on this station; and I should feel myself guilty of neglect of duty, were I not to represent his zeal, ability, and courage, which shine conspicuous on every occasion which offers. Inclosed, I send you a list of killed and wounded, and also of the Vessels taken, and have the honour to be, Sir,

> With great respect,
> Your most obedient servant
> HORATIO NELSON.

A List of Killed and Wounded in His Majesty's Squadron under the command of Commodore Horatio Nelson, on the 31st of May, 1796.

> Agamemnon—one killed; two wounded.
> Blanche—one wounded.
> > HORATIO NELSON.

A List of Vessels of War and Transports, taken by the Squadron under the Command of Commodore Horatio Nelson, on the 31st of May, 1796.

VESSELS OF WAR.

Le Genie (Ketch), three eighteen-pounders, four swivels, and sixty men.

Le Numero Douze (Gun-boat), one eighteen-pounder, four swivels, and thirty men.

TRANSPORTS.

La Bonne Mère, two hundred and fifty tons, Brig-rigged, laden with brass twenty-four pounders, thirteen-inch mortars, and gun carriages.

La Vierge de Consolation, one hundred and twenty tons, Ketch-rigged, laden with brass guns, mortars, shells, and gun carriages.

Le Jean Baptiste, one hundred tons, Ketch-rigged, laden with brandy, and a small quantity of bread.

Name unknown, one hundred tons, Ketch-rigged, laden with Austrian prisoners.

St. Anne de Paix, seventy tons, Ketch-rigged, laden with wheel-barrows and intrenching tools, destroyed.

> HORATIO NELSON.

"A LIST OF PRIZES" TAKEN BETWEEN THE 1ST OF JUNE, 1794, AND THE 1ST OF JUNE, 1796.

[Autograph, in the Nelson Papers.]

TIME WHEN.	VESSEL'S NAME.	ESTIMATE.	RECEIPT. Part.	RECEIPT. Total.	REMARKS.
Between June 1st and August 1st .	(Vanneau . . ⎰ L'Eclair . . ⎱ (Privateer . .	£ s. d. 43 00 0	£ s. d. . . .	£ s. d. 35 00 0	
	Prince Royal . .	57 00 0	52 04 0	. . .	{ Another payment to be made.
	Madᵐ· Bisson . .	250 00 0	. . .	250 00 0	
	Madᵐ· de la Mercie	400 00 0	. . .	352 00 0	
	Corsican Boat . .	100 00 0	Nothing.	. . .	Released improperly.
	Corsican Boat . .	25 00 0	. . .	25 00 0	
	Genoese Polacca .	25 00 0	Nothing.	. . .	Released.
	L'AimableCatherine	33 00 0			
	Tartane	13 00 0	. . .	13 00 0	
	Tartane	78 00 0	. . .	78 00 0	
	Small Vessels off ⎰ Bastia . . . ⎱	80 00 0	. . .	80 00 0	
	St.Fiorenzo,shar- ⎰ ing with C. W. ⎱	25 00 0 ⎫			
	Bastia	100 00 0 ⎬ 200 00 0			
	Calvi	150 00 0 ⎭			
	Spanish Brig; re- ⎰ capture . . ⎱	100 00 0	. . .	5 00 0	Given upon Salvage.
1795.					
January . .	Spanish Brig . .	80 00 0			
Do.	Some others . . .	10 00 0			
Do.	Revolution . . .	50 00 0	. . .	47 10 0	
March 14th .	(Ça Ira . . . ⎰ Le Censeur . ⎱ (Speedy . . .	600 00 0	. . .	682 10 0	
July 13th. .	L'Alcide	20 00 0			
— 21st. .	Belvidere	1000 00 0	. . .	318 10 0	
August 26th .	Alassio	150 00 0	88 04 0		
— 13th .	Bombard	20 00 0	. . . .	. . . .	(£923 remitted to Eng- ⎰ land by M'Arthur (and Capt. Nelson.
October 18th	Venetian Brig . .	50 00 0	. . . .	. . . .	In Pollard's hands.
— 28th	Danish Brig . . .	30 00 0	. . . .	. . . .	Littledale and Broderip.
— 29th	Two Tartans . .	10 00 0	. . . .	. . . .	Pollard.
November 3rd	Sᵗ· Aʸ· de Padua .	80 00 0	. . . .	. . . .	(£2100 remitted to ⎰ England by M'Ar- (thur and Nelson.
1796.					
January 28th	Spartano	250 00 0	. . . .	. . . .	(£1157 remitted to ⎰ England by M'Ar- ⎱ thur and Captain (Nelson.
— 24th	. . . .	250 00 0	. . . .	. . . .	£1140 ditto, as above.
February 11th	Volunta de Dio . .	80 00 0	. . . .	. . . .	Pollard.
— 16th	St. Giovanni . . .	30 00 0	. . . .	. . . .	Pollard.
— 23rd	Buona Sorte . .	60 00 0	. . . .	. . . .	Pollard.
	Bombard omitted .	20 00 0			
				200 00 0	Omitted for Corsica.
April 25th .	(Fortuna . . . ⎰ Conception . . ⎱ ⎰ Name unknown . ⎱ (Ditto	100 00 0			
				318 10 0	⎰ To be added for Bel- (videre.
		4349 00 0 [4369]	340 8 0	1908 8 0 [2405 0 0]	£2226 18 0 Total received.

This Account to May 11th, 1796, three years from my sailing from Spithead.

HORATIO NELSON.

May 31st . .	Le Genie . . .	
	Numº· 12. . .	
At Torre dell	La Bonne Mère .	150 00 0
L'Arnea .	Misericordia .	
	St. Giov. Baptista	
	St. Anne de Paix	

TO ADMIRAL SIR JOHN JERVIS, K.B.

[From Clarke and M'Arthur, vol. i. p. 286.]

Off Nice, June 2nd, 1796.

I have sent the Diadem, with all the prizes, except the armed Ketch, first to San Fiorenzo, where the Brig, and, if not too leaky, the Ketch, laden with ordnance stores, are to be left; and I have written to the Viceroy, that if he wants any of them for the Island, I will direct them to be landed. The mortars are wonderfully fine, thirteen and a half inch : but the number of either cannon or mortars we know not. The Vessel with brandy, and the Gun-boat, if not wanted in Corsica, I have desired Captain Towry to carry to Leghorn. I have kept the Ketch with me, and put a Mate and a few men into her, and occasionally shall send her in-shore, where she may be of great use; she sails and rows exceedingly well, had been just hove down, and completely refitted. By papers found, sixteen sail of Transports are destined for Vado, with ordnance stores for the siege, and cannoniers. I wish we may get any, but the chance is much against us : I can only promise, that I will not miss an opportunity. I have an account of the exact force of the Enemy on the 6th of February, which was sent to General Buonaparte : it consists, including the garrison of Toulon and the whole Coast, of 65,000 men. The Army, when Buonaparte took the command, was effective 30,875. Probably many of the 65,000 are gone forward; but still, on the whole, the force is not so great as I believed. I have got the charts of Italy sent by the Directory to Buonaparte, also Maillebois' Wars in Italy, Vauban's Attack and Defence of Places, and Prince

N 2

Eugene's History; all sent for the General. If Buonaparte is ignorant, the Directory, it would appear, wish to instruct him : pray God he may remain ignorant.

In my public letter it was impossible to enumerate every individual; but next to Captain Cockburn stands Captain Stuart[4] of the Peterel : Spicer[5] commanded the Boats which first boarded the Ketch, under the heavy fire, and had a little skirmish when on board, and to him the Commander surrendered.

I am, &c.

HORATIO NELSON.

TO ADMIRAL SIR JOHN JERVIS, K.B.

[From Clarke and M'Arthur, vol. i. p. 287.]

June 3rd, 1796.

I feel obligations to you on every occasion, since I have had the pleasure of serving under your command; and I endeavour, by an assiduous attention to my duty, to merit the continuance of your good opinion. I shall not go to Pisa at present, we may be useful here; and, to say the truth, when I am actively employed, I am not so bad. My complaint is as if a girth were buckled taut over my breast, and my endeavour, in the night, is to get it loose. If the service will admit of it, I shall, perhaps, at a future day take your leave. I wish, Sir, that Captain Cockburn had the Minerve;[6] he is worthy of her, or a better Ship. My poor Soldier-officer (Lieutenant Pierson) wishes much to go with me ; if it be possible, pray indulge us.

I am, &c.

HORATIO NELSON.

---

[4] Captain Charles Stuart: he was Posted in 1796.

[5] Lieutenant Spicer, Second Lieutenant of the Agamemnon : he became a Post Captain in 1802.

[6] On the 1st of July, Sir John Jervis wrote to Commodore Nelson :—"I believe Captain Hotham will decline La Minerve, and Captain Cockburn shall, in that case, have her: She carries the new builder to Ajaccio, who has promised me to fit her well." The Admiral added — "While the French exercise the Government of Leghorn, it is a joke to suppose it a Tuscan Port, and you will of course act accordingly. I heartily wish you health; increase of honour, &c."—*Tucker's Memoir of Earl St. Vincent*, vol. i. p. 187.

TO THOMAS POLLARD, ESQ., LEGHORN.

[Autograph, in the possession of John Luxford, Esq.]

St. Fiorenzo, June 4th, 1796.

Dear Pollard,

Pray send Hoste[7] by the Tartar or Diadem, the first Ship, or he may possibly lose his passage to England. I shall write you fully when it is settled, whether Agamemnon goes or not.

Yours truly,

HORATIO NELSON.

TO ADMIRAL SIR JOHN JERVIS, K.B.

[From Clarke and M'Arthur, vol. i. p. 287.]

Fiorenzo, June 4th, 1796.

I feel highly flattered by your desire to have me continue to serve under your command, which I own would afford me infinite satisfaction ; and I therefore beg leave to propose some measures that may still give me that pleasure.

The first is, although the Agamemnon can certainly remain in this Country for the next three months, she must be in England before the winter. Another is, that if a Sixty-four is ordered to go, although Diadem is certainly in better plight than Agamemnon, yet in point of sailing she is much inferior. The third is, if you really think that the Admiralty will order my Flag to be hoisted in this country, that you would direct me to hoist my Pendant on board any Ship you judge proper. You will easily perceive, that my wishes to stay are sincere; were they not, after your kindness to me, I should be ungrateful. June 5th.

I am not, dear Sir, less anxious than yesterday, for having slept since my last letter : indeed, I cannot bear the thoughts of leaving your command. You have placed an unbounded confidence in me, and, I own, I feel that no exertion of mine has been wanting for a moment, to merit so great an honour.

I am, &c.

HORATIO NELSON.

[7] Young Hoste having been attacked by fever, was placed by Captain Nelson under the care of Mr. and Mrs. Pollard, for whose kindness he expressed a deep sense of gratitude in a letter to his father, dated Leghorn, 5th June, 1796.—*Memoirs of Captain Sir William Hoste*, vol. i. p. 56.

TO ADMIRAL SIR JOHN JERVIS, K.B.

[From Clarke and M'Arthur, vol. i. p. 289.]

5th June, 1796.

Two days after we took the Vessel with Austrian troops on board, who had been made prisoners by the French, a Boat came off to Captain Cockburn, with a Genoese Master and the crew of the Vessel, and papers, to say, they were chartered by the Spanish Consul at Savona, to carry these troops to Barcelona for the Swiss regiment. I have examined some of the Austrians, who assert, that they were marched by a guard to the Vessel, and, when on board, a person gave them thirty sous each, and told them they were going to Spain, where they would find many of their comrades. The men declared it was against their inclination, and that they wished to return to their own service, or to serve with the English until there was an opportunity. Knowing, as I do, that the French absolutely sell them to the Spaniards,[8] I have no scruple in keeping them, to be sent back to their own sovereign; and, if you, Sir, approve, I will discharge the Genoese vessel, and put the men, with Admiral Linzee's permission, into the Mignonne. They want a change of apparel, and a bed each, which, if we get no work for, the German Government ought to provide: they are as fine healthy-looking men as I ever saw, the oldest of one hundred and fifty-two is thirty-four years of age. Until we have an opportunity of sending them to General Beaulieu, I think they would add to the strength of our Ships, five

---

[8] Sir John Jervis thus indignantly alluded to these disgraceful proceedings in a Letter to Mr. Jackson, Secretary of Legation at Turin, dated Victory, off Toulon, 15th August, 1796:—

"From a Swiss dealer in human flesh, the demand made upon me to deliver up 152 Austrian grenadiers, serving on board his Majesty's Fleet under my command, is natural enough; but that a Spaniard, who is a noble creature, should join in such a demand, I must confess astonishes me; and I can only account for it by the Chevalier Camano being ignorant that the persons in question were prisoners of war in the last affair with General Beaulieu, and are not deserters, and they were most basely sold by the French Commissaries in the Western Riviera of Genoa, to the vile crimps who recruit for the Foreign regiments in the service of Spain. It is high time a stop should be put to this abominable traffic, a million times more disgraceful than the African slave trade; and I trust the strong remonstrances about to be made by the Court of Vienna to the Court of Madrid will produce the desired effect."— *Tucker's Memoirs of Earl St. Vincent*, vol. i. p. 201.

Ships, thirty each: this is submitted with deference to your better judgment. As the Speedy is come in with one of our prizes, I take the liberty of sending her to receive your final directions. I have written so fully by the Egmont, which I hope will be with you to-morrow, that I shall not venture to urge my request—viz., that you would contrive that I may still serve with you. I may have been impertinent in suggesting so many ways, by which I might still remain ; but do not, Sir, imagine that I meant anything by my propositions, than what an anxious disposition pointed out.

I am, &c.

HORATIO NELSON.

TO THE RIGHT HON. SIR GILBERT ELLIOT.

[Autograph, in the Minto Papers.]

Dear Sir,　　　　　June '9th, 1796.

I am sorry to say one of our Ordnance vessels foundered at sea in the late western gale. Mr. Pollard will not sell the cargo of the Brig till he knows what part your Excellency may please to order. I have just heard from Sir John Jervis, who is in great spirits: eleven Sail of the Line in the outer Road,[9] with eight Frigates, one other of the Line nearly ready, five in the Arsenal, fitting. The Admiral hopes for a glorious Naval campaign (his own words)—that is, hoping they will come out. I am ordered to hoist my Pendant in the Captain, 74. Believe me ever,

Your Excellency's most faithful,

To his Excellency the Vice-Roy.　　　　　HORATIO NELSON.

TO THE RIGHT HON. SIR GILBERT ELLIOT.

[Autograph, in the Minto Papers.]

Sir,　　　　　Agamemnon, 10th June, 1796, San Fiorenzo.

Having here forty French prisoners on board the Diadem, one of my Squadron, I have to request your Excellency will be pleased to direct that they shall be received on shore.

I have the honour to remain, &c.

To his Excellency the Vice-Roy.　　　　　HORATIO NELSON.

[9] Of Toulon.

TO THE RIGHT HON. SIR GILBERT ELLIOT.

[Autograph, in the Minto Papers. About the 11th of June, 1796, Commodore Nelson left the Agamemnon, and hoisted his Distinguishing Pendant in the Captain, of 74 guns.]

Captain, June 12th, 1796.

Dear Sir,

I was honoured with your Excellency's letter this morning. By letters yesterday from the Admiral, he has directed me to carry all the Austrian soldiers to him. I ever feel proud of your Excellency's good opinion, which on every occasion which may offer in future I shall endeavour to merit. With every kind wish for your health and happiness, believe me,

Your Excellency's most faithful
and obedient Servant,
HORATIO NELSON.

To his Excellency the Vice-Roy.

TO MRS. NELSON.

[From Clarke and M'Arthur, vol. i. p. 290.]

Captain, at Sea, 13th June, 1796.

You will see, my dear Fanny, by the date of this letter, that I have at last left poor old Agamemnon. Whether it is right or wrong, time must determine. I have remained in a state of uncertainty for a week; and had the Corn-ships, which were momentarily expected from Naples, arrived, I should have sailed for England. The Admiral has on every occasion behaved with the greatest attention to me; and if I am to serve, it is better I should serve in this Country, where I am known and respected, than to take my chance of being sent Home, and ordered to another station. All Agamemnon's Officers are changed,[1] except Suckling, and the Master, who has a wife and large family. Suckling wishes, as his elder brother is dead, to return: I do not believe any one person in the world has a better heart than he has, or who would do more real good, if Providence ordains that he should be master of the Wooton

---

[1] The following Officers served with Captain Nelson in the Captain, from June 11th, 1796 :—Lieutenants—Richard Dalton, Peter Spicer, James Summers, James Noble, Henry Compton, and Edward Berry. Surgeon—Thomas Eshelby. Master —Philip Thomas.—*Clarke and M'Arthur.*

estate. I have sent my small present for you by him, and also something for my father. What is become of George Tobin ?[2] He is a fine young man: it is a pity he has not got more forward.

June 19th, 1796.

I have just left Sir John Jervis: the French are fitting, and, if Richery joins from Cadiz, they may come out: but we shall certainly beat them, if it pleases God to give us the opportunity. Indeed, the French say, they are Masters on shore, and the English at sea. The Pope has paid largely to save Rome : Naples, I suppose, must pay also. Both the Emperor, and Spain are trying which shall succeed with Naples—one for war, the other for peace. The Emperor must either directly have 100,000 men in Italy, or make peace; how that will affect England, I know not. If we can make a good peace, I wish for it, but hope we shall not be so pusillanimous as to give up all our conquests.

Yours, &c.

HORATIO NELSON.

TO WILLIAM LOCKER, ESQ., LIEUTENANT-GOVERNOR,
GREENWICH HOSPITAL.

[Autograph, in the Locker Papers.]

Captain, at Sea, June 20th, 1796.

My dear Friend,

For this last fortnight my destination has been so often changed, that I have been very uncertain whether I was to go home or stay. The Egmont, Captain Sutton,[3] was under orders for England with Admiral Linzee's flag on board,[4] and had carried the Convoy from Leghorn to Corsica. At this time, orders came out for a second-rate and the worst Ship of the Line to go home with the Convoy: there could be no doubt but Agamemnon must be the Ship. Sir John, knowing Sutton's anxiety to get home and the interest which had been made for that purpose, ordered me to St. Fiorenzo to take

---

[2] Query George Tobin, who was made a Post Captain in April, 1802.

[3] Afterwards Admiral Sir John Sutton, K.C.B.

[4] Vice-Admiral Robert Linzee : he died an Admiral of the Blue in September, 1804.

Egmont, and Sutton to take my Ship, when, to my great astonishment, Sutton declined going home unless his Ship went,—
the best conditioned and best manned of all who came first out
of England.   For more than a week Agamemnon stood for
England, and had the Corn-ships, which were momentarily
expected, arrived, I must have gone.   However, when it was
known in the Fleet, many wished to go, and the Captain
of this Ship had the preference,[5] he being in a very bad state
of health.   If I hoist my Flag here, the Goliah, I fancy, will
be my Ship: she is new coppered, but, I fear, wretchedly
manned and worse ordered.   However, the latter I don't
mind, if I have but good stuff to work upon.   I have sent by Lieutenant Suckling, of Agamemnon, the quarter cask of Sherry.
Pray write him a line what he is to do with it: he intends at present to ask Mr. Delafons, who he knows is your acquaintance.   I
left Sir John yesterday, off Toulon, in good health and spirits: he
most particularly desired me to make his kindest remembrances
to you, and to say that he would write, but that I must say the
truth, he had not a moment from writing.   This Station is particular for correspondence, for our Ministers at all the Italian
Courts are ever writing.   Should the French come out, I am
satisfied we should give a very good account of them.   As to
the news of the Armies, the French so far outnumber General
Beaulieu, that he has been obliged to retreat into the Tyrol.
Mantua is besieged, but we hope it will hold out a very long
time.   With kindest remembrances to every part of your
family, believe me ever,

Your most faithful,

HORATIO NELSON.

TO THE REVEREND MR. NELSON, HILBOROUGH.

[Autograph, in the Nelson Papers.]

Captain, at Sea, June 20th, 1796.

My dear Brother,
    Whilst you were absent on your tour, you had amusement
in plenty, without my writing; but long before this, I suppose
you are arrived at Hilborough to attend hay-harvest.   I have

---

[5] Captain J. S. Smith.

been very near sailing for England. Captain Sutton, of the Egmont, wishing to go home, the Admiral sent commissions for us to exchange Ships, taking for granted it was, of all things, what Captain Sutton wished ; but he declined, unless his own Ship went home. Till the present arrangement took place, I stood for England, and, had the Corn-ships arrived at St. Fiorenzo, from Naples, I must have sailed. The Admiral thinks I shall be ordered to hoist my Flag here, and wishes to keep me. If the Admiralty do order my Flag out, it is well done ; if not, it is ill done, for it will be near £500 out of my pocket.

I left the Fleet yesterday, off Toulon, twelve Sail of the Line. The Enemy have eleven ready, and five or six fitting. I think it possible we shall get another battle with them; if so, I have little doubt of its being more successful than the others. Reports here are full of a Spanish war. If that should be the case, we shall probably draw towards Gibraltar, and receive large reinforcements. Our Corsican brethren have (at least, a great part of them) behaved so ill, that I hope our Ministry will have no scruple in leaving them most perfectly free and independent. The French have still a large Republican party in the Island, which take every opportunity of making disturbances. As to the progress of the French in Italy, it has astonished me, not from the extraordinary valour and good conduct of the French, but from the imbecility and fear of the Italian States. Poor General Beaulieu has never been reinforced, and is retreated into the Tyrol, with 14,000 men, the remains of his Army. Mantua is now besieging, but I dare say it will make a vigorous defence. The French have levied vast riches in Italy, and the Church is to pay dearly for his peace, even if they are so kind as to grant him one. Naples must do the same. I suppose England will be the last to make peace ; and whilst she trusts to her Wooden Walls, she [will] be more successful than any other Power. This has ever been proved, yet we continue blindly to be attached to an Army.

If my Flag comes out, I shall most probably hoist it in the Goliah, as she is new coppered. In other respects, she is not so desirable as this Ship, for I hear she is wretchedly manned, and worse disciplined. The latter I don't mind, if I have but the stuff to work upon. I have selected a Captain Miller[6] to be my Captain, about thirty-five years of age: in my opinion a most exceeding good Officer and worthy man. If we have a Spanish war, I shall yet hope to make something this war. At present, I believe I am worse that when I set out—I mean in point of riches, for if credit and honour in the service are desirable, I have my full share. Opportunities have been frequently offered me, and I have never lost one of distinguishing myself, not only as a gallant man, but as having a head; for, of the numerous plans I have laid, not one has failed, nor of opinions given, has one been in the event wrong. It is this latter which has perhaps established my character more than the others; and I hope to return in as good health as I set out with. Indeed, this Country agrees much better with my constitution than England, and I fear the cold damps of England.

Genoa, June 22nd.

I can write no more; therefore must conclude with most kind remembrances to Mrs. Nelson, my Aunt, &c., &c., and believe me your most affectionate Brother,

HORATIO NELSON.

TO THE FRENCH MINISTER AT GENOA.

[From a Copy sent to Mrs. Nelson, on the 2nd of August, 1796, in a Letter printed by Clarke and M'Arthur, vol. i. p. 304.]

Sir,   Genoa Mole, 22nd June, 1796.

Generous Nations are above rendering any other damage to individuals than such as the known Laws of War prescribe. In a Vessel lately taken by my Squadron was found an *imperiale* full of clothes belonging to a General Officer of Artillery. I therefore send you the clothes as taken and some papers which may be useful to the Officer, and have to request you will have the goodness to forward them.

I am, &c.

HORATIO NELSON.

---

[6] A slight notice of this very gallant Officer, with an account of the singular accident that deprived the Country of his services, at the early age of thirty-seven, will be found at the end of the Volume. *Vide* Note B.

TO ADMIRAL SIR JOHN JERVIS, K.B.

[From Clarke and M'Arthur, vol. i. p. 291.]

Genoa Mole, 23rd June, 1796.

I came in here on Tuesday, and shall get to sea this day, when I shall lose no time in proceeding with the Meleager to Leghorn, the situation of which is very critical. An additional treaty has been made between the King of Sardinia and the French; it was signed at their head-quarters at Tortona, on the 17th of June. Oneglia and Loano are absolutely to be given up to the King of Sardinia, as are the other fortresses. The King, by constant guards, is to protect the baggage and stores of the French, who appear to want every man in Italy and have therefore made exactly the same terms with the Genoese, and declare that they will evacuate the whole Riviera. Report says, General Beaulieu has given the French a check, and that the peasantry have killed full 15,000 men; pray God it may be true.

The complaints of the Genoese Government are so ridiculous, that I hardly know what to say. If we are to allow the free passage of the Enemy coastways, we are useless. The best mode, in my opinion, is to speak openly—that so long as the French are in possession of batteries on the Coast, which fire on our Ships, so long we shall consider it as an Enemy's Coast. I have the pleasure to declare, our conduct has so completely alarmed the French, that all their Coasting trade is at an end; even the Corvettes, Gun-boats, &c. which were moored under the fortresses of Vado, have not thought themselves in security, but are all gone into Savona Mole, and have unbent their sails.

I am, &c.

HORATIO NELSON.

TO ADMIRAL SIR JOHN JERVIS, K.B.

[Original, in the Admiralty.]

Captain, at Sea, June 24th, 1796.

Sir,

Having yesterday received from Mr. Brame three Notes from the Genoese Secretary of State to him, complaining of the conduct of His Majesty's Squadron under my orders, and which Mr. Brame has transmitted to Lord Grenville, one of his Majesty's Principal Secretaries of State, without affording me an opportunity of refuting, or even explaining my conduct, a measure which I not only consider as more precipitate than is necessary, but tending in a certain degree to injure my character, by the possibility of an impression lying on the mind of my Sovereign of my having acted wrong.

The Complaints are, for a constant breach of the Neutrality of the Republic of Genoa; for firing on the Neutral territory; for attacking and taking French Ships on the Coast; for searching and taking possession of Genoese Vessels, and ill-treating the Crews, as is particularly set forth in the Notes, dated May 28th, June 11th, and 16th.

I have no scruple in declaring that I have considered, do consider, and shall consider the Western Riviera of Genoa, whilst it is in possession of the French, and whilst it acts hostilely towards his Majesty's Squadron, as the Coast of a declared Enemy. It is needless to enumerate the various acts of hostility committed on his Majesty's Squadron. I do most solemnly declare that every Point, Town, and Bay from Savona to Ventimiglia has fired, and do continue to fire, with shot, on his Majesty's Ships whenever they approach the Coast; and this fact must be well known to the Serene Republic of Genoa, and that not one place on the whole Coast from Savona to Ventimiglia is neutral for an English Ship.

In answering particular complaints of ill-treatment and of the searching Genoese vessels, I am perfectly ready to give every explanation in my power, for ill-treatment of crews of Vessels searched by his Majesty's Ships is as contrary to his Majesty's orders as it is to my duty as an Officer, or repugnant to my feelings as a gentleman.

The Note of May 28th, states ill-treatment to a Greek Vessel under the Tower of Marini. I have made every inquiry of every Ship of my Squadron, and all the Captains solemnly declare to me that they know of no such circumstance, or anything similar, in the smallest degree, to what is represented; and I do firmly believe that the Vessel boarded and the crew ill-treated could not have been by any of his Majesty's Ships, and as the Vessel carried the tri-coloured

Flag, it would have been but fair to conclude she was a French
Vessel. The conduct as represented is so scandalous, that
I am assured no English ship-of-war ever did act in the
smallest degree resembling it. No time is mentioned for this
act having been committed, or I would state the exact situation of every Ship in my Squadron on that day.

The Note of June 11th, states, firing at a Genoese vessel
under the guns of Castle Franco, at Finale, on the 7th of
May, and that the same night the Boats of the Ships boarded
and took some Vessels out of the Road of Finale, and ill-treated
the mariners and robbed the Vessels of money and effects. I
shall relate a plain tale, and declare on my honour to the truth
of it:

On the morning of May 7th, I made the signal for the
Peterel to chase a Ship in-shore. On her getting near the
Vessel, but at two or three gun-shots from the shore, she fired
a shot to bring her to, which the Vessel not obeying, two or
three more were fired. But the Vessel getting under the
guns of the fortress of Finale, she fired no more. On her
standing towards Finale, a battery on the western side of the
Town fired many shot at the Peterel, and Commodore Nelson
was informed the next day that the battery which fired was in
possession of the French, and that the Governor of Finale had
sent to the battery requesting the French not to fire, as it
might draw the fire of the English Squadron on the Town,
but to which the French paid no regard.

In the evening of the same day, having chased some French
Vessels into Loano, the batteries of La Pietra opened on us;
but I would not return a shot, although I knew the Town and
battery to be in possession of the French, as it might injure
innocent Genoese, who could not, unless authorized by their
Government, prevent the French from erecting batteries, and
firing on his Majesty's Ships. In the night I sent my Boats to
bring off [for] my examination, the Vessels in the Road of Finale,
which they did without being discovered by the batteries; and
next morning, the 8th, finding them all Neutrals, I liberated
the whole, four or five in number. The Master of the Felucca
told me that he had lost a pair of silver buckles, and that a keg
of wine, of ten gallons, had been drunk: at the same time, he
owned he could not say it was our seamen who took his buckles,

which he valued at forty livres. The keg of wine I offered to return to him, as it had been taken to refresh our people, but this he declined. The Master breakfasted on board, and carried a Note from me to the Governor of Finale; and I declare, on my honour, that I heard no complaint whatever, except as above stated, and he appeared to me to leave the Ship perfectly contented.

The next Note, dated June 16th, and which the Secretary declares shall be the last, which I am glad to hear, never having in any one case given the least cause for any complaint of my conduct. The Serene Government of Genoa may know, on inquiry, that so far from my conduct having been oppressive, it has been constantly marked by a forbearance and humanity never exceeded.

I shall relate the plain matter of fact, and with so great a regard to truth, that I freely wish the case to be examined, and those who have been guilty of falsehood, stigmatized as they deserve. Nearly the whole facts, as stated by the Secretary, are false, as I am ready to prove by the declaration of the French Commander of the Convoy taken by me at L'Arena, delivered by him at Leghorn.

On May 31st, between the hours of two and three in the afternoon, a French vessel with her colours flying, then at anchor under the Tower of L'Arena, which had Genoese colours hoisted, fired on his Majesty's colours. I instantly directed the Squadron to anchor in L'Arena, and to take the French vessels. In running in, a gun went off from the Agamemnon, by accident, but did not, I believe, go near the shore—certainly not near the Tower. The French vessels of war and the Squadron exchanged a few guns, when our Boats resolutely boarded the Enemy and took them. During this contest, to my astonishment, the Tower of L'Arena opened a fire on his Majesty's Ships having their colours flying, it being notorious that the French commenced the attack; and, therefore, had all the Coast been actually in the possession of the Genoese, I had every reason to expect an exact Neutrality, and not that the Genoese fortress would have assisted the Enemies of England in their attack on his Majesty's Ships, which I most solemnly declare they did. But such was my humanity and forbearance, that so far from returning the fire to a fortress bearing the Genoese flag, and which had killed and wounded several of his Majesty's subjects, and fired through the Agamemnon, that I patiently received the fire, and sent a Boat, with an Officer and a Flag, to ask the reason of their firing on the English colours, and that if the Governor continued to fire, I should most certainly return it. The Governor's answer to the Officer was, that he thought we had fired first, but now he knew it was the French, he should fire no more, and hoped I would not fire on the fortress or the Town, which I did not, although a heavy fire of musketry continued to be kept up on our Boats from the houses, and which it was in my power to have destroyed in ten minutes.

These facts, most truly related, will shew who has real cause of complaint. I have confined myself to the subject of complaint in the three Notes ; but I can bring forward, for almost every day, complaints of a nearly similar conduct, but (as I know the French are in actual possession of the whole Coast, although the Genoese are allowed by them, for convenient reasons, I have no doubt, to have certain fortresses with their colours flying on them) it is useless to mention them. The Serene Government will not, I am sure, say they can afford protection to any English Ship, in any Bay or Port on the Coast, from Savona to Ventimiglia.

I am, &c.
HORATIO NELSON.

TO ADMIRAL SIR JOHN JERVIS, K.B.

[From Clarke and M'Arthur, vol. i. p. 291.]

25th June, 1796.

My dear Sir,

I send you, a full reply to the three complaints of the Genoese Secretary of State ; a copy of which I have also enclosed for Mr. Drake, that he may answer the Government of Genoa, if he thinks it right. The Genoese can only make these complaints to please the French ; but I cannot think it right, that we are to be traduced to please any Nation on earth.

I am, &c.
HORATIO NELSON.

TO (APPARENTLY) HIS EXCELLENCY FRANCIS DRAKE, ESQ.,
MINISTER AT GENOA.

[Autograph, in the Nelson Papers. The precise date of this Letter does not
appear, but it was probably written about this time.]

Captain Macnamara, of his Majesty's Ship Southampton,
is, I understand, the Officer who took from the Village of
Aranzano a Polacca ship named [sic], which he sent into
Vado Bay, and which immediately I ordered to be restored
to her Master and Crew, on the principle that she was taken
from the Neutral territory of the Republic of Genoa.

The circumstances attending his taking the Tartan, or his
reason for firing, I am totally ignorant of, as the Southampton
is absent by orders from the Commander-in-Chief; but I shall,
as soon as possible, transmit to Captain Macnamara the complaint made against his conduct at Aranzano, and shall desire
his reasons and account of the circumstances, which, so soon
as I receive, I shall transmit to your Excellency.

I am, &c.

HORATIO NELSON.

TO ADMIRAL SIR JOHN JERVIS, K.B.

[From Clarke and M'Arthur, vol. i. p. 292.]

Leghorn Roads, June 28th, 1796.

Sir,

I made the best of my way to this place, as I wrote you
word from Genoa was my intention ; but from calms, and contrary winds, it was yesterday morning before I anchored in the
northern road of this Port. The French took possession of
the Town about one o'clock, and immediately fired on the
Inconstant, and a Prize of Captain Hood's, laden with timber,
but without doing them any damage. The exertions of Captain Fremantle[7] must have been very great, for the Consul,

---

[7] Captain Fremantle's Official Report of his proceedings was published in the
London Gazette of the 23rd of August, 1796. On transmitting it to the Admiralty,
Sir John Jervis said that "the retreat of the British Factory with most of their
property," was owing "to the unparalleled exertions of Captain Fremantle ; Commodore Nelson, owing to calms and light winds, not having reached Leghorn Roads
until the Enemy was in possession."

and Mr. Fonnereau tell me, that except bad debts, and the loss of furniture, nothing of any great consequence was left in the Town. I hear the Governor behaved with all the attention in his power to the English, by doubling the guards on the Mole to prevent them from being molested in getting out their Vessels; and, that when it was represented to him that 200 bullocks and some bread were shipping for the English, his answer was, Leghorn is a free Port, and shall remain so, until I receive contrary orders from the Grand Duke.

I have just detained a Fishing-boat from the Town: the troops entered at Porta Pisa, and marched through Via Grande to the Mole battery. General Buonaparte went to the palace of the Grand Duke, and thence made a visit to the Governor, and took possession of the house of the English Consul. A French sentinel is mounted at the gates with a Tuscan. Except the French troops necessary for the batteries, the rest lie outside the Town, on the glacis ; for not one has a tent. The governor set off directly for Florence. I have written to say, that whatever may be their policy, in withholding a few vegetables and fruit from me, yet that their Fishing-boats might safely go out as usual ; for we never wished to distress innocent inhabitants. I intend remaining here for a day or two, in order to prevent any English ship from entering, until the news may spread about. It is then my intention to proceed to St. Fiorenzo, to get wine, wood, &c., and thence to go to Genoa. I find my Ship well manned, although not active.

I am, &c.
HORATIO NELSON.

TO THE RIGHT HON. SIR GILBERT ELLIOT.

[Autograph, in the Minto Papers.]

Captain, San Fiorenzo, July 1st, 1796.

Dear Sir,
I know you must be anxious to hear what has been passing at Leghorn, therefore I send you information just as I received it, without form or order. You may depend Buonaparte[8] is gone, and I hope on the account supposed, that General

---

[8] Nelson usually wrote, *Buona Parte.*

Beaulieu is reinforced. The English are under infinite obligations to Spannochi,[9] who is suffering for it. And to Captain
Fremantle they are much obliged, for his great exertions in
getting all their shipping out of the Mole. I will not say that
any exertions of my own were wanting to get to Leghorn
sooner, for it was Thursday noon before we heard the rumour
at Genoa, and it was the same day they knew it at Leghorn,
when an express was sent to me. Calms prevented my arrival
till the Monday morning; fortunately, my assistance was not
wanting, and it was to these (apparently to me unfortunate)
calms that so much property was saved. So soon as I get a
little provision and wood, which will be two days, I shall go
over to Genoa, to inquire for letters and to hear the news, but
pray keep this secret, or I shall be tormented with applications
for passages, and I have as many on board as is convenient to
me. Whatever commands or letters you may have, I shall
take great care of them. From Genoa, I shall proceed directly
to the Fleet, and I sincerely hope they may be induced to come
out before they know of Buonaparte's retreat; for I have no
doubt but the destination of the French Army was Corsica,
and it is natural to suppose their Fleet was to amuse ours
whilst they cross from Leghorn. Ever believe me, dear Sir,
    Your Excellency's most obliged and faithful servant,
                                    HORATIO NELSON.
      His Excellency the Vice-Roy.

P.S. Your Excellency may wish to send the Vanneau or
Sardine to some place with your dispatches. I will order them
to Bastia to receive your commands the moment I receive your
wishes; they are perfectly ready for sea.

MEMORANDA.

[Inclosed in the preceding Letter.]

June 20th.—Sent and got a small Fishing-boat on board;
the crew were much frightened, and said, if the French knew

---

[9] Governor of Leghorn : he was a Neapolitan, and had commanded the Guiscardi,
74. Buonaparte's complaint to the Grand Duke of Tuscany against Spannochi,
dated on the 29th of June, 1796, for favouring the English, and in his whole conduct
displaying a decided hatred against the French, and the Grand Duke's answer, are
given in the *Annual Register* for that year. A very curious English letter from
him to Captain Collingwood, while Captain of the Guiscardi, dated 15th January,
1796, is printed in the *Correspondence of Lord Collingwood*, ed. 1837, vol. i. p. 40.

they came on board an English Ship they would shoot them. They said the Governor went off to Florence yesterday afternoon, and that, except the cavalry, the French were laying on the glacis. I told the man, Giovanni Neri, not to be afraid, but to bring me information; he had some letters, which he carried on shore, and several messages.

June 29th.—About ten o'clock, Giovanni Neri, having been apparently fishing, came on board, with an answer to the letter sent yesterday, and also to the several messages to different people in the Town. He says the Governor was sent off as a prisoner, but for what reason he does not know; his wife and children were sent off this morning. More than 1000 of the inhabitants had quitted the place yesterday, but the French would allow nothing to pass the gates, and that they searched every Boat which comes out of the Mole. The French entered at Porta Pisa, passed through the great street to the Mole, when Buonaparte went to the palace of the Grand Duke, which was prepared for his reception, from thence he went with Mr. Bellville, the Consul, to the Governor, and from thence to the English Consul's, where is the head quarters. The Municipality, last evening, ordered a general illumination. The French have been proving the muskets, and have taken possession of one large store belonging to the English. A great number of troops arrived last evening and this morning; they are many of them at St. Giacomo; the whole Coast on both sides of Leghorn is full of them.

June 30th.—Giovanni Neri came on board at daylight, and Macevena (one of the people employed by Mr. Udney) with him. Last night, Buonaparte set off with all the Cavalry: it was reported General Beaulieu was reinforced, had marched towards Manteau, and that the troops from that Town had joined him. The troops which are at Leghorn and on their march was 15,000 men, all but 3000 are retiring; the first act of the French was to shut the gates. Buonaparte, on his arrival at the Mole battery, told the Officer commanding there to fire on the English; and, on the Officer saying he had no orders, he struck him on the breast, and called him a scoundrel. The first order was, that if any communication was held with the English Shipping in the road, the people concerned would be shot; the next was, that every person who had or

knew of any effects belonging to the English, and did not
directly reveal the same, would suffer death. An order was
given for every house to deliver up their arms, and afterwards
they were searched by the French soldiers. All spare mat-
tresses were taken for the French soldiers, who live in the great
street and sleep there, and it is ordered to be lighted every
night; not a shop is opened, nor a thing brought to market,
but the French help themselves. Yesterday, it was noticed
that workmen would be wanted, but they would be regularly
paid. The soldiers are promised to be new clothed at Leghorn. The Grand Duke gave a dinner to Buonaparte, after
which he asked the Grand Duke to send an Officer to shew him
the nearest way to Rome, and that he was going to join his
Army at Osteria Bianca. On his arrival there, he told the
Officer he might go back again, and immediately pushed on
with the 4000 cavalry. It is also said that the Governor of
Leghorn said, 'I thought you came as friends, but I find you are
enemies and, as that is the case, I wish to go to Florence.' On
this, Buonaparte called him a Neapolitan scoundrel, a macca-
roni eater, &c. &c., and said, ' I will send you to Florence,'
which he did, as a prisoner.

Commodore Nelson has given Giovanni Neri a certificate,
and recommends him to the good offices of the English.

TO THE RIGHT HON. SIR GILBERT ELLIOT.

[Autograph, in the Minto Papers.]

Captain, San Fiorenzo, July 2nd, 9 P.M., 1796.

Dear Sir,

By the arrival of the Inconstant, I have received directions
from the Admiral to blockade the Port of Leghorn, and to be
aiding and assisting to your Excellency in preventing any
attempts of the French on the Island of Corsica, and in such
other matters as you may wish, and is in my power.

You will give me credit, I am sure, for my fullest exertion
in the execution of this duty, and that if, on every occasion, I
do not comply with all your wishes, that it is the want of the
means, and not the want of inclination.

Having promised this, I shall relate my present intentions,

which time and a variety of circumstances must occasionally alter. Blanche, I hope, is at Leghorn; Meleager sails to-morrow morning; at farthest, I shall sail on Monday morning, and shall take Sardine with me. I purpose anchoring myself with Sardine in the northern road of Leghorn, and that two Ships shall always cruise to the southward of the Town, and to anchor all Vessels near me till I consider or receive farther directions about them; the very sight of forty or fifty Sail must be mortifying to the French, and shew the Tuscans the happy effects of their rigid neutrality. Every day I intend to have a Vessel passing between Bastia and Leghorn to Genoa. You will of course direct the Vanneau and Rose to hold the communication with me; and should Convoy be wanted for Civita Vecchia, Gaeta, or Naples, I shall, if possible, furnish good ones.

You will, I am sure, see the necessity of these Convoys being as seldom as possible, by a proper number of vessels being collected before the Convoy is desired: this will enable me better to attend to all the services.

I shall send to Genoa directly on my arrival off Leghorn. Believe me, dear Sir,

Your Excellency's most faithful and obedient Servant,

HORATIO NELSON.

To the Vice-Roy.

TO THE RIGHT HON. SIR GILBERT ELLIOT.

[Autograph, in the Minto Papers.]

Captain, San Fiorenzo, July 2nd, 1796, 10 A.M.

Dear Sir,

I have this moment received your Excellency's letter, and have given orders to the Sardine and Vanneau to sail directly for Bastia, and having communicated with you, to proceed, and watch such places as you think most likely for the embarkation to take place, and to pay the strictest attention to every requisition and desire of your Excellency. The way to Corsica, if our Fleet is at hand, is through Elba; for if they once set foot on that Island, it is not all our Fleet can stop their passage to Corsica. Pray God, General Beaulieu may draw

them back again. If we had the troops, the possession of
Porto Ferrajo would be most desirable for us. The moment
I get the Speedy, I will send her on the same service as the
Sardine and Vanneau.

Believe me ever, your Excellency's most faithful,

HORATIO NELSON.

His Excellency the Vice-Roy.

TO ADMIRAL SIR JOHN JERVIS, K.B.

[Original, in the Admiralty.]

Captain, San Fiorenzo, July 3rd, 1796.

Sir,

Yesterday evening, by the Inconstant, I was honoured with
your order for the blockade of Leghorn, and for rendering
every assistance to the Vice-Roy for preventing the Enemy
from landing in the Island of Corsica, all which I shall attend
to in the strictest manner, having sent Meleager with the
Convoy, and the Blanche, I take for granted, will lay off the
Port. I have sent Meleager with orders for the blockade, and
shall sail, if possible, to-morrow myself, with the Sardine.

I wish much to have your ideas of the blockade, as the one
we had of Genoa was of little consequence. The Vessels were
told, ' you must not enter Genoa,' but the first night or brisk
wind never failed to carry them in; and if we stopped them,
it only became an expense, for which Mr. Udney[1] has not
been paid. My present intention is to anchor with Captain
and Sardine (which is not fit to cruise, for want of men) in
the northern Road, to keep two Frigates cruising to the southward of the Town, and to anchor all Vessels bound to Leghorn near me, or see that they steer clear of the Port. I am
this day equipping the French Gun-boat No. 12, which I intend always to have near me. She carries one eighteen
pounder in her bows : she will, of course, be very useful. I
intend to have her valued to-morrow morning. The Ketch of
three eighteen pounders I have not lately heard of, but I
have not much fear for her safety. She shall be valued when

---

[1] The British Consul at Leghorn.

I get her. I mean, not only to prevent all Vessels from entering, but also from sailing, giving them notice that they shall not sail without coming on board me for permission and examination. This will lower the French, and raise us in the opinion of the Leghornese.

I shall keep a constant communication with Genoa, and shall write Mr. Brame to notify to the Serene Government and to all the Consuls that Leghorn is blockaded, and that all Vessels attempting to enter will be fired on. I have written the Vice-Roy, and send you a copy of my letter. Believe, Sir, nothing shall be wanting on my part to do everything possible to distress the French. The possession of Porto Ferrajo may be desirable for us, but I trust General Beaulieu will yet give a good account of these marauders.

This moment I have received your letters by the Sincere respecting bullocks. Mr. Heatly,[2] also, has just been with me. He has had a conversation with the Vice-Roy about them; and the issue is, that Mr. Littledale is going in the Sincere to look out on the coast of Rome and Naples, and having found them, Transports are then to be sent. The Vice-Roy has not written to me on the subject of the Packets for Barcelona; but I most perfectly agree with you that four are better than two, but the impression of a very close blockade of Leghorn for a fortnight, may have the happy effect of rousing the inhabitants. I shall not fail to sow as much inveteracy against the French as is possible. From Turin is the only place we can expect news of either Army, England, or France. Therefore, I must keep something of force every week to go to Genoa, and I shall not fail to communicate everything to you. In point of force I want but little, but in point of numbers, you will see, more than probably can be spared from other services. The northern passage and the southern must be guarded, and the more I can anchor in sight of the place, the more effect it will have, for if we send them directly away, the loss of trade will not be so conspicuous to the lower class, and it is from them I hope an insurrection.

Lord Garlies,[3] by the suggestion of the Vice-Roy, stopped

---

[2] Agent Victualler to the Navy.

[3] Captain of the Lively frigate. He succeeded as 8th Earl of Galloway in 1806, and died an Admiral of the Blue and K.T. in 1834.

the Southampton's departure for Gibraltar. I most perfectly agree in the propriety of the measure, for several Ships will want convoy to Gibraltar, and numbers of French emigrants passages in the Transports; therefore, Captain Macnamara[4] waits your further orders. An application will also, I hear, be sent you for a Convoy to Naples. The Ships are not quite ready, and I wish that all vessels bound that way may take the same Convoy.

I sent you a daily report from Leghorn, by the Comet. It is natural to suppose that if any one man comes off expressly to give us information, he will expect to be paid. I paid him for the day he came to me. I pray God for good news from Beaulieu, then all will be well.

I have only to hope, that when it is reduced almost to a certainty that Mr. Martin[5] means to give you a meeting, that I may be called to assist at the ceremony. Ever believe me, Sir, with the greatest respect,

Your most faithful servant,

HORATIO NELSON.

How much pleased I am with Colonel Graham's letter.[6] It is owing clearly to the Navy that the Siege of Mantua is raised.

TO DAVID HEATLY, ESQ.

[From a Copy in the Nelson Papers. Mr. Heatly was Agent Victualler to the Navy in Corsica.]

Captain, San Fiorenzo, July 4th, 1796.

Sir,

As the Vice-Roy has desired a passage and every accommodation to Mr. Gouthier and his family, it is necessary that they

---

[4] Captain James Macnamara, of the Southampton, of 32 guns. This gallant officer obtained an unenviable celebrity from having killed Colonel Montgomery in a duel, in April 1803. At his trial, Lord Nelson bore strong testimony to his amiable disposition and honourable character. He died a Rear-Admiral of the Red early in 1826.

[5] Vice-Admiral Martin, Commander of the French Fleet in Toulon. He commanded the Enemy's Fleet in the Actions with Admiral Hotham of the 13th and 14th of March, and of the 13th of July, 1795.

[6] The Siege of Mantua was not raised until the 30th of July. See Colonel Graham's (afterwards Lord Lynedoch) Dispatch, dated "Head-Quarters of Field-Marshal Wurmser's Army, Vallegio, 1st August, 1796," announcing that event, in the *London Gazette* of the 27th of August, 1796.

should be victualled for their passage to Gibraltar; therefore,
I send you a copy of the Vice-Roy's letter to Captain Craven.
If you have any doubts of the propriety of victualling them for
their passage to Gibraltar, I must refer you to the Vice-Roy
for the intention of his letter.

I am, Sir, &c.

HORATIO NELSON.

TO THE RIGHT HON. SIR GILBERT ELLIOT.

[Autograph, in the Minto Papers.]

Captain, San Fiorenzo, July 5th, 1796, 10 A.M.

Dear Sir,

Captain Fremantle has this moment given me your letter of
yesterday's date. I have wrote to the Admiral for more precise
instructions as to the blockade, and have pointed out the in-
utility of such a blockade as that of Genoa. I have a letter
ready to send to Mr. Brame, desiring him to acquaint the
Serene Government of Genoa that Leghorn is blockaded, and,
of course, that no Vessel will be permitted to enter that Port;
and, should they attempt it, they will be fired upon. I have
desired the same communication to all the Foreign Ministers
and Consuls residing in that City. Respecting the Tartan
fishermen from Leghorn, I mean not to molest them, at least for
the present; they will give us frequent communication with the
Town, and will mark our good will to the inhabitants, which I
shall, in scraps of paper, always send amongst them, and of my
readiness to assist them in liberating Leghorn from its present
tyrannical Rulers.

As you have had the goodness to tell me of your Regulations
for the Corsican Privateers, I shall make my observations on
them freely. The first Article, (till we can, by post from
the Coast, make known the determination by a letter to all
the Foreign Consuls at Leghorn, some of which will doubtless
get safe, and desire each to signify the contents,) may be thought
as hard; it might be altered ' to be brought into Bastia, for the
consideration of the Vice-Roy,' &c.

To the 2nd Article, I agree most fully is proper.

3rd.—Is it not meant to make prize of provisions going to

Leghorn ? I should think this as necessary as any other stores, for the provisions cannot be for the inhabitants.

4th.—The time of the 20th of the month appears sufficient, but this to be judged by yourself; and

To the last I agree most perfectly. If two or more Corsican Privateers join me, I agree, and am sure none of my Squadron will differ from me; whilst they remain under my orders, each Vessel shall share alike, that is, if I have six Vessels and the Corsicans two, they shall share one quarter; and if more or less, the same proportion.

I will immediately, on my arrival off Leghorn, send you an account of the Vessels I have, and what Convoy I can order for Naples; only let the Vessels be ready the moment the Ships of war come to Fiorenzo.

I shall add to my letter to Mr. Brame, that all Vessels, after this notice, which sail from Leghorn, will be made prize of; and also, that no Vessel will be suffered to pass inside the Melora.

The wind, yesterday, was a hurricane. We have been under sail, but are obliged to anchor again.

Believe me ever, Dear Sir,

Your Excellency's most obedient servant,

HORATIO NELSON.

His Excellency the Vice-Roy.

TO THE RIGHT HON. SIR GILBERT ELLIOT.

[Autograph, in the Minto Papers.]

Captain, San Fiorenzo, July 5th, 1796.

Dear Sir,

It blows such a storm of wind that I cannot yet get out; I hope it will moderate in the morning.

I shall send your bills to Genoa by some Frigate, as soon as possible. By letters from the Admiral, of old date, received last night, brought by Sincere, he desires me to concert with your Excellency the arrangement of the Packets to Barcelona. I take for granted the Admiral has wrote fully to your Excellency on the subject. Whenever you please to desire my opinion in any matters, you will believe I shall give the

openest opinion. I feel every day more and more honoured
by the confidence of Sir John Jervis in my conduct, and it will
ever be my study to deserve the continuance of his and your
good opinion. Being, with the greatest respect,

Your Excellency's most faithful,

HORATIO NELSON.

His Excellency the Vice-Roy.

If your Excellency has an opportunity, I beg you will send
my letter to Mr. Drake.

EXTRACT OF A LETTER FROM COMMODORE NELSON TO ADMIRAL SIR JOHN JERVIS, K.B.

[Inclosed in a Letter from Sir John Jervis to Evan Nepean, Esq., dated " Victory,
off Toulon, 22nd July, 1796;" now in the Admiralty.]

5th July, 1796.

Herewith I send you the valuation of the small Gun-boat.
No. 12,[7] as she will be much wanted in the Road of Leghorn.
It is clear she is not over-valued, for she is almost new. The
brass guns and swivels are only considered as old brass.

TO JOSEPH BRAME, ESQ., HIS MAJESTY'S CONSUL AT GENOA.

[From a Copy in the Admiralty, and original Draught, in the Nelson Papers.]

Captain, at Sea, July 6th, 1796.

Sir,

Being ordered to blockade the Port of Leghorn, I have to
desire that you will officially inform the Government of Genoa,
and all the Foreign Ministers and Consuls, that the Port of
Leghorn is in a state of blockade, and that any Vessels which
may clear out from Genoa for Leghorn, or attempt to enter
it after this public declaration, which I desire you will give in
its fullest force and form, will be made Prizes of, or fired on,
and sunk, as circumstances may make proper: and you will also
signify, that the entry of the Road, which includes the space
inside the Melora, will be considered as the Port of Leghorn.
The Genoese Government will of course make this known to

[7] Vide p. 177, ante.

all the Towns in the Riveira of Genoa, as you will write to all your Vice-Consuls, from Port Especia to Ventimiglia.

I have also further to desire that you will acquaint the Government of Genoa, and all the Foreign Ministers and Consuls, that no Vessel will be permitted to leave the Port of Leghorn until it is delivered from the hands of its present tyrannical Rulers, and restored to its legal Government; and you will desire the several parties mentioned to write to their Consuls at Leghorn of this my determination. And as I think it honourable to make known this determination, that no person may plead ignorance, so it will be credited, if my character is known, that this blockade will be attended to with a degree of rigour unexampled in the present war.

I am, Sir,
Your obedient servant,
HORATIO NELSON.

TO THE CONSULS OF THE DIFFERENT NATIONS AT LEGHORN.

[From a Copy in the Admiralty, and the original Draught in the Nelson Papers.]

His Britannic Majesty's Ship Captain, off Leghorn, July 7th, 1796.
Sir,
I have to acquaint you that no Vessel will be permitted to enter or leave the Port of Leghorn till it is restored to its legal Government. I beg leave to recommend that all Ships should be taken from the Road into the Mole, as it may prevent disagreeable consequences.

I have the honour to be, Sir,
With great respect, your most obedient servant,
HORATIO NELSON.

TO THE RIGHT HON. SIR GILBERT ELLIOT.

[From a Copy, in the Nelson Papers.]

Captain, off Porto Ferrajo, July 9th, 1796.
Sir,
Although I saw the Inconstant weigh anchor from Fiorenzo, on Wednesday evening, and also saw her off Cape Corse on the next morning, when, Captain Fremantle writes me, he made

the Captain's signal to come within hail, which I did not see, nor if I had, should I have believed it could have been made to me, as the Inconstant did not make any effort to speak me. Thus I pursued my route off Leghorn, without being informed what was your Excellency's intention.

Yesterday morning, at seven o'clock, I received your letter, and having dispatched the Meleager to Genoa, for information, and directed Captain Sawyer to pursue the proper methods for the effectual blockade of Leghorn, taking under his direction the Sardine, Le Genie, and a Gun-boat I fitted out at San Fiorenzo, I proceeded, with the Peterel, off this place, where I arrived last night, and sent in a Boat to examine if the French or English had possession. We found the Southampton there. This morning, I saw the Convoy to the westward, and the Inconstant is making sail to join me; therefore I have only to assure your Excellency that every effort of mine shall be used to fulfil your intentions, when I know them, being, with the greatest respect,

Your most obedient servant,
HORATIO NELSON.

His Excellency the Vice-Roy.

I send you a copy of my letter to Mr. Brame, and also to the Foreign Consuls at Leghorn.

TO ADMIRAL SIR JOHN JERVIS, K.B.

[From a Copy, in the Nelson Papers.]

Captain, off Porto Ferrajo, July 9th, 1796.

Sir,

It was yesterday, at seven in the morning, I received the Vice-Roy's letter, acquainting me of his intention to possess Porto Ferrajo,[8] then close off the Melora. I instantly dis-

---

[8] Sir Gilbert Elliot's reasons for taking possession of Porto Ferrajo in the Island of Elba, are fully shewn by his Letter to the Governor of that place, dated Bastia, 6th July, 1796 :—

" Sir,—The French troops have taken possession of the City of Leghorn, the cannon of the fortresses have been directed against the Ships of the King, in the Road, and the property of his Majesty's subjects at Leghorn has been violated, notwithstanding the neutrality of His Royal Highness the Grand Duke of Tuscany, and the reiterated

patched the Meleager to Genoa, with my letters, the one to Mr. Brame, and to the Foreign Consuls at Leghorn. I inclose copies, and directed Captain Cockburn to remain in that Port forty-eight hours, in order to receive all the information which is to be collected.

The Blanche, Sardine, Le Genie, a Gun-boat, and two Corsican privateers, I left, to continue the blockade of Leghorn, and proceeded, with the Peterel, off this place, where I arrived last night. The Convoy hove in sight this morning, and the Inconstant is working up to join me. In the night I sent a boat into Porto Ferrajo, where they found his Majesty's Ship Southampton.

I have the honour, &c.

HORATIO NELSON.

TO ADMIRAL SIR JOHN JERVIS, K.B.

[From " The London Gazette," of the 20th of August, 1796.]

Captain, Porto Ferrajo, 10th July, 1796.

Sir,

I have the pleasure to inform you, that the Troops under the command of Major Duncan took possession of the Forts and Town of Porto Ferrajo, this day, at ten o'clock. On my joining the Convoy from Bastia, yesterday forenoon, Major Duncan having done me favour to come on board, we concerted on the most proper methods for speedily executing the Vice-Roy's instructions to the Major. The Troops were landed last night, about a mile to the westward of the Town, under the direction of Captain Stuart, of the Peterel ; and the Major immediately

protestations of the French to respect it. There is likewise reason to believe, that the French have the same design upon the fortress of Porto Ferrajo, hoping by such means to facilitate the designs which they meditate against the Kingdom of Corsica. These circumstances have determined us to prevent the plans of the Enemies of the King, which are equally hostile to his Royal Highness, by placing at Porto Ferrajo a garrison capable of defending that place, our only intention being to prevent that fortress, and the whole of the Island of Elba, from being taken possession of by the French. We invite and request you, Sir, to receive the troops of his Majesty which will appear before the place, under the following conditions."—According to these conditions, Porto Ferrajo and its dependencies were to remain under the government of the Grand Duke ; and a solemn promise was given, that the troops should retire, and the place be restored, at the peace.—*Annual Register*, vol. xxxviii. " State Papers," p. 133.

marched close to the gate on the west side, and at five
o'clock this morning sent in to the Governor the Vice-Roy's
letter, containing the terms which would be granted to the
Town, and gave him two hours for the answer.　At half-past
five I came on shore, when we received a message from the
Governor, desiring one hour more to consult with the principal
inhabitants.　We took this opportunity to assure the Tuscan
inhabitants, that they should receive no injury whatever in
their persons or property.

Having ordered the Ships into the harbour, to their several
stations, before appointed, the Major and myself determined,
should the terms offered be rejected, to instantly open the fire
of the Ships, and to storm the place, on every point from the
land and sea.　The harmony and good understanding between
the Army and Navy employed on this occasion, will I trust be
a farther proof of what may be effected by the hearty co-operation of the two services.

I cannot conclude without expressing my fullest approbation
of the zeal and good conduct of every Captain, Officer, and
Man in the Squadron ; and also, that during the time I was
necessarily employed on shore, that my First Lieutenant,
Edward Berry, commanded the Ship, and placed her opposite
the grand bastion, within half-pistol shot; and in such a manner
as could not have failed, had we opened our fire, to produce
the greatest effect.

　　　　　　I have the honour to be, &c.

　　　　　　　　　　HORATIO NELSON.

N. B. The Place is mounted with one hundred pieces of
cannon and garrisoned by 400 Regulars, besides Militia.

　　　　　　SHIPS' NAMES.
　　Captain, 74 guns.
　　Inconstant, 36 guns, Captain Fremantle.
　　Flora, 36 guns, Captain Middleton.
　　Southampton, 32 guns, Captain Macnamara.
　　Peterel, 16 guns, Captain Stuart.
　　Vanneau, Brig, Lieutenant Gourly.
　　Rose, Cutter, Lieutenant Walker.

TO THE RIGHT HON. SIR GILBERT ELLIOT.

[From a Copy, in the Nelson Papers.]

Captain, Porto Ferrajo, July 10th, 1796.

Sir,

I am happy in congratulating your Excellency on the success of your plan for the possessing ourselves of the Forts and town of Porto Ferrajo. The perfect harmony and good understanding subsisting between Major Duncan[1] and myself would not, I trust, have failed to gain the possession of this invaluable post and harbour, even had the handsome terms offered by your Excellency been rejected. Major Duncan, than whom his Majesty has not a more zealous Officer, will detail to your Excellency his proceedings. I have the honour to be, with the greatest respect,

Your Excellency's most faithful and obedient servant,

HORATIO NELSON.

His Excellency the Vice-Roy.

TO HIS EXCELLENCY THE HON. WILLIAM F. WYNDHAM.

[From a Copy, in the Nelson Papers.]

Captain, Porto Ferrajo, July 11th, 1796.

Sir,

I have the pleasure to inform you that the King's troops took possession of this place yesterday forenoon. This measure was judged expedient, in order to prevent the French from possessing it, and thereby have an easy access to Corsica.

The Governor of this place (for except the guarding the fortifications all is left as before) sends off a letter for the Grand Duke to-morrow morning, and of course he will send copies of the Vice-Roy's letter to him; and also, of all the letters and declarations which have passed between him and Major Duncan, and myself. You will credit, Sir, that the utmost attention will be paid to the declarations, &c., and I trust that the Tuscan subjects will feel that protection by the assistance of his Majesty's forces by sea and land, which will give an increase to their happiness. The inhabitants

---

[1] Vide, vol. i. p. 373.

seem sensible of the great difference between their situation
and that of the unfortunate Livornese; and happy, indeed,
shall I be, to see the necessity of withdrawing our Troops when
the Enemies of all Italy shall be driven out of it, and all the
Dominions of his Royal Highness restored to the tranquillity
experienced before the flagrant breach of faith in the French.
All is not only quiet, but as the Vice-Roy expresses himself, better than quiet in Corsica.
I am honoured with the direction of the blockade of Leghorn. I have already granted permission to several persons
to bring their Vessels to Porto Ferrajo, to trade from hence to
any neutral Country they please.

I am, Sir, with the greatest respect,
Your most obedient and very humble servant,
HORATIO NELSON.

TO ADMIRAL SIR JOHN JERVIS, K.B.

[From a Copy, in the Nelson Papers.]

Captain, off Leghorn, July 15th, 1796.

Dear Sir,
I send Meleager to Bastia, to tell the Vice-Roy all the
Genoese news, and also to take with him all the letters and
papers I have received, which the Vice-Roy will forward to
you so soon as read. I may congratulate you on the soreness
which the French feel for your strict blockade of the Port of
Toulon. We have fairly got to be masters from one end of
the Coast to the other. I wish Government had given you full
answers about stopping corn and merchandise going to France.
It is on this point the French Minister lays his stress. We
feel much by not having a Minister at Genoa at this particular
time, that Government not having the smallest notice taken of
their complaints, although they must know they are without
foundation. I intend to go to Genoa so soon as Meleager
returns, and I have wrote to the Vice-Roy for his advice
respecting my making a visit to the Doge, and of introducing
the subject matters of complaint, and of assuring him of our
respect for the real independence of Genoa; and that I have
declared to Mr. Drake, that whilst the French are in possession

P 2

of the western Riviera of Genoa, and act hostilely against the English, I should consider it the Coast of an Enemy.

We cannot get rid of the stoppage of provisions going to France. As to the rest, I can say, on paper and by mouth, some soothing things to the Doge; and as to a breach of the rights of Nations, the French have the whole coast fortified, and their present breach of all honour and faith, by the cruel invasion of Tuscany.

General Wurmser,[2] you will see, commands the Army. They have beat the French near Mantua: not less than 13,000 have been killed or taken. On the Rhine, and with the Prince of Condé's Army, where is Louis the Eighteenth, all is victorious: not less than 40,000 French have been destroyed—their Army is annihilated.

Jourdan writes, he cannot stop without reinforcements till he gets to the gates of Paris. The Prince Charles has behaved with great resolution and conduct, and gained immortal honour: he was everywhere.

I shall make the minds of the English easy, at Genoa, by assuring them I shall come to their help whenever they are ready to embark, but that we have not Shipping to embark their effects. If they please, they may send to Fiorenzo and have any Merchantmen, but not a Transport can be spared.

Four P.M.—I am just anchored in Leghorn Roads. I have had a Fishing-boat on board. All quiet at Leghorn.

Yesterday, the Tree of Liberty was planted in great form, and the Goddess of Liberty was carried in great procession; 2500 Troops in the place. I have not yet had an opportunity of having the Genie valued: she is at present chasing to the southward. The Sardine cannot move in light airs, she is so very foul; and, to say the truth, she has not men to manage her, although I am sure Captain Killwick[3] does all in his power. Believe me, dear Sir,

With the greatest respect,

Your most faithful and obedient humble servant,

HORATIO NELSON.

As Sardine is also to the southward, I cannot send his state and condition.

---

[2] Field-Marshal Wurmser, a veteran then in his eightieth year, succeeded General Beaulieu in the command of the Austrian Army.

[3] Captain Edward Killwick: he was Posted in 1797, and died before 1802.

TO THE RIGHT HON. SIR GILBERT ELLIOT.

[Autograph, in the Minto Papers.]

Captain, off Leghorn, July 15th, 1796.

Dear Sir,

I send the Meleager, that Captain Cockburn may tell you all the news from Genoa, and also Mr. Trevor's,[4] Mr. Brame's, and every paper I have received, which you will be so good as to forward to the Admiral, when read.   On the subject of Mr. Fairpoult's Note, I wish very much for your advice.   We feel the loss of having no Minister at Genoa : our Consul has no power to answer these Notes, of either the Genoese Secretary of State, or to refute the infamous lies which are fabricated by the French Minister to irritate the Genoese against us.   It is certainly notorious that we endeavour to stop all intercourse between Genoa and France, and here it is the French Minister lays his stress ; and at the same time gives out that the British stop all Vessels belonging to the Genoese, to whatever place they may be bound.   By the influence, or rather fear of the French, the Genoese Government have made several of the most frivolous complaints of the breach of neutrality in the Western Riviera.   I have answered all the notes, and I hope they will reach Mr. Drake.   Duplicates I sent to request you to forward, when I was last at St. Fiorenzo, but in the meantime the Genoese get no answer whatever ; this they must feel, and the French are making the most of it.

I mean to go to Genoa so soon as Cockburn returns to me, and I will visit the Doge, and tell him that I have received the various Notes sent to Mr. Brame, and have answered them all ; that the facts are either totally false, or so much misstated, that they bear not the smallest resemblance of truth ; that I have

---

[4] Apparently the letter from Mr. Trevor, (now in the Nelson Papers,) dated June 30, 1796, wherein, after acknowledging the receipt of Commodore Nelson's letter of the 22nd of that month, and promising to send him the earliest notice he might receive of his promotion : " on which event," Mr. Trevor said, he should " drink with equal zeal and confidence to the Admiral of the Van," he asked Nelson's opinion " as to the *extent* of the inconvenience which the loss of the Port of Leghorn will be to his Majesty's Fleet, and to our establishment in that *cursed* Corsica ;" and warned the Viceroy against some "*foul play*" in that Island.   Mr. Trevor added— " Rome is said to have bought a peace.   Naples is making her's at Basle, and the Emperor trying to make the best he can."

declared to Mr. Drake, that whilst the French are in possession of the Western Riviera, and act hostilely against His Britannic Majesty's Ships, that I must consider it as the Coast of an Enemy, but that so far from wishing to act with the smallest degree of harshness against the Genoese, that neither my orders or my inclination will allow me to do it. The Doge will naturally put a question, why we stop vessels loaded with merchandise bound to France. It is here I shall find the difficulty in answering, and he will of course desire to have what I say put in writing. Do you think, Sir, I had better take no manner of notice of what is going on, and let these assertions of the French be unrefuted, for the Genoese commerce is suspended, and defer my visit to the Doge for a future day? Pray, Sir, give me your advice. My Admiral is at a distance, and I well know the delicacy of intermeddling with the Diplomatic functions. The blockade of Leghorn is as complete as is possible. Pray God the successes of the Austrians may be such as to make the Tuscans rise on the French, and open the Mole Gate, when I will most assuredly assist them by landing myself. Do you think, Sir, Mr. Drake will come to Genoa? We must suffer by his absence.

Ever believe me, dear Sir,

Your Excellency's most faithful

HORATIO NELSON.

His Excellency the Vice-Roy.

TO THE DANISH CONSUL AT LEGHORN.

[Enclosed in the preceding Letter of the 17th of July.]

Captain, Leghorn Roads, July 17th, 1796.

Sir,

I wrote to all the Consuls at Leghorn by way of Genoa, and have every reason to believe you have received my letter, (but I send a copy.) If you have, I am surprised you should send a Danish vessel out of a blockaded Port, which Leghorn is, till it is restored to its legal Government.

Respect for the Danish flag, and humanity to the owners of this Vessel, impel me to return her into the Port, and not pro-

ceed to those extremities which the laws of Nations allow in
the case of a declared blockaded port.

I have the honour to be, Sir, with great respect,

Your most obedient Servant,

HORATIO NELSON.

TO THE RIGHT' HON. SIR GILBERT ELLIOT.

[Autograph, in the Minto Papers.]

Captain, Leghorn Roads, July 18th, 1796.

Dear Sir,

The Rose joined me in half an hour after the Comet, and
I sent off directly the Sardine, Peterel, and Comet. I fear
the Pope has altered his intentions since the news was sent to
the Admiral; if not, I have still hopes his Holiness may commence war against the French; for I never heard he was in
actual hostility against them. Should, however, the Sloops not
be wanted, I will thank you to recommend to the Captains to
join me; they are wanted here. I have now only Blanche
and Meleager with me. The Rose must go to refit, and I
ought to send a Ship every week to Genoa. The Corsican
privateers keep at such a distance that I cannot communicate
with them. I wish two could be directed to be always at my
elbow. I think I have heard there is a person who directs their
proceedings.

Yesterday morning a Danish vessel came out, loaded with
oil and wine for Genoa : with some difficulty I persuaded the
gentleman to go in again. I believe it was a trial to know if I
was in earnest ; for on his positively refusing and my taking
possession [of] him, to deliver him to a Corsican privateer, he
in about two hours altered his note, and begged I would allow
him to return. I wrote a letter to the Danish Consul, of which
I send you a copy. Mr. Brame's letter will tell you of his
communication, on the 9th, I suppose, to all the Foreign
Ministers and Genoese Government; and my letter to all the
Consuls at Leghorn, if they were put in the post at Genoa,
must have got to Leghorn on the 11th or 12th; but on the
8th, I sent a similar letter to the Venetian Consul, by a Ship
I ordered to return ; therefore you may be assured they knew
it long ago. The French have laid powder under all the

works, which has alarmed the inhabitants, and nearly all the women have quitted the place. The cannon and mortars are mounted on the ramparts, and they say they expect more troops, but I trust, by their wishing to get into fortified Towns, they are at their last shifts, and that this will yet be the most glorious of any campaign this war. I purpose going to Genoa the moment Meleager arrives, and so soon as I return will send your Excellency all the news.

Believe me ever
Your Excellency's most obedient Servant,
HORATIO NELSON.

2000 French arrived yesterday, and Tartans are fitting with heavy cannon to fire on us: therefore, I wish more than ever for two privateers. A camp is forming at Monte Neva.

TO ADMIRAL SIR JOHN JERVIS, K.B.

[From Clarke and M'Arthur, vol. i. p. 300.]

Leghorn Roads, 18th July, 1796.
Dear Sir,

I hope his Holiness the Pope may yet wage war against the French. I have never heard that he has been in actual hostility against them. The blockade of Leghorn is complete, not a Vessel can go in or come out without my permission. Yesterday a Dane came out laden with oil and wine for Genoa : I told him he must return, or I should send him to Corsica. His answer was, ' I am a Neutral, and you may take me, but I will not return.' I therefore took possession, and intended giving him to a Corsican privateer ; when, in about two hours, he begged I would allow him to return. On this, I sent him back with a letter to the Danish Consul, whence the following is an extract :—' Respect for the Danish flag, and humanity to the owners of this Vessel, impel me to return her into their possession, and not proceed to those extremities which the laws of Nations allow in case of a declared blockaded Port.' This, I am satisfied, was a trial of what I intended ; for he said, all the Neutrals were determined to come out. If we are firm, the Grand Duke will sorely repent his admission of the French : his repeated proclamations for the people to be quiet, have given time to the French to lay powder under all the works; and, in case of any disturbance, they say, ' up shall go the works.' Cannon are pointed from the wall to every street, and all the cannon and mortars are mounted : the famous long brass gun is on the Mole-head, and also a mortar. The Grand Duke declares he yet hopes the Directory will order Buonaparte to leave Leghorn; but I believe the French now wish to get into fortified Towns, to prolong the campaign.

The Captain has her wants, but I intend she shall last until the autumn; for I know, when once we begin, our wants are innumerable. I hope the Admiralty will send out fresh Ships. The French are fitting out here from four to six Tartans, with thirty-six pounders, to drive me out of the Roads; but I am prepared against Fire Vessels, and all other plans, as well as I am able. The Tartans, it is said, will be out to-night : two thousand French are arrived, and more are expected. I have only now to beg, that whenever you think the Enemy will face you on the water, that you will send for me; for my heart would break to be absent at such a glorious time.

I am, &c.

HORATIO NELSON.

MEMORANDUM.

[From a Copy, in the Nelson Papers.]

[About the 20th July, 1796.]

Sir John Jervis, K.B., Admiral and Commander-in-Chief of the Fleet, is so well satisfied (from the representations of Commodore Nelson,) of the exceeding good conduct and alacrity shewn by persons of every description in the Fleet, in the possessing ourselves of Porto Ferrajo, that Commodore Nelson is directed by the Commander-in-Chief, to return his thanks to the Captains, Officers, and Ships' Companies employed on that service, for their good conduct, to which the Commodore begs leave to add his confidence that, had the town not surrendered on terms, it would have fallen by the bravery of the Seamen and Soldiers.

TO HIS ROYAL HIGHNESS THE DUKE OF CLARENCE.

[From Clarke and M'Arthur, vol. i. p. 301.]

Captain, Leghorn Roads, under sail for Genoa, 20th July, 1796.

Sir,

I was this morning honoured with your Royal Highness's letter of May 30th ;[5] and it gives me real satisfaction to be assured of the continuance of your good opinion. Indeed, I can say with truth, that no one whom you may have been pleased to honour with your notice, has a more sincere attachment for you than myself. It has pleased God this war, not only to give me frequent opportunities of shewing myself an Officer worthy of trust, but also to prosper all my undertakings in the highest degree. I have had the extreme good fortune, not only to be noticed in my immediate line of duty, but also to obtain the repeated approbation of His Majesty's Ministers at Turin, Genoa, and Naples, as well as of the Vice-Roy of Corsica, for my conduct in the various opinions I have been called upon to give ; and my judgment being formed from common sense, I have never yet been mistaken.

You will hear of our taking possession of Porto Ferrajo : if we had not, to a certainty the French would, and then they would have been too near Corsica, where I fear we have an ungrateful set of people ; and one party acknowledged friends to the French, which, although greatly outnumbered by our

"Richmond, May 30, 1796.

[5] "Dear Sir,

"I am to acknowledge the receipt of your various obliging and instructive letters since I wrote last : pray continue your invaluable correspondence. I wish the Austrian Army had afforded you better news ; but I am dreadfully alarmed the fate of Italy is sealed, and that the Italian States must bow to the French. In short, my good friend, when I compare the want of energy of the old Governments, the treachery and blunders made by the Austrians, with the enthusiasm and activity of the French, and the ability of their conductors, I can see no end to their conquests on the Continent. I am apprehensive the Emperor must make peace, and that flagitious Monarch of Prussia will have reason to be on his guard against his friends in France. As for this Country, thank God, our Navy can, and will protect us ; but Fleets cannot root out the accursed doctrines of the French.

"I hope you enjoy your health : and I trust you will soon return, as your Ship must be in a state more fit for a Dock than the Ocean : wherever you are, rely upon my friendship and regard, and believe me, Dear Sir, yours sincerely, WILLIAM."— *Autograph*, in the Nelson Papers.

friends, constantly makes disturbances. The armistice of the
Pope and King of Naples will, I believe, come to nothing; it
was only done to gain time, and they will be guided by the
success or defeat of the Austrians. The King of Naples is
firm; he has been by far the most faithful Ally of England.[6]
He is at the head of 80,000 men at Velletri, only two posts
from Rome, where the people are ripe for a revolt, and
already declare that the busts, statues, and manuscripts, shall
not go out of Rome. The French possessing themselves of
Leghorn, so contrary to the repeated pledges of the Directory,
will afford such an opportunity for all the Italian States to
break with them again, that perhaps they may be induced to
give it up: the King of Naples, if they refuse, would march
to attack it, and we are sure of the lower order at Leghorn.
The garrison is reinforced to 5000 men, and provisions are
getting into the Citadel. The French General has told the
inhabitants, that if they are not quiet, he would blow all the
works up round the Town, which in fact would blow half the
Town up: the mines are laid; large Vessels are also fitting
with forty-two pounders, and furnaces, to annoy me; but I am
prepared, as much as possible, against whatever may happen.

Genoa, July 23rd.—I arrived here yesterday, and rejoice
to hear that Marshal Wurmser has commenced offensive operations. I have no doubt but the French will retire to Piedmont
as fast as they advanced from it; and I fear they may force
the King of Sardinia into an alliance against us. To-morrow
I return to Leghorn.

I am, &c.

HORATIO NELSON.

TO THE RIGHT HON. SIR GILBERT ELLIOT.

[Autograph, in the Minto Papers.]

Captain, at Sea, July 20th, 1796.

Dear Sir,

I feel very much obliged by your advice not to have any
explanation with the Genoese Government; I have at the

---

[6] Peace was, however, made between the King of Naples and the French Republic
on the 10th of October following.

same time taken every pains to convince the Genoese they
have nothing to fear bound to any other places except France,
and I hope it will have its effect, for not a Wood-vessel bound
to Piombino would go out of the Port. I send you copies of
Mr. Drake's letters to me, and also the French Minister's
Note to the Genoese Government. I wish Mr. Drake was at
Genoa, for such threats may, unless counteracted, have its
effect. The lower order certainly hate the French; amongst
the proscribed are some of the Senate, Second Order, and
Clergy; and those who the Minister demands should be rein-
stated, are several younger sons of Noble families, who for
their conspiracies about a year or half past were proscribed
from having a seat in the Councils. The Arms which he
mentioned were found loaded—in short, matters are fast approaching to a crisis, and will be favourable or otherwise to
us, as the successes or defeats of the Austrians point out; inclination from all I hear, is for us in the Senate.

Yesterday evening, an express came in from Vienna; nothing
certain is known; but report says, it is an assurance that the
Emperor will change his Minister for one more acceptable to
the Republic. It seems the Siege of Mantua was not raised by
the sortie on the 15th, but has been since vigorously attacked;
a second sally is spoke of, but it is not confirmed. I should
hope the Austrian Army must be there before this time. Mr.
Jackson's[7] letter to the Admiral says they will take the field
about the 15th, with 50,000 foot and twenty-two squadrons of
Cavalry.

I have received a letter which you will see the Swedish
Minister wrote to Mr. Brame, to allow light Swedes to leave
the Port of Leghorn. I did not give any encouragement
that it would be done; something may be said in favour of
letting them out, and other Neutrals without cargoes, but the
great line of punishing (if I may use the expression) the
Grand Duke will [be] done away, for I consider that all
the neutral Powers to Tuscany will represent to the Grand
Duke the injury they sustain by his admission of the French
into the Town of Leghorn, and will consider the blockade as
the natural consequence of such conduct. This will, I trust,

---

[7] Secretary of Legation at Turin.

make the Ministry of Tuscany use every effort with the
Directory, to order the French to retire out of Tuscany, or in
failure thereof, that the Neapolitans will finish their truce,
and being joined by the Tuscans, commence hostilities against
the French; for the faith of the Directory any more than of
the former leaders of France will never pass current again:
by the continuance of a close blockade, this is the fruit I
promise myself, but I shall be guided by your Excellency;
but if you once open the door, it will never be shut again ;
some will bring little, some much.

I have got from Messrs. Heath the money for your Excellency, and £8000 for the Deputy Commissary General; this
is all I could get in so short a time as my stay. Mr. Heath
tells me the one per cent. is customary: indeed, this is the
trade, for remittances are not now wanted for London.

He tells me he is almost sure he can supply Corsica with
£10,000 sterling, per week, but it is necessary they should
know if it is wished they should collect money for this purpose. You will be so good as to direct them what to do, and
Mr. Buckholm will do the same. I shall every week send a
Frigate to Genoa; pray direct Mr. Buckholm, if he wants
money, to make the bills payable to Mr. Heath instead of me;
for should there be any irregularity in the drawing or payment, it may give some trouble to myself.

Some Genoese merchants have asked me if they may go to
Corsica to purchase Prize-goods, and they intend to take
money with them. I have given them encouragement,
and told them the first Frigate should take them and money
to Bastia, and that I will take an opportunity of conveying
them safe back again.

If I have done wrong, pray say so; but I think you will like
to have these ready-money gentry come amongst you. With
the greatest regard, believe me, dear Sir,

Your Excellency's
Most faithful
HORATIO NELSON.

His Excellency the Vice-Roy.

TO ADMIRAL SIR JOHN JERVIS, K.B.

[From Clarke and M'Arthur, vol. i. p. 302.]

27th July, 1796.

I have recommended to the Merchants at Genoa, whenever they are alarmed, to ship their goods in time on board such Neutral vessels as they may find in the Port; for that it would be impossible, however much you might be inclined, to send Transports to receive their effects, which in Heath's house amount to £160,000 sterling. Things are fast approaching to a crisis, and will probably be determined before you receive this.   I am, &c.

HORATIO NELSON.

TO THE RIGHT HONOURABLE SIR GILBERT ELLIOT, VICE-ROY OF CORSICA.

[Autograph, in the Minto Papers.]

Captain, Leghorn Roads, July 28th, 1796.

Dear Sir,

Many thanks for your letters; do with every Vessel as you like. I am sure you will recollect the various services we want them all for, and at this moment it is most particularly interesting: we should have something off Genoa, the friends of the English say it may turn the scale in our favour. Mr. Drake sees the necessity of it, and so do I, therefore I am more interested that a Privateer or two should come under my orders. I shall keep the Blanche from sailing for Genoa for a few days, if you desire any more money from thence. I thought I had wrote you fully as to the time the blockade must have been known at Leghorn. We can only judge of the fair time, for of course the Masters will not acknowledge they know anything about it. The Venetian Consul knew it the 8th; all at Genoa knew it the 9th; and if the Foreign Ministers did not send my letters to their respective Consuls, and the notification to themselves, it does not rest with us. By post, it must have been at Leghorn on the 12th, in the morning, although there cannot be a doubt but all knew it before, although they may plead not officially. I have a private

letter from the Admiral, containing his full approbation of my
letter to the Consul, and of mine to Mr. Brame. I think I
sent your Excellency copies, and the Admiral will send me
his public approbation so soon as he has leisure. I have
wrote to him on the subject of the Swedes. We must be first,
or the blockade will be as useless as the Genoa one. I grieve
to hear you have been indisposed, but good news from the
Army will make us all merry. I have just received an odd
letter from Mr. Trevor,[8] in which he assures me of the determination of the French to invade England. I beg my best
thanks to Lady Elliot for her remembrance, and that she will
accept my sincere good wishes for her health; and ever believe me, dear Sir,

Your Excellency's most faithful servant,

HORATIO NELSON.

His Excellency the Vice-Roy.

MEMORANDUM.

[Autograph draught, in the Nelson Papers.]

Captain, Leghorn Roads, July 31st, 1796.

The Fishing-vessels from Leghorn not to be molested or
put into quarantine by the Ships of War, or Corsican Privateers.

N.B. If any Fishing-vessel is known to carry any cargo or
passengers, she is to be seized.

HORATIO NELSON.

TO CAPTAIN COLLINGWOOD, H.M.S. EXCELLENT, ST. FIORENZO.

[Autograph, in the possession of the Hon. Mrs. Newnham Collingwood.]

On H. M.'s Service.

Captain, Leghorn Roads, August 1st, 1796, half-past eight, P.M.

My dear Coll.,

The Viceroy tells me you are at Fiorenzo; therefore I take
my chance of this finding you. My date makes me think I
am *almost* at Leghorn; soon I hope to be there in reality.

---

[8] This letter is not in the Nelson Papers.

Except 1700 poor devils, all are gone to join the Army.
Sometimes I hope, and then despair of getting these starved
Leghornese to cut the throats of this French crew. What an
idea for a Christian! I hope there is a great latitude for us
in the next world. I know by myself how anxious all must
be for authentic news, therefore I will tell you. My letters are
from Mr. Drake, at Venice, copy of one from Colonel Graham, the Resident at the Austrian Army, and from our
Minister at Turin.

The sortie from Mantua was great, but I do not find the
siege has been raised; but I have nothing later than
20th July. General Buonaparte is wounded in the thigh.
The Austrian Army, 50,000 foot, twenty-two squadrons of
cavalry, besides the garrison of Mantua, and 20,000 at
Triest, coming forward, would commence operations about the
18th or 20th of July. Every moment I expect news from
Genoa: it can, I hope, hardly fail of being good.

This blockade is complete, and we lay very snug in the
North Road, as smooth as in a harbour. I rejoice with you
our English Post is open again to us. I have letters only to
the middle of June: all well, and as to Public affairs, Mr.
Pitt seems as strong as ever. What have we to do with the
Prince's private amours? The world say there are faults on both
sides: like enough. Thank God, I was not born in high
life. The promotion of Flags seems deferred, but I suppose
it must take place soon. I have this moment received accounts that the post from Naples, (say Capua,) which arrived
to-day, has brought an account that the truce with Naples
finishes to-day, and hostilities commence to-morrow. Pray
God it may be so. With a most sincere wish for driving the
French to the Devil, your good health, an honourable Peace,
us safe at home again, I conclude, by assuring you, my dear
Collingwood, of my unalterable friendship and regard, and
that I am, in the fullest meaning of the words,

Yours most truly,

HORATIO NELSON.

TO ADMIRAL SIR JOHN JERVIS, K.B.

[From Clarke and M'Arthur, vol. i. p. 303.]

1st August, 1796.

Sir,

I experience the highest degree of pleasure which an Officer is capable of feeling, the full approbation of his Commander-in-Chief; which must not be a little increased by knowing that his Commander is such a character as Sir John Jervis, without disparagement or flattery, allowed to be one of the first in the service.

All goes well here, nothing gets in or comes out, except a Privateer, which our Boats cannot come up with; yet I do not say but that in a westerly gale Vessels may get in, notwithstanding all our endeavours : I will, however, answer for my exertions to prevent them; rowing Vessels are the most useful against the French privateers. The lower Orders at Leghorn are miserable; several have been on board, wishing to serve for provisions: they have a plan for rising, but the Grand Duke almost every day tells them the French will go away, and therefore orders them to be quiet.

August 2nd.

Before any more letters arrive, I must give you the trouble of reading some omissions which I have made in my former ones. Respecting the Corsican privateers, my answer was on a supposition that two of the Privateers would give up every other consideration, and absolutely put themselves under my orders : in that case, and in that case only, did I mean to alter the established rule for sharing. However, not one has obeyed, or put himself under my orders: it has been an age since I have seen any of them. I had last night a great deal of conversation with an old fisherman ; he says, 300 light cavalry, Tuscans, are coming into Leghorn, that forage for cavalry is providing about three miles from Pisa, and that the people of Leghorn will not be put off any longer than the 10th or 15th. The French must go. I have made up my mind, that when Marshal Wurmser forces the French, and especially if the King of Naples comes forward, that the Grand Duke will order a number of troops into Leghorn, and say to the French, ' We choose to keep our own Town :' when the

French would go quietly off. These people represent them
as a miserable set of boys, without clothes or shoes; so the
Commissaries must have done well for themselves: all the best
men are gone to the Army.

The day before yesterday, Vice-Consul Udney's things were
all returned into his house: the French are grown very civil
to the inhabitants, who, on the contrary, grow more impertinent.
The other day they drove the guard from Pisa gate with sticks,
and told them they should not stay beyond the 10th : a revolt
against the Ministry of the Grand Duke would be the consequence of their stay. That said Major de Place, who came
on board the Victory to pay his respects to you, is the Governor
appointed by the French, and who will certainly lose his head
if there is an insurrection: they call him traitor. I have sent
to Mr. Wyndham, to know if the Grand Duke means to make
good the losses of the English; for till I receive his official
letter, desiring me to take off the blockade, I shall not feel at
liberty so to do; unless the entire property, or the value of it,
is restored, or until I receive directions from you. No property
has been sold, for there were no buyers : it may be made over,
but that certainly will not do. I shall in this event permit
light Vessels to pass, but not a cargo on any account ; for the
Grand Duke may say, in that Vessel went the English property, and shew as permitted by the English Officer : you will
think I am beforehand, but a regular plan can never do harm;
and then, when the event takes place, and take place it soon
will, I have not this part to think of.

Almost all Tuscany is in motion : the whole of this day
they have told the French, 'You shall go away; we will not
be starved for you.' The French are sending many things
out of the town, but the generality of English goods are safe :
they have been repeatedly put up for sale, but none would
buy.

August 3rd.

The Leghornese have given notice to the French, that they
shall not make their grand Fête on the 10th of August, by
which time their new clothes are to be ready. All work, such
as repairing gun-carriages, &c., is left off. I have no doubt but
by the 15th we shall have Leghorn, and then I look forward to

our settling with the Pope. The appearance of a Squadron off Cività Vecchia, and respectful yet firm language, will, I have no doubt, induce his Holiness to open his Ports as usual.

I am, &c.

HORATIO NELSON.

TO THE RIGHT HON. SIR GILBERT ELLIOT.

[Autograph, in the Minto Papers.]

Captain, Leghorn Roads, Aug. 1st, 1796.

Dear Sir,

I am much favoured by your letter of July 30th, and the Blanche is gone for Genoa, and have great hopes she will bring us good news. Enclosed I send you a copy of my letter to the Swedish Minister at Genoa, which I hope you will approve: my intention is to keep these gentlemen in good humour with us. Your reasons are strong, and I give up my opinion, and prefer yours, as most consonant to keep up good will with Neutral Powers. The Admiral's answer, I think, will be with you, therefore I have adopted a signal, that these people may suffer as little inconvenience as possible. I have every inclination to befriend every Neapolitan: the good faith of the King of Naples demands and ensures it of us; but I fear the permitting cargoes will draw us into scrapes with other Powers; and we cannot exactly say, such a tonnage may carry their cargoes before purchased, and to others, the Vessels I will liberate whenever they come to me, but with Cargoes I fear we must not. A little time, I hope, must induce the French to quit Leghorn. The Great Duke sends messages for the people to remain quiet, and all will end well; but in the meantime, the lower Orders are, from their former plenty, absolutely in great want. Two nights ago, a man came off to say, that the fishermen had a place assigned them to attack; the' shoemakers, bricklayers, and other trades, different places. The Venetians were to liberate the slaves, and possess themselves of the place where the colours were hoisted, they thought about the 10th; but they must be sure the French would not be able to return in force: they all speak disrespectfully of the Grand Duke's Ministry. I send your Excellency the disposition of my Squadron: so soon as I can get any of them

about me, I will instantly send a Frigate for the Convoy—the
Blanche is in my mind; but some small Vessel, such as Vanneau, or Rose, which rows, is absolutely necessary against
these small Privateers : some of the small ones from here are
gone to the eastward. Almost every day Vessels come from
the westward for Leghorn, and I ought not to have less
than four Vessels to block the port; indeed, they are too few.
In six days you may be sure, as far as I can say, a Convoy
will be ready. I am glad they are coming round to Bastia.
The first Vessel which comes, if English—I don't call Sardine
one—shall immediately sail for Bastia, to take the Convoy.
If a Privateer or two could be induced to attend the Convoy
in sight of Naples, I do not think they would lose much, for
along the Roman coast they would pick up something. I dare
say you want Speedy to send to Barcelona; but you see, Sir,
my state, therefore do not take it amiss she has not yet gone
to you. I will not keep her a moment longer than I can help :
in everything, it is my endeavour to meet your wishes. We
are not likely to suffer for want of fresh beef. I have sent the
Admiral an offer from Genoa, to supply the Fleet with 100
Roman bullocks every week, onions, lemons, biscuit, &c., &c.
Our money will do much for us. I am glad the Sincere has
taught the Romans good manners. Not wishing to keep the
Rose, as Mr. Walker tells me you so much want him, you
must take my letter as it is. Believing me, ever

Your Excellency's most faithful and obliged,

HORATIO NELSON.

His Excellency the Vice-Roy.

LIST OF COMMODORE NELSON'S SQUADRON, AND HOW
DISPOSED OF.

[Autograph, in the Minto Papers.]

Captain . .	Leghorn Roads, to blockade the North Passage.
L'Eclair . .	South Passage.
Gun-boat . .	Under the Melo.
Sardine . .	With the Vice-Roy.
Peterell . .	Ajaccio.
Blanche . .	No water—gone to Genoa—will return in five or six days.

Meleager . . Ordered to the Fleet.
Speedy . . Gone to Genoa for information; expected
                 to-morrow, to go to the Vice-Roy for
                 Barcelona packet.
Le Genie . . Heaving down, Porto Ferrajo.

I have not room in my letter, but the Sincere is not certainly a sufficient Convoy for such valuable Vessels.

                                                      H. N.
August 1st, 1796.

TO WILLIAM LOCKER, ESQ., ROYAL HOSPITAL, GREENWICH.

[Autograph, in the Locker Papers.]

Captain, Leghorn Roads, August 2nd, 1796.

My dear Sir,

I shall confine my present letter principally to the subject
of your recommendation, with many other friends of Mr.
Summers. Very soon after his arrival, Admiral Hotham appointed him, in what was considered at the time as a real
vacancy, for it was certain Lieutenant Wenman Allison could
not survive, and he died a very few days after his arrival in
London. Lieutenant Summers feels, and so do I, that after
having been a year with me, and in a good vacancy, that he
is not confirmed; and I feel it the more, as those made since
him in invaliding vacancies, are confirmed. Indeed, the Admiralty have confirmed a Mr. Compton to a vacancy, when
they had actually sent out another Lieutenant, and two are
now serving in the vacancy of Lieutenant, now Captain Andrews. This business, I am sure, wants nothing but a fair
explanation, which I beg you to do. I have sent one certificate to Mr. Summers's agents, Marsh and Creed, and send
you another, which pray present to some of our friends at the
Board. I have every reason to believe Admiral Young[9] will
state the matter fairly to Lord Spencer.

I may almost congratulate you on our re-entry into
Leghorn; the country, from the Grand Duke, downwards,
is so completely in distress by the blockade of Leghorn, that

---

[9] Admiral William Young, then one of the Lords of the Admiralty; one of Nelson's early Naval friends. Vide vol. i. p. 89.

all is in motion, and if the French are not out of Leghorn before the 15th, there will be a general insurrection. The Leghornese have told the French, they shall not celebrate their Fête of August 10, to which the French must submit: they say the Grand Duke is a young man, but they do not spare his Ministry. The present Governor of Leghorn, who is fixed since the French came, they say is a traitor, and, if there is an insurrection, his head will go off: but I believe we shall manage all without blood—the French will go off. No person in Leghorn will buy the English property, for they could not send it away; therefore, except what is destroyed, all is safe. Some English merchants compromised with Buonaparte for their effects; they will lose, which I am not sorry for. Fear of the French has been the cause of all their successes in Italy. With kindest remembrances to every one of your family, believe me,

Ever your affectionate and obliged,

Horatio Nelson.

TO MRS. NELSON.

[From Clarke and M'Arthur, vol. i. p. 304.]

2nd August, 1796.

Had all my actions, my dearest Fanny, been gazetted, not one fortnight would have passed during the whole war without a letter from me: one day or other I will have a long Gazette to myself; I feel that such an opportunity will be given me. I cannot, if I am in the field for glory, be kept out of sight. Probably my services may be forgotten by the great, by the time I get Home ; but my mind will not forget, nor cease to feel, a degree of consolation and of applause superior to undeserved rewards. Wherever there is anything to be done, there Providence is sure to direct my steps. Credit must be given me in spite of envy. Even the French respect me : their Minister at Genoa, in answering a Note of mine, when returning some wearing apparel that had been taken, said, 'Your Nation, Sir, and mine, are made to show examples of generosity, as well as of valour, to all the people of the earth.' The following is a copy of the Note I had sent him.[1]

[1] Vide p. 188, ante.

I will also relate another anecdote, all vanity to myself, but you will partake of it : A person sent me a letter, and directed as follows, ' Horatio Nelson, Genoa.' On being asked how he could direct in such a manner, his answer, in a large party, was, ' Sir, there is but one Horatio Nelson in the world.' The letter certainly came immediately. At Genoa, where I have stopped all their trade, I am beloved and respected, both by the Senate and lower Order. If any man is fearful of his Vessel being stopped, he comes and asks me ; if I give him a Paper, or say, ' All is right,' he is contented. I am known throughout Italy ; not a Kingdom, or State, where my name will be forgotten. This is my Gazette.

Lord Spencer has expressed his sincere desire to Sir John Jervis, to give me my Flag. You ask me when I shall come home ? I believe, when either an honourable peace is made, or a Spanish war, which may draw our Fleet out of the Mediterranean. God knows I shall come to you not a sixpence richer than when I set out. I had a letter a few days since from H. R. H. the Duke of Clarence, assuring me of his unalterable friendship.[2] With kindest love to my father, believe me your most affectionate husband,

HORATIO NELSON.

TO THE MARQUIS DE SILVA, AT NAPLES.

[From Clarke and M'Arthur, vol. i. p. 306.]

3rd August, 1796.

Sir,

I am only this moment honoured with your letter of July 16th, requesting my permission for the departure of some Neapolitan vessels without cargoes. The honour and steadfast faith of his Sicilian Majesty in the good cause which all people ought to have espoused, make the situation of Neapolitan vessels very different from those of any other Nation : I feel that I shall fulfil the wishes of my Sovereign, and of my Admiral, in permitting the departure of Neapolitan vessels

---

[2] There is no letter from his Royal Highness between the dates of May 30th and September 2nd, 1796, now in the Nelson Papers.

without cargoes. Therefore, if you will order the Vessels to come to me, I will furnish them with proper passports to prevent their being molested.[3]

I am, &c.
HORATIO NELSON.

TO THE RIGHT HON. SIR GILBERT ELLIOT.

Autograph, in the Minto Papers.]

Captain, Leghorn Roads, August 3rd, 1796.

My dear Sir,

You must take the trouble of reading all my packet from Genoa and letter for the Admiral, I will not keep Peterel to select. One *old* lady tells me all she hears, which is what we wish. The moment we have any other Vessel, I will send Speedy, and she shall go now if you want her. The strength of Peterel is sufficient, if she has Vanneau, Rose, or one or two Corsican privateers; if not, I do not conceive the Captain would be a sufficient Convoy against the Row-boats. I have a letter of July 16th, from the Neapolitan Consul at Leghorn, and shall endeavour to get a letter to him this evening, desiring the small Vessels (without) cargoes to come to me. He only asks me without cargoes.

Believe me your Excellency's
Most faithful and much obliged,
HORATIO NELSON.

His Excellency the Vice-Roy.

---

[3] On the 17th of August, Sir William Hamilton communicated to Commodore Nelson "his Sicilian Majesty's sincere thanks for this act of friendship," and added— "Hitherto Naples deserves everything from us. It would have never made an armistice if it could have been avoided. It was to gain time; and be assured they will never make peace with the French, if they insist upon excluding the British ships from the Ports of the Two Sicilies, and their not supplying the King's Fleet with provisions." —*Original*, in the Nelson Papers. Sir William Hamilton was, however, mistaken; for by the third article of the Treaty of Peace between Naples and France, concluded on the 10th of October following, the King of Naples engaged himself to "observe the most strict neutrality towards all the belligerent Powers: in consequence, he pledges himself to prevent, indiscriminately, access to his Ports of all armed Ships of war belonging to the said Powers which shall exceed four, according to the regulations acknowledged by the said neutrality; and all stores or merchandise known by the name of 'contraband of war' shall be refused them."

TO THE RIGHT HON. SIR GILBERT ELLIOT.

[Autograph, in the Minto Papers.]

Leghorn Roads, August 4th, 1796.

Dear Sir,

The Admiral has sent orders for the Peterel to proceed to the Adriatic. If he has sailed, pray send something after him, and so soon as he has dropped the Convoy at Naples, he will proceed on his voyage. Lieutenant Walker, I hear from Captain Dixon, did not make the best of his way off Bastia, but chased and took possession of a Danish brig from Amsterdam. If so, I shall most probably try him by a Court Martial; and the L'Eclair means to lay in her claim.

Ever your most obliged,

HORATIO NELSON.

His Excellency the Vice-Roy.

TO THE RIGHT HON. SIR GILBERT ELLIOT.

[Autograph, in the Minto Papers.]

Captain, Leghorn Roads, August 5th, 1796.

My dear Sir,

If you can send Speedy instantly to me, she is most useful; if not, I submit, and will guard Leghorn as long as I can. I have directed Captain Elphinstone to obey your desires. I had wrote to the Neapolitan Consul, and I sincerely rejoice that my letter was, as far as I was able, very similar to yours.

Ever yours most faithfully,

HORATIO NELSON.

His Excellency the Vice-Roy.

TO THE RIGHT HON. SIR GILBERT ELLIOT.

[Autograph, in the Minto Papers.]

Captain, Leghorn Roads, August 5th, 1796.

My dear Sir,

Leghorn is, from all accounts last night, in such a state, that a respectable force landed, would, I have every reason to suppose, insure the immediate possession of the Town. I know many things must be considered. Not less than 1000 troops should be sent, to which I will add every soldier in my Squadron, and a party of seamen to make a show. In every way, pray consider this as private, and excuse my opinions. I well know the difficulty of getting a proper person to command this party. Firmness, and that the people of Leghorn should know the person commanding, will most assuredly have a great effect. A cordial co-operation with me (for, vanity apart, no one is so much feared or respected in Leghorn as myself) is absolutely necessary. A declaration from your Excellency would, I am sure, have the happiest effect.

I am going further: we know the jealousy of the Army against the Navy, but I am by the King's Commission a Colonel in the Army[4] from June 1st, 1795. I should like such a man as Duncan, he receiving your directions to consult no one but myself; but I have most unfortunately a Major, now I fancy Lieutenant-Colonel . . . . . . on board, who could [not] serve under Major Duncan. If I landed as Colonel, of course I should command the whole, and I most certainly should not call Mr. . . . . . . to my councils; but I feel almost the impossibility of your settling this business, although I am sure it would be for his Majesty's service ; and if my character is known, the internal regulations of the troops should rest by order under the Major, Duncan ; and I should only interfere in the great scale. I will, however it may hurt the feelings of Major . . . . . . , keep him on board, with six soldiers; he shall never command in co-operation with me ; therefore, do not let this be an objection. You will consider, Sir, all these points, and form a much better judgment than I can, only give me credit that the nearest wish of my heart is to serve my King and Country, at every personal risk and consideration.

Believe me ever your Excellency's most faithful

HORATIO NELSON.

It has ever pleased God to prosper all my undertakings, and I feel confident of His blessing on this occasion. I ever consider my motto, *Fides et Opera.*[5]

---

[4] Being Colonel of the Marines.

[5] It does not appear that Nelson used any Armorial Ensigns until after he was made a Knight of the Bath, in May, 1797, when Arms were assigned to him, (vide

N.B. Twenty-four hours will do the business.　Send an active Officer.

His Excellency the Vice-Roy.

TO ADMIRAL SIR JOHN JERVIS, K.B.

[From Clarke and M'Arthur, vol. i. p. 306.]

Leghorn Roads, 5th August, 1796.

Dear Sir,

If I write too much, say so, and I will hold my pen; for myself, I feel a comfort in knowing everything on which each Vessel of my Squadron is employed; and as but few of my letters require answers, I hope you do not think it gives you too much trouble to read them, occupied as I know you are with greater concerns. I would not stop the Comet one moment, as I was anxious she should find Peterel at Bastia. As to stores, she is just come from Ajaccio, but was absolutely refused those supplies which she stood in need of. If a Ship goes into an arsenal, she not only ought to have her damages made good, but her wants should also be supplied according to the discretion of the proper officers : the Peterel was sent shamefully away, and Mr. James[6] was treated, from his account, with a most unwarrantable incivility. Do these Naval Civilians, of all descriptions, mean to separate themselves from our authority? If they be not punishable by Martial law, other punishments, although more slow, will, I trust, assuredly fall upon them. I mean not this as a public complaint, for I would not have every Captain take what stores he pleases; but, at the same time, the fair wants of a Vessel, whatever is the rank of her Commander, ought to be supplied, and the Officer treated with civility. You well know, Sir, what to do, to settle both sides of the question, therefore I shall say no more; the Peterel's sails are rags, and none have been supplied her.

I know, dear Sir, the Vice-Roy's worth and wisdom, and

---

a subsequent page,) and he then adopted the Motto mentioned in the above letter. Before that time he generally used a seal with the cipher " A. N.," which probably belonged to his sister, " poor Ann Nelson;" or a large seal with the head of Neptune engraved on it.

[6] Commander of the Peterel.

you will, as he does, give me credit for having only one point in view, to serve my King and Country faithfully; and as both you and he have the same consideration, I shall not, as far as my abilities will allow me, think very differently from either. You are ever adding, Sir, to my obligations, and I can only endeavour to repay you by the way most agreeable to yourself, a most assiduous attention to my duty.

I have given permission to some Neapolitan vessels to leave the Mole for Naples, but without cargoes. The worth and good faith of the King of Naples demand of us everything we can grant; and it was a real pleasure for me to find, the day after I had granted the permission, that the Vice-Roy had written a very similar letter to the Marquis de Silva. I have also permitted, by desire of Mr. North, some goods to pass, and the American tribute to the Dey of Algiers. A Venetian vessel is to come here, and load under my guns. The Dey's Lord of the Bedchamber, or some such great man, has been on board my Ship: he was highly pleased with my entertainment of him, and declared he would supply us with bullocks of 600 lbs. each, for ten Spanish dollars; he was never tired of looking about him.

I must relate an anecdote: I asked him why he would not make peace with the Genoese and Neapolitans, for they would pay the Dey? His answer was, 'If we make peace with every one, what is the Dey to do with his Ships?' What a reason for carrying on a Naval war! but has our Minister a better one for the present? I have sent great news to Bastia; but (I wish the word was out of our language) I am not fully contented: we beat the Enemy on the 29th, 30th, 31st, 1st, and 2nd; and because I do not know whether we beat them on the 3rd, I am not satisfied;[7] such is human nature. Guns are sounding from the ramparts, and I am wicked enough to wish that all these fellows' throats may be cut before night.

[7] After raising the siege of Mantua on the 30th of July, Buonaparte joined his army at Breschia. The French had then recently gained many advantages over the Austrians, particularly at Lonado; but on the 31st, the French were driven out of it, and beaten in an engagement. On the 1st of August, the Austrians were routed at Breschia, and took refuge in the mountains of the Tyrol. On the 3rd, Marshal Wurmser, who had advanced to the assistance of the other divisions of the Austrian army, was defeated at Castiglione. The Austrians were worsted at Gavardo on the

August 11th.

Yesterday the French had their fête, but they seemed fearful of a riot : by proclamation, all Tuscans were ordered to remain in their houses, and every possible precaution taken. The French say they have no orders from their Government to quit Leghorn ; therefore they shall remain.

I am, &c.

HORATIO NELSON,

TO . . . .

[Autograph Draught in the Nelson Papers.]

Captain, Leghorn Roads, August 5th, 1796.

My Lord,

From the total deprivation of trade in Leghorn, more than 50,000 people are thrown out of employment, and I believe it is within compass when we include the whole canal trade to every part of Italy. Hundreds have been on board in small boats, to beg bread. All agree they have repeatedly represented to the Grand Duke the miserable state to which they are reduced, and the answer they have repeatedly received, was to beg of them to remain quiet. All this, your Lordship knows most probably from our Minister ; but the lower Order in Leghorn assure me, that they can nor will any longer be put off by promises ; that the French shall quit Leghorn, and that they are determined to rise on them if they are not out of the Town on the 15th August, and that they shall not celebrate their fête of August 10th. I do not fail to give every en couragement to these good dispositions, and assurances of my hearty assistance in case the French do not go off. The plans are laid, but it would be wrong to put them on paper in this uncertain state of the safety of posts. The French here are grown complaisant ; the inhabitants, of course, very insolent : they tell them, ' You shall go by the 15th.' The soldiers every night desert by ten and twenty. The other night, an

4th ; and on the 5th, Buonaparte gained a decisive victory over Wurmser near Lonado. Such is the condensed narrative in the *Annual Register*, vol. xxxviii. pp. 105—107 ; but Colonel Graham's Reports of the proceedings of the Austrian army from its head quarters, published in the "London Gazette" of the 27th of August, 1796, give a much more favourable account of those Actions.

Officer and twenty cavalry went off. We will not go to Mantua to be killed, is their common talk.

I am not sanguine without good reason, but I have at present not the smallest doubt but by the 16th, Leghorn will be free. The English property has been repeatedly put up for sale, but no one will purchase; therefore, except some which is plundered, all is safe; and the French possessing themselves of Leghorn has been of the greatest detriment to themselves, and not the smallest to us. Our Fleet wants for nothing. Naples and Genoa supply us to the utmost of our wishes, while France is effectually cut off from those great supplies of stores of all kinds, and corn, which she used to receive from Leghorn. Tartans, with furnaces and heavy cannon, and fire-vessels, are prepared for my destruction; but I feel so well guarded against all attempts, that I shall not move from my anchorage. Not a Vessel, large or small, has sailed or entered the Port since the day the French entered.

I have the honour to be, &c.

HORATIO NELSON.

TO THE RIGHT HONOURABLE SIR GILBERT ELLIOT.

[Autograph, in the Minto Papers.]

Captain, Leghorn Roads, August 10th, 1796.

My dear Sir,

So true it is that to men who have only the good of their King and Country at heart, the same ideas must strike them. I feel the highest degree of pleasure from your letter. If you think it right to communicate to the General[8] that you have opened your mind to me, pray assure him there is nothing I feel greater pleasure in than hearing he is to command. Assure him of my most sincere wishes for his speedy success, and that he shall have every support and assistance from me. Guns we may land, but our stock of shot is very small. We may be sure of all the country people being our friends. I send you great news, and have no doubt but the battle of the

---

[8] Lieutenant-General John Thomas de Burgh, Commander of the Forces in Corsica: he succeeded as thirteenth Earl of Clanricarde, in December, 1797, and dying in July, 1808, was succeeded in his honours by his son, the present Marquis of Clanricarde.

3rd was favourable to our friends. L'Eclair is gone to Genoa
for more news, which I shall instantly send you. I do not
keep the Speedy ten minutes, so anxious am I that you should
hear of this success. You will be so good as to send to the
Admiral when opportunity offers, for I do not keep Speedy
to write more than this line.

Ever believe me your most faithful

HORATIO NELSON.

Not a word will escape me.

His Excellency the Vice-Roy.

TO THE RIGHT HON. SIR GILBERT ELLIOT.

[Autograph, in the Minto Papers.]

Captain, Leghorn Roads, August 11th, 10 P.M.

My dear Sir,

Major Logan is just come on board, and I have had a long
conversation with him, as you wished, and I believe the Major
sees the attempt in the same favourable point of view in which
I do. I have satisfied Major L. that there is no danger in
the attempt—that the troops can be landed and embarked
without danger, even should a superior force come against
them, a thing not very likely to happen. Being on shore,
there can be no doubt but that nearly every Tuscan is friendly
to us. The Grand Duke, to keep the Venetians quiet, has
employed them, at three pauls a day, to clear the Pisa canal,
and they are at work under my guns. More, perhaps, is to
be done by conciliatory measures, than open force (not
that I mean force is not to be used; I am sure it must, but
that I will come to hereafter). What is our object? To dis-
possess the French of Leghorn; not to keep it I suppose, but
free the Leghornese from a foreign garrison. This is the
point.

If your Excellency declares that our object is only to
restore Leghorn to its legal Government, and that, so soon as
that is done, that the English troops shall leave the garrison,
and offer, at the same time, honourable terms to the French,
(which the General can meliorate, or the contrary, as things
alter,) this must make even our enemies in Leghorn wish the

French to quit the place. I suppose the French will, as is usual with those gentlemen, determine to die in [the] works—at least, they say so; a mortar battery will probably bring them to reason. A regular siege I take to be entirely out of the question. Every house that is destroyed must make all the Leghornese urgent with the French, and probably the rich may pay the Commander well for a capitulation; which, if I know Frenchmen right, he will not be averse to; so that he can say mortars, shot, fire, &c. &c.—in short, to hold out long enough to make a letter. On the first landing, a proclamation of our intentions must strengthen our interest. I wish to make it also the interest of the friends of the French for them to quit Leghorn. It would be impertinent in me, but I rely on your goodness to say a word about the cannons, mortar, &c. A few guns may be necessary. I have 18-pounders and 32-pounders; the Diadem, 18 and 24-pounders. I can land two 32-pounders and 1000 shot, the same of 18-pounders, and two guns; Diadem, two 18-pounders and 1000; in all, two 32-pounders, 1000 shot; four 18-pounders, 2000 shot. Something must be left to chance. Our only consideration, is the honour and benefit to our Country worth the risk? If it is (and I think so), in God's name let us get to work, and hope for his blessing on our endeavours to liberate a people who have been our sincere friends.

Ever, my dear Sir,

Your Excellency's most obedient servant,

HORATIO NELSON.

This is wrote, as Major Logan will tell you, in an instant; therefore you must take my ideas as they flow, and excuse them. I have no copy, and will not keep the Major; pray, at a future day, let me have it.

TO ADMIRAL SIR JOHN JERVIS, K.B.

[From Clarke and M'Arthur, vol. i. p. 308. It appears that in the former part of this letter, Nelson informed the Admiral that he was going to Bastia, to consult with the Vice-Roy on the subject of the Leghorn expedition.]

15th August, 1796.

All will be well, I am satisfied, in our Leghorn expedition, provided Wurmser is victorious; upon this ground only have

I adopted the measure. We are impatient for the battle of
the 3rd. There are reports at Florence that the Austrians are
checked; but no account of this had been published by the
French at Leghorn on the 14th. All the heavy stores are
shipping here and at St. Fiorenzo, and twenty-four hours,
when the opportunity offers, will be sufficient. I hope we
shall have settled Leghorn before the Dons, if they intend it,
arrive. I have still my doubts as to a Spanish war; and if
there should be one, with your management I have no fears.
Their Fleet is ill-manned and worse Officered, I believe; and
they are slow. Lord Bute's letter paves the way very clearly
for your line of acting: Ministers seldom commit themselves
in an opinion. Should the Dons come, I shall then hope I
may be spared, in my own person, to help to make you at
least a Viscount.

[Apparently in continuation.]

August 17th, Bastia.

It is possible that the Spanish frigate bound to Civitá
Vecchia may be intended to carry money from his Holiness,
with the famous Apollo, &c. &c., for the French. It is allowable
to seize the property of Enemies, even on board Neutral Ships
of War. Mr. North tells me, that in the late war two or three
Danish Ships of War were seized by the Spaniards, carrying
stores to Gibraltar; and, on the remonstrance of the Danish
Minister at Madrid, the answer he received was, that it was
not Men of War which were stopped, but Vessels which had
made themselves Merchantmen for the time. This hint may
be useful: the times are critical.

I am, &c.

HORATIO NELSON.

TO THE REVEREND MR. NELSON, HILBOROUGH.

[Autograph, in the Nelson Papers.]

Captain, between Bastia and Leghorn, August 18th, 1796.

My dear Brother,

I always have very great pleasure in receiving a letter from
you, and I have only to beg that you will write more frequently. I laugh at your fancying my being able to buy, at
least, Tofts; and don't you be uneasy when I assure you that

if I have saved my Ship-pay, the Marine I throw in, I shall
be content; but I verily believe that will not be the case. It
is true I have taken numbers of prizes, but I have always
shared with my Squadron, none of whom have I ever received
sixpence from; or, had so many Vessels in sight, that they
run away with the greater part. I believe had I trusted to
my own good fortune and enterprising spirit, I might have
been able to think of Tofts; but that gives me not a moment's
concern. Happy, happy shall I be to return to a little but
neat cottage!

I may tell you as a *secret*, that probably the next letter you
see from me will be in the Public Gazette. An expedition[1]
is thought of, and of course I shall be there, for most of
these services fall to my lot. I have just been arranging
shot, shells, &c. &c., for to give our Enemies. As to rewards, I expect none. I shall not, perhaps, return till a
peace, when our services are forgot. I am not surprised that
the Linen draper should sell his estate. Almost every one
lives beyond his income, and attempts to imitate his neighbour who is richer. However, now, I am a real Commodore
having a Captain under me,[2] I shall share for all prizes, whoever is the taker. A Spanish galleon taken now in this
Country will be a capital stroke, but I can hardly bring myself to believe they will venture on a war. If they do, we
must give up Corsica, and that is all. Our Fleets will cover
every sea but the Mediterranean. The Dons will expect it
at home and abroad. America will readily join against them,
and they will lose Mexico and Peru. America will find
soldiers and privateers, and we must find Ships-of-war. I
have my eye on a Spaniard who is gone, I fancy, to the
mouth of the Tiber, to bring away the tribute of the Pope for
the French. I hope to catch her on her return, if she has
really their busts and money on board.

I rejoice to hear Aunt Mary is so well recovered. Tell her

---

[1] Against Leghorn.

[2] He was appointed a full Commodore, having Captain Ralph Willett Miller as
his Captain, on the 11th of August, three days before the date of this letter. It
appears from the " Order of Battle" of the 19th of August, 1796, that Captain
Charles Stuart was his Captain until Captain Miller joined.—*Original* in the Nelson Papers.

I hope yet to take her by the hand before the year comes round. Tell me all the Norfolk news that is interesting. How are all our friends at Swaffham? Does Mr. Rolfe live at (I have forgot the name) Saham. I shall keep this letter open till I get to Leghorn, which I keep very warm with my blockade, and hope to be able to tell you good news. I thank my nephew[3] for his letter, and if he works as hard in the Church as I have done on the sea, he may become a Bishop.

August 19th.

I am sorry to tell you the Austrians have had a check in Lombardy, by fancying themselves too powerful. It disappoints my hopes for the present. Remember me most kindly to Mrs. Nelson and Aunt Mary, Miss Charlotte, Horace, our friends at Swaffham, and everywhere else. Perhaps you may meet Maurice Suckling: he will now marry Miss Framingham. He may be odd, but I believe none will do more real good with the estate when he comes to it, which I hope he will.[4] Josiah thanks you all for your inquiries: he is not the least altered.

Ever, your most affectionate brother,

HORATIO NELSON.

TO THE RIGHT HON. SIR GILBERT ELLIOT.

[Autograph, in the Minto Papers.]

Captain, at Sea, August 18th, 1796.

My dear Sir,

Our news is not very good, but it is best to know the worst. You have probably the means of knowing what is going on at Leghorn; as to any rendezvous at Monte Christo, I have no idea of that place, or that 4000 men can be embarked in Boats. I shall send a Ship to Genoa, almost directly, for news. I hope it will be better.

Ever yours most faithful,

HORATIO NELSON.

His Excellency the Vice-Roy.

[3] Horatio, only son of the Rev. William Nelson, who was then but seven years old.

[4] Vide vol. i. p. 108. Lieutenant Maurice Suckling did marry that lady.

TO THE RIGHT HON. SIR GILBERT ELLIOT.

[Autograph, in the Minto Papers.]

Captain, off Bastia, August 18th, 1796.

My dear Sir,

Seeing your Excellency's boat coming on board, I beg leave to suggest that one of your privateers should look at Cività Vecchia and the mouth of the Tiber, to see if the Spanish frigate is there, and to endeavour to find out if she is taking the riches of Rome on board: if she is, I shall seriously think of getting hold of her, but I believe I shall get the Admiral's opinion before she sails.

Ever your most faithful,

HORATIO NELSON.

His Excellency the Vice-Roy.

TO THE REVEREND MR. NELSON, BATH.

[Autograph, in the Nelson Papers.]

Captain, August 19th, 1796.

My dear Father,

Your most affectionate letter of July 4th gave me infinite pleasure, and I assure you that no small part of the satisfaction I feel in doing my duty, is knowing the pleasure it will give you and my dear wife. As to the rewards, I think it very possible those who are on the spot will get them, whilst we who fag at a distance are forgot. The *last* service is always the best, for it is natural. This gentleman had a Victory two years ago, the fruits of which we enjoyed, and perhaps have lost again. The other is on the spot to receive his reward before the newer object presents itself. But all cannot be employed near home, and half the rewards are useless. God forbid I should ever lose myself so much as to be Knighted. Fame says we are to have a Spanish war in this Country. The only consequence it can be to us may be the necessary evacuation of Corsica, and that our Fleet will draw down the Mediterranean. The Dons will suffer in every way for their folly, if they are really so fool-hardy as to go to war to please the French.

I am now an established Commodore, having a Captain

appointed to the Ship ; therefore my professional rise is regular
and honourable. My brother William thinks I have been
making a fortune, but I have assured him of the contrary. I
am glad to hear Aunt Mary is so well recovered, and as all
the world will make peace, I cannot be very long before my
arrival in England, and shall rejoice to have a neat cottage.
I am not surprised at the selling of estates : each man imitates
his richer neighbour. As to our news here, the Austrians do
not seem victorious anywhere, and the consequence is, the
French force friends where they are superior. Corsica is
threatened and will probably fall, for the French have a very
strong party in the Island. This is not strange. All their
connexions are with the French. Great numbers of Corsican
officers are in high stations in their Army, which cannot be
the case with ours

[*torn*]

always asks after you. He must take his chance as I have
done before him. Last year, from various causes, I missed the
opportunity of sending something to the poor. I send it in
time this year, and at the proper time you will dispose of it.
As to Aunt Mary, I wish to send some little thing she may
want. Maurice sent her wine some time back, and the credit
of it

[*torn.*]

TO HIS ROYAL HIGHNESS THE DUKE OF CLARENCE.

[From Clarke and M'Arthur, vol. i. p. 309.]

19th August, 1796.

Sir,

In the present situation of affairs I will not let slip an opportunity of writing to your Royal Highness. The check
which the Austrians have met with in Italy on the 3rd, 4th,
and 5th, must give another unfavourable turn to the affairs of
our Allies. The French have made the most of it, and they
were no doubt masters of the field of battle. I wish to say
more than I dare to trust to the post, of the object of an expedition that was to have taken place the moment Wurmser
became victorious, in which I was to have been a principal

actor.—Our affairs in Corsica are gloomy; there is a very strong Republican party in that Island, and they are well supported from France; the first favourable moment, they will certainly act against us. The French are endeavouring to get over from the continent twenty and thirty men at a time, and they will accomplish it in spite of all we can do. Gentili, a Corsican, who commanded in Bastia when we took it, is arrived at Leghorn, to command in Corsica. Twenty field pieces have been sent from here, and are landed near Ajaccio.

As to our Fleet, under such a Commander-in-Chief as Sir John Jervis, nobody has any fears. . . . We are now twenty-two Sail of the Line, the combined Fleet will not be above thirty-five Sail of the Line, supposing the Dons detach to the West Indies. I will venture my life Sir John Jervis defeats them; I do not mean by a regular battle, but by the skill of our Admiral, and the activity and spirit of our Officers and seamen. This Country is the most favourable possible for skill with an inferior Fleet; for the winds are so variable, that some one time in twenty-four hours you must be able to attack a part of a large Fleet, and the other will be becalmed, or have a contrary wind, therefore I hope Government will not be alarmed for our safety—I mean more than is proper. I take for granted they will send us reinforcements as soon as possible, but there is nothing we are not able to accomplish under Sir John Jervis. I am stationed, as you know, to blockade Leghorn; and now Corsica may prevent my going to the Fleet, which I feel very much, but all cannot be as we wish. I assure your Royal Highness that no small part of my pleasure in the acknowledgment of my services, has arisen from the conviction that I am one of those of whom from your early youth you have been pleased to have a good opinion; and I have to beg that your Royal Highness will ever believe me your most faithful,

HORATIO NELSON.[5]

[5] His Royal Highness replied to this letter from Richmond on the 3rd of October following:—

"Dear Nelson,

"I received yours of 19th August, from Leghorn Roads, a few days ago, and must lament, in common with you and every good wisher of his country, the constant

TO THE SWEDISH CONSUL AT LEGHORN.

[From Clarke and M'Arthur, vol. i. p. 310, who state that in the first part of this letter, Commodore Nelson assured the Swedish Consul that the Commander-in-Chief of his Majesty's Fleet in the Mediterranean, wishing to alleviate the calamities which the French, by their possessing themselves of the Neutral port of Leghorn, had brought on the Swedish Nation, had, in consideration of the near approach of winter, when the Baltic Sea would be frozen over, authorized him to permit the departure of Swedish vessels without cargoes.]

20th August, 1796.

You will therefore direct such Swedish vessels as may wish to quit the port of Leghorn, to come out of the Mole, and anchor near me, when I will furnish them with passports, to prevent their being molested on their voyage.

I am, &c.

Horatio Nelson.

defeats the Austrians have suffered in Italy. It is a lamentable circumstance how victory has attended the French in their different expeditions on the Continent. The Archduke, I hope, in Germany will exterminate these monsters ; in which case, I yet trust Italy will be once more freed from requisitions and devastation.

"It is a pleasant circumstance to every Englishman, and particularly to professional men, to see the Navy of this Country ride triumphant in all quarters of the globe : Still, dear Nelson, I never wish to hear of twenty-two British Sail of the Line being opposed to thirty-five of the Enemy, though a Combined Fleet. I venerate and esteem Jervis's abilities as high as any man, and I am well acquainted with the intrepidity and valour of the English sailor, and the knowledge and experience of their officers ; and, as a seaman myself, I can easily understand the advantages to be taken from variable winds and calms. However, the risk, believe me, between such unequal force, is too great.

"You very properly shew your discretion by your caution ; and, therefore, you will understand mine if I do not by letter enter into the future destination of your Fleet, and of the intentions of our Government towards the Mediterranean. A Spanish war is inevitable, and I look forward with an anxious eye to the conquests which our Navy will make ; and render themselves if possible more the terror and the admiration of the world.

"I feel very sensibly the flattering expressions you use in your letter to me, relative to being so many years my acquaintance. I loved and esteemed you from the beginning as an ornament to the service, and must ever regard you as such. The time must come when we shall be where both my birth and my experience in the Navy ought to place me—I mean when I am entrusted with the executive management of the Admiralty. It then will be both my duty and my inclination to serve the deserving—amongst whom you will stand ever one of the foremost. For the present, adieu, and ever believe me to be, Dear Nelson, your most affectionate friend, William."—*Original* in the Nelson Papers.

TO THE RIGHT HON. SIR GILBERT ELLIOT.

[Autograph, in the Minto Papers.]

Captain, Leghorn Roads, August 20th, 1796.

My dear Sir,

I send you all my letters which you will be so good as to forward to Sir John Jervis when read; nothing new at Leghorn; the same paper is stuck up at Leghorn as at other places, it is extraordinary they should have been so long writing this famous victory—half, I hope, is not true. Mr. Heatly, the great victualler, writes me that the supply he is now procuring, will be the first and last, for the port of Genoa will be shut. If this should be the case, I really think we ought, in the moment they shut their Port, to seize the Island of Capraja. We shall find stores, arms, &c., for the use of the Corsican expedition, for by Mr. Drake's account, and it is more probable than Monte Christo, that Island is now to be the road to Corsica. I have sent the Blanche to Genoa, but my numbers are so small, that I may not always be able to convey my news to your Excellency the moment I receive it. I expect her by the 23rd, for she is not to enter the Port; if one of your Hired-vessels could be here by that time, and occasionally call on me at other times, you will get news from Genoa very quickly.

Ever your Excellency's
Most obedient servant,
HORATIO NELSON.

His Excellency the Vice-Roy.

TO ADMIRAL SIR JOHN JERVIS, K.B.

[From Clarke and M'Arthur, vol. i. p. 310.]

Leghorn Roads, August 20th, 1796.

We are anxious indeed to receive news. All our expected hopes are blasted, I fear, for the present, by Wurmser's feeling too sure. Austria, I suppose, must make peace, and we shall, as usual, be left to fight it out: however, at the worst, we only give up Corsica, an acquisition which I believe we cannot keep, and our Fleet will draw down the Mediterranean. The Dons will pay most severely, if they are fools enough to involve themselves in a war. The way to Corsica is to be through the Island of Capraja. Should Genoa shut her Port against us, I shall presume to advise the Viceroy instantly to seize Capraja, where he will find all the arms, &c. for Corsica, and probably French troops. I send you a letter from Mr. Drake, not very favourable for a successful campaign.

[Apparently in Continuation.]

August 22nd.

On Thursday last, 1225 French left Leghorn with General Vaubois, and almost all the Officers; the French Major de Place commands the remainder, which is not more than eight or nine hundred men, that is the utmost. Seventy or eighty sailors are gone with the Army, to manage, as they say, some flat-bottomed Boats that are prepared for crossing the inundations about Mantua, which place they are determined to storm. Another very extraordinary thing has taken place here; all the cannon that had been mounted on the works, except on the Mole, has been dismounted, and put into the same stores whence it was taken. What does this mean? an evacuation, I should rather think; yes, and that they are ordered to replace things as they found them. Mr. Wyndham, my reports say, is gone to Rome, and thence to the King of Naples,[6] to endeavour to induce his Majesty to recommence hostilities. Lively is sent to examine the coast to the southward, to see if any number of boats are collected to carry over troops to Corsica. Lord Garlies is active, and I feel a real pleasure in having him with me, I only hope for an opportunity of giving him some real service.

August 23rd.

I again hope that the defeat of the French is at hand, they are surrounded at Verona. The Austrians on the 15th got a reinforcement of 20,000 men. Buonaparte is reported to have been wounded.

I am, &c.

HORATIO NELSON.

[6] An Armistice between Naples and France had been signed on the 5th of June, which lasted until the Treaty of Peace, concluded on the 10th of November following.

TO SIGNOR JAQUES DE LAVELETTE, GOVERNOR OF LEGHORN.

[From Clarke and M'Arthur, vol. i. p. 311.]

Leghorn Roads, 22nd August, 1796.

Your Excellency, from the great length of time you have been at Leghorn, well knows that it is the pride of the English to relieve and alleviate the misfortunes even of their enemies. Much more, then, would it be a pleasure to England to assist the Tuscans in their distress, from the breach of faith of the French, and their most extraordinary conduct towards a Neutral State. I therefore had given passports to every fisherman to go out as usual with their tartans; and it is with astonishment I find that these poor fishermen, who are obliged to come on board my Sovereign's Ship to obtain that permission, which not only maintains a number of poor Tuscan families, but also supplies the Town of Leghorn with fish, are by your Excellency, as President of the Health-office, subjected to a quarantine of ten days, although I have given my word of honour, which until now was never doubted, that I am with my Squadron *in libera practica*.

I must desire, Sir, that you will represent my liberal conduct, contrasted with yours, to his Royal Highness, your Sovereign. You must have noticed my long forbearance, in not having repelled the firing of the batteries against his Britannic Majesty's Ships; you must have known that it has been humanity, and not want of power, towards a Town and its innocent inhabitants belonging to your Sovereign, whose situation I have pitied: but now, as the Enemy have withdrawn such numbers of their troops, and the Tuscan soldiers being so superior to the French, I beg leave to acquaint you, that if in future one shot is fired at his Britannic Majesty's Ships, I shall chastise the battery; and whatever damage may happen to the Town, your Sovereign and the inhabitants of Leghorn must lay the entire blame on his Excellency Jaques de Lavelette, and not on your Excellency's most obedient servant,

HORATIO NELSON.

TO THE RIGHT HON. SIR GILBERT ELLIOT.

[Autograph, in the Minto Papers.]

Captain, Leghorn Roads, August 22nd, 1796.

My dear Sir,

I have no means of sending to you, and my numbers are now so small, that I much fear I cannot send to you so often as I wish. On Thursday and Friday, they say 1225 French marched out of the Town, and with them 78 or 80 sailors, which they want to use in the flat Boats they have prepared for crossing the river and inundations about Mantua. There does not remain here more than 800 or 900 of the worst of the troops. General Vaubois and all the superior Officers are gone. The French Major de Place commands, and every day small parties go off. There is also another very extraordinary circumstance: all the cannon which the French had taken from the Arsenal to mount on the works, are all taken from thence, and replaced in the storehouses where they came from, except on the Mole-head. What can all this mean? Is it a prelude to an evacuation? But I shall have further particulars this evening. You will have heard from Mr. Wyndham: my reports say he is gone to Rome, and to the King of Naples at Monte Casino, to endeavour to induce him to recommence hostilities. I take this to be in consequence of your letter. The 400 Corsican soldiers which were in Leghorn are gone to Mantua, and I am assured that no Tuscan boat will carry a Frenchman over to Corsica. However, I have sent the Lively to examine minutely the coast. Although the French had the field of battle, yet I am confident, from all I hear, that their loss of men was very many more than the Austrians. I am to have to-night particulars of the action of the 13th, near Corona. Pray, Sir, when Sardine comes to Bastia, if the Gorgon is arrived, send her to me.

23rd.—I am in great fear my reporter is taken: something extraordinary must have happened, or he would have been on board this morning. Twenty tartanes from Leghorn are round me; they all agree that very few French remain in Leghorn, that the cannon are all replaced in the storehouse, and that no paper has been stuck up since the

Action of the 3rd and 4th; and they are all inveterate against
Mr. Villettes, who is certainly in the French interest. You
will form an opinion what is proper to be done. Nearly all
the Light-horse are gone off this morning. The Ragusa
boat tells me that a courier arrived yesterday, which says that
the French are surrounded in Verona, that the Austrians had
got all their Army united, and kept the French in. It was
said last night that Gentili was arrived at Leghorn, but he
does not know if it actually was so. This is the time to strike
our blow; and even if we could not succeed, of which I have
not the smallest doubt, what an Army the French must send
to dislodge us from the water-side! The Danes say there are
reports that the French, on the 20th, lost 9000 men near
Verona. All agree the Austrians received a great reinforcement on the 15th: they report 20,000 men. I hope Blanche
will arrive for me to send you Genoa news, but L'Eclair
must go.

Ever believe me, dear Sir,
Your Excellency's most faithful servant,
HORATIO NELSON.

His Excellency the Vice-Roy.

May I beg my private letters may go, when opportunity
offers, for England—by post, I mean.

TO MRS. NELSON.

[From Clarke and M'Arthur, vol. i. p. 312. In this letter he informed Mrs.
Nelson that as soon as affairs were settled with the Grand Duke, he should pay his
Holiness the Pope a visit, and he added—]

Leghorn Roads, August 23rd, 1796.

I do not think that he will oppose the thunder of the Vatican
against my thunder; and you will, I dare say, hear that I am
at Rome in my barge. If I succeed, I am determined to row
up the Tiber, and into Rome.

Yours, &c.
HORATIO NELSON.

TO THE RIGHT HON. SIR GILBERT ELLIOT.

[Autograph, in the Minto Papers.]

Captain, Leghorn Roads, August 23rd, 1796.

My dear Sir,

I have the honour to transmit your Excellency a letter from [the] Ragusan Consul; my answer has been that I would immediately send it to you and Sir John Jervis, but that whatever indulgence is granted must be to Ships without cargoes. All proper representation has been made to the Grand Duke, and the answer they have received has been, you are at liberty to quit the Port. If your Excellency is still of opinion, that in the present situation of affairs, it will be more political in us to allow the departure of Vessels without cargoes to those Nations who ask it of us, I shall, without waiting for the answer of my Admiral, permit their departure. I have the honour to perfectly agree with your Excellency's former sentiments, that on all considerations it would be honourable in us to allow of the departure, and that to the lower Order in Leghorn the desolation and misery which the French have brought on them would be more apparent.

I am, with the highest respect,
Your Excellency's most obedient Servant,
HORATIO NELSON.

His Excellency the Vice-Roy.

Pray forward the enclosed to the Admiral; the Danish Consul has sent the same : he has fifteen Danes.

TO THE RIGHT HON. SIR GILBERT ELLIOT.

[Autograph, in the Minto Papers.]

Captain, Leghorn Roads, August 25th, 1796.

My dear Sir,

The Blanche is not yet arrived from Genoa, but I shall keep the letters open till she does. Our Leghorn news becomes every day interesting; you will see, even by the Governor's letter, that a number of the French have quitted the place, the remainder are in the three forts of Fort Nova, Marata, and the Old Fort; they send certificates to the gates, but the

forts are shut up every night. Gentili, with a number of
Corsicans, are here, and are certainly intended to be carried
to Bogniano; they have sent some few from towards Piombino ; these went first to Capraja, from thence to the coast of
Ajaccio, from whence, two nights ago, came a French Row-
boat, with four or five Frenchmen, supposed to be Officers.
Whatever distress they may feel, yet Corsica seems a great
object to them, more, perhaps, to keep us in hot water, than
with any real hope of conquest. Nor do these Privateers go
to the southward and through the Straits of Bonifaccio, or
do they go round by Cape Corse ; nothing has a chance of
stopping these Boats but Vessels like themselves; the only
way is to cut at the root, for whilst Leghorn is open, this
communication must always be going on. There has certainly been a battle between the 12th and 20th, and as the
French have published nothing, we may hope it has been
favourable to us.[7]   I am sure Leghorn would be no very difficult task : the inhabitants, to a certainty, would admit us into
the Town, when we should soon master these forts.   This
moment brings to my eyes a body of about 200 men, with the
Corsican flag carrying before them; they are partly from
Nice, and joined by Genoese, &c., on the road.   The time approaches when we shall either have to fight them in Corsica
or Leghorn.   I believe they are by far less dangerous here
than in Corsica.

Thursday night.—I have had my reporter off, and a
Tunisian, with a Leghorn merchant, to beg a Venetian for
Tunis may be allowed to sail with her cargo.   I send you
his letter, but I cannot think we can open the door for
allowing any Nation to quit the Port with cargoes.   I explained to him the great difference respecting goods and
money actually belonging to the Dey of Algiers, that we were
actuated by the love of justice, and that he must be sensible
that our blockade was the natural consequence of the French
taking Leghorn, and that it must be blockaded till they
quitted it, when the Port would again be neutral ; but I submit
to your Excellency the propriety of allowing this cargo, which,

---

[7] Buonaparte defeated Marshal Wurmser in two Engagements, on the 11th and
12th of August.

perhaps, may be English property, to sail from this place. All the English property is collected into proper warehouses and the French say it will shortly be sold. This merchant says it is believed there was a great battle on the 16th, 17th, and 18th, and that the French army is now only 22,000 men, and retreated to Lodi,[8] but nothing is published. All agree about Gentili and the Corsicans. The Leghornese will, if they are sure of the French being beat, to a certainty join us, and enable us to get into the Town, when we could soon get the forts. I am anxious for the Blanche.

August 26th.—Last night came on board a letter from the Spanish Consul, requesting leave for the Ships of his Nation to quit the Port, in particular one which is loaded with construction timber for Carthagena ; this Ship, of all others, should not pass me. If I thought it would be a Spanish war, I would get hold of her, but at present that would be going too great lengths. The Blanche is in sight. Reports, by the man last night, that the French say more Corsicans are coming from Nice, to embark for Corsica. They all bring their wives and children. As my letter is merely of news, pray forward it [to] Sir John Jervis, with the enclosures. The Lively had two men killed and two wounded, the other day, by a shot striking her, yet I do not, unless forced, like to fire into Leghorn.

Ever believe me,
Your Excellency's most faithful humble Servant,
HORATIO NELSON.

His Excellency the Vice-Roy.

Now is the time for the Corsican privateers to act, but I fear they will not.

TO THE RIGHT HON. SIR GILBERT ELLIOT.

[Autograph, in the Minto Papers.]

Captain, off the Gorgona, August 27th, 1796.

My dear Sir,

I am on my way to the Fleet, it is a great object that the Ship should join, and as there is no Captain joined her, I

---

[8] This report was untrue.

think it advisable to go in her myself. If the Spaniards go
to war with us, which I own I cannot even yet bring myself
to believe, I hope to be in time to assist our worthy Admiral,
and at all events I shall wish to talk a little with him. I
wrote you so fully by the Gorgon, Leghorn news, and
Blanche has such packets of Genoa news, that there is little
for me to say. I hear many of these Corsicans from France
are to be carried by Greek vessels from Genoa, Port Especia,
Piombino, and, in short, the whole coast; if each takes eight or
ten, it is almost impossible we can stop any of them, but if
they are sure of being taken care of when they land in
Corsica, the part of the Kingdom where they are so concealed
or assisted must be rotten at heart. Others say Monte Christo
is the rendezvous; this can be easily ascertained, as all the
people from Leghorn believe there has been a battle between
the 12th and 20th. Why should we not hope it is so, for why
should Leghorn have had so very large a part of its force
taken away, if the French have entirely forced the Austrians
out of Italy?

I shall desire the Privateer to call on board the Lively,
who is in Leghorn Roads, and commands the blockade
till my return, to receive from Lord Garlies such news as
he may have picked up. I take for granted the Admiral
will send me back in a Cutter, but I shall give him a good
ordered Seventy-four, and take my chance of helping to
thrash Don Langara,[9] than which few things, I assure you,
would give me more real pleasure. This will nearly be their
force from Cadiz: Spanish, ten; French, seven; Carthagena,
not more than seven; Toulon, not more than eight or ten.
Suppose them all united, thirty-two or thirty-four; our Fleet,
twenty-two Sail of such Ships as hardly ever before graced
the Ocean, but I will suppose it is to be a Spanish war—they
know Man has joined. I do not think they will come up the
Straits. Solano may be gone to the West Indies. Langara
and Richery, I really think they would do us more damage
by getting off Cape Finisterre; it is there I fear them. Oh,
our Convoy, Admiral Man, how could you quit Gibraltar?[1]

---

[9] Admiral Don Juan de Langara, Commander-in-Chief of the Spanish Fleet.

[1] The conduct of Rear-Admiral Man, an Officer of reputation, excited the astonishment of the whole Navy. In October 1795, he was sent from the Mediterranean.

Sir John, however, is a man of political courage, no less neces-
sary than warlike—will certainly, in my humble opinion, beat
Don L., if he attempts to come this side San Sebastian's,
with Richery in company. Whatever the Don may say, we
must not trust. Believe me, dear Sir,
　　Your Excellency's most obedient, faithful servant,
　　　　　　　　　　　　　　　　　　HORATIO NELSON.
Pray forward my private letters.

His Excellency the Vice-Roy.

Lord Garlies has the necessary directions about the light
vessels.

Fleet by Admiral Hotham, with six Sail of the Line and a Frigate, in pursuit
of Admiral Richery's Squadron, and continued detached until the declaration of
War with Spain, in October, 1796, when he was expressly commanded to join
Sir John Jervis, both by the Admiral and the Admiralty. From the inferiority of the English Fleet to that of the Enemy, his arrival was anxiously
expected; but instead of obeying his orders, he cruised for a short time off
Cape St. Vincent, and then actually proceeded with his Squadron to England,
where he arrived on the 30th of December. Nelson's opinion of his conduct is
shewn by his Letters; and the Commander-in-Chief, writing to the Secretary of the
Admiralty, on the 11th of November, said—" I have greatly to lament the measure
Rear-Admiral Man has taken, in proceeding to cruise off Cape St. Vincent with the
Squadron under his orders, for a limited time, and then of repairing to Spithead."
To Earl Spencer, on the same day, Sir John Jervis expressed himself in still
stronger terms:—" The conduct of Admiral Man is incomprehensible: he acknow-
ledges to have received my orders and the duplicates, and that he opened the
dispatches which directed my continuance in the Mediterranean. I had taken the
liberty of cautioning him against consulting with the Captains under his orders, who
all wanted to get to England; and yet, by a passage in his public letter, it appears
that he acted with their concurrence." ＊ ＊ ＊ " I cannot describe to your Lordship the disappointment my ambition and zeal to serve my Country has suffered by this
diminution of my Force; for had Admiral Man sailed from Gibraltar on the 10th
October, the day he received my orders, and fulfilled them, I have every reason to
believe the Spanish Fleet would have been cut to pieces."—*Tucker's Life of Earl
St. Vincent*, vol. i. pp. 239, 240.
　　Captain (afterwards Lord) Collingwood, writing from Gibraltar on the 5th of
December, observed—" The Spanish Fleet, nearly double our numbers, were cruising
almost in view, and our reconnoitring Frigates sometimes got amongst them,
while we expected them hourly to be joined by the French, who had already possession of the harbour in which we lay. But no Man appeared, and as the Enemy
began to annoy us from the shore, we sailed on the 2nd of November. We arrived
here on the 1st instant, and judge of our surprise to find that Admiral Man and his
Squadron had gone off to England. He is well known to be as brave a man as any
in the world, and no one has more anxiety to do what is right. I am confident he

TO THE RIGHT HON. SIR GILBERT ELLIOT.

[Autograph, in the Minto Papers.]

Captain, Leghorn Roads, September 3rd, 1796.

My dear Sir,

I left our good Admiral two days ago, all well, and send by Lord Garlies a letter from him. Whatever fears we may entertain for Corsica, it is certain Government at home have none, by taking so very respectable a part of your force away. I have only to say that you can propose no way in which I can be useful to you that I shall not most readily concur in, and have desired Lord Garlies to converse with your Excellency how we can be most beneficially employed. The other service his Lordship is ordered upon, you will, if possible, I well know, most readily assist him in. For Leghorn news, and for all others from this quarter, I beg leave to refer you to his Lordship.

Believe me with the most perfect respect,
Your Excellency's most faithful,
HORATIO NELSON.

His Excellency the Vice-Roy.

I send you a letter to read in which your expedition to Leghorn is glanced at; please to forward it to the Admiral.

May I beg the favour of my private letter for England.

TO ADMIRAL SIR JOHN JERVIS, K.B.

[From Clarke and M'Arthur, vol. i. p. 313.]

Leghorn Roads, 3rd September, 1796.

I arrived yesterday, and now send you two copies of letters from Mr. Wyndham. Lord Garlies goes over to Bastia this

always means the best; but the thing is incomprehensible, and God knows by what arguments he will justify it."—*Correspondence of Lord Collingwood*, vol. i. p. 45.

When Rear-Admiral Man arrived in England, the Admiralty wrote to him, dated on the 2nd of January, 1797—" That they cannot but feel the greatest regret that you should have been induced to return to England with the Squadron under your orders, under the circumstances in which you were then placed;" and their Lordships signified their displeasure by adding, that " orders will be sent to you, either by this or to-morrow's post, to strike your flag and come on shore."—*Tucker's Memoirs of Earl St. Vincent*, vol. i. p. 216.

How he escaped a Court-martial is very surprising. Admiral Man does not appear ever to have been again employed; and he died an Admiral of the Red, in September, 1813.

day, to converse with the Vice-Roy, who, Captain Cockburn tells me, has apparently no fears for Corsica: his information, I must suppose, is good, and that he knows of every
additional scoundrel who sets foot in the Island. You will
comment on the day when Mr. Wyndham says the treaty[2] was
signed—the very day Langara sailed from Cadiz; but the
sudden return, and all Mr. Duff's[3] letters, give us a large field
for conversation, which may amuse your Vice-Admirals, and
drive away ennui.

I have before told the Vice-Roy, how impossible it is
for us to stop boats which row faster than our barges; but
that, whatever he proposes, I should most readily concur in
for sending him every assistance. I enclose an official
answer from the Grand Duke to my letter, which I forgot
to show you. Some parts border a little on impertinence;
however, it has made us laugh; and the King of England
cannot, although I hear he is one of the best masons in
his Dominions, stop shot-holes half so soon as I can make
them. I yet hope for a good and glorious campaign by sea
and land, and I wish that Mr. Wyndham's fears may be
realized, and that the Toulon Fleet may come out; but I fear
they will not.

　　　　　　　　　　　　　I am, &c.
　　　　　　　　　　　　　HORATIO NELSON.

NOTE ADDRESSED TO THE GENOESE GOVERNMENT.

[From a Copy in the Admiralty.]

Commodore Nelson is surprised and astonished to hear that
some bullocks, the actual property of his Britannic Majesty,
have been prevented from being embarked in the Port of
Genoa. This case is so new and extraordinary, that the Commodore hopes there is some mistake in the matter, which will
be rectified on this representation, for the Commodore cannot
conceive that the property of his Sovereign or Subjects can be
stopped by a friendly Power on any pretence whatsoever. It

---

[2] Offensive and defensive between France and Spain, which was signed on the
19th of August.

[3] James Duff, Esq., British Consul at Cadiz.

is usual for all Nations, when they think it right to prohibit
the exportation of provisions, to give notice that after a certain
time no provisions will be allowed to be exported.

The Commodore hopes, for the happiness of the Genoese
Nation, as also for that of the English, that the Serene Government will take no measure which may intercept the harmony
which so happily subsists between his Sovereign and the
Serene Republic of Genoa, and which the Commodore has at
all times so studiously endeavoured to preserve.

Dated on board his Britannic Majesty's Ship Captain,
    Mole of Genoa, September 4th, 1796.

                                HORATIO NELSON.

NOTE ADDRESSED TO THE GENOESE GOVERNMENT.

[From a Copy in the Admiralty, transmitted in Admiral Sir John Jervis's letter
of the 17th of September, 1796.]

                                About September, 1796.

The Commodore [not] having yet received any answer to his
Note of September 4th, is induced to trouble the Doge with a
visit, to request his influence for a speedy answer being given,
and at the same time to assure the Doge that the oxen are
bought under the full sanction of the Proclamation of October,
1795; and the Commodore gives his word of honour that it
has been proved to him that not one of the beasts have been
bred or purchased in the Republic of Genoa.

Therefore, as this sudden prevention of their embarkation,
contrary to the proclamation of October, 1795, must have
arisen from some gross misrepresentation, the Commodore
hopes now he has had the honour of explaining to the Doge
the whole affair, that a favourable answer will be given to his
application, for the cattle being the property of his Britannic
Majesty, can never be sold to any person, and they must at
present be considered as sequestered by order of the Serene
Government, and at a time when the Commodore, by order
of his Admiral, Sir John Jervis, Commander-in-Chief of the
British Fleet, is showing every attention to the subjects of
Genoa, in permitting several of their Vessels to leave Leghorn
with their cargoes, and permitting wood to be embarked from
the Tuscan State for the City of Genoa.

TO HIS EXCELLENCY FRANCIS DRAKE, ESQ.

[From a Copy in the Admiralty.]

September 9th, 1796.

My dear Sir,

Mr. Brame, or rather Mr. Bird, will detail to you the whole history about the bullocks, and what steps have been taken on my part. I hope you will not think I have gone too far. I assure you it has gone much against me to fish in Diplomatic water, for there must be many forms in getting through these matters which I am unacquainted with. I shall endeavour to have something here to wait your answer. The French seem to dictate to this Government what they shall do. I was present yesterday at the meeting of the Merchants, and told them what I knew of the return of the Spanish Fleet into Cadiz. However, they say they will be prepared; and if they let me know in time, I will most certainly afford them every protection in my power; and if the Genoese Government seize (sequestered they have) the property of the King, God knows how long they will regard the property of the Subject.

The Russian Minister has just sent me word that, last night, the Doge put the question to the Senate to give me thirty bullocks, but it was overruled, and I am not to have one. The principal argument was, we shall offend the French, and we had better offend the English than them, for they will not injure us so much. I have desired that all your papers may be sent on board me ; if not, Mr. Brame will destroy them.

Mr. Brame is unfit for business.

[Not signed.]

TO THE GENOESE SECRETARY OF STATE.

[From a Copy in the Admiralty.]

His Britannic Majesty's Ship Captain, Genoa Mole,
September 10th, 1796.

Sir,

I have to request that you will inform me whether an answer is to be given this day to the repeated applications for the embarkation of his Britannic Majesty's cattle. If I receive none, I shall, in the evening, send off an express to his Excellency Mr. Drake, and another to his Excellency Sir John Jervis, Admiral of the British Fleet, and withdraw his Majesty's Ships from the Port of Genoa; and I believe that their Excellencies will take such measures as are proper in this extraordinary conjuncture, in the detention of his Britannic Majesty's property. Hoping, for the happiness of the two Nations, that the Government of Genoa will take no step which may for a moment intercept the harmony which has lately prevailed between his Britannic Majesty and the Serene Government,

I have the honour to be, Sir,

Your most obedient servant,

HORATIO NELSON.

TO MRS. NELSON.

[From Clarke and M'Arthur, vol. i. p. 316.]

September 10th, 1796.

I have memorialized the Senate, and had an audience of the Doge, but still these wise heads are puzzled. The Doge was very curious about me; he asked my age, said he had heard much of me, that the blockade of Leghorn was strict beyond what he could have thought possible; at the same time, he publicly thanked me for my goodness on many occasions to Genoese vessels. It has hitherto, my dearest Fanny, been my good fortune to have combined the strictest rigour of my duty with gaining the good-will of the parties interested. My conduct has been open: that has been my secret, and it has answered.

Yours, &c.

HORATIO NELSON.

TO ADMIRAL SIR JOHN JERVIS, K.B.

[From a Copy in the Admiralty.]

Captain, off Genoa, September 11th, 1796.

Sir,

You know of my orders for L'Eclair, to come to Genoa for a Convoy of bullocks, which Mr. Heatly had bought for the use of the Fleet. Last Sunday I was surprised to meet the L'Eclair at sea, and more so, to find that the Government of Genoa had refused the embarkation. I send you Mr. Brame's [letter]—I should say, Mr. Bird's (his son-in-law), for Mr. B. is scarcely able to write—which is a faithful detail of all that has passed.

As I send every paper, I shall not trouble you with a repetition of them. This Government is in terror of the French: many of its Members are bought over, and all, I believe, think that the English would be a far more generous Enemy than the French: therefore, they would rather offend us than them. In my conversation with the Doge, I hinted (on his rather insinuating that a great Army close to their gates might cut off all supplies of meat for the City), that we had the power to cut off supplies of corn and wood which come by sea. His answer was, what was true, that a small Country like Genoa, was in a terrible situation between great Powers at war. I urged our claim to justice, having conformed to the laws of Genoa. He admitted we had justice and right on our side.

You will, Sir, I am sure, do what is right, for a more flagrant disregard for the English can never be told. If the property of the Sovereign is sequestered, God knows how long the property of the Subject will be safe: certainly no longer than it suits their convenience.

I hope you will think I have done what is proper, and shall be happy to receive your commands how to act. I should think a firm demand from you, with a threat of detaining Genoese provisions so long as they detain his Majesty's, will have its proper effect.

Every day French vessels come to Genoa laden with powder, shot, &c., and land them at St. Pierre d'Arena,[4] where the French have large magazines of powder, and other stores. They have four guns mounted on the beach, for their protection, and are going to erect a large battery and have one thousand men to defend it. They have demanded one of the large palaces for an hospital, and taken it. If the war continues, it

---

[4] In Commissary Sucy's letter to the Commandant of the Lanthorn Battery, he said that the agents of the Government there had guaranteed the French landing " goods" in the harbour of St. Pierre d'Arena.

must end in the French taking possession of Genoa, (supposing their success continues.)   Such an event has happened!
which I must reserve for another letter.   Whatever may be
the consequence, my mind tells me I have done perfectly
right, and I hope you will also think so.

Believe me, Sir,
With the greatest respect,
Your most obedient servant,
HORATIO NELSON.

TO ADMIRAL SIR JOHN JERVIS, K.B.

[From a Copy in the Admiralty.]

Captain, off Genoa, September 11th, 1796.

Sir,

As I wish only to be supported by truth, I send you every
Paper relative to the subject, and firmly believe I shall receive
the approbation of your judgment.[5]   I shall only declare to
you, on my honour, that I had not the smallest intention to
attack the French vessel, had not the French themselves
forced me to it.   I do not think neutrality can be all on one
side.

I have the honour to be, &c.

HORATIO NELSON.

Sent another letter to the Consul, desiring him to exert
himself, and not to give way one inch; that I felt I had acted
right; and desired he would look out for inhabitants of St. P.
d'Arena to state the truth, and also the soldiers in the Lanthorn Battery.

About seven o'clock the Town began, ceased for half an

---

[5] This affair, which is the subject of many subsequent Letters, was complained of
by the Commissary Director, Sucy, to the Commandant of the Lanthorn Battery, in
a letter dated St. Pierre d'Arena, 25 Fructidor, (11th September,) in which he
said that the Commandant did not fire on the English sloops, [boats,] for violating
the neutrality, until their prize was at a distance, and that he discontinued it when
the English ships were within reach.   In reply, the Commandant stated, that he
could not suppose the English sloops of war, which came out of the harbour, would
be guilty of a violation of neutrality, and the more so as they had given their word
of honour not to make reprisals for twenty-four hours after their departure; adding,
that he had directed the batteries to fire as soon as he was aware of the attack on
the French tartan.   These Letters are in the *Annual Register*, vol. xxxviii. "State
Papers," pp. 199, 200.

hour between ten and eleven o'clock, when they recommenced, and amused themselves till one P.M. (I did not return one shot) over us, under us, and on all sides, shot and shells. Not a man hurt, or the Ship touched.

I have had several Genoese boats off; they are very riotous, but the lower Genoese are our friends.

Six P.M.—My Boat is come off that went with a Flag of Truce to the southward of Genoa. The Captain told the Officer verbally that the Ports of the Republic were shut to the English. I must observe, that all communication with the Government of Genoa is in writing: they [neither] receive, nor usually send, anything but in writing.

TO JOSEPH BRAME, ESQ., BRITISH CONSUL AT GENOA.

[From a Copy in the Admiralty.]

September 11th, 1796.

Sir,

I have to desire that you will immediately go to the Government, and acquaint them that the French have a battery at St. Pierre d'Arena, which has commenced an attack on his Majesty's boats sent to St. Pierre d'Arena, to look out and inquire for our Boat which some deserters took away last night; and I gave the Officer orders if the French fired on him, to make reprisals, which he has done, by bringing off a French Vessel discharging her cargo of Ordnance Stores; and I am not a little surprised to find the battery at the Lanthorn firing on the English boats for their just reprisal.

I only mention the above circumstance to mark the fact more strongly, for I believe myself perfectly justifiable by the laws of Nations, to attack the Enemy's batteries wherever they may be placed; and I believe it is the first time the Serene Government has taken a decided part of one Enemy against another. I shall acquaint Sir John Jervis with the whole circumstance, and the Vessel will await his orders.

I am, &c.

HORATIO NELSON.

FACTS.

[From a Copy in the Admiralty.]

September 11th, 1796.

A French battery at St. Pierre d'Arena—the French landing all sorts of warlike stores under the guns of Genoa—the
French battery fired on his Britannic Majesty's Boats—the
Boats board and take a French Vessel landing warlike stores
abreast of the French battery, on which, all the guns of
Genoa open a fire on his Britannic Majesty's *Ships,* and not a
shot fired in return to the Genoese fortresses, and only three
fired at the French battery, to mark the power of the English, and their humanity in not destroying the houses and
innocent Genoese inhabitants.

How can the Serene Government of Genoa mark this conduct as strictly Neutral? Where the French erect batteries
cannot be considered as Neutral ground.

Everything in Genoa and under its guns or parts of the
Coast which are really Neutral, the Commodore ever has, and
will most inviolably respect.

The inhabitants of St. Pierre d'Arena, the Genoese soldiers
on the batteries will, if they declare the truth, support the
whole of my assertions, that the French fired first, and that
the English Boats had committed no act good or bad, before
the French fired.

Dated on board his Britannic Majesty's Ship, Captain, off
Genoa, September 11th, 1796.

HORATIO NELSON.

For,

The knowledge of every person in Genoa, and its neighbourhood.

TO HIS EXCELLENCY FRANCIS DRAKE, ESQ.

[From a Copy in the Admiralty.]

Captain, at Sea, September 12th, 1796.

Dear Sir,

Having transmitted the whole of my correspondence in the
very extraordinary affair of yesterday, I shall only endeavour to
relate some few circumstances and observations as they strike

me, for I cannot doubt but on proper representation by you, that the affair will redound to my credit, instead of appearing against me.　No one, as you will do me the justice (I flatter myself) to say, ever more studiously endeavoured to keep out of scrapes with the Genoese than myself, knowing the influences of terror which the French have in their councils; but there are bounds beyond which insolence cannot be borne.　I know it is the common language of the Senators to hold England as a better enemy than the French; and I believe it is the first time that any Neutral State, which one of the Powers at war in part possesses, in the least interfered between the belligerent Powers, but allowed them to fight it out.　But if the Neutral State thought fit to preserve its neutrality, surely the parties attacked had the most undoubted right to expect assistance, and not the attackers.　This must be allowed by all interested parties; and if the Genoese find one person who saw the fact, that will say my two Boats committed any act, either good or bad, unless rowing towards San Pierre d'Arena would be so considered, (the Boats were not 100 yards from the Lantern Battery when the French opened their fire,) I will permit all the world to say I am wrong.

Had I intended to take French vessels, I could have sent out our Boats in the night and carried them off without any person's knowledge; but when I weighed from Genoa, I had not a knowledge that any Vessel was at St. Pierre d'Arena; nor, when our two Boats went away, did I know of what Nation the Vessels were, for I was not one cable's length from the Mole, with a land wind which would have carried any Ship, in half-an-hour or less, to the spot.　Had my intentions been hostile, the two Ships could have sent nine Boats and 100 soldiers, and as many seamen; but I had not, on my first ordering the Boats which had been rowing round the Moles, the smallest idea of any firing.　My Boats have always cutlasses, and each Boat two or three muskets in them.　The Lieutenant asked me what he should do if the French fired?　I told him to take the Vessel lying there, if she was laden with warlike stores; but even if she were French, and laden with common merchandize, not to bring her off.

I again assure you, that our two Boats could not have been

more than 100 yards from the Lantern Battery (for I do not think the French Battery is 300, in a straight line) before the French fired, as I have related.

I immediately sat down to write Mr. Brame (No. 1), which I sent by a Lieutenant.[6] Whilst I was writing, the firing continued from the French, and began by the Genoese; but you will mark my forbearance in your representation. They will acknowledge, that from half-past seven A.M. to one P.M., with the intermission of about half an-hour, the batteries kept a continual fire of shot and shells. I should have been more pleasantly situated had I returned the fire; for my Ship would have been covered with smoke. The lives which must have been lost in the Town, and the damage done, would have been immense; but, as at Larnea, not one shot did I fire at Genoa. This, the whole Town will say is true; and that it was in my power is to be presumed, or they would not have fired on me for such a length of time. That Being who has ever protected me, did not permit, wonderful to tell, one shot to strike the Ship: over us, under us, and on all sides of us, even to throwing the water upon our decks, (by the shot striking the sea,) but no, not one hurt us.

I lay off Genoa with as perfect ease as usual. At half-past one P.M. I sent a Flag of Truce on shore, to the southward of the Town. Lieutenant Pierson was taken into the Guard-room, and the Captain of the Port sent for to receive him. Mr. P. desired to go into the Town, but was told the Government could not be answerable for his safety, on which he delivered my letter, directed to the Secretary of State, in-closing a letter for Mr. Brame, (Nos. 2 and 3.) At six P.M. the Captain of the Port returned, and said that my letter had been delivered, and that he was told by the Secretary of State to say, that the Ports of the Republic of Genoa were shut for the present against the English, but that the Government would find ways to send me an answer. I had a letter from Lieutenant Compton, by a Genoese boat, telling me, that while he was with Mr. Brame, a party of armed French attacked the four boys who row the Jolly-boat, but that the guard at Porta Reale defended them, and fired on the

----

6 Vide p. 265, ante.

French, killed one Frenchman by putting three balls through him, and wounding some others.

The Genoese boat-people told me, that the rage of the French was excessive. They declared they would cut the Volunteers into pieces the size of tunny-fish. All was riot; the Government had reinforced the guards at all the gates and batteries, and the drawbridges were all up, and the gates shut. Some ladies and gentlemen who came to Mr. Pierson at the Guard-room, from their villas, to ask what was the matter and real truth, said, the Officer[7] who commanded at the Lantern was a strong Jacobin. Therefore, this, my dear Sir, ought to be the man punished: our Boats were under his protection. You will do what is right. I shall trouble you no more, only to assure you, that I am your most obliged and faithful servant,

HORATIO NELSON.

TO ADMIRAL SIR JOHN JERVIS, K.B.

[From Clarke and M'Arthur, vol. i. p. 319.]

September 14th, 1796.

I assure you, dear Sir, on the most mature reflection, I feel nothing in this affair to reproach myself with; and I shall much rejoice to find you think the same. Some steps must necessarily be taken. You have formerly said you would pardon my writing opinions to you; therefore, should not a Squadron demand of the government of Genoa the free admission of their Ports? (the insult and cruelty of firing on our Boats is, I suppose, more a Ministerial affair;) and in case of refusal, then comes the consideration, what is next to be done? are the French to be attacked at S. Pierre d'Arena? is the trade of Genoa to be stopped? I mean, are all Genoese vessels to be sent into St. Fiorenzo, and there ordered to remain with the masters and crews on board, in full possession of their Vessels, until the Government of Genoa open their Ports and give satisfaction for what has happened? This last, to be sure, may be easily got over: I have in some measure taken upon myself to chastise the French, although supported by Genoa. I shall close this letter with whatever conversation I may have with the Vice-Roy.

[7] Lieutenant-Colonel Bediani.

[In continuation.]

September 15th.

It is no small degree of pleasure for me to tell you, that the Vice-Roy most fully approves of every measure I have taken. He also wishes that the taking and securing Genoese Ships be adopted, as a pledge for the safety of the English property at Genoa, and as a measure of reprisal for the conduct of the Government. As the Vice-Roy will write more fully, I shall not touch on our intended expedition.

I am, &c.

HORATIO NELSON.

TO . . . .

[From a Copy in the Admiralty.]

[About 17th September, 1796.]

Gentlemen,

This Government seeming determined not to give any answer to the representation made by the Consul and myself, and you having asked my opinion how you are to act with the cattle ordered by Mr. Heatly, the Agent-Victualler, for the account of his Majesty, I have no doubt but it will be proper for you to keep the cattle at the least possible expense till you receive your directions from Sir John Jervis, K.B., Commander-in-Chief of his Majesty's Fleet, either through Mr. Heath, or some other person ordered by the Admiral to deliver his orders.

I am, &c.

HORATIO NELSON.

TO ADMIRAL SIR JOHN JERVIS, K.B.[8]

[From a Copy in the Admiralty, and the original draught in the Nelson Papers.]

Captain, Harbour of Capraja, September 19th, 1796.

Sir,

Having received on board the Captain and Gorgon the Troops ordered for the attack of the Island of Capraja, under

[8] On transmitting this letter to the Admiralty, Sir John Jervis said—"I enclose, for the information of the Lords Commissioners of the Admiralty, Commodore Nelson's report of the expedition against, and capture of the Island Capraja; the

the command of Major Logan,[9] I sailed from Bastia on the evening of the 14th, with these, Vanneau, and Rose, and was joined next day by La Minerve, Captain Cockburn. From excessive calm weather, it was the 17th before we arrived off the Island, which afforded time to prepare every means for the prevention of our landing, there not being more than three places where it is possible for troops to get on shore. The length of passage, which was unexpected, induced Major Logan to divide his forces, in order to distract the attention of the Enemy, and it had the most complete effect; and a landing was made at the north end of the Island, under cover of the Rose, Lieutenant Walker, and Vanneau, Lieutenant Gourly, who conducted themselves very much to my satisfaction. At six o'clock, on the morning of the 18th, we sent in a Flag of Truce, with our Summons, No. 1; received Answer, No. 2; our Reply, No. 3; Capitulation, No. 4; and, at four o'clock in the afternoon, the troops took possession of the Fortresses. I landed from the Squadron 100 troops, under the command of Lieutenant Pierson, of the 69th Regiment, whom Major Logan and myself hold ourselves much pleased with for his management of the Capitulation, and also a party of seamen under Lieutenant Spicer, who carried cannon up the mountain with their usual spirit and alacrity. It would be doing injustice were a distinction to be made between the two services; all had full employment, and I am confident

conduct of which reflects the highest honour on his skill, judgment, and enterprise, and on the good training of those under his command, among whom Captain Cockburn of his Majesty's Ship Minerve, stands eminently distinguished, as do Lieutenants Berry, Spencer, and Noble of the Captain. The latter was desperately wounded in one of the successful enterprises in the western Riviera of Genoa, and the two first-named have exposed their persons on all occasions, with that cool, deliberate courage which forms so prominent a feature in the Commodore's character, and I beg leave to recommend them to their Lordships' favour and protection." —*Tucker's Memoirs of Earl St. Vincent*, vol. i. p. 230. The attack on Capraja was not, however, quite so satisfactory as would appear from the official accounts of the affair; for General de Burgh, in a letter to Commodore Nelson, dated Bastia, September 20, 1796, thanking him for his zealous co-operation with the troops, said—" I am, however, mortified to learn that there should have been any check in the business, which, although but a temporary one, places the British troops in a light they do not usually appear in. Any Corsican failures I can easily make my mind up to, never expecting much good from our worthy fellow-subjects of this Island."—*Original* in the Nelson Papers.

[9] Major James Logan, of the 51st Foot; he was made a Lieutenant-Colonel in 1800.

but one opinion prevailed, that of expediting the surrender of the Island by every means in their power.

I cannot conclude without assuring you of my most sincere approbation of the conduct of Captain Cockburn of La Minerve, Captain Dixon of the Gorgon, and Lieutenant Berry, who had the temporary command of the Captain, and of every officer and man in the Squadron.

> I have the honour to be, Sir,
> Your most obedient servant,
> HORATIO NELSON.

N.B.—Two French Privateers are taken, and two ditto destroyed with several Vessels, their prizes, and some magazines of French property on shore.

INCLOSURE No. I.

TO THE GOVERNOR OF THE FORTRESS AND ISLAND OF CAPRAJA.

Commodore Horatio Nelson, and Major James Logan, Commanders of the Forces by Sea and Land of His Britannic Majesty before the Island of Capraja, Summon the Fort and Island of Capraja to surrender to the Arms of His Britannic Majesty.

The Commissary, the Commandant, and other Officers, Civil and Military, in the service of the Serene Republic of Genoa, and all the Garrison shall receive all Military Honours, and be treated with all regard and attention, with liberty to stay in the Island, whilst their conduct is not prejudicial to the British Garrison; or retire to Genoa, as they may please.

All people in the Civil Department to be continued in the Offices which they at present hold, if they are not found acting contrary to the tranquillity of the Island.

All the inhabitants of the Town and Island, are assured of perfect security for their persons, property, and religion; and the British Government will not fail to take every measure for promoting their interest and their prosperity, whilst the Island remains in their Administration : the present laws will be preserved.

No Contribution will be demanded, nor any Taxes which they do not at present pay to the Government of Genoa.

All the Public effects will be demanded and taken into custody. Commissaries will be appointed by us to take an exact inventory, which the British Government will account for to the Serene Republic, directly the differences between them shall be happily terminated.

All French property, public and private, shall be given up to us, and be at our disposal till further orders from the Vice-Roy of Corsica, and the Admiral.

If the present favourable terms are not immediately acceded to, the Commander of the Fort rests responsible for the effusion of blood, and all the other consequences of his refusal.

Dated in Camp, before the Town of Capraja, this 11th day of September, 1796.

HORATIO NELSON.
JAMES LOGAN.

INCLOSURE, No. II.

TO THE GOVERNOR OF THE FORTRESS AND ISLAND OF CAPRAJA.

Dated at Camp, before the Town of Capraja, September 18th, 1796.

Sir,

Had your answer been a refusal to treat, before this time, our attack by Land and Sea would have commenced, and the lives and property of innocent inhabitants would have been sacrificed by your fruitless attempt against the superior forces attacking you. We will not permit any delay beyond one hour, for you to take your resolution of treating with us; and we assure you such favourable terms will never again be offered by, Sir,   Your very humble servants,

HORATIO NELSON.
JAMES LOGAN.

CAPITULATION OF THE FORT AND ISLAND OF CAPRAJA.

First.—The Troops to march out of their works with the Honours of War, and the Garrison to go to Genoa, or stay in the Island, on their parole.

Secondly.—The Religion and Laws shall be preserved.

Thirdly.—No more Taxes shall be paid to the English than have been paid to the Serene Republic of Genoa.

Fourthly.—All the Officers of the Municipality to hold their present situations, so long as they conduct themselves properly.

Fifthly.—Possession to be taken of the Fortress at four o'clock this afternoon.

Sixthly.—Inventories to be taken of the Stores which belong to the Serene Republic of Genoa.

Seventhly.—The property of the Inhabitants, as well as that of the Officers of the Garrison, shall not be touched.

Eighthly.—All French property shall be given up to the English.

Ninthly.—The Officers with the Garrison shall be embarked and carried in security to Genoa, as by the first Article.

Dated September 18th, 1796.

HORATIO NELSON.   AGOSTINO AGNOLO, COMSᴿ.
JAMES LOGAN.   BROS MAGGIORE.
                        ⎰ PASQUAL SOSSOSS.
                        ⎱ DOMᴷ. CORRIO.
                          GEO. SALERI.
                          Tutti li Padri del Commune.

———

TO THE RIGHT HON. SIR GILBERT ELLIOT.

[Autograph, in the Minto Papers.]

Captain, Harbour of Capraia, September 19th, 1796.

My dear Sir,

I congratulate you most sincerely on the capture of this Island,[1] which I hope will give additional security to the King-

---

[1] Sir Gilbert Elliot's instructions to Commodore Nelson respecting the capture of Capraja, a small Island about nine miles E.N.E. of Cape Corse, dated on the 15th of September, contain a full explanation of his motives for adopting that strong measure. After stating the provocations of the Genoese government, which had not only refused satisfaction for its insult and hostility on the 11th, but had intimated, in answer to the representations made on that subject, that all the Ports of the Republic were shut against the British ships; that hostilities had also been committed against Corsica, and his Majesty's subjects, by Vessels fitted out at Capraja during the last two years, contrary to the laws of neutrality; that so far from any satisfaction having been obtained, the Genoese Government had even refused to admit a British Vice-consul at Capraja, who might have given information of such injurious proceedings, and have restrained the abuses of which we had reason to complain; that an Agent of the French Republic had also been constantly established and avowed at Capraja, who had carried on every species of depredation and hostility; and that the Enemy had made a practice of coming over to that Island with stores and ammunition destined for the re-conquest of Corsica, the Viceroy proceeded : "I

dom of Corsica. I shall only say how much I am satisfied
by having had to act with an officer of so much zeal and
ability as Major Logan, and that I do not believe the two
services ever more cordially united than on the present occasion. Believe me, dear Sir,

Your most faithful and obedient servant,

HORATIO NELSON.

His Excellency the Vice-Roy.

P.S. I received your Excellency's letter at half-past one
this day, for which I most sincerely thank you. We could not
send to make the fire, as that Town did not know of the surrender. I hope Mr. Udney's news of victory is true, and not
the French account.

H. N.

have for these reasons judged it expedient to take possession of the Fort and Island
of Capraja in his Majesty's name, and to place a British garrison there, until due
satisfaction is made by the Government of Genoa for the above-mentioned injuries,
and a sufficient security is obtained against a repetition of them in future. I should
have wished extremely to know the Admiral's pleasure on this occasion; but having
already had an opportunity of being acquainted with his general sentiments on the
subject, and the facility of executing this enterprise depending very much on dispatch
and secrecy, I am well assured that Sir John Jervis will not disapprove of my carrying this measure into immediate effect. Under these circumstances, I do not scruple,
Sir, to request your assistance and co-operation, having had many opportunities of
knowing your zeal and readiness on every occasion of public service. For particulars respecting the troops to be embarked on this expedition, and all other matters
relative to its execution, I beg leave to refer you to Lieutenant-General de Burgh,
Commander-in-Chief. Major Logan, who commands the troops, will concert every
point with you, and will join you in the summons, capitulation, or any other correspondence which you may find it necessary to have with the Commissioner or
Commandant of the place.

" It remains only to point out the footing on which I deem it expedient to take
possession. The place must be summoned to surrender to his Majesty's arms ; the
most favourable terms may be offered to the Officers civil and military, and to the
garrison ; they may be carried to Genoa if they think proper, or may remain at
Capraja on their parole, but not to take any part hostile to the English garrison.
Every degree of protection must be promised to the inhabitants, and assurances that
every attention will be paid to their interests and prosperity, during our occupation
of the place. The public stores are to be delivered up on inventory, and are to be
accounted for to the Genoese government, if an accommodation should hereafter
take place. All French property is to be delivered up to the English, and the
British flag is to be hoisted on the fort or towers. Wishing you success in this
enterprise, and reposing entire confidence in your zeal and abilities, as well as in the
spirit of your Officers and men, I have the honour to be, &c., GILBERT ELLIOT."—
Clarke and M'Arthur, vol. i. p. 320.

TO THE COMMANDER OF THE SPANISH FRIGATE.

[This Correspondence is taken from the Official Dispatch in the Admiralty: the original draughts of some of the Letters are in the Nelson Papers. Commodore Nelson fell in with a Spanish Frigate on his passage from Capraja to Leghorn, on the 20th of September, which first hauled her wind to the eastward, and afterwards bore down to the Commodore. The following correspondence then took place between Commodore Nelson and the Spanish Captain, Don Juan de Sannava.]

His Britannic Majesty's Ship Captain, at Sea, 20th September, 1796.

Sir,

Having heard that several English Ships have been detained in the Ports of Spain, and also that the Court of Spain has made an Alliance, offensive and defensive,[2] I desire to know of you, on your honour, if you know that there is a war between England and Spain?

I am, Sir,
Your very humble Servant,
HORATIO NELSON.

REPLY OF THE CAPTAIN OF THE SPANISH FRIGATE.

[From a Copy in the Admiralty.]

Abord.de la Fregate Espagnole La Vengeance, le 20ᵉ 7bre, 1796.

Monsieur le Commandant,

Je suis parti de Carthagène le 4 de ce mois; il n'y avoit alors rien d'extraordinaire, et je n'ai connoissance d'aucune déclaration de guerre ni d'aucune alliance défensive ou offensive avec la France; et quant à la difficulté que vous me faites de me laisser entrer à Livourne, elle m'étonne d'autant plus que c'est une affaire qui devrait être traitée entre les Cours; on ne m'a point absolument parlé de semblable difficulté, et au contraire il m'a été recommandé de maintenir la bonne intelligence entre elles; il ne m'est absolument pas possible d'attendre, comme vous désirez, une réponse du Vice-Roy de Corse, ainsi, dans le cas où vous ne pourrez pas abso-

---

[2] A Treaty of Peace, offensive and defensive, between France and Spain, was signed at Ildephonso, on the 19th of August, 1796; and on the 11th of October following, War was declared by Spain against Great Britain.

lument me donner le passage sans cette formalité, je me
retirerai, et j'informerai ma Cour de tout ce que s'est passé dans
cette occasion.

J'ai l'honneur d'être,
Monsieur le Commandant,
Votre trés humble et trés obéissant serviteur,
JUAN DE SANNAVA.

TO DON JUAN DE SANNAVA, CAPTAIN OF THE SPANISH
FRIGATE LA VENGEANCE.

[From a Copy, in the Admiralty.]

His Britannic Majesty's Ship Captain, at Sea, 20th September, 1796.

Sir,

It is not possible for me to desire a Spanish Officer to do
what would be considered in the smallest degree dishonourable.

I am in doubt, Sir, whether it is War or Peace between the
two Courts. You, Sir, say you are sure that all is Peace,
and that the most perfect good understanding subsists between
the two Courts.

Thus circumstanced, I have to request as a mark of your
desire to cement that harmony, that you will attend me to
Bastia, to speak with the Vice-Roy of Corsica on this very
delicate question.

Should, Sir, you refuse to comply with this most reasonable
request, the fatal consequences must rest with you, and I
must do my duty in using force.

I have the honour to be, Sir,
Your most obedient Servant,
HORATIO NELSON.

Don Juan de Sannava.

TO COMMODORE NELSON.

[From a Copy in the Admiralty.]

Abord de la Fregate Espagnole La Vengeance, la 20e 7bre, 1796.

Monsieur,

Puisque vous vous opposez à ce que j'arrive à Livourne, je
n'y irai pas; mais d'aucune manière je ne puis aller à Bastia, à

moins que vous ne m'y obligiez par force, et le parti que vous
prenez est un acte de violence, et si vous ne voulez pas com-
promettre les deux Nations, vous ne pouvez pas vous refuser à
ajouter foi à ma première lettre ; et si l'incertitude où vous êtes
sur la bonne harmonie que régne entre les deux cours vous
parait une raison suffisante pour vous déterminer à un acte
d'hostilité, vous serez responsable de toutes les suites que
pourra entrainer une semblable détermination.

Si ce que j'ai l'honneur de vous dire ne vous suffit pas, per-
mettez moi de reprendre la route d'Espagne. Si vous vous
opposez encore à ce dernier parti, veuillez envoyer votre balandre
à Bastia avec une lettre que je vous adresse pour le Vice-Roy,
j'attendrai avec vous que la réponse arrive, mais je ne pourrai
me dispenser de faire part à ma Cour du retard que vous aurez
mis à ma commission, et de l'obstacle que vous mettez à mon
retour.

J'ai l'honneur d'être avec respect,

Monsieur le Commandant,

Votre trés humble et trés obéissant serviteur,

JUAN DE SANNAVA.

TO DON JUAN DE SANNAVA.

[From a Copy in the Admiralty.]

His Britannic Majesty's Ship the Captain, at Sea,
20th September, 1796.

Sir,

From the repeated assurances you have given me, on your
honour, that there is no offensive alliance entered into by
Spain with France against England, I am induced to shew
your Court how desirous an English officer is to preserve
that harmony and good understanding which ought ever to
subsist between our two Countries, by allowing you to return
to Spain, instead of enforcing my reasonable request for you
to proceed to Bastia, to speak to the Viceroy of Corsica.

Therefore, Sir, if you will pledge me your word of honour
that the harmony between our two Courts is uninterrupted, I
will, on your giving me your honour that you will proceed
direct for Spain, allow you to proceed. I am, Sir,

Your most obedient servant,

To Don Juan de Sannava.   HORATIO NELSON.

TO COMMODORE NELSON.

[From a Copy in the Admiralty.]

Abord de la Fregate Espagnole La Vengeance, 20ᵉ 7bre, 1796.

Monsieur,

Puisque vous l'exigez, je consens à ne pas entrer à Livourne, et à m'en retourner en Espagne, où je serai forcé de rendre compte des difficultés que vous me faites, et de tout ce que s'est passé entre nous au sujet de ma mission, et de l'obstacle que vous avez mis à son exécution ; vous demeurez, Monsieur, responsable de toutes les suites qu'il peut entrainer; et quant à la parole d'honneur que vous exigez de moi de ne pas entrer à Livourne, je vous la donne.

J'ai l'honneur d'être,

Monsieur le Commandant,

Votre trés humble et trés obéissant serviteur,

JUAN DE SANNAVA.

TO ADMIRAL SIR JOHN JERVIS, K.B.

[From a Copy in the Admiralty.]

Captain, at Sea, September 21st, 1796.

Sir,

Yesterday morning I saw a Spanish Frigate coming from the southward, who, when she raised our hull, hauled her wind to the eastward. In about one hour after this she bore down to us, and I sent on board the letter No. 1; on which the letters to No. 6 passed between us. As to permitting him to go into Leghorn, that was out of the question with me ; but I chose to have a good deal of communication with him, that I might draw my final opinion if it was War when he sailed, which I am certain it was not. The Second Captain, who came on board, admitted that an English Ship was detained at Carthagena, but that it was in consequence of several Spanish ships having been detained by the English, particularly in Corsica, and that Lord Bute had made representations of the subject. On the other hand, his circuitous route through the Straits of Bonifaccio, wishing to get into Leghorn from the southward, led me to fancy he had cause for not wishing to meet any English Ships of War.

I had before me Mr. Drake's, Mr. Wyndham's, and the
Russian Minister at Genoa's letters, saying that an Alliance,
offensive and defensive, had been entered into between Spain
and France; also Mr. Budd's letter, with Mr. Gregory's.

On the other hand, I had your letter, sending Mr. Gregory's
and Mr. Budd's, but no insinuation that it was actually a war;
the Vice-Roy's, that he considered the Spanish Question still
in suspense, although an embargo had been laid on the English
shipping at Cadiz and Carthagena; that war was not generally expected at Gibraltar, and that it was not to be wished
for by us.

Thus circumstanced, I thought it most proper not to take
him (although I own my fingers itched for it), which I hope
you will approve of. The Don is not aware that it is this
question that was working in my mind, but that it was that I
wanted him to go to Bastia, to know from the Vice-Roy
whether I might allow him to go into Leghorn, and that I
would force him to go to Bastia to have this answer, before
I would allow him to return to Spain.   I am, Sir,

Your most obedient servant,

HORATIO NELSON.

TO THE RIGHT HON. SIR GILBERT ELLIOT.

[Autograph, in the Minto Papers.]

Captain, off Porto Ferrajo, September 24th, 1796.

My dear Sir,

By the Rose at three o'clock on Tuesday morning, I received your letter about Castiglione, and immediately weighed
from Capraja, where, indeed, all my business was not finished,
but I never can rest idle if anything is to be done.   I ordered
Lieutenant Walker to keep by me as I was totally ignorant
of the navigation, and his Cutter would have been most
useful in taking out the Privateers; however, Mr. Walker
thought proper to part from me the next night.   It was last
evening before I got near to Castiglione, having had bad
weather and dangerous navigation, as is rarely met with in the
Mediterranean.   I stood under Cape Troya, when I sent my
boat on board some Neapolitan vessels, and afterwards on
shore to some Neapolitan towers, when I learnt that the

French had taken possession of Castiglione on Wednesday evening with five hundred men, and the Neapolitan officer expected them every moment to take possession of his towers. I have therefore been obliged to bring back your letters, which I have desired Colonel Montresor[3] to forward to Bastia, for my presence is absolutely necessary at Leghorn, where I think I shall be able to get a person known to Mr. Wyndham, of the name of Pensa, to forward your letter; I therefore keep it, and return the others. The Blanche is going to the Fleet, her Captain being to be tried by a Court Martial; and should he come to Bastia, is not fit to be seen by your Excellency till he clears his character. *I send it on a slip of paper*, which please to tear in pieces.[4] I mention this, as I believe the Ship must come for bread.

I send you my letter to the Admiral about a Spanish frigate; I longed to take her, but dare not. You will see that the Don fancies the business hangs in my refusing him leave to enter Leghorn, and not daring, he should return to Spain to make his complaints, without speaking to your Excellency; whereas, in truth, I wished to have brought him to Bastia, to ask your advice whether I should not take him. However, I have acted on the safe side: if we are not to have a war, this *act* of *violence* will easily be got over; and if we are, I hope my not taking this fine Frigate will redound to the honour of some of our active Frigate commanders. The Captain is so much distressed for bread, that if you have the Cutter or Brig to send to Leghorn, pray direct their Commanders to bring us some, as I learn it is baked at Bastia for the Fleet.

Ever, my dear Sir, believe me,
Your Excellency's most faithful

His Excellency the Vice-Roy.   HORATIO NELSON.

Lieutenant Walker just in sight, off Porto Ferrajo. I am very angry with him.

[3] The late General Sir Henry Tucker Montresor, K.C.B., G.C.H., who commanded the Corsican Regiment, and had been nominated Commandant of Elba: he died in March, 1837.

[4] Captain Charles Sawyer of the Blanche was tried by a Court-martial on the 18th of October 1796, for odious misconduct, and for not taking public notice of mutinous expressions uttered against him: being found guilty, he was sentenced to be dismissed from his Majesty's service, and rendered incapable of ever serving in any military capacity whatever. He was superseded in the command of the Blanche by Captain (now Admiral) D'Arcy Preston.

TO THE RIGHT HON. SIR GILBERT ELLIOT.

[Autograph, in the Minto Papers.]

Leghorn Roads, September 25th, 1796.

Dear Sir,

I have with me Diadem and Lively; Captain goes to Ajaccio, Blanche to the Fleet. Yet if you want another Ship besides Gorgon, I must, and will with pleasure, spare you one. Captain Cockburn has great concerns to settle at Porto Ferrajo. I have wrote him, that I wish him, for his own sake, to go there and settle them. I believe all the Privateers on the coast are here, full twenty in number. From what I hear, some were on their passage to Capraja when this S.S.E. wind came on, last Monday night, or we should have had them. I will come over to you when Captain Cockburn joins; but he has my directions to attend to your wishes.

I shall not let L'Eclair sail till midnight, in hopes some person will come off and give us good news. Lord Garlies tells me you are now likely to be quiet with the Corsicans, and that the most sensible part begin now to find it is their interest to adhere to the British Government. Nothing came on board; but, as the Captain calls at St. Fiorenzo, I will send what I hear by her. About 2000 Corsicans are, by report from the Blanche, in the Town. Believe me ever your Excellency's most faithful,

HORATIO NELSON.

His Excellency the Vice-Roy.

TO THE RIGHT HON. SIR GILBERT ELLIOT.

[Autograph, in the Minto Papers.]

September 26th, 1796.

My dear Sir,

I send you the account of Wurmser's success as I receive it, and only hope it is true: if it is, we shall do better than ever. There are about 1000 Corsicans here, who are to be pushed over in the Privateers, as they say, with Gentili, &c.

Ever your most faithful,

HORATIO NELSON.

His Excellency the Vice-Roy.

Since writing the above, I have confirmèd accounts that the paper is true, and, also, that Frankfort is in possession of the Austrians, with all the tribute raised by the French. General Jourdan is reported to have shot himself. Thirty millions of florins.

TO ADMIRAL SIR JOHN JERVIS, K.B.

[Original draught, in the Nelson Papers.]

Diadem,⁵ at Sea, 28th September, 1796.

Sir,

Yesterday morning the Captain sailed from Leghorn, according to your orders, as did L'Eclair, from necessity, the day before—both for Ajaccio. During the course of yesterday, I received repeated information of the movements of the Privateers with the Corsicans on board; the whole number of Corsicans is nine hundred, including all the Officers; six brass twelve-pounders are embarked, thirty-five cases of small arms, and various other articles, in from fifteen to twenty Privateers, and I am certain they mean to sail the first favourable moment. [On the 25th, each Corsican was paid 100 livres.⁶] The Corsicans behave so ill at Leghorn, that the French are determined to send them off, upon the general principle of action of the French—'If you succeed, so much the better for us; if you do not, we get rid of a set of scoundrels.'

Now, Sir, the point for me to consider is, where will the French land in Corsica? the twelve-pounders can only be to possess a Post, (that they meant to have gone by Capraja, at least to possess it, is now certain; the French Commissary was heard to say to Gentili, I told you long ago to possess Capraja; you now see what you have lost.) This, you will say, the Viceroy, from his information and means of knowledge of every part of his kingdom, ought to know better than any one of us. I am on my way to concert with his Excel-

---

⁵ The Captain being sent from Leghorn to Ajaccio, under the command of Lieutenant Berry, Commodore Nelson hoisted his Broad Pendant on board the Diadem, 64, Captain George Henry Towry.

⁶ The passages within brackets occur in the Copy in *Clarke and M'Arthur*, vol. i. p. 325, but are not in the draught: and there are other, though] unimportant variations between them.

lency how I can best use my small force to his advantage,
considering the other services I have to look to.

My idea runs strong that Porto Vecchio, which is reported
to me to be neglected by us, and in which is a fort, is the
object the Enemy mean to possess, which, if their friends in
the Island support them, is sure refuge for their Vessels, and
an opening for the introduction of more troops and supplies.
If the Viceroy will put some men in the fort, and I find
Sardine, I will, with the Venom, which I have ordered from
Leghorn, place them as Guard-ships in the harbour; and I will
endeavour to have a Frigate off that part of the coast. If the
Enemy land nearer Bastia, the Vice-Queen's Yacht (but this
I don't build upon) may be useful. Vanneau, Rose, and the
four small Feluccas, which the Vice-Roy has purchased, must
. . . . . . our communication, and be the searchers for the
Enemy about the Islands between the Main and Corsica.
[These Vessels, with those which may be there, will be sure
to destroy them; although it is possible the men may get
on shore: but I hope, from the small craft which may be
sent about the Islands between Corsica and the main, we may
get accounts of their approach.] If their intention be to land
on the western coast of Corsica, I take for granted they will
never attempt the route by Cape Corse, which would every
hour expose them to the sight of some of our Ships, which
of course would be their destruction. In either case, I think
I shall act upon the idea that they will proceed to the southward, passing the passage of Piombino to Castiglione, the last
place in their possession : but if I can find them on that coast,
I believe (having knowledge of the whole Coast,) I can
destroy their *flota*. But, supposing they pass the Islands, if
we possess Porto Vecchio, although the people may land, yet
there is not shelter for the Vessels the whole Coast to Bastia.
But perhaps they will push for the Coast of Sardinia, Mada-
lina Islands, &c. and pass the Straits of Bonafaccio. This
must be a work of time, and we shall have I hope many
chances for their destruction; [no opportunity for which shall
be omitted by, Sir, your most obedient servant,

                                    HORATIO NELSON.]

What will the Vice-Roy do? Would it not be well to give

notice to the Island that 900 refugee Corsicans are forced by
the French to embark, and to attempt the [*imperfect.*]

[P.S. The French are very angry at our taking Capraja:
the Commissioner was heard to say to Gentili, 'I told you we
should have sent 300 men, and taken Capraja; you now see
the consequence.']

29th September, in sight of Bastia.

The Austrians, under the Archduke, took possession of
Frankfort on the 8th; and it is expected that Wurmser will
once more attack the French: Mantua stopped him again.
All hope for another and younger General. The Neapolitan
property is detained by the French at Leghorn.]

TO ADMIRAL SIR JOHN JERVIS, K.B.

[From Clarke and M'Arthur, vol. i. p. 327.]

Sir,   Bastia, 30th September, 1796.

Last night, on my arrival, I received your most secret
orders ;[7] but I believe many people on this Island have an idea

---

[7] In consequence of the defensive alliance with Spain, it was determined by our
Government that Corsica should be evacuated; a measure which Southey denounces as
"disgraceful;" and he adds, that the Viceroy "deeply felt the impolicy and ignominy
of the evacuation," though it appears to have been highly expedient. On the 25th of
September, Sir John Jervis wrote to Commodore Nelson:—"Having received
orders to co-operate with the Viceroy in the evacuation of the Island of Corsica,
and afterwards to retreat down the Mediterranean with his Majesty's Fleet under
my command, I desire you will lose no time in going over to Bastia, and consulting
with the Viceroy upon the best means of performing the operation, and to give every
assistance in your power towards the completion of it; leaving the blockade of Leghorn under the direction of Captain Cockburn." Soon after the Government had issued
those orders it changed its intentions; and on the 21st of October, a Dispatch was
sent to Sir John Jervis, "signifying his Majesty's pleasure relative to the keeping
possession of Corsica, should the troops, stores, &c., not have been withdrawn; but,
in that event, to occupy Porto Ferrajo in Elba." This Dispatch arrived, however,
too late; and in reply to it, Sir John Jervis said that "the maintenance of the
Sovereignty of the Island of Corsica, under the circumstances of the moment, was
next to impossible, and that he was happy that the removal of the troops, provisions,
and stores to Porto Ferrajo, was an anticipation of his orders." In a Letter to Earl
Spencer, on the 11th of November, Sir John Jervis observed—"I consider it a great
blessing that the evacuation of Corsica had taken place before I had received the
orders to maintain the Viceroy in the Sovereignty of it, which could not have been
effected for any length of time, as the moment the Enemy had landed in force, every
man in the interior of the Island would have taken part with him, and there was not
a tenable part in it."—*Tucker's Memoirs of Earl St. Vincent,* vol. i. pp. 239, 240.

that something like your orders is going forward. I shall not fail to arrange what Transports may be necessary for each Port, which is all that I can do until matters are brought to greater maturity.

The Vice-Roy thinks that there will not be more than about 600 émigrés, Corsicans and French, and the stores I do not believe are very numerous; for the ordnance which we found in the different fortifications, the Vice-Roy will not, I imagine, think it right to take away. His Excellency is very much distressed by this measure, and believes the Island is at this moment in a most perfect state of loyalty to the King, and affection for the British Nation : but what strikes me as a greater sacrifice than Corsica, is the King of Naples : if he has been induced to keep off the Peace,[8] and has perhaps engaged in the war again by the expectation of the continuance of our Fleet in the Mediterranean, hard indeed is his fate : his Kingdom must inevitably be ruined.

I am, &c.

HORATIO NELSON.

[Apparently in continuation.]

Bastia, 3rd October, 1796.

I have arranged upon paper—for more, whilst the affair is to be kept secret, cannot be done—the disposition and number of Transports which will be wanted at each Port ; it must not be considered as exact, for the reason before stated, but it is very near the mark. No cannon or stores taken in the Island are to be touched. Corsica is to be left entirely independent, and with means of defence against any power. God knows what turn the minds of the Corsicans may take when the measure comes to be known. Their love of plunder, and a desire to make peace with their former tyrants the French, may induce them to disturb us, and in that event an embarkation of stores, especially from hence, is by no means easy : but this is a digression. I send you the account of Ships necessary, made out from returns of stores to the General, and by communi-

---

[8] It has been already stated that an Armistice between the King of Naples and the French was signed on the 5th of June, 1796 ; and on the 10th of October, when Corsica was evacuated, and our Fleet was about to withdraw from the Mediterranean, his Neapolitan Majesty concluded a Peace with the Republic.

cation with the Vice-Roy. It will at least shew you that my
mind has not been idle, however my abilities, without a soul
to speak to in the different departments, may fall short of my
wishes.

I am, &c.

HORATIO NELSON.

MEMORANDA RESPECTING THE EVACUATION OF CORSICA

[Autograph, in the possession of James Young, Esq., of Wells, in Norfolk. Commodore Nelson sent an autograph copy of these Memoranda, though not quite so
circumstantial in details, to Sir Gilbert Elliot, which the Vice-Roy received on the
4th of October, 1796. The variations or additions in brackets are from the last
mentioned Copy.]

BASTIA.

1200 Barrels of Powder	} One large Ship.
300 Tons of Stores of all kinds	
600 Emigrés and their effects	{ Three ; at least two.
1500 Troops of all descriptions and baggage, including Capraja	} Five.
Hospital Staff and Sick	{ Boreas Arm. H. T. Ship.
Staff and Effects	One.

For Bastia . . Eleven Sail.

FERRAJO.

Stores and Troops [and English effects], 200,   Two—Three.

FIORENZO.

Stores and Troops 200,   say Two.

CALVI.

Stores and Troops [and Emigrés] . . . . say Three.

AJACCIO.

Stores and Troops [and Emigrés] . . . - Seven.

BONAFACCIO.

Stores and Troops [very few] . . . . . . One.

Merchants are supposed to have Vessels, and the Navy to
take all their own Stores: therefore the above is for the Army
and dependents.

Twenty-eight Sail . . . . . Thirty.

The Vice-Roy proposes, with the approbation of Sir John Jervis, to embark the British Troops on board the Ships of War, which will secure to the Nation this most valuable part of the Embarkation, in the case of a very superior Fleet attacking our Convoy.

French prisoners, about 600, near Bastia . . . . proposed to be sent to Calvi.

Ships of War necessary for the attendance on the Transport:—

Bastia	Captain and two Frigates.
Ferrajo	One Frigate.
Capraja	One Sloop. [One Frigate, which will carry the whole Garrison.]
Fiorenzo	Any Vessels of War. [Not necessary to mention.]
Calvi	One Frigate.
Ajaccio	One Ship of the Line: two or three other Vessels of War. [Two Frigates and Sloops.]
Bonafaccio	Speedy. [Sloop.]

TO ADMIRAL SIR JOHN JERVIS, K.B.

[From Clarke and M'Arthur, vol. i. p. 328.]

October 15th, 1796.

As far as my powers and abilities go, you may rely on me that nothing shall be left undone which ought to be done, even should it be necessary to knock down Bastia. Last night I took the Vice-Roy and Secretary of State afloat; and at daylight this morning, went to General de Burgh, and told him, that from the embarkation of the Vice-Roy, the evacuation and regulation of the Town became entirely military, and of course devolved on us. I hope the General will join me cordially. I have been to the magazines, and have arranged, as far as I have the means, the embarkation of provisions; and

the General says he will have proper guards to keep off the
populace. I have recommended to him to send for the
Municipality, and to tell them that the direction of affairs was
in our hands, and that it would be at their peril were they to
interfere in the embarkation of any property belonging to us.
Had not the Ships arrived when they did, yesterday would
have lost us Bastia: the Ships are laid opposite the Town,
with springs. I am sorry to say the Convoy with Southampton is not in sight, and it is calm; the Captain is not at
anchor: it is the terror of the Ships which will keep order
here. If you could order a Ship round and two Transports,
they would be very useful. I have detached a Felucca to
prepare Capraja, and shall send Southampton to attend at
Elba, but that evacuation not to take place until we are
finished here, which, according to the present appearances,
will be some time. Had not Elba been ours, our Smyrna
Convoy and Transports, I believe, would have been lost. I
purpose taking the Ships from Leghorn when we are absolutely all afloat, or we shall have swarms of Privateers to
torment us.

[In continuation.]

17th October, 1796.

I have received your letter, and am going on as well as a
heavy surf will permit. The dispatches of this morning[1] are
wonderful: do his Majesty's Ministers know their own minds?
If you stay, we are sure of the coast opposite to Elba, and the
fine bay of Telamon. It does not become me to say a word :
the national Honour and the fate of Italy cannot, I am confident, be placed in better hands than yours. The whole
weight is left on you.

---

[1] These Dispatches are said by Clarke and M'Arthur to have contained counter
Orders respecting the proceedings of the Fleet, which had been previously directed
to leave the Mediterranean. It would appear from the following passage in a Letter
from Sir William Hamilton to Commodore Nelson, dated Naples, 31st October, 1796,
that Nelson and Sir Gilbert Elliot had been instrumental in preventing the Fleet
from leaving the Mediterranean. Speaking of the late Vice-Roy of Corsica, Sir
William observed, "A great point indeed was gained by your joint endeavours to
prevent the King's Fleet from abandoning the Mediterranean, and by which I verily
believe these Kingdoms and all Italy are saved from the absolute ruin with which
they were immediately threatened."—*Autograph*, in the Nelson Papers.

18th October.

We are smoother than we have been, but still there is a good deal of surf. I shall strictly attend to all your orders, and will write more fully to-morrow.

I am, &c.

HORATIO NELSON.

TO MESSRS. HEATH AND CO., GENOA.

[Autograph in the possession of J. B. Heath, Esq.]

Bastia, October 17th, 1796.

Dear Sir,

. . . . . I am sorry that you, or any Englishman, should have thought I acted without thought on the 11th September.[2] Whether the measure was right or wrong in itself, is not for me to say. I certainly thought a good deal before I ordered the reprisal. The King's honour was, I conceive, too much insulted to forbear. I ordered my Officers to be prepared for the event. However, we all regret what an innocent Merchant suffers from public measures. The Vice-Roy and Admiral both think I acted perfectly right, even had I attacked the French vessel and battery before they fired. The Genoese were bound in duty to have fired on the French battery, and not on his Majesty's flag. But I mention this, as I really wished to have retained your, and every Englishman's, good opinion. You will hear that we are evacuating Corsica. The inhabitants all in grief, but it is by no means certain we shall leave the Mediterranean. The Spanish are up, but what can they do against us?

I am, dear Sir, your very humble servant,

HORATIO NELSON.

TO MRS. NELSON.

[From Clarke and M'Arthur, vol. i. p. 329.]

About 17th October, 1796.

We are all preparing to leave the Mediterranean, a measure which I cannot approve. They at home do not know what this Fleet is capable of performing; anything, and everything.

---

[2] In the affair of St. Pierre d'Arena.

Much as I shall rejoice to see England, I lament our present
orders in sackcloth and ashes, so dishonourable to the dignity
of England, whose Fleets are equal to meet the World in
arms; and of all the Fleets I ever saw, I never beheld one in
point of officers and men equal to Sir John Jervis's, who is a
Commander-in-Chief able to lead them to glory.

Yours, &c.

HORATIO NELSON.

TO ADMIRAL SIR JOHN JERVIS, K.B.

[From Clarke and M'Arthur, vol. i. p. 330.]

19th October, 1796.

We shall attend chiefly, to that most important article,
ordnance stores: all English guns, mortars, and stores should
most assuredly be removed at every place. My present intention is to embark the troops on the morning of the 21st:
I am sorry to be obliged to take the Line-of-battle ships to
Elba, as I am anxious to have them with you; but they are
so full of stores, and will perhaps be of troops, that I can only
say, twelve hours shall be the outside for Egmont and Excellent, and I shall bring the Viceroy probably in a few hours
afterwards to talk with you. Sardine is under weigh for
Naples, and only waits to make sail until the Viceroy's letter
is finished. Dido is gone to Elba, to acquaint Colonel Montresor, the Commandant, of the great change. Everything
may be done at Porto Ferrajo: you will be delighted with
that Port.   Noon, 19th of October.

We have just received accounts from the Municipality, that
a number of French have landed near Cape Corse, and have
sent to demand of the Municipality what part they mean to
take. The Viceroy has informed the Municipality, that we
wish to quit them amicably, and in the state we promised;
but if they permitted the French to enter the Town, or in any
way embarrassed our embarkation, that it would end in the
destruction of the batteries, and would be highly detrimental
to Bastia. We shall act, I see, with prudence, and retreat in
time. The garrison of Capraja is arrived.

I am, &c.

HORATIO NELSON.

TO ADMIRAL SIR JOHN JERVIS, K.B.

[Autograph, in the possession of Josiah French, Esq.]

Captain, Port Ferrajo, October 21st, 1796.

Sir,

I have the honour to acquaint you that I arrived at Bastia on the 14th, and was joined between that time and the 19th by the Egmont, Captain, Excellent, and Southampton. The Ships-of-the-line were moored opposite the Town, the embarkation of provisions and stores commenced on the 15th, and was continued without intermission till the 19th at sunset. In that night every soldier and other person were brought off with perfect good order from the north end of the Town.[3]

It is unnecessary for me to mention to you the fatigue of the whole of this duty, but I cannot omit to state the merits of every officer employed on it, and most particularly that of Lieutenant Day, Agent for Transports; and much which has been saved may be fairly attributed (without disparagement to any one) to his indefatigable attention and ability. The Captains of all the Ships-of-war, although not particularly in their line of duty, never omitted, night or day, their personal exertions.

[3] Admiral Sir John Jervis, in his Dispatch to Earl Spencer, dated, "Victory, in San Fiorenzo Bay, 23rd October, 1796," gave the following account of the evacuation of Corsica: "Soon after the Viceroy communicated to the Municipality of Bastia that the Island was to be evacuated, the reins of Government were wrested from him, and a Committee of Thirty nominated to carry it on. At this moment a gale of wind at west, which rushed in violent gusts from the mountains, drove the Southampton and the Transports from their anchors. Upon this the Committee of Thirty insisted that an equal number of Corsicans should mount guard with the British at the citadel and barriers, and refused to allow the Viceroy to send a messenger with letters to the Corsican Generals in the French service at Leghorn, having determined to send delegates of their own. The instant I was apprised of this I detached the Captain with orders to the Egmont, (in case Captain Stuart fell in with her,) to proceed to Bastia. Happily, Commodore Nelson arrived there in the Diadem at this most interesting period, and by the firm tone he held, soon reduced these gentlemen to order, and quiet submission to the embarkation; but he wrote to me, that another Line-of-battle ship and a Transport or two would accelerate the work much. I therefore dispatched the Excellent with two Troop-transports, and they had an uncommon quick passage. By the unwearied labour of Commodore Nelson, and those under his command, everything was embarked on the 19th, and he sailed for Port Ferrajo at midnight. On the 20th, the Spanish Fleet, consisting of thirty-eight Sail of the Line and ten Frigates, was abreast of Cape Corse.—*Tucker's Memoirs of Earl St. Vincent*, vol. i. p. 234.

The cordiality with which the whole of this service was carried on between His Excellency the Vice-Roy, Lieutenant-General de Burgh, and myself, I cannot but think it right to inform you of; and that I have the honour to be with the greatest respect,

Your most obedient servant,

HORATIO NELSON.

TO HIS ROYAL HIGHNESS THE DUKE OF CLARENCE.

[From Clarke and M'Arthur, vol. i. p. 332.]

Captain, 25th October, 1796.

Sir,

I was honoured with your Royal Highness's letter of 2nd of September,[4] a few days past, in the midst of a very active scene, the evacuation of Bastia; which being our first post, was entrusted to my direction, and I am happy to say that not only Bastia, but every other place in the Island is completely evacuated. The Corsicans sent to Leghorn for the

---

[4] "Richmond, September 2nd, 1796.

"Dear Sir,

"I am to acknowledge the receipt of yours of 20th and 23rd July, which came safe to hand. I congratulate you on being at last in the command of a Ship of 74 guns, and I believe you did not make the exchange before it was requisite. I always was persuaded you would make the best use of any opportunity to distinguish yourself; you have had many, and I hope you will have more, in which the same good fortune, I trust, relative to your person, will attend you. As for the execution, I am confident the King's service will benefit always under your direction.

"Since your last letter, the Austrian affairs both in Italy and Germany have suffered seriously. I am not yet so blind to the French Revolution, as not to be convinced there must be treachery amongst the Imperial Officers, which, it is to be lamented, the Emperor will not or cannot detect. I should think our Fleet, situated as Italy now is, from these repeated defeats of the Austrians, cannot be of any more use in the Mediterranean; and, indeed, as a Spanish war seems to be inevitable, the West Indies will require a great Naval force, and it will be proper to augment the Fleet which protects our own coasts, and is known under the denomination of the Channel Fleet. I therefore suppose the Mediterranean Fleet will be divided—part to the West Indies, and the rest come home, leaving a few Frigates, under a very active Officer, at Gibraltar.

"We cannot say dear old England is as we could wish it: however, we are better off than any other Nations; and, thank God, there is no treachery amongst our Military, or conspiracy amongst our people! I wish for the best; and, being clear of all kind of party, I care not who is the Minister, provided he is active, and really anxious to make peace the moment he can. Adieu, my dear friend, and ever believe me, yours sincerely, WILLIAM."—*Autograph*, in the Nelson Papers.

French, as was natural for them, in order to make their peace;
and the Enemy was in one end of Bastia, before we had
quitted the other. The exertions of the Navy on this occasion, as on all others which I have seen, have been great, and
beyond the expectations of those who never will believe what
we are capable of performing. Our troops are ordered to
Porto Ferrajo, which can be defended against any number of
the Enemy for a length of time; and the Port, although small,
will hold with management our whole Fleet and Transports.

As soon as all our Transports are arrived at Elba, we are to
go out to look for Man, who is ordered to come up: we shall
then be twenty-two Sail of such Ships as England hardly ever
produced, and commanded by an Admiral, who will not fail
to look the Enemy in the face, be their force what it may: I
suppose it will not be more than thirty-four Sail of the Line.
We may reasonably expect reinforcements from England; for
whilst we can keep the combined Fleet in the Mediterranean,
so much more advantageous to us; and the moment we retire,
the whole of Italy is given to the French. Be the successes
of the Austrians what they may, their whole supply of stores
and provisions comes from Trieste, across the Adriatic to the
Po, and when this is cut off, they must retire. If the Dons
detach their Fleet out of the Mediterranean, we can do the
same—however, that is distant. I calculate on the certainty
of Admiral Man's joining us, and that in fourteen days from
this day we shall have the honour of fighting these gentlemen:
there is not a seaman in the Fleet who does not feel confident
of success. If I live, your Royal Highness shall have no
reason to regret your friendship for me, and I will support
Sir John Jervis to the utmost of my power. . . . I hope soon
to hear that your Flag is flying, which I am sure will be most
honourable for yourself, and I trust most advantageous for
our King and Country. I am, as ever, your most faithful,

HORATIO NELSON.

TO THE GENOESE GOVERNMENT.

[From an Autograph Draught in the Nelson Papers.]

[About October or November, 1796.]

Commodore Nelson has the honour to acquaint the Serene
Government of Genoa, that he is charged by his Excellency

the Vice-Roy of Corsica, and Sir John Jervis, K.B., Commander-in-Chief of his Britannic Majesty's Fleet in the Mediterranean, to come to Genoa, and to demand from the Serene Government the immediate restitution of the British shipping and property sequestered in the Port of Genoa; satisfaction for the insults offered his Majesty's Flag, by the firing of cannon on it on the 11th day of September last, and that this conduct is considered more insulting, as it was entirely unprovoked by any conduct on the part of his Majesty's Officers and Men, who were employed on a legal service near the shore of St. Pierre d'Arena, in possession of the French, and a French battery erected on it; and also for the subsequent conduct of the Government on that day, by shutting the Ports of the Republic to the British, at the instigation of his Majesty's Enemies.

These open Hostilities left no choice with the Servants of his Majesty in these Seas, but that of vindicating His honour by immediate reprisals. The consequence has been, that Capraja is at present occupied by British troops, and that a great number of Genoese Vessels, have been seized at sea and in our harbours, and which will every day increase, are sequestered.

I am also instructed by his Excellency the Vice-Roy to state to the Government of the Serene Republic that Capraja had offered many provocations to His Majesty's Government in Corsica anterior to the late events at Genoa. That Island had been, for these last two years, the constant haunt of Vessels calling themselves French privateers, fitted out in the harbour of Capraja, under the eye of the Genoese Government, by a French agent, received and acknowledged as such.

These Vessels lay in wait at Capraja, for the Trade of his Majesty's Subjects, and exercised a piratical warfare against the English and Corsicans, under the protection of a Genoese fort, and harbour in a manner entirely contrary to the laws of Neutrality : that no redress has been obtained from the Serene Republic by any representations which were made by his Majesty's Minister at Genoa; that although a French Agent was not only received at Capraja, but was avowedly the instrument of these hostilities, the Serene Republic declined the reasonable and just request that was made to them on our part, to admit an English Vice-Consul at the same place.

I am also directed by the Vice-Roy and Admiral to inform the Serene Republic that they would still have persevered in the same system of moderation and forbearance, from a sincere regard for the Serene Republic, and from an ardent desire to maintain, even with great sacrifices, the harmony which has so long been preserved, through difficult and delicate times, between the two Governments, if the violent and insulting transaction of the 11th of September had not committed the honour of his Majesty, as well as the interest and just claims of his Subjects, too deeply to admit of further forbearance.

I am further instructed, at the same time, to inform the Serene Republic, that neither desire of conquest nor avidity of gain, by a war against the extensive trade of the Genoese, have influenced their councils on this occasion ; and that the only objects they have in view are to obtain reparation for the late insults committed at Genoa, and a security against a repetition of those injuries which have been experienced from the conduct of the Genoese Government at Capraja.

When these objects are accomplished, it is their Excellencies' desire, and they will think it their duty, to restore everything to its former footing, and to revert to that friendly intercourse with Genoa which it has been so much the wish of his Majesty, and the study of all his Servants to maintain, notwithstanding many provocations which perhaps the nature of the times and circumstances have rendered unavoidable.

I trust that these, their Excellencies' sentiments, will sufficiently evince to the Genoese Government and to the whole world, their amicable and pacific disposition and will render the Serene Republic alone responsible for the events that have ensued from the present differences, or for those measures which their Excellencies may be justly called upon to employ for vindication of his Majesty's honour and the protection of his Subjects. I have the honour to be, &c.

HORATIO NELSON.

TO JOSEPH BRAME, ESQ., BRITISH CONSUL AT GENOA.

[From a Copy in the Admiralty.]

Dear Sir,   Captain, at Sea, November 4th, 1796.

The night before last, I received, through the hands of Mr. Bertram, your letter of October 12th, transmitting an Answer

of the Genoese Secretary of State to the Admiral's letter, and
my Memorial, also their Note to you; and you say you have
sent me a copy of your Note to the Government of Genoa,
which you hope I shall approve of. This latter Paper you
have omitted to send, which I am sorry for, as I hoped to have
seen in it Mr. Secretary of State most severely taken to task,
for daring to tax me with a breach of my Word of Honour.[5]
You must know, from your own acquaintance with me, that I
am incapable of such conduct, and you had my Report of the
transaction, which was sufficient for you to resent, as becomes
your station, and my hitherto unimpeached honour; but, if
you have so far forgotten yourself and station as to permit such
an infamous lie to be uncontradicted, it is my desire, and I
demand it of you, that you go immediately to the Secretary of State, and state that I say, the scandal of a breach of
honour lies with him for writing an untruth, with his Government for permitting it, and with their Officer, who pledged
himself for the Republic's being neutral, when I gave my
Word of Honour to observe the Neutrality of Genoa, and that
I would attack no Vessel in its Port, or under the guns of
Genoa.

This reciprocal pledge was given in your room, and yourself
interpreted; and of course you will recollect, that I would not
give my Word of Honour till the Officer gave his for the
Neutrality of the Republic. I call on the Government of
Genoa to say, if they understood my pledge of Honour to be
otherwise than that I would not commence an attack, and
[not] that I would abstain from repelling or chastising one.

You will mark the flagrant breach of honour in the Republic of Genoa. They permitted the French to enter the
Port of Genoa, contrary to their Edict of Neutrality, with
Vessels loaded with gunpowder: they permit all kinds of
warlike stores for the attack of Neutral Powers to be landed
within 300 yards of the walls of Genoa: they permit guns to
be mounted by the Enemies of England within the same distance.

The consequence of this conduct on the part of the Government of Genoa, was, that the French fired on his Majesty's
Boats; and, on the Boats resenting the insult, from what had

---

[5] In the affair of St. Pierre d'Arena. Vide ante.

heretofore been considered as a Neutral Territory, by taking
a French Vessel, the Government of Genoa, instead of supporting its Neutrality by opening a fire upon the French
battery, turned the guns of Genoa, first on his Majesty's Boats,
and then on the Ships; and, in addition to this hostile act,
they permitted a number of French armed Vessels to come
out of the Port of Genoa, to attack his Majesty's colours.

This statement of facts, which I dare them to contradict,
but which it was your bounden duty to have supported long
since, will show the Genoese Nation, and the whole World,
who has broken their Parole of Honour.

I am, &c.

HORATIO NELSON.

TO WILLIAM LOCKER, ESQ., LIEUTENANT-GOVERNOR, ROYAL
HOSPITAL, GREENWICH.

[Autograph, in the Locker Papers. On the 2nd of November, Admiral Sir John
Jervis with the Fleet, (of which the Captain formed part,) sailed from Mortella
Bay for Gibraltar, and arrived there on the 1st of December following.]

Captain, at Sea, November 5th, 1796.

My dear Friend,

It is true that my time has lately been so fully employed,
that I have not had that time I wished for, to write to all my
friends. However, as I am attached to the Fleet, I have not
so many affairs in hand. Sir John desires me to say, when I
write you, that he is sorry he cannot, so much as he wishes,
write to you himself. We have now done with Corsica; I
have seen the first and the last of that Kingdom. Its situation
certainly was most desirable for us, but the generality of its
inhabitants are so greedy of wealth, and so jealous of each
other, that it would require the patience of Job, and the riches
of Crœsus to satisfy them. They say themselves they are only
to be ruled by the Ruling Power shooting all its Enemies, and
bribing all its Friends. They already regret our departure
from them, for no more silver harvests will come to their lot.
I remember when we quitted Toulon we endeavoured to
reconcile ourselves to Corsica; now we are content with Elba
—such things are: however, we have a fine Port, and no
expenses for the Government of the Island.

We are anxious to hear what the King of Naples has determined on, in consequence of our remaining to support him:

if he is marched, I hope soon to be in possession of Leghorn again. The conduct of the Pope is extraordinary; although he is at war with the French, yet he has not opened his Ports to us: he is fearful of a turn in the present happy prospects. In short, Italy has been lost by the fears of its Princes; had they expended half the money to preserve their Territories, which they have paid the French for entering them, their Countries would have been happy, instead of being filled with present misery and diabolical notions of Government. I have received the third volume of Charnock's book,[6] but how it came to me I know not, but suppose by the Queen. As the book gets forward, it naturally becomes more interesting. I am in your debt for the subscription.

We left St. Fiorenzo on the 2nd, at night, and are now seeing our Smyrna convoy part of the way down the Straits, and hope to meet Admiral Man, who has, more than a month past, known the situation of our gallant Admiral. Orders have been sent, which fame says, were received October 10th; but Admiral Man could not have sailed on the receipt of them, as Swedes have been spoke only eight, nine, and ten days through the Gut.

So soon as our Fleet is united, I have no doubt but we shall look out for the Combined Fleet, who I suppose are about thirty-four Sail of the Line, badly manned, and worse ordered; whilst ours is such a Fleet as I never before saw at sea. There is nothing hardly beyond our reach. I need not give you the character of Sir John Jervis, you know him well; therefore I shall only say, he is worthy of such a Fleet, for he knows how to use us in the most beneficial manner for our Country. You will not forget me kindly to every part of your family, and also to Mr. Bradley and our Naval friends; also to Simon Taylor. As I read in the paper, St. Domingo is to be evacuated, I hope Jamaica will be safe. All the French Army in Italy is going to the Devil very fast. We are on shore, upon *velvet.* Ever believe me, your most affectionate,

HORATIO NELSON.

I write this to go when opportunity offers.

November 11th, off Minorca.

Have you done the business for Mr. Summers?

6 " Biographia Navalis."

TO MRS. NELSON.

[From Clarke and M'Arthur, vol. i. p. 335.]

November 7th, 1796.

You will, by this time, have known the determination that has been made for this Fleet to remain in the Mediterranean. As soon as we have defeated the Spanish Fleet, which I doubt not, with God's help, we shall do, I have two or three little matters to settle in Italy, and then I care not how quickly I return to you. Do not flatter yourself that I shall be rewarded; I expect nothing, and therefore shall not be disappointed: the pleasure of my own mind will be my reward. I am more interested, and feel a greater satisfaction, in obtaining yours and my father's applause, than that of all the world besides.

Yours, &c.
HORATIO NELSON.

TO HIS ROYAL HIGHNESS THE DUKE OF CLARENCE.

[From an autograph in the Nelson Papers.[7]]

Captain, at Sea, November 11th, 1796.

Sir,

What may be thought in England of our embarkation from Bastia I know not, but I conceive myself to have a fair right to be well spoken of, as the few facts which I shall state will evince. [I shall relate them to your Royal Highness, to give you an idea of the state of our Army and the Viceroy on my arrival.]

On the 14th of October I was close in with Bastia, [before daylight,] in the Diadem, Captain Towry. Before the Ship anchored, I went on shore to the Viceroy, landing opposite his house. I found his Excellency very happy at my arrival, and immediately requested me to send off his most valuable papers, and acquainted me with the plan of some Corsicans to take his person that night; that, except the guard which was at his house, our troops were in the citadel; that a Committee of Thirty had taken the Government of the Town,

---

[7] The passages within brackets are not in the draught, but they occur in the copy in Clarke and M'Arthur, vol. i. p. 332, and may have been taken from the Letter itself.

had sequestered the property of the English, and had refused
to suffer any vessel or boat to quit the Mole, [and also that
a plan was laid to seize his person; that the Town was full
of armed Corsicans who had mounted guard at every place,
and that our troops were in the citadel, except the guard at
his house.]

From the Viceroy I went to General de Burgh, where
I learnt that as many armed Corsicans as British were in
the Citadel; that they had mounted guard with the British at
the Citadel gate, on the batteries, barrier gates, and at the
storehouses of Government, and every magazine of the English
Merchants; and that it was necessary for the troops to stand
to their arms for self-defence;—in short, that there was not
a prospect of saving either stores, cannon, or provisions. I
submitted to the General the propriety of shutting the Citadel
gate in order to prevent any more armed men from getting
into it, [and that I would moor the Ships opposite to the
Town.] On my return from the General to the Viceroy, the
Merchants, Owners, and Captains of Privateers came to me with
tears, stating the fact of even their trunks with wearing apparel
being refused to them, and that they were beggars without my
help, not a prize would these people allow to quit the Mole:
[a Transport's boat had, they said, been refused permission
to leave the Mole until she was searched, and on nothing being
found in her, they suffered her to pass; a Privateer was moored
across the Mole heads.] I requested them to be quiet, and
that nothing should be left undone by me for their relief. About
ten A.M., the Egmont, Captain Sutton, had arrived, and I
anchored the Ships close to the Mole head, abreast of the
Town, sent all our boats, manned and armed, to tow the Ships
out of the Mole, sending a message to the Committee, that
if there was the smallest molestation to every species of
English property being removed from the Town and out of the
Mole, that I would open the fire of the Ships and batter the
Town down. This message had its desired effect. The Corsicans on guard down muskets and ran; and the Mole, upwards
of sixty sail, was soon clear [At noon, having made the signal
for boats manned and armed, I ordered Captain Towry to
proceed into the Mole with them, and to open the passage
for all the Vessels who chose to come out; with instructions

to take the first English Vessel he came to in tow, and
if he met with the smallest molestation, he was to send to the
Municipality in my name, and inform them that if the least impediment were thrown in the way in getting any Vessel out of
the Mole, or embarking any property belonging to the English
from the Town, I would instantly batter it down.   Captain
Sutton very handsomely went to Towry's assistance, for on the
approach of the latter to the Mole, the privateer pointed her
guns, and 100 muskets were levelled from the Mole head.
On this Captain Sutton sent my message, and pulling out his
watch, gave them one quarter of an hour for an answer, when
the Ships would in five minutes open their fire.   Upon this
the people on board the Privateer, and from the Mole heads,
and even the Corsican sentries, quitted the place with the
utmost precipitation, and of course every vessel came out of
the Mole.]

In the afternoon, an owner of a Privateer came to me to
say, he had goods in the custom-house, which they refused
to deliver: I ordered him to go to the Committee, and say
I sent him for the things, [which if not instantly delivered
I would open my fire.]   In five minutes, he returned with the
keys, and said they were as white as sheets, and said not a word.
At night they made one more effort to get duty paid for some
wine [landed, and of course going to be embarked by an English
merchant.]   I had only occasion to send word that I would
come to them myself; from this moment all was quiet, and
no people could behave better.   Bastia, it was agreed on all
hands, never was so quiet; not an armed man was found in
the streets to the night of our embarkation, [since we had been
in possession of the Island.]

The Viceroy consented to go on board my Ship that night,
which took off from the General and myself much concern;
and we set heartily to work to save what time would permit,
which may fairly be estimated at £200,000 sterling.   The
seamen were employed on shore to work and my soldiers
landed to guard the north end of the Town.   The French
Troops landed near Cape Corse on the 18th; and [on the
15th in the morning, I landed my troops to take post at the
Viceroy's house, which covered our embarking place, and a
hundred seamen as a working party; the General ordered
about another hundred men from the troops for the same pur-

pose, and the rest kept post in the Citadel. We set heartily to work, and continued without intermission until the 19th at sunset; when I calculate we had saved about £200,000 sterling worth of cannon, powder, stores, and provisions, exclusive of baggage, household stuff, &c., &c., for the poor émigrés could not afford to leave a rag. Our boats never ceased night nor day.]

On the 19th they sent a message to the Municipality, desiring to know how they intended to receive them; if as friends, they demanded that the English should be prevented from embarking. In this state, nothing more could be attempted to be saved; and therefore at [twelve at] night the troops quitted the Citadel, and came to the north end of the Town, where was an open piece of ground, and from whence I embarked every man in a heavy gale of wind, with the two field-pieces which the troops brought from the Citadel to protect their retreat—the General and myself being the last men in the boat. [The French passing at the back of the Town were in the Citadel at one, A.M. From its blowing a gale of wind, it was dawn of day when the General and myself[8] went into the barge, not one man being left ashore ; and we took with us the two field-pieces brought down to cover our retreat.] It is impossible I can do justice to the good dispositions of the General, or the good management of the Viceroy with the Corsicans, not a man of whom but cried on parting with him; even those who had opposed his Administration could not but love and respect so amiable a character. It was clear that dread of the French was more predominant in their minds, than dislike to us ; and it was this perhaps that greatly contributed to their first resolves, which were not to be justified. The French took possession of the Citadel at one A.M., and it was near 6 A.M., before the last of us was afloat, but we kept too good a countenance for an attack. At this time the Spanish Fleet was off Cape Corse, but we had a fine wind, and before night I had every man and vessel safe moored in Porto Ferrajo, for its size the most complete port in the world. I am, &c.

HORATIO NELSON.

[8] Clarke and M'Arthur state that "Commodore Nelson was the last person who left the shore. On getting into his boat, he turned round to the Corsican mob, and, with the coolness of a sailor, anathematized the whole of their ungrateful race, adding, 'Now, John Corse, follow the natural bent of your detestable character, plunder and revenge.'"

TO CAPTAIN COLLINGWOOD.

[Autograph, in the possession of the Honourable Mrs. Newnham Collingwood.]

My dear Coll.,   November 20th, 1796.

Many thanks for your newspapers which were a very great treat. From them I do not build much on the prospect of peace. The French will try the Dons before they submit to any humiliation. I see we are ready to give up our conquests, except the Mynheers: they must pay the piper.

I rejoice with you that all your home are well. It is a great comfort to hear from those folks in England: I had not that satisfaction. The mode now of sending letters is new, and it must take time to have it known, although William Young [9] has sent several for me, and would, I am sure, continue so to do.

We are not I fear soon to get a fair wind. How tedious is our voyage: besides, it will take some time at Gibraltar to repair our damages. We have all of us some when the truth comes out. I was lucky in sending my letters for England if Cygnet is gone home, but is that certain? and I was also *lucky* in getting a cask of porter from her, which you shall have part of, when drawn off. Perhaps Lively is going for Gibraltar for dispatches. I expect no change of wind before the 29th. God bless you, and believe me ever

Your most faithful,

HORATIO NELSON.

We have reports that Man is gone through the Gut—not to desert us, I hope, but I have my suspicions.

TO THE REV. DIXON HOSTE.

[Autograph, in the possession of Captain Sir William Hoste, Bart.]

Captain, at Sea, November 25th, 1796.

My dear Sir,

Our friends in England sometimes accuse us of not writing so frequently as they wish us: on many occasions we can retort the charge—so says your good son, William. I can

---

[9] Rear-Admiral William Young, then one of the Lords of the Admiralty.

say, which will be enough for a letter, that I have never once had cause to wish him anything *but what he is.* His accidents, I can truly say, have so happily turned out that I hope he is in no way the worse for them, but I have strongly recommended for him not to break any more limbs.

Although this is writing at sea, yet most probably it will leave us at Gibraltar, for which place we are steering ; and you will, perhaps, expect a little news from near the fountain-head, did you not know that our future movements are too important to be trusted to a letter; and our past ones, every newspaper tells you *more* than I can, for what is not known they happily guess at. Our evacuation of Corsica was effected beyond our most sanguine expectations, and contrary to the belief of our absent friends, the part allotted to me, the evacuation of Bastia, considered the most important, ended, as our world here, say, much to my credit; for the French and their adherents were round the Town, and the Spanish Fleet only thirty-six miles from us ;[1] but I left not a man behind, and saved two hundred thousand pounds' worth of cannon, stores, and provisions, and landed the whole Army, &c. &c. safe at Porto Ferrajo, a place of shelter I had contributed to take a few months before. Our gallant Admiral, Sir John Jervis, in vain expected Admiral Man from Gibraltar, but we have been disappointed, and you know where he is by this time, instead of coming to our help who so much needed it, but in this world nothing ought to surprise us. We are only fifty leagues from Gibraltar, and hope there to find reinforcements from England, when, if we are twenty-five Sail of the Line, you may rest perfectly assured under our present Commander, we shall beat the Combined. God send our meeting may be soon, for I should be sorry to have a Peace before we make

---

[1] Towards the end of September, Admiral Don Juan de Langara, with the Spanish Fleet, consisting of nineteen Sail of the Line, ten Frigates, and some Corvettes, put to sea from Cadiz, and proceeded to Carthagena, where they were joined by seven Line-of-battle Ships, thus making twenty-six Sail of the Line. With this imposing force, Langara appeared off Cape Corse in Corsica, on the 15th of October, at which time Sir John Jervis's Squadron, amounting to only fourteen Sail of the Line, (the "Captain" being at Bastia,) were at anchor in Mortella Bay. Instead, however, of attacking the English Fleet, the Spanish Admiral went to Toulon ; and on his arrival there, on the 26th of that month, the Combined Fleets formed thirty-eight Sail of the Line and nearly twenty Frigates.

the Dons pay for meddling. When you see Mr. and Mrs. Coke, I beg you will make my compliments, and present mine to Mrs. Hoste. William tells me he is writing a long letter: therefore, perhaps, he will tell you more news than I can.

November 28th.—I this day delivered to William your letter of October 31st: he says you seem to regret his not going home in the Agamemnon; had I thought so, I certainly should not have taken him from her. I am, dear Sir,

Your very obedient servant,

HORATIO NELSON.

TO WILLIAM SUCKLING, ESQ.

[From " The Athenæum."]

Captain, off Gibraltar Bay, November 29, 1796.

My dear Sir,

It would, you may believe, have given me no small satisfaction to have received a letter from your own hand, and to have conveyed to me that you enjoy that good health which I most sincerely wish you, as well as a continuance of every family felicity: it is not in my nature to forget, for an instant, the many acts of kindness you have shewn me during the whole course of my life. I can only endeavour to give you the satisfaction of knowing that it has not been thrown away on an unworthy object. My professional reputation is the only riches I am likely to acquire in this war; what profit that will bring me time only can determine, however, it is satisfactory to myself, and I believe will be so to you. This day has brought me from Lord Spencer, the fullest and handsomest approbation of my *spirited*, *dignified*, and *temperate* conduct, both at Leghorn and Genoa, and my first Lieutenant[2] is made a Captain; a share of a galleon, and I want no more— but, God knows, ambition has no end!

How is Mrs. Suckling, Mr. Rumsey, Miss Suckling, and every part of your family? I am interested that all should be happy, and contribute to make you so. You will hear how we are deserted, but our Commander-in-Chief is a host

---

[2] Lieutenant Martin Hinton.

in himself, and I hope yet to assist him in beating the Dons, which we shall do if we have a proper force to seek them out. The Admiralty have confirmed me as an established Commodore : they have done handsomely by me. The Smyrna convoy goes on for England ; we have towed them from Corsica, and I hope they will arrive safe. I venture to tell you the Admiralty always forward letters to the Mediterranean by the Cutters, which almost every week come to us—therefore pray write me a line.

December 2nd.—It was yesterday before we anchored, and I am sorry to hear of several Fish-ships being taken by the Spaniards. The Admiral has sent out a Squadron to secure our Newfoundland convoy, which is hourly expected. As to our future movements I am totally ignorant—nor do I care what they are. I shall continue to exert myself in every way for the honour of my Country; and in every situation, believe me your most affectionate nephew,

HORATIO NELSON.

You will not forget to remember me to Mrs. Suckling, Miss Suckling, Mr. Rumsey, and family, Mr. Merce,[3] and all other friends.

TO CAPTAIN COLLINGWOOD.

[Autograph, in the possession of Mrs. Newnham Collingwood.]

December 1st, 1796.

My dear Coll.,

I hope you heard from home by the Brig. Man is certainly gone to England, and the consequences, after Cornwallis may be guessed at. I send you some papers of Troubridge. You will like to run them over.

Ever yours most truly,
HORATIO NELSON.

If we are at anchor, will you dine here at three o'clock?

---

[3] *Sic.* Query—" Muntz ;" vide ante.

TO ADMIRAL SIR JOHN JERVIS, K.B.

[From a Copy in the Admiralty, and a draught in the Nelson Papers. This
Letter was transmitted to the Secretary to the Admiralty, on the 4th of December,
by Sir John Jervis, who said, " Although I sent you for the Lords Commissioners
of the Admiralty, by the Fox (2nd) Cutter, on the 27th September, all the documents transmitted to me by Commodore Nelson, relative to the transaction which
the Marquis Spinola has so grossly misrepresented in his Memorial to Lord Grenville, I felt it due to the Commodore to put him in possession of the Memorial, and
I enclose his animated and able refutation of the whole case."]

Captain, Gibraltar Bay, December 3rd, 1796.

Sir,

I am honoured with your letter of yesterday's date,[4] enclosing
an extract of a letter from the Marquis of Spinola, the Genoese
Minister to the Court of London, and desiring my Report of
the Transaction.

I shall do little more that I have already done, sending you
the exact Report of the Transaction, for the truth of which

[4] This Letter, with the Marquis of Spinola's Note, is now in the Nelson Papers.
The affair of St. Pierre d'Arena (which has been sufficiently described) forms the
first part of Spinola's complaint ; and he then makes the following statements, which
naturally excited Nelson's indignation :—" The Commodore, in addition to this
breach of faith, and to render himself still more unworthy of the rank he bears, has
disgraced himself with the assertion of what was not true, by colouring this
aggression with the pretence of searching upon the beach of San Pierre d'Arena for
a launch, carried away by some deserters, which was never seen at that place. This
was evident to the Commodore, from the little distance he was off, and was also
proved by the attestation of many witnesses who were sworn and registered in the
Process Verbal, and who at the same time declared the taking the Tartan to have
been made prior to the firing.

" In consequence of this recent fact, the Envoy and Minister Plenipotentiary at the
Court of his Britannic Majesty, by order of his own Government, has done himself the
honour to present to the King, by means of his Minister, a Memorial, showing how
much the Republic has always studied to deserve the good-will of England; the ungrateful
return she has met with from her Agents in the Mediterranean ; her expectation of that
recompence which justice requires for the great injuries she has sustained; and, finally,
the declaration of a measure which the Republic hath judged indispensably necessary
to take upon this occasion—that is, to secure, by a guard of soldiers, the sequestration
of four English merchant Ships, with the view of recovering from their effects the
compensation demanded for what she has lost—a compensation which shall be
estimated according to the rules of right, and which, were this measure not adopted,
ought to be made good to the Republic. Moreover, to preserve the Republic from
the danger of being again exposed and placed in the most perilous situations, and
also from the vicinity of the victorious French armies, she has thought it necessary
to adopt the measure of informing the British Commanders that, until further deli-
beration, English Ships will not be admitted into the Ports of the said State."

you have the declared testimony of two Lieutenants, which they are ready to confirm with their oaths.

But I cannot allow the Marquis's Note to pass without severe reprobation. It is couched in language unbecoming a gentleman, whatever privilege he may plead as a Minister, and is what the declaration of his own Government (for they sent me a copy of their Report to him) by no means warranted. Whatever my unworthiness may be, I shall show myself his superior by abstaining from language which his rank as a Nobleman and Representative of the Republic of Genoa, ought to have made it impossible for him to use. I dare him or his superiors to deny the following facts—viz. :

The French are in possession of every foot of Sea-coast from the gates of Genoa to Ventimiglia (except the citadels of Savona Finale and St. Remo), not that those Citadels have commanded neutrality for upwards of ten years past. That the beach of St. Pierre d'Arena was covered with shot, shells, guns, waggons, carriages, store-houses filled with powder, and every other Military store landed from French vessels within 300 yards of the walls of Genoa. That four guns were mounted on the high part of the beach of St. Pierre d'Arena, and French sentinels placed over them; that not one anchoring place from Genoa to Ventimiglia was accessible to an English Ship, as the French had erected batteries which commanded every one.

In pledging my honour, it never could be understood that I meant to debar myself from destroying the Enemy wherever he insulted me ; nor do I conceive that if the French had taken possession of Genoa, my Word of Honour would have been any longer sacred for that City, for it was given reciprocally that the Republic would not permit her Neutrality to be broken. I send a copy of my letter to Mr. Consul Brame, which more fully expresses my feelings.

The Secretary to the Republic states *one* fact in his Report to the Marquis—viz., that I offered to restore the French Vessel to any Genoese Officer if the Government would pledge itself to make reparation for the insult which Mr. Secretary says I pretend to call it.

It will appear clear to any mind, that desire of making a prize or insulting the Republic of Genoa could not have

influenced my conduct, for I was placing the Republic in the
most independent and respectable situation by making Her
the judge between two Enemies, and by my declaring that if
any man, on a fair examination, would say that his Majesty's
Boats had committed any act, good or bad, before the French
fired, I would submit to be considered as wrong. But the
Government of the Republic did not choose so close an investigation, when I should have been present. The reason is
clear : my Statement could not have been contradicted by such
an examination, and their Officer must have been made answerable for his assisting the French in an attack on his Majesty's
Boats and Ships, who were inflicting proper chastisement on
the Enemy for firing on the English flag, then under the
fancied protection of the battery of the Lanthorn, from which
it was not 100 yards distant.

The Marquis states how much the Republic has *always*
studied to deserve the good will of England. I deny the fact
of *always*. Does She not acknowledge detaining the bullocks
purchased out of the Dominions of the Republic by British
Agents, for the use of his Majesty's Fleet ? Is not this un-
friendly, and very nearly a hostile act ? And the Marquis
states the ungrateful return which the English Agents have
made for their kindnesses. This, I think, Mr. Secretary could
not have sent him, for the Vessels of Genoa had particular
privileges, both at Leghorn and other places in the Tuscan
States, by directions from Sir John Jervis, and for which I
had the acknowledgment of his Serenity the Doge in person.

I respect and esteem the greatest part of the Genoese
Nation, and am ready to confess that I have been admitted
into Genoa and Port Especia and nowhere else, and have
been allowed freely, till the first week in September last, to
take goods for my money ; and so far from my conduct being
oppressive to the sea-faring part of the Nation, which is all I
could have to do with, it is impossible any one could even
be received with more attention than I have always been by
the seamen of Genoa. They knew that I seized all Vessels
going to France, but that all others were sure of my good will.

The Marquis concludes with a truth which is clearly to
me the cause of all the hostile conduct of the Government
of Genoa—*fear of the French ;* and had his Excellency only

mentioned this fact at first, he would have saved himself much trouble, as well as, Sir,

Your most obedient Servant,

HORATIO NELSON.[7]

TO MRS. NELSON.

[From Clarke and M'Arthur, vol. i. p. 336. Government having determined to withdraw the garrison from Porto Ferrajo, Commodore Nelson was ordered by Sir John Jervis, on the 10th of December, 1796, to hoist his Distinguishing Pendant on board La Minerve Frigate, to take the Blanche under his command, and to proceed from Gibraltar to Porto Ferrajo. Upon his arrival there, or meeting with them, he was also to take under his command the seventeen Ships or Vessels named, and " to carry into execution His Majesty's commands relative to the disposition of the troops and stores lately removed to that garrison from the Island of Corsica," a transcript of which was enclosed to him. The British Artillery and the 1st Regiment, or Royal Scotch, were to be disembarked at Gibraltar ; and all the other Troops, British and Foreign, were to be landed at Lisbon. Sir John Jervis's order concluded in these words :—" Having experienced the most important effects from your enterprise and ability, upon various occasions since I have had the honour to command in the Mediterranean, I leave entirely to your judgment the time and manner of carrying this critical and arduous service into execution."—*Original*, in the Nelson Papers.]

[About the 10th December, 1796.]

I am going on a most important Mission, which, with God's blessing, I have little doubt of accomplishing: it is not a

---

[7] Commodore Nelson's explanations proved entirely satisfactory to the Government; and in February, 1797, he had the gratification of receiving a copy of the following letter from Lord Grenville, Secretary of State for Foreign Affairs, to the Lords of the Admiralty :—

Downing Street, 2nd February, 1797.

To the right Honourable the Lords Commissioners of the Admiralty.

My Lords—I have had the honour of laying before the King the different papers relative to the complaint preferred by the Marquis de Spinola, in the name of the Genoese Government, against Commodore Nelson, together with the two letters from that Officer relating thereto, which were transmitted to this Office by Mr. Nepean the 28th ult. His Majesty had not thought it proper that I should enter into any discussion or explanations with the Marquis de Spinola in question, until due reparation shall have been made for the acts of hostility committed by the Republic against his Majesty's Ships, and against the property of his Majesty's subjects ; but as this circumstance deprives Commodore Nelson for the present of that public testimony in favour of his conduct, which must result from such a discussion, whenever it may be entered into, I esteem it an act of justice due to that Officer, considering the nature of the charge brought against him, to inform your Lordships, that his Majesty has been graciously pleased entirely to approve of the conduct of Commodore Nelson in all his transactions with the Republic of Genoa. I have the honour to be, my lords, you lordships' most obedient humble servant, GRÈNVILLE.—*Clarke and M'Arthur.*

fighting Mission, therefore be not uneasy. I feel honoured in being trusted, as I am, by Sir John Jervis. If I have money enough in Marsh and Creed's hands, I wish you would buy a Cottage in Norfolk. I shall follow the plough with much greater satisfaction than viewing all the magnificent scenes in Italy.

Yours, &c.

HORATIO NELSON.

TO ADMIRAL SIR JOHN JERVIS, K.B.

[From the London Gazette, of February 28, 1797. The gallant action described in the following dispatch, took place during Commodore Nelson's passage from Gibraltar to Porto Ferrajo ; and it is remarkable that neither in James's " Naval History," nor in any one of the numerous " Memoirs of Lord Nelson," is the precise place where the action occurred mentioned, each writer merely saying it was on the passage to Porto Ferrajo. It appears, however, from La Minerve's Log,[8] that she and the Blanche sailed from Gibraltar on the 15th, that on the 19th at Noon, Cape de Gatte bore " N.N.W. five or six leagues," and that at Noon, on the 20th, she was " off Carthagena."]

20th December, 1796.

Sir,

Last night, at ten o'clock, I saw two Spanish Frigates, and directed Captain Cockburn, in the Minerve, to attack the

---

[8] The following extract from La Minerve's Log is inserted, because it seems to have been written by Commodore Nelson himself, and because it contains a fuller account of the Action than the Official Dispatch :—

" Tuesday 20th, off Carthagena, P.M. Fresh gales and cloudy weather. At 5, spoke H.M. Ship Blanche, and ordered her to steer 20 miles N.E. by E. Shortened sail, and at ½ past 6, brought to on the starboard tack. At 10, the Blanche made signal to speak us : bore down to her. The Captain told me he saw two Spanish Frigates to leeward : cleared for action and bore down. At 20 minutes before 11, I passed under the stern of one of them, which I hailed. Knowing it to be a Spaniard, and not being answered, I commenced action with her by firing a broadside into her. At 11, saw the Blanche engage the other. At ½ past 11, saw the mizen mast of the Ship I was engaged with, fall. Wore ship occasionally, to prevent her getting to leeward, which I saw she endeavoured to effect. At 20 minutes past 1, she hailed us, and struck her colours. I sent the Lieutenant to take possession of her. He sent the Spanish Captain on board, who surrendered himself, and gave up his sword : told me his name was Don Jacobo Stuart, and that the Frigate was the Santa Sabina, mounting 40 guns, 20 18-pounders on the main-deck, 280 men. Took her in tow, and made sail to the S.E. Sent the Second Lieutenant and 24 men on board her to clear her decks, &c. The people on board La Minerve employed repairing damages, &c. At ½ past 3, saw another Frigate standing towards us, which supposed to be H.M. Ship Blanche : ¼ past 4, she hailed our Prize in Spanish, and fired a broadside into her ; in consequence of which we cast off the Prize, which stood to

Ship which carried a poop light: the Blanche bore down, to attack the other. I have not yet received from Captain Preston[9] an account of his Action; but as I saw the Blanche this morning to windward, with every sail set, I presume she has not suffered much damage.

Captain Cockburn brought his Ship to close action at twenty minutes before eleven, which continued without intermission until half-past one, when La Sabina, of forty guns, twenty-eight eighteen pounders on her main-deck, 286 men, Captain Don Jacobo Stuart, having lost her mizen-mast (as she did after the Action), her main and fore-masts, 164 men killed and wounded, struck her colours. You are, Sir, so thoroughly acquainted with the merits of Captain Cockburn, that it is needless for me to express them; but the discipline of the Minerve does the highest credit to her Captain and Lieutenants, and I wish fully to declare the sense I entertain of their judgment and gallantry. Lieutenant Culverhouse,[1] the First Lieutenant, is an old Officer of very distinguished merit. Lieutenants Hardy,[2] Gage,[3] and Noble,[4] deserve every praise which gallantry and zeal justly entitle them to, as do every other officer and man in the Ship. You will observe, Sir, I am sure, with regret, amongst the wounded, Lieutenant James

the eastward. At ½ past 4 commenced action with her. At 5 she wore Ship and stood from us. Saw three other Ships astern, which, as daylight cleared away, proved to be two Line-of-battle Ships and a Frigate, which the Ship we had last engaged joined, and they all made sail in chase of us. Light airs and baffling weather: made all sail possible; our Prize in sight, bearing about E.N.E., Blanche bearing west. At 7, do. weather: the people employed repairing damages, fishing lower masts, which were badly wounded. Sabina hoisted English colours over the Spanish, and stood to the N.E., which induced the largest Line-of-battle Ship to give up the pursuit of us and follow her. At ½ past 9, she brought the Santa Sabina to, when her mizen masts went over the side, and she was re-taken. The other Line of Battle Ship and two Frigates continued in chase of us. Saw a Fleet bearing E., supposed them to be the Spanish Fleet. Made signal for the Blanche to join us, which she did not answer. In the first action, had 7 seamen and marines killed, and 34 wounded: second action, 10 wounded. At noon, fresh breezes and hazy weather: one Line of Battle Ship and two Spanish Frigates in chase of us."

[9] Captain, now Admiral D'Arcy Preston.
[1] Vide, ante.
[2] The late Vice-Admiral Sir Thomas Hardy, G.C.B.
[3] Now Vice-Admiral Sir William Hall Gage, G.C.H., one of the Lords of the Admiralty.
[4] Now Rear-Admiral James Noble.

Noble, who quitted the Captain to serve with me, and whose merits and repeated wounds received in fighting the Enemies of our Country, entitle him to every reward which a grateful Nation can bestow. The Minerve's opponent being commanded by a gallant Officer, was well defended, which has caused her list of killed and wounded to be great, as also her masts, sails, and rigging to be much damaged.

I have the honour to be, Sir,

With the greatest respect,

Your most obedient servant,

HORATIO NELSON.

Killed, 7.

Wounded, 34.

Missing, 4, supposed to be in the Prize.

Officers Wounded: Lieutenant J. Noble, Mr. Merryweather, boatswain.

Petty Officers Killed and Wounded :

One Midshipman killed.

Wounded, Captain's Clerk; and the Serjeant of the 11th Regiment, serving as Marines.

Damages : All her masts shot through, and furniture much cut.

HORATIO NELSON.

TO ADMIRAL SIR JOHN JERVIS, K.B.

[From the London Gazette of February 28, 1797, and original draught in the Nelson Papers.]

December 20th, 1796.

Sir,

In addition to my letter of this morning, I have to aquaint you that Lieutenant Culverhouse and Hardy, with a proper number of men, being put in charge of La Sabina, and she taken in tow, at four A.M. a Frigate was seen coming up, which by her signals was known to be Spanish. At half-past four, she came into action with the Minerve, who cast off the Prize ; and Lieutenant Culverhouse was directed to stand to the southward. After a trial of strength of more than half an hour, she wore and hauled off, or I am confident she would have shared the fate of her companion : at this time three other Ships were seen standing for the Minerve. Hope was alive that they were only Frigates, and also that the Blanche was one of them ; but when the day dawned, it was mortifying to see there were two Spanish Ships of the Line and two Frigates, and the Blanche far to windward.

In this situation, the Enemy frequently within shot by bringing up the breeze, it required all the skill of Captain Cockburn, which he eminently displayed, to get off with a crippled Ship: and here I must also do justice to Lieutenants Culverhouse and Hardy, and express my tribute of praise at their management of the Prize ; a Frigate repeatedly firing into her without effect: and at last the Spanish Admiral quitted the pursuit of the Minerve for that of La Sabina, who was steering a different course evidently with the intention of attracting the notice of the Admiral, as English colours were hoisted over the Spanish. The Sabina's main and foremast fell overboard before she surrendered. This is, Sir, an unpleasant tale, but the merits of every officer and man in the Minerve and her Prize, were eminently conspicuous through the whole of this arduous day. The Enemy quitted the pursuit of the Minerve at dark.

I have the honour to be, Sir,
Your obedient servant,
HORATIO NELSON.

P.S.—Killed, none.
Wounded, ten.
Officer wounded—Mr. Hinton, Gunner.
Mainmast much damaged, sails and rigging cut.

TO HIS EXCELLENCY DON MIGUEL GASTON, CAPTAIN GENERAL OF THE DEPARTMENT OF CARTHAGENA.

[From Harrison's "Life of Lord Nelson," vol. i. p. 149.]

His Britannic Majesty's Ship the Minerve at Sea,
December 24, 1796.

Sir,

The fortune of war put La Sabina into my possession after she had been most gallantly defended : the fickle Dame returned her to you with some of my officers and men in her.

I have endeavoured to make the captivity of Don Jacobo Stuart, her brave Commander, as light as possible ; and I trust to the generosity of your Nation for its being reciprocal for the British Officers and men.

I consent, Sir, that Don Jacobo may be exchanged, and at full liberty to serve his King, when Lieutenants Culverhouse and Hardy are delivered into the garrison of Gibraltar, with such others as may be agreed on by the Cartel established between Gibraltar and St. Roche for the exchange of prisoners.

I have also a domestic taken in La Sabina; his name is Israel Coulson. Your Excellency will, I am sure, order him to be immediately restored to me, for which I shall consider myself as obliged to you.

I also trust that those men now Prisoners of War with you, will be sent to Gibraltar. It becomes great Nations to act with generosity to each other, and to soften the horrors of war.

I have the honour to be, with the most perfect esteem, your most obedient servant,

HORATIO NELSON.

TO ADMIRAL DON JUAN MARINO.

[From Harrison's " Life of Lord Nelson," vol. i. p. 150.]

[Apparently about December 24th, 1796.]

Sir,

I cannot allow Don Jacobo to return to you without expressing my admiration of his gallant conduct. To you, who have seen the state of his Ship, it is needless to mention the impossibility of her longer defence. I have lost many brave men; but in our masts I was most fortunate, or probably I should have had the honour of your acquaintance. But it pleased God to order it otherwise, for which I am thankful. I have endeavoured to make Don Jacobo's captivity as easy as possible, and I rely on your generosity for reciprocal treatment towards my brave officers and men, your prisoners.

I am, &c.,

HORATIO NELSON.

TO ADMIRAL SIR JOHN JERVIS, K.B

[From Clarke and M'Arthur, vol. i. p. 339.]

24th December, 1796.

You will, I am sure, forgive me for interesting myself for our friend Cockburn; he is now near ninety short of complement, although I have some hopes that those taken in the Prize may be returned to Gibraltar; they are all good men. The Gunner of the Peterel is amongst the missing; we hope he is on board the Prize: good men were wanting, and probably he pushed himself forward. My Coxswain, an invaluable man, is also a prisoner. If you can, pray, Sir, procure some good men for Cockburn; he deserves every favour you are pleased to bestow on him. I take it for granted the Admiralty will promote Lieutenant Culverhouse, and I hope Lieutenant Noble will also be promoted. I find that both a Spanish Squadron of seven Sail of the line, and a French Squadron of five, are out, but where I cannot learn. The French I have on board speak much of the misery in France; they do not, however, think the Directory will make peace: its Members and the Generals eat, and take everything.

I am, &c.

HORATIO NELSON.

TO ADMIRAL SIR JOHN JERVIS, K.B.

[From a Copy in the Admiralty.]

December 24th, 1796.

Sir,

Yesterday the Minerva took, off the south end of Sardinia, a French Privateer, called the Maria, of six nine-pounders and sixty-eight men, three days from Marseilles, on a cruise, taken nothing.

I am, Sir, &c.

HORATIO NELSON.

TO THE RIGHT HON. SIR GILBERT ELLIOT, BART.

[Autograph, in the Minto Papers.]

La Minerve, East side of Sardinia, December 24th, 1796.

My dear Sir,

I begin my letter by telling you that your box of papers is found, and now on board this Ship under my care. This I rejoice at. It was on board the Diadem. The Fleet arrived safe at Gibraltar, December 1st, since which it has blown very hard easterly. Ten or twelve sail of Merchant ships are lost, three Sail of the Line drove out of Gibraltar Bay, and reports say that the Courageux is lost, and every man except five (and Captain Hollowell, who was attending a Court-martial,) perished;[5] but I hope and believe that, although she might have struck, which caused the boat to break from her stern, yet as a ship was seen passing the gut without a main mast, I think it is her. The Gibraltar struck, carried away her fore-top mast, but went off the Pearl rock, and is safe. The Zealous struck on the Barbary shore, but is arrived at Gibraltar.

On the 14th, at night, I left the Admiral. On the 19th, at night, took a Spanish frigate of 40 guns, 18-pounders, larger than Minerve. On the 20th, in the morning, fought another as large, beat her, and she run from us: but there is no certainty in this world: two Sail of the Line and two Frigates surrounded us, took our Prize from us, and we very narrowly escaped visiting a Spanish prison. Two Lieutenants and a number of our men are taken, and we have lost near fifty killed and wounded; but 'tis well it's no more. Yesterday we took a French privateer, three days from Marseilles. Lady Elliot sailed October 23rd, from Gibraltar, in good health and spirits. I shall finish at Porto Ferrajo. I have reserved a place for you on board the Minerve; I long to see you, for your advice is a treasure, which I shall ever most highly prize. Only tell me when and where to send a Ship, and she shall attend you. The Admiral has told you the object of my mission, therefore I shall not repeat it.

---

[5] The report was unfortunately true. The Courageux was wrecked on the rocks at the foot of Apes Hill, on the Coast of Barbary; but the loss was not so heavy as was reported, though upwards of 460 of her men perished.

December 27th. I arrived at Porto Ferrajo yesterday, and as Fremantle tells me you will certainly be at Naples by the 1st January, I send him for you. I shall see the General[6] this morning, and will add a postscript of how he feels. I have wrote Sir W. H.,[7] as I have to Mr. Drake, and Mr. Trevor, to ask for a public letter of my conduct, as has come under their knowledge. To Sir William I made use of your name, and I trust, that when you come here, I shall not want for your testimony. I feel a fair right to state my services, such as they are, at the end of the war, to our Sovereign, who, I believe, is not slow to reward arduous endeavours to serve him.

Believe me ever, dear Sir,

Your affectionate

HORATIO NELSON.

TO . . . . .

[Fragment.　From a Copy, in the Nelson Papers.　Perhaps to Mr. Wyndham.]

[Apparently about December, 1796.]

. . . . from us, but there is no certainty in this world. Two Sail of the Line and two Frigates surrounded us, took our prize from us, and we very narrowly escaped visiting a Spanish prison. Two Lieutenants, and a number of our men are taken, and we have lost near fifty in killed and wounded, but it is well it's no worse. Yesterday[8] we took a Privateer, three days from Marseilles.

I have wrote Sir William Hamilton, to Mr. Drake,[9] and Mr.

---

[6] Lieut.-General de Burgh.

[7] Sir William Hamilton, at Naples.

[8] On the 23rd of December, 1796, La Minerve, off Sardinia, captured the French Privateer Maria. Vide p. 317.

[9] Mr. Drake wrote to Commodore Nelson, in reply to this request, on the 25th of January, 1797:—"As our Public correspondence will in all probability finish here, I cannot refrain from expressing to you the very high opinion entertained by our Allies of your conspicuous merit; and indeed it is impossible for any one who has had the honour of co-operating with you, not to admire the activity, talents, and zeal which you have so eminently displayed on all occasions, during the course of a long and arduous service. These sentiments I have frequently had occasion to state to his Majesty's Ministers, as the real ones of all those who have had an opportunity of estimating the value of your services, of which I myself can never fail to bear the most honourable testimony."—*Clarke and M'Arthur.*

Trevor, to ask for a Public letter of my conduct, as has come under their knowledge. To Sir William I made sure of, from home, and I trust when you come here, I shall not want for your testimony. I feel a fair right to state my services, such as they are, at the end of the War, to our Sovereign, who, I believe, is not slow to reward arduous endeavours to serve him. Believe me, &c.

                                        HORATIO NELSON.

TO THE RIGHT HON. SIR GILBERT ELLIOT.

[Autograph, in the Minto Papers.]

La Minerve, December 27th, 1796.

My dear Sir,

I have been with the General, and communicated my orders, which probably you are acquainted with. I dare not write fully, as it is not impossible but the letters may be stopped on the road. The General seems uncertain how to act, but as Naples has made her peace, the Admiral thinks we have *almost* done with Italy. I have not mentioned my orders yet to Sir William Hamilton, therefore I am sure you will not, for whatever we may do cannot be too secret. I long to talk with you. Fremantle sails on Thursday morning: he shall stay forty-eight hours at Naples; this is the full stretch I can allow him, and I trust you will find it sufficient; if not, I will send something else for you, but I feel I have nothing so pleasant. Ever believe me,

                    Your most affectionate,

                                        HORATIO NELSON.

Sir Gilbert Elliot, Bart.

The Spanish and French fleet are certainly gone down the Mediterranean.[1] I saw, I am now sure, more than twelve of the Line.

---

[1] About the 1st of December, the Spanish Fleet, accompanied by five French Sail of the Line, under Rear-Admiral Villeneuve, quitted Toulon, and a few days after the Spaniards entered Carthagena, while the French Squadron, owing to the gale of wind which proved so fatal to the Courageux, escaped through the Gut of Gibraltar, and reached Brest in safety.

TO ADMIRAL SIR JOHN JERVIS, K.B.

[From a Copy in the Admiralty.]

December 29th, 1796.

Sir,

I have fitted the Fortuna as a Flag of Truce, given the command of her to Lieutenant John Gourly, and hope she will sail to-morrow for Carthagena, with all the Spanish prisoners now here, which I hope you will approve of. I send a copy of my letter to the Captain-General of Carthagena.

I am, Sir,
Your most obedient Servant,
HORATIO NELSON.

TO THE CAPTAIN-GENERAL OF CARTHAGENA.

His Britannic Majesty's Ship La Minerve, Port Ferrajo,
29th December, 1796.

Sir,

I send to your Excellency a Flag of Truce, which carries away every Spanish prisoner from this place, and I request that your Excellency will direct the English prisoners with you to be immediately put on board the Flag of Truce. I shall not urge the humanity attending the frequent exchange of unfortunate people. It will appear, I am sure, in the same light to you, as it does to your Excellency's

Most obedient Servant,
HORATIO NELSON.

TO ADMIRAL SIR JOHN JERVIS, K.B.

[From the London Gazette, of the 28th February, 1797.]

La Minerve, Port Ferrajo, 29th December, 1796.

Sir,

Herewith I send you Captain Preston's letter to me, of his Action on the 19th December, at night;[3] and I have the honour to be, &c.

HORATIO NELSON.

[3] Captain D'Arcy Preston's Letter is a necessary illustration of the Action with the Spanish Frigates:—

Blanche, at Sea, December 20th, 1796.

Sir,

I have to acquaint you, that last night, after having hailed the Minerve, immediately as her hauling her wind across me to attack the larger ship would permit

TO LIEUTENANT-GENERAL DE BURGH.

[From a Copy in the Admiralty.]

December 29th, 1796.

Dear Sir,

I received your private and public letters at the Court
Martial this day, and feel very much your very handsome
manner in communicating with me.

I fear I shall scarcely have time to-morrow to answer, so
fully as I wish, your public letter, but my answer will be full
to the point, that my instructions, written and verbal, are
clear, that this place is not to be kept on the consideration of
its being any longer useful to his Majesty's Fleet, that the
Fleet has no longer any inducement to come on the Coast of
Italy.

I shall withdraw nearly all the supplies from this place
whether the troops quit it or not, and reduce the Naval force
here as much as possible. The object of our Fleet in future
is the defence of Portugal, and keeping in the Mediterranean
the Combined Fleets. To these points my orders go, and I
have no power of deviating from them. I intend, after to-
morrow, sending the Transfer to Gibraltar. I must take for
granted that Sir John Jervis will take care to cover the Convoy down in such a way as he shall judge fit. However,

the Blanche to wear, I bore up, and in three or four minutes after the Minerve's
first broadside, brought the frigate to Leeward to close action, the two ships just
clear of each other: the enemy made but a trifling resistance, and eight or nine
broadsides completely silenced her, when they called for quarter, and their colours
were hauled down. I am sorry to add, that the very near approach of three fresh
ships (two of which were discovered nearly within gun-shot before we went into
action) rendered my taking possession of her impracticable; when I wore to join
the Minerve, but finding the ships did not then close with the frigate I had left
much damaged in her sails and rigging, I again stood after her, but she had by
this time got her fore-sail, fore-top sail, fore-top-gallant sail set, and not only out-
sailed the Blanche before the wind, but was joined by another ship standing from
the land. Nothing could exceed the steadiness and good conduct of the first
lieutenant, Mr. Cowan, the whole of the officers and ship's company I have the
honour to command; and I have great pleasure in informing you not one person
was hurt, or the rigging the least damaged.

I have the honour to be, &c. &c.,

D'ARCY PRESTON.

P.S.—I beg leave to add how much obliged I am to Captain Maitland, who is on
board, a passenger, to join his ship, for his very great assistance on the quarter-
deck during the action. D. P.—*London Gazette*, of 28th February, 1797.

some orders must turn up before I can probably collect my
Ships. I shall endeavour to call on you in the forenoon.
Believe me, dear Sir,

Your much obliged,

HORATIO NELSON.

TO LIEUTENANT-GENERAL DE BURGH.

[From Clarke and M'Arthur, vol. i. p. 341.]

La Minerve, 30th December, 1796.

Sir,

I am honoured with your letter of the 28th, and have most
seriously attended to every part of the very wise reasoning contained in it: the difficulty of your deciding on the contrary
orders of Government, and of guessing what may be their intentions at present, I clearly perceive.[4] But my instructions
from Admiral Sir John Jervis, both written and verbal, are so
clear, that it is impossible for me to mistake a tittle of them,
or the sentiments of my Commander-in-Chief; and I am
therefore ready to meet the responsibility. I am positively
ordered to execute the King's instructions for carrying the
troops to the places destined for them. I am advised that the
British Fleet will never come to Porto Ferrajo, and that all
our Naval establishments here are to be immediately withdrawn, which I shall do as expeditiously as possible.

The King of Naples having made a Peace, the Admiral
considers his business with the Courts of Italy as terminated;
and that the point he is now instructed to attend to is the
protection of Portugal; therefore the utility of Porto Ferrajo,
as far as relates to a safe place for our Fleet, is at an end;
what its further political consequence may be, does not come
within the sphere of my supposed knowledge; nor of what
may happen both in Portugal and Gibraltar from the want of
this Army. I have sent to collect my Squadron, and as soon

---

[4] General de Burgh did not think himself authorized to abandon Porto Ferrajo
until he had received specific instructions to that effect; and in the Letter to Commodore Nelson, to which the above was the reply, he said:—"I will at the same
time confess that my only motive for urging delay, arises from a wish to have my
proceedings in some measure sanctioned by orders we ought to expect, and by no
means from an idea that we assist the service by staying here; for I have always
held the opinion, that the signing of a Neapolitan peace with France ought to be
our signal for departure."—*Clarke and M'Arthur*, vol. i. p. 341.

Y 2

as they arrive, unless I should receive other orders, I shall offer myself for embarking the troops, stores, &c. ; and should you decline quitting this Post, I shall proceed down the Mediterranean with such Ships of war as are not absolutely wanted for keeping open the communication with the Continent, supposing the Enemy to have no more Naval force in this neighbourhood than at present.

I am, &c.

HORATIO NELSON.

MEMORANDA.

[The following Memoranda, in Nelson's own hand, occur in the Nelson Papers. They are without a date, and it is impossible to ascertain to what precise year they belong. They were, however, written before the loss of his arm in July 1797, and probably while in the Captain, in April or May of that year. The date is unimportant; but as a specimen of the attention which he paid to *details*, and of his habit of arrangement and of committing everything to paper, they are deserving of insertion.]

SURGEON.

Healthy, fourteen; in the Sick List, three men, objects for invaliding.—Necessaries to the 19th June, only.

PURSER.

Provisions for nine weeks full, of all species, except wine, of that only thirty-nine days.

MASTER.

One hundred and thirteen tons of water, beef very good, pork sometimes shrinks in the boiling, the rest of the provisions very good. In cutting up provisions, Master's Mate, Boatswain's Mate, Captain [of the] Forecastle, Captain [of the] Tops, and Quarter-masters. Pretty well supplied with stores; rigging and sails in good order ; two pair of main-shrouds cut in the eyes.

GUNNER.

Eighteen rounds of powder filled; plenty of wads, forty rounds.

CARPENTER.

Hull in good state. Knee of the head supported by two cheeks. Masts and yards in good state. Pretty well stored.

CAPTAIN AND FIRST LIEUTENANT.

Watches, three. In five divisions : well clothed.

MARINES.

Sixty-six.—Lent sixteen.

TO THE REVEREND EDMUND NELSON.

[From Clarke and M'Arthur, vol. i. p. 342.]

La Minerve, 1st January, 1797.

My dear Father,

On this day I am certain you will send me a letter; may many, very many happy returns of it attend you. My late Action will be in the Gazette, and I may venture to say it was what I know the English like. My late prisoner,[5] a descendant from the Duke of Berwick, son of James II., was my brave opponent; for which I have returned him his sword, and sent him in a Flag of truce to Spain. I felt it consonant to the dignity of my Country, and I always act as I feel right, without regard to custom: he was reputed the best Officer in Spain, and his men were worthy of such a Commander; he was the only surviving Officer. It has ever pleased Almighty God to give his blessing to my endeavours. With best love to my dear wife, believe me your most dutiful Son,

HORATIO NELSON.

TO MRS. NELSON.

[From Clarke and M'Arthur, vol. i. p. 342.]

Porto Ferrajo, January 13th, 1797.

I expect Sir Gilbert Elliot here every hour, he goes down to Gibraltar with me; he is a good man, and I love him. As to peace, I do not expect it, Lord Malmesbury[6] will come back as he went; but the people of England will, I trust, be more vigorous for the prosecution of the war, which can alone insure an honourable peace. Naples is alarmed at hers. The French Minister is travelling thither with a train of 300 persons, a printing press, &c., and a company of comedians, &c. The Pope has not made his peace, and is most seriously alarmed.[7]   Yours, &c.

HORATIO NELSON.

[5] Don Jacobo Stuart, Captain of the Sabina.

[6] Lord Malmesbury was sent to Paris to negotiate a Peace, but as Nelson anticipated, "came back as he went."

[7] On the 25th of January, Mr. Graves, the British Agent at Rome, informed Commodore Nelson that all the ports in the Dominions of the Pope were open to the English Ships.

TO THE REVEREND MR. NELSON, HILBOROUGH.

[Autograph, in the Nelson Papers.]

La Minerve, Port Ferrajo, January 13th, 1797.

My dear Brother,

Although I know I can tell you nothing more than my public letters will, of our actions, yet I feel you like to receive a private one, merely if it contains only, ‘We are well,’ which is literally all I can write, for what is past the Papers tell you—what is to come, I must not. However, if self-approbation is a comfort, which I readily admit, I am receiving inexpressible pleasure to be received in the way I ever have been in this Country, and particularly since our last business. You love particulars : therefore for your *private* journal I shall relate some circumstances which are most flattering to me and make our Action stand amongst the foremost of any this war.

When I hailed the Don, and told him, ‘This is an English Frigate,’ and demanded his surrender or I would fire into him, his answer was noble, and such as became the illustrious family from which he is descended—‘ This is a Spanish Frigate, and you may begin as soon as you please.’ I have no idea of a closer or sharper battle : the force to a gun the same, and nearly the same number of men ; we having two hundred and fifty. I asked him several times to surrender during the Action, but his answer was—‘ No, Sir ; not whilst I have the means of fighting left.’ When only himself of all the Officers were left alive, he hailed, and said he could fight no more, and begged I would stop firing. The next Frigate was La Ceres of forty guns, who did not choose to fight much : not a mast, yard, sail, or rope but is knocked to pieces. Main and mizen masts with main yard are new, and every shroud and rope in the Ship fore-mast and fore-yard are fished

On my arrival here, it was a ball night, and being attended by the Captains, was received in due form by the General,[8] and one particular tune[9] was played : the second was ‘ Rule Britannia.’ From Italy I am loaded with compliments—it is

---

[8] De Burgh.

[9] Perhaps “ See the Conquering Hero,” &c., the name of which he may not, from modesty, have liked to write.

true, these are given on the spot; what England may think I
know not. *We* are at a distance. In about a week I shall
be at sea, and it is very probable you will soon hear of
another Action, for I am very much inclined to make the
Dons repent of this war. You will not fail to remember me
kindly to Mrs. Nelson, your children, Aunt Mary, who I
shall rejoice to see, all our friends at Swaffham, &c. ; and believe me ever

Your most affectionate brother,

HORATIO NELSON.

TO MRS, POLLARD, NAPLES.

[Autograph, in the possession of John Luxford, Esq. Mrs. Pollard was the wife
of Mr. Pollard, a Merchant at Leghorn, to whom many of Nelson's letters were
written. When the English were driven from Leghorn, Mr. and Mrs. Pollard proceeded to Naples.]

La Minerve, January 25th, 1797.

My dear Madam,

Many thanks for your kind remembrance of me. The box
is very handsome, as is the sample of Naples ware you sent
me by L'Utile. It is just the thing I wished ; and if any
opportunity offers, I wish to get it here, when Captain Fremantle will, I hope, take care of it. I beg you will tell
Pollard I am very angry with him, for fancying I had, in any
way, or at any time, neglected his interest or convenience ;
so far from it, I assure you, my opinion has ever been uniform
that I think him a most honest merchant ; and that was [what]
we all at Leghorn [thought] ; and [if] I had any interest in
naming Agents,[1] I should certainly name Pollard as *one*.
Besides, my personal obligations are such to him, that I shall
not readily forget. I freely forgive his strong language to
Cockburn about me, as my heart tells me I am perfectly
innocent of the charge he has laid against me. I am glad to
hear Naples agrees with you; and very soon, I believe, Leghorn will be at liberty. In every place, and in every situation, believe me, my dear Madam,

Your most obliged,

HORATIO NELSON.

[1] For Prizes.

Since writing my letter, I have seen some very handsome things which Fremantle has; and have, therefore, to request that, as far as ten or twelve pounds, you will buy for Mrs. Nelson some silk shawls, particular large handkerchiefs of silk, and such other pretty things as a most elegant woman may like. Pray, excuse all this trouble, and believe me ever,

Your obliged,

HORATIO NELSON.

TO LIEUTENANT-GENERAL DE BURGH.

[Autograph draught, in the Nelson Papers.]

La Minerve, Porto Ferrajo, [about 20th] January, 1796 [1797.]

Sir,

The whole of the Ships of War which Sir John Jervis has appropriated for the service of the evacuation of this place being now either in the Port or near approaching it, I have therefore to request that you will be pleased to inform me, with as little delay as possible, whether it is your intention to embark the troops and stores now here, or any part of them.

Should your answer be in the affirmative, every measure shall be taken by me for the speedy arrival of the troops in Gibraltar and Portugal; and should it be a negative, in that case I shall, according to my instructions, withdraw all our Naval stores and establishment, and as many Ships of War as I think can possibly be spared from the service which may be required of them here, our Fleet being now particularly instructed to attend to the preservation of Portugal.

[*Imperfect.*]

TO ADMIRAL SIR JOHN JERVIS, K.B.

[From a Copy in the Admiralty. Commodore Nelson sailed from Porto Ferrajo in La Minerve on the 29th of January 1797, and proceeded to reconnoitre Toulon and Carthagena, on his way to Gibraltar, and thence to Lisbon, to join Admiral Sir John Jervis. The Romulus, Captain George Hope, the Southampton, Captain Macnamara, and some other Vessels of War, in charge of a convoy of Transports, also sailed for that place, but they were directed to form two divisions and to take different courses, so that one of them might certainly escape the Enemy's Fleet. On board La Minerve, Sir Gilbert Elliot, late Vice-Roy of Corsica, Monsr. Pozzo de Borgo (who had been Secretary of State in that Island under the British Government, and who was afterwards so well known as a diplomatist), and several persons of the Vice-Roy's suite were embarked. His Private Secretary, Mr. Hardman, and Colonel Drinkwater were sent in the Romulus, but on her arrival at Gibraltar they joined their Chief on board La Minerve.]

La Minerve, Porto Ferrajo, January 25th, 1797.

Sir,

Although I hope to be with you before Southampton, yet it is possible that may not be the case, as I mean to look into Toulon, Mahon, and Carthagena, that I may be able to tell you the apparent state of the Combined Fleet.

The General having declined to evacuate Porto Ferrajo,[2] as you will observe by the copy of the letter transmitted herewith, I have, notwithstanding, withdrawn all our Naval establishment from this place, having first completed every Ship to as much stores as her Captain pleased to take. Every Transport is completely victualled, and arranged, that every soldier can be embarked in three days.

The way in which I have sent down the Storeship and Dolphin, as also the Convoy, eight or nine Sail, with my intention of looking into the Enemy's ports, I hope you will approve of.

I shall not enter into further particulars till I have the honour of seeing you, but believe me, with the greatest respect,

Sir,

Your most obedient servant,

HORATIO NELSON.

P.S. I have sent orders for Pallas to join you by the Dido and Southampton, and have left similar orders at this place.

---

[2] Colonel Drinkwater says, " On the 27th December, Nelson reached Porto Fer-rajo. Sir Gilbert Elliot was then absent on his visit to the Italian States, but intelligence of the Commodore's arrival was immediately sent to him. On the return of the Vice-Roy to Elba, a consultation was held between Sir Gilbert Elliot, Lieutenant-General de Burgh (who commanded the Troops), and Commodore Nelson, respecting the late orders from Government at home, which Nelson had been specially deputed by the Admiral to carry into effect. The subject was one of great difficulty, involving many interests, and had of course the most deliberate consideration, the result of which was that, under existing circumstances, it was deemed of paramount importance that the British Troops should, notwithstanding those orders, continue in possession of Elba until his Majesty's Ministers could be fully apprised of the many cogent reasons for that course of proceeding."—Narrative, pp. 6, 7.

Ships left at Porto Ferrajo :—

Inconstant	Rose	} Gun-boats.
Blanche	Venom	
Peterel	Mignonne	
Speedy	} Sloops.	
L'Utile		

TO MRS. NELSON.

[From Clarke and M'Arthur, vol. i. p. 343.]

27th January, 1797.

My next letter will probably be dated from Lisbon, where I hope to arrive safe with my charge, but in war much is left to Providence : however, as I have hitherto been most successful, confidence tells me I shall not fail : and as nothing will be left undone by me, should I not always succeed, my mind will not suffer; nor will the world, I trust, be willing to attach blame, where my heart tells me none would be due. Sir Gilbert Elliot and his suite, amongst whom is Colonel Drinkwater,[3] go in La Minerve, therefore I shall be sure of a pleasant party, let what will happen.

Yours, &c.,

HORATIO NELSON.

TO EDWARD HARDMAN, ESQ., PRIVATE SECRETARY TO HIS EXCELLENCY SIR GILBERT ELLIOT.

[Autograph, in the possession of John Hardman, Esq. Finding at Carthagena that the Spanish Fleet had left that Port, Commodore Nelson became extremely anxious to join Sir John Jervis. La Minerve arrived at Gibraltar on the 9th of February, when Nelson learnt that the Spaniards had passed the Rock, to the west-

---

[3] Colonel Drinkwater (who afterwards assumed the name of Bethune), was an eye-witness of the Battle of St. Vincent; and finding that Sir John Jervis's official letter was "little calculated to gratify the legitimate anxiety of the Nation, and did not render justice to Nelson," he wrote the NARRATIVE of that évent, to which Lord Nelson particularly refers in the "Sketch of his Life," (vide vol. i. p. 13.) That very interesting Tract was first published anonymously, in 1797, and again, in 1840, with the author's name, (the profits of which he appropriated to the funds of the Nelson Column,) entitled, "A Narrative of the Battle of St. Vincent, with Anecdotes of Nelson, before and after that Battle." Colonel Drinkwater Bethune is also well known for his History of the Siege of Gibraltar, of which he was supposed to be the last survivor. He died in January 1844, aged 81.

ward, on the 5th, and had sent Le Terrible and two other Sail of the Line and a
Frigate with supplies for their Lines before Gibraltar, which Ships were then at
anchor at the head of the Bay. His two Lieutenants, Culverhouse and Hardy,
taken in La Sabina, were then prisoners on board Le Terrible, but an exchange
being effected, they rejoined La Minerve. Nelson could remain only one day at
Gibraltar, and as the Romulus was left there for repairs, Colonel Drinkwater was
removed to La Minerve, and she weighed in the forenoon of the 11th of February.]

La Minerve, February 11th, 1797.

Dear Sir,

The Minerve was most certainly ready for sea, and it is as
true, that had Sir Gilbert been on board, the Minerve would
have been at sea before the lee-tide made. Hope's[4] Barge
attended instead of Minerve's. Now the tide is made against
us; therefore, I most heartily wish you all a good appetite,
and only beg you will be on board as early in the evening as
possible—say eight o'clock—for I shall sail the first moment
after; but I fear a *westerly* wind.

Yours most truly,

HORATIO NELSON.

P.S. I took my leave of the Governor, and refused to dine
on shore.

BATTLE OF ST. VINCENT.

[The preceding Letter is the last that has been found until the Battle of St.
Vincent, which took place three days after it was written. But some very interesting circumstances occurred in that short interval, which are graphically described
in Colonel Drinkwater's *Narrative.*

As soon as La Minerve sailed from Gibraltar, she was pursued by Le Terrible and
another of the Spanish Line-of-battle Ships. The headmost of the Spanish Ships
gaining on the Frigate, she prepared for action; and Colonel Drinkwater having asked
Nelson's opinion as to the probability of an engagement, he said he thought it very
possible, and looking up at his Broad Pendant, added, "But before the Dons get
hold of that bit of bunting, I will have a struggle with them, and sooner than give
up the Frigate I'll run her ashore." Soon after this conversation, Commodore
Nelson and his guests sat down to dinner, and while Colonel Drinkwater was congratulating Lieutenant Hardy on his being no longer a Prisoner of War, the ap-
palling cry was heard of "a man overboard!" There is perhaps no passage in
Naval history of more thrilling interest than the following account of what then
occurred :—" The Officers of the Ship ran on deck; I, with others, ran to the stern-
windows to see if anything could be observed of the unfortunate man; we had
scarcely reached them before we noticed the lowering of the jolly-boat, in which was
my late neighbour Hardy, with a party of sailors; and before many seconds had

---

4 Captain George Hope, of the Romulus.

elapsed, the current of the Straits, (which runs strongly to the eastward,) had carried the jolly-boat far astern of the Frigate, towards the Spanish Ships. Of course, the first object was to recover, if possible, the fallen man, but he was never seen again. Hardy soon made a signal to that effect, and the man was given up as lost. The attention of every person was now turned to the safety of Hardy and his boat's crew; their situation was extremely perilous, and their danger was every instant increasing, from the fast sailing of the headmost ship of the chase, which by this time had approached nearly within gun-shot of the Minerve. The jolly-boat's crew pulled 'might and main' to regain the Frigate, but apparently made little progress against the current of the Straits. At this crisis, Nelson, casting an anxious look at the hazardous situation of Hardy and his companions, exclaimed 'by G——, I'll not lose Hardy: back the mizen topsail.' No sooner said than done; the Minerve's progress was retarded, having the current to carry her down towards Hardy and his party, who seeing this spirited manœuvre to save them from returning to their old quarters on board the Terrible, naturally redoubled their exertions to rejoin the Frigate. To the landsmen on board the Minerve an action now appeared to be inevitable; and so, it would appear, thought the Enemy, who surprised and confounded by this daring manœuvre of the Commodore, (being ignorant of the accident that led to it,) must have construed it into a direct challenge. Not conceiving, however, a Spanish Ship of the Line to be an equal Match for a British Frigate, with Nelson on board of her, the Captain of the Terrible suddenly shortened sail, in order to allow his consort to join him, and thus afforded time for the Minerve to drop down to the jolly-boat to take out Hardy and the crew; and the moment they were on board the Frigate, orders were given again to make sail. Being now under studding-sails, and the widening of the Straits allowing the wind to be brought more on the Minerve's quarter, the Frigate soon regained the lost distance, and in a short time we had the satisfaction to observe that the dastardly Don was left far in our wake; and at sunset, by steering further to the southward, we lost sight of him and his consort altogether."—*Narrative*, pp. 14, 15.

During the night of the 11th, La Minerve found herself surrounded by several large Ships, which Nelson believed to be the Spanish Fleet, but from which he extricated himself with his usual skill. Nothing was seen of the Spaniards the next day, and on the 13th, La Minerve joined Sir John Jervis's Fleet; Sir Gilbert Elliot and Commodore Nelson immediately waited on the Admiral, on board the Victory, who, on learning that the Enemy was so near, made the signal to "prepare for Action."

Commodore Nelson then left La Minerve, and hoisted his Broad Pendant on board of his own Ship, the Captain, commanded by Captain Miller. Sir Gilbert Elliot requested to remain with the Admiral in the Victory, but was refused; and he with his suite were transferred to the Lively Frigate, Captain Lord Garlies, who had orders to proceed to England. Sir John Jervis, however, yielded to the joint entreaties of Sir Gilbert Elliot and Lord Garlies, that the Lively might remain with the Fleet until she could carry home the intelligence of the expected engagement. Thus Sir Gilbert and Colonel Drinkwater became spectators of one of the most important events of their time, and thus too the Battle fortunately found an able historian.

As Nelson's "Remarks," in pp. 340, 344, relate almost entirely to his own proceedings in the Captain, it is proper to insert Sir John Jervis's Official Dispatch, with a list of the two Fleets, shewing their comparative force, &c.

TO EVAN NEPEAN, ESQ., SECRETARY TO THE ADMIRALTY.

[From the " London Gazette Extraordinary" of the 3rd of March, 1797.]

" Victory, Lagos Bay, February 15, 1797.

" Sir,

" The hopes of falling in with the Spanish Fleet, expressed in my letter to you of the 13th instant, were confirmed that night, by our distinctly hearing the report of their signal guns, and by intelligence received from Captain Foote, of his Majesty's Ship the Niger, who had, with equal judgment and perseverance, kept company with them for several days, on my prescribed rendezvous, (which, from the strong south-east winds, I had never been able to reach,) and that they were not more than the distance of three or four leagues from us. I anxiously awaited the dawn of day, when, being on the starboard tack, Cape St. Vincent bearing east by north eight leagues, I had the satisfaction of seeing a number of Ships extending from south-west to south, the wind then at west and by south. At forty-nine minutes past ten, the weather being extremely hazy, La Bonne Citoyenne made the signal that the Ships seen were of the Line, twenty-five in number. His Majesty's Squadron under my command, consisting of fifteen Ships of the Line, named in the margin,[5] happily formed in the most compact order of sailing, in two lines. By carrying a press of sail, I was fortunate in getting in with the Enemy's Fleet at half-past eleven o'clock, before it had time to connect and form a regular Order of Battle. Such a moment was not to be lost; and confident in the skill, valour, and discipline of the Officers and Men I had the happiness to command, and judging that the honour of his Majesty's arms, and the circumstances of the War in these seas, required a considerable degree of enterprise, I felt myself justified in departing from the regular system; and, passing through their Fleet, in a line formed with the utmost celerity, tacked and thereby separated one-third from the main body, after a partial cannonade, which prevented their re-junction till the evening; and by the very great exertions of the Ships, which had the good fortune to arrive up with the Enemy on the larboard tack, the Ships named in the margin[6] were captured, and the Action ceased about five o'clock in the evening.

" I enclose the most correct list I have been able to obtain of the Spanish Fleet opposed to me, amounting to twenty-seven Sail of the Line, and an account of the Killed and Wounded in his Majesty's Ships, as well as in those taken from the Enemy. The moment the latter (almost totally dismasted) and his Majesty's Ships, the Captain and Culloden, are in a state to put to Sea, I shall avail myself of the first favourable wind to proceed off Cape St. Vincent, in my way to Lisbon.

" Captain Calder, whose able assistance has greatly contributed to the public

[5] Victory	100	Excellent	74
Britannia	100	Orion	74
Barfleur	98	Colossus	74
Prince George	98	Egmont	74
Blenheim	90	Culloden	74
Namur	90	Irresistible	74
Captain	74	Diadem	64
Goliath	74		
[6] Salvador del Mundo	112	San Nicolas	80
San Josef	112	San Ysidro	74

service during my command, is the bearer of this, and will more particularly describe to the Lords Commissioners of the Admiralty the movements of the Squadron on the 14th, and the present state of it.

"I am, Sir, &c.

"J. JERVIS."

"LIST OF THE SPANISH FLEET OPPOSED TO THE BRITISH, THE 14TH OF FEBRUARY, 1797.

Santissima Trinidad . . .	130	Pelayo	74
Mexicana	112	San Genaro	74
Principe de Asturias . . .	112	San Ildephonso	74
Concepcion	112	San Juan Nepomuceno . .	74
Conde de Regla	112	San Francisco de Paula . .	74
Salvador del Mundo . . .	112 taken	San Ysidro	74 taken
San Josef	112 taken	San Antonio	74
San Nicolas	84 taken	San Pablo	74
Oriente	74	San Firmin	74
Glorioso	74	Neptuno	74
Atlante	74	Bahama	74
Conquestador	74	Name unknown [San Domingo]	74
Soberano	74	Name unknown [Terrible]	74
Firme	74		

"LIST OF THE BRITISH FLEET OPPOSED TO THE SPANISH, THE 14TH OF FEBRUARY, 1797.

		KILLED.	WOUNDED.
Victory	Admiral Sir John Jervis, K.B., 1st Captain, Robert Calder . 2nd Captain, George Grey .	1	5
Britannia . . .	Vice-Admiral Thompson . . Captain Thomas Foley . .	0	1
Barfleur	Vice-Admiral Hon. William Waldegrave . . . . . Captain James Richard Dacres	0	7 *
Prince George . .	Rear-Admiral William Parker Captain John Irwin . . .	8	7
Blenheim. . . .	Thomas Lenox Frederick . .	12	49
Namur	James Hawkins Whitshed . .	2	5
Captain	Commodore Nelson . . . Captain Ralph Willett Miller	24	56
Goliath	Sir Charles Henry Knowles .	0	8
Excellent . . .	Cuthbert Collingwood	11	12
Orion	Sir James Saumarez	0	9
Colossus	George Murray	0	5
Egmont	Captain John Sutton	0	0
Culloden	Thomas Troubridge	10	47
Irresistible . . .	George Martin	5	14
Diadem	George Henry Towry	0	2
		73	227

"OFFICERS KILLED.

Captain.—Major William Norris, of the Marines; Mr. James Godinch, Midship man.

Excellent.—Mr. Peter Peffers, Boatswain.

Culloden.—Mr. G. A. Livingstone, Lieutenant of Marines.

Irresistible.—Sergeant Watson, of the Marines.

"OFFICERS WOUNDED.

Blenheim.—Mr. Edward Sibby, Acting Lieutenant; Mr. Peacock, Boatswain; Mr. Joseph Wixon, Master's Mate, since dead.

Captain.—Commodore Nelson, bruised, but not obliged to quit the deck; Mr. Carrington, Boatswain, wounded in boarding the San Nicolas; Mr. Thomas Lund, Midshipman.

Excellent.—Mr. Edward Augustus Down, Master's Mate.

Orion.—Mr. Thomas Mansel, Midshipman.

Irresistible.—Mr. Andrew Thompson, Lieutenant; Mr. Hugh M'Kinnon, Master's Mate; Mr. William Balfour, Midshipman.

LIST OF THE KILLED AND WOUNDED ON BOARD THE SPANISH SHIPS TAKEN BY THE SQUADRON UNDER THE COMMAND OF ADMIRAL SIR JOHN JERVIS, K.B., ON THE 14TH OF FEBRUARY, 1797:

San Ysidro.—4 Officers, 25 Artillerists, Seamen, and Soldiers killed; 8 Officers, 55 Artillerists, &c., wounded.

Salvador del Mundo.—5 Officers, 37 Artillerists, &c., killed; 3 Officers, 121 Artillerists, &c., wounded.

San Nicolas.—4 Officers, 140 Artillerists, &c., killed; 8 Officers, 51 Artillerists, &c., wounded.

San José.—2 Officers, 44 Artillerists, &c., killed; 5 Officers, 91 Artillerists, &c., wounded.

Note.—Among the killed is the General Don Francisco Xavier Winthuysen, Chef D'Escadre."—*London Gazette Extraordinary*, 3rd March, 1797.

Though there were two Vice, and one Rear-Admiral, and a Commodore in the Fleet, no other Officer was mentioned in Sir John Jervis' Dispatch than Captain Calder, the First Captain of the Victory, (or Captain of the Fleet,) afterwards so well known as Admiral Sir Robert Calder. The omission of the Flag Officers was as unusual, as the total disregard shewn to the brilliant services of Nelson, Troubridge, Collingwood, and Frederick, was unjust. That injustice was, however, partially remedied by the following *Private* Letter to Earl Spencer, the First Lord of the Admiralty, dated on 16th of February; but, as it did not appear in the "London Gazette," it was a very inadequate compensation to their wounded feelings:—

"H.M.S. Victory, in Lagos Bay, 16th February, 1797.

"My Lord,

"The correct conduct of every Officer and man in the Squadron on the 14th inst. made it improper to distinguish one more than another in my public Letter, because I am confident that had those who were least in action been in the situation of the fortunate few, their behaviour would not have been less meritorious; yet to your Lordship it becomes me to state that Captain Troubridge, in the Culloden, led the Squadron through the Enemy in a masterly style, and tacked *the instant the Signal flew*, and was gallantly supported by the Blenheim, Prince George, Orion, Irresistible, and Colossus; the latter had her fore and fore-top-sail yards wounded, and they unfortunately broke in the slings in stays, which threw her out, and impeded the tacking of the Victory.

"Commodore Nelson, who was in the rear on the starboard tack, took the lead on the larboard, and contributed very much to the fortune of the day, as did Captain Collingwood; and in the close, the San Josef and San Nicolas having fallen foul of each other, the Captain laid them on board, and Captain Berry, who served as a volunteer, entered at the head of the boarders, and Commodore Nelson followed immediately, and took possession of them both; the crippled state of these Ships, and of the Captain, entangled as they were, and that part of the Enemy's Fleet, which had been kept off in the morning (as described in the public letter) joining at the instant, it became necessary to collect the Squadron, to resist an attempt to wrest those Ships, and the Salvador del Mundo and the San Ysidro, from us, which occasioned the discontinuance of the Action.

"The Enemy has still twenty-two Ships of the Line and nine Frigates in condition for service off Cape St. Vincent, and the moment our damaged Ships are repaired, and proper jury-masts, &c., raised on board the Prizes, I shall face him in my way to Lisbon. The Ships' returns of killed and wounded, although not always the criterion of their being more or less in Action, is, in this instance, correctly so. If I succeed in getting our Trophies into the Tagus, it is my intention to place Masters and Commanders in them all. Captain Hallowell, whose conduct on board the Victory during the Action has made him more dear to me than before, declining this sort of service on account of the idleness it is likely to produce, I request, as the greatest favour your Lordship can confer on me, that you will have the goodness to give him the command of a large Frigate, manned, and allow him to serve under my Command.

"It is with great repugnance I say anything to your Lordship about promotions, knowing how much you must be pressed upon at home; but Commodore Nelson being uncommonly anxious to reward Lieutenants Spicer and Noble, the former now First of the Captain, and the latter most desperately wounded in the belly and shoulder on board La Minerve, in her Action with the Sabina, in addition to a shot he got in his neck on the Coast of Genoa, his father an Officer in the Army, and a brother a Midshipman in the Navy, having died on service in the West Indies, will, I trust, excuse my naming them to you a second time. Sensible as I am of the just attention paid to the merits of all who have happened to share in successful Actions with the Enemy since you have been at the head of the Board of Admiralty, I do not presume to call your attention to others.

"I have omitted to notice that Rear-Admiral Sir William Parker, whose Flag was on board the Prince George, in the Van on both Tacks, made his Signals in a very officer-like manner; for the rest I beg leave to refer you to Captain Calder, who is thoroughly master of the subject, and I desire to recommend him and Captain Grey to your protection. I had a conversation with Admiral Waldegrave on the subject of his carrying a duplicate of these Dispatches, which, as there existed a possibility of our bringing the Spanish Fleet to action a second time, he very commendably declined; perhaps your Lordship will think it due to him to send the Romney to Lisbon, to convey him, his suite, and baggage, (rather too much for a Frigate,) to England. I have the honour to be, &c.

"J. JERVIS."

No one can read that Letter without being surprised that the paragraphs at its commencement, respecting Captain Troubridge and Commodore Nelson, did not find their proper place in the Public Dispatch. Even in this Private Letter only one of the Flag Officers is praised for his conduct in the Action, and he merely for "having made his signals in a very Officer-like manner." This withholding of praise is the more remarkable, from Lord St. Vincent having, on other occasions, in his

Dispatches, expressed his admiration of gallantry and good conduct in the strongest, and sometimes in extravagant terms.

Sir John Barrow, one of the Secretaries to the Admiralty, (whose authority on such a point is very high,) states, that " It is known that in Jervis's original letter, he had given to Nelson all due praise, but was prevailed on by Sir Robert Calder, the Captain of the Fleet, to substitute another in which it was left out, on the ground that as Nelson had disobeyed the signal of recall, [the signal to tack,] any eulogy on his conduct would encourage other Officers to do the same, while the exclusive praise of one individual would act as a discouragement of the rest ;" and Sir John Barrow very justly adds, " The surprise is, that a man of Lord St. Vincent's sagacity should not have detected the lurking jealousy that gave rise to such a recommendation."—(*Life of Admiral Earl Howe*, p. 249.)　The surprise is, however, still greater that a man so pre-eminently distinguished for firmness and self-government as Lord St. Vincent, should have yielded to a recommendation to act unjustly, not to Nelson only, but to his Admirals, and to the Captains who had so highly distinguished themselves.　This surprise will be increased, when it is remembered that, " after the battle, Sir John Jervis received Nelson on the quarter-deck of the Victory, took him in his arms, said he could not sufficiently thank him, and insisted on his keeping the sword of the Spanish Rear-Admiral which he had so bravely won." —(*Brenton's Life and Correspondence of the Earl of St. Vincent*, vol. i. p. 313 ; and see p. 346, post.)　Another of Lord St. Vincent's biographers relates a piquant, and, for the reason afterwards stated, an *important* anecdote of the Admiral and his First Captain: " In the evening, while talking over the events of the day, Captain Calder hinted that the spontaneous manœuvre which carried those *duo fulmina belli*, Nelson and Collingwood, into the brunt of battle, was an unauthorized departure by the Commodore from the prescribed mode of attack !　' It certainly was so,' replied Sir John Jervis, ' and if ever you commit such a breach of your orders, I will forgive you also.'　The flattering reception which, immediately after the Action, Sir John Jervis had given to the Commodore, is well known."—(*Tucker's Memoirs of Earl St. Vincent*, voi. i. p. 262.)

Though the Commander-in-Chief's praise of his Officers was cold and private, their and his rewards were great and general.　Parliament voted them its thanks in the most cordial manner.　Admiral (of the Blue) Sir John Jervis was created Baron Jervis, of Meaford, in the county of Stafford, and Earl of St. Vincent, by Patent, on the 27th of May, 1797, to him and the heirs male of his body, with a pension of £3000 a-year.　Vice-Admiral (of the Blue) Charles Thompson, and Rear-Admiral (of the Blue) William Parker, the second and fourth in command, were made Baronets.　Vice-Admiral (of the Blue) the Honourable William Waldegrave, the third in command, being a Peer's son, and having thus higher rank than a Baronet, did not immediately receive any honours, but on the 29th of December, 1800, he was created an Irish Peer, by the title of Baron Radstock, Castletown, Queen's County.　Commodore Nelson was invested with the Order of the Bath ; Captain Robert Calder, the Captain of the Fleet, was Knighted ; and the Naval Medal, instituted after Lord Howe's victory, in 1794, was given to the Admirals and Commodore, and to the Captain of every Ship of the Line in the Fleet, being a very different principle of distribution from that adopted in 1794, when the gallant Collingwood found himself among those excluded from the distinction.　His noble conduct on being offered the Medal for the Battle of St. Vincent, is well known.

The elevation of Sir John Jervis to an *Earldom*, for the Battle of St. Vincent, has been often remarked upon ; but it is explained by a letter from Lord Spencer, of the 1st of February, 1797, fourteen days before the Battle, intimating the King's intention to raise him to the Peerage, so that he was, in fact, a *Baron* when it was fought.—(*Tucker's Memoirs of Earl St. Vincent,* vol. i. p. 225.)

To these Remarks it is requisite to add some observations on the account of the Battle, in Mr. James's " *Naval History*," as that writer has ventured to say that Nelson's boldness and decision in wearing the Captain, quitting the Line, and attacking the Leewardmost Division of the Spanish Fleet, was not his own spontaneous act, but arose from a signal made by the Commander-in-Chief. That assertion, which is not only a detraction from the merits of one of Nelson's most brilliant exploits, but an impeachment of his veracity, is, however, without the slightest foundation.

In the account of the proceedings of the Captain on the 14th of February, signed by Nelson, Captain Miller, and Captain Berry (vide p. 340, post), it is said—

" At one P.M., the Captain having passed the sternmost of the Enemy's Ships, which formed their Van, and part of their Centre, consisting of seventeen Sail of the Line—they on the larboard, we on the starboard tack—the Admiral made the signal to tack in succession; but I, perceiving the Spanish Ships all to bear up before the wind, or nearly so, evidently with an intention of forming their Line going large, joining their separated Division, at that time engaged with some of our centre Ships, or flying from us,—to prevent either of their schemes from taking effect, I ordered the Ship to be wore; and passing between the Diadem and Excellent, at a quarter past one o'clock was engaged with the headmost, and, of course, leewardmost of the Spanish Division." This is repeated in the " Remarks," in Nelson's autograph, (vide p. 344, post,) except that he does not there mention that the Admiral had made the signal " to tack."

Mr. James's statement is as follows:—" At about 1h. P.M., just as the rearmost Ship of that part of the British Line, which was still on the Starboard Tack, had advanced so far ahead, as to leave an open sea to Leeward of the Spanish weather Division, then passing in the contrary direction, the advanced Ships of the latter, as the last effort to join their Lee Division, bore up together. Scarcely was the movement made, ere it caught the attention of one, who was as quick in foreseeing the consequences of its success, as he was ready, in obedience to the spirit, if not, the letter, of a signal just made, in devising the means for its failure. That signal (No. 41,) had been hoisted on board the Victory, at 51 m. past Noon, and directed the Ships of the Fleet ' to take suitable stations for mutual support, and engage the Enemy, as coming up in succession.'[7] Commodore Nelson, accordingly directed Captain Miller to wear the Captain." James then adds in a note, " That the Captain wore out of the Line in compliance with any signal is, we know, contrary to received opinion, but the following stands as an entry in the log-book of a Flag-Ship then at no great distance from her,—' At 1, Sir John Jervis made the signal for the English Fleet to form Line as most convenient. On this, the Captain pressed all sail from her station of sailing, and stood on, and fell into our Van, ahead of us.' Although the signal here specified was No. 31, instead of 41, there is every reason

---

[7] The Editor has failed in obtaining the General Signal Book used in 1797, and in finding a list of the Signals made by the Victory on the 14th of February. In 1798, the Code of Signals was changed, when the signal for " The Ships to take suitable stations for their mutual support, and engage the Enemy as they get up with them," became " No. 28 ;" and the signal to " form a Line of Battle astern and ahead of the Admiral, as most convenient from the accidental position of the Ships, without regard to the prescribed form," became " No. 48."

to suppose that the latter, the first signal not having been made since 11 A.M., was the signal to which the entry had reference."—*Naval History*, vol. ii. p. 37.

Whether the signal was " No. 31," or " No. 41," the Log of that Ship (whose name is improperly withheld, but which was probably the Prince George, Rear-Admiral Parker,) does not state that in consequence of its being made, the Captain wore, quitted the Line, and pursued a Division of the Enemy's Fleet; but it states, (as was no doubt the case,) " that she made all sail, left her station in the Line, and stood on, and fell into the Van, ahead" of the said Flag Ship; a proceeding perfectly consistent with the signal "No. 31," " to form Line as most convenient," but inconsistent with the signal, " No. 41," i. e., " to take stations for mutual support," &c. Mr. James therefore not only supposes one signal was *another* signal, but he wishes it to be believed that the signal which he thinks was wrongly described, led to an evolution, totally different from that which the signal (" No. 31") is expressly stated to have produced. Moreover, how can the proceeding of the " Captain," in wearing and quitting the Line, instead of obeying the Admiral's signal " to tack," be said to be " *in obedience to the spirit*" of the signal " No. 41, to take suitable stations for mutual support, and engage the Enemy on coming up in succession ?"

Mr. James's assertion is thus shewn to have been made without any authority whatever; and it is proved to be untrue by—

First, the " Remarks" signed by Captains Miller and Berry, as well as by Nelson himself, and by the "Remarks"in Nelson's own autograph. *Secondly*, by the admission of the Commander-in-Chief, as is shown by the two anecdotes just related, the very foundation of both of which is, that Nelson's proceedings were unauthorized and irregular; by, to a great extent, Sir John Jervis's private letter to Lord Spencer, and by his reception of Nelson after the Battle. *Thirdly*, by the general admission of the whole Fleet, and, indeed, of the whole British Navy. *Fourthly*, by Captain Collingwood's letter, " you formed the plan of attack," (vide p. 349, post.) *Fifthly*, by Colonel Drinkwater's Narrative. And, *Sixthly*, by its not being disputed in Rear-Admiral Parker's Statement, addressed to Nelson, though that Statement was written, because Admiral Parker's friends considered that in Nelson's Remarks on the Battle, Parker had not the credit that properly belonged to him. A copy of Admiral Parker's Statement is inserted in the APPENDIX to this Volume, and Nelson's laconic, if not contemptuous Answer to it is in p. 437, post. Southey, in a long Note on the omission of Nelson's name in the Dispatch, justly says, "the decisive movement by which the Action became a victory, was executed in neglect of orders, upon his own judgment, and at his peril."

Not satisfied with trying to divest Nelson of the merit of one exploit, Mr. James suggests that he claimed more credit than he deserved for another. After quoting the concluding passages of Nelson's " Remarks," but of the former part of which (as in his account of the Agamemnon's proceedings on the 13th and 14th of March, vide p. 10, ante,) he takes no notice, he says, " There is, it appears, a doubt whether the San Josef got foul of the San Nicolas just before, or during, Commodore Nelson's possession of the latter: at all events, it seems certain that the San Josef fell on board by the stern, and afterwards dropped broadside-to ; in which position she was boarded from the San Nicolas, as already described. But a more serious doubt attaches to the statement of the San Josef's surrender having been the consequence of that boarding. As far as our researches have gone, it appears to be clearly established, that the Prince George was engaging the San Josef at the moment she got foul; and that the former Ship only suspended her fire until, having edged away to leeward of the Captain and San Nicolas, she was able to resume it ahead and clear of the Captain ; that the San Nicolas at this moment fired into the Prince George, who accordingly bestowed part of her return fire upon the San Nicolas, and continued her fire upon both Spanish Ships until, at the end of some minutes, hailed from the Captain to announce that they had struck."—*Naval History,* vol. ii. p. 41.

As Mr. James gives no authority for these doubts, they might fairly have been left unnoticed. There is, however, no wish to avoid the question. Mr. James's "*researches*" on the subject seem to have begun and ended with Admiral Parker's Statement, where nearly the same words occur. (Vide the APPENDIX.) The answer to Admiral Parker and Mr. James is short and conclusive. The Prince George may have been firing into the San Josef before, or even at the time when she was boarded by Nelson from the San Nicolas, (though Nelson's letter to Admiral Parker makes it very doubtful,) and if it were so, it may have convinced the Spaniards of the hopelessness of contending against their new assailant; but it is indisputable that *the San Josef did not surrender until Nelson was in her main-chains, at the head of his boarders.* That the Spanish Captain considered Nelson as his conqueror is proved by his having presented the Spanish Admiral's sword to *him.* Common sense would shew that the San Josef, a First-rate, with a thousand men, would have received the Boarders in a very different manner—little resistance having been offered to Nelson and his followers—had she not been previously severely handled by our Ships. Nor did Nelson ever assert the contrary: his words are, " I ordered my people to board the First-rate, which was done in an instant, Captain Berry assisting me into the main-chains. At this moment a Spanish Officer looked over the quarter-deck rail, and said they had surrendered." (Vide pp. 343, 346, post.) In his Letter to Captain Locker, (p. 355, post,) sending him an account of the battle, he says, " I pretend not to say that those Ships might not have fell had I not boarded them ; but truly it was far from impossible but they might have forged into the Spanish Fleet, as the other Ships did."

A FEW REMARKS RELATIVE TO MYSELF IN THE CAPTAIN, IN WHICH MY PENDANT WAS FLYING ON THE MOST GLORIOUS VALENTINE'S DAY, 1797.[8]

[From a Copy in the Nelson Papers, corrected by Nelson, and with the autograph signatures of Commodore Nelson, Captain Miller, and Captain Berry. Clarke and M'Arthur state that Commodore Nelson sent a Copy of this Narrative to H.R.H. the Duke of Clarence, with the following Note :—" The praises and honours of my Admiral tell me I may relate my tale : I therefore send your Royal Highness a few Remarks relative to myself in the Captain, in which my Pendant was flying on the most glorious Valentine's Day." It appears from a Letter to Captain Locker (vide p. 355, post) that a Copy was sent to him for publication.]

At one P.M., the Captain having passed the sternmost of the Enemy's Ships which formed their van and part of their centre, consisting of seventeen Sail of the Line, they on the larboard,

---

[8] These " Remarks" were published soon after they were written, and were reprinted in the Naval Chronicle, in 1799, (vol. ii. p. 500.) The copy in Clarke and M'Arthur (vol. i. p. 349) differs verbally in many places from the above, and they say that they had made " some additions" from the Original found in the Nelson Papers. That " original" is now given *verbatim.*

we on the starboard tack, the Admiral made the signal to
'tack in succession;' but I, perceiving the Spanish Ships all to
bear up before the wind, or nearly so, evidently with an intention of forming their line going large, joining their separated
Division, at that time engaged with some of our centre Ships,
or flying from us—to prevent either of their schemes from
taking effect, I ordered the ship to be wore,[9] and passing
between the Diadem and Excellent, at a quarter past one
o'clock, was engaged with the headmost, and of course leewardmost of the Spanish division. The Ships which I know were,
the Santissima Trinidad, 126; San Josef, 112; Salvador del
Mundo, 112; San Nicolas, 80; another First-rate, and Seventy-
four, names not known. I was immediately joined and most
nobly supported by the Culloden, Captain Troubridge. The
Spanish Fleet, from not wishing (I suppose) to have a decisive
battle, hauled to the wind on the larboard tack, which brought
the Ships afore-mentioned to be the leewardmost and sternmost
Ships in their Fleet. For near an hour, I believe, (but do not
pretend to be correct as to time,) did the Culloden and Captain
support this apparently, but not really, unequal contest; when
the Blenheim, passing between us and the Enemy, gave us a
respite, and sickened the Dons. At this time, the Salvador del
Mundo and San Isidro dropped astern, and were fired into in
a masterly style by the Excellent, Captain Collingwood, who
compelled the SanIsidro to hoist English colours, and I thought
the large Ship Salvador del Mundo had also struck; but Captain Collingwood, disdaining the parade of taking possession
of beaten enemies, most gallantly pushed up, with every sail
set, to save his old friend and messmate, who was to appearance in a critical state. The Blenheim being ahead, and the
Culloden crippled and astern, the Excellent ranged up within
ten feet of the San Nicolas, giving a most tremendous fire,
The San Nicolas luffing up, the San Josef fell on board her,
and the Excellent passing on for the Santissima Trinidad, the
Captain resumed her situation abreast of them, and close alongside. At this time the Captain having lost her foretop-mast,
not a sail, shroud, or rope left, her wheel shot away, and
incapable of further service in the line, or in chase, I directed

---

[9] Vide the preceding Observations.

Captain Miller to put the helm a-starboard, and calling for the
Boarders, ordered them to board.[1]

The Soldiers of the 69th Regiment, with an alacrity which
will ever do them credit, and Lieutenant Pierson of the same
Regiment, were amongst the foremost on this service. The
first man who jumped into the Enemy's mizen-chains was
Captain Berry, late my First Lieutenant;[2] (Captain Miller
was in the very act of going also, but I directed him to remain;)[3]
he was supported from our spritsail-yard, which hooked in the
mizen-rigging. A soldier of the 69th regiment having broke
the upper quarter-gallery window, jumped in, followed by
myself and others as fast as possible. I found the cabin-doors
fastened, and some Spanish Officers fired their pistols; but
having broke open the doors, the soldiers fired, and the
Spanish Brigadier (Commodore with a Distinguishing Pendant)
fell, as retreating to the quarter deck, on the larboard side,
near the wheel. Having pushed on the quarter-deck, I found
Captain Berry in possession of the poop, and the Spanish ensign hauling down. I passed with my people and Lieutenant
Pierson on the larboard gangway to the forecastle, where I
met two or three Spanish Officers prisoners to my seamen,
and they delivered me their swords.

At this moment, a fire of pistols or muskets opened from the
Admiral's stern gallery of the San Josef, I directed the soldiers
to fire into her stern; and, calling to Captain Miller, ordered

---

[1] James (vol. i. p. 40) says, there was then "no alternative but to board the
Spanish two-decker." If he meant that to *Nelson*, there could be no other choice,
he was correct; but many Captains had, under similar circumstances, (as no one
knew better than Mr. James,) found an *alternative* in leaving their antagonist
alone.

[2] Captain Berry was then a passenger in the Captain, having lately been promoted
to the rank of Commander; and he was Posted on the 6th of March following, for
his gallantry at St. Vincent's.

[3] The following interesting anecdote has been obligingly communicated by Captain
Miller's sister, Mrs. Dalrymple:—"While Captain Miller was leading his men to the
San Nicolas, Commodore Nelson said 'No, Miller; *I* must have that honour;' and
on going into the cabin, after the contest, Nelson said, 'Miller, I am under the
greatest obligations to you,' and presented him with the Spanish Captain's sword;
and then, as if he could not sufficiently shew his sense of his Captain's services, he
again expressed his obligations, and drawing a ring from his finger, placed it on
Captain Miller's. The ring, rather a large topaz, set round with diamonds, and the
Spanish Officer's sword, are now in the possession of Miss Miller, Captain Miller's
only surviving child.

him to send more men into the San Nicolas, and directed my people to board the First-rate, which was done in an instant, Captain Berry assisting me[4] into the main chains. At this moment a Spanish Officer looked over the quarter-deck rail, and said—'they surrendered;' from this most welcome intelligence it was not long before I was on the quarter-deck, when the Spanish Captain, with a bow, presented me his Sword, and said the Admiral was dying of his wounds below. I asked him, on his honour, if the Ship were surrendered? he declared she was; on which I gave him my hand, and desired him to call to his Officers and Ship's company, and tell them of it—which he did; and on the quarter-deck of a Spanish First-rate, extravagant as the story may seem, did I receive the Swords of vanquished Spaniards; which, as I received, I gave to William Fearney, one of my bargemen, who put them with the greatest sangfroid under his arm. I was surrounded by Captain Berry, Lieutenant Pierson, 69th Regiment, John Sykes, John Thomson, Francis Cook, all old Agamemnons, and several other brave men, seamen and soldiers: thus fell these Ships.

N.B.—In boarding the San Nicolas, I believe, we lost about seven killed and ten wounded, and about twenty Spaniards lost their lives by a foolish resistance. None were I believe lost, in boarding the San Josef.

HORATIO NELSON.
RALPH WILLETT MILLER.
E. BERRY.

[Added in Nelson's Autograph.]

Don Francisco Xavier Winthuysen, Rear-Admiral, died of his wounds on board the San Josef. Don Tomas Geraldino, killed on board the San Nicolas when boarded by the Captain.

---

[4] Charnock, Harrison, and Southey, state that Nelson led the way into the San Josef, vehemently exclaiming, "Westminster Abbey, or Victory!"—a gasconade very inconsistent with his character.

A FEW REMARKS RELATIVE TO MYSELF IN THE CAPTAIN, IN
WHICH MY PENDANT WAS FLYING ON THE MOST GLORIOUS
VALENTINE'S DAY, 1797.

[Autograph draught, in the Nelson Papers. Though this Paper is in many places
in the same words as the preceding, yet as it is a document of a different character,
the former being merely signed by Nelson, while this is wholly in his own hand, and
as, moreover, it contains some interesting additions, both are printed entire.]

On the 13th February, at 6 P.M., shifted my Pendant from
from La Minerve Frigate to the Captain.

Valentine's day, at daylight, signal to prepare for Battle:
at 10, saw some strange Ships standing across the van of our
Fleet, on the larboard tack, which was sailing in two divisions,
eight in the weather, seven in the lee, on the starboard tack.
About 11, signal to form the Line, as most convenient. At
twenty-five past 11, the Action commenced in the Van, then
passing through the Enemy's Line. About 1 A.M., the Captain having passed the sternmost of the Enemy's Ships,
which formed their Van, consisting of seventeen Sail of the
Line, and perceiving the Spanish Fleet to bear up before the
wind, evidently with an intention of forming their Line, going
large—joining their separated division,—or flying from us ; to
prevent either of their schemes from taking effect, I ordered
the Ship to be wore, and passing between the Diadem and
Excellent, at ten minutes past 1 o'clock, I was in close Action
with the Van, and, of course, leewardmost of the Spanish
Fleet. The Ships which I know were the Santa Trinidad,
San Josef, Salvador del Mundo, San Nicolas, San Isidro,
another First-rate and Seventy-four, names not known. I was
immediately joined and most nobly supported by the Culloden, Captain Troubridge. The Spanish Fleet, from not
wishing, I suppose, to have a decisive Battle, hauled to the
wind on the larboard tack, which brought the Ships above
mentioned to be the leewardmost Ships in their Fleet. For an
hour the Culloden and Captain supported this apparently, but
not in reality, unequal contest, when the Blenheim, passing
to windward of us and ahead, eased us a little. By this time
the Salvador del Mundo and San Isidro dropped astern, and
were fired into in a masterly style by the Excellent, Captain
Collingwood, who compelled them to hoist English colours,

when, disdaining the parade of taking possession of beaten
Enemies, he most gallantly pushed up to save his old friend
and messmate, who was to appearance in a critical situation :
the Blenheim having fallen to leeward, and the Culloden
crippled and astern, the Captain at this time being actually
fired upon by three First-rates and the San Nicolas and a
Seventy-four, and about pistol-shot distance of the San
Nicolas. 'The Excellent ranged up with every sail set, and
hauling up his mainsail just astern, passed within ten feet of
the San Nicolas, giving her a most awful and tremendous fire.
The San Nicolas luffing up, the San Josef fell on board her,
and the Excellent passing on for the Santa Trinidad, the
Captain resumed her situation abreast of them, close alongside.

At this time, the Captain having lost her fore-topmast, not
a sail, shroud, or rope standing, the wheel shot away, and
incapable of further service in the Line or in chase, I directed
Captain Miller to put the helm a-starboard, and calling for the
Boarders, ordered them to Board.

The Soldiers of the 69th Regiment, with an alacrity which
will ever do them credit, with Lieutenant Pierson, of the same
Regiment, were amongst the foremost on this service. The
first man who jumped into the Enemy's mizen-chains was
Captain Berry, late my First-Lieutenant. He was supported
from our spritsail-yard ; and a soldier of the 69th Regiment
having broke the upper quarter-gallery window, jumped in,
followed by myself and others, as fast as possible. I found the
cabin-doors fastened, and the Spanish Officers fired their
pistols at us through the windows, but having broke open the
doors, the soldiers fired, and the Spanish Brigadier (Commodore, with a distinguishing Pendant) fell as retreating to the
quarter-deck. Having pushed on the quarter-deck, I found
Captain Berry in possession of the poop, and the Spanish
Ensign hauling down. The San Josef at this moment fired
muskets and pistols from the Admiral's stern-gallery on us.
Our seamen by this time were in full possession of every part :
about seven of my men were killed, and some few wounded,
and about twenty Spaniards.

Having placed sentinels at the different ladders, and ordered
Captain Miller to push more men into the San Nicolas, I

directed my brave fellows to board the First-rate, which was done in a moment. When I got into her main-chains, a Spanish Officer came upon the quarter-deck rail, without arms, and said the Ship had surrendered. From this welcome information, it was not long before I was on the quarter-deck, when the Spanish Captain, with a bended knee, presented me his Sword, and told me the Admiral was dying with his wounds below. I gave him my hand, and desired him to call to his Officers and Ship's Company that the Ship had surrendered, which he did; and on the quarter-deck of a Spanish First-rate, extravagant as the story may seem, did I receive the Swords of the vanquished Spaniards, which as I received I gave to William Fearney, one of my bargemen, who placed them, with the greatest sang-froid, under his arm. I was surrounded by Captain Berry, Lieutenant Pierson, 69th Regiment, John Sykes, John Thompson, Francis Cook, and William Fearney, all old Agamemnons, and several other brave men, Seamen and Soldiers. Thus fell these Ships. The Victory passing saluted us with three cheers, as did every Ship in the Fleet. The Minerve sent a boat for me, and I hoisted my Pendant on board her, directing Captain Cockburn to put me on board the first uninjured Ship of the Line, which was done ; and I hoisted my Pendant in the Irresistible, but the day was too far advanced to venture on taking possession of the Santa Trinidad, although she had long ceased to resist, as it must have brought on a night Action with a still very superior Fleet. At dusk, I went on board the Victory, when the Admiral received me on the quarter-deck, and having embraced me, said he could not sufficiently thank me, and used every kind expression which could not fail to make me happy. On my return on board the Irresistible, my bruises were looked at, and found but trifling, and a few days made me as well as ever.

H. N.

N.B. There is a saying in the Fleet too flattering for me to omit telling—viz., ' Nelson's Patent Bridge for boarding First-Rates,' alluding to my passing over an Enemy's 80-gun Ship; and another of a Sailor's taking me by the hand on board the

San Josef, saying he might not soon have such another place to do it in, and assuring me he was heartily glad to see me.[6]

TO CAPTAIN COLLINGWOOD, H.M.S. EXCELLENT.

[Autograph, in the possession of the Honourable Mrs. Newnham Collingwood. Upon this letter Captain Collingwood wrote, "Nelson shifted his Broad Pendant into the Irresistible, his own Ship being so mauled."]

Irresistible, February 15th, 1797.

My dearest Friend,

' A friend in need is a friend indeed,' was never more truly verified than by your most noble and gallant conduct

---

[6] On the morning after the Battle, the 15th of February, Nelson went on board the Lively to see Sir Gilbert Elliot, but the late Viceroy had just gone to the Victory, to congratulate Sir John Jervis on the events of the preceding day. Nelson found, however, Colonel Drinkwater, whose relation of the substance of their conversation is of great interest:—"'Where is Sir Gilbert?' was his first inquiry. 'Gone with Lord Garlies to the Victory,' was my reply. 'I hoped,' he rejoined, 'to have caught him before he saw the Admiral; but come below with me.' And he led the way to the cabin. Seated alone with the Commodore, I renewed, in the most expressive terms, my congratulations on his safety from the perils of such a fight, and on the very distinguished part he had personally taken in the Action, of which many particulars had by this time reached the Lively. He received my compliments with great modesty, though evidently with great satisfaction. I then remarked that, as the Lively would bear the glorious news to England, I should feel much obliged by his giving me as many particulars of the proceedings of his Ship, the Captain, and of his own conduct in the capture of the two Ships, as he was disposed to communicate. Our intimacy was such, that I felt no difficulty in drawing from him these details; and this circumstance will be an apology for my making these remarks with such great freedom. I observed to him, that the position of the Captain appeared to all of us in the Lively, to be for a long time most extraordinary and unaccountable. We had expected every instant to see the Ship annihilated by the overpowering force to which she was singly opposed. In the animation of conversation, I went so far as to ask, 'How came you, Commodore, to get into that singular and perilous situa-tion?' He good-naturedly replied, 'I'll tell you how it happened. The Admiral's intention, I saw, was to cut off the detached Squadron of eight Sail, and afterwards attack the main body, weakened by this separation. Observing, however, as our Squadron advanced, and became engaged with the Enemy's Ships, that the main body of the Enemy were pushing to join their friends to leeward, by passing in the rear of our Squadron, I thought, unless, by some prompt and extraordinary measure, the main body could be diverted from this course, until Sir John (at that time in Action in the Victory) could see their plan, his well-arranged designs on the Enemy would be frustrated. I therefore ordered the Captain to wear, and passing the rear of our Squadron, directed Captain Miller to steer for the centre of the Enemy's Fleet, where was their Admiral-in-Chief, seconded by two three-deckers, hoping by

yesterday in sparing the Captain from further loss; and I beg,
both as a public Officer and a friend, you will accept my most
sincere thanks. I have not failed, by letter to the Admiral,
to represent the eminent services of the Excellent. Tell me
how you are; what are your disasters? I cannot tell you
much of the Captain's, except by Note of Captain Miller's, at
two this morning, about sixty killed and wounded, masts bad,

this proceeding to confound them, and, if possible, make them change their course
(as he did,) and thus afford Sir John Jervis time to see their movements, and take
measures to follow up his original intention.' I do not say that Nelson expressed
himself in exactly the above words, but his statement was to the same effect.

"In compliance with my request, he then gave me the details of his boarding the
St. Nicolas, and afterwards the St. Josef, which are given in the original Narrative,
adding the following particulars:—'I saw (and then he spoke with increased animation) that from the disabled state of the Captain, and the effective attack of the
approaching British Ships, I was likely to have my beaten opponent taken from me;
I therefore decided to board the St. Nicolas, which I had chiefly fought, and considered to be my Prize. Orders were given to lay the Captain aboard of her: the
spritsail-yard passed into her mizen-rigging. Lieutenant Berry, with the Ship's
Boarders, and Captain Pearson, with the 69th Regiment, (acting as Marines on
board the Captain,) soon got possession of the Enemy's Ship. Assisted by one of
the Sailors, I got from the fore-chains into the quarter-gallery, through the window,
and thence through the cabin to the quarter-deck, where I found my gallant friends
already triumphant.' He then gave me the details of the extraordinary circumstances
attending his afterwards getting possession of the St. Josef. Of course, my high
admiration of his conduct was often expressed, as he proceeded in giving me these
very interesting particulars, of which I made pencil notes on a scrap of paper I
found at hand; and these communications from my gallant friend were the more
valuable from their being made before he had seen any other Officer of the Fleet,
except Captain G. Martin, of the Irresistible, to which Ship he had repaired for
refreshment and repose, until the Captain, his own Ship, almost a wreck in her
rigging, &c., could be put into manageable order.

"Towards the conclusion of this interesting interview, I repeated my cordial
felicitations at his personal safety, after such very perilous achievements. I then
adverted to the honours that must attend such distinguished services. ' The
Admiral,' I observed, ' will of course be made a Peer, and his seconds in command
noticed accordingly. As for you, Commodore,' I continued, ' they will make you a
Baronet.' The word was scarcely uttered, when placing his hand on my arm, and,
looking me most expressively in the face, he said, ' No, no : if they want to mark
my services, it must not be in that manner.' ' Oh !' said I, interrupting him, ' you
wish to be made a Knight of the Bath ;' for I could not imagine that his ambition, at
that time, led him to expect a Peerage. My supposition proved to be correct, for he
instantly answered me, ' Yes ; if my services have been of any value, let them be
noticed in a way that the public may know me, or them.' I cannot distinctly
remember which of these terms was used, but, from his manner, I could have no
doubt of his meaning, that he wished to bear about his person some honorary
distinction, to attract the public eye, and mark his professional services."—Narrative, pp. 83, 88.

&c. &c. We shall meet at Lagos; but I could not come near you without assuring you how sensible I am of your assistance in nearly a critical situation. Believe me, as ever, your most affectionate

HORATIO NELSON[7]

TO THE RIGHT HON. SIR GILBERT ELLIOT, BART.

[Autograph, in the Minto Papers. Not having found Sir Gilbert Elliot on board the Lively, Nelson, on his return to the Irresistible, immediately wrote to him.][8]

My dear Sir,　　　　　　　　　　　Irresistible, 15th February, 1797.

You will naturally, I know, be anxious for the safety of your friends, amongst whom I feel a pride to be numbered. I

---

[7] This Letter ought not to be separated from the gallant Collingwood's Reply:—

"My dear good Friend,　　　　　　　"Excellent, 15th February, 1797.

"First let me congratulate you on the success of yesterday, on the brilliancy it attached to the British Navy, and the humility it must cause to its Enemies; and then let me congratulate my dear Commodore on the distinguished part which he ever takes when the honour and interests of his Country are at stake. It added very much to the satisfaction which I felt in thumping the Spaniards, that I released you a little. The highest rewards are due to you and Culloden; you formed the plan of attack,—we were only accessories to the Dons' ruin; for had they got on the other tack, they would have been sooner joined, and the business would have been less complete. We have come off pretty well, considering: eleven killed, and fourteen wounded. You saw the four-decker going off this morning to Cadiz,—she should have come to Lagos, to make the thing better, but we could not brace our yards up to get nearer. I beg my compliments to Captain Martin: I think he was at Jamaica when we were. I am ever, my dear friend, affectionately yours, C. COLLINGWOOD.'
—*Correspondence of Vice-Admiral Lord Collingwood*, 5th ed., vol. i. p. 55.

[8] Sir Gilbert Elliot's Reply to this Letter is fortunately preserved:

"My dear Sir,　　　　　　　　　　　Lively, 15th February, 1797.

"You will easily believe, I trust, the joy with which I witnessed your glory yesterday. To have had any share in it is honour enough for one man's life, but to have been foremost on such a day could fall to your share alone. Nothing in the world was ever more noble than the transaction of the Captain from beginning to end, and the glorious group of your Ship and her two Prizes, fast in your gripe, was never surpassed, and I dare say never will. I am grieved to learn that you are wounded, however slightly you talk of it. May you speedily recover, and enjoy your honours and the gratitude and admiration of your Country for many years, without any abatement or rubbers of any kind! I was in hopes you were unhurt, by seeing you on board the Minerva, and hearing the cheers you were saluted with. I am happy to find Miller is not amongst the hurt. God bless you, my dear friend! since you let me call you so, for I am not likely to decline a title so honourable to me, and believe me, &c.

"To Commodore Nelson.　　　　　　　　　"GILBERT ELLIOT."

am proud in my Admiral thinking that my reputation has not been diminished by the events of yesterday. The Captain is a wreck in hull and masts. We know not, exactly, but suppose near sixty killed: amongst the slightly wounded is myself, but it is only a contusion and of no consequence, unless an inflammation takes place in my bowels, which is the part injured. But they who play at balls must expect rubbers. Remember me to all my friends in the Lively, and

Believe me ever your most faithful

HORATIO NELSON.

TO THE RIGHT HON. SIR GILBERT ELLIOT.

[Autograph, in the Minto Papers.]

Irresistible, February 16th, 1797.

My dear Sir,

Your affectionate and flattering letter is, I assure you, a sufficient reward for doing (what to me was a pleasure) *my duty*. My Admiral and others in the Fleet think nearly the same as you do of my conduct. To receive the Swords of the vanquished, on the quarter-deck of a Spanish First-rate, can seldom fall to the good fortune of any man. Miller is doing for you two Sketches of the Action, sufficient, I am sure, to please you, from your knowledge of its correctness.

You will now, I am sure, think me an odd man, but still I hope you will agree with me in opinion, and if you can be instrumental in keeping back what I expect will happen, it will be an additional obligation, for very far is it from my disposition to hold light the Honours of the Crown; but I conceive to take hereditary Honours without a fortune to support the Dignity, is to lower that Honour it would be my pride to support in proper splendour.

On the 1st of June, 12th of April,[9] and other Glorious days, Baronetage has been bestowed on the Junior Flag Officers: this Honour is what I dread, for the reasons before given, and which I wish a friend to urge for me to Lord Spencer, or such other of his Majesty's Ministers as are supposed to advise the

---

[9] The Battles of Lord Howe, in 1794, and Lord Rodney, in 1782.

Crown. There are other Honours, which die with the possessor, and I should be proud to accept, if my efforts are
thought worthy of the favour of my King.[1] May health and
every blessing attend you, and I pray for your speedy passage
and a happy meeting with Lady Elliot and your family. And
believe me ever,

Your most obliged and faithful

HORATIO NELSON.

Sir Gilbert Elliot, Bart.

TO THE REVEREND MR. NELSON, HILBOROUGH.

[Autograph, in the Nelson Papers. On the 16th of February, the Fleet anchored,
with the Prizes, in Lagos Bay, to repair damages, and to prepare for another Action,
the Enemy being still at sea with twenty-three Sail of the Line, while the English
had only fifteen.]

Irresistible, Lagos Bay, February 17th, 1797.

My dear Brother,

As reports may get abroad concerning me, I know it will
be satisfactory to hear immediately from myself. I am, in
reality, not near so much hurt as the Doctors fancied, and
two days will restore me to perfect health. I shall only send
you an extract of a letter from Sir Gilbert Elliot, who was a
spectator of the battle, viz. :—' You will easily believe, I trust,
the joy with which I witnessed your glory yesterday. To
have had any share in it is honour enough for one man's life,

---

[1] See Colonel Drinkwater's *Narrative* in p. 348, ante. The Colonel's memory
seems to have failed him, when he said that the discovery of Nelson's wishes, in his
conversation on the 15th of February, "was not forgotten, or without consequences:"—
"As was expected, his Majesty, in reward for Nelson's distinguished conduct, had
intended to create him a Baronet. Sir Gilbert Elliot, who took a warm interest in
Nelson's welfare, called on me in London, to impart this news ; when I made
known to him the purport of my conversation on board the Lively, and suggested
that it was advisable to make this circumstance known to the Government. Sir
Gilbert saw the matter in the same light. He lost no time in communicating what
had passed on this subject to some member of the Cabinet, Lord Spencer, I believe,
who was then at the head of the Admiralty Board, and his Lordship took steps to
meet Nelson's wishes, in the manner most likely to gratify his feelings, by obtaining for him, instead of a Baronetcy, the Order of the Bath, although for that purpose
it was necessary to make him an Extra Knight." — *Narrative*, p. 88. But the
above Letter shews that Sir Gilbert Elliot was acquainted with Nelson's wishes
as early as the 16th of February, and it is highly probable that he represented
them in the proper quarter. He was not made an *Extra* Knight of the Bath,
there being a vacancy at the time of his nomination.

but to have been foremost on such a day could fall to your share alone. Nothing in the world was ever more noble than the transaction of the Captain from beginning to end, and the glorious group of your Ship and her two Prizes, fast in your gripe, was never surpassed, and I dare say never will. I am grieved to learn that you are wounded, however slightly you talk of it. May you speedily recover, and enjoy your honours and the gratitude and admiration of your Country for many years, without any abatement or rubbers of any kind! I was in hopes you were unhurt, by seeing you on board the Minerva, and hearing the cheers you were saluted with.'

The Admiral's letter[2] will tell the rest. With kindest remembrances to Mrs. Nelson, [and] family, and Aunt Mary, and all our friends at Swaffham, believe me, my dear brother,

Your most affectionate

HORATIO NELSON.

TO THE REVEREND DIXON HOSTE.

[From the Memoirs of Captain Sir William Hoste, Bart., vol. i. p. 67.]

Irresistible, Lagos Bay, February 17th, 1797.

My dear Sir,

You will be anxious to hear a line of your good and brave William after the sharp services of the Captain on the 14th. I have hitherto said so much of my dear William, that I can only repeat, his gallantry never can be exceeded, and that each day rivets him stronger to my heart.

With best respects to Mrs. Hoste, believe me, my dear Sir,

Your most obedient servant,

HORATIO NELSON.

The Captain is so cut up that I am obliged to shift my Pendant.

---

[2] This remark shews how confidently Nelson expected that full justice would be done to him in the *Dispatch*.

TO WILLIAM LOCKER, ESQ., LIEUTENANT-GOVERNOR, ROYAL
HOSPITAL, GREENWICH.

[Autograph in the Locker Papers.   On the day preceding the date of this Letter,
—viz., the 20th of February, a Promotion took place, when Nelson became a
REAR ADMIRAL OF THE BLUE.   On the same occasion, the late Admiral of the
Fleet, Sir Charles Edmund Nugent, G.C.H., obtained his Flag, so that had Nelson
lived to the present time, he would only have succeeded to the highest rank in his
profession in January, last year.[3]]

My dear Friend,   Irresistible, Lagos Bay, February 21st, 1797.

I was too unwell to write you by the Lively; but as I know
how anxious you are for my welfare, both in health and repu-

[3] Though numerous Letters from Nelson to his Wife are inserted, only one extract
has yet been given from Mrs. Nelson's Letters to him.   The exemplary character of
that amiable woman is little known to the world; and it is only justice to her to
state that her Letters, which in their style are perfectly simple and unaffected, are
filled with expressions of warm attachment to her husband, great anxiety for his
safety, lively interest in his fame, and entire submission to his wishes.   His father,
whom she always calls " our father," lived with her to the end of his life, and no
daughter ever watched the declining health of her own parent, with more care and
affection than she shewed to him.   Of her purity of conduct her husband, even when
the slave of a passion as romantic as it was unfortunate and criminal, bore the
strongest testimony; and it was cruel, when honours were bestowed upon his Family,
that no mark of National respect should have been shewn to his virtuous and neglected
Widow.   Some extracts from a few of her Letters, cannot fail to excite respect for
her character and sympathy in her subsequent misfortunes; but before inserting
them, it is impossible to resist giving the following pleasing notice of Lady Nelson,
which occurs in a Letter to the Editor from a venerable Lady, the personal and intimate friend both of Lord and Lady Nelson, and the widow of one of his bravest and
most distinguished followers :—
   " I will only say on this sad subject, that Lord Nelson always bore testimony to
the merits of Lady Nelson, and declared, in parting from her, that he had not one
single complaint to make—that in temper, person, and in mind, she was everything
he could wish.   They had never had a quarrel; but the Syren had sung, and cast
her spell about him, and he was too guileless in his nature, and too unsuspecting, to
be aware of his danger until it was too late.   I am aware of your intention not to
touch upon this delicate subject: I only allude to it, in order to assure you, from
my personal knowledge, in a long and intimate acquaintance, that Lady Nelson's
conduct was not only affectionate, wise, and prudent, but admirable, throughout her
married life, and that she had not a single reproach to make herself.   The affections
of her Lord were alienated, not when they were together, but at a distance, and
beyond the reach of her mild and feminine virtues.   I say not this to cast unnecessary blame on *one* whose memory I delight to honour, but only in justice to that
truly good and amiable woman, the residue of whose life was rendered so unhappy by
circumstances over which she had no control.   If mildness, forbearance, and indulgence to the weaknesses of human nature could have availed, her fate would
have been very different.   No reproach ever passed her lips; and when she parted

tation, I send you a short Detail[4] of the transactions of the Captain; and if you approve of it, are at perfect liberty to insert in the newspapers, inserting the name of Commodore

from her Lord, on his hoisting his Flag again, it was without the most distant suspicion that he meant it to be final, and that in this life they were never to meet again. Excuse my troubling you with these observations, as I am desirous that you should know the worth of her who has so often been misrepresented, from the wish of many to cast the blame anywhere, but on him who was so deservedly dear to the Nation. There never was a kinder heart than Lord Nelson's; but he was a child in the hands of a very designing person, and few, perhaps, could have resisted the various artifices employed to enslave the mind of the Hero, when combined with great beauty, extraordinary talents, and the semblance of an enthusiastic attachment." Lady Nelson survived her husband many years, and died in her sixty-eighth year, on the 4th of May, 1831.

On her husband's promotion as a Rear-Admiral, Mrs. Nelson thus wrote to him:

February 23rd, [1797.]

" My dearest Husband,—Yesterday's Gazette authorizes our good Father and myself to congratulate you on your being a Flag-Officer. May it please God your fame and successes continue and increase under this Promotion! I never saw anything elevate our Father equal to this. He repeated with pleasure the last words your good Uncle [Captain Maurice Suckling] told him, ' that he would live to see you an Admiral.' "

On the same occasion he heard from his Father:—

" My dear Rear-Admiral,

" I thank my God with all the power of a grateful soul, for the mercies he has most graciously bestowed on me, in preserving you amidst the imminent perils which so lately threatened your life at every moment; and, amongst other innumerable blessings, I must not forget the bounty of Heaven in granting you a mind that rejoices in the practice of those eminent virtues which form great and good characters. Not only my few acquaintances here, but the people in general met me at every corner with such handsome words, that I was obliged to retire from the public eye. A wise Moralist has observed, that even bliss can rise but to a certain pitch; and this has been verified in me. The height of glory to which your professional judgment, united with a proper degree of bravery, guarded by Providence, has raised you, few sons, my dear child, attain to, and fewer fathers live to see. Tears of joy have involuntarily trickled down my furrowed cheek. Who could stand the force of such general congratulation? The name and services of Nelson have sounded throughout the City of Bath, from the common ballad-singer to the public theatre. Joy sparkles in every eye, and desponding Britain draws back her sable veil, and smiles. It gives me inward satisfaction to know, that the laurels you have wreathed sprung from those principles and religious truths which alone constitute the Hero; and though a Civic Crown is all you at present reap, it is to the mind of inestimable value, and I have no doubt will one day bear a golden apple: that field of glory, in which you have long been so conspicuous, is still open. May God continue to be your preserver from the arrow that flieth by day, and the pestilence that walketh by night! I am your affectionate father, EDMUND NELSON."—*Clarke and M'Arthur*, vol. i. p. 359. The honorary Freedom of the City of Bath was voted to Admiral Nelson on the 20th day of March, 1797. He also received the Freedom of the Cities of London, Norwich, Bristol, and of several other Corporations.

[4] The " Remarks," in p. 340.

instead of ' I. ' Captains Miller and Berry, &c., have authen-
ticated the truth, till my quitting the San Josef to go on
board the Minerve, and farther than this the Detail should not
be printed. As I do not write for the press, there may be
parts of it which require the pruning-knife, which I desire you
will use without fear. I pretend not to say that these Ships
might not have fell, had I not boarded them ; but truly it was
far from impossible but they might have forged into the
Spanish Fleet as the other two Ships did. I hope for a good
account of the Santissima Trinidad ; she has been seen
without masts, and some of our Frigates near her.

February 21st.—Sir John has just sent me word the Hope
goes for England in a few minutes ; therefore, I can only say,
believe me ever

Your most affectionate friend,
HORATIO NELSON.

Captain Martin[5] desires I make his best respects. My
Pendant is in this Ship.

TO WILLIAM SUCKLING, ESQ.

[From " The Athenæum." The Fleet sailed from Lagos Bay on the 23rd, and
anchored in the Tagus on the 28th of February. The Spanish Fleet arrived at Cadiz
on the 3rd of March.]

Irresistible, off Lagos Bay, February 23rd, 1797.

My dear Sir,

It was not till yesterday that I heard from Captain Naylor,
of the Marines, and by a letter of November 21st, from Mrs.
Nelson, that I heard of my friend Miss Suckling's marriage,
or I should not have been so long in sending my congratulations on what I hope will turn out so pleasing an event.[6] I
have known her from her earliest days, and know that a better
heart does not inhabit any breast : pray write to her from me,
and assure her from my heart I wish her every felicity.

---

[5] The Captain of the Irresistible, now Admiral Sir George Martin, G.C.B.,
G.C.M.G.

[6] Miss Suckling, a natural daughter of his uncle, Mr. Suckling, married, on the
10th of November 1796, Henry Wigley, Esq., then of Worcester, afterwards of
Malvern Hall, in Warwickshire, who assumed the name of Greswolde, in 1833, on
succeeding to the estates of that family.

A A 2

The event of the late Battle has been most glorious for England, and you will receive pleasure from the share I had in making it a most brilliant day, the most so of any I know in the Annals of England. " *Nelson's patent Bridge* for boarding First-rates"[7] will be a saying never forgotten in this Fleet, where all do me the justice that I deserve. The Victory, and every Ship in the Fleet, passing the glorious group, gave me three cheers. My hurt at the moment was nothing, but since, it has been attended with a suppression of urine, but the inflammation is gone off, and I am nearly recovered. It is not impossible but we may meet the Dons again on our route to Lisbon, but I fancy I am to stay at sea when the Fleet enters the Tagus. You will observe that I have changed my Ship; the Captain will never be fit to receive me again, and the Admiralty must send me a new Ship. I beg my best and kindest remembrances to Mrs. Suckling, Mr. Rumsey, and all our friends at Hampstead; and believe me ever your most obliged and affectionate Nephew,

HORATIO NELSON.[8]

TO WADHAM WINDHAM, ESQ., M.P. FOR NORWICH.

[From Clarke and M'Arthur, vol. i. p. 354.]

Irresistible, off Lisbon, 26th February, 1797.[8]

Sir,

Particular circumstances having put the Spanish Rear-Admiral's Sword, Don Xavier Francisco Winthuysen, into my hands, on the most glorious 14th of February, and Admiral

---

[7] Vide p. 346, ante.

[8] About this period Nelson received the following Letter from H. R. H. the Duke of Clarence :—·

" Richmond, January 6th, 1797.

" Dear Sir,

" I am to acknowledge the receipt of yours of 25th October, November 11th, and November 28th, all which came safe to hand, and which I would have answered sooner, but I have been very much engaged in Parliament. I will begin by replying to your account about the evacuation of Corsica, as it is partly mentioned in yours of 25th October, and contains the whole of November 11th. I rejoice with all my heart the Island is no more ours, and particularly, as under your judicious arrangement, we have left nothing behind. The inhabitants were never our friends, and as the ports were bad, I·think the expense was of no use; indeed, our Fleet always considered Leghorn as the best place to refit. I am confident you will ever dis-

Sir John Jervis having done me the honour of insisting on my keeping possession of it, I know no place where it would give me or my family more pleasure to have it kept, than in the Capital City of the County in which I had the honour to be born.

If, therefore, you think, Sir, that the Mayor and Corporation of Norwich would wish to accept such a present, I have to request that you, as a Representative of Norwich, would send my Letter, and the box containing the Sword, to the Mayor.

I am, &c.

HORATIO NELSON.

TO THE MAYOR OF NORWICH.[9]

[From the Assembly Book of the Corporation of Norwich.]

Irresistible, off Lisbon, 26th February, 1797.

Sir,

Having the good fortune, on the most glorious 14th of February, to become possessed of the Sword of the Spanish

tinguish yourself: therefore your exertions may and must have astonished the world, but not me, who am so well acquainted with your merits. So far for Corsica, which I hope we shall in future leave to its fate. I believe in the abilities of Jervis, and in the good order and discipline of any Fleet under his command and more particularly of one so well Officered—still, however, even had Man joined you, *twenty-two* British Ships *ought not* to be risked against *thirty-four* of the Enemy. Man's name introduces your's of 28th November, and I shall begin with him first. I perfectly agree with you that he has acted wrong, though I must differ from you that his reasoning is right. As he received positive orders from home, and from Jervis, to join you up the Mediterranean, he *ought* to have gone: still, however, the Government were injudicious in keeping the Fleet up the Mediterranean after the Pope and King of Naples had made Peace, and Corsica was no more ours. I rejoice you are at Lisbon, and hope you will never go farther again than Gibraltar. As for Man's conduct about victualling his Fleet, it proves his insanity. I have the highest opinion of Jervis, and make no doubt he will do everything in his power. As for you, my dear Friend, I hope and believe you have long known my opinion of you, and whenever I am where I ought to be, namely, at the Head of the Navy, it will be both my duty and inclination to distinguish you. Write as circumstances arise; for your letters are invaluable. For the present, Adieu; and ever believe me, Dear Sir, Yours sincerely, WILLIAM.—*Autograph*, in the Nelson Papers.

[9] "NORWICH.—At a Quarterly Assembly, held the 3rd May, 1797:—Ordered, That the Honorary Freedom of this City be presented to His Royal Highness Prince William Frederick (Son of His Royal Highness the Duke of Gloucester) now resident in this City, and that His Royal Highness be sworn at any Court of Mayoralty. This day the Chamberlain brought into the Assembly the Sword lately sent by Rear

Rear Admiral Don Xavier Francisco Winthuysen, in the way
set forth in the paper transmitted herewith, and being born
in the County of Norfolk, I beg leave to present the Sword
to the City of Norwich, in order to its being preserved as a
Memento of the Event, and of my Affection for my Native
County.

I have the honour to be, Sir,

Your most obedient Servant,

HORATIO NELSON.

TO MRS. NELSON.[9]

[From Clarke and M'Arthur, vol. i. p. 355.]

Irresistible, Lisbon, 28th of February, 1797.

We got up here with our Prizes this afternoon: the more I
think of our late Action, the more I am astonished; it absolutely appears a dream. The Santissima Trinidad, of four

---

Admiral Nelson to Mr. Mayor, with the following Letter. [Vide above.] And this
Assembly do unanimously return Thanks to Admiral Nelson for his attention to his
Native County: And it is ordered that the Honorary Freedom of this City be pre-
sented to him, as a Testimony of the sense entertained of his gallant conduct in the
Action on the glorious 14th February, and of the services he has rendered to his
King and Country on various occasions, and that he be sworn a Freeman at any
Court of Mayoralty: And the Assembly request the Mayor to transmit a Copy of
this Order to Admiral Nelson."—*From the Assembly Book of the Corporation of
Norwich.*

[9] It appears from the following Extracts from Mrs. Nelson's Letter of the 11th of
March, that Commodore Nelson had written to her on the 16th of February, when
the Dispatch containing an account of the Victory left the Fleet, and again on the
22nd. To a wife's, were united a mother's fears for the effect of a Battle, as her
son, Josiah Nisbet, was a Midshipman of the Captain:—

" My dearest Husband,

" Yesterday I received your Letter of February 16th. Thank God you are well,
and Josiah. My anxiety was far beyond my powers of expression. M. Nelson and
Captain Locker behaved humanely, and attentive to me. They wrote immediately,
Captain Locker assuring me you were perfectly well, Maurice begging me not to
believe idle reports, the Gazette saying you were slightly wounded. Altogether, my
dearest husband, my sufferings were great. Lady Saumarez [whose husband, Captain Sir James Saumarez, commanded the Orion in the Battle,] came running to tell
me she had Letters from her husband—all this was on this day week. He speaks
generously and manly about you, and concluded by saying, ' Commodore Nelson's
conduct is above praise.' You were universally the subject of conversation."

Mrs. Nelson then described the polite speeches made to her, and thus naturally
expressed her alarm about *boarding*:—

" I shall not be myself till I hear from you again. What can I attempt to say

decks, lost five hundred killed and wounded; had not my Ship been so cut up, I would have had her; but it is well, thank God for it! As to myself, I assure you I never was better, and rich in the praises of every man from the highest to the lowest in the Fleet. The Spanish War will give us a Cottage and a piece of ground, which is all I want. I shall come one day .or other laughing back, when we will retire from the busy scenes of life : I do not, however, mean to be a hermit; the Dons will give us a little money.

If my Father should at any time wish for any part that is in my Agent's hands, I beg he would always take it, for that would give me more real pleasure than buying house or land. I go to sea the day after to-morrow in this Ship, with a Squadron to be off Cadiz, consisting of the Irresistible, Orion, &c. Sir John Jervis has already spread the Frigates ; and I shall return by the time his Fleet is ready for sea.

Yours, &c.

HORATIO NELSON.

to you about Boarding? You have been most wonderfully protected : you have done desperate actions enough. Now may I—indeed I do—beg that you never Board again. *Leave* it for *Captains.* How rejoiced Jo. must have been to have seen you, although it was but an absence of two months. To-morrow is our wedding-day, when it gave me a dear husband, my child the best of fathers. I hope he will deserve all the blessings Providence has bestowed on him." . . . "Do come home this summer, or in the autumn. It is said a change in Administration would certainly have taken place, had not this wonderful and fortunate Victory taken place. Admiral Parker, it seems, had written the Captain and Culloden bore the brunt of the Action. This instant have I received a letter from Lord Hood, telling me Sir Robert Calder was gone to Portsmouth. Thank you, my dearest husband, a thousand times, for your letter of February 22nd. God bless and protect you, and my Jo.—crown all your endeavours with success, and grant us a happy meeting. I can bear all my extreme good fortune. Your affectionate Wife, FRANCES H. NELSON."—*Autograph,* in the Nelson Papers.

The fears for his safety which his exploits had excited, again shew themselves in her Letter of the 20th of March :—" I sincerely hope, my dear husband, that all these wonderful and desperate ʼactions—such as boarding Ships—you will leave to others. With the protection of a Supreme Being, you have acquired a character, or name, which all hands agree cannot be greater : therefore, rest satisfied. What does Josiah say to all this? he is seasoned."—*Ibid.*

TO SIR JAMES SAUMAREZ, CAPTAIN OF H.M.S. ORION.

[Original, in the possession of the Dowager Lady de Saumarez. The object of Nelson's Squadron, was to watch the Spanish Fleet, and to intercept the Viceroy of Mexico, who was expected at Cadiz with a large treasure, escorted by two First Rates and a Seventy-four.]

Rendezvous,—Secret.

By Horatio Nelson, Esquire, Commodore, &c.

S. S. West from Cape St. Vincent's, about 25 leagues ; Latitude from 35° 50′ N. to 36° 10′ N., stretching from thence towards Lavache, on the Coast of Barbary. A Ship will always be kept on the Rendezvous, in case I should leave it ; *not finding me by the 17th, to return to Lisbon.*[1]

Given on board the Irresistible at Lisbon, March 2nd, 1797.

HORATIO NELSON.

[Indorsed by Commodore Nelson.]

Rendezvous not to be opened, but in case of separation.

MEMORANDA RESPECTING PRIZE MONEY.

[Autograph, in the Nelson Papers.]

[Apparently about March, 1797.]

From August 10th 1796, Commodore Nelson has a right to share as a Flag-Officer.

A Privateer taken by Minerve,[2] sold for one thousand dollars.

A Dutchman by ditto, condemned at Gibraltar, from Cette.

A ditto by Diadem, and at Porto Ferrajo.

Spanish Prizes known:

Augustus Frederick	2,000
Mahonesa . . . . ·	10,000
Spanish Polacca	2,000
Ditto, ditto, by Minerve	500
Carry forward	14,500

[1] The words in italics were added in Nelson's own hand.
[2] On the 23rd of December, 1796.

Brought forward	14,500
St. Antonio	2,000
Jesu Maria	15,000
Virgen del Carmen	1,000
Active	1,000
Nostra Signora	26,000
Negro Arigo	6,000
Signora Misericordia	16,000
Cubano.	25,000
Santa Natolia	100,000
Foudroyant	25,000
Spanish Brig from Porto Rico, by Transfer	4,000
Ditto, ditto, by Caroline and Seahorse	12,000
French and Spanish Brigs, by Pallas	8,000
Spanish Brig, by Southampton	2,000
Four Spanish Ships of War	180,000
	537,500[3]

Thus far known : more are taken, but no particulars known.

TO VICE-ADMIRAL THE HON. WILLIAM WALDEGRAVE.[4]

[From the "Naval Chronicle," vol. x. p. 280.]

March 5, 1797.

My dear Admiral,

I send you a Narrative[5] of the transactions of the Captain on the 14th of February, and also the Sword of one.of the Officers (I believe Second Captain of the San Nicolas) with whîch he killed one of my seamen.

How hard this wind is not to let us out, but I hope it is at its last gasp. Believe me, my dear Sir,

Your most obliged and affectionate humble servant,

HORATIO NELSON.[6]

[3] *Sic*, but the total is properly 437,500.

[4] Third in Command on the 14th of February, afterwards created Lord Radstock, for his services on that day. Many Letters to Lord Radstock from Nelson, will be found in subsequent parts of this Work.

[5] Vide p. 340, ante.

[6] The news of the Victory of the 14th of February reached London on the 3rd of March; and about the 21st of that month Sir John Jervis and his Officers and

TO ADMIRAL SIR JOHN JERVIS, K.B.

[From Clarke and M'Arthur, vol. i. p. 355.]

[On or about 12th March, 1797.]

It is almost a pity to give the Viceroy a chance of eluding our vigilance; as yet we have never covered a less space than from twelve to twenty-eight leagues. Respecting myself, I wish to stay at sea, and as I have directed Captain Miller to provide me with everything necessary, whether in the Captain or in any other Ship, I beg if any Line-of-Battle Ships are left out either on this side of the Straits, or to the eastward of Gibraltar, that I may be the man : and this brings forward a subject which I own is uppermost in my mind—the safety of our Troops.[5] Should they embark from Elba, the French have a number of Ships at Toulon, and may get two, three, or four ready, with a number of Frigates, and make a push for our Convoy. I am willing, as you know, to go eastward to cover them even to Porto Ferrajo, or off Toulon, or Minorca, as you may judge proper; and if they are on their passage, you will not, I presume, go to the westward until they arrive at Gibraltar. I have said much, but you have spoiled me by allowing me to speak and write freely ; yet be assured I mean nothing further than my wish to undertake this service, if you approve of it.

I am, &c.,

HORATIO NELSON.

Men received the approbation of the King for their services, which he thus conveyed to Nelson :—

"Victory, Tagus, 21st of March, 1797.

"Sir,

"In obedience to the commands of the Lords Commissioners of the Admiralty by far the pleasantest I ever received, I have the honour to convey to you personally His Majesty's most gracious approbation of your distinguished services in the Action with the Fleet of Spain, on the 14th of February, signified through Earl Spencer to the Lords Commissioners of the Admiralty."—Sir John Jervis also transmitted to him the thanks of both Houses of Parliament, and of the Corporation of London.— *Clarke and M'Arthur*, vol. i. p. 356. It was probably on the same occasion that he was informed of his promotion to the rank of Rear-Admiral.

[5] Left at Elba, vide p. 323, ante.

TO JOHN M'ARTHUR, ESQ.

[Autograph, in the possession of Mrs. Conway. Mr. M'Arthur, while Lord Hood's Secretary, was one of Nelson's Agents for Prizes.]

Irresistible, off Lagos Bay, March 16th, 1797.

My Dear Sir,

Your letter of November 30th, by Aurora, I only received the beginning of this month before I left Lisbon, and the various claims of Ships for Corsica. I believe if every Ship can be stated exactly as they state themselves, an opinion might be taken from an eminent lawyer. For instance, Tartar assisted in landing stores, and in drawing up one gun from such a time to such a time; the Scout was in sight of Bastia from the 3rd to the 7th, and was fired at—and so of the others. I do not believe that these claims ought greatly to diminish *us* who had the whole service. I think when each Ship states her services, that we ought to resort to the King in Council; as to Ships hearing the guns, it is ridiculous. I heard the guns which were fired at San Fiorenzo—the Ships in Porto Ferrajo heard both. I wish you had told me about our Genoese vessels, which money we have lodged, I hope, on interest—pray tell me about it.

I am here looking for the Viceroy of Mexico, with three Sail of the Line, and hope to meet him. Two First Rates and a 74 are with him; but the larger the ships the better the mark, and who will not fight for dollars?[6] The Spanish Fleet are in Cadiz, the Officers hooted and pelted by the mobility. Their first report was, the Action happening on a foggy day, when the fog cleared up, they only saw fifteen Sail of the Line, therefore concluded at least five were sunk in the Action. My usual good fortune attended me which I know will give you, amongst my other friends, satisfaction. I only,

---

[6] Among the numerous Verses written on the Victory of St. Vincent were the following. In consequence of the scarcity of specie, Spanish Dollars were issued from the Bank on the 10th of March, 1797, of the value of 4s. 6d., but they were recalled on the 1st of October, in the same year. On each Dollar the King's bust was struck on the neck of the King of Spain:

The additional head on the Dollar impress'd
Is to circulate Jervis's fame;
To his valour 'tis owing, it must be confess'd,
England made an impression on Spain.

got on board the Captain at seven o'clock in the evening of the 13th. I shall write Lord Hood when anything here occurs. In the meantime I beg you will make my most kind remembrances to him and Lady Hood; and do you believe me,

Your most faithful humble servant,

HORATIO NELSON.

TO HIS ROYAL HIGHNESS THE DUKE OF CLARENCE.

[From Clarke and M'Arthur, vol. i. p. 356.]

Off Cape St. Vincent, March 22nd, 1797.

Sir,

The Spanish fleet went into Cadiz on the 3rd of the month, the Santissima Trinidad with them. They acknowledge she had struck, but that a Seventy-four sent a boat on board, and hoisted her colours again, which they give as a reason why she did not lay her head towards our Fleet.[7] I feel a great satisfaction in this account being confirmed, as I believe all will allow that I had more action with her than any Ship in our Fleet; and I am sure your Royal Highness will have pleasure in likewise knowing, that my conduct has not escaped the notice of the Spanish Fleet, who now in Cadiz do justice to the Broad Pendant.

I am looking out with an anxious eye for the Viceroy of Mexico, but I fear he will go to Teneriffe. The Spanish Fleet is, fit and unfit, thirty Sail of the Line in Cadiz, and I

---

[7] It appears almost certain that the Santissima Trinidad did surrender herself. Colonel Drinkwater says—

"In the original Narrative, I mentioned the circumstance doubtfully, although I can affirm that, in an interval of the clearing away of the smoke, I saw a white flag flying over the Spanish Ensign, importing her surrender. I mentioned the fact to those near me at the time; but the discomfited Ship, being at that moment supported by the division of eight Ships cut off in the morning, but which had now rejoined their friends to windward, drifted away under their protection, dismasted, and a log on the water. Such was her crippled state, that she was allowed to separate from the main body of the Enemy's Fleet, and was seen (as was reported before the Lively left the British Squadron) alone, off Cape St. Mary's, making the best of her way into Port, where she eventually arrived. Many years, however, did not elapse before the same Santissima Trinidad became a prize to the Hero, who engaged her so gallantly on the 14th of February, in the still more memorable and tremendous Battle off Cape Trafalgar, in October, 1805."—*Narrative*, p. 81.

suppose twenty will be ready for sea by the first week in April. I am assured fifteen Sail of the Line are ordered to Ferrol, and both Squadrons are destined for Brest, making thirty Sail from the two Ports of Cadiz and Ferrol. I trust Sir John Jervis will be reinforced; at present his situation is not very pleasant. Eighteen two-decked Ships are to perform two services; at least this is what strikes me as necessary, viz. to see our Army safe from Elba, and to prevent the Spanish Fleet sailing with impunity from Cadiz. If Sir John stays off Cadiz, the French will push out two or three Sail of the Line, and most probably take our Army; if he goes into the Straits, the Detachment from Cadiz gets unmolested to Ferrol: here is a choice of difficulties. I have ventured to propose to the Admiral, letting me go with two or three Sail of the Line, off Toulon, or to Elba, as may be necessary, and for the Fleet to stay outside. I beg your Royal Highness will not think that I am in the habit of advising my Commander-in-Chief; but Sir John Jervis has spoiled me by encouraging me to give my opinion freely; knowing that it is not impertinence in me, I have thought it right to say thus much.

An American who left Cadiz two days past tells us, that Cordova[8] is sent to Madrid as a prisoner, and that every Admiral and Captain are under arrest until their conduct can be inquired into; and it is said they are determined to fight us again. Captain Oakes is now at my elbow, and desires me to say everything respectful for him.

　　　　　　　　　　　　I am, &c.,
　　　　　　　　　　　　HORATIO NELSON.

SERVICES PERFORMED THIS WAR BY CAPTAIN NELSON, OF
HIS MAJESTY'S SHIP AGAMEMNON.

[Autograph, in the Nelson Papers. There is another Paper in the same Collection, containing similar Notes; and the few facts stated in it, which do not occur in these Memoranda, are here added within brackets.]

　　　　　　　　　　　　　　　[Apparently written in March, 1797.]
　　1793.

August 19th.—Received the fire of Fort Cavaliere, and took a Ship from Marseilles bound to Smyrna.

---

[8] The late Commander in Chief of the Spanish Fleet.

October 21st.—Engaged the Melpomene, of 40 guns, 420 men; La Minerve, 40 guns, 420 men; La Fortunée, 40 guns, 350 men; La Flêche, 28 guns, 220 men; when being much disabled, the Enemy left me.

1794.

January 21st.—Landed about four miles from San Fiorenzo : burnt the only water mill in that part of the Country, and destroyed a magazine of corn and flour. Four French frigates were lying in San Fiorenzo.

February 6th.—Landed at Centuri : burnt four Polacca ships, loaded with wine for the French, at San Fiorenzo.

February 8th.—Landed at Magginagio, burnt eight Sail of Vessels, took four, and destroyed about 2000 tons of wine. Captain Nelson struck the French colours with his own hand.

February 12th.—Attacked a French courier-boat, whose crew got on shore at Capraja : after a very smart contest, in which I lost six men, carried her.

February 19th.—Landed at Lavizena, took the tower of Miomo, distant three miles from Bastia, and drove the French within gun-shot of the walls of Bastia.[9]

February 24th.—Run down the town of Bastia, and cannonaded it for two hours.

February 26th.—Drove the French from a work they were making to the southward of Bastia.

March 18th.—Landed at Erbalonga, stayed on shore alone with the Corsicans for two days, and reconnoitred the whole works of Bastia, from which I gave my decisive opinion as to the practicability of taking the Town.

April 3rd to May 26th.—Landed, for the Siege of Bastia, jointly with Colonel Villettes, 1000 Marine troops, 300 seamen; the Town surrendered May 22nd, after our batteries had been open forty days.

June 18th to August 12th.—Landed for the Siege of Calvi : batteries opened July 5th. Town surrendered August 10th; batteries open twenty-six days.

[9] " Gave it up to the friendly Corsicans."

[October 1st.—Took a Brig under the French battery of Cape Martin.]

1795.

March 13th.—Engaged the Ça Ira for two and a half hours; killed on board her 110 men.

March 14th.—Engaged with the Fleet.

[July 8th.—Fired at by the French Fleet.]

July 13th.—Engaged with the Fleet.

[August 14th.—Took some Enemy's vessels under the Forts of Alassio.]

August 26th.—Took eleven Sail out of Alassio.[1]

[September 6th.—Took a Brig from under the Fort of Oneglia.]

1796.

April 25th.—Took four Sail of Frenchmen from under the batteries of Loano, after a smart contest.

[May 8th.—Took two Vessels from under the batteries of Pietra.]

May 31st.—Took six Sail of Frenchmen from the batteries of Torre dell'Areno, after some resistance.

CAPTAIN.

July 10th.—Took in conjunction with Major Duncan, the Fortresses and Town of Porto Ferrajo.

[September 11th.—Fired at by the batteries of Genoa.]

September 18th.—Took in conjunction with Major Logan, the Island of Capraja, the Garrison surrendering prisoners of war.

October 19th.—Embarked the Vice-Roy, and all our troops from Bastia, the French being in possession of the Citadel, and landed them the same day at Porto Ferrajo.

LA MINERVE.

December 19th.—Fought and took La Santa Sabina of 40 guns; twenty-eight 18-pounders on her main deck, 286 men, after an action of two hours and fifty minutes.

December 20th.—Fought the Santa Matilda of 34 guns. She ran away, or I am confident we should have taken her,

---

[1] In the other Memoranda, "August 26th, took nine Sail of Vessels."

we being at the same time closely pursued by two Spanish Ships of the Line and two Frigates.

[1797.]

February 14th.—Engaged with the Fleet.

TO EARL SPENCER, FIRST LORD OF THE ADMIRALTY.

[Autograph draught, in the Nelson Papers.]

Captain, off Cape St. Mary's, April 2nd, 1797.

My Lord,

Yesterday I had the honour of receiving your Lordship's letter[2] of March 17th, signifying to me his Majesty's most gracious intention to confer on me the Most Honourable Order of the Bath, as a mark of his Royal approbation of my conduct on several occasions during the present War. May I presume, through your Lordship, who have so favourably represented my services to the King, to present my most profound and humble acknowledgments to his Majesty for this most distinguished mark of his Royal Favour?

I feel it would be presumptuous in me to say more than to acknowledge the very handsome manner in which your Lordship has been pleased to execute his Majesty's commands, and that I am,

Your Lordship's most obliged Servant,

HORATIO NELSON.

[2] TO REAR-ADMIRAL NELSON.

"Admiralty, 17th March, 1797.

" Sir,

"I have His Majesty's commands to acquaint you, that in order to mark his Royal approbation of your successful and gallant exertions on several occasions during the course of the present War in the Mediterranean, and more particularly of your very distinguished conduct in the glorious and brilliant Victory obtained over the Fleet of Spain by His Majesty's Fleet, under the command of Admiral Sir John Jervis, on the 14th of February last, His Majesty has been pleased to signify his intention of conferring on you the Most Honourable Order of the Bath, with which it is His Majesty's pleasure that you should be Invested, when the proper measures can be taken for that purpose. I have great satisfaction in communicating to you this very distinguished mark of the Royal approbation.

"I am, &c.

"SPENCER."

TO HIS ROYAL HIGHNESS THE DUKE OF CLARENCE.

[From Clarke and M'Arthur, vol. ii. p. 6.]

2nd April, 1797.

Your Royal Highness, who has known me for every hour upwards of sixteen years, will do me justice in saying, that at no one period of my life did my zeal and duty to my King and Country abate ; and I must rejoice in having gained the good opinion of my Sovereign, which I once was given to understand I had no likelihood of enjoying.[3] With every sentiment of the most dutiful attachment, believe me to be your Royal Highness's faithful servant,

HORATIO NELSON.

TO MRS. NELSON.

[From Clarke and M'Arthur, vol. ii. p. 6.]

April, 1797.

Though we can afford no more than a Cottage—yet, with a contented mind, my dearest Fanny, my Chains, Medals, and Ribbons are all-sufficient. We must be contented with a little, and the cottage near Norwich, or any other place you like better, will, I assure you, satisfy me. Do not mention this mark of the Royal Favour[4] to any one except my Father. Be assured, whether my letters are long or short, yet still that my heart is entirely with you. With love to my father, believe me your most affectionate husband,

HORATIO NELSON.

TO THE REVEREND MR. NELSON, HILBOROUGH.

[Autograph in the Nelson Papers.]

Captain, off Cape St. Vincent's, April 6th, 1797.

My dear Brother,

Many thanks for your kind letter of March 13th, and I beg you will thank all our friends for their kind congratulations; and I must be delighted, when, from the King to the Peasant, all are willing to do me honour. But I will partake of no-

---

[3] Vide vol. i. p. 294.

[4] The Order of the Bath. Though he was appointed on the 17th of March, the Honour was not notified in the London Gazette until the 27th of May.

thing but what shall include Collingwood and Troubridge.[5] We are the only three Ships who made great exertions on that glorious day: the others did their duty, and some not exactly to my satisfaction. We ought to have had the Santissima Trinidad and the Soberano, seventy-four. They belonged to us by conquest, and only wanted some good fellow to get alongside them, and they were ours. But it is well; and for that reason only we do not like to say much.

Sir John Jervis is not quite contented, but says nothing publicly. An anecdote in the Action is honourable to the Admiral, and to Troubridge and myself. Calder[6] said, ' Sir, the Captain and Culloden are separated from the Fleet, and unsupported: shall we recall them?'—' I will not have them recalled. I put my faith in those Ships: it is a disgrace that they are not supported and separated.'

Success hides a multitude of faults. We have just spoke a Vessel from Cadiz: Cordova and three Captains are condemned to be shot; but it is said Cordova's sentence will not be carried into execution, but I should think it will, to appease the people; but he certainly does not deserve it, although many of his Fleet do. The Admiral joined me from Lisbon on the 2nd, and on the 3rd, we looked into Cadiz. Their West India Convoy was to have sailed that day: now I do not expect they will sail this summer; for I have no idea they will fight us again. However, they may, in a month or two, be forced out. I am come off here to look for the Viceroy, with Culloden and Zealous, and La Minerve; but I do not expect any success. You will not be surprised to hear I have declined all hereditary Honours; and as to entailing a Title, unless you have a good estate to send with it, you send misery; and, till I became a Flag-officer, I had not made both ends meet. Chains and Medals are what no fortune or connexion in England can obtain; and I shall feel prouder of those than all the Titles in the King's power to bestow. Pray remember me kindly to Mrs. Nelson, our Aunt, your Children, the Rolfes, and all our friends at Swaffham, and believe me ever, your most affectionate brother,

HORATIO NELSON.

---

[5] Alluding to the partial distribution of Medals for Lord Howe's Victory in 1794.

[6] First Captain to Sir John Jervis, or Captain of the Fleet.

Captain Berry, who is a Post-Captain, late my First Lieutenant, has promised to call upon you. He is going to visit
a sister, who is married, and lives at or near Tofts. You will
find him a very pleasant and gentlemanlike man.

TO JOHN M'ARTHUR, ESQ.

[Autograph, in the possession of Mrs. Conway.]

Captain, off Cadiz, 10th April, 1797.

My dear Sir,

Many thanks for your most kind congratulations on our late
success; but I hope soon the good people of England will have
something else to talk about—more recent victories; for if our
Ships are but carried close by the Officers, I will answer for a
British Fleet being always successful. I have to thank you
for your account of Prizes pending in the Admiralty Court,
and will, as soon as I have time, and get hold of Cockburn,[1]
send you the names of the Ships who share for them, and also
the power to take the money for distribution, but we had
better be sure of no appeals before we hurry the payment.

The Spaniards threaten us they will come out, and take their
revenge: the sooner the better; but I will not believe it till I
see it; and if they do, what will the mines of Mexico or Peru
signify, compared with the honour I doubt not we shall gain
by fighting an angry Don? They will have thirty Sail of the
Line, we twenty or twenty-two; but fear we shall have a peace
before they are ready to come out. What a sad thing that will
be! We have reports of great expected changes; whoever is
Minister, will, I hope, get us an honourable peace. I suppose
a Ship is to be sent out for me, but I hope not the Gibraltar.
The Captain is little better than a wreck. When you see
Lord Hood, I beg you will make my kindest remembrances
to his Lordship and Lady Hood; and believe me, my dear
Sir, your much obliged,

HORATIO NELSON.

---

[1] Captain, now Admiral Sir George Cockburn, so often mentioned; he then commanded La Minerve.

TO JOHN M'ARTHUR, ESQ.

[Autograph, in the possession of Mrs. Conway.]

Captain, off Cadiz, April 10th, 1797.

Dear Sir,

In answer to your circular letter of January 31st, just received, I send you my opinion relative to Bastia and Calvi; and desire that should the unjust claims of the Windsor Castle and Inflexible, with many others, be attended to, that a claim is laid in for San Fiorenzo for the Agamemnon, as she was one of the Ships actually employed in the blockade of the Port, and without which no Frigates could have been taken, and also never being out of hearing of the guns, and making a diversion of the Enemy's Force by two landings on the opposite side of the Island, about twelve miles distant, and cannonading Bastia, &c. &c.

I am, dear Sir, your very humble Servant,

HORATIO NELSON.

This claim is only just, if the others, far less so, are complied with.
H. N.

Meleager, Amphitrite, Leda, &c. &c., Billet, and innumerable gun-boats, must not be forgot, should all ridiculous claims be allowed.
H. N.

If Captains Hunt and Bullen share, I insist that Hallowell do the same, I am ready to bear testimony he did more service than *most* of us.

TO JOHN M'ARTHUR, ESQ.

[Original, signed by Rear Admiral Nelson, in the possession of Mrs. Conway.]

BASTIA.

Victory, Princess Royal, Fortitude, Agamemnon, Gorgon, are the only Ships employed, first to the last, at Bastia. The Illustrious and Tartar, with the L'Imperieuse, had more of the Siege than any other Ships except those first mentioned. The others came and went occasionally to the Commander-in-Chief; and, of course, if any service was to be performed during their stay, or they could bring anything from the places they came from, of course they could not do otherwise than do so. The Terrible came one day, and several other Ships; but I cannot conceive they can have a right to share equal to every Ship and man who was employed, at the imminent risk of his life, from the first to the last. But, so far from throwing any impediment in the way, I am ready they should share in the manner as follows:—Let each Ship state the number of days she was actually employed in the Siege of Bastia, which will, of course, give the number of men, and let it be divided in this manner. It may give a little trouble; but then the man who served forty-nine days will be paid, and the man who served one day will also be paid, each according to his labour. If the Officers who are interested, being there the whole Siege, agree with me, I desire the point may not be given up.—*Answer to the First.*

Answer to the Second.—The Troops serving as Marines, and the Marines of every Ship of the Line and Frigate in the Fleet being ordered ashore for the Siege of Bastia, by Sir William Scott's opinion every Ship ought to share, who had any men belonging to her on shore, on the principle, I suppose, that those on board did their duty. It appears very fair; and is Sir William Scott prepared to say, that as the Ships are to share with us who are on shore, that we shall share with those who are afloat, and took prizes? If it is justice to one, it is so to the other. The Alcide and Egmont are in the same state as other Ships in the Fleet, except bringing part of the Troops from San Fiorenzo, and, of course, having the trouble of landing them, and assisting from April 4th to April 11th, by landing Officers and Seamen which were then embarked, and only the Soldiers remained during the Siege.

Answer to the Third.—The Windsor Castle can have less right to share than almost any Ship. She was laying in San Fiorenzo. If a Commander-in-Chief chooses to order one hundred men out of every Ship in his Fleet, can this entitle those men to share for prizes taken by that Ship? Most of the Ships brought out of Toulon had men lent from different Ships: I will be bold to say, not one of those men were in any Prize List for those Ships; nor, if those Ships they were lent to had taken a Prize, would the Ships they belonged to have presumed to claim as aiding and assisting at the capture? For instance, the Captain has fifty men on board the San Josef, late her Prize, but now commissioned: should the San Josef take a Prize going home, by Sir William Scott's opinion the Captain has a right to claim, on the ground that part of the company of the Captain were on board at the capture, and the Prize could not have been taken but by the assistance of men lent from different Ships. By the Proclamation, those men cannot share for what the Captain takes, nor can the Captain share for what those men may take: at all events the Officers are different. I dispute the Windsor Castle sharing.

Answer to the Fourth.—The Scout to be allowed the number of days. Dido and L'Aigle not one moment employed during the Siege. They probably brought something from Leghorn which we wanted. They are different from Romney and Tartar, who had some hard fag; and for a number of days every Ship in the Mediterranean was part of the hostile Force, as Sir William Scott calls it; for each had some men on shore.

Answer to the Fifth.—Captain Ferris has no claim, but just as much as the Windsor Castle and many other Ships.

Answer to the Sixth.—Captain Bullen and Captain Hunt were employed during the Siege, and, in justice, have a right to share; but what does the Proclamation say? I suppose these gentlemen to be Volunteers on board Ship—how would they share?—not with the Captains, but as Volunteers, with the last class; nor can a Commander-in-Chief order two Captains to share for the same Ship. But, for my part, I desire that these gentlemen may be put upon the Prize List, as Captains. Why is Captain Hallowell omitted? He rendered more service than almost any other Officer. If these share, I insist that he does.

Answer to the Last.—Every Ship that is commissioned by Great Britain must, in a certain degree, contribute to the success of her Arms, in every quarter of the Globe, although not actually present. For instance, had there been no Fleet in the Channel, the French might have come up the Mediterranean and taken us all: therefore the Home Fleet certainly took care of us and covered us. The farther they kept the Enemy off, the more to their credit. This reasoning of Sir William Scott's is carried too far. On the whole I desire the opinion of the first-named Ships may be taken, and I agree with the majority.

But how will Lieutenant Colonel Villettes, Major Brereton, two Lieutenants Duncan, Lieutenant de Butts, and twenty-five Artillery-men feel? The Army at San Fiorenzo may claim for being present at the surrender; for I saw them peeping over the rocks like so many eagles, and certainly within hearing of the guns during the whole Siege.

I once before said I thought it must be laid before the King in Council.

HORATIO NELSON.

CALVI.

Answer to the First.—The Sincere, Captain Shields, most certainly entitled to share.

Answer to the Second.—The L'Aigle, Captain Hood, most certainly entitled.

Answer to the Third.—Not correctly stated. The St. Fiorenzo not one moment employed, or even in sight of Calvi, during the Siege. Sir Charles Hamilton was Captain of the Dido part of the time—then Captain Towry. The Dido most certainly entitled to share, but not *two* Captains.

Answer to the Fourth.—The Britannia, No. Mis-stated her situation. The Commander-in-Chief being cruizing off Calvi in the latter end of July, the Britannia, Admiral Hotham, came to him: on her return to Port from off Gourjean, Lieutenant Gourly came on shore with some empty wine-pipes when I was mounting the very last gun. Our batteries had been open upwards of three weeks. This is all I know of the Britannia, or all the assistance I received from her. I never will consent to her sharing, if any one will join me.

Answer to the Fifth.—La Lutine, Captain M'Namara, clearly entitled to share.

Answer to the Sixth.—The Inflexible, No. When going to the Siege of Calvi, I ordered thirty men and a Midshipman of that Ship to be lent to the Agamemnon, and the people are borne as part of the Agamemnon's crew. The Captain, nor Officers, or other part of the crew, shall never share with my consent.

Answer to the Seventh.—Captain Hallowell and Captain

Serocold are, by their gallantry, entitled to share as Field
Officers; but being not in commission, how far, by the King's
Proclamation, can they share with the Navy? Ought they
not to be paid jointly out of the whole capture? It was not
particularly Naval service, but joint service. But, however
this may be, I desire my consent may be given to their sharing
equal to myself. Captain Cook was employed in landing the
Troops, and erecting batteries, and of course is much more
entitled than the Britannia, or any Ship who only came to the
Commander-in-Chief.

The other Ships are not stated; therefore I know not who
claims.

HORATIO NELSON.

TO ADMIRAL SIR JOHN JERVIS, K.B.

[From Clarke and M'Arthur, vol. ii. p. 7.]

April 11th, 1797.

I shall endeavour by fair means to accomplish your wishes
in the blockade. I have myself no idea that the Spanish Fleet
will be ready for sea for some months; and I own, Sir, that
my feelings are alive for the safety of our Army from Elba.
If the French get out two Sail of the Line, which I am confident they may do, our Troops are lost, and what a triumph
would that be to them! I know you have many difficulties to
contend with, but I am anxious that nothing should miscarry
under your orders. If you think a Detachment can be spared,
I am ready to go and do my best for their protection. At all
events, I trust you will not imagine that my taking the great
liberty of thus mentioning my thoughts, arises from any other
motive than affection towards you.

I am, &c.

HORATIO NELSON.[5]

[5] About this date he received the following Letter from the Commander-in-
Chief:—

"Ville de Paris, Lisbon, 31st March, 1797.

" My dear Admiral,

"Many thanks for your letters, and the intelligence sent you from Lagos. By a
letter I received yesterday from the neighbourhood of it, I learn that Gravina is
working hard to get the Fleet forward: eighteen Sail of the Line and several Frigates

TO THE AMERICAN AND DANISH CONSULS AT CADIZ.

[From a Copy in the Admiralty.]

His Britannic Majesty's Ship Captain, off Cadiz, 11th April, 1797.

Sir,

In consequence of the unprovoked declaration of War by the King of Spain, against his Britannic Majesty and the British Nation, it is thought right that Spain should no longer have any Trade:

I have, therefore, the honour to acquaint you, that no

appeared ready for sea on the 23rd, and the report at Cadiz was, that they would sail to-morrow; therefore keep a sharp look-out. The arrival of Sir Robert Calder has detained me three days longer than I intended, to deliver his Ship from a large quantity of useful stores, and to remove myself and suite into the Ville de Paris. I hope to get over the bar with most of the Squadron in the course of this day. The rich Ships from La Vera Cruz and the Havannah are certainly on their passage, and much agitation is felt in Spain on that account: therefore Gravina may be forced out. The Spanish Chargé here sent an express to Madrid on Monday, to give an account of the reinforcement from England, and of my dropping down below the castle in the Victory: whether this will produce a change of intention we shall soon see. All here send you their best regards: say everything proper for us to Captain Miller and your worthies, and be assured I am yours most truly, J. JERVIS." —*Clarke and M'Arthur.*

Sir Robert Calder brought Nelson this beautiful Letter—so characteristic of the wife of a Naval Veteran—from Lady Parker, the wife of his early patron, Sir Peter Parker, Bart., then an Admiral of the White and Commander-in-Chief at Portsmouth:—

"Portsmouth, 15th March, 1797.

"My dear Nelson,

"I cannot let Sir Robert Calder sail from hence without writing you a few lines. There are no expressions in the English language, that I am acquainted with, equal to convey the idea which I have of your gallant and meritorious exertions in your Country's cause upon all occasions. Your conduct on the memorable 14th of February, a proud day for Old England, is above all praise; it never was nor ever can be equalled. All that I shall say is, that your mother could not have heard of your deeds with more affection, nor could she be more rejoiced at your personal escape from all the dangers to which you were exposed on that glorious day. Long may you live, my dear Nelson, an ornament to your Country and your Profession, is the sincere wish of your old commander Sir Peter and myself, and every branch of our family. Pray offer my most affectionate regards to your truly able and gallant Commander-in-Chief; he shall henceforth be my Valentine. I must request you also to remember me to dear, good Collingwood, in the kindest manner; I am very happy at the glory he has gained: remember me also to George Martin, and the whole of the invincible Fifteen that I have the honour of knowing. God bless you, my dear Nelson, your affectionate and sincere friend, MARGARET PARKER."—*Autograph,* in the Nelson Papers.

Neutral Vessel will be permitted in future to enter or leave the Port of Cadiz, unless by leave obtained from me, or the Commander-in-Chief of the British Fleet; and that, from this moment, Cadiz is to be considered as a blockaded Port. I have the honour to be, Sir,

> Your most obedient servant,
> HORATIO NELSON.

TO THE RESPECTIVE CAPTAINS UNDER THE ORDERS OF REAR-ADMIRAL NELSON.

[From a Copy, in the Admiralty.]

By Horatio Nelson, Esq., Rear-Admiral of the Blue, &c. &c. &c.

Admiral Sir John Jervis having directed me to form the blockade of Cadiz, and to prevent the entrance or departure of the Trade to and fro, with all the precision in my power—

You are therefore hereby directed, when you board any Ships bound to Cadiz, to acquaint the Master of such Ship that the Port is blockaded, and that he must seek another market; and in case of boarding any Vessel from Cadiz, you are to direct their return into that Port, unless they should be in ballast, when they may be allowed to proceed .on their voyage.

You will, I am confident, execute this service with all civility and attention to the Nations in amity with Great Britain.

> Given on board the Captain, off Cadiz,
> the 11th April, 1797.
> HORATIO NELSON.

TO ADMIRAL SIR JOHN JERVIS, K.B.[7]

[From Clarke and M'Arthur, vol. ii. p. 7.]

12th April, 1797.

My dear Sir,

Troubridge talked to me last night about the Viceroy at Teneriffe. Since I first believed it was possible that his Ex-

---

[7] On the 12th of April, Sir John Jervis thanked him for his friendly hint about Porto Ferrajo, and for his offer to go in quest of it, of which he said he availed himself by sending him orders to proceed with the Captain, Colossus, and Leander,

cellency might have gone there, I have endeavoured to make myself master of the situation and means of approach by sea and land. I shall begin by sea.

The Spanish Ships generally moor with two cables to the sea, and four cables from their sterns to the shore; therefore, although we might get to be masters of them, should the wind not come off the shore, it does not appear certain we should succeed so completely as we might wish. As to any opposition, except from natural impediments, I should not think it would avail. I do not reckon myself equal to Blake;[8] but if I recollect right, he was more obliged to the wind coming off the land, than to any exertions of his own : fortune favoured the gallant attempt, and may do so again. But it becomes my duty to state all the difficulties, as you have done me the honour to desire me to enter on the subject.

The approach by sea to the anchoring place is under very high land, passing three valleys; therefore the wind is either in from the sea, or squally with calms from the mountains. Sometimes in a night a Ship may get in with the land-wind and moderate weather. So much for the sea attack, which, if you approve, I am ready and willing to look at, or to carry into execution. But now comes my plan, which could not fail of success, would immortalize the undertakers, ruin Spain,

---

to Gibraltar, and thence up the Mediterranean. Sir John Jervis said he had reason to think that the Garrison was on its way to Gibraltar, under the escort of the Inconstant, Captain Fremantle. He added that the Dido and Terpsichore were going to Santa Cruz, Teneriffe, to ascertain whether the Vice-Roy of Mexico was actually there ; that there was no other news from England than that Earl Howe was going to leave Bath to be invested with the Garter, "which event was made known to him by letter under His Majesty's own hand." Upon this passage in Sir John Jervis's Letter it may be remarked, that glorious as were the Naval Victories of the reign of King George the Third, no Admiral except Lord Howe ever obtained the Garter, and that it was the great object of Earl St. Vincent's ambition to the last hour of his life. Several eminent military Commanders have been made Knights of the Garter, but probably none of them except the Duke of Wellington would have been honoured with the distinction had they not been Peers by descent.

[8] In April, 1657, Admiral Blake having received information that six Spanish galleons laden with silver, and ten other Ships, had put into Santa Cruz at Teneriffe, immediately resolved to attempt destroying them. He succeeded in the attack, and burnt the whole Spanish Fleet down to the water's edge, except two Ships which sunk ; and then the wind veering to the south-west, he passed with the Fleet safe out of port again.—*Campbell's Admirals*, vol. ii. p. 245. See also Clarendon's *History of the Rebellion*, ed. 1826, vol. vii. p. 214.

and has every prospect of raising our Country to a higher
pitch of wealth than she ever yet attained : but here soldiers
must be consulted, and I know from experience, excepting
General O'Hara, they have not the same boldness in undertaking a political measure that we have ; we look to the
benefit of our Country, and risk our own fame every day to
serve her : a Soldier obeys his orders, and no more. By
saying Soldiers should be consulted, you will guess I mean
the army of 3700 men from Elba, with cannon, mortars, and
every implement now embarked ; they would do the business
in three days, probably much less. I will undertake with a
very small Squadron to do the Naval part. The shore,
although not very easy of access, yet is so steep, that the
Transports may run in and land the Army in one day. The
water is conveyed to the Town in wooden troughs : this
supply cut off, would probably induce a very speedy surrender : good terms for the Town, private property secured
to the Islanders, and only the delivery of public stores and
foreign Merchandise demanded, with threats of utter destruction if one gun is fired. In short, the business could not miscarry.

Now it comes for me to discover what might induce
General de Burgh to act in this business. All the risk and
responsibility must rest with you. A fair representation
should also be made by you of the great National advantages
that would arise to our Country, and of the ruin that our
success would occasion to Spain. Your opinion besides
should be stated, of the superior advantages a fortnight thus
employed would be of to the Army, to what they could do in
Portugal; and that of the six or seven millions sterling, the
Army should have one half. If this sum were thrown into
circulation in England, what might not be done ? It would
ensure an honourable Peace, with innumerable other blessings. It has long occupied my thoughts.

Should General de Burgh not choose to act, after having
all these blessings for our Country stated to him, which are
almost put into our hands, we must look to General O'Hara.
The Royals, about 600, are in the Fleet, with Artillery sufficient for the purpose. You have the power of stopping the

Store-ships; 1000 more men would still insure the business, for Teneriffe never was besieged, therefore the hills that cover the Town are not fortified to resist any attempt of taking them by storm; the rest must follow—a Fleet of Ships, and money to reward the Victors. But I know with you, and I can lay my hand on my heart and say the same—It is the honour and prosperity of our Country that we wish to extend.

I am, &c.

HORATIO NELSON.

TO SIR JAMES SAUMAREZ, COMMANDER OF HIS MAJESTY'S SHIP ORION.

[Original, in the possession of the Dowager Lady de Saumarez. The Command of the Squadron blockading Cadiz, was transferred to Sir James Saumarez, on Admiral Nelson's proceeding to Porto Ferrajo.]

By Horatio Nelson, Esquire, Rear-Admiral of the Blue, &c. &c. &c.

In obedience to directions from Admiral Sir John Jervis, K.B., You are hereby required and directed to take under your command, the Ships named in the margin,[1] and to carry into execution the orders you will herewith receive respecting the Blockade of the Port of Cadiz.

Given on board the Captain, off Cadiz, April 12th, 1797.

HORATIO NELSON.

TO ADMIRAL SIR JOHN JERVIS, K.B.

[From a Copy, in the Admiralty.]

Captain, 20 Leagues W. by S. of the Southern end of Corsica,
April 21st, 1797.

My dear Sir,

You will rejoice to hear I am with the Convoy,[2] all safe and well. I shall now trouble you with a detail of my proceedings, which you may read or not, as you like. The day after I left

---

[1] Culloden, Irresistible, Zealous.
[2] With the troops from Elba.

you in the evening, Seahorse, Caroline, and Southampton, joined me off Cabrita Point. I sent Gibson with the Gibraltar letters, and wrote a line to General O'Hara, to say, that if he could dispense with the Emperor of Morocco's present for a little while, I should like to have the Meleager. His answer was, he did not care if the Emperor did not get his present this month; and, therefore, Meleager joined me, with Gibson, at noon, on Saturday the 15th. I lost no time, speaking everything to get information in getting to the eastward. Repeated Vessels confirmed to me that a French Squadron of four Sail of the Line, one Frigate, and a Brig, were off the south end of Minorca. The Southampton parted company, in chase, I fancy, of a Spaniard; but I hope we shall either pick him up, or he will get to Gibraltar in time to execute your orders relative to his Convoy. On the 18th and 19th, I passed Ivica, Majorca, and within gun-shot of Port Mahon, with a strong wind at N.W., which I fancy blew the French Ships under St. Peter's, in the Island of Sardinia; and this morning, at 7 A.M., with inexpressible pleasure, I saw the Convoy, which I shall hope to see safe in Gibraltar; and I detach Gibson to tell you this good news.[1] By what I learn, all is lost in Italy. The whole state of Venice is actually French. Trieste is said to be also in their possession, and Buonaparte is within 150 miles of Vienna, with 150,000 men. The Archduke Charles is fortifying some pass to make a stand; but there seems no prospect of stopping these extraordinary people. I will not take up more of your time than to say, I have written to Gibraltar for the Agent of Transports and the Agent-Victualler to be prepared to expedite my departure, that I may join you, and be ready for other service.

Believe me ever,

Dear Sir,

Your most faithful servant,

Horatio Nelson.

I have sent Seahorse and Meleager to go on the north side of the Islands, to endeavour to get hold of some Spanish Frigates

---

[1] In the imperfect copy of this Letter in Clarke and M'Arthur, (vol. ii. p. 9,) the following words occur here, " I hope you will press General O'Hara about Tene-- riffe."

which are thereabout. I must take the liberty of saying, I
believe the weather was the entire cause of Oakes's long delay
at Gibraltar : it was worse than when we were there in December. However that may be, the Seahorse is one of the
very best ordered Ships I have ever met with. Captain Oakes
intends to speak to you about going on shore to Lisbon for his
health, or quitting and going home. He is most exceedingly ill.

TO HIS ROYAL HIGHNESS THE DUKE OF CLARENCE.

[From Clarke and M'Arthur, vol. ii. p. 10.]

Off Cape de Gatte, 30th April, 1797.

Sir,

The French Squadron, of four Sail of the Line, one Frigate,
and a Brig, were seen from Minorca only twenty-two hours
before I passed it on the 19th, in my way up. I observed a
Man-of-War Brig evidently looking at us ; but my charge was
too important to separate one Ship in chase of her, especially
as the Seahorse, Southampton, and Meleager had parted
company ; for until this Garrison is safe down, I do not think
our business is well finished. I spoke a Danish Frigate just
now, six days from Malaga, who says the Spanish Fleet is
certainly ordered to come out of Cadiz; this redoubles my
anxiety to join my Admiral, for I should seriously lament
being absent on such an occasion, especially as I believe it
will be the last on many accounts; first, that I think we should
finish their Marine, and next, that my health is getting so indifferent from want of a few months' repose, and the pains I
suffer in my inside, that I cannot serve, unless it is absolutely
necessary, longer than this summer.

In October I intend to ask permission to return to England
until February, should the war still continue ; and when it is
considered that I have been four years and nine months without
one moment's repose for body or mind, I trust credit will be
given me that I do not sham. I have sent poor Captain
Oakes[2] with the Meleager to look for some Spanish frigates ;

[2] Captain George Oakes of the Seahorse.

his health is most distressing, and I have strongly recommended
to him to go home, and, if he is fortunate in taking a Frigate,
I am in hopes he will.   As I know your Royal Highness's
regard for this Officer, I must be interested about him.

I am, &c.

HORATIO NELSON.

TO ADMIRAL SIR JOHN JERVIS, K.B.

[From Harrison's Life of Lord Nelson, vol. i. p. 183.   Another Copy with some
variations is in Clarke and M'Arthur.]

Captain, off Cape Pallas, 1st May, 1797.]

Dear Sir,

As I shall send away the Rose Cutter the moment I see
the Rock, you will know from her arrival that we are in a
fair way for arriving safe at Gibraltar.   I spoke a Danish
Frigate on the 27th of April, from Malaga four days.   He
says the Spanish Fleet has most positive orders to come to sea
and fight you.   This makes me doubly anxious to join you.[3]
I have not interfered with Captain Fremantle's charge and
arrangement of the Convoy, it could not be in better hands;
therefore I only overshadow them with my wings.   I have
the satisfaction to tell you, that all the Troops—except the
Royals, who were always intended to be embarked in the
Ships of War—are embarked in the Transports, with the
exception of twenty, and General Horneck,[4] who are in two
Vessels loaded with wine.   I offered to take a hundred into
each Ship of my Squadron, but I found there was not the
smallest necessity for it.

I hope, Sir, you will state this point at Home, as it would
have been a severe reflection on me, not to have left what was
necessary for the embarkation of the Army.   I rejoice in this
opportunity of vindicating my conduct; and beg leave again to

[3] Clarke and M'Arthur omit the preceding passage, and insert here, "The Sea ·
Horse and Meleager are ordered to be there on the 4th, Meleager landing the
Emperor of Morocco's clock in her way," which does not occur in Harrison, whose
Copy bears strong evidence of being correct.

[4] Major General Charles Horneck: he died a Lieutenant General in 1804.

recommend Lieutenant Day, Agent for Transports, to your notice. I placed my reliance on his judgment not to leave a Ship more than was necessary, and I am not deceived. A more zealous, active Officer as Agent for Transports I never met with. General de Burgh also speaks of him in the highest terms, and I hope the Transport Board will keep their promise of recommending those Officers in their service who eminently distinguish themselves, which I take upon myself to say, Lieutenant Day has not only done at Bastia, but at Porto Ferrajo. For his conduct at the former place you were so good, on my stating his services, to recommend him to the Admiralty; I should not do justice to his Majesty's service, were I not to urge it again. I have the pleasure to add, that all the Captains under my orders have conducted themselves like zealous good Officers.

I have the honour to be, &c.,
HORATIO NELSON.

TO JAMES SIMPSON, ESQ., AMERICAN CONSUL AT MALAGA.

[From Clarke and M'Arthur, vol. ii. p. 12. In reply to the American Consul's request that he would protect twelve American Vessels at Malaga, which were unable to proceed, on account of three French Privateers that were watching them.]

Sir,   Gibraltar, 20th May, 1797.

I shall immediately grant the protection you have requested, by sending the Andromache, Captain Mansfield, to-morrow off Malaga, who will protect the Vessels close to the coast of Barbary, where you tell me they will consider themselves safe. In thus freely granting the protection of the British flag to the subjects of the United States, I am sure of fulfilling the wishes of my Sovereign, and I hope of strengthening the harmony which at present so happily subsists between the two Nations.

I am, &c.,
HORATIO NELSON.

TO CAPTAIN RALPH WILLETT MILLER.

[Autograph, in the possession of Miss Miller. Captain Miller was then Admiral Nelson's Flag Captain in the Captain.]

Ville de Paris, May 24th, 1797.

Dear Sir,

We are to go into the Theseus;[4] therefore the Admiral desires the Captain to be anchored near her. She is next Ship to the Vice-Admiral; therefore pray direct my things to be in readiness—I mean my Store Room. Such Officers as wish to go with me are to get ready: Mids., Hoste and Bolton, &c., and such men as came from Agamemnon, if they like it; but this we can soon settle. Sir John desires you will dine here. It is believed the Peace is signed. I send your letters, and be assured I am ever

Your obliged,

Horatio Nelson.

TO HIS ROYAL HIGHNESS THE DUKE OF CLARENCE.

[From Clarke and M'Arthur, vol. ii. p. 12.]

Sir,　　　　　　　　　　　　　　　　Off Cadiz, May 26th, 1797.

I beg leave to return you my most sincere acknowledgments for the three letters I have received from your Royal Highness.[5] Whatever confidence you are pleased to repose in me,

---

[4] On rejoining Sir John Jervis off Cadiz, he shifted his flag to the Theseus, and was appointed to command the In-shore Squadron, a service of constant activity, as the Mortar, and Gun-boats were incessantly firing on the Spanish Ships, Batteries, and Flotilla. Preparations were, at the same time, making for the attack on Teneriffe.

[5] The following are the three Letters alluded to; and, like all the preceding ones, cannot be read without inspiring respect for his late Majesty's sagacity and patriotism:—

" Dear Nelson,　　　　　　　　　　" Richmond, March 13th, 1797.

" I am, believe me, very happy to own myself in the wrong, and in future to acknowledge that the British Fleet when *well* disciplined, *well* Officered, and *nobly* commanded, *can* beat *any* number of *Spaniards*. I rejoice, my good friend, with all my heart, at the splendid Victory Jervis and his fine fellows have gained over the Dons. Your conduct has been, as usual, meritorious, and you really need not to have been wounded to complete your fame; for amongst all ranks of people your character has *long* been established. I am happy to inform you that his Majesty has expressed himself in the most gracious manner about you; and it is but justice to Spencer, *though I hate him*, to say that in his speech he did you the credit you so amply merited. You, my dear Friend, have long known my sentiments about

will not, I trust, be misplaced; but my conduct and not my words must prove this. . . . . Our western Ports in Ireland might surely be more used, and stores procured as easily as at Gibraltar, Lisbon, &c. A plan with little expense might be formed, for always having a large Squadron to the westward of England. We rejoice here at the certainty of soon receiv-

Jervis, and I am happy they coincide with yours; the Action and its result speak for themselves, and must give every Englishman sincere pleasure—more particularly those who belong to the British Navy, and have the happiness, as I have, of possessing intimate friends in that gallant Fleet. I am very sorry to see by the Returns, that you was wounded, and still more so by your silence, am I alarmed that you have severely suffered; for I am persuaded otherwise, after such an event, so glorious to the English Name, and, particularly, so highly honourable to the British Navy, you would certainly have wrote to one who is attached to the Service, and particularly interested in your welfare. My best wishes for your health and happiness attend you, and ever believe me, yours sincerely, WILLIAM."

" Dear Nelson, " St. James's, April 7th, 1797.
" Yesterday I received yours of 3rd March, from Lisbon, giving me no news either from Portugal or Spain, but commenting on your late glorious Victory. I certainly should have been better pleased, if the Santissima Trinidada had arrived at Portsmouth, instead of reaching Cadiz, and I am clearly of opinion that had Man and his Squadron, *as they ought*, have been with Jervis, the Victory would have been more to the advantage of this Country, though at the same time it could not have been more to the credit of the gallant Officers and Men. I am sorry Jervis's ill state of health has made it requisite for Thompson to carry on the Harbour duty. I sincerely hope Jervis is, by this time, as well as this Country, and all his friends in particular, must be anxious to see him: give him my best compliments. I trust your Cruise with the Frigates will be this time as fortunate as your last was glorious. You will, of course, be permitted to choose your Ship, which, whether a three or a two-decker, will be, I am sure, well managed. I feel proud of your friendship and regard, and believe me, whatever trust his Majesty may honour me with, it will be both my duty and inclination to fill with care and attention. Adieu, and ever believe me, dear Sir, yours sincerely, WILLIAM."

" Dear Sir, " Richmond, April 30th, 1797.
" I am to acknowledge the receipt of your two letters, the one of the 22nd March, and the other of 2nd April. I lament with you the return of the Santissima Trinidada into Cadiz, and am not surprised to find the Admirals and Captains of the Spanish Fleet in disgrace. I am sorry by your last letter to find Jervis has joined you before you fell in with the Vice-Roy of Mexico. I wish the reinforcement from hence had been stronger, because I highly approve of your reasoning relative to the Spanish and French Fleets, and likewise see the necessity of our troops being removed from Elba. I am perfectly satisfied with your silence, though at the time it made me uneasy. I rejoice at the King's having conferred the Bath on you; for I am sure you deserve the Royal approbation.
" You my good friend, conclude your last letter by saying you are a *Gallant Fleet*. Gracious God, what a difference in this Country! The Ships at Spithead for a whole week in a perfect state of mutiny—the Men commanding their Officers, and a Parliament consisting of Delegates from each Ship of the Line, sitting all that time

ing large reinforcements, which, as the Combined Fleet will very soon be forty Sail of the Line, must be acceptable ; and we found our belief on the abundance of spare Ships that are at the disposal of the Admiralty ; for, although we are so inferior, we find that a Squadron under Lord Hugh Seymour is actually cruising on our station.

I am, &c.,

HORATIO NELSON.

TO MRS. NELSON.

[From Clarke and M'Arthur, vol. ii. p. 12.]

27th May, 1797.

How Government can answer for this act,[1] I cannot guess ; but I have done. We are to anchor off Cadiz, in sight of the whole Spanish Fleet. I am barely out of shot of a Spanish Rear Admiral.

Yours, &c.,

HORATIO NELSON.

TO ADMIRAL DON JOSEF DE MAZAREDO, CADIZ.

[From Harrison's Life of Nelson, vol. i. p. 186.]

Theseus, May 30th, 1797.

Sir,

I have the honour of sending your Excellency a packet from Sir John Jervis; and I embrace the opportunity of assuring

on board the Queen Charlotte, and issuing Orders to his Majesty's Fleet. I hope, though I have not a good opinion of Lord Spencer, that the Admiralty have acted with discretion. The King, with the advice of his Ministers, has very properly pardoned the Seamen and Marines. A Squadron has proceeded to Sea, and, for the present, discipline is once more restored to that part of the British Navy ; but the Mutiny has spread to Plymouth, and still rages there. The business, of course, must come before Parliament ; therefore, till the investigation, I shall say no more. But paint to yourself the Fleet at Spithead, during a War, for a whole week, in a complete state of Mutiny, and the necessity of the pardon for the whole from the Sovereign ! As for Ireland, that Country is in a state of rebellion ; therefore, the worst consequences from the *now necessary* want of discipline, would arise in the Sister Kingdom, should the French seriously turn their thoughts to the Invasion of Ireland. Pardon my gloom ; but I have a very great stake in this Country, and a family of young children to protect. In all situations, I am yours sincerely, WILLIAM."—*Autographs*, in the Nelson Papers.

[1] "This act" seems to have been the sending out a Squadron under Lord Hugh Seymour, instead of reinforcing Sir John Jervis' Fleet.

you of my high esteem of your character. The 4th of June being the birthday of my Royal Master, Sir John Jervis intends firing a *feu de joie*, at eight o'clock in the evening; and has desired me to mention it to your Excellency, that the Ladies at Cadiz may not be alarmed at the firing. Believe me your Excellency's most faithful servant,

HORATIO NELSON.[6]

TO ADMIRAL SIR JOHN JERVIS, K.B.[7]

[From Clarke and M'Arthur, vol. ii. p. 13.]

My dear Sir,　　　　　　　　　Theseus, 31st May, 1797.

I never have a letter from the Duke of Clarence, but H. R. H. mentions you. I have mislaid that of April 5th, or I should have thought it my duty to have sent it. His Royal Highness therein said, 'My best wishes and compliments attend the illustrious Jervis; tell him I admire him, I envy him, and I sincerely hope his Fleet will now fall in with the Dollars.' A letter from a humbler pen came to me at Gibraltar—Collingwood; and his sentiments are, I am confident, those of the whole Fleet—'I have a great desire our Admiral should be a Marquis this summer, his bright honours will reflect on all of us.'　　　　　　I am, &c.

HORATIO NELSON.

[6] To this Letter the Spanish Admiral replied :—

"On Board the Conception, off Cadiz, 1st June, 1797.

"My dear Sir,—I correspond to the urbanity merited by the letter with which you honoured me, the 30th May last. The Ladies of Cadiz, accustomed to the noisy sounds of salutes of the vessels of war, will sit, and will hear what Sir John Jervis means to regale them with, for the evening of the 4th current, in honour of his Britannic Majesty's birthday; and the general wish of the Spanish nation cannot but interest itself in so august a motive.

"God preserve you many years. I kiss your hands.

"Your attentive Servant,
"JOSEF DE MAZEREDO."

[7] In a Letter dated on the 6th of May, Sir John Jervis, after saying that Teneriffe was no longer the important object it was when Nelson suggested it, that he must concentrate all his force, and that he had written strongly for reinforcements, added :— "We seldom disagree, but in the instance of the letter from Rear-Admiral Parker which foolishly got into the papers, I totally differ with you; for it appears by the letter that Moreno covered Cordova in the evening; and the Rear-Admiral shall go to Leon, and prove the letter, if Moreno requires it; this is due to a brave man under persecution. I very much approve the letter you propose to send with the newspapers." Vide p. 393.

CASE FOR THE OPINION OF COUNSEL.

[Autograph draught, in the Nelson Papers.]

[Apparently written in May or June, 1797.]

Admiral Sir John Jervis, with the British Fleet, blockades Cadiz; and, the more effectually to perform that service, appoints an Inner Squadron to lay at anchor, or keep under sail, as the case may require; and four Ships are appointed for the Inner Squadron.

On the afternoon of the 27th, [of April, 1797,] a Convoy, under a Venetian Frigate and several other Neutral Vessels, came out of Cadiz; and the more effectually to examine them closely, and to prevent any of them from eluding a search, two of the Inner Squadron were ordered by the Commander of the Inner Squadron to keep under sail. During the night, the boats of all the Ships were employed in examining the Convoy, the whole British Fleet being in sight in the offing.

During the night, two Spanish Frigates passed through the Fleet; and in the morning of the 28th, soon after daylight, the Commander of the Inner Squadron made the signal for the two Ships, who had been under sail during the night, to chase the Frigates, which they did, then in sight of the whole Fleet.[8] The two Frigates run close to the shore, anchored, and fired their guns at the two Ships sent in chase, for about

---

[8] The affair here alluded to is best described in the brief official report of Captain Martin, of the Irresistible, (now Admiral Sir George Martin, G.C.B., G.C.M.G.,) to Admiral Sir John Jervis, who said that the "skilfulness" and "decision" shewn by Captain Martin, rendered this "one of the most notable actions that ever came under my observation:"—

"Irresistible, off Lador, April 28th, 1797.

"Sir,—I beg leave to acquaint you, that on the morning of the 26th, at six A.M., I gave chase, in his Majesty's ship under my command, to two ships in the S.E., in company with the Emerald, and that at half-past two P.M. we attacked them in Coral Bay, near Trafalgar, where they had anchored; that at four they struck to his Majesty's ships, and proved to be the Spanish frigates Elona and Ninfa, mounting thirty-six guns and three hundred and twenty men each, from the Havannah, bound to Cadiz. The former cut her cable after she had struck, and ran on shore; and notwithstanding we got her off, from the damage she received, we were not able to keep her afloat. Part of the crews left the ships, and got on shore.

"From every account I have been able to collect, the two frigates had eighteen men killed and thirty wounded. The Irresistible had one man killed and one wounded. I have the honour to be, &c., GEORGE MARTIN."—*London Gazette.*

one hour and a half, when one Frigate cut her cable and drove
on shore. The other hauled down her colours, and was immediately taken possession of and towed out to sea. The
other Frigate who had run on shore was also got afloat, but
soon afterwards sunk at her anchors.

Your Opinion is desired, who by Law are entitled to the
Head-money, the value of the Prize being acknowledged the
property of the whole Fleet,—whether the whole Fleet, the
Ships who occupied the Inner Squadron, or only the two Ships
who fired and took possession of the two Frigates?

TO JOHN M'ARTHUR, ESQ.

[The "Naval Chronicle," vol. iii. p. 304. This Letter is reprinted with some
additions, but very imperfectly, in Clarke and M'Arthur, vol. ii. p. 13.]

My dear Sir,　　　　　　　　　　Theseus, June 1st, 1797.

*　*　*　*　*　*　*　*　*

We are off Cadiz with a greater inferiority than before. I
am barely out of shot of a Spanish Rear-Admiral. We have
every day Flags of Truce; the Dons hope for peace, but must
soon fight us, if the war goes on. I wish it was all over, for
I cannot fag much longer; and, to please our Fleet, I hear
that a Squadron is looking out, in the limits of this station,
for the galleons daily expected: what a special mark of favour
to us, who are enabling them to cruise so much at their ease!
Believe me, dear Sir, your obliged and faithful servant,

HORATIO NELSON.

P.S. Sam Hood[9] is gone, I hope, to get riches; sure to
get honour.

TO SIR JAMES SAUMAREZ, CAPTAIN OF
HIS MAJESTY'S SHIP ORION.

[Autograph, in the possession of the Dowager Lady de Saumarez.]

My dear Sir,　　　　　　　　　　Theseus, June 1st, 1797.

Some of your people yesterday said that they heard some
Ship in the Fleet had served the whole allowance. Sir John

---

[9] Captain of the Zealous, afterwards Rear-Admiral Sir Samuel Hood, K.B., Bart.,
one of the most distinguished Officers in the Service: he is again often mentioned.

Jervis wishes to know the Ship they have heard has done it. I must therefore request you will have the goodness to inquire if they know the Ship, or what made them fancy it was so, or if any person, and who, told them. I forgot it this day; therefore pray excuse this trouble, and believe me,

Ever your obliged,

HORATIO NELSON.

TO ADMIRAL SIR JOHN JERVIS, K.B.

[From Clarke and M'Arthur, vol. ii. p. 14.]

About 6th June, 1797.

My dear Sir,

Mr. Jackson[1] has delivered me your confidential letter: you may depend upon me. I want nothing but what we have, except two five-inch howitzers, two four or six-pounders, field-pieces, 500 shells, some cases of fixed ammunition, and two or three artillerymen (no Officer) to fix the fusees, and a devil-cart. With this, and what you propose, I have no doubt of doing the job as it ought to be, the moment the Ships come in sight. I also want twenty ladders; the size and dimensions I will get from the Carpenter of the Blenheim, late of the Captain, who has made proper ones, which one man could carry for escalade, for my use in former times.

I am, &c.

HORATIO NELSON.

TO ADMIRAL SIR JOHN JERVIS, K.B.

[From Clarke and M'Arthur, vol. ii. p. 14, who have so mangled this interesting Letter that there is no other way of giving its contents than in their own unsatisfactory manner:—" In writing to his Admiral on the same day (7th June, 1797), he informed him, that, according to the intelligence received from an American, the Town's-people at Cadiz were fearful of an attack, and that not one half of the guns were mounted on the walls. "*I long to be at them!*" exclaimed the gallant seaman. He also at the same time, touched upon the Teneriffe expedition.]

7th June, 1797.

You must think, my dear Sir, of giving me 200 Marines in addition to what I can land; the whole business is arranged

[1] Master of the Ville de Paris.

in my mind, and I can point out to you the absolute necessity. Captain Oldfield of the Marines, who was with Dacres[2] in the Sceptre at the beginning of the war, is a very worthy man; and under Captain Troubridge ashore, and myself afloat, I am confident of success.

I am, &c.
HORATIO NELSON.

TO VICE-ADMIRAL MORENO, OF THE SPANISH NAVY.

[From Clarke and M'Arthur, vol. ii. p. 15, Vide p. 389, ante, whence it would seem that this Letter was written early in May.]

Theseus, 8th of June, 1797.

Sir,

A Spanish Officer having said, that you had expressed a wish to obtain a Letter supposed to have been written from his Majesty's Ship Egmont, and inserted in an English News-paper, relating to the Action of February 14th, every inquiry has been made to obtain the Newspaper, and hitherto without effect. Captain Sutton of the Egmont has also done every-thing in his power, but without being able to learn whether any Letter from that Ship has been published. The inquiry has, however, produced from my Commander-in-Chief, Sir John Jervis, the most handsome testimony of the gallant con-duct of a Three-decked Ship, bearing the Flag of a Vice-Admiral, who did everything which a good Officer could do, to attempt to cut through the British line, between the Victory and the Egmont.

I am, &c.
HORATIO NELSON.

TO ADMIRAL SIR JOHN JERVIS, K.B.

[From Clarke and M'Arthur, vol. ii. p. 16.]

9th June, 1797.

My dear Sir,

The Newspaper was at last found in the night, on the quarter-deck, and is gone as you desired: it will, I fear,

---

[2] Captain James Richard Dacres.

militate against Cordova, if any weight be given to a News-paper account. Your testimony of Moreno's conduct will no doubt be of service to him; the Trials are commenced, and every day an account is sent off to Madrid. The heavy charge against Cordova is, not coming into Cadiz with his Convoy, which they say he could have done the day after he had passed the Straits. Morales, it is expected, will be shot, Cordova broke, Moreno acquitted. The long trial of the Officers who gave up Figueras is just finished, and five are to be shot. All the Officers who composed the Council of War are to be degraded in their public and private rank. According to reports, the French have been refused a passage through Spain to Portugal ; and a Minister of ours is at Paris. The Venetians are suffering every misery from the French. I was in great hopes the salute was from an Admiral from England. The number of men you propose to give me, I have no doubt are all-sufficient; but I well know that a few more red coats have their use in dazzling the eyes of the Enemy.

I send you the State of the Swiftsure; even the sight of the two poor men[3] in irons on board her has affected me more than I can express : if Mr. Weir[4] would look at them, I should be glad. The youth may, I hope, be saved, as he has inter-vals of sense, his countenance is most interesting. If any mode can be devised for sending him home, I will with pleasure pay fifty pounds to place him in some proper place for his recovery ; the other, I fear, is too old. Your manage-ments are always good, and nothing shall be wanting in the execution. Martin[5] has got an idea that I am likely to move; and should it be proper to enlarge the Squadron, I beg he may go, but not to displace one of the others. I hope the reinforcement will soon arrive. I do not build much on the acts of the Portuguese Squadron,[6] even if they go off Spartel.

I am, &c.,

HORATIO NELSON.

---

[3] These men were suspected of having simulated derangement, to obtain their dis-charge.

[4] Dr. Weir, Physician to the Fleet.

[5] Captain George Martin of the Irresistible.

[6] Under Rear Admiral, the Marquis de Niza.

TO CAPTAIN SIR JAMES SAUMAREZ, HIS MAJESTY'S SHIP ORION.

[Autograph, in the possession of the Dowager Lady de Saumarez.]

Theseus, June 9th, 1797.

My dear Sir James,

Send, I beg, whatever you think fit towards San Lucar: all you do is right, and can hardly want my sanction. I hope your Boats will be rewarded for their trouble: they take all the Prizes for our Squadron. Believe me ever,

Your most faithful

HORATIO NELSON.

TO ADMIRAL SIR JOHN JERVIS, K.B.

[From Clarke and M'Arthur, vol. ii. p. 17.]

10th June, 1797.

My dear Sir,

I hope, for the poor men's sakes, that they are imposing on me; but depend on it, that God Almighty has afflicted them with the most dreadful of all diseases. They do not sham; indeed, you will find I am not mistaken, and all the Commissioners in the World cannot convince me of it. For what purpose can these poor wretches attempt to destroy themselves? for what purpose can one of them have spoken to me as rationally as any person could do? Do let Mr. Weir look at them: I am sure he will think with me, from the order to represent those who are objects unfit for the service, I could not do otherwise than I did; but if you think I have said too much, pray curtail my Report. But I will get to pleasanter subjects. I am forming a ladder for the escalade, which when finished, I will send to the Ville de Paris, that we may have twenty at least. Ten hours shall make me either a conqueror, or defeat me. I long to be at work, for I begin to think these fellows will not soon come out, at least not whilst negotiations are going on.

I am, &c.

HORATIO NELSON.

TO ADMIRAL SIR JOHN JERVIS, K.B.

[From Tucker's Memoirs of Earl St. Vincent, vol. i. p. 411.]

H.M.S. Theseus, 12th June, 1797.

My dear Sir,

The Flag of Truce was only to bring the letters sent herewith; but it brought out in conversation a circumstance which, though believed by many, I have my doubts about—at least, that the Spaniards would have acknowledged it—viz. that the Trinidad not only struck her Colours, but hoisted *un Pavillon Parliamentaire ;*[7] the fact is now so well established that it cannot be done away. The next morning, when attended by the Frigate, seeing some of our Ships not far off, I suppose Egmont and Namur, she hoisted an English Jack over the Spanish Flag, to induce the English to suppose she was a prize. Everybody, their Officer says, expects Peace to be settled, and that it will be known here by the end of the month.[8]

Believe me your most faithful,

HORATIO NELSON.

TO ADMIRAL SIR JOHN JERVIS, K.B.

[From Clarke and M'Arthur, vol. ii. p. 17.]

13th June, 1797.

The ladder sent is not so light as I wished, but we could not do any better with the stuff we had. Three men can rear it with pleasure, and, if possible, there should be ten men at a time on it : in short, the actors in our performance must not be too anxious to mount. Wishing that I may soon see them used,

Believe me yours faithfully,

HORATIO NELSON.

-----

[7] See Colonel Drinkwater's *Narrative*, p. 364, ante.

[8] Clarke and M'Arthur added to their version of this Letter (but it does not appear upon what authority) this paragraph : " I have one ladder finished, thirty-two feet long, and when you think the time draws near to make people guess, I should like one from every Ship in the Fleet."

TO ADMIRAL SIR JOHN JERVIS, K.B.

[From Tucker's Memoirs of Earl St. Vincent, vol. i. p. 412.]

H.M.S. Theseus, June 13th, 9, P.M.

My dear Sir,

What the intentions of the Dons are, I know not; but their movements would assure me, if English, that they are on the eve of coming out. We see that thirteen Sail of the Line are unmoored and hove short. I saw Gravina cat his anchor, and they did it briskly; but the accommodation ladder of his Ship was not in at sunset. The signals which they have been making this day are not their usual Harbour-signals. I will give them credit for their alertness, if they come out in the morning. This Squadron have their bulkheads down, and in perfect readiness for battle, and to weigh, cut, or slip, as the occasion may require. I have given out a Line of Battle,—myself to lead; and you may rest assured that I will make a vigorous attack upon them, the moment their noses are outside the Diamond. Pray do not send me another Ship, for they may have an idea of attacking the Squadron; and if you send any more, they may believe we are prepared, and know of their intention. It will, Sir, be my pride to show the world that your praises of my former conduct have not been unworthily bestowed. Believe me ever, my dear Sir,

Your most affectionate and faithful,

HORATIO NELSON.

TO MRS. NELSON.

[From Clarke and M'Arthur, vol. ii. p. 19.]

15th June, 1797.

A few nights ago a Paper was dropped on the quarter deck, of which this is a copy:—' Success attend Admiral Nelson! God bless Captain Miller! We thank them for the Officers they have placed over us. We are happy and comfortable, and will shed every drop of blood in our veins to support them, and the name of the Theseus shall be immortalized as high as the Captain's. SHIP's COMPANY.'

Yours, &c.

HORATIO NELSON.

TO ADMIRAL SIR JOHN JERVIS, K.B.[9]

[From Tucker's Memoirs of Earl of St. Vincent, vol. i. p. 414.]

Theseus, June 21st, 1797.

My dear Sir,

The history of women was brought forward, I remember, in the Channel Fleet last War. I know not if your Ship was an exception, but I will venture to say, not an Honourable but had plenty of them; and they always will do as they please. Orders are not for them—at least, I never yet knew one who obeyed.

Your most faithful,
HORATIO NELSON.

TO ADMIRAL SIR JOHN JERVIS, K.B.

[From Clarke and M'Arthur, vol. ii. p. 21.]

June 29th, 1797.

My dear Sir,

The two Vessels which came out of Cadiz this day nearly agree in the same story, that the Spanish Fleet, twenty-eight Sail of the Line, is full manned, chiefly Soldiers, and is ready for sea, and there are two Sail also nearly fitted out which are not manned; the Toulon Ships and those from Carthagena are expected the first Levanter. The people of Cadiz have petitioned Government to order the Fleet to sail; for that, whatever may be the event, it must force us to quit this ground; and as three Ships from Lima are momentarily expected, and the Havannah Convoy (for every morning the Merchants are on the walls to see if they are in our Fleet), they declare if they should fall into our hands, that the Merchants in Spain would be ruined. They know we have a Bomb-vessel fitting at Gibraltar, and are in terror of a bom-

---

[9] Sir John Jervis' reply to this Letter, dated on the 21st, commenced thus :— "I perfectly agree with you that the overflow of Honourables and the Disciples they have made among the Plebeians has been the ruin of the Service. I never permitted a woman to go to sea in the Ship," &c.—*Autograph*, in the Nelson Papers.

bardment. I will write to Don Josef Mazaredo, and he shall have the letter soon after daybreak to-morrow : he is a Biscayner—they are not famed for politeness or gallantry. I hope I shall always have to boast, and truly, of your unalterable friendship, which it shall ever be my study to deserve.

I am, &c.

HORATIO NELSON.

TO MRS. NELSON.

[From Clarke and M'Arthur, vol. ii. p. 21.]

29th June, 1797.

Rest assured of my most perfect love, affection, and esteem for your person and character, which the more I see of the world, the more I must admire. The imperious call of honour to serve my Country, is the only thing which keeps me a moment from you, and a hope, that by staying a little longer, it may enable you to enjoy those little luxuries which you so highly merit. I pray God it may soon be peace, and that we may get into the cottage.

I have to thank many friends for their kind congratulations, and have had a long letter and genealogy from the York Herald, Mr. Nayler, whom I have referred to my brother Maurice. I have sent my brother my Supporters, Crest, and Motto : on one side a Sailor properly habited, holding in his hand the Broad Pendant on a staff, and trampling on a Spanish flag; on the other side the British Lion tearing the Spanish flag, the remnants hanging down, and the flag in tatters. Motto, what my brother William suggested, turned into English—"Faith and Works."[1]

---

[1] It being necessary for the erection of his Banner as a Knight of the Bath in Westminster Abbey, that he should have Armorial Ensigns, and not having a right to any by descent, he obtained two Grants ; one, of his Crest and Arms ; the other, of his Supporters, copies of which documents are printed in Clarke and M'Arthur, vol. ii., Appendix, Nos. 4 and 5. The Grant, dated on the 28th October, 1797, recited that he was by tradition descended from the Family of Nelson, registered in the Heralds' Visitation of 1664, " his family having borne the Arms so registered, [viz. ' Or a Cross, sable, surmounted by a Bend, gules,'] but that he was unable, from the want of family evidences, to ascertain his connexion with the said family," and it proceeded to " grant, exemplify, and confirm to SIR

I hope you will like them. I intend my next winter's gift at Burnham should be fifty good large blankets of the very best quality, and they will last for seven years at least. This will not take from anything the Parish might give. I wish inquiry to be made, and the blankets ordered of some worthy man; they are to be at my father's disposal in November. I have received my dear father's letter. God bless him and you.

Yours, &c.

HORATIO NELSON.

TO GEORGE NAYLER, ESQ., YORK HERALD AND GENEALOGIST OF THE ORDER OF THE BATH.

[Autograph, in the possession of Albert William Woods, Esq., Lancaster Herald.]

Theseus, off Cadiz, June 29th, 1797.

Sir,

I am honoured with your letter of May 29, relative to my Pedigree; and I have desired my Brother to deliver you this letter, and to arrange such matters as are proper with you. As Government have always, I believe, on occasions like the present, paid all the Fees of Office, Installation, &c., I expect they will do it on the present occasion, for I cannot think of

HORATIO NELSON the Arms following; that is to say, Or, a Cross flory, sable, a Bend, gules, surmounted by another engrailed of the field, charged with three Bombs, fired, proper. And for a Crest, on a wreath of the colours, the stern of a Spanish Man-of-War, proper, thereon inscribed, '*San Josef,*' being the name of one of the Line-of-Battle Ships, taken in the Engagement with the Spanish Fleet, off Cape St. Vincent, on the 14th day of February, 1797, by His Majesty's Fleet under the Command of Sir John Jervis, Knight of the Most Honourable Order of the Bath, (now Earl of Saint Vincent,) to be borne and used for ever hereafter by him the said Rear-Admiral Sir Horatio Nelson (as a memorial of his distin-guished services and merits, which will be more particularly stated in his Patent of Supporters) and his descendants, and by those of his said father, Edmund Nelson, with due and proper differences according to the laws of Arms, without the let or interruption of any person or persons whatsoever." His Supporters, (but whether suggested by the Heralds or by himself, is doubtful,) as described in the Grant of them, were, " On the Dexter, a Sailor, armed with a cutlass, and a pair of pistols in his belt, proper, the exterior hand supporting a Staff, thereon hoisted a Commo-dore's Flag, gules; on the Sinister, a Lion, rampant, reguardant, proper, in his mouth a broken Flag-staff, therefrom flowing a Spanish Flag, or and gules."

being at one sixpence expense :[2] but my Brother will express my sentiments fully on this head, and I have the honour to be, Sir,

Your most obedient servant,
Horatio Nelson.

TO THE REV. DIXON HOSTE, GOODWICKE, NEAR ROUGHAM.

[Autograph, in the possession of Sir John Bickerton Williams.]

Theseus, June 30th, 1797.

My dear Sir,

As I have desired my dear William to write you, I shall only express my anxiety that his Time should be sent to me. I hear he was borne some short time on the Grampus' books, but of this you know more than I can do. My health is so very indifferent, that longer than the 30th September I cannot serve without a short respite from fatigue ; but I hope the War will be over by that time ; for, unless we are united at Home much good cannot be expected,—let it be a War of the Nation, and what signify France, Holland, and Spain.

We are looking at the Ladies walking the walls and Mall of Cadiz, and know of the ridicule they make of their Sea Officers. Thirty Sail are now perfectly ready, and, the first east wind, I expect the Ships from the Mediterranean, which will make them forty Sail of the Line. We are now twenty; some of our Ships being always obliged to be absent for water, provisions, &c. However equal we may be to do the business, yet I cannot bring myself to believe that it is good policy to leave us so inferior, whatever honour there may be in it. The merchants of Cadiz have repeatedly petitioned Government to force out the Fleet; and say truly, that ten Sail of the Line had better be sacrificed than the loss of their three Ships from Lima, and their Homeward Convoy, which must fall into the hands of the English, if they are not forced from

---

[2] Nelson's refusal to pay any Fees for the Honour conferred upon him, calls for a much longer Note than the fact might seem to justify, because it relates to a still existing abuse, equally repugnant to the feelings of distinguished Officers, injurious to the Public ,and derogatory to the dignity of the Crown. See the Appendix, p. 467.

before the harbour. I am of opinion that some morning, when least expected, I shall see them tumbling out of Cadiz. We in the advance are, night and day, prepared for battle : our friends in England need not fear the event. At present we are all quiet in our Fleet ; and, if Government hang some of the Nore Delegates, we shall remain so. I am entirely with the Seamen in their first Complaint. We are a neglected set, and, when peace comes, are shamefully treated; but, for the Nore scoundrels, I should be happy to command a Ship against them. We have reports through Spain that Pitt is out: it is Measures must be changed, and not merely Men. I beg my respects to Mr. Coke and Mrs. Coke, and believe me, dear Sir,

Your very obedient servant,
HORATIO NELSON.

TO ADMIRAL DON JOSEF DE MAZAREDO, CADIZ.

[From Harrison's Life of Nelson, vol. i. p. 188.]

30th June, 1797.

Sir,

I am directed by my worthy Commander-in-Chief to inform your Excellency, that numbers of the Spanish fishing-boats are found at such a distance from the land as plainly to evince that they have something farther in view than catching fish ; and, therefore, that orders are given, that no Fishing-vessel be in future, permitted to go farther from the shore than their usual fishing-ground, which, we understand, is in about thirty-five fathoms water.

Your Excellency, I am confident, will receive this communication as an addditional mark of attention from my Commander-in-Chief to the inhabitants of Cadiz, and its environs, and will take measures for the information of the fishermen, that their boats will be sunk, if found acting in contradiction to this notification of the British Admiral. With every sincere good wish towards your Excellency, believe me, your most obedient,

HORATIO NELSON.

TO ADMIRAL SIR JOHN JERVIS, K.B.

[From Clarke and M'Arthur, vol. ii. p. 22.]

3rd July, 1797.

We will begin this night by ten o'clock;[3] and I beg that all the launches of the Fleet may be with me by eight, or half-past at farthest, also all the barges or pinnaces. I wish to make it a warm night at Cadiz. The Town and their Fleet are prepared, and their Gun-boats are advanced; so much the better. If they venture from their walls, I shall give Johnny his full scope for fighting. Mazaredo will be more than human, if he can keep the Merchants of Cadiz in good humour. I am inclined to think he has been out this afternoon. I intend, if alive, and not tired, to see you to-morrow, and ever to the last believe me your faithful,

HORATIO NELSON.

TO ADMIRAL SIR JOHN JERVIS, K.B.[4]

[Original in the Admiralty. Published in the London Gazette, of the 1st August, 1797.]

Theseus, July 4th, 1797.

Sir,

In obedience to your orders, the Thunderer Bomb was placed, by the good management of Lieutenant Gourly, her present Commander, assisted by Mr. Jackson, Master of the Ville de

---

[3] The preparations mentioned in this Letter were made for the bombardment of Cadiz, which took place in the night of the 3rd of July. On that day Sir John Jervis issued the following General Order:—" All the barges and launches, *without exception*, with their carronades properly fitted, and plenty of ammunition and pikes, are to be with Admiral Nelson at half-past 8 o'clock this night, for a particular service. The watering must cease for to-night." The particulars of the Affair are fully detailed in Nelson's official Dispatch.

[4] This Letter was transmitted to the Admiralty, with the following Dispatch, from the Commander-in-Chief:—

" Ville de Paris, off Cadiz, July 5th, 1797.
" Sir,

" I desire you will acquaint the Lords Commissioners of the Admiralty, that the Terpsichore, with the Thunder bomb, having a detachment of Artillery on board, and the Urchin Gun-boat from Gibraltar, joined on the 2nd Instant, and the night following, Rear-Admiral Nelson, having made his dispositions, the Bomb, covered by the Gun-boat, Launches, and Barges of the Fleet, was placed near the Tower of

Paris, who volunteered his able services within 2500 yards of the walls of Cadiz; and the shells were thrown from her with much precision, under the directions of Lieutenant Baynes, of the Royal Artillery; but, unfortunately, it was soon found that the large Mortar was materially injured, from its former services; I therefore, judged it proper to order her to return under the protection of the Goliath, Terpsichore, and Fox, which were kept under sail for that purpose, and for whose active services I feel much obliged.

The Spaniards having sent out a great number of Mortar Gun-boats and armed Launches, I directed a vigorous attack to be made on them, which was done with such gallantry, that

San Sebastian, and fired some shells into the Town, when an attempt was made by the Gun-boats and Launches of the Enemy to carry her. The Rear-Admiral, who is always present in the most arduous enterprises, with the assistance of some other Barges, boarded and carried two of the Enemy's Gun-boats, and a Barge launch of one of their Ships of War, with the Commandant of the Flotilla. In this short conflict eighteen or twenty Spaniards were killed, the Commandant and several wounded; he and twenty-five men were made prisoners; the rest swam ashore.

" This spirited Action was performed with inconsiderable loss on our part, as per enclosed. The Launch of the Ville de Paris was sunk by a raking shot from the Enemy's gun-boats; but, by the active, intelligent mind of Captain Troubridge, got up yesterday morning, and repaired on board the Culloden.

" Rear-Admiral Nelson's actions speak for themselves; any praise of mine would fall very short of his merit.   " I am, Sir, &c.

                                                          "J. JERVIS.

" P.S. The inclosed Report from Rear-Admiral Nelson has just reached me."

" RETURN OF THE KILLED AND WOUNDED IN THE ATTACK OF THE SPANISH
         GUN-BOATS, THE NIGHT OF THE 3RD JULY, 1797.

Theseus	5 wounded.
Irresistible	1 wounded.
Seahorse . . .	1 wounded.
Ville de Paris , . .	5 wounded.
Prince George . . .	1 killed; 5 wounded.
Diadem . . .	1 wounded.
Barfleur	1 wounded.
Egmont	1 wounded.

               Total: 1 killed; 20 wounded.

                    " OFFICERS WOUNDED.

Seahorse.—Captain Fremantle, slightly.
Ville de Paris.—Lieutenant William Selby, ditto.
Diadem.—Lieutenant W. J. Rowe, ditto.
Prince George.—Lieutenant Gregory Grant, ditto.
Ditto.—Mr. R. Tooley, Midshipman, ditto.
Barfleur.—Mr. Hugh Pearson, Master's Mate.
Theseus.—John Sykes, Admiral's Coxswain.

                                                   J. JERVIS."

they were drove and pursued close to the walls of Cadiz, and must have suffered considerable loss: and I have the pleasure to inform you, that two Mortar-boats and an armed Launch remained in our possession.

I feel myself particularly indebted, for the successful termination of this contest, to the gallantry of Captains Fremantle and Miller, the former of whom accompanied me in my Barge; and to my Coxswain, John Sykes,[5] who, in defending my person, is most severely wounded; as was Captain Fremantle, slightly, in the attack.[6] And my praises are generally due to every Officer and man, some of whom I saw behave in the most noble manner; and I regret it is not in my power to particularize them. I must also beg to be permitted to express my admiration of Don Miguel Tyrason, the Commander of the Gun-boats. In his Barge, he laid my Boat alongside, and his resistance was such as did honour to a brave Officer; eighteen of the twenty-six men being killed, and himself and all the rest wounded. Not having a correct list of killed and wounded, I can only state, that I believe about six are killed and twenty wounded.

I have the honour to be, &c.,

HORATIO NELSON.

[5] Lord St. Vincent rewarded this gallant fellow with a Gunner's warrant, and appointed him to the Andromache. Captain Miller, writing to Nelson, towards the end of 1797, said, " I wish that Sykes had served time sufficient, as I would have endeavoured to prevail on Lord St. Vincent to make him a Lieutenant; his manners and conduct are so entirely above his situation, that Nature certainly intended him for a gentleman."—*Clarke and M'Arthur.* Sykes was killed by the bursting of a cannon, before October 1799.

[6] Speaking of the Blockade of Cadiz, and of this Affair, in the " Sketch of his Life," Nelson says, " It was during this period that perhaps my personal courage was more conspicuous than at any other part of my life. In an attack of the Spanish Gun-boats, I was boarded in my Barge with its common crew of ten men, cockswain, Captain Freemantle, and myself, by the Commander of the Gun-boats; the Spanish Barge rowed twenty-six oars, besides Officers, thirty men in the whole. This was a service hand to hand with swords, in which my Coxswain, John Sykes, now no more, twice saved my life. Eighteen of the Spaniards being killed and several wounded, we succeeded in taking their Commander." (Vide vol. i. p. 13.) Clarke and M'Arthur state that Sykes saved his Admiral's life by parrying the blows aimed at him, and that he once actually interposed his own head to receive the full force of a Spanish sabre, which, fighting hand to hand, he could in no other way prevent from falling on Nelson.

TO ADMIRAL SIR JOHN JERVIS, K.B.

[From Clarke and M'Arthur, vol. ii. p. 24.]

July 5th, 1797.

My dear Sir,

I am thankful, for your flattering letter,[7] which, as we all like, I will believe as much of as I can. To-night[8] my plan is for Cadiz, on the outside of the lighthouse: Jackson knows a good berth. If the Brigs come out, we will have a dash at them, and, as the Boats will be in three divisions under Captains, we may expect a little more regularity, in case of any unforeseen event. Your encouragement for those Lieutenants who may conspicuously exert themselves, cannot fail to have its good effect in serving our Country, instead of their thinking that if a Vessel is taken, it would make the son of some great man a Captain, in the place of the gallant fellow who

[7] " My dear Admiral,

" I congratulate you most heartily on the events of last night. Every service you are engaged in adds fresh lustre to the British arms, and to your character. (*) Examine strictly your prisoners, to discover if any of them are under the convention of Trinidad or Lagos, and make the Spanish Officers clearly understand the object of your investigation. (†) Most truly yours,

" Ville de Paris, 4th July, 1797."   " J. Jervis.

The unjustifiable manner in which Clarke and M'Arthur have printed documents, is strikingly shewn by their copy of this Letter. At the place marked (*) they have *interpolated* this paragraph, " The letter is characteristic of your noble soul, and cannot be improved by the ablest pen in Europe;" and at (†) they have *added*, " Johnson, First-lieutenant of the Emerald, is a man after your own heart; put him in a way of taking a Gun-boat, and I will answer he succeeds, or loses his life in the attempt. I think the Barges and Launches should come to you to-morrow after the night has closed, and you will make your arrangements accordingly ; perhaps it would be better to try to carry some more Gun-boats, without the Bomb-ketch. The Lieutenant, who has the greatest merit in taking a Brig shall be made Captain of her immediately"—*neither of which passages is to be found in the Original Letter*, now in the Nelson Papers.

[8] Of this second bombardment of Cadiz, the Commander-in-Chief gave the following official account to Mr. Nepean, the Secretary to the Admiralty. (*London Gazette*, 1st August, 1797.)

" Ville de Paris, off Cadiz, the 10th July, 1797.

" Sir,

" I desire you will acquaint the Lords Commissioners of the Admiralty, that Rear-Admiral Nelson ordered a second Bombardment of Cadiz, on the night of the 5th, under the direction of Captain Bowen of the Terpsichore, Captain Miller of the Theseus, and Captain Waller of the Emerald ; and appointed Mr. Jackson, Master of the Ville de Paris, to place the Thunderer, Terror, and Strombolo; and that the

captured her. At present the Brigs lie too close to each other to hope for a dash at them, but soon I expect to find one off her guard, and then———. We have eighty-seven living prisoners now on board, and near thirty have since died of their wounds. News from Cadiz this morning is, that some people were killed in the Town, and fifteen were killed, and a great number wounded in the Spanish gun-boats.

I am, &c.
HORATIO NELSON.

TO ADMIRAL SIR JOHN JERVIS, K.B.

[From Tucker's Memoirs of the Earl of St. Vincent, vol. i. p. 418.]

H.M.S. Ship Theseus, 7th July, 1797.

My dear Sir,
The Officer who came out with the Flag of Truce says, that our Ministers at Lisle are Lords Grenville, Malmesbury,

Bombardment produced considerable effect in the Town and among the Shipping. Ten Sail of the Line, among them the Ships carrying the Flags of Admirals Mazarredo and Gravina, having warped out of the range of shell, with much precipitation the following morning; and it is with great satisfaction I inform you, that this important service was effected with very little loss on our side, as per enclosed return of killed and wounded. The Rear-Admiral meditated another operation on the night of Saturday the 8th, under his own direction; but the wind blew so strong down the bay, he could not get his bomb-vessels up to the point of attack in time.
    "Mr. Hornsey, Master's Mate of the Seahorse, distinguished himself in a very remarkable manner. I am, &c.

"ST. VINCENT."

A RETURN OF THE OFFICERS AND MEN BELONGING TO THE SQUADRON, WHO WERE KILLED OR WOUNDED ON THE NIGHT OF THE 5TH INSTANT, ATTENDING THE BOMB-VESSELS AND ATTACKING THE SPANISH GUN-BOATS:

    "Victory, William Cuming, Commander.—1 officer wounded.
    Blenheim, W. Bowen, Commander.—1 seaman killed.
    Theseus, R. W. Miller, Commander.—1 seaman killed; 2 officers, 5 marines or soldiers wounded.
    Culloden, T. Troubridge, Commander.—1 seaman killed; 2 seamen wounded.
    Irresistible, G. Martin, Commander.—1 seaman wounded.
    Audacious, D. Gould, Commander.—1 officer, 3 seamen wounded.
    Seahorse, T. F. Fremantle, Commander.—1 officer wounded.

OFFICERS WOUNDED.

    Victory.—Lieutenant Collins, much bruised.
    Theseus.—John Oldfield, Captain of Marines.
    Ditto.—John Coltier, Midshipman.
    Audacious.———— Stephenson, ditto.
    Seahorse.—John Hornsey, Acting-Assistant.

"J. JERVIS."

and St. Helens; Dell' Campo and Camporosa, on the part of
Spain; and De la Croix, Le Turneur, and another on the
part of France: that Peace is expected every day,—that
with the Emperor is ratified and finished; also, that the
Government of Genoa is completely altered,—many of the
Senators were massacred, and their palaces plundered. News
from Cadiz, by a Market-boat, that our Ships did much
damage; the Town was on fire in three places; a shell that
fell in a Convent destroyed several priests (that no harm, they
will never be missed); that plunder and robbery was going
on—a glorious scene of confusion; that representations have
been made to Mazaredo, and to the Admiral, to come out
with the Fleet. I see an Admiral moving forwards, and now
I perceive it is Mazaredo. The bombs and mortars will be
finished to night, but I cannot part with the Isis. I have
arranged about the change of howitzers: to-morrow I will
write on that subject. I wish you had mentioned about Zealous: we hear nothing of her.

Ever yours most faithfully,
HORATIO NELSON.

Please God, I hope the Spanish Fleet are coming out, and
the Admiral is under sail; and I open my letter to say they
are all on the move.

TO ADMIRAL SIR JOHN JERVIS, K.B.

[From Tucker's Memoirs of the Earl of St. Vincent, vol. i. p. 327.]

Theseus, July 9, 1797.

My dear Sir,

In the first place, I congratulate you on the finish, as it
ought, of the St. George's business,[9] and I (if I may be per-

---

[9] Symptoms of mutiny having shewed themselves on board some of the Ships
of Sir John Jervis's Fleet off Cadiz, he suppressed them with his characteristic
vigour and decision. On Friday the 7th, and Saturday the 8th of July, four mutineers of the Saint George were tried by a Court-Martial; and on the latter day, Sir
John Jervis wrote two Notes respecting them to Nelson. In the first he said, "If
these four unfortunate men receive sentence of death, as there is every reason to believe they will, from the strong and direct evidence which came home to the bosoms
of all yesterday, and the Court Martial ends this day, they will suffer at 6 o'clock in
the evening, therefore," &c. As the trial did not terminate until after sunset, the

mitted to say so) very much approve of its being so speedily carried into execution, even although it is *Sunday.* The particular situation of the service requires extraordinary measures. I hope this will end all the disorders in our Fleet : had there been the same determined spirit at home, I do not believe it would have been half so bad, not but that I think Lord Howe's sending back the first petition was wrong.

Yours most affectionately and gratefully,
HORATIO NELSON.

TO SIR ROBERT CALDER, KNIGHT, FIRST CAPTAIN TO
ADMIRAL THE EARL OF ST. VINCENT, K.B.

[From Tucker's " Memoirs of the Earl of St. Vincent," vol. i. p. 328.]

My dear Sir,   Theseus, July 9th, 1797.

I am sorry that you should have to differ with [Vice-Admiral Thompson] but had it been Christmas Day instead of Sunday, I would have executed them.

sentence was not carried into execution on the 8th, and Sir John Jervis conse-quently wrote to Rear-Admiral Nelson: " The sentence must be carried into execu-tion to-morrow morning, although it is Sunday, and you will take care to have the Boats of the detached Squadron up in time."—*Autographs* in the Nelson Papers. In a Letter to Nelson, dated " Ville de Paris, Sunday Evening, 9th July, 1797," Sir John Jervis said:—" Vice-Admiral Thompson has presumed to censure the execution on the Sabbath, in a public letter; and I have insisted on his being removed from this Fleet immediately, or that I shall be called home; and I have *stipulated for no more Admirals.*"—*Autograph* in the Nelson Papers. Writing to Earl Spencer on that day, the Commander-in-Chief observed, " The Court-Martial on the mutineers of the St. George did not finish before sunset yesterday, *or they would have been executed last night.* The most daring and profligate of them con-fessed to the Clergyman who attended him, that the plan had been in contempla-tion six months, in concert with the Britannia, Captain, Diadem, and Egmont. I hope I shall not be censured by the Bench of Bishops, as I have been by Vice-Admiral [Thompson,] for profaning the Sabbath : the criminals asked five days to prepare, in which they would have hatched five hundred treasons ; besides that, we are provoking the Spanish Fleet to come out by every means in our power; and seven and twenty Gun and Mortar boats did actually advance, dastardly enough, it must be confessed, and cannonaded the advanced Squadron, now composed of ten Sail of the Line, on seeing twenty Barges and Pinnaces go to attend the execution of the sentence."—*Tucker's Memoirs of Earl St. Vincent,* vol. i. p. 327. On the 22nd of September, the Admiralty acknowledged the receipt of Lord St. Vincent's letter announcing the execution of the mutineers on the Sunday, and their Lord-ships expressed " their very high approbation" of his " conduct on that unpleasant and urgent occasion."—*Ibid.* p. 329.

We know not what might have been hatched by a Sunday's grog: *now* your discipline is safe. I talked to our people, and, I hope, with good effect: indeed, they seem a very quiet set. Ever your most faithful,

HORATIO NELSON.

TO ADMIRAL SIR JOHN JERVIS, K.B.

[From Clarke and M'Arthur, vol. ii. p. 26, who thus abridge the former part of this Letter:[1]—"On the 9th of July, 1797, he informed Lord St. Vincent, that, although he hoped enough had been done to force out the Spanish Fleet, yet in case there had not, he would try them again, 'when,' he added,"]

9th July, 1797.

Down comes Cadiz; and not only Cadiz, but their Fleet, if Mazaredo will not come out. The people of Cadiz are told, that they have made great destruction amongst us, and believe it; and reports say their gun and mortar-boats are to attack our advanced Squadron the very first calm night. If they succeed in either destroying some of us, or crippling our masts, then Mazaredo puts to sea, and destroys you: therefore do not be surprised, my dear Sir, if you hear a cannonade; I am prepared.

I am, &c.

HORATIO NELSON.

TO ADMIRAL SIR JOHN JERVIS, K.B.

[From Tucker's Memoirs of the Earl of St. Vincent, vol. i. p. 419.]

H.M.S. Theseus, July 10th, 1797.

My dear Sir,

I will send Mr. Yawkins off San Pedro, and hope it will answer its intended purpose. I was in hopes the gentry would have enabled me to have a run at them, but they are too much on their guard. If the King of Spain goes on this way, and the Mexican Fleet fall into our hands, he will be like Billy Pitt, give nothing but paper. As for those shots flying about the Theseus, it will do her good, and make her the

---

[1] Clarke and M'Arthur introduced into this Letter, two paragraphs out of the following Letter of the 10th of July.

better for your support in some proud day, not far distant, I
hope. Portugal ought to be grateful for your attention to her
interest, and so ought little England.

Believe me ever your most faithful,

HORATIO NELSON.

The Dons will be tired enough to take a good *nap* this
afternoon.

TO SIR JAMES SAUMAREZ, CAPTAIN OF HIS MAJESTY'S SHIP ORION.

[Autograph, in the possession of the Dowager Lady de Saumarez.]

Theseus, July 10th, 1797.

Dear Sir,

I beg you will have the goodness to immediately send in my
Letter for Don Josef de Mazaredo: his Letter of yesterday
does not please the Admiral.

Ever your most obedient Servant,

HORATIO NELSON.

TO CAPTAIN JOHN NICHOLSON INGLEFIELD, COMMISSIONER OF THE NAVY AT GIBRALTAR.

[From Clarke and M'Arthur, vol. ii. p. 27.]

July 11th, 1797.

My dear Sir,

I am sorry to find, from General O'Hara's letter, that he
has the smallest alarm for our success in anything my great
Commander-in-Chief plans : had my orders been well executed, not a Spanish gun or mortar boat would have been left
at Cadiz. Our loss of men is most trifling; but, however
that might have been, I had rather see fifty shot by the
Enemy, than one hanged by us. It is good at these times to
keep the Devil out of their heads.

Mazaredo is alarmed; has drawn all his Ships between St.
Mary's and Cadiz; and if you make haste with the sea-mor-
tar, I will bomb him out of Cadiz bay. Three fires were seen
in the Town, but they were got under without much difficulty.
I laid myself with the Bomb on the strong face of Cadiz, seventy

guns and eight mortars. They expected me on the weak side. The next night I took them on the soft side, and eighty shells fell in the Town, and some over it amongst their Shipping. Yesterday, in the Theseus, I had the honour of every gun from the southern part of Cadiz, and of every Gun and Mortar-boat. I could not get them out so far as I wished, or some of them should have paid me a visit. I sent ninety-one prisoners into Cadiz, whom I took on the night of the 3rd; and, as to killed, I know nothing about them : eighteen were killed in the Commanding Officer's boat, that had the presumption to lay my Barge aboard, manned with some of the Agamemnon's people. My Squadron is now ten Sail of the Line. If they come out, there will be no fighting beyond my Squadron.

I am, &c.,

HORATIO NELSON.

TO MRS. NELSON.

[From Clarke and M'Arthur, vol. ii. p. 28.]

July 12th to the 14th, 1797.

I should be glad if the house were bought : and if you do not object, I should like Norfolk in preference to any other part of the Kingdom; but do you choose. I am sure the time is past for doing anything for George Tobin; had he been with me, he would long since have been a Captain, and I should have liked it, as being most exceedingly pleased with him. My late Affair here will not, I believe, lower me in the opinion of the world. I have had flattery enough to make me vain, and success enough to make me confident. When you know I am sent from the Fleet, never calculate on a letter until you hear I am returned. I am always sorry when you are disappointed; and as I may now be absent for a short time,[2] do not be anxious about letters, for you cannot hear from me. Ever believe me your most affectionate husband,

HORATIO NELSON.

---

[2] The Commander-in Chief having received intelligence that a Spanish Ship called "El Principe d'Asturias," richly laden, from Manilla to Cadiz, was at Santa Cruz, it was determined to carry Nelson's favourite design of attacking that place into effect; but it must not be forgotten, that a principal cause of its failure was, that, an essential

MEMORANDA.

[Autograph, in the Nelson Papers. This Paper appears to contain certain Questions relating to the attack on Teneriffe, which Nelson submitted to Admiral Sir John Jervis, whose decision upon them is added.]

When the Summons is sent in to demand the immediate Surrender of Santa Cruz, or the whole Island, with the entire Cargoes of such Ships as may have landed them at that place, and every species of property, together with Cannon, Stores, &c., which is not *bonâ fide* the actual growth of the Island of Teneriffe, or such goods as may be the property of shopkeepers for the consumption of the inhabitants of the Island— I wish to know if it is your directions, that I do, at the same time, demand a contribution of dollars for the preservation of all other property in the Island of Teneriffe, together with the Vessels employed on the fishery on the African Coast?

Not to demand any contribution if all is given up.

Is it your opinion, that the Summons should be for the

part of his original plan was not carried out, namely the assistance of a large body of Troops. (Vide pp. 379, 380, ante.) On the morning of the 14th of July, he quitted the in-shore Squadron, and joined the main body of the Fleet. He then, it appears, submitted the above-mentioned points for Sir John Jervis's consideration, and received the following order for the Expedition :—" By Sir John Jervis, Knight of the Bath, Admiral of the Blue, and Commander-in-Chief of his Majesty's Ships and Vessels employed, and to be employed, in the Mediterranean, &c. &c. &c. You are hereby required and directed to take the Ships named in the margin[3] under your command, their Captains being instructed to obey your orders, and to proceed with the utmost expedition off the Island of Teneriffe, and there make your dispositions for taking possession of the Town of Santa Cruz, by a sudden and vigorous Assault. In case of success, you are authorized to lay a heavy contribution on the inhabitants of the Town and adjacent district, if they do not put you in possession of the whole cargo of El Principe d'Asturias, from Manilla, bound to Cadiz, belonging to the Philippine Company, and all the treasure belonging to the Crown of Spain; and you are to endeavour to take, sink, burn, or otherwise destroy, all Vessels of every description, even those employed in the Fishery, on the Coast of Africa, unless a just contribution is made for their preservation, by the inhabitants of the Canary Islands ; and having performed your mission, you are to make the best of your way back, to join me off this Port. Given on board the Ville de Paris, off Cadiz, the 14th July, 1797. J. JERVIS."—*Original* in the Nelson Papers.

On the 15th of July, Sir John Jervis thus affectionately expressed his wishes for Nelson's success :—" God bless and prosper you. I am sure you will deserve success. To mortals is not given the power of commanding it."—*Ibid.*

[3] " Theseus, Culloden, Zealous, Leander, Seahorse, Emerald, Terpsichore, Fox (1), Cutter."

whole Island of Teneriffe, or only for the Town of Santa Cruz, and the district belonging to it?

For the whole Island.

What contribution do you wish me to demand for the preservation of private property, with the exceptions as before, for the Grand Canary?

Palma, Gomera, Ferro, Forte Ventura, Lancerote.

And, in case of a refusal to what I may think reasonable Terms, to what length may I proceed with propriety?

[The answer to this Question is not given.]

MEMORANDUM.

[Autograph, in the Nelson Papers.]

The Culloden and Zealous to each make a Platform[4] for one 18-pounder. The Theseus to make a slay for dragging cannon.

Each Ship to make as many iron ram-rods as possible, it being found that the wooden ones are very liable to break when used in a hurry.

The Seahorse to make a platform for one nine-pounder.

July 17th, Delivered.

[4] The annexed Section of the Platform is among the Nelson Papers:—

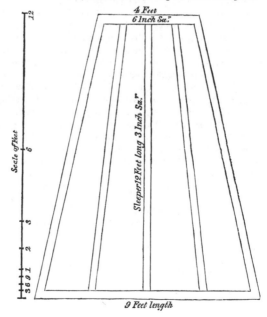

9 Feet length

QUESTIONS WHICH APPEAR TO HAVE BEEN SUBMITTED TO
ONE OR MORE OF THE CAPTAINS OF THE SQUADRON.

[Autograph, in the Nelson Papers.]

QUESTION 1st.

Is it your opinion that from the information we have been
able to collect, and from Lieutenant Wably's plan, that the
landing should be made in the valley marked E., known by
the name of Lion's Mouth, and endeavour to get over the
mountain marked F. and attack the fort marked G? Or is it
your opinion that, at least, 600 men should be landed under
the Line Wall, and to escalade that wall?

2nd.

Supposing the escalade of the Line Wall to be successful,
is it your opinion that an immediate attack should be made
on the Town and Mole, by turning to the left, or should the
attack be made by turning to the right, and attacking the
battery G.?

THE FOLLOWING REGULATIONS ARE RECOMMENDED BY
REAR-ADMIRAL NELSON.

[Autograph, in the Nelson Papers.]

July 17th, [1796.]

1st.

That each Ship's Boats should be kept together by towing
each other, which will keep the people of each Ship collected,
and the Boats will be in six divisions, and nearly got on shore
at the same moment.

2nd.

The Marines of each Ship of the Line to be put in their
Launches, which will carry them.

3rd.

The moment the Boats are discovered by a firing being
made on them, the Bomb-vessel to commence her fire on the
Town, and to keep it up till the flag of truce is hoisted from
either the Enemy or from us.

4th.

That a Captain should be directed to see the Boats put off

from the beach, that more men may be speedily got on shore
with the field-pieces.

5th.

Frigates to anchor, as soon as possible after the alarm is
given, or the forces ashore, near the battery in the N.E. part
of the Bay.

6th.

Immediately as the forces get on shore, they are to get in the
rear of the battery marked G., in the N.E. part of the Bay,
and to instantly storm it, and also to take post on the top of
the hill which is above it.

Every Ship to land the number of men as against their
names expressed,[5] with a proper proportion of Officers and Midshipmen, exclusive of Commissioned Officers and servants.

And the Captains are at liberty to send as many more men
as they please, leaving sufficient to manage the Ship, and to
man the launch and another boat. Every Captain that
chooses, is at liberty to land, and command his seamen, under
the direction of Captain Troubridge.

It is recommended to put as many Marine coats or jackets
on the seamen as can be procured, and that all should have
canvas cross-belts.

The Marines to be all under the direction of Captain
Oldfield, the senior Marine Officer; and he is directed to put
himself under the direction of Captain Troubridge, as is
Lieutenant Baynes, of the Royal Artillery, with his Detachment.

TO THOMAS TROUBRIDGE, ESQ., CAPTAIN OF H.M. SHIP CULLO-
DEN, AND COMMANDER OF THE FORCES ORDERED TO BE
LANDED FOR TAKING SANTA CRUZ.

[Autograph draught, in the Nelson Papers.]

Sir,   Theseus at Sea, 20th July, 1797.

I desire you will take under your command the number of
Seamen and marines named in the Margin,[6] who will be under

[5] Theseus, 200.   Zealous, 200.   Terpsichore, 100.
    Culloden, 200.   Seahorse, 100.   Emerald, 100.
           Exclusive of Officers and Servants, 900.

[6] [As above.]

the command of Captains Hood, Fremantle, Bowen, Miller, and Waller, and the Marines under the command of Captain Thomas Oldfield, and a detachment of the Royal Artillery under the command of Lieutenant Baynes, all of whom are now embarked on board his Majesty's Frigates, Seahorse, Terpsichore, and Emerald.

With this detachment you will proceed as near to the Town of Santa Cruz as possible, without endangering your being perceived; when you will embark as many men as the Boats will carry, and force your landing in the north-east part of the Bay of Santa Cruz, near a large battery. The moment you are on shore, I recommend you to first attack the battery; which when carried, and your post secured, you will either proceed by storm against the Town and Mole-head battery, or send in my Letter, as you judge most proper, containing a Summons, of which I send you a copy; and the terms are either to be accepted or rejected in the time specified, unless you see good cause for prolonging it, as no alteration will be made in them : and you will pursue such other methods as you judge most proper for speedily effecting my orders, which are to possess myself of all cargoes and treasures which may be landed in the Island of Teneriffe.

Having the firmest confidence in the ability, bravery, and zeal of yourself, and all placed under your command, I have only to heartily wish you success, and to assure you that I am your most obedient and faithful servant,

HORATIO NELSON.

[Autograph, in the Nelson Papers.]

Theseus, July 20th, 1797.

The Culloden's Officers and men, with only their arms, to be ready to go on board the Terpsichore, at 1 P.M., this day ; to carry with them four ladders, (each of which to have a lanyard four fathoms long,) a sledge-hammer, wedges, and a broad axe.

The Boats' oars to be muffled with either a piece of canvas or kersey.   H. N.

Delivered July 20th, to the Culloden, Zealous, and Theseus.

TO LIEUTENANT BAYNES,[1] ROYAL ARTILLERY.

[From a Copy, in the Nelson Papers.]

Theseus, July 20th, 1797.

Sir,

As I have directed Captain Thomas Troubridge, of his Majesty's Ship Culloden, to command the Forces destined to take the Town of Santa Cruz, I have to request that you will attend to all his desires, for the more speedily executing my orders, and I send you the third Article of the Regulations I have recommended. I have the honour to be, &c.

HORATIO NELSON.

ARTICLE 3rd.

The moment the boats are discovered by a firing being made on them, the Bomb-vessel to commence her firing on the Town, and to keep it up till a Flag of Truce is hoisted either from the Enemy or from us.

TO CAPTAIN THOMAS OLDFIELD, SENIOR CAPTAIN OF THE MARINES ORDERED TO DISEMBARK.

[From a Copy, in the Nelson Papers.]

Theseus, July 20th, 1797.

Sir,

You will take the command of all the Marines of the Squadron, and put yourself under the command of Captain Troubridge of H.M.S. Culloden, who has my order to command the Forces landed for the taking the Town of Santa Cruz.

I am, &c.

HORATIO NELSON.

[1] Lieutenant Baynes, who is afterwards so highly spoken of, obtained the rank of Lieutenant-Colonel, in December 1814, and died on the 18th of January 1818.

TO THE GOVERNOR, OR COMMANDING OFFICER OF SANTA CRUZ.

[Autograph draught, in the Nelson Papers.]

By Sir Horatio Nelson, Knight of the Most Honourable
Order of the Bath, Rear-Admiral of the Blue, and
Commander-in Chief of his Britannic Majesty's Forces by
Sea and Land, before Santa Cruz.

Sir,　　　　　　　　　　　　　Theseus, 20th July, 1797.

I have the honour to acquaint you, that I am come here
to demand the immediate surrender of the Ship El Principe
d'Asturias, from Manilla bound to Cadiz, belonging to the
Philippine Company, together with her whole and entire
cargo; and also all such other cargoes and property as may
have been landed in the Island of Teneriffe, and not intended
for the consumption of its Inhabitants. And, as it is my
earnest wish that not one individual inhabitant of the Island
of Teneriffe should suffer by my demand being instantly complied with, I offer the following most honourable and liberal
Terms; which if refused, the horrors of war, which will fall on
the Inhabitants of Teneriffe, must be by the World imputed
to you, and to you only; for I shall destroy Santa Cruz,
and the other Towns in the Island, by a bombardment, and
levy a very heavy contribution on the Island.

ARTICLE 1st.

The Forts shall be delivered to me; and instantly a party of
the British troops shall be put in possession of the gates.

ARTICLE 2nd.

The Garrison shall lay down their arms; but the Officers
shall be allowed to keep their swords, and the Garrison, without the condition of being prisoners of War, shall be tran-
sported to Spain, or remain in the Island whilst their conduct
is orderly and proper, as the Commanding Officer pleases.

ARTICLE 3rd.

Upon the express condition that the full and entire cargoes of
El Principe d'Asturias, and all such other cargoes and property as may have been landed on the Island of Teneriffe,
and not intended for the consumption of its Inhabitants, [shall
be surrendered,] and the first Article complied with, not the
smallest contribution shall be levied on the Inhabitants; but

E E 2

Sir,

I have the honor to acquaint that I am sent here to demand the Surrender of the Ship Hamilla with all her Cargoe and also all property whatsoever which may belong to the King of Spain. I am been landed in the Island of Tenerife and not intended for the Consumption of it

the Alarm; As it is my earnest Wish
that no one Individual Inhabitant
of the Island of Teneriffe should suffer by
my demands being in I hastily concluded with
So Hon the following most honorable and
liberal terms, which if refused by your
Excellency, the honours of War which
were fixed on the Inhabitants of Teneriffe
must be by the World imputed to
You, and of You only.

Prostitution when changing employment,
to intemperance & to turn'd character made
in Holy Catholic Religion the principles
of Handrace & Religious orders where
be considered as might by experienced care
prostitution. The laws of Prayer, States
to be continued as at present unless
by the general and of the Islandery.—
Of these Terms are not subscribed to
with thy Seven miles again spent over
Servants terms

they shall enjoy the fullest protection in their persons and properties.

ARTICLE 4th.

No interference whatever shall be made in the Holy Catholic Religion; the Ministers of it, and and all its Religious Orders, shall be considered as under my especial care and protection.

ARTICLE 5th.

The Laws and Magistrates shall be continued as at present, unless by the general wish of the Islanders. These Terms subscribed to, the Inhabitants of the Town of Santa Cruz shall lodge their arms in one house, under the joint care of the Bishop and Chief Magistrate; and it will be my pride to consult with those Gentlemen, what may be most advantageous for the Inhabitants.   HORATIO NELSON.

I allow half of one hour for acceptance or rejection.

HORATIO NELSON.[7]

TO ADMIRAL SIR JOHN JERVIS, K.B.

[From a Copy in the Nelson Papers. A full account of the proceedings and failure of the Squadron at Teneriffe will be found in Nelson's Journal, and in Captain Troubridge's Report. (Vide p. 427, post.) It is, therefore, only necessary to observe here, that the first attempt against Santa Cruz was intended to have been made in the night of the 21st, but the Ships were discovered before they effected a landing. The following Letter, which announced Nelson's intention to renew the attack in person, during the night of Monday, the 24th of July, is supposed to be the last he ever wrote with his right hand, and Clarke and M'Arthur have given a *fac simile* of it. Those writers state that previous to the attack, Nelson, with some of the Captains of his Squadron, supped on board the Seahorse, Captain Fremantle, at whose table the lady, whom he had lately married in the Mediterranean, presided, and add that " Nelson, on leaving the Theseus, being sensible of the extreme danger to which he was about to be exposed, had called his son-in-law, Lieutenant Nisbet, who had the watch on deck, into the cabin, that he might assist in arranging and burning his Mother's letters; when perceiving that the young man was armed, he had begged of him earnestly to remain behind, adding, ' Should we both fall, Josiah, what would become of your poor Mother? The care of the Theseus falls to you; stay, therefore, and take

---

[7] On the Paper containing the draught of this Letter, Nelson wrote the following Memoranda:—

50, Launch.	20, Frigate's Launch.	
28, Barge.	25, Barge.	
14, Yawl.	13, Cutter.	416
16, Pinnace.		174
108	58	590

charge of her.' ' Sir,' replied Nisbet, ' the Ship must take care of herself.   I will
go with you to-night, if I never go again.'"—*Clarke and M'Arthur*, vol. ii. 35.
Whatever other arrangements Nelson may have made, he certainly did not destroy
his Wife's Letters, because they still exist among the Nelson Papers.]

My dear Sir,   Theseus, off Santa Cruz, July 24th, 8 P.M.
I shall not enter on the subject while we are not in possession of Santa Cruz ; your partiality will give credit, that all
has hitherto been done which was possible, but without effect :
this night I, humble as I am, command the whole, destined to
land under the batteries of the Town, and to-morrow my
head will probably be crowned with either laurel or cypress.
I have only to recommend Josiah Nisbet to you and my
Country.   With every affectionate wish for your health, and
every blessing in this world, believe me your most faithful,
                                        HORATIO NELSON.
The Duke of Clarence, should I fall in the service of my
King and Country, will, I am confident, take a lively interest
for my Son-in-Law, on his name being mentioned.

TO HIS EXCELLENCY DON ANTONIO GUTIERREZ,
COMMANDANT-GENERAL OF THE CANARY ISLANDS.

[From Harrison's " Life of Nelson," vol. i. p. 215.]

His Majesty's Ship Theseus, opposite Santa Cruz de Teneriffe,
Sir,   26th July, 1797.
I cannot take my departure from this Island, without returning your Excellency my sincerest thanks for your attention towards me, by your humanity in favour of our wounded
men in your power, or under your care, and for your generosity towards all our people who were disembarked, which I
shall not fail to represent to my Sovereign, hoping also, at a
proper time, to assure your Excellency in person how truly I
am, Sir, your most obedient, humble servant,
                                        HORATIO NELSON.

P.S.—I trust your Excellency will do me the honour to
accept of a Cask of English beer and a cheese.

TO ADMIRAL SIR JOHN JERVIS, K.B.

[From a Copy in the Nelson Papers, printed in the London Gazette of September 2nd, 1797. It is remarkable that in this, his official Dispatch, Nelson does not mention his own wound, of which his biographers give the following account:—
"Attended by his son-in-law, Nelson had proceeded from the Seahorse to the Mole of Santa Cruz, and had there received his severe wound [a grape-shot] through the right elbow, [the same fire having wounded seven other men in their right arms,] as he was in the act of drawing his Sword and stepping out of the Boat. This Sword, which he had so long and deservedly valued from respect to his uncle Maurice Suckling, was grasped, when falling, in his left hand, notwithstanding the agony he endured. Lieutenant Nisbet, who had remained close to him, saw his father-in-law wounded from the tremendous fire of the Spaniards, and heard him exclaim, ' I am shot through the arm, I am a dead man.' Nisbet placed him at the bottom of the Boat, and observing that the sight of the quantity of blood which had rushed from the shattered arm seemed to increase the faintness, he took off his hat to conceal it. He then with great presence of mind examined the state of the wound, and holding the shattered arm so as to stanch the blood, he took some silk handkerchiefs from his neck, and bound them tightly above the lacerated vessels ; but for this attention, Nelson, as he afterwards declared, must have perished. Mr. Nisbet was assisted by a seaman of the name of Lovel, one of the Admiral's Bargemen ; who, having torn his shirt into shreds, constructed a sling for the wounded arm. They then collected five other seamen, and at length, with their assistance got the Boat afloat, which had grounded from the falling of the tide. Having thus far succeeded, Lieutenant Nisbet took one of the oars that remained, and ordered the man who steered to go close under the guns of the batteries, that they might be safe from their tremendous fire. The voice of his son-in-law enforcing this judicious order, roused Nelson from his fainting state, and he immediately desired to be lifted up in the boat, that, to use his own words, ' he might look a little about him :' he was accordingly raised by Nisbet. The scene of destruction and the tempestuous sea were sublimely dreadful : a painful uncertainty prevailed respecting the fate of his brave companions ; when, on a sudden, a general shriek from the crew of the Fox, which had sunk from a shot she had received under water, made the Admiral forget his own weak and painful state. Many were rescued from a watery grave by Nelson himself, whose humane exertions on this occasion added considerably to the agony and danger of his wound. Ninety-seven men, including Lieutenant Gibson, were lost, and eighty-three were saved. The first Ship which the Boat could reach, happened to be the Seahorse ; but nothing could induce the Admiral to go on board, though he was assured that it might be at the risk of his life, if they attempted to row to another Ship : ' Then I will die,' he exclaimed, ' for I would rather suffer death than alarm Mrs. Fremantle by her seeing me in this state, and when I can give her no tidings whatever of her husband. They accordingly proceeded without further delay for the Theseus ; when, notwithstanding the increased pain and weakness which he experienced, he peremptorily refused all assistance in getting on board : ' Let me alone, I have yet my legs left, and one arm. Tell the surgeon to make haste and get his instruments. I know 1 must lose my right arm, so the sooner it is off the better."—*Clarke and M'Arthur*, vol. ii. p. 35.

Some account of what passed after the Admiral had been wounded, is contained in a letter from Mr. Hoste, one of the midshipmen, to his father. " At two o'clock [in the morning] Admiral Nelson returned on board, being dreadfully wounded in the right arm with a grape-shot.　I leave you to judge of my situation, when I beheld our boat approach with him who I may say has been a second father to me, his right arm dangling by his side, whilst with the other he helped himself to jump up the Ship's side, and with a spirit that astonished every one, told the surgeon to get his instruments ready, for he knew he must lose his arm, and that the sooner it was off the better.　He underwent the amputation with the same firmness and courage that have always marked his character."—*Memoirs of Captain Sir William Hoste*, vol. i. p. 73.]

Theseus, off Santa Cruz, 27th July, 1797.

Sir,

In obedience to your orders to make a vigorous attack on Santa Cruz, in the Island of Teneriffe, I directed from the Ships under my command, 1000 men, including Marines, to be prepared for landing, under the direction of Captain Troubridge, of his Majesty's Ship Culloden, and Captains Hood, Thompson, Fremantle, Bowen, Miller and Waller, who very handsomely volunteered their services ; and although I am under the painful necessity of acquainting you that we have not been able to succeed in our attack, yet it is my duty to state that I believe more daring intrepidity was never shewn than by the Captains, Officers, and Men you did me the honour to place under my command.[8]

Enclosed I transmit to you a list of the killed and wounded, and amongst the former, it is with the deepest sorrow, I have to place the name of Captain Richard Bowen, of his Majesty's Ship Terpsichore, than whom a more enterprising, able, and gallant Officer does not grace his Majesty's Naval service ; and with great regret I have to mention the loss of Lieutenant John Gibson, Commander of the Fox cutter, and a great number of gallant Officers and men.

I have the honour to be, Sir,
With the greatest respect,
Your most faithful and obedient Servant,
HORATIO NELSON.

[8] In the Copy in the Nelson Papers the following paragraph occurs here, but it is not in the Letter in the London Gazette :—" And the Journal which I transmit you herewith will, I hope, convince you that my abilities, humble as they are, have been exerted on the present occasion."

LIST OF KILLED, WOUNDED, DROWNED, AND MISSING, OF HIS MAJESTY'S SHIPS UNDER-MENTIONED, IN STORMING SANTA CRUZ, IN THE ISLAND OF TENERIFFE, ON THE NIGHT OF THE 24TH OF JULY, 1797.

Theseus.—8 seamen, 4 marines, killed; 25 seamen wounded; 34 seamen and marines drowned.

Culloden.—1 seaman, 2 marines killed; 12 seamen, 6 marines, wounded; 36 seamen and marines drowned.

Zealous.—3 seamen, 2 marines, killed; 19 seamen, 2 marines, wounded.

Leander.—1 seaman, 5 marines, killed; 1 seaman, 4 marines, wounded; 1 ditto missing.

Seahorse.—2 seamen killed; 13 seamen, 1 marine, wounded.

Terpsichore.—8 seamen killed; 9 seamen, 2 marines, wounded; 4 seamen and marines missing.

Emerald.—5 seamen, 3 marines, killed; 11 seamen wounded; 10 seamen and marines drowned.

Fox Cutter.—17 seamen and marines drowned.

Total: 28 seamen, 16 marines, killed; 90 seamen, 15 marines, wounded; 97 seamen and marines drowned; 5 seamen and marines missing.

OFFICERS KILLED.

Richard Bowen, Captain of the Terpsichore.

George Thorpe, First Lieutenant of ditto.

John Weatherhead, Lieutenant of the Theseus.

William Earnshaw, Second Lieutenant of the Leander.

Raby Robinson, Lieutenant of Marines, of ditto.

Lieutenant Basham, Marines, of the Emerald.

Lieutenant John Gibson, of the Fox cutter, drowned.

OFFICERS WOUNDED.

Rear-Admiral Nelson, his right arm shot off.

Captain Thompson, of the Leander, slightly.

Captain Fremantle, of the Seahorse, in the arm.

Lieutenant J. Douglas, of ditto, in the hand.

Mr. Waits, Midshipman, of the Zealous.

HORATIO NELSON.

A DETAIL OF THE PROCEEDINGS OF THE EXPEDITION AGAINST
THE TOWN OF SANTA CRUZ, IN THE ISLAND OF TENERIFFE.

[From a Copy in the Nelson Papers, the original having apparently been transmitted in the preceding Letter.]

On Friday, the 21st instant, (July,) I directed to be embarked on board the Seahorse, Terpsichore, and Emerald
Frigates, one thousand men, (including 250 Marines, under
the command of Captain Thomas Oldfield,) the whole commanded by Captain Troubridge, attended by all the boats of
the Squadron, scaling-ladders, and every implement which I
thought necessary for the success of the enterprise. I directed
that the Boats should land in the night, between the Fort on
the north-east side of the Bay of Santa Cruz and the Town,
and endeavour to make themselves masters of that Fort, which
when done, to send in my Summons, the liberal terms of which
I am confident you will approve.

Although the Frigates approached within three miles of the
place of debarkation by twelve o'clock, yet from the unforeseen circumstance of a strong gale of wind in the offing, and
a strong current against them in shore, they did not approach
within a mile of the landing-place when the day dawned,
which discovered to the Spaniards our force and intentions.
On my approach with the Line-of-Battle Ships, Captains
Troubridge and Bowen, with Captain Oldfield, of the Marines, came on board, to consult with me what was best to be
done, and were of opinion, if they could possess themselves of
the heights over the Fort above mentioned, that it could be
stormed, to which I gave my assent, and directed the Line-
of-Battle Ships to batter the Fort, in order to create a diversion; but this was found impracticable, not being able to get
nearer the shore than three miles, from a calm and contrary
currents, nor could our men possess themselves of the heights,
as the Enemy had taken possession of them, and seemed as
anxious to retain &c. as we were to get them. Thus foiled
in my original plan, I considered it for the honour of our
King and Country not to give over the attempt to possess
ourselves of the Town, that our enemies might be convinced
there is nothing which Englishmen are not equal to; and

confident in the bravery of those who would be employed in the service, I embarked every person from the shore on the 22nd at night.

On the 24th, I got the Ships to an anchor about two miles to the northward of the Town, and made every shew for a disposition of attacking the heights, which appeared to answer the end, from the great number of people they had placed on them. The Leander, Captain Thompson, joined this afternoon, and her Marines were added to the force before appointed, and Captain Thompson also volunteered his services.

At 11 o'clock at night the Boats of the Squadron, containing between six and seven hundred men, one hundred and eighty men on board the Fox, Cutter, and about seventy or eighty men in a Boat we had taken the day before, proceeded towards the Town. The divisions of the Boats conducted by all the Captains, except Fremantle and Bowen, who attended with me to regulate and lead the way to the attack; every Captain being acquainted that the landing was to be made on the Mole, and from whence they were to proceed, as fast as possible, into the Great Square, where they were to form, and proceed on such services as might be found necessary. We were not discovered till within half gun-shot of the landing-place, when I directed the Boats to cast off from each other, give an hurra, and push for the shore.

A fire of thirty or forty pieces of cannon, with musketry, from one end of the Town to the other, opened upon us, but nothing could stop the intrepidity of the Captains leading the divisions. Unfortunately, the greatest part of the Boats did not see the Mole, but went on shore through a raging surf, which stove all the Boats to the left of it.

For the detail of their proceedings, I send you a copy of Captain Troubridge's account to me,[9] and I cannot but express

---

[9] TO HORATIO NELSON, ESQ., REAR-ADMIRAL OF THE BLUE.

[Original, in the Nelson Papers.]

"Culloden, 25th July, 1797.

"Sir,

"From the darkness of the night, I did not immediately hit the Mole, the spot appointed to land at, but pushed on shore under the Enemy's battery, close to the southward of the Citadel. Captain Waller landed at the same instant, and two or

my admiration of the firmness with which he and his brave associates supported the honour of the British Flag.

Captains Fremantle, Bowen, and myself, with four or five Boats, stormed the Mole, although opposed apparently by 400 or 500 men, took possession of it, and spiked the guns; but such a heavy fire of musketry and grape-shot was kept up

three other boats. The surf was so high, many put back : the boats were full of water in an instant, and stove against the rocks, and most of the ammunition in the men's pouches wet. As soon as I had collected a few men, I immediately pushed, with Captain Waller, for the Square, the place of Rendezvous, in hopes of there meeting you and the remainder of the people, and waited about an hour, during which time I sent a Sergeant with two gentlemen of the Town, to summons the Citadel. I fear the Sergeant was shot on his way, as I heard nothing of him afterwards.

The ladders being all lost in the surf, or not to be found, no immediate attempt could be made on the Citadel. I therefore marched to join Captains Hood and Miller, who, I had intelligence, had made good their landing to the S.W. of the place I did, with a body of men. I endeavoured then to procure some intelligence of you, and the rest of the officers, without success. By day-break, we had collected about eighty Marines, eighty Pike-men, and one hundred and eighty small-arm Seamen. These, I found, were all that were alive that had made good their landing. With this force, having procured some ammunition from the Spanish prisoners we had made, we were marching to try what could be done with the Citadel without ladders ; but found the whole of the streets commanded by field-pieces, and upwards of eight thousand Spaniards and one hundred French under arms, approaching by every avenue. As the boats were all stove, and I saw no possibility of getting more men on shore—the ammunition wet, and no provisions—I sent Captain Hood with a Flag of Truce to the Governor, to say I was prepared to burn the Town, which I should immediately put in force if he approached one inch further; and, at the same time, I desired Captain Hood to say it would be done with regret, as I had no wish to injure the inhabitants ; that if he would come to my terms, I was ready to treat, which he readily agreed to : a copy of which I had the honour to send you by Captain Waller, which, I hope, will meet your approbation, and appear highly honourable.

From the small body of men, and the greater part being pike and small-arm seamen, which can be only called irregulars, with very little ammunition in the pouches but what was wet in the surf at landing, I could not expect to succeed in any attempt upon the Enemy, whose superior strength I have before mentioned. The Spanish Officers assure me they expected us, and were perfectly prepared with all the batteries, and the number of men I have before mentioned under arms : with the great disadvantage of a rocky coast, high surf, and in the face of forty pieces of cannon, though we were not successful, will shew what an Englishman is equal to.

I have the honour to be,
With great respect, Sir,
Your most obedient humble servant,
T. TROUBRIDGE.

P.S. I beg to say, that when the Terms were signed and ratified, the Governor,

from the Citadel and houses at the head of the Mole that we could not advance, and we were all nearly killed or wounded.[1]

The Fox, Cutter, in rowing towards the Town, received a shot under water, from one of the Enemy's distant batteries, immediately sunk, and Lieutenant Gibson, her Commander, with ninety-seven men, were drowned.

I must not omit to acquaint you of the satisfaction I received from the conduct of Lieutenant Baynes, of the Royal Artillery, not only from the ardour with which he undertook every service, but also from his professional skill.

JOURNAL.

REMARKS ETC. ON BOARD HIS MAJESTY'S SHIP THESEUS.

[From a Copy, in the Nelson Papers.]

1797.

Friday, July 14th.—Wind S.S.W. Moderate breezes and cloudy weather. At half-past 8, I weighed, and made sail towards the Fleet. At noon, I received my orders from Sir John Jervis, K.B., Commander-in-Chief, &c. to take under my command H.M. Ships Theseus, Culloden, Zealous, Leander, Seahorse, Terpsichore, Emerald, and Fox Cutter, and Mortar boat.

July 15th.—Wind S.S.W. Moderate breezes and cloudy. At 5 A.M., made signal for the Captains of the Squadron under my command (except the Leander and Terpsichore, who were to join me at sea) and gave them orders to put them-

in the handsomest manner, sent a large proportion of wine, bread, &c., to refresh the people, and shewed every mark of attention in his power.

A copy of this Letter, in the Nelson Papers, contains the following additional paragraph, after the words " is equal to," but it is not in the Original Letter :—

" I have the pleasure to acquaint you, that we marched through the Town on our return, with the British Colours flying at our head."

[1] Clarke and M'Arthur state that—" This last sentence is only found in the rough MS. copy of this Journal dictated by the Admiral, and drawn up by the Secretary ; and has a pen drawn across it, as if Nelson had resolved not to speak himself of the wound he had received ;" but their statement is not borne out by the Copy *now* in the Nelson Papers.

selves under my command, and delivered them the Rendezvous, in case of separation. At 6, weighed, and made sail to the westward, with H.M. Ships Culloden, Zealous, Seahorse, Emerald, Fox Cutter, and Gun-boat in tow. Received on board several scaling-ladders from the Fleet. At 9, spoke his Majesty's [Ship] Alcmene and Convoy from England. Sent the Emerald to look out W.N.W. for the Terpsichore. At 11, wore the Squadron, and made all sail to W.N.W.

Sunday, July 16th.—Wind W.N.W.; Cape St. Vincent distant 30 leagues; light airs and clear weather. At 5, I was joined by his Majesty's Ships Terpsichore and Blanche. Gave Captain Bowen orders to put himself under my command. Parted company with the Blanche, and stood on with the Squadron under my command. At 1 A.M., ordered the Emerald and Seahorse to chase in the S.S.E. : made and shortened sail occasionally : Squadron in company.

Monday, July 17th.—Wind N.W. North point of Teneriffe S. 46° W. distant 166 leagues. Moderate breezes and clear weather. Stowed the anchors: shortened sail occasionally. At 10 A.M., made signal for the Captains of the Squadron to come on board and receive my further instructions. At 11, bore up with the Squadron in company.

Tuesday, July 18th. Wind N.E. North part of Teneriffe S. 47 W., distant 117 leagues. Moderate breezes and clear weather. Made and shortened sail occasionally. General signal for Midshipmen: directed the Small-arm-men to exercise themselves, and fire at a target. At noon, fresh breezes and cloudy. Squadron in company.

Wednesday, 19th.—Wind N.E. by E. Teneriffe bears S. 43° W., distant 63 leagues. Fresh breezes and clear weather. Made and shortened sail occasionally : Squadron in company. Directed the Theseus to make a slay for an eighteen-pounder; the Culloden and Zealous each to make a platform, and the Seahorse to make a platform for a nine-pounder.

Thursday, July 20th.—Wind N.N.E. : Teneriffe S. 33° W., distant 13 leagues : fresh breezes and clear weather. Made and shortened sail occasionally : Squadron in company. Made a general signal for Captains.

Friday, July 21st.—Wind N.N.E.: North-East point of

Teneriffe W. by S., ½ S. distant 9 leagues: moderate breezes and cloudy weather. Made and shortened sail occasionally. At four P.M. shortened sail, and hove to, to the N.W. At six, saw the Island of Teneriffe bearing W. ½ S., distant 10 or 12 leagues. At eight A.M. made the signal for the Squadron to wear to the eastward, and hoist out their Boats to take the Marines and Small-armed-men on board the Seahorse, Terpsichore, and Emerald. Made a general signal for Captains, gave them Rules, Orders, and Regulations for their landing at Santa Cruz. Sent Captains Troubridge, Hood, and Miller, with the rest of the Officers, Marines, and small-armed men on board the Frigates. Wore the Line-of-Battle Ships to the eastward: in sight at noon—the Seahorse, Terpsichore, and Emerald; Culloden and Zealous in company.

Saturday, July 22nd.—Wind N.E. by E.: Santa Cruz N.W. by W., distant 10 or 12 miles. Fresh breezes and cloudy weather. Squadron in company. Tacked and made sail to the eastward. North end of Teneriffe W. by N., 10 or 11 leagues. At seven, bore up for the Island. At half-past one A.M. shortened sail, and hove to with our heads to the eastward. At half-past three, bore up for Santa Cruz. At half-past four, saw the Seahorse, Terpsichore, and Emerald off Santa Cruz, with the Mortar-boat and the Ships' boats pulling off shore. At six, Captains Troubridge and Bowen, with Captain Oldfield of the Marines, came on board to consult with me what was best to be done, and represented to me, although the Frigates approached within three miles of the place of landing by twelve o'clock, yet from the unforeseen circumstance of a strong gale of wind in the offing and a strong current against them in shore, they did not approach within a mile of the landing-place when the day dawned, which discovered to the Spaniards their force and intentions; and were of opinion, if they could possess themselves of the heights over the Fort, that it could be stormed, to which I gave my assent. At nine, the Frigates anchored in shore, off the east end of the Town, and landed their men. Stood off and on Santa Cruz, with the Line-of-Battle Ships, and wore occasionally. At ten o'clock, made the signal to prepare for battle, intending to batter the Fort with the Line-of-battle

Ships, in order to create a diversion, but this was found impracticable, not being able to get nearer the shore than three miles, from a calm and contrary currents: nor could our men possess themselves of the heights, as the Enemy had taken possession of them, and seemed as anxious to retain as we were to get them.

Sunday 23rd.—Santa Cruz distant eight or ten miles. Strong gales and cloudy weather. At four, struck top-gallant masts. A.M. at half-past one, wore the Line-of-Battle Ships. At day-light, the Zealous took a Boat from the Grand Canaries, bound to Santa Cruz with stock. At seven, Captain Troubridge came on board, and acquainted me of his not being able to get possession of the heights over the Fort, and that he had embarked the Troops on board the Frigates the preceding evening. At nine, made the signal for the Frigates to weigh and join me. At noon, employed the Boats carrying the men from the Frigates to the Line-of-battle Ships. Standing off and on: Squadron in company.

July 24th.—Santa Cruz N.W. by W., distant five or six miles. Fresh gales and cloudy weather. Employed taking the Seamen and Marines on board from the Frigates: hoisted all the Boats in: made and shortened sail occasionally. Standing off and on Santa Cruz: Squadron in company. A.M. at eight, Santa Cruz N. four leagues. Answered the Terpsichore signal for a strange sail N.E.; made the private signal, which proved his Majesty's ship Leander, who joined the Squadron at noon. Made the Terpsichore's signal to anchor.

Tuesday, July 25th.[3]—Wind E.N.E. Santa Cruz distant ten or twelve miles. Strong gales and clear weather. At one, made the general signal to anchor. At half-past five the Squadron anchored a few miles to the northward of Santa Cruz. At six, made the signal for Boats to prepare to proceed on service, as previously ordered. At eleven o'clock, between 600 and 700 men embarked in the Boats of the Squadron, 180 men on board the Fox Cutter, and about 70 or 80 men in a Boat we had taken, who proceeded in six

---

[3] In fact the 24th. A Ship's Log is kept from Noon to Noon, so that the events which happened after Noon of the 24th, would be entered under the 25th.

divisions, under Captains Troubridge, Hood, Thompson, Miller, and Waller, Captains Fremantle and Bowen attending the Admiral to regulate the attack. At half-past one A.M., we got within half gun-shot of the Mole head, without being discovered, when the alarm bells rang, and 30 or 40 pieces of cannon, with musketry from one end of the Town to the other, opened upon us. The night being extremely dark, it was only the Admiral, Captains Thompson, Fremantle, and Bowen, with four or five boats in the whole, who found the Mole, which was instantly stormed and carried, although defended by 400 or 500 men, and the guns (six 24-pounders,) were spiked; but such a heavy fire of musketry and grape-shot was kept up from the Citadel and houses at the head of the Mole, that we could not advance, and nearly all were killed or wounded.

Captains Troubridge, Hood, Miller, and Waller, landed with part of the Boats just to the southward of the Citadel, passing through a raging surf, which stove all the Boats, and wet all the ammunition. Notwithstanding these difficulties, they pushed over the Enemy's line wall and batteries, and formed in the Great Square of the Town, about 80 marines, 80 pikemen, and 180 small-armed seamen, (total 340,) where they took possession of a convent, from whence they marched against the Citadel, but found it far beyond their power to take. At daylight, from prisoners taken, Captain Troubridge found there were 8000 Spaniards in arms, and 100 French, with five field-pieces, assembled at the entrance of the Town; and seeing the impossibility of getting any assistance from the Ships, at seven o'clock, he sent Captain Hood with a message to the Governor, that if he should be allowed, freely and without molestation, to embark his people at the Mole-head, taking off such of our Boats as were not stove, and that the Governor should find others to carry off the people, the Squadron now before the Town would not molest it. The Governor told Captain Hood he thought they ought to surrender prisoners of war, to which he replied that Captain Troubridge had directed him to say, that if the terms he had offered were not accepted in five minutes, he would set the Town on fire, and attack the Spaniards at the point of the bayonet, on

which the Governor instantly closed with the Terms,[3] when
Captain Troubridge with his party, marched, with the British
colours flying, to the Mole, where they embarked in such of
our Boats as were not stove, the Spaniards finding others to
carry them off to the Ships. And here it is right that we should
notice the generous and noble conduct of Don Juan Antonio
Gutierrez, the Spanish Governor. The moment the terms
were agreed to, he directed our wounded men to be received
into the hospitals, and all our people to be supplied with the
best provisions that could be procured; and made it known
that the Ships were at liberty to send on shore and purchase
whatever refreshments they were in want of during the time
they might lie off the Island.

The Fox Cutter, in approaching towards the Town, received
a shot under water from one of the Enemy's batteries, on
which she immediately sunk, and Lieutenant John Gibson,
her commander, and ninety-seven men were drowned. At
seven, got under weigh. Squadron in company, standing off
and on.

July 27th.—Received the remainder of the Officers, Seamen, and Marines on board. Ordered the body of Captain
Richard Bowen[4] to be committed to the deep with the honours
of war.

---

[3] TERMS AGREED UPON WITH THE GOVERNOR OF THE CANARY ISLANDS.

"Santa Cruz, 25 July, 1797.

"That the Troops, &c. belonging to his Britannic Majesty shall embark with all
their arms of every kind, and take their Boats off, if saved, and be provided with
such other as may be wanting; in consideration of which it is engaged on their
part they shall not molest the Town in any manner by the Ships of the British
Squadron now before it, or any of the Islands in the Canaries; and prisoners shall
be given up on both sides.

"Given under my hand and word of honour,
"SAM^L. HOOD.

"Ratified by
"T. TROUBRIDGE, Commander of the British Troops.
"J^N. ANTONIO GUTIERREZ, Com^te. Genl. de las Yslas de Canaria.'

—*Original*, in the Nelson Papers, in the hand-writing of Captain Hood, and signed
by him, Captain Troubridge, and the Spanish Governor.

[4] A Memoir and Portrait of this gallant Officer, who had frequently distinguished
himself, are given in the *Naval Chronicle*, vol. xxiii. p. 353. The Earl of St.
Vincent and Nelson used great exertions to induce the Government to place a monument to his Memory in Westminster Abbey, but without success, there being *no
precedent!*

Joined Lord St. Vincent,[4] Wednesday, August 16th, at 11 A.M.

[To this Narrative the annexed rough Sketch is added:]

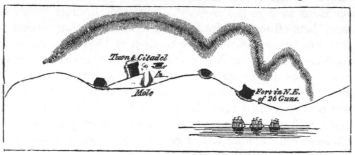

TO ADMIRAL SIR JOHN JERVIS, K.B.

[From a *Fac-simile* in Clarke and M'Arthur, vol. ii. p. 41.]

Theseus, July 27th, 1797.

My dear Sir,

I am become a burthen to my friends, and useless to my Country; but by my letter wrote the 24th, you will perceive my anxiety for the promotion of my son-in-law, Josiah Nisbet. When I leave your command, I become dead to the World; I go hence, and am no more seen. If from poor Bowen's loss, you think it proper to oblige me, I rest confident you will do it; the Boy is under obligations to me, but he repaid me by bringing me from the Mole of Santa Cruz.

---

[4] The following Letter was Lord St. Vincent's official account of the Expedition, published in the *London Gazette* of the 2nd of September, 1797:—

"Sir,   "Ville de Paris, off Cadiz, August 16th, 1797.

"I desire you will acquaint the Lords Commissioners of the Admiralty, that I detached Rear-Admiral Nelson, and the Squadron named in the margin,[5] with orders to make an attempt upon the Tower of Santa Cruz, in the Island of Teneriffe, which, from a variety of intelligence, I conceived was vulnerable. On Saturday the 15th of July, the Rear-Admiral parted company, and on Tuesday the 18th, the Leander having joined from Lisbon, I sent her after the Rear-Admiral, under instructions left by him.

"The Emerald joined yesterday, with the enclosed dispatch and reports from the Rear-Admiral; and although the enterprise has not succeeded, his Majesty's arms have acquired a very great degree of lustre. Nothing from my pen can add to the

[5] Theseus, Culloden, Zealous, Seahorse, Emerald, Terpsichore, Fox (first) Cutter.

I hope you will be able to give me a frigate, to convey the remains of my carcase to England. God bless you, my dear Sir, and believe me, your most obliged and faithful,

HORATIO NELSON.

You will excuse my scrawl, considering it is my first attempt.

Sir John Jervis, K.Bth.

TO ADMIRAL SIR JOHN JERVIS, K.B.

[Autograph, in the Nelson Papers.]

Theseus, August 16th, 1797.

My dear Sir,

I rejoice at being once more in sight of your Flag,[6] and with your permission will come on board the Ville de Paris, and pay you my respects. If the Emerald has joined, you know my wishes. A left-handed Admiral will never again be considered as useful, therefore the sooner I get to a very humble cottage the better, and make room for a better man to serve the State; but whatever be my lot, believe me, with the most sincere affection, ever your most faithful,

HORATIO NELSON.

Turn over.

The papers I sent by Waller were, I find, neither *correct* or all which I wished to send. I send you the total by Captain Miller.[7]

---

eulogy the Rear-Admiral gives of the gallantry of the Officers and men employed under him. I have greatly to lament the heavy loss the Country has sustained in the severe wound of Rear-Admiral Nelson, and the death of Captain Richard Bowen, Lieutenant Gibson, and the other brave Officers and Men who fell in this vigorous and persevering assault.

"The moment the Rear-Admiral joins, it is my intention to send Seahorse to England with him, the wound Captain Fremantle has received in his arm also requiring change of climate; and I hope that both of them will live to render important services to their King and Country.

"I am, Sir, your most obedient humble servant,

ST. VINCENT."

[6] The Theseus joined Sir John Jervis's Fleet on that day.

[7] Nothing could be more kind or encouraging than Lord St. Vincent's answer:—

"My dear Admiral,　　　　　"Ville de Paris, 16th August, 1797.

"Mortals cannot command success; you and your Companions have certainly deserved it, by the greatest degree of heroism and perseverance that ever was exhibited. I grieve for the loss of your arm, and for the fate of poor Bowen and Gib-

TO LADY NELSON.

[From a Copy, in the Nelson Papers.]

Theseus, at Sea, August 3rd [to 16], 1797.

My dearest Fanny,

I am so confident of your affection, that I feel the pleasure you will receive will be equal, whether my letter is wrote by my right hand or left. It was the chance of war, and I have great reason to be thankful; and I know that it will add much to your pleasure in finding that Josiah, under God's Providence, was principally instrumental in saving my life. As to my health, it never was better; and now I hope soon to return to you; and my Country, I trust, will not allow me any longer to linger in want of that pecuniary assistance which I have been fighting the whole war to preserve to her. But I shall not be surprised to be neglected and forgot, as probably I shall no longer be considered as useful. However, I shall feel rich if I continue to enjoy your affection. The cottage is now more necessary than ever. You will see by the papers, Lieutenant Weatherhead is gone. Poor fellow! he lived four days after he was shot. I shall not close this letter till I join the Fleet, which seems distant; for it's been calm these three days' past. I am fortunate in having a good surgeon on board; in short, I am much more recovered than [I] could have expected. I beg neither you or my father will think much of this mishap: my mind has long been made up to such an event. God bless you, and believe me

Your most affectionate husband,

HORATIO NELSON.

son, with the other brave men who fell so gallantly. I hope you and Captain Fre-mantle are doing well; the Seahorse shall waft you to England the moment her wants are supplied. Your Son-in-law is Captain of the Dolphin Hospital-ship, and all other wishes you may favour me with shall be fulfilled, as far as is consistent with what I owe to some valuable Officers in the Ville de Paris. We expect to hear of the Preliminaries of Peace being agreed on every hour. I have betted 100l. that they were settled on or before the 12th, and that the Definitive Treaty is signed before that day month. Give my love to Mrs. Fremantle. I will salute her and bow to your stump to-morrow morning, if you will give me leave. Yours most truly and affectionately, ST. VINCENT." *Autograph* in the Nelson Papers.

August 16th.

Just joined the Fleet perfectly well, and shall be with you, perhaps, as soon as this letter. Good Earl St. Vincent has made Josiah a Master and Commander. I shall come to Bath the moment permission comes from the Admiralty for me to strike my Flag. Sir Peter feels himself authorized to give me leave of absence, when the first you hear of me will be at the door. God bless you and my father, and ever believe me,

Your most affectionate,

HORATIO NELSON.[8]

[8] About this time he received the following Letter from his Royal Highness the Duke of Clarence:—

"Dear Nelson,　　　　　　　　　　　　　　　　4th July, 1797.

" I was very happy to find you had executed with so much success and promptitude Lord St. Vincent's order for the evacuation of Porto Ferrajo. I feel for poor Oakes on every account, and sincerely wish he was safe at home; and believe me, I am also much concerned at the state of your own health. After such long and distinguished service, you will of course get leave to return. In answer to your last letter, I can only say, that I hope and believe our confidence is mutual; therefore in future no more apology on either side is wanted. Under this idea, I must begin by defending an Officer against whom you have become prejudiced......Want of discipline in some of our home Squadrons, and the energy of infamous incendiaries, had for many months thrown the whole Fleet into a state of democracy and absolute rebellion. I rejoice that the Theseus has fallen into such good hands, and I shall shortly hear that she is in the best order of the Mediterranean fleet. One word more about what has passed at Spithead, Plymouth, and the Nore, and I will never mention the disgraceful business again; but I cannot pass over unnoticed your remark about short weights and measures. Every Officer must know that by the old allowance, the men on board the King's ships had more provisions than they could consume, and that they always sold a part; therefore an increase of provisions was not wanted. I will not hurt your mind by relating the horrid particulars of the late events, but shall conclude the subject by observing, that in your next you will unsay what you have too hastily expressed. I dread nothing, as the government here appear to pursue proper measures, and I am convinced St. Vincent will keep up his Fleet in discipline. Lenity at first is severity at the last. My best wishes and compliments attend your gallant Commander: my only acquaintance with him is as an Officer. His very great attention and abilities were shown to me during the Spanish armament, since which time I have, and always shall, respect him.

" You will, I am sure, always distinguish yourself: and I am afraid, from the exorbitant demands of the Directory, that for some time your fleet will be constantly employed. I am happy to find you are at last come over to my way of thinking. As circumstances arise, pray write; and ever believe me, dear Sir, yours sincerely— WILLIAM." *Clarke and M'Arthur,* vol. ii. p. 26. This Letter is not now in the Nelson Papers.

TO REAR-ADMIRAL WILLIAM PARKER.[9]

[From the "Naval Chronicle," vol. xxi. p. 304.]

Dear Sir,   August 19th, 1797.

I must acknowledge the receipt of your letter of the 25th July; and, after declaring that I know nothing of the Prince George till she was hailed from the forecastle of the San Nicolas, it is impossible I can enter into the subject of your letter, &c.   I am, &c.,

HORATIO NELSON.

TO ADMIRAL SIR JOHN JERVIS, K.B.

[From Clarke and M'Arthur, vol. ii. p. 43. On the 20th of August, Nelson obtained his Chief's permission to return to England, and was directed on that day to strike his Flag in the Theseus, and hoist it on board the Sea-horse, taking Captain Fremantle under his command (whose wound also rendered it necessary that he should go on shore), and to proceed to Spithead—*Original* Orders in the Nelson Papers.]

[Between the 20th and 30th August, 1797.]

I cannot let Dido pass, without beginning to express my thanks for your unvaried goodness to me, which I hope I shall never forget. As to myself, I am exactly as I left you. Fremantle I think very bad, and a month hence he may lose his arm.[1] We have a fine fair wind.

I am, &c.

HORATIO NELSON.

TO WILLIAM SUCKLING, ESQ.

[From "The Athenæum."]

Seahorse, off Scilly, August 30th, 1797.

My dear Sir,

As I can write but slowly, I am forced to begin my letter a great way from Portsmouth, where, please God, I am bound. I have ever been a trouble to you, and am likely so to continue, as I have now to request you will have the goodness to

⁹ Vide p. 339, 340, *ante*, and the APPENDIX.

¹ Though Captain Fremantle did not lose his arm, he suffered so severely as to be unable to serve for more than a year.

ask the Collector of the Customs at Portsmouth to take care
of my wine, and such things as I may place under his care,
till I can find a hut to put my mutilated carcase in.

It is my intention to set of directly for Bath, if the Admiral[3]
can give me leave of absence, but to be in London in one
week. Pray, remember me kindly to Mrs. Suckling, and all
my good friends near you, and believe me,

Your most affectionate Nephew,

HORATIO NELSON.

TO EVAN NEPEAN, ESQ., SECRETARY TO THE ADMIRALTY.

[Original, in the Admiralty.]

Seahorse, Spithead, 1st September, 1797.

Sir,

I have the honour to acquaint you of my arrival here,
agreeable to orders, of which the enclosed is a copy. And I
have to request their Lordships' permission to go on shore[4] for
the recovery of my wounds.[5]

I have the honour to be, &c.,

HORATIO NELSON.

[3] His old friend and early patron, Sir Peter Parker, Commander-in-Chief at
Portsmouth.

[4] Having received permission to strike his Flag on the 3rd of September, Sir Horatio Nelson immediately proceeded to Bath, where he joined his Wife and Father.

[5] The Order for him to strike his Flag is in the Nelson Papers, and the form of
such documents may be new to unprofessional readers :—

"We, the Commissioners for executing the Office of Lord High Admiral of
　　Great Britain and Ireland, &c.

"Whereas we think fit that you shall strike your Flag, and come on shore. You
are hereby required and directed to strike your Flag, and come on shore accordingly.
Given under our hands, the 2nd September, 1797.

"H. SEYMOUR.
"J. GAMBIER.
"W. YOUNG.

"To Sir Horatio Nelson, K.B., Rear-Admiral
　　of the Blue, on board His Majesty's ship
　　Seahorse, at Spithead.

"By Command of their Lordships,

"EVAN NEPEAN."

TO JOHN PALMER, ESQ.

[Original, in the possession of Mrs. Palmer.]

Bath, September 4th, 1797.

Dear Sir,

I left Lord St. Vincent perfectly well, fifteen days ago, and he begged me to assure you, that the moment your son[6] has served his Time, he will instantly promote him.

Believe me, Dear Sir,
Your most obedient servant,
HORATIO NELSON.

TO THE REVEREND MR. NELSON, HILBOROUGH.

[Autograph, in the Nelson Papers.]

Bath, September 6th, 1797.

My dear Brother,

Yesterday brought me your truly affectionate letter. As to [my] personal health, it never was better, and my arm is in the fairest way of soon healing. Next week, I intend to be in Town, and it is not impossible, but I may visit Norfolk for a few days, especially if a decent house is likely to be met with near Norwich; but Wroxham very far indeed exceeds my purse. Bath will be my home till next spring. I think our good Father is not in the smallest degree altered. Lady Nelson[7] joins me in kind love to Mrs. Nelson, our Aunt, and

---

[6] The late Captain Edmund Palmer, C.B., who when commanding the Hebrus, of 38 guns, captured, on the 27th of March, 1814, L'Etoile, French frigate, an Action as remarkable for its gallantry, as for being the last in which the Tri-Colour Flag was struck to that of England. Captain Palmer was rewarded with the Naval Medal, and afterwards with the Cross of Companion of the Bath. He presented the Ensign of L'Etoile to Earl St. Vincent, whose grand-niece, Henrietta Mary Elizabeth, daughter and co-heiress of Captain Jervis, he married in 1817, and who has obligingly contributed the above and some other Letters. Captain Palmer died in September, 1834.

[7] The following account of the wounded Admiral, in a Letter from Lady Nelson to his uncle, Mr. Suckling, will be read with much interest:—

" My dear Sir,   " Bath, Wednesday, September 6th, 1797.

" I beg you will accept the united thanks of my dear husband and myself for your kind inquiries and truly friendly invitation to your house, which we would have accepted had it not been for the necessity of my husband's arm being dressed every

friends at Swaffham, and believe me, your most affectionate
brother,

HORATIO NELSON.

I left Captain Nisbet perfectly well.　He saved my life
by his recollection in stopping the bleeding.

TO HIS ROYAL HIGHNESS THE DUKE OF CLARENCE.[8]

[From Clarke and M'Arthur, vol. ii. p. 45.]

Sir,　　　　　　　　　　　　September 7th, 1797.

I trust your Royal Highness will attribute my not having
sent a letter since my arrival to its true cause—viz., the not
being now a ready writer.　I feel confident of your sorrow for
my accident; but I assure your Royal Highness, that not a
scrap of that ardour with which I have hitherto served our King
has been shot away.　　　　　　I am, &c.,

HORATIO NELSON.

day by a surgeon.　We purpose being in London the middle of next week.　I have
written to Mr. M. Nelson to take us a lodging, and as soon as my husband can do
without a surgeon, we shall spend some time with you.　Earl Spencer has written a
handsome letter, and is to be in town next week.　My husband's spirits are very
good, although he suffers a good deal of pain—the arm is taken off very high, near
the shoulder.　Opium procures him rest, and last night he was pretty quiet.　The
Corporation have handsomely congratulated him on his safe arrival.　Such a letter
from Lord Hood!—it does him honour, and I have forgot the ill treatment of former
years which my good man received from him.　Everything which concerns my
husband I know you feel interested in, therefore shall not make any excuses for
what I have told you."—*From " The Athenæum."*

[8] The Duke of Clarence wrote to Nelson on the same day:

" TO SIR HORATIO NELSON, K.B.

" Dear Sir,　　　　　　　　　　Dover, September 7th, 1797.

" I congratulate you with all my heart upon your safe arrival at last, covered with
honour and glory.　As an old friend, I cannot but lament the very severe loss you
have sustained in losing your right arm.　I hope your health is good, and that you
are gone, as I am informed, more for the purpose of joining Lady Nelson, than for
the re-establishment of a constitution in which I am doubly interested, both as a
friend, and as one who is anxious to see the country have restored to her a brave and
excellent Officer.　Excuse my anxiety, as it proceeds from friendship and admiration
of your public character, and I must request you will allow Lady Nelson to write to
me how you are, and when you will be able to be in London, that I may be one of
the first to shake you by the hand.　My best wishes and compliments attend you
and Lady Nelson, and ever believe me, Dear Sir, yours sincerely, WILLIAM."—
Autograph in the Nelson Papers.

TO — MANLEY, ESQ.

[Autograph, in the possession of Miss Miller.]

Bath, September 8th, 1797.

My dear Manley,

Ralph Willett Miller I left most perfectly well; he is not only a most excellent and gallant Officer, but the only truly virtuous man that I ever saw. He longs to get home to his wife and family. Lord St. Vincent has been so good as to promote Josiah to be Master and Commander, and will, if he deserves it, in proper time do more for him. His Lordship has been always so partial to me, that I should be an ingrate was I not on every occasion to support his honour and glory at all personal risk. I regret not the loss of my arm in the cause it fell from me.

God bless you, and believe me
Your most affectionate,
HORATIO NELSON.

Lady Nelson desires her kind love.

TO THE REVEREND DIXON HOSTE.

[Autograph, in the possession of Captain Sir William Hoste, Bart. This Letter is without a date, but as it bears the Post mark, "Bath," it must have been written in September, 1797.]

[Bath, September, 1797.]

My dear Sir,

I did write a line to Mr. Coke to tell him how I had disposed of his recommendations, both of whom have done him so much honour; but one gallant fellow is gone.[8] Your dear good son is as gallant; and I hope he will long live to honour Norfolk and England. I grieved to have left him; but it was necessary, and Lord St. Vincent will continue to be his kind protector and friend. His worth both as a man, and as an Officer, exceeds all which the most sincere friend can say of him. I pray God to bless my dear William. Happy father in such a son! As to myself, I suppose I was getting well too fast, for I am beset with a Physician, Surgeon, and Apothecary, and,

---

[8] Lieutenant Weatherhead, who was killed at Teneriffe.

to say the truth, am suffering much pain with some fever ; but time, I hope, will restore me to tolerable health.　Captain Ralph Willet Miller is Captain of the Theseus—one who loves William, and is the only truly virtuous man that I ever saw. I beg my best respects to Mrs. Hoste, and believe me,

　　　　　Dear Sir,

　　　　　　Your most obedient servant,

　　　　　　　　HORATIO NELSON.

Lady Nelson desires her compliments.

TO CAPTAIN SIR ANDREW SNAPE HAMOND, BART.,
COMPTROLLER OF THE NAVY.

[Autograph, in the possession of his son, Vice-Admiral Sir Graham Eden Hamond,
Bart., K.C.B.]

　　　　　　　　　　Bath, September 8th, 1797.

　My dear Sir Andrew,

　I have ever been fully sensible that you have spoken of my services in the most flattering manner, and for this last mark of your kindness, I cannot sufficiently thank you.　Success covers a multitude of blunders, and the want of it hides the greatest gallantry and good conduct.　You will see by my Journal the first attack on the 21st, under Troubridge, completely failed ; and it was the 25th[9] before it could be again attacked, which gave four days for collecting a force to oppose us.　Had I been with the first party, I have reason to believe complete success would have crowned our endeavours.　My pride suffered ; and although I felt the second attack a forlorn hope, yet the honour of our Country called for the attack, and that I should command it.　I never expected to return, and am thankful.　I shall not go to Town till the 20th, or my arm is well : I suffer a good deal of pain, owing to a cold falling on it.[1]　Lady Nelson and myself most

---

　[9] On the night of the 24th and morning of the 25th.

　[1] The following curious facts, respecting the loss of his Arm, have been obligingly communicated by Sir George Magrath, K.H., Medical Inspector of Hospitals and Fleets, who was Lord Nelson's Surgeon in the Victory, in the years 1803 and 1804, and of whose professional abilities, it will be seen by a subsequent Letter, his Lordship had the highest opinion.　After stating that in 1804 Lord Nelson was valetudi-

sincerely hope your tour will perfectly re-establish your health, and beg to be kindly remembered to Lady Hamond. Believe me, ever

Your obliged and affectionate,

HORATIO NELSON.

TO ADMIRAL THE EARL OF ST. VINCENT, K.B.

[From Clarke and M'Arthur, vol. ii. p. 46.[1]]

London, 18th September, 1797.

My dear Lord,

I shall be brief at first. I had a very miserable passage home, and this day am not the least better than when I left

---

nary, that the capillary system was easily influenced by the weather which produced derangement of the stomach and indigestion, causing nervous irritability in different parts of the body, but which Nelson called rheumatism, Sir George Magrath writes— " I think this *neuralgic* predisposition, was originally induced by the clumsy application of the ligature (including I presume the seive) to the humeral artery of his arm, when it was amputated; and from its long and painful retention, producing agonizing spasms of the stump, which seriously affected his general health, through the medium of the nervous system. Yet, of all the sufferings of the operation, and its subsequent facts, so strongly pressed upon his mind, he complained most of 'the coldness of the knife,' in making the first circular cut through the integuments and muscles. So painfully and deeply was the recollection engrafted on his feelings, that I had general instructions, in consequence, whenever there was a prospect of coming to Action, to have a hanging stove kept in the gally, for the purpose of heating water, in which to immerse the knife, in the event of his being the subject of operation, and on which he always calculated. His Lordship's abhorrence of the cold instrument was practically illustrated off Toulon, when expecting to come into action with Monsieur Latouche Treville. In the hurry of clearing the Ship, the Cockpit had become the recipient of much of the moveable lumber. I applied to the executive Officers to have my Quarters cleared, but, from the bustle on the occasion. ineffectually. In a state of despair, I was compelled to appeal to his Lordship on the Quarter-Deck, who promptly sent for the First Lieutenant (Quillam), to whom he gave peremptory orders instantly to see the Cockpit in a proper state, accompanied with the significant remark, that ' he (Quillam) might be amongst the first to require its accommodation.' When I thanked his Lordship for his interference, and was departing for my Quarters, he called me back, and good-naturedly said—' Doctor, *don't forget the warm water;*' I then intimated to him, that a hanging stove was in readiness in the gally, when he signified his approbation by a smile, and an approving nod." Sir George Magrath's interesting account of Lord Nelson's health, while under his care, will be given in its proper place.

[1] He left Bath for Town a few days before the date of this Letter. The principal object of his coming to London was to be Invested with the Ensigns of the Order

good Dr. Weir;[3] and Cruikshanks[4] has me now in hand. I found my domestic happiness perfect, and I hope time will bring me about again; but I have suffered great misery. My general reception from John Bull[5] has been just what I wished,

of the Bath, which Ceremony took place at St. James's Palace, on the 27th of that month. It was intended that he should have been Invested by the Earl of St. Vincent, to whom the following Letter was written on the subject by the Duke of Portland, Secretary of State for the Home Department; but his absence on the Expedition against Teneriffe when it reached the Earl, and his wound, after his return to the Admiral, prevented the King's instructions from being carried into effect: he had therefore the gratification of being Invested by the Sovereign himself, with the usual formalities, on the 27th of September. Strictly speaking, the attribution of the Title of " Sir" to him, in the meantime, was incorrect, as he did not receive Knighthood until that occasion. He was Installed in May, 1803. It is a remarkable circumstance, that the Duke of Wellington (who had been appointed an *Extra* Knight in 1804,) succeeded Nelson as one of the *Constituent* Knights of the Order of the Bath.

" TO ADMIRAL THE EARL OF SAINT VINCENT.

" My Lord,   " Whitehall, June 22nd, 1797.

" His Majesty having been graciously pleased, as a mark of his Royal approbation of the eminent services of Rear-Admiral Nelson, to nominate him to be one of the Knights Companions of the Most Honourable Order of the Bath, and it being necessary that he should be Invested with the Ensigns of the said Order, which are transmitted to him by this opportunity, I am to signify to your Lordship the King's pleasure that you should perform that Ceremony: and it being His Majesty's intention that the same should be done in the most honourable and distinguished manner that circumstances will allow of, you will concert and adjust with him such time and manner for Investing him with the Ensigns of the Order of the Bath, as shall appear to you most proper for showing all due respect to the King's order; and as may at the same time mark in the most public manner His Majesty's just sense of the zeal and abilities which Rear-Admiral Nelson has exerted in the service of his King and Country. I have the honour to be, my Lord, your lordship's most obedient, humble servant, PORTLAND."—From a *Copy* in the Nelson Papers.

[3] Physician to the Earl of St. Vincent's Fleet.
[4] " The eminent Surgeon. Previous to his leaving Bath, Lady Nelson at the earnest request of her husband, had attended the dressing of his arm, until she had acquired sufficient skill and resolution to perform it herself, which she afterwards did continually. On his arrival in London, he was attended by Mr. Cruikshanks, and his nephew, Mr. Thomas; by Mr. Jefferson, who had been Surgeon of the Agamemnon; and, at the request of Mr. Bulkely, one of the two surviving Officers who had been on the San Juan expedition, Dr. Moseley was afterwards called in. But the wound becoming still more painful, and his spirits very low, it was also shown to other eminent Surgeons, and amongst the rest to Mr. Keate; who strongly recommending that the cure should be left to time and nature, it was accordingly preferred to more violent methods."—*Clarke and M'Arthur*, vol. ii. p. 46.
[5] As a proof of the kind feeling of "John Bull" towards him during his illness, Clarke and M'Arthur relate, that "During the month of October, whilst he con-

for I assure you they never forget your name in their honest praises. I have now a favour to beg of you.

After George Cockburn's gallant action with the Sabina, I directed a gold-hilted Sword to be made for him, which I had hoped to present to him myself in the most public and handsome manner; but as Providence has decreed otherwise, I must beg of you to present it for me. My good friend Grey[6] will, I hope, inquire, and get it out of the Argo. I feel confident of your goodness. Good Captain Locker has just been with me, and made the most kind inquiries after you. I am not to go to the Levée until the end of next week. Lady Nelson sends her love. God bless you.

I am, &c.

HORATIO NELSON.

TO MAJOR SUCKLING, THIRD REGIMENT DRAGOON GUARDS.

[Autograph, in the possession of Captain Montagu Montagu, R.N. It has no date, but is endorsed, and has the Post mark of " 25 September, 1797."]

141, Bond-street, [about September 24th, 1797.]

My dear Sir,

I feel very much obliged by your kind inquiries. I am at present under the care of Mr. Cruikshanks, but may be some time before I am perfectly recovered. Your good father tells me you are [in] great [hopes] of the Lieutenant-Colonelcy. I

---

tinued in this state of suffering, at the lodgings of Mr. Jones, in Bond-street, Nelson had one night retired to his bed-room, after a day of constant pain, hoping with the assistance of laudanum to enjoy a little rest; when the exhilarating news of Admiral Duncan's victory threw the whole metropolis into an uproar. The first idea that presented itself to the family, was an alarm of some dreadful fire. The mob knocked repeatedly and violently at the door, as the house had not been illuminated. It was at length opened by a servant, who informed them, that Sir Horatio Nelson, who had been so badly wounded, lodged there, and could not be disturbed. A general interest for the valuable life of their honoured Admiral, for an instant repressed the joy which Duncan's victory had occasioned: 'You will hear no more from us to-night,' exclaimed the foremost of the party; and that universal sympathy for the health of Nelson which pervaded even the minds of the lowest of his countrymen was clearly shown, no subsequent visit being paid by the mob, notwithstanding the tumult that prevailed."— Ibid.

[6] Captain, afterwards the Honourable Sir George Grey, Bart., K.C.B., then Captain of the Victory. He died in 1828.

sincerely wish you success. Lady Nelson joins me in best respects to Mrs. Suckling, and believe me, dear Sir, your most obliged,

HORATIO NELSON.

You must excuse short letters.

[It being intended to grant Nelson a Pension of £1000 a-year, custom rendered it necessary that he should state his Services in a Memorial to the King.]

TO THE KING'S MOST EXCELLENT MAJESTY,
THE MEMORIAL OF SIR HORATIO NELSON, K.B., AND REAR-ADMIRAL IN YOUR MAJESTY'S FLEET,

Humbly Sheweth,

That, during the present War, your Memorialist has been in four Actions with the Fleets of the Enemy—viz., on the 13th and 14th of March 1795, on the 13th of July 1795, and on the 14th of February 1797; in three Actions with Frigates; in six Engagements against Batteries; in ten Actions in Boats employed in cutting out of Harbours, in destroying Vessels, and in taking three Towns. Your Memorialist has also served on shore with the Army four months, and commanded the Batteries at the Sieges of Bastia and Calvi;

That, during the War he has assisted at the Capture of seven Sail of the Line, six Frigates, four Corvettes, and eleven Privateers of different sizes, and taken and destroyed near fifty Sail of Merchant Vessels; and your Memorialist has actually been engaged against the Enemy upwards of one hundred and twenty times. In which Service your Memorialist has lost his right eye and arm, and been severely wounded and bruised in his body. All of which Services and wounds your Memorialist most humbly submits to your Majesty's most gracious consideration.

HORATIO NELSON.

About October, 1797.

TO ADMIRAL THE EARL OF ST. VINCENT, K.B.

[From Clarke and M'Arthur, vol. ii. p. 47.]

London, 6th October, 1797.

My dear Lord,

The King asked after your general health.[7] I told his Majesty that, considering the great fatigue you were undergoing, your health was tolerable. Lord Howe made many of not only handsome, but kind inquiries after you. Lord Spencer says, my pension will be the same as those for the 1st of June, £712 with the deductions. My poor arm continues quite as it was, the ligature still fast to the nerve, and very painful at times. The moment I am cured I shall offer myself for Service ; and if you continue to hold your opinion of me, shall press to return with all the zeal, although not with all the personal ability, I had formerly,

I am, &c.,

HORATIO NELSON.

TO EVAN NEPEAN, ESQ., SECRETARY TO THE ADMIRALTY.

[Original, in the Admiralty.]

London, 9th October, 1797.

Dear Sir,

I have this moment received the enclosed from Lieutenant Withers[8] who served with me in the Agamemnon and Cap-

[7] Clarke and M'Arthur say (vol. ii. p. 45), that the King's gracious manner, on Investing him with the Order of the Bath, made a lasting impression on his mind ; but Nelson nowhere speaks of the King's reception of him. Of the many accounts of his Majesty's remarks to him on his first appearance at Court after the loss of his arm, and of his answers, the following has been verified by Lady Berry, who, in reply to the Editor's inquiry, obligingly informed him that "the fact is as stated of Nelson's having emphatically called Berry his 'right hand,' on presenting him to the King, in reply to His Majesty's expression of concern at the loss of his right arm; and though the words may not be exactly correct, they are essentially the same." "'You have lost your right arm,' observed the King—'but not my right hand,' replied Sir Horatio, 'as I have the honour of presenting Captain Berry to you ; and, besides, may it please your Majesty, I can never think that a loss which the performance of my duty has occasioned ; and, so long as I have a foot to stand on, I will combat for my country and King.'" The latter part of this speech, like the exclamation of "Victory, or Westminster Abbey," on boarding the San Josef, seems much too *melodramatic* to be true. Lord Eldon relates that the King, after acknowledging his great *services*, added, "But your Country has a claim for a bit more of you."—*Twiss's Memoirs of Lord Eldon*, vol. i. p. 103.

[8] Lieutenant Thomas Withers died a Post Captain.

tain, very much to my satisfaction.   Should any Ship be commissioned for the East Indies, I would willingly recommend him to any Captain.

⁀ I am, &c.

HORATIO NELSON.

TO LIEUT.-GOVERNOR LOCKER, ROYAL HOSPITAL, GREENWICH.

[Autograph, in the Locker Papers.]

October 11th, 1797.

My dear Sir,

Many thanks for your kind letter, I sincerely wish my arm

[The remainder is in Lady Nelson's hand-writing.]

Thus far my husband has begun his letter to you, but an appointment with a friend of his prevents his concluding ; therefore, in his name and my own, we shall rejoice to see you on Thursday.   I thank Lord St. Vincent for his notice. I wish my Captain⁹ had wrote us a line.

Yours very sincerely,

FRANCES H. NELSON.

Sir H. Nelson attends the Drawing-room, therefore you are sure of him.

Pray give our Compliments to Mr. L., and ask him to take a family dinner on Thursday or Friday with us.   We expect you.

TO THE RIGHT HONOURABLE THE LORD CHANCELLOR.[1]

[From a Copy, in the Nelson Papers.]

141, Bond-street, October 12th, 1797.

My Lord,

In addressing a letter to you some persons may think me wrong, and that I ought to have chosen the interference of a friend ; but, feeling a conviction that if what I have to ask is proper for your Lordship to grant, that I require, on the present occasion, no interest but your own opinion of my endea-

---

⁹ Her son, Captain Nisbet.
[1] Alexander Lord Loughborough, afterwards created Earl of Rosslyn.

Oct. 11. 1797

My Dear Sir

Many thanks for your
kind letter, I sincerely with my own

ment with a friend of his however
his concluding — therefore as his
name and my own we shall rejoice
to see you on Thursday — I thank you?
A. Vincent from his notice, saving My
Capt... had waste us a line —
Sir H. Nelson
G.M. Very sincerely
attends of the
Treasurer H Nelson
saving I am sure
of living —
Thursday from

vours to serve the State. I therefore enclose my request,[1] which, if your Lordship has the goodness to comply with, will be a small provision for the youngest son of my venerable father, and a lasting obligation conferred upon

Your most obedient servant,

HORATIO NELSON.

TO JOHN HALKETT, ESQ., SECRETARY OF PRESENTATIONS TO
THE LORD CHANCELLOR.

[From a Copy, in the Nelson Papers.]

141, Bond-street, October 23rd, 1797.

Sir,

The Lord Chancellor having been so good as to write me that he will comply with my request in giving my brother, the Reverend Suckling Nelson, A.B., of Burnham in Norfolk, the Rectory of Burnham St. Albert's, (*alias* Sutton,) with the mediety of Burnham St. Margaret's, (*alias* Norton,) with the mediety of Burnham All Saints, (*alias* Ulph,) County Norfolk, Diocese of Norwich, when it shall be vacant by the resignation of my father, the Reverend Edmund Nelson, which it now is, he having wrote to the Bishop of Norwich for that purpose, I have, therefore, to request the favour of you (or that you will have the kindness to put me in the way) to expedite the forms it is necessary to go through in order to obtain the Presentation as speedily as possible. Your compliance with this request will very much oblige

Your most obedient servant,

HORATIO NELSON.

[1] To give his youngest brother, the Reverend Suckling Nelson, one of the Livings held by his father on his father's resignation of it. Lord Loughborough's consent was conveyed in terms that did him honour :

" Sir,

" You have judged perfectly right in the mode of your application to me. Any interference would have much diminished the satisfaction I feel in acknowledging the perfect propriety of your request, and the just title your great services have gained to every mark of attention which, in the exercise of a public duty, it is in my power to express. Yours, &c., LOUGHBOROUGH."—*Autograph* in the Nelson Papers.

TO THE REVEREND MR. WEATHERHEAD, SEDGEFORD, NORFOLK.[2]

[Autograph.]

141, Bond-street, October 31st, 1797.

Dear Sir,

Believe me, I have largely partaken in our real cause for grief in the loss of a most excellent young man. Whether he is considered in his moral character, or as an Officer, he was a bright example to all around ; and when I reflect on that fatal night, I cannot but bring sorrow and his fall before my eyes. Dear friend, he fought as he had always done, by my side, and for more than one hundred times with success; but for wise reasons (we are taught to believe) a separation was to take place, and we must, however hard the task, be resigned. With most sincere good wishes for your future happiness without alloy, believe me, dear Sir,

Your most faithful servant,

HORATIO NELSON.

TO CAPTAIN KNIGHT, H.M. SHIP MONTAGU, SHEERNESS.

[Autograph, in the Nelson Papers.]

My dear Sir,

Most heartily do I congratulate you on your hard-earned and gl—

[The remainder, except the signature, is not in Sir Horatio Nelson's hand.]

—orious Victory.[3] I take the opportunity of sending, by a most particular friend of mine, Mr. George Preston, 319½ dol-

---

[2] The Letter to which this was an answer, is in the Nelson Papers, and was printed by Clarke and M'Arthur. It is dated 26th October, 1797, and expressed the liveliest gratitude for Sir Horatio Nelson's favours to his late son.

[3] The Battle of Camperdown, in which Captain Knight (afterwards Admiral Sir John Knight, K.C.B.) commanded the Montagu and obtained the Medal. This Letter does not appear to have been forwarded ; and unless the dollars were for Prize Money due to some of the crew of the Montagu, while serving in the Agamemnon or Captain, in the Mediterranean, it is difficult to say for what the payments were made. Colonel Drinkwater states, that on his acquainting Nelson that an engagement was hourly expected between Admiral Duncan's Fleet, and that of Holland, "he started up in his peculiar energetic manner, notwithstanding Lady Nelson's attempt to quiet him, and stretching out his unwounded arm—'Drinkwater,' said he, 'I would give this other arm to be with Duncan at this moment.'"—*Narrative of the Battle of St. Vincent*, p. 97.

lars, being 2½ for each common man, and 10½ for each Petty Officer. Any civility you can show Mr. Preston I shall consider as an obligation conferred upon,

My dear Sir,
Your most obedient humble servant,
HORATIO NELSON.

I return the List you sent me.

TO THE REVEREND HENRY CROWE, SMALLBURGH, NORWICH.

[Autograph, in the possession of the Reverend Henry Crowe, son of the gentleman to whom the Letter was addressed.]

London, 141, Bond-street, November 16th, 1797.

Dear Sir,

The First Lord of the Admiralty cannot assure to you that any particular Ship shall be kept in Commission after a Peace. Chaplains, after so many years' service, are entitled to half-pay, but which only extends to a certain number. Lady Nelson and myself thank you for your congratulations, and believe me,

Dear Sir,
Your faithful servant,
HORATIO NELSON.

TO THE CHAMBERLAIN OF THE CITY OF LONDON.[4]

[Autograph, in the possession of John Wild, Esq.]

Sir Horatio Nelson presents his most respectful Compliments to the Chamberlain of the City of London, and begs leave to acquaint him, that he will attend at his Office on Tuesday next, at one o'clock, unless any other hour should be more agreeable.

Wednesday, November 22nd, 1797.

[4] On the 28th December, 1797, Sir Horatio Nelson received the Freedom of the City of London, in a Gold box, of the value of one hundred Guineas. On that occasion, the Chamberlain (the celebrated John Wilks) thus addressed him :—

" Rear-Admiral Sir Horatio Nelson, I give you joy, and with true satisfaction I

TO CAPTAIN BERRY, R.N., DR. FORSTER'S, NORWICH.

[Autograph, in the possession of Lady Berry.[5]]

My dear Sir,　　　　　　November 28th, 11 P.M. [1797.]
Any event which has the prospect of adding to your felicity
cannot but afford me pleasure; and I most heartily congratulate you on becoming one of *us,* and we shall have great pleasure in being known to Mrs. Berry. I am confident nothing
will alter you for the worse, and I wish you to be no better:
therefore we will leave off further complimenting.

The Foudroyant will be launched in January, and in commission early in February. I am not perfectly at liberty about
a First-lieutenant, but I believe Galwey[6] will be the man; Mr.
Vassall[7] second, although a much older Officer; but if they do

return you thanks, in the name of the Lord Mayor, Aldermen, and Common-Council
assembled, who have unanimously voted you the Freedom of the Capital, for your
distinguished valour and conduct in the favourite service of the Navy, and particularly against a very superior force of the Enemy off Cape St. Vincent, on the 14th
February last. Many of our Naval Commanders have merited highly of their
country by their exertions, but in your case there is a rare heroic modesty, which
cannot be sufficiently admired. You have given the warmest applause to your
Brother-Officers and the Seamen under your command; but your own merit you
have not mentioned, even in the slightest manner, and the relation of the severe
and cruel wounds you suffered in the service of your country is transmitted by your
noble Commander-in-Chief. May you long live to enjoy the grateful benedictions
of the Country which you honour and protect."

To this Speech Sir Horatio Nelson replied:—

" Sir, nothing could be more gratifying to me (as it must be to every Sea Officer)
than receiving the high honour this day conferred upon me, in becoming a Freeman
of the great City of London; and I beg you to believe, and to assure my Fellow-
Citizens, that my hand and head shall ever be exerted, with all my heart, in defence
of my King, the Laws, and the just liberties of my Country, in which are included
everything which can be beneficial to the Capital of the Empire. I beg leave, Sir,
to return you my sincere thanks for the very flattering expressions you have honoured me with on this occasion."

　[5] The late Rear Admiral Sir Edward Berry, Bart., K.C.B., married on the 12th of
December 1797, Louisa, daughter of Samuel Forster, M.D., of Norwich. To this
Lady, the Editor is indebted for much valuable information, conveyed to him in Letters alike charming from their unaffected grace and simplicity, their true womanly
feeling, and the affectionate interest they display for the fame of Lord Nelson and
of her distinguished Husband. Lady Berry was the intimate friend of Lady Nelson,
to whose merits she has rendered such ample justice.

　[6] The late Rear-Admiral Edward Galwey, who died a few months ago.

　[7] Lieutenant Nathaniel Vassall, who obtained that rank in November 1780, about
three years before Lieutenant Galwey.

not choose to stand as I like in the Ship, they may stay away; and so I have told Mr. Vassall. We are fearful of undertaking our trip to Bath, as Lord Spencer says I must be in Town to attend the Procession on the 19th of December,[8] which is to be very fine. I enclose you the Arms,[9] and I beg you will make my best respects to the Mayor; also, to Doctor Forster and family, and believe me ever,

Your most faithful,

HORATIO NELSON.

TO EVAN NEPEAN, ESQ., SECRETARY TO THE ADMIRALTY.

[Original, in the Admiralty.]

Sir,   London, November 28th, 1797.

I beg you will inform their Lordships that, on the 31st of March last, I sent my Agents, Messrs. March and Creed, an order from Sir John Jervis, now Lord St. Vincent, dated 4th of April 1796, for my hoisting a Distinguishing Pendant, and desired that the same might be presented to their Lordships, for the purpose of procuring the necessary order for payment of the usual allowance. This, they inform me, was done; but, on inquiry at the Admiralty, I find that the order is nowhere to be found, and I can therefore only conclude that Messrs. March and Creed's letter, enclosing the Commander-in-Chief's order, never was delivered, or that if it has, it must have been by some means mislaid. In either case, I trust their Lordships will regard my assurance that I *did* hoist my Distinguishing Pendant under a *positive order* from Sir John Jervis, and the acknowledgment of my Agents that such order was actually received by them, as proof sufficient for their Lordships to grant me an order for payment of the customary allowance; and I have to flatter myself that such an order will, in consequence, be issued.

I am, Sir, &c.,

HORATIO NELSON.

---

[8] Vide p. 458, post.

[9] A drawing of his Arms, probably as a pattern for those to be placed over the Sword of the Spanish Admiral, which he gave to the Corporation of Norwich.

P.S.　I have been paid as a Rear-Admiral from August
11th, 1796, when a Captain was appointed to the Ship in
which my Pendant flew; but from April 4th to August 11th,
I pray to be allowed for the Distinguishing Pendant ten
shillings per day.

H. N.

TO THE RIGHT HONOURABLE THE LORD CHANCELLOR.

[From a Copy, in the Nelson Papers.]

141, Bond-street, December 2nd, 1797.

My Lord,

Your goodness in further offering to serve my relatives was
much more than I had any reason to hope or expect; but, in
consequence of it, I wrote to my brother, the Reverend
William Nelson, of Christ's College, Cambridge, and Rector
of Hilboro', in Norfolk. His wish and mind was for a Stall
at Norwich; but as that is out of the question, any Resi-
dentiary Stall will be acceptable, the nearer Norfolk the more
agreeable.

I have the honour to be, with the highest respect and
obligation,

Your lordship's most obedient servant,
HORATIO NELSON.

THANKSGIVING IN ST. GEORGE'S CHURCH, HANOVER-SQUARE,
LONDON.

[This most interesting Paper is taken from a *fac-simile* which was in the possession of the family of the Rev. Mr. Greville, then Minister of St. George's, Hanover-
square.]

An Officer desires to return Thanks to Almighty God for
his perfect recovery from a severe Wound, and also for the
many mercies bestowed upon him.

[For next Sunday.]

December 8th, 1797.

TO CAPTAIN BERRY, R.N., DR. FORSTER'S, NORWICH.

[Autograph, in the possession of Lady Berry.]

Secret, except to Dr. Forster and Miss.

December 8th, [1797.]

My dear Sir,

If you mean to marry, I would recommend your doing it
speedily, or the to be Mrs. Berry will have very little of your
company; for I am well, and you may expect to be called
for every hour.   We shall probably be at sea before the
Foudroyant is launched.   Our Ship is at Chatham, a Seventy-
four, and she will be choicely manned.   This may not happen,
but it stands so to-day

Ever yours most faithfully,

HORATIO NELSON.

TO CAPTAIN RALPH WILLETT MILLER.

[Autograph, in the possession of Miss Miller.]

December 11th, [1797.]

My dear Sir,

As I have not the hand of a ready writer, my friends must
put up (at the best) with short letters, and oftener excuse my
writing anything.   I could say nothing of you anywhere, or
to any person, that was not pleasant to your friends, and
strictly true.   John Bull does not forget the Captain on the
14th February, for both at the London Tavern and Guild-
hall after ' Lord Duncan' (the last Action being the best) ' and
his Fleet,' comes ' Earl St. Vincent and the glorious 14th
February'; then ' Sir H. N., and the brave Officers and men
who fought on board the Captain on the 14th February'; and
had our Battle been in the Channel, it would have been so
much the better for us.

[The following, except the Signature and Postscript, is in Lady Nelson's writing.]

Lady Nelson and myself called to see your little girl at
Mr. Taylor's.   She is a very fine girl, and a great favourite
with Mr. and Mrs. Taylor, who seem very fond and kind to
her.   They are, I am sure, good people, and spoke in most

affectionate terms of Mrs. Miller. It is fixed I am to have
the Vanguard. She will be out of dock in ten days; and as
there are many Ships paying off at Chatham, I shall be well
manned and soon; therefore I am in hopes of joining Lord
St. Vincent some time in February. Lady Nelson begs you
will accept her compliments.

Believe me, your sincere,
HORATIO NELSON.

Berry is married, but still goes with me. Many thanks for
your letters.

TO THE REVEREND MR. MORRIS, THESEUS, LISBON.

[Autograph, in the possession of Dawson Turner, Esq., F.R.S.]

December 11th, 1797.

My dear Sir,

I can assure you that nothing could give me greater pleasure than to have you once more with me. The Foudroyant[8]
is at present the Ship named for my Flag, and she will be
commissioned by Captain Berry about the middle of February.
It is my wish to go to Lord St. Vincent; but, as that must be
uncertain, and I am determined not to go to sea again without a Chaplain, I must leave the matter to your consideration,
how far it may be eligible for you to come home for such an
appointment. I shall not engage myself till the Ship is commissioned, unless I hear first from you. I beg my best regards
to Captain Oldfield,[9] and thank him for his kind letter; and
believe me ever your obliged,

HORATIO NELSON.

P.S. The Vanguard is my Ship; and she will [be] next
week in commission: this change must for the present deprive
[me] of you.

---

[8] On the 13th of December, Sir Horatio Nelson being pronounced fit for Service,
the Foudroyant was intended to receive his Flag, but the Ship not being in a sufficiently forward state, the Vanguard was substituted for her.

[9] Of the Marines, who is particularly mentioned in the account of the attack on
Santa Cruz, *ante.* He obtained his Majority, and, to use the words of the official
Dispatch, " fell gloriously" in command of the Marines of the Theseus, at Acre, in
April, 1799.

TO CAPTAIN ALBEMARLE BERTIE, OF H.M. SHIP BRAKEL.

[From the " Naval Chronicle," vol. xxvi. p. 10.]

My dear Bertie,   141, Bond-street, December 11th, 1797.

You have reason to abuse me, for not long ago answering your affectionate letter; but truly, till last Monday, I have suffered so much, that I hope for your forgiveness. I am now perfectly recovered, and on the eve of being employed. You are on a most unpleasant service,[1] but the Country demands a strict scrutiny, and we rest confident that you will do ample justice, be that what it may. Remember me kindly to your worthy President,[2] and such of those with you that I know, and believe me ever,

Your affectionate friend,

HORATIO NELSON.

TO WILLIAM MARSDEN, ESQ., SECRETARY TO THE ADMIRALTY.

[Original, in the Admiralty.]

Sir,   December 13th, 1797.

I am honoured with your letter of yesterday, and beg leave to acquaint you, that I am ready to attend at St. Paul's, on the 19th,[3] in such manner as their Lordship's may be pleased to direct, and also that Captains Berry and Noble[4] will attend with me. I am, Sir, your most obedient servant,

HORATIO NELSON.

---

[1] Sitting as a Member of the Court Martial at Sheerness, for the trial of Captain John Williamson, charged with misconduct in command of the Agincourt, in the Battle of Camperdown, on the 11th of October, of which charge he was found Guilty, and sentenced to be placed at the bottom of the List of Post Captains, and rendered incapable of ever serving on board any of his Majesty's ships.

[2] Admiral Skeffington Lutwidge.

[3] On the 19th of December, His Majesty and the Royal Family attended at St. Paul's "to return thanks to Almighty God, for the many signal and important Victories obtained by His Majesty's Navy, during the present War." Seats were provided for those Flag Officers who had commanded, or been present in a General Action in which any Ships of the Enemy's Line had been captured, and Nelson was one of the Admirals who were invited by the Lords of the Admiralty to attend. One of the original programmes of the Ceremony is now in the Nelson Papers; and it will also be found in the *Annual Register*.

[4] Before mentioned as a Lieutenant of the Agamemnon and Theseus. He was then a Commander, was Posted in April 1802, and is now a Rear-Admiral of the Red.

AGREEMENT OF THE ADMIRALS SERVING UNDER THE EARL
OF ST. VINCENT, TO INSTITUTE LEGAL PROCEEDINGS FOR
THE RECOVERY OF PRIZE AND FREIGHT MONEY.

[Original, in the Nelson Papers. This Paper was drawn up by Rear-Admiral Sir
William Parker, but it appears that Nelson raised many objections to the proposition.]

October and 13th December, 1797.

We, the undersigned, Sir Charles Thompson, Vice-Admiral
of the Blue, the Honourable Vice-Admiral William Waldegrave, Rear-Admirals Sir William Parker, Sir Horatio Nelson,
serving in the Fleet, under the command of the Right Honourable the Earl St. Vincent, conceiving, and having no
doubt (except the Table-money allowed to the Commander-
in-Chief) that all the emoluments—viz , Prize-money and
Freight-money, belonging or appertaining to the Admiral or
Flag-Officer in a Fleet, where there is only one, must and
does by right belong to the Flag-Officers jointly, in a Fleet
where there are many, to be divided in proportions, agreeable to his Majesty's Order in Council for the distribution of
Prize-money.   And as it has been customary to divide
Freight-money in this manner, in Fleets where there are more
Flag-Officers than one, and been invariably practised in every
instance as far back as the highest Officer upon the Naval
List, the Earl St. Vincent, notwithstanding, arrogates[5] to himself a right to the whole of the Flag-Officers' share of the
Freight-money, as Commander-in-Chief, and retains the same
to his own use.

We, the undersigned, do hereby engage and bind ourselves
respectively, to have recourse to the Laws of our Country, to
obtain that justice we are not likely to obtain otherwise; and
as the times of our coming under the said Earl St. Vincent's
command has happened at different periods, the proportion of
Freight-money due to each of us respectively, of course, is
different also; the said Parties do therefore hereby further
agree that each and every one shall, immediately upon signing
their names to this agreement, deposit the sum of one hundred pounds, and so on, more if requisite, in equal proportions,
afterwards, to carry on the Law-suit: but that in the end,

---

[5] Nelson wrote, in the margin, " claims."

upon obtaining a Decree, each Party's expense shall be proportioned according to the sum each respectively recovers—viz., if from the difference of time either party recovers a sum double to that which either of the others recover, that person is to stand at double the expense of the other, and so on, in a like proportion with respect to each other, agreeably to the sums respectively recovered.

To which we hereunto set our Hands and Seals, at the times, and in the presence, as against our names expressed.

[Added in Nelson's handwriting.]

Lord Howe, paid.
    Hood, paid, but not certain as to right.
    Duncan, ditto   ditto.
    Hotham, paid.
    Harvey, paid.

[In Nelson's Autograph.]

December 13th.—From inquiry, have my doubts.

I think the opinion of three Lawyers should be taken as to our right to share in Freights, if any can be found supposed capable of judging for us, before we embark ourselves in a Law-suit which they are to determine. I recommend asking Admirals Lord Howe, Barrington, Hood, Hotham, Duncan, &c., how they have acted, before we involve in Law. Lord St. Vincent, on being informed of their opinion, will no doubt act accordingly.

TO EVAN NEPEAN, ESQ., SECRETARY TO THE ADMIRALTY.

[Original, in the Admiralty.]

14th December, 1797.

Sir,

As it is my wish that Lieutenant Edward Galwey should be First Lieutenant of the Vanguard, and as he is now under sailing orders on board the Arethusa, at Spithead, I have to request their Lordships will be pleased to order his immediate discharge, without waiting till he be relieved.

I have the honour to be, &c.

HORATIO NELSON.

TO EARL SPENCER, FIRST LORD OF THE ADMIRALTY.

[Autograph, in the Admiralty.]

Admiralty, Noon, Monday, [apparently December 18th, 1797.]

My Lord,

I am just from Chatham. The Vanguard will be out of dock at half-past one this day, and ready to receive men whenever your Lordship is pleased to direct her being Commissioned.

Ever your most obedient,

HORATIO NELSON.

APPENDIX.

NOTE A, page 10.

The proceedings of the Agamemnon on the 13th of March are thus incorrectly related by Mr. James:—" At 10 h. 45 m. the Agamemnon got upon the quarter of the Ça Ira, still in tow by the Vestale, and, aided for a short time by the Captain, continued a distant engagement with the crippled 80, until about 2 h. 15 m. P.M., when several of the French Ships bearing down to the protection of their disabled companion, the Agamemnon ceased firing, and dropped into her station in the line," (*Naval History*, vol. i. p. 258,) whereas the "*distant engagement*" commenced *within one hundred yards*, and towards its close was *within half pistol shot*. In point of time, too, James is incorrect, as the firing ended at half-past one, instead of at half-past two. Nor did the Agamemnon cease firing on account of the approach of the French Ships, but returned to the Fleet in obedience to the Admiral's signal. Here, however, James may have been misled by Admiral Hotham's *Dispatch*, as he does not state that he recalled the Van-ships, but merely says, that the Agamemnon and Inconstant were "*obliged to quit*" the Enemy, as if it had been the spontaneous act of their Captains, and not done in obedience to his own signal. Justice will, however, be best rendered to the Agamemnon's services on the 13th and 14th of March, by a copy of her Log of those days.

" Friday, 13th March.—Light breezes and hazy; at $\frac{3}{4}$ past 1, wore Ship to the Westward. The Admiral made the signal to bear North West of each other. At $\frac{1}{4}$ past 2, Genoa Light House, N.E. by E. Wore and made sail after the Enemy. At $\frac{1}{4}$ past 3 the Admiral made the signal to prepare for Action. At 6 minutes past 4, to form the Line of Battle on the Larboard Tack; at $\frac{1}{4}$ past 4, for the Bedford and Captain to make more sail; Ditto for them to get in their stations. At $\frac{3}{4}$ past ditto the Princess Royal made the Captain's signal to get in her station. Ditto to make more sail, and for every Ship to carry lights during the night. At 5, the Bedford and Captain's signal repeated. The Admiral made the signal to keep in close order of sailing; Ditto for the Mozelle to keep within sight of the Enemy, and Fox Cutter to pass within hail. At 16 minutes past 5, the Admiral made the signal to engage the Enemy as coming up with them. At 20 minutes before 6, the signal to tack together. At $\frac{1}{4}$ before 8, the Mozelle made the signal that the Enemy had either tacked or wore. Made and shortened sail per signal, the Enemy in sight. A.M. at 4, all our Fleet in company; eight sail to the windward. At daylight saw one of the Enemy's Line-of-Battle Ship's carry away his topmasts. The Inconstant coming fast up with this disabled Ship, (which afterwards proved to be Le Ça Ira, of 80 guns.) Hove seven live bullocks overboard, clearing the decks. At $\frac{1}{4}$ past 9, the

Inconstant began firing at the disabled Ship—made all possible sail: at $\frac{1}{4}$ before 1 l we began our fire upon ditto; at Noon, the Action continuing.

" Saturday, 14th.—Nearly calm : we kept up a constant fire upon the Ça Ira; at this time several of the Enemy's Ships bearing down upon us; at $\frac{1}{4}$ past 1, the Admiral made our signal to discontinue the Action; answered ditto; hauled off, and stood for the Fleet. At the same time, for the Fleet to come to the wind upon the Larboard Tack. At $\frac{1}{4}$ before 4, to form the Order of Battle on the Larboard line of bearing; at $\frac{1}{4}$ past 4, for the Mozelle to keep sight of the Enemy during the Night. At 5, the preparative signals to tack and for all Ships to carry a light; made and shortened sail. At 1, A.M., the Princess Royal west $\frac{1}{2}$ a mile : all the Fleet in company. At 6, the Admiral made the signal for a general chase in close Line of Battle. At $\frac{1}{4}$ past do., to form the Line of Battle S.E. and N.W.; ditto for the White Division to make more sail, Cape Delle Melle, W.N.W. 5 or 6 leagues. At 40 minutes past ditto, the signal for the Bedford and Captain to attack the Enemy; at 7, the signal repeated; ditto, for the Bedford to engage closer; ditto for the Captain to engage closer. At 5 minutes past ditto, for a general engagement. At $\frac{1}{4}$ past ditto, to come to the Wind on the Larboard Tack. At 20 minutes past, to annul ditto. At 25 minutes past ditto, for Courageux and Illustrious to make more sail; at $\frac{1}{4}$ past 7, for them to get in their stations. At 8, for ditto to wear. The Enemy's Ships began firing on the Van of our Line, which they returned. At $\frac{1}{4}$ past 8, we began to engage on our Starboard side, as did the Princess Royal. As the Ship got up, the engagement became general, but at a great distance on the Larboard side, the Enemy having the wind. At $\frac{1}{4}$ past [9], we began to engage on both sides, as did the Princess Royal. At 5 minutes past 10, two of the Enemy's Ships struck their colours; boarded them, and hoisted English colours. They proved to be Le Ça Ira, of 80 guns and 1300 men, Le Censeur, of 74 guns, 1000 men. The engagement continued, but at a great distance from the centre to the rear. Saw that the Courageux and Illustrious had lost their main and mizen masts. The carpenters and seamen employed repairing our damages."

Mr. Hoste's (then a Midshipman of the Agamemnon) account of her proceedings on the 13th of March, in a letter to his father, dated on the 20th of that month, agrees both with Captain Nelson's Narrative and with the Agamemnon's Log. " The French Fleet were then standing to windward, carrying a press of sail. We had not chased long, when one of the French Ships carried away her topmasts and fell to leeward. The Agamemnon being one of the fast sailers, soon came up with her, and engaged her for three hours. We were obliged to leave her, or the whole French Fleet would have tacked and bore down upon us in a Line of Battle abreast, to save their disabled Ship. The Admiral seeing us in danger, made our signal to join our Fleet, the French being then within random shot, and firing at us. We joined our Fleet, and the French Fleet hauled their wind on the larboard tack, formed in a Line of Battle ahead standing from us, having their disabled Ship in tow. The Ship we engaged was the Ça Ira, of 84 guns, and 1300 men; she had 110 men killed and wounded in the Action with us, and she was otherwise much disabled in her masts and rigging. We very luckily had not a man hurt. I assure you the Agamemnon was the sole cause of the French Fleet being brought to Action the day following, as we disabled the Ça Ira so much on the 13th, that she could not get topmasts up in the night. We were at quarters all that night, hoping to have another brush with them in the morning.

" At daylight the wind shifting, gave us the weather-gage. Admiral Hotham immediately made the signal to form the Line ahead, and prepare for Action. The English Fleet consisted of fourteen Sail of the Line. At forty minutes past six, part of our Van was engaged with the Enemy, and about half-past nine the whole Fleet was in Action. We continued engaging them for five or six hours, and the day ended with the taking of the Ça Ira and Le Censeur, of 74 guns and 1000 men. The Agamemnon had not a man killed; two slightly wounded. The number of men killed on board the two French Ships, I have not been able to hear exactly, but I believe about 800 killed and wounded."—*Memoirs of Sir William Hoste*, vol. i. p. 39,

---

NOTE B, p. 188.

CAPTAIN RALPH WILLETT MILLER.

The following account of this gallant Officer, who is twice emphatically described by Nelson, after many years of intimacy, as "the only truly virtuous man he ever knew," is founded on an affectionate notice of him in the *Naval Chronicle*, (vol. ii. p. 581,) signed " C. V. P.," (apparently the late Vice-Admiral Sir Charles Vinnicombe Penrose, G.C.M.G., K.C.B.)

Captain Miller was born in New York on the 24th of January, 1762, and was the only son of an American gentleman, who sacrificed the whole of his property to his zeal and steady attachment to Loyalty, by his wife, Miss Martha Willett. He was sent early to England for education, and was entered on board the Ardent in 1778, where his zeal and abilities were so conspicuous as to recommend him to the particular attention of Admiral Gambier, who appointed him his Aide-de-camp, and frequently employed him in the flat-bottomed boats against the rebels in America. He volunteered for every service, was in all the actions fought by Admirals Barrington, Rodney, Hood, and Graves, and was three times wounded. In 1781, he was made a Lieutenant by Lord Rodney; and, while Lieutenant of the Windsor Castle, he was at the destruction of the French ships on the evacuation of Toulon, in 1793. His zeal and enterprise on that occasion, which nearly proved fatal to him, are shewn by Sir Sidney Smith's public letter. Lieutenant Miller was soon after removed to the Victory by Lord Hood, and was actively employed in the boats and on shore at the reduction of St. Fiorenzo, Bastia, and Calvi. Having volunteered to set fire to the French fleet in Gourjean Bay, in July 1794, Lord Hood immediately appointed him to command La Poulette, with orders to fit her out as a Fireship for that purpose. He attempted that object five times, but, owing to the failure of the wind, without success. In January, 1796, he was promoted to the rank of Post-Captain, and appointed to the command of the Mignonne, but Earl St. Vincent on assuming the command in the Mediterranean, being informed of his merits, removed him to the Unité, and sent him on an important service to the Adriatic. In August, 1796, Commodore Nelson selected him, solely from his reputation, to be his Captain in the "Captain," which Ship he commanded, and greatly distinguished himself, on the 14th of February, 1797. During the blockade of Cadiz, he was frequently employed in the Captain's boats against the Spanish Gun-boats. When the expedition against Teneriffe was undertaken, Captain Miller was removed to the Theseus, and in the attack on the town of Santa Cruz, was the first who entered the Enemy's works at the Mole. Having driven the Enemy from those works, he narrowly escaped, his clothes being torn, and himself much bruised and cut by the stones which the Enemy's shot threw over him. After Sir Horatio Nelson's return to England, he continued in the Theseus, was again employed in the blockade of Cadiz, and was twice engaged with the Enemy's gun-boats in

Gibraltar Bay. He again distinguished himself in command of the Theseus at the Battle of the Nile, when he was wounded in the face; and at the Siege of Acre, he commanded the Naval operations with great credit and success.

His melancholy fate is fully described in the official Report of the First Lieutenant of the Theseus, Mr. England, to Sir Sidney Smith, dated "Theseus, at Sea, off Mount Carmel in Syria, 15th of May, 1799 :"—

"It is with extreme concern I have to acquaint you that yesterday morning, at half past nine o'clock, twenty 36-howitzer shells and fifty 18-pounder shells had been got up and prepared ready for service by Captain Miller's order—the Ship then close off Ceserea, when in an instant, owing to an accident that we have not been able to discover, the whole was on fire, and a dreadful explosion took place. The Ship was immediately in flames : in the main-rigging and mizen-top, in the cockpit, in the tiers, in several places about the main-deck, and in various other parts of the Ship. The danger was very imminent, and required an uncommon exertion of every one to get under so collected a body of fire as made its appearance ; and I have the happiness to add, that our exertions were crowned with success, the fire got under, and the Ship most miraculously preserved." * * * " Our loss from the explosion, I here lament, has been very great; and Captain Miller, I am sorry to add, is of the number killed, which amount to twenty; drowned, nine ; and forty-five wounded. The whole of the poop and after-part of the quarter-deck is entirely blown to pieces, and all the beams destroyed : eight of the main-deck beams also broke, which fell down and jammed the tiller, all the ward-room bulk-heads and windows entirely blown to pieces, and the Ship left a perfect wreck. In short, a greater scene of horror or devastation could not be produced ; and we are all truly grateful to God Almighty for His most signal preservation, in saving us from a danger so very great and alarming."

In transmitting this Report to Earl St. Vincent, Sir Sidney Smith thus alluded to Captain Miller:—" The service suffers from this loss at this conjuncture, in the proportion by which it gained advantage from his gallant example, his indefatigable zeal, and consummate skill, in conducting the operations for the defence of the north side of this Town, committed to his management. He had long been in the practice of collecting such of the Enemy's shells as fell in the Town without bursting, and of sending them back to the Enemy better prepared, and with evident effect. He had a deposit on board the Theseus ready for service, and more were preparing, when, by an accident, for which nobody can account, the whole took fire, and exploded at short intervals."

Captain Miller's character, as drawn by one of his professional brethren, is the best conclusion to this Sketch of his services:—" I have often had occasion to admire the dashing intrepidity of Nelson, and the judicious determined conduct of Troubridge ; but these united characters are so firmly blended in that of my excellent friend, Miller, that words fall far below my estimation of his virtues and abilities—humanity, benevolence, and the accomplished gentleman, form the features of his countenance and character in so eminent a degree, that no one can see him without admiration."

At the suggestion of Captain Sir Edward Berry in 1801, a Monument by Flaxman was erected to Captain Miller's memory in St. Paul's Cathedral by his brother Officers; and Lord Nelson's feeling letter on the subject, written in January 1801, will be found under that year. He left a widow and two daughters, only one of whom, Miss Miller, is now living.

NOTE C, p. 401.

THE ORDER OF THE BATH.

In 1725, Sir Robert Walpole advised King George the First to revive the ORDER OF THE BATH; and he thus, to use Horace Walpole's words, created "an artful bank of thirty-six Ribbands, to supply a fund of favours in lieu of places." Another *job*, though of an inferior kind, arose out of that measure, by the appointment of the Duke of Montagu as Great Master, and of a Corps of unnecessary Officers, which Officers were entitled, by the Statutes, to demand from each Knight an immediate payment of £329 10s. 6d. on his nomination, £76 16s. 8d. on his Installation, and £16 per annum.

The annual payments have long been discontinued, and the Crown has ever since paid Salaries to the Officers instead. As no Great Master has been appointed since the death of the Duke of Montagu in 1749, the Fee to that Officer has ceased; but all the other Fees, amounting to £330 11s. 2d., are still demanded of every Knight Grand Cross, on his nomination. To this are to be added £52 10s. for a Grant of Supporters, but which is "optional;" and if (like Nelson) he had no Family Arms, to which to affix the said Supporters, Arms must also be granted to him—the cost of which Grant in Nelson's time, was £42 12s. 6d., but is now £70. When the Order was made the reward of *actual* Naval and Military Services, the Officers on whom it was conferred, naturally and justly declined paying the Fees, as such a payment had the appearance of *paying for Honours* that had been fairly and hardly earned. The Crown was therefore obliged, in such cases, to take upon itself to discharge those Fees; thereby virtually admitting that the Order is sometimes *not* given for distinguished *Services*, creating a broad and invidious distinction between the merits of the Knights, and *doubly* paying its own Servants. The amount demanded of Nelson, £428 7s. 5d., was paid by the Treasury; and from 1800 to 1832, no less a sum than £7913 was paid by the Public to the Officers of the Order, (besides their Salaries,) for the Fees of Naval and Military Officers, or on the nomination of Members of the Royal Family and Foreigners, as Knights of the Order.

On the enlargement of the Order of the Bath in 1815, another and still more disgraceful *job* occurred by the demand of £21 19s. from each Knight Commander, for his Banner and Plate of Arms to be placed in Westminster Abbey, for recording his Pedigree, and for a Copy of the Rules and Ordinances; and £6 17s. 8d. from each Companion for a Plate of his Name and Style in the Abbey, recording his Services, and for the Rules and Ordinances. As there have been more than 380 Knights Commanders, and more than 900 Companions, (supposing that 100 of the one class, and 300 of the other, but which is certainly too large a proportion, were wise enough not to pay those Fees,) at least £9000 has been taken from Officers, most of whom had far more merits than money; and to this hour *no Banner nor Plate has ever been placed in Westminster Abbey, and no Rules or Ordinances have ever been issued, nor even written!*

This *fraud*, and the original *abuse* of Fees, having at last attracted the attention of the Government, Mr. Secretary Stanley brought down a Message from the Crown to the House of Commons, on the 17th of April 1834, announcing that "His Majesty deemed it proper that measures should be taken for relieving the persons on whom the Order might in future be conferred from the payment of Fees and Charges, as authorized by the existing Statutes and Regulations, and expressing His Majesty's confidence that "his faithful Commons will direct the inquiry to be instituted as to the loss which will be sustained." On the following day, Mr. Stanley, in a very able speech, alluded to a wish that had been lately expressed by the House, that Military Officers should be relieved from those Fees, which, he said, were " of no public utility whatever;" and he proceeded to observe that the sum of £386 was really most inconvenient to be paid by many of them; that it was proposed to reduce the Officers of the Order from nine to four, to pay them salaries out of the Civil List, and to do away with the Fees altogether; but he added, that for the accomplishment of this "great public object," in an equitable manner, it was necessary to give compensation to those persons whose Offices were to be abolished. Mr. Stanley afterwards observed, " I only wish for inquiry in order to ascertain what Fees may, without injustice, be abolished, and what persons are entitled to compensation? If any, then to consider *whether you will continue the abuse of making persons pay for Honours granted to them on the ground of merit,* or will impose a charge of some few hundred pounds upon the Public, and by doing so, get rid of *a National grievance, and a National dishonour.*" The House, and particularly the Whig and Liberal Members, highly approved of the abolition of the Fees, but they seemed to demur to give compensation where none might be justly due—one of the said Fees being, as Mr. Stanley informed them, £6 to the King's barber! Admiral Sir Edward Codrington, G.C.B., said the subject was of very great importance to Naval Officers; that he held in his hand the Bill presented to him; that he was shocked on receiving it, to find that any Officer having received such an Honour from his Sovereign should be called upon to pay for it; that he would never pay one farthing of the money; and that the Order was lessened in his estimation from the moment he received this Bill. Mr. O'CONNELL called the Fees " absolute piracy;" and SIR ROBERT PEEL spoke in support of Mr. Stanley's motion. On the 21st of April, the following Resolution was agreed to by the House, " That the Lords of the Treasury be authorized to make compensation out of the Consolidated Fund to such Officers of the Order of the Bath as may be deprived of their Salaries and Fees;" and a Bill was accordingly ordered to be brought in.

Extraordinary as it must appear, *nothing more was done;* and though the distinguished person who supported the motion on that occasion is now Prime Minister, and though the Minister who brought forward the measure, and who then so emphatically and so justly described those Fees as " *a National disgrace and a National dishonour,*" again presides over the Department to which the Order of the Bath belongs, the *Fees,* on the appointment of a Knight Grand Cross, *remain in precisely the same state as in* 1834. Even a vacancy in one of the nine Offices, which, as the House of Commons were informed, it was intended to abolish, has been lately filled up, (thus perpetuating the chief obstacle to a better system;) and the only improvement that has taken place is the very proper and obvious one (the merit of which is due to Lord Stanley) of discontinuing to demand of the new Knights Commanders and Companions a Fee for Banners and Plates which will never be made, and for Rules and Ordinances which will probably never be written. Eight of the nine Officers (one, but who had neither salary nor Fees, having, without either his knowledge or consent, been removed) retain their sinecures; and the Officers of Her Majesty's Service, Civil, Naval, and Military, who eminently distinguish themselves by their talents or prowess, are still compelled (unless the Country pays the absurd demand) to contribute out of their personal resources to the maintenance of the Porter, Trumpeter, Cook, and Barber of the Royal Household!

That the Officers of the Navy and Army, and the Public, may know exactly how those Fees, which reflect " *disgrace*" and " *dishonour*" on the Nation, are distributed, a Copy of the *Bill* sent to Nelson is here given:

AN ACCOUNT OF FEES PAID BY VIRTUE OF THE KING'S SIGN MANUAL FOR
REAR-ADMIRAL HORATIO NELSON.

	£	s.	d.
Secretary of State's Office	6	7	6
Lord Chamberlain's Office	26	14	6

To the Seven Officers of the Order, viz.—

	£	s.	d.
Dean	22	6	8
Genealogist	22	0	0
Bath King of Arms	22	0	0
Register	22	0	0
Secretary	22	0	0
Gentleman-Usher	22	0	0
Messenger	18	13	4
	£151	0	0

	£	s.	d.		£	s.	d.
Bath King of Arms, for Book of Statutes	6	13	4				
Secretary for Notice of Election	6	13	4				
Seal of the Order to the Book	0	10	6				
					£164	17	2
To the Garter, and the Officers of Arms for the Patent of Supporters,					40	12	6
To the King of Arms, and other Officers of Arms, for the Patent of Confirmation and Exemplification of the Arms					42	12	6
To Fees of Honour to the King's Household					128	6	0
Warrant for dispensation for wearing the Star					7	13	6
Two suits of Ribbons					0	13	9
Soliciting the same, &c.					10	10	0
					£428	7	5

The last Item has rather an awkward appearance in a Bill relating to *Honours.*

"The Fees of Honour to the King's Household" appear to have been thus distributed:

LIST OF FEES ON RECEIVING KNIGHTHOOD.[1]

	£	s.	d.
Earl Marshal of England	3	13	4
Garter and Heralds at Arms	8	10	0
Lyon and Heralds of Scotland	8	10	0
Gentlemen Ushers of the Privy Chamber	5	0	0
Gentlemen Ushers Daily Waiters	5	0	0
Gentlemen Usher Assistant	1	5	0
Gentlemen Ushers Quarter Waiters	4	0	0
Grooms of the Privy Chamber	5	0	0
Exons to the Yeomen of the Guard	5	0	0
Knight Harbinger	3	6	8
Gentlemen and Yeomen Harbingers	5	6	8
Office of Robes	4	0	0
Removing Wardrobe	2	5	4
Carried forward	£60	17	0

[1] Copied from the original Bill delivered to Sir James Duff, in May 1779, now in the possession of Thomas Willement, Esq.

	£	s.	d.
Brought forward	60	17	0
Pages of the Bed Chamber	7	0	0
Sergeants at Arms	5	0	0
Sergeant Porter	1	0	0
Sergeant and Office of Trumpets	3	0	0
Barber	1	0	0
Sewers of the Chamber	2	0	0
Grooms of the Great Chamber	1	0	0
Household Drums	0	13	4
Pages of the Presence	0	10	0
Surveyor of the Ways	0	10	0
Yeomen of the Mouth	1	16	0
Gentlemen of the Buttery and Cellar	1	12	0
Surveyor of the Dresser	0	10	0
Yeomen Ushers	1	0	0
Master Cook	1	5	0
Keepers of the Council Chamber	1	0	0
Footmen and Coachmen	2	10	0
Porters at Gate	1	0	0
Closet Keeper	0	10	0
Registrar of the College of Arms	1	8	2
Principal Usher of Scotland	3	6	8
	£98	8	2

The Fees on Knighthood are at the present time £108, but it has not been ascertained how the additional *ten* pounds are distributed, no *Bill* being at present furnished to the Knight, who merely receives an immediate demand in writing from the Lord Chamberlain's Office for the money, and unless it be paid, the Honour is not notified in the " London Gazette." Nor has it been discovered in what manner the difference between the Fees to the Royal Household for making a Knight of the Bath, and those on simple Knighthood, were applied. Probably the Cook and the Barber were more highly remunerated by the Knights of the Bath, to whom, in former ages, those important functionaries rendered actual, though ridiculous, services.

REAR-ADMIRAL SIR WILLIAM PARKER'S LETTER AND STATEMENT RESPECTING THE BATTLE OF ST. VINCENT.

[From the " Naval Chronicle," vol. xxi. p. 301. Referred to pp. 339, 340, 439, ante.]

" Blenheim, off Cadiz, September 1, 1797.

" Dear Bingham,

" I have heard some time back, by some of my friends in England, that from a statement of the Action of the 14th February, by then Commodore Nelson, I had not that credit that properly belonged to me. I have had no power to do myself the justice I might be entitled to, for want of a sight of that Letter, which I did not get until the 20th of July. It is of no moment to me to make any observations further than concerns myself; I have written to him upon the subject, which, least any of my friends may not have considered me in the situation I really stood, in the success of that day from that cause also, I here send you the copy of what I have written, with his answer.

" He was absent from the Fleet at the time I wrote, and when he returned, had lost his arm. I had no immediate answer; it was left with the Commander-in-Chief, by whom he desired it to be delivered to me after he was gone to England, as I was told to prevent a rejoinder; but with assurances that no offence was meant by him to me, and that he never thought it could be understood that both Ships had struck to him.

" This answer is little to the purpose, though after what he had written it could not be much otherwise. He has got my observations as far as respects myself; and I receive in words, what I suppose was thought he should not commit to paper, for I believe he had advice upon the occasion. I have no other object or wish than to be considered by my friends in the way I am entitled, or any intention of making comments upon Admiral Nelson's Letter, but what concerned my own situation, and the Ships he did not mention.

" Dear Bingham,
" Your friend and well-wisher,
" W. Parker.

" P.S. You may shew this, with its enclosure, to any of my friends whom you may suppose have read Admiral Nelson's Letter."

" TO REAR-ADMIRAL NELSON.

" My dear Sir,   " Blenheim, off Cadiz, 25th July, 1797.

" It was not until the 21st of this Inst. July, that I saw the Letter in the Sun, dated the 20th March, with Remarks upon the proceedings of his Majesty's Ship the Captain, in the Action of the 14th February, to the whole of which, from a near situation, I was an eye witness.

" I very readily admit that you have all the credit that belongs to an able Officer and a brave man; but in support of myself, the Officers of the Prince George and Orion (and Blenheim, previous to your acknowledging her) I cannot but express my surprise at the statement contained in your Letter.

" You say, ' After wearing, that at a quarter past one o'clock you were engaged, and immediately joined, and most nobly supported by the Culloden, Captain Troubridge. For near an hour, did the Culloden and Captain support this apparently, though not really, unequal contest, when the Blenheim passing between you and the Enemy, gave you a respite,' &c.

" I must here take the opportunity of pointing out to you, that after passing through the Enemy's disordered Line upon the star-board tack—viz., the Culloden, Blenheim, Prince George, Orion, and Colossus—the Culloden and Colossus more to windward than the other three Ships, which were in an exact line close to each other, tacked per signal in succession, and stood after the Enemy upon the larboard tack in the following order—viz., Culloden, Blenheim, Prince George, and Orion— Colossus having lost her fore and fore-top-sail yards, missed stays, and remained astern; during the progress towards the Enemy upon the larboard tack, you were observed to wear from the rear of our line, and stand towards the Enemy also, the Culloden by the minutes on board the Prince George, began to engage first—viz., twenty minutes past one o'clock—and you fell in a-head of her some time after, and began to engage at half-past one. Soon after you began, the Blenheim was advanced upon the Culloden's larboard quarter as far ahead as she could be, keeping out of her fire, and began also; and not long afterwards the Prince George was the same with respect to the Blenheim, and Orion with respect to the Prince George. The Prince George began at thirty-five minutes past one, but for some time could not get advanced enough to bring her broadside to bear without yawing, occasionally; the

Orion in the Prince George's rear began as soon as she could get sufficiently advanced; therefore, so different to your statement, very soon after you commenced your fire, you had four Ships pressing on, almost on board of each other, close in your rear; but the Ships thus pressing upon each other, and the two latter not far enough ahead to fire with proper effect, besides having none of the Enemy's Ships left in the rear for our succeeding Ships, at thirteen minutes past one I made the signal, No. 66 (fill and stand on), the most applicable as I thought to the occasion, which, though occasionally shot away, was re-hoisted, and kept flying the greater part of the Action.

"From the time stated that the Prince George began to engage the Enemy upon the larboard tack, until the San Josef struck her Colours (say about five or ten minutes past four), after falling on board the San Nicolas, the fire of the Prince George was without intermission, except a small space of time, edging under your lee when dividing from the San Josef, her then antagonist, not being able to pass to windward of your Ship, and the San Nicolas, then on board each other—viz., your larboard bow upon her lee quarter—the San Josef mizen-mast being gone, and main-top-mast head below the rigging shot away, fell on board the San Nicolas to windward, the Prince George in the meantime edging to leeward of you and the San Nicolas, and advancing sufficiently ahead of the Captain to fire clear of her, recommenced her fire both upon the San Nicolas and San Josef, from receiving shot from the San Nicolas upon passing ahead of the Captain, then on board of her; this continued pretty heavy eight or ten minutes, until the San Josef struck her Colours; then, upon ceasing to fire, we were hailed from the Captain, saying both Ships had struck. The Prince George endeavoured to proceed on ahead, leaving the San Josef, as also the other, to be taken possession of by you, assisted by such succeeding Ships, as the Commander-in-chief, who had arrived up, might direct.

"The first Ship that came within my observation, except the five Ships alluded to, was the Excellent, whose Captain neither requires your testimony or mine in proof of his bravery and good conduct; he closed with the San Isidro at twelve minutes past three, and she soon struck: he had all his Sails set, passing on ahead; the Namur some time came up, fired at some Ship in the rear, and passed on ahead also; and about this time the Orion, in my rear, lowered her boat down to take possession of a three-decker (the Salvador), which she had been some time opposed to, after the Prince George had passed her; this was, I think, about the time the Prince George was edging under your lee, and the Commander-in-chief arriving up.

"Of this Action, my dear Sir, I felt conscious at the time, and feel so now, that every exertion was used on my part as a Flag Officer, and by the Captain and Officers, and Company of the Prince George, in which I was embarked, to take and destroy the Enemy, and believe me, neither they or myself expected to meet an account so different to the real statement of that Action as is observed in your Letter. I am well aware that people in Action know but little of occurrences in their rear, yet when a Letter is written to be exposed to public view, positive assertions should be made with great circumspection.

"I observed nothing but gallantry and good conduct in every Ship that came under my observation, from first to last, and think myself equally entitled to an acknowledgment of a proportion of the success of that day, with any man present at it.

"I feel much concern at the occasion of this Letter, but remain, &c.

"W. PARKER.

"To Admiral Nelson."

"Dear Sir, "August 19th [1797.]

"I must acknowledge the receipt of your Letter of the 25th July; and after declaring, that I know nothing of the Prince George till she was hailed from the forecastle of the San Nicolas, it is impossible I can enter into the subject of your Letter, &c.

"HORATIO NELSON."

"NARRATIVE OF THE PROCEEDINGS OF HIS MAJESTY'S FLEET UNDER THE COMMAND OF ADMIRAL SIR JOHN JERVIS, K.B. AND COMMANDER-IN CHIEF, ETC. THE 14TH OF FEBRUARY, 1797.

"In the night of the 13th we heard the Signal Guns of the Enemy, and at daylight the signal to prepare for battle. The morning being pretty hazy, we did not get sight of them by our Frigates until seven o'clock, and then only partially; at thirty-eight minutes past nine, the signal for general chase; at half-past ten a Frigate made known, per signal, twenty-five Sail of the Line were in sight, and soon after, eight Sail more; at a quarter past eleven, the signal for the order of battle, without regard to the Order prescribed; the Enemy now being open to our view, and in disordered line upon the larboard tack, the King's Fleet upon the starboard; at forty-two minutes past eleven, the signal to cut through the Enemy's Line, I being the only Flag Officer in the van; this was effected by the Culloden, Blenheim, myself in the Prince George, Orion, and Colossus, the Culloden passed through, leaving some Ships of the Enemy between the Prince George and herself, the other four of us were close after each other, which occasioned the Enemy's Ships left in their rear, though the two headmost were three-deckers, to tack, and soon after they wore about, and made a good deal of sail. At forty-eight minutes past eleven, the signal to engage, which continued during our passing through a number of the Enemy's Ships upon the contrary tack, in no regular order, close on board of some, and others more distant; and until eighteen minutes past twelve, when we tacked, per signal, in which time the Colossus lost her fore and fore top-sail yards, and the Enemy a good deal disabled; and at twenty minutes past one o'clock, the signal to cut back through the Enemy's Line and engage them to leeward: when we tacked, the two three-deckers tacked after us, and which the rest of the Enemy's rear were about to do; but the Commander-in-chief, with the Ships of centre and rear, following close, covered us from their attack upon the rear of the Ships with me, and obliged them to re-tack, engaging that part of the Enemy's Fleet, and effectually divided it; Commodore Nelson, in the Captain, being in the rear of our Line upon the starboard tack, tacked, and joined the Ships with me in the van. The Enemy's van, now consisting of considerably the larger number of their Fleet, in great disorder, we got up with, and began to engage upon the larboard tack; at half-past one o'clock close on board of them; at forty-three minutes past one, the signal, per my order, for the Ships ahead to fill and stand on, and which I found necessary again to repeat at three o'clock; the Commander-in-chief arriving up in the rear of the Orion, my second astern, at a quarter past, repeated it also. This part of the Action was supported until this time by the Culloden, Captain, Blenheim, Prince George, and Orion, during which time the Enemy never formed; therefore, though we sometimes had the fire of two or three Ships together, yet, from their disordered state, our fire had great effect upon them, for it could not be lost, even if it had not the full effect upon the Ship we happened to be most particularly opposed to; they were generally huddled together in a very irregular manner, and I have no doubt but they did each other a great deal of injury. By this time, five of them became very much disabled, and at twenty-three minutes past three, the Excellent, Captain Collingwood, coming up closer with one of them most to windward, and she struck her Colours; and at half-past, the Victory up astern of the Orion, when one of the three-deckers, which we had engaged, and left in a rear very much disabled, struck her Colours, I believe, to the Victory; soon after, from the disabled state of the Captain, fore-top-mast gone, she fell on board one of the Ships she had been opposed to; but whether from the exact intention of Commodore Nelson, I am to learn; however, he boarded her and made her strike; and a three-decker, bearing a Rear-Admiral's Flag, struck to the fire of the Prince George, and, from her disabled state, fell on board the same Spanish Ship Commodore Nelson was on board of, upon the quarter on the other side. The Namur by this time came up to windward, and passed between the Prince George, Culloden, and the St. Trinidad, of 130 guns, Don Cordeva, the Commander-in-chief, which Ship was very much beaten at that time, and in apparently a sinking state. But the support very opportunely given to her by the two three-deckers, in the early part alluded to, just arriving up, saved her from the necessity of striking, though it had been asserted she did strike. The four Ships that we in the van had left in our rear that had struck, were taken possession of by our succeeding Ships : at sun-set, the signal to wear and come to the wind upon the other tack, and soon after to form in order of battle, in close order to cover the Prizes. Too much cannot be said of the bravery displayed in the conduct of the Ships with me, and I certainly feel it incumbent on me to say, that the Captain, Culloden, and Blenheim, but more particularly the two former, bore more of the brunt of the Action than the Prince George and Orion, from their being more in the van. The Commander-in-chief certainly displayed great Naval abilities in conducting this Attack, and management throughout, and I do not believe the King has a more competent Officer. I am in the full belief that more acts of gallantry and good conduct were displayed than possibly could come within my observation.

"W. Parker.

"Mem.—The Prince George expended 197 barrels of powder; lost ten men killed and nine badly wounded, slightly wounded innumerable."

British Navy.—Number of their Guns, 1,244.
Spanish Navy.—Number of their Guns, 2,408.

LETTERS

INSERTED IN THE SECOND EDITION

OF

𝔗𝔥𝔢 𝔉𝔦𝔯𝔰𝔱 𝔙𝔬𝔩𝔲𝔪𝔢,

WHICH DO NOT OCCUR IN THE FIRST EDITION.

ADVERTISEMENT

SECOND EDITION.

SINCE the publication of the First Volume of this Work, the Editor has been favoured with many communications, which have caused some additional Letters to be inserted in the present Edition.

Through the influence of a friend, access has been obtained to the Papers of the late Dr. M‘Arthur, which are now in the possession of his daughter, Mrs. Conway; but they contain few original documents relating to Lord Nelson, and scarcely any of the Manuscripts that were used in Clarke and M‘Arthur's " Life of Nelson." If no other Papers of Dr. M‘Arthur are in existence, the suggestion in the Preface that his family had retained Letters which were lent to him is without foundation; and the Editor, therefore, willingly recalls it. The fact, however, remains, that many of the persons who lent original Letters to Dr. M‘Arthur, never recovered them. It is therefore possible that they may have been lost.

Though the examination of Dr. M‘Arthur's Papers was not attended with the expected result, some valuable original Letters, and Copies of a few others, have thereby been obtained. The original Letters were addressed to Lord Hood, during the Sieges of Bastia and Calvi, or to Dr. M‘Arthur; and (together with two Letters from other sources) are inserted in their proper places in this Volume.

The most important document in Mrs. Conway's possession is, the *original* Manuscript of Lord Nelson's autobiographical "Sketch of his Life," which is now for the first time printed exactly as it was written.

The Editor is much indebted to Lady Bolton, a niece of Lord Nelson, for many Letters and Papers of great interest, which were obligingly communicated by James Young, Esq., of Wells in Norfolk. He has also to offer his best acknowledgments to the Dowager Lady de Saumarez, and to Lord de Saumarez, for Lord Nelson's Letters to that distinguished ornament of the Naval Service, the late Admiral Lord de Saumarez; to Mrs. Ellis, daughter of Admiral Sir Peter Parker, (Nelson's early patron and friend;) to Admiral Sir Robert Otway, Bart., K.C.B.; to Colonel Hugh Percy Davison; to Captain Sir Andrew Pellet Green, K.C.H.; to the Reverend Henry Girdleston; to Captain Sir George Augustus Westphal, R.N.; to Captain Widdrington, R.N.; to Captain Robert Fitz-Gerald Gambier, R.N.; to Nathaniel Young, Esq.; and to the Reverend Edward Bushby, of St. John's College, Cambridge.

He also begs leave to thank Lord Stanley for his permission to print Lord Nelson's Letters to the Secretary of State for War and Colonies, in the years 1803, 1804, and 1805, which, as stated in the Preface, are now in the Colonial Office.

Advantage has been taken of this Edition to supply some particulars of Lord Nelson's family, as well as of himself; to insert additional Notes; and to correct typographical and other errors.

January 13, 1845.

TO WILLIAM SUCKLING, ESQ.

[From the "Gentleman's Magazine," vol. xcv. part i. p. 196.]

My dear Uncle,   January 14th, 1784.

There arrives in general a time in a man's life (who has friends), that either they place him in life in a situation that makes his application for anything farther totally unnecessary, or give him help in a pecuniary way, if they can afford, and he deserves it.

The critical moment of my life is now arrived, that either I am to be happy or miserable:—it depends solely on you.

You may possibly think I am going to ask too much. I have led myself up with hopes you will not—till this trying moment. There is a lady I have seen, of a good family and connexions, but with a small fortune,—1000*l.* I understand.[1] The whole of my income does not exceed 130*l.* per annum. Now I must come to the point:—will you, if I should marry, allow me yearly 100*l.*[2] until my income is increased to that sum, either by employment, or any other way? A very few years I hope will turn something up, if my friends will but exert themselves. If you will not give me the above sum, will you exert yourself with either Lord North or Mr. Jenkinson, to get me a Guard-ship, or some employment in a Public Office where the attendance of the principal is not necessary, and of which they must have such numbers to dispose of. In the India Service I understand (if it remains under the Directors) their Marine force is to be under the command of a Captain in the Royal Navy : that is a station I should like.

You must excuse the freedom with which this letter is dictated; not to have been plain and explicit in my distress had been cruel to myself. If nothing can be done for me, I know what I have to trust to. Life is not worth preserving without happiness; and I care not where I may linger out a miserable existence. I am prepared to hear your refusal, and

---

[1] Apparently Miss Andrews. Vide vol. i. p. 91.

[2] The gentleman who, under the signature " P.," i. e., the late William Pearce, Esq., of the Admiralty, communicated this letter to the " Gentleman's Magazine," states that Mr. Suckling immediately complied with the request. If so, Nelson was probably refused by the fair object of his affections.—See vol. i. p. 90.

have fixed my resolution if that should happen; but in every situation, I shall be a well-wisher to you and your family, and pray they or you may never know the pangs which at this instant tear my heart. God bless you, and assure yourself, I am, Your most affectionate and dutiful nephew,

HORATIO NELSON.

TO COMMODORE LINZEE.

[Autograph, in the possession of the Honourable Mrs. Gregory, sister of the present Viscount Hood. The Agamemnon joined Commodore Linzee at Cagliari, on the 24th of October. Vide p. 331.]

Agamemnon, October 24th, 1793.

My dear Sir,

I am sorry to have been so long in joining you, as I feel great satisfaction in being put under your orders. What has contributed to delay me a little, was four French Frigates and a Brig crossing me. A few shot was exchanged with one of them, who I left in a sinking state. We having lost the use of our main topmast, could not haul the wind to them, and they seemed to have got enough: therefore would not come down to me. Believe me yours most faithfully.

HORATIO NELSON.

Sailmakers would be of great service to us for a day, and some Carpenters with their tools: 24 hours will fit us for service.

Ten days past we boarded a Ship from Smyrna, but I think we ought not to be put into quarantine.

TO VICE-ADMIRAL LORD HOOD.

[Autograph, in the possession of Mrs. Conway.]

Agamemnon, at anchor, off Porto Novo, February 8th, 1794.

My Lord,

Yesterday at this place, they hoisted National colours as I passed, as also the Vessels in the harbour. I went to l'Avasina, but there is no Ship there. Captain Freemantle tells me, a Ship under Ragusa colours is in Bastia. This morning being very fine, I anchored here, and sent on shore a message to say I was come to deliver them from the Republicans, and wished to be received as friends, but that if a musket was fired, I would burn the Town. The answer[3] is literally as translated, viz.,

'We are Republicans ; that is sufficient. It is not at Maginaggio you ought to address yourself. Go to St. Fiorenzo, Bastia, or Calvi :—they will give you an answer such as you desire. The soldiers which I command are true soldiers of France. The Commander of the Military of Cape Corse."

From this answer, I landed, and struck the National colours with my own hand, and ordered the Tree of Liberty to be cut down. The Commander retiring to a hill, with National colours, and his troops. We destroyed about five hundred tuns of wine ready to be shipped, and ten sail of Vessels.

Just as we were coming .   .   [*The Remainder is lost.*]

TO ADMIRAL LORD HOOD.

[Autograph, in the possession of Mrs. Conway.]

Agamemnon, February 22nd, 1794, between Cape Corse and Bastia.

My Lord,

I was honoured by your letter of the 19th, yesterday morning, by the Cutter, and beg leave most sincerely to congratulate your Lordship on the taking Fiorenzo.[6] We saw plainly, when evening set in on the 19th, the fire at Fiorenzo,

---

[3] The *original* Letter of the French Commandant is in the Nelson Papers :
"Nous sommes Republicains. Ce mot seul doit suffire. Ce n'est point au Maginaggio, lieu sans deffence, à qui il faut vous adresser. Allez à St. Fiorent, Bastia, ou Calvi, et l'on vous repondra, selon vos desirs. Pour la trouppes que je commande elle est prête à vous montrer qu'elle est composé de Soldats Francais.
                                    " Le Command^t. Militaire du
                                                        " Cape Corse."

[6] St. Fiorenzo was taken on the 17th of February ; and the French having retreated to Bastia, Lord Hood proposed to Lieutenant-General Dundas (afterwards General Sir David Dundas, K.B.,) the Commander of the Forces, to reduce it. General Dundas, however, considering the plan impracticable, refused his co-operation without a reinforcement of 2000 men from Gibraltar. Lord Hood determined to take Bastia with the Naval force only, and gave the command of the Seamen employed in the batteries to Nelson. Clarke and M'Arthur have printed the

and had no doubts but it was the Frigates on fire. We were close to Bastia. On receiving your letter, I bore away for the Cape, and at 4 P.M. joined Romulus. Captain Sutton had landed the arms, &c., before I got to him at the place he was ordered. I hope my letter sent by the Tartar, and, by Captain Fremantle put on board the Terpsichore, will convey to your Lordship the information you wanted about Bastia. I am now going to take another look at the place, when I shall send this letter. To the northward of the Town, at three miles distance, troops may be safely landed; and a good road for marching all the way to Bastia, but not for heavy artillery; but probably landing-places may be found to the northward of Bastia, much nearer than three miles. I see the little Camp with two guns, *en barbette*, is intended to prevent landing to the southward, as I dare say the shot will reach to the opening of the Lagoon : but then troops may land under cover of Gun-boats and other small Vessels, although Ships cannot get in. But every defence of Bastia is plainly to be seen from the sea, and in my opinion will soon fall. Yesterday morning, a very large Swedish ship from the Levant, loaded with corn, was within two miles of Bastia. I believe he intended for that Port; but if [he] had not, the boats would have carried her in, but we were between her and the Town. We could not get to his papers, except the common ones, as he is in quarantine. Nothing shall get in, you may be assured.

following remarkable Extract from Lord Hood's Letter to General Dundas respecting the operations against Bastia, dated Victory in Martello Bay, 6th March 1794: " I am honoured with your Letter of yesterday's date, in which you are pleased to say, ' after mature consideration, and a personal inspection for several days of all circumstances, local as well as others, I consider the Siege of Bastia, with our present means and force, to be a most visionary and rash attempt, such as no Officer could be justified in undertaking.' In answer to which, I must take the liberty to observe, that however visionary and rash an attempt to reduce Bastia may be in your opinion, to me it appears very much the reverse, and to be perfectly a right measure; and I beg here to repeat my answer to you, upon your saying, two days ago, that I should be of a different opinion to what I had expressed were the responsibility upon my shoulders, ' that nothing would be more gratifying to my feelings, than to have the whole responsibility upon me ;' and I am now ready and willing to undertake the reduction of Bastia at my own risk, with the force and means at present here, being strongly impressed with the necessity of it."

Saturday evening. I have just had a boat off from Erbalonga : they say that our landing at l'Avasina, and marching so near Bastia, has been of the greatest service to them, as the Enemy intended that night coming with Gun-boats and troops, and burning all the revolted villages. All the Corsicans, to the very walls of Bastia, have now declared for us, and they tell me not much less than 1000 are now under the outworks of Bastia; indeed, we have seen the firing of musketry the whole evening.

Sunday noon. It is only just now I have been able to examine Bastia more closely. I find the Enemy every hour are strengthening their works. The two guns mounted *en barbette* are now making a half-moon battery. I passed close with Romulus and Tartar,[7] the Enemy opened their fire from the battery. We directly dislodged them, and they to a man quitted the works. The Town opened on us with shot and shells, but without doing us any damage of consequence : our guns were so exceedingly well pointed, that not one shot was fired in vain ; a parcel of powder for one battery blew up, and did apparently considerable damage. Indeed, my Lord, I wish the troops were here : I am sure, in its present state it will soon fall. I don't think the Corsicans have the strong post General Paoli mentions, or, I think I must have known it. They tell me the garrison of Fiorenzo is got into Bastia.

I am, &c.,

HORATIO NELSON.

TO THE RIGHT HONOURABLE ADMIRAL LORD HOOD.

[Autograph, in the possession of Mrs. Conway.]

Agamemnon, June 7th, 1794.

My Lord,

I have cleared our between decks of all our Ordnance stores, and sent them to the Dolphin. I have not touched those in our hold, which, unless your Lordship chooses we should be entirely cleared of, all the stores will, I think, be no

[7] Romulus, 36, Captain John Sutton, afterwards Vice-Admiral Sir John Sutton, K.C.B. The Tartar, 28, was commanded by Captain, afterwards Vice-Admiral Sir Thomas Francis Fremantle, Bart., G.C.B., G.C.M.G.

great inconvenience for a short cruize. We are unmoored and short on our other anchor: will send for the Troops directly.

I am with great respect,
Your Lordship's most faithful servant,
HORATIO NELSON.

I have wrote Captain Inglefield to request some of the Transports' boats may take some wads and platforms from us.

TO ADMIRAL LORD HOOD.

[Autograph, in the possession of Mrs. Conway.]

Agamemnon, near Calvi, 19th June, 1794.

My dear Lord,

Believing that what I should do would be of service to our Country, and of course meet with your Lordship's approbation, I have the honour to acquaint you that on my arrival in Mortella Bay, on the 15th instant, General Stuart was anxious to proceed on our expedition against Calvi, in which I own I most heartily concurred with him, believing ourselves safe under your Lordship's wing. I sailed on the 16th, in the evening, from Mortella Bay, and anchored here on the 17th at night. Yesterday was taken up in looking at the Enemy, and this morning at daylight, the troops 1450 were landed, together with seventy volunteers from the Transports, thirty men which I took out of the Inflexible, and one hundred Seamen from the Agamemnon. I was obliged to use every effort to forward the service. The General, after looking at Calvi, wished to have some additional force; therefore I sent the Fox to Fiorenzo, with orders to Captain Wallis[8] to proceed to Bastia, for such troops as General Stuart wished to have. As the Gorgon had not men enough left her by your Lordship to take care of her, I was obliged to solicit volunteers from the Transports to bring her round with

---

[8] Captain James Wallis, who served with Nelson as First Lieutenant of the Boreas. He then commanded the Gorgon, Store Ship.

me, and therefore was under the necessity of desiring Inflexible to lend twenty men to assist in navigating the Ship. The Fox is to bring 150 of the Royal Louis. If the Victory does not join us before the Lutine is cleared, I must send her for guns from the Commerce de Marseilles,[9] which are much wanted. Captain Cooke, who I found at Fiorenzo, with a zeal which will ever do him credit, wished to accompany me on the present Expedition. I not only have the greatest pleasure in having him with me, but his assistance to me has been very great: and as he is anxious to remain, I hope he will be allowed by your Lordship to stay with me till the Siege is over. I have much to say, but wish not to keep the Scout.

Believe me, with highest respect,

Your Lordship's most faithful,

HORATIO NELSON.

General Stuart requests me to say that nothing particular has happened since our landing, and that he is really so busy that he cannot find time to write to your Lordship; but begs to refer you to me for particulars, which I have given in my letter.

TO ADMIRAL LORD HOOD.

[Autograph, in the possession of Mrs. Conway.]

Camp, June 21st, 1794.

My Lord,

I did myself the honour of writing your Lordship by the Scout, who was in search of you here, to acquaint you of our situation. You will know from my letters to Captain Tyler[1] and Captain Wallis, of what I thought it right to order, in consequence of General Stuart's finding this place much stronger than he expected. As the General will write to tell

---

[9] The Commerce de Marseilles, of 120 guns, was one of the Ships brought from Toulon by Lord Hood, in December 1793.

[1] Captain Tylor, of the Meleager of 32 guns. This gallant Officer, who was severely wounded in command of the Tonnant, at the Battle of Trafalgar, died Admiral Sir Charles Tyler, G.C.B., in September, 1835.

you his wants and wishes, it is only necessary for me to say, that had not the weather been so bad as to preclude all intercourse with Ships for the last twenty-four hours, and still continues very bad, the Lutine would have been cleared of her stores and sent to Fiorenzo to request ten more guns from the Commerce de Marseilles, the general intending to have seventeen guns of the French against the Enemy, and three or four of my 24-pounders to fire shells from. Our landing place is very bad; the rocks break in this weather so far from the shore, and the mountain we have to drag the guns up so long and so steep, that the whole of yesterday we were only able to get one gun up, and then we have one mile and a half at least to drag them. I hope before long we shall be able to land some to the eastward of Cape Revellata; but it being within half gun-shot of the Enemy, it cannot at present be done. General Stuart wishes much for the Fortunée Gun-boat to lay in this Bay, to the eastward of Revellata, to prevent the Enemy's Gun-boat from coming in there to annoy our intended Battery, and proposes to place a heavy gun as a defence for her. She can lay with another small Vessel under a high point of land between her and the Enemy. I wrote to Lieutenant Fennell to try and get some volunteers, and to bring the Gun-boat to me. Your Lordship[2] so well knows our want of seamen here, that I am sure I need not mention it: we shall have more than forty pieces of ordnance to drag over these mountains : my numbers are two hundred, barely sufficient to move a twenty-four pounder. The two Vessels laden with powder at Fiorenzo, the General

<hr>

[2] On the 21st of June, Lord Hood wrote officially to Captain Nelson from the Victory in Mortella Bay :—

" Sir,—I am waiting with great impatience to hear from you, not knowing what Stores you took with you, and what more may be wanted. The additional troops General Stuart ordered from Bastia embarked this morning, and I expect to see the Ariadne and Transports to-morrow, when I shall join and proceed with him. In addition to the men from this Ship already on the expedition, I have sent fifty more under the command of Captain Hallowell, who is accompanied by Captain Serocold, both very able, willing, and zealous Officers, from whom you will have much assistance, and they are directed to follow your orders, which I am confident they will both do with great alacrity, and that all will go on with equal cordiality and good humour as at Bastia. I am, Sir, with great regard, &c., HOOD. P.S. I tremble for what may have happened from last night's wind."—From a *Copy* certified by Nelson, in the Hood Papers.

will write you, I take for granted, about. He says he shall want the powder they have on board. Had not the weather been bad, I am sure one battery against Monachesco would have opened to-morrow morning. Twenty-four hours, I think, will put us in possession of it. We seem here determined to act with vigour, and it is the only thing to get us on. The Enemy are hard at work making batteries. I wrote your Lordship that Captain Cooke is with me, who with great zeal and activity could not think of laying idle at Fiorenzo, therefore offered his services to me, which I cheerfully accepted. If it is not contrary to your Lordship's plan for him, I believe he wishes much to stay with me. He begs I will present his respects; and believe me your Lordship's most faithful servant,

HORATIO NELSON.

The Dolphin is in the greatest distress for men—not having enough to weigh an anchor, so Captain May tells me. The Lutine shall sail the moment she is cleared of her stores.

Many of the Transports have been obliged to leave this anchorage, from the badness of the anchoring ground, none of which are now in sight.

TO ADMIRAL LORD HOOD.

[Autograph, in possession of Mrs. Conway.]

Camp, June 23rd, 1794.

My Lord,

The Agamemnon who put to sea in the evening of the 21st, is, I hope, at Fiorenzo, and hope very soon to see her again with the Store-ships, who put to sea the day before. Not one Ship is returned to us. The General this morning sent Captain Stephens,[3] of the Artillery, to ask me, as more French twenty-pound shot could not be got, to give him my opinion what other guns could best be spared, and shot for them, to make up the original demand, all of which, I am told,

---

[3] Captain Edward Stephens of the Artillery, was the Senior Officer of that Corps at the Siege: he became a Lieutenant-Colonel in January 1794, and a Lieutenant-General in June, 1813.

will certainly be wanted. I endeavoured to fix on those sizes which I thought most likely to be obtained; and as the General wishes to write your Lordship, I send the Fox Cutter. The Lutine, if the weather moderates, will be cleared to-morrow, when I shall immediately send her to your Lordship at Fiorenzo, for these guns, &c. No more guns have been able to be landed, the swell has been so great: therefore the battery against Manachesco cannot be opened till another battery of four twenty-four pounders is erected to draw off the Enemy's fire. Twelve guns are judged necessary for the first parallel. If we cannot get on faster, we shall be a long while in getting possession, if the Enemy make an obstinate resistance. The Vessels with the powder having gone to sea, I have been obliged to order the Dolphine and Lutine to land powder, and Wolseley[4] having twenty-four barrels of prize powder, that is bought of him.

I am, with highest respect,
Your Lordship, your most faithful servant,
HORATIO NELSON.

Captain Cooke desires to present his respectful compliments.

TO THE HON. LIEUTENANT-GENERAL STUART.

[Autograph, in the possession of Mrs. Conway.]

June 23rd, 1794.

Two thirty-six pounders from Commerce de Marseilles and 3000 shot.

Two twenty-four pounders from Agamemnon, and 2000 shot.

N.B.—The Agamemnon has not 900 shot of this calibre.

Four eighteen-pounders French, and 6000 shot, supposed from Pearl and Fiorenzo.

Three twelve pounders French, and 4500 shot.

Two twenty-four pounders from Agamemnon for shells.

---

[4] Captain of the Lowestoffe, vide p. 350, ante.

These wanted, exclusive of the five guns and ten-inch howitzer on board the Victory.

I think these guns are more likely, with the shot, to be got than any others.

HORATIO NELSON.

TO ADMIRAL LORD HOOD.

[Autograph, in the possession of Mrs. Conway.]

Camp, June 25th, 1794.

My Lord,

I am sorry your Lordship has not received my letters as I have wrote three since my landing. We go on well; and although we have, in appearance, a great deal of hard work to get through, yet I have no doubt but it will be accomplished in a proper manner.

The seamen are in want of tents, except the Agamemnon's ten, all the others (Victory's, who came yesterday, excepted) are lodged in sail tents, which are wanted for the Artillery Stores, Commissaries, and Hospitals. There being no houses near us, makes the application to the Navy very frequent and urgent. If those Ships who have tents can send us thirty, we want them. I have landed the Purser of the Agamemnon to issue provisions for the seamen. I have also to request that 300 pair of shoes may be ordered directly. I had not shoes more than sufficient for the Transport's people, and mine are barefooted.

I can assure your Lordship that I believe all will go on here with harmony and spirit. The General has an opinion of his own which is not to be drawn from its proper object by the talking of any people, and he keeps his opinion and intentions to himself; therefore prevents any opinions being given.

Captain Cooke goes in the Lutine to join your Lordship. His merits your Lordship is fully acquainted with, and I have only to say that they are certainly not lessened by his services under me. I send a Return of seamen. I am, with highest respect,   Your Lordship's most faithful servant,

HORATIO NELSON.

Since writing, Lieutenant Fennell is just arrived in the Fortunée Gun-boat. No account of stores or troops being given me, it was impossible I could give your Lordship any account, or of what stores when wished, to be followed. I shall never omit writing your Lordship every occurrence.

The Tisiphone is just arrived. I have desired Captain Elphinstone to join Wolseley. Many thanks for the newspapers.

TO ADMIRAL LORD HOOD.

[Autograph, in the possession of Mrs. Conway.]

Camp, June 30th, 1794.

My Lord,

The General has thought, as we all did, of the necessity of landing two 12-pounders on the point near Revellata. A battery is made there, and I have put a Midshipman and twelve men to fight it. The General tells me he cannot afford men to encamp there for its defence. The 36-pounders, so soon as the Dolphin is cleared of shot and shells, I shall take out of the Gun-boat and put on board her. They are not to [be] landed at present, nor do I think they ever will. Two 26-pounders are to be landed from Lutine this morning, and the day after to-morrow our battery is to open against Monachesco ; for it is found we cannot carry on our batteries against the Mozelle till that post is damaged. To our battery against Mozelle from the landing place is three miles. Wolseley, as soon as he has completed getting up the 12-pounders, tells me he shall go on board the Victory and acquaint your Lordship of his proceedings.

I am with highest respect,

Your Lordship's most obedient Servant,

HORATIO NELSON.

We want provision for the seamen on shore, particularly meat : our consumption of that article is very great. What Vessel would your Lordship wish me to find for it ? if only to Fiorenzo, the Fox Cutter would very soon get it for us.

TO ADMIRAL LORD HOOD.

[Autograph, in the possession of Mrs. Conway.]

Battery, July 31st, 1794.

My dear Lord,

I own I rejoiced when our fire opened against the Enemy, being thoroughly convinced, all we have to guard against is unnecessary delay : the climate is the only Enemy we have to fear; that we can never conquer. The garrison knew it, and wished to make use of their knowledge. Our fire has had all the effect which could be hoped for. Except one general discharge, and a gun now and then still at us, we have had no opposition. Every creature (very few excepted) of the Troops are in the lower Town, which we are to respect, it being full of black Flags.[5]   Far be it from me to cast a reflection on the General's humanity—I admire it; but there are times, and I think the present is one, when it would be more charitable to our Troops to make the Enemy suffer more, than for our brave fellows to die every hour, four or five of a day. Why might not the General send notice, that they must remove from the lower Town all their sick to the upper Town, for that it might be a necessary measure to destroy it? In that case, they would be so crowded, the casements being filled with sick, that a few hours must make them submit to any terms. We cannot fire at the small craft which lay under the walls, for the lower Town, and these Vessels I dare say are filled with people or Troops.

The General is very unwell, not able to remain here last night; I have not heard of him this morning. This is my ague day, but I hope this active scene will keep off the fit. It has shook me a good deal; but I have been used to them, and don't mind them much. Lieutenant Byron,[6] heir to the title of Lord Byron, with an Ensign of the 51st, were killed yesterday afternoon, and one Officer wounded. I hope our

---

[5] Indicating the Hospitals.

[6] Lieutenant William Byron, of the Royal Irish Regiment, only son of the Honourable William Byron, (who died in 1776,) son of William, 5th Lord Byron, was on his decease, heir apparent of his grandfather to the Peerage. The other Officer who fell was Ensign Boggis.

Naples friend, Pierson,[7] will get a Commission: he is a very good young man. The Dolphin's men are on board; and both her and the Agamemnon I ordered to be ready to weigh against they should receive your Lordship's directions. Hallowell is very well, and joins in best respects with your most faithful,

HORATIO NELSON.

One Seaman slightly wounded.

TO ADMIRAL LORD HOOD.

[Autograph, in the possession of Mrs. Conway.]

Camp, August 2nd, 1794.

My dear Lord,

I am just come from the General: asking him if he had any letter or message to send to your Lordship, as I was going to send the Cutter, his answer was, Nothing. I therefore conclude you know of this Truce, and how it will end: probably till the time you granted them for receiving succours; if so, five days are elapsed. The Officers who came out were very inquisitive about the terms which were granted Bastia—whether they were not allowed to carry their Arms to the water-side. If there is no chance of firing, the keeping our seamen on the Batteries in the heat of the day is cruel. Sixteen fell ill yesterday, absolutely from the heat. I hope the Cutter has brought good news. Believe me your most faithful,

HORATIO NELSON.

The General is quite recovered.

I would not wish anything to be said to the General about our seamen. Hallowell and myself are always on the batteries with them, and our Jacks don't mind it.

---

[7] He is frequently mentioned in subsequent Letters.

TO ADMIRAL LORD HOOD.

[Autograph, in the possession of Mrs. Conway.]

Agamemnon, Genoa Mole, September 23rd, 1794.

Mr. Drake is not yet arrived, nor have we any account of his movements since the Letter he wrote the Consul, saying he expected to be here on the 20th. On Sunday evening I waited on the Doge, and, as Mr. Drake was not arrived, I found it absolutely necessary to say something civil, which I did in the following words : ' That I was come to pay my respects to his Serenity, and to assure him, that both by duty and inclination I should pay the strictest attention to the neutrality of Genoa ; and should be happy in doing everything in my power to cement the harmony which sub- sisted between the two Nations.'   The Doge was much pleased, and very civil; saying, ' That he thanked me for my expressions of friendship, and begged to assure me, that it should be reciprocal on his part; and that from so pleasing a beginning of our renewal of friendship, he had no doubt of its being lasting ; that he was always happy to see English Men-of-War in Genoa ; and whatever I found a difficulty in getting, by making it known to him, he would be happy in removing it ; and that the gates were always at my disposal.' I was received in some State, the Doge advancing to the middle of the room to receive me, and I had the honors of a Senato.   On my departure from the Palace, the orders of the Doge had preceded me to the gates, where the Cap- tain of the Guard told me he had the decree for the gates at whatever time I pleased.   I hope your Lordship will think I did right in expressing myself in the manner I did.   I can tell your Lordship for your private ear, that never man was so unpopular as Mr. Drake in Genoa—the Nobles, Middle class and Lowest, equally hate him.   Even the boat people speak of him as being so unlike any other Englishman.   Yesterday evening I had an application from the Master of an English brig, taken by the French privateers under the guns of a Genoese fort, in March last, and kept with his people in one of the Lazzarettos, till the Genoese Courts determine whether she was taken within the limits of their Coasts.   The Master and crew wish my application for them to be liberated in the first instance, and secondly, that an immediate examination of the case may take place, as they are sure, they say, of proving that the Vessel was taken under the guns of the Genoese fort. I told the Merchants that this was more a business for Mr. Drake than myself, but that if Mr. Drake did not soon arrive, I would apply for the Master and crew to be liberated. The Consul, from late circumstances, has no weight. I shall acquaint Mr. D. of the circumstance so soon as he arrives.

TO JOHN M'ARTHUR, ESQ.

[Autograph, in the possession of Mrs. Conway.]

Agamemnon, Leghorn, November 28th, 1794.

My dear Sir,

I dare say you inquired at Gibraltar about the expense of the Corn vessel, and have directed Littledale and Broderip to pay the amount, although the letter is not yet arrived. This letter is on the subject of our Bastia and Calvi Prize-money.

What I have got at present is nothing : what I have lost is, an eye, 300*l.*, and my health, with the satisfaction of my Ship's company being completely ruined : so much for debtor and creditor. It is absolutely necessary you should know how the Prize-money is to be distributed. It may be necessary, and I think must be finally determined by the King in Council. Shall those who were present at the commencement, those who only came time enough to see the Enemy's flags struck, share equal to us who bore the burden of the day ? It must be considered as very different to sharing Prize-money at sea. There the object, if resistance was made, could be assisted : with us it was quite different. Far be it from me to be illiberal. Those Ships who rode guard the whole time, as Victory, Princess Royal, and Fortitude, and Agamemnon, are the only Ships who remained the whole Siege ; Gorgon, great part ; L'Imperieuse, certain ; and Fox Cutter. How the others are to be discriminated, I cannot say.

I think you ought to get the opinion of two good Counsel, and from their opinion you may form some judgment what may be necessary to be done. Colonel Villettes and myself have talked the matter over, and think, as we were joined together in the same service, that we should be considered as different from the others. Then Brereton and the Captains who block- aded the Port, and served on shore—under what head those [Ships] who accidentally assisted for one moment and were gone the next, is not for me to determine. If it is thought right these points ought, and I must desire may be, inquired into. I know no reason why every one that pleases is to share with us. It may be necessary to speak to Lord Hood on the subject, who, I am sure, will recommend what is just, and that I would have you pursue.   Believe me,

Your very obedient humble Servant,

HORATIO NELSON.

END OF VOL. II.